STATA BASE REFERENCE MANUAL
VOLUME 1
A-F
RELEASE 8

A Stata Press Publication
STATA CORPORATION
College Station, Texas

Stata Press, 4905 Lakeway Drive, College Station, Texas 77845

The suggested citation for this software is

StataCorp. 2003. *Stata Statistical Software: Release 8.0*. College Station, TX: Stata Corporation.

Full Contents of Reference Volumes 1–4

Contents of Reference Volume 1

Contents of Reference Volume 2

Contents of Reference Volume 3

Contents of Reference Volume 4

Subject Table of Contents

This is the complete contents for all of the Reference manuals.

Getting Started

Data manipulation and management

Basic data commands

Functions and expressions

Dates

Inputting and saving data

Combining data

Reshaping datasets

Labeling, display formats, and notes

Changing and renaming variables

Examining data

Miscellaneous data commands

Utilities

Basic utilities

Error messages

Saved results

Internet

Data types and memory

Advanced utilities

Graphics

Statistics

Basic statistics

Logistic and probit regression

Pharmacokinetic statistics

Survival analysis

Time series

Cross-sectional time series (panel data)

Auxiliary regression and related commands

Commands for epidemiologists

Analysis of survey data

Transforms and normality tests

Nonparametric statistics

Simulation/resampling

Cluster analysis

Factor analysis and principal components

Do-it-yourself maximum likelihood estimation

Quality control

Other statistics

Matrix commands

Basics

Programming

Other

Programming

Basics

Program control

Parsing and program arguments

Console output

Commonly used programming commands

Debugging

Advanced programming commands

Special interest programming commands

File formats

Interface features

Cross-Referencing the Documentation

When reading this manual, you will find references to other Stata manuals. For example,

[U]   **29 Overview of Stata estimation commands**
[P]   **matrix define**
[XT]   **xtabond**

The first is a reference to Chapter 29, *Overview of Stata estimation commands* in the *Stata User's Guide*, the second is a reference to the `matrix define` entry in the *Stata Programming Reference Manual*, and the third is a reference to the `xtabond` entry in the *Stata Cross-Sectional Time-Series Reference Manual*.

All of the manuals in the Stata Documentation have a shorthand notation, such as [U] for the *User's Guide* and [P] for the *Stata Programming Reference Manual*.

The complete list of shorthand notations and manuals is as follows:

[GSM]   *Getting Started with Stata for Macintosh*
[GSU]   *Getting Started with Stata for Unix*
[GSW]   *Getting Started with Stata for Windows*

[U]   *Stata User's Guide*

[R]   *Stata Base Reference Manual*

[G]   *Stata Graphics Reference Manual*

[P]   *Stata Programming Reference Manual*

[CL]   *Stata Cluster Analysis Reference Manual*
[XT]   *Stata Cross-Sectional Time-Series Reference Manual*
[SVY]   *Stata Survey Data Reference Manual*
[ST]   *Stata Survival Analysis & Epidemiological Tables Reference Manual*
[TS]   *Stata Time-Series Reference Manual*

Detailed information about each of these manuals may be found online at

`http://www.stata-press.com/manuals/`

Title

> **intro** — Introduction to base reference manual

Description

This entry describes the layout of the *Stata Base Reference Manual*.

Remarks

The complete list of *Reference* manuals is as follows:

[R]	*Stata Base Reference Manual*
	Volume 1, A–F
	Volume 2, G–M
	Volume 3, N–R
	Volume 4, S–Z
[G]	*Stata Graphics Reference Manual*
[P]	*Stata Programming Reference Manual*
[CL]	*Stata Cluster Analysis Reference Manual*
[XT]	*Stata Cross-Sectional Time-Series Reference Manual*
[SVY]	*Stata Survey Data Reference Manual*
[ST]	*Stata Survival Analysis & Epidemiological Tables Reference Manual*
[TS]	*Stata Time-Series Reference Manual*

When we refer to the "*Reference* manuals", we mean all eight manuals listed above. When we refer to the "*Base Reference Manual*", we mean just the 4-volume *Base Reference Manual*.

Detailed information about each of these manuals may be found online at

http://www.stata-press.com/manuals/

Arrangement of the Reference manuals

The Stata *Reference* manuals are each arranged like an encyclopedia—alphabetically.

At the beginning of Volume 1 of the *Stata Base Reference Manual* is a full table of contents for all four volumes. After this is a subject table of contents for all the *Reference* manuals and the *User's Guide*. At the end of Volume 4 is a combined index for all the *Reference* manuals, except the *Graphics* manual, and for the *User's Guide*. Each of the *Reference* manuals, other than the *Base Reference Manual*, has its own index.

Most entries in the *Reference* manuals are Stata commands. Be sure to see the subject table of contents, located immediately before this entry.

The `search` command can also be used to find the Stata commands that relate to a particular statistical topic; see [R] **search**.

The Stata user community has written many additions to Stata, which are available on the Internet. Use `search, all` to widen the search to the Internet.

1

Arrangement of each entry

Each entry in the *Reference* manuals is generally arranged in the following format:

Syntax

Entries begin with a syntax diagram. A command's syntax diagram shows how to type the command, indicates all possible options, and gives the minimal allowed abbreviations for all the items in the command. For instance, the syntax diagram for the summarize command is

summarize [*varlist*] [*weight*] [if *exp*] [in *range*] [, [detail | meanonly]

[format] [separator(#)]]

by ... : may be used with summarize; see [R] **by**.

Items in the typewriter-style font should be typed exactly as they appear in the diagram, although they may be abbreviated. Underlining is used to indicate the shortest abbreviations where abbreviations are allowed. For instance, summarize may be abbreviated su, sum, summ, etc., or it may be spelled out completely. Items in the typewriter font that are not underlined may not be abbreviated; thus, if and in may not be abbreviated.

The square brackets denote optional items. In the first line of the syntax diagram, *varlist*, *weight*, if *exp*, and in *range* are optional. Nested square brackets are used to denote optional items within optional items. Thus, the last half of the syntax diagram (from the comma through separator(#)) is optional, as is any part of it. The part that reads

[detail | meanonly]

means that either detail or meanonly may be specified, but not both. A vertical bar in a syntax diagram separates alternatives.

To make the diagrams easier to read, we will often omit the plethora of brackets around the options, since you are supposed to know that each of the options is itself optional. Thus, a cleaner but less precise form of the above syntax diagram is

summarize [*varlist*] [*weight*] [if *exp*] [in *range*] [, [detail | meanonly]

format separator(#)]

by ... : may be used with summarize; see [R] **by**.

Items typed in *italics* represent arguments for which you are to substitute variable names, observation numbers, and the like.

(*Continued on next page*)

The diagrams employ the following symbols:

#	Indicates a literal number, e.g., 5; see [U] **15.2 Numbers**.
[ ]	Anything enclosed in brackets is optional.
{ }	At least one of the items enclosed in braces must appear.
|	The vertical bar separates alternatives.
%*fmt*	Any Stata format, e.g., %8.2f; see [U] **15.5 Formats: controlling how data are displayed**.
exp	Any algebraic expression, e.g., (5+myvar)/2; see [U] **16 Functions and expressions**.
filename	Any filename; see [U] **14.6 File-naming conventions**.
newvar	A variable that will be created by the current command; see [U] **14.4.2 Lists of new variables**.
numlist	A list of numbers; see [U] **14.1.8 numlist**.
oldvar	A previously created variable; see [U] **14.4.1 Lists of existing variables**.
options	A list of options; see [U] **14.1.7 options**.
range	An observation range, e.g., 5/20; see [U] **14.1.4 in range**.
"string"	Any string of characters enclosed in double quotes; see [U] **15.4 Strings**.
varlist	A list of variable names; see [U] **14.4 varlists**. If *varlist* allows time-series operators, a note to that effect will be shown below the syntax diagram; see [U] **14.4.3 Time-series varlists**.
varname	A variable name; see [U] **14.3 Naming conventions**.
weight	A [*wgttype*=*exp*] modifier; see [U] **14.1.6 weight** and [U] **23.16 Weighted estimation**.
xvar	The variable to be displayed on the horizontal axis.
yvar	The variable to be displayed on the vertical axis.

If a command allows the by prefix—and most commands do—this will be indicated immediately following the syntax diagram. The summarize command allows by.

Description

Following the syntax diagram is a brief description of the purpose of the command.

Options

If the command allows any options, they are explained here.

Remarks

The explanations under *Description* and *Options* are exceedingly brief and technical; they are designed to provide a quick summary of the command. The remarks explain in English what the preceding technical jargon means.

Saved Results

Commands are classified as e-class, r-class, s-class, or n-class, according to whether they save calculated results in e(), r(), s(), or not at all. These results can then be used in subroutines by other programs (ado-files). Such saved results are documented here; see [U] **21.8 Accessing results calculated by other programs** and [U] **21.9 Accessing results calculated by estimation commands**.

Methods and Formulas

The techniques and/or formulas used in obtaining the results are described here, as tersely and technically as possible. If a command is implemented as an ado-file, that is indicated here.

References

Published sources are listed that either were directly referenced in the preceding text or might be of interest.

Also See

Other manual entries are listed that, if this entry interested you, might also interest you. These entries are labeled as "Complementary", "Related", or "Background". Complementary entries are for commands that you might use with the command at which you are looking. Related entries are for commands that you might use instead of the command at which you are looking. Background entries provide background information that you may need in order to use the command at which you are looking.

Also See

Complementary:	[R] **net search**, [R] **search**
Background:	[U] **1.1 Getting Started with Stata**

Title

> **about** — Display information about my version of Stata

Syntax

```
about
```

Description

about displays information about the Stata that you are running.

Remarks

about displays information about the release number, flavor, serial number, and license for your Stata. If you are running Stata for Windows, information on memory is also displayed:

```
. about
Stata/SE 8.0 for Windows
Born 01 Dec 2002
Copyright (C) 1985-2003
Total physical memory:      64948 KB
Available physical memory:  11292 KB
10-user Stata for Windows (network) perpetual license:
       Serial number:  8198040000
         Licensed to:  Alan R. Riley
                       StataCorp
```

or

```
. about
Intercooled Stata 8.0 for Macintosh
Born 01 Dec 2002
Copyright (C) 1985-2003
Single-user Stata for Macintosh perpetual license:
       Serial number:  48040001
         Licensed to:  Chinh Nguyen
                       Stata Corporation
```

Also See

Related:	[R] **which**
Background:	[U] **4 Flavors of Stata**

5

Title

adjust — Tables of adjusted means and proportions

Syntax

adjust $\left[var \left[= \# \right] \dots \right]$ $\left[if\ exp \right]$ $\left[in\ range \right]$, by(*varlist*) $\left[\ \left[\ \text{xb} \mid \underline{\text{pr}} \mid \text{exp}\ \right] \right.$

$\left[\ \text{se} \mid \text{stdf}\ \right]$ generate(*newvar1* $\left[newvar2 \right]$) ci level(*#*) vertical

equation(*eqno*) nooffset replace label(*text*) selabel(*text*) cilabel(*text*)

nokey noheader format(%*fmt*) *tabdisp_options* $\left. \right]$

Description

After an estimation command (see [R] **estimation commands**), adjust provides adjusted predictions of $\mathbf{x}\beta$ (the means in a linear-regression setting), probabilities (available after some estimation commands), or exponentiated linear predictions. The estimate is computed for each level of the by() variable(s), setting the variable(s) specified in [*var* [= #] ...] to their mean or to the specified number if the = # part is specified. Variables used in the estimation command but not included in either the by() variable list or the adjust variable list are left at their current values, observation by observation. In this case, adjust displays the average estimated prediction (or the corresponding probability or exponentiated prediction) for each level of the by variables.

Options

by(*varlist*) is required, and specifies the variable(s) whose levels determine the subsets of the data for which adjusted predictions are to be computed. The variables in by() are not required to be involved in the original estimation command. A maximum of seven variables may be specified in the by() option.

xb indicates that the linear prediction from the estimation command is to be displayed. This produces predicted values (means in the linear-regression setting), and is equivalent to the xb option of predict. Realize that, depending on the estimation command, the xb values may not be in the original units of the dependent variable. The default is xb if pr or exp are not specified.

pr is an alternative to xb, and indicates that predicted probabilities are to be displayed. The pr option is not available after all commands.

exp is an alternative to xb, and indicates that exponentiated linear predictions, $\exp(x\beta)$, are to be displayed. Depending on the estimation command, the resulting quantities might be called "incidence rates", "hazard ratios", etc.

se indicates that the standard error of the linear prediction is to be displayed. This is equivalent to the stdp option of predict.

stdf indicates that the standard error of the forecast of the linear prediction is to be displayed. This is equivalent to the stdf option of predict, and is only available after estimation commands that support the stdf predict option.

6

generate(*newvar1* [*newvar2*]) generates one or two new variables. If one variable is specified, then the adjusted linear predictions for each observation are generated in *newvar1* (holding the appropriate variables to their means or to other specified values). If pr is specified, then the adjusted linear predictions are transformed to probabilities. If exp is specified, then the exponentiated predictions are returned. If *newvar2* is specified, then the standard errors from either the se option or the stdf option are placed in the second variable.

ci specifies that confidence intervals are to be displayed. The confidence intervals are for the displayed estimates as determined by the choice of the xb, pr, or exp options—producing intervals for the adjusted linear prediction, probability, or exponentiated linear predictions. When stdf is specified, prediction intervals are produced. These are, by definition, wider than the corresponding confidence intervals.

level(*#*) specifies the confidence level, in percent, for confidence or prediction intervals. The default is level(95) or as set by set level; see [R] **level**.

vertical requests that the endpoints of confidence or prediction intervals be stacked vertically on display.

equation(*eqno*) specifies which equation in a multiple-equation system is to be used in the adjust command. This option is allowed only following multiple-equation estimation commands.

nooffset is relevant only if you specified offset(*varname*) or exposure(*varname*) when you fit your model. It modifies the calculations made by adjust so that they ignore the offset or exposure variable.

replace specifies that the data in memory are to be replaced with data containing one observation per cell corresponding to the table produced by the adjust command.

label(*text*), selabel(*text*), and cilabel(*text*) allow you to change the labels for the displayed predictions (from the xb, pr, or exp options); error terms (from the se or stdf options); and confidence intervals (from the ci option). label() and selabel() also change the variable labels for the variables created by the generate() option.

nokey and noheader suppress the display of the table key and header information.

format(*%fmt*) specifies the display format for presenting the numbers in the table; see [U] **15.5 Formats: controlling how data are displayed**. format(%8.0g) is the default. Standard errors and confidence intervals are further formatted for output by automatic enclosure within parentheses or square brackets.

The allowed *tabdisp_options* are center, left, cellwidth(*#*), csepwidth(*#*), scsepwidth(*#*), and stubwidth(*#*); see [P] **tabdisp**.

Remarks

adjust is a post-estimation command; see [U] **23 Estimation and post-estimation commands**. adjust is really a front-end process for predict; see [R] **predict**. It sets up the values at which predictions are desired and then displays the predictions in tabular form; the data remain unchanged. adjust's options control the labeling of the predictions, errors, and confidence intervals. tabdisp is used to produce the final table. Several options from tabdisp are available for control over the final appearance of the table.

If you restricted your estimation command to a portion of the data using if or in, then you will generally want to use the same conditions with adjust. This is easily done by including if e(sample) with the adjust command. However, there may be legitimate reasons for using different data to perform the estimation and to obtain adjusted predictions (i.e., out-of-sample adjusted predictions).

Note: If you performed an estimation command using weights and follow that with the `adjust` command letting some of the variables vary observation by observation, the weights will not be used in constructing the adjusted table. This is not a concern when all variables of the estimation command are specified in `adjust`'s variable list and `by()` option variable list.

An interesting way to use `adjust` is after using `xi` with the estimation command. Another interesting use of `adjust` is to specify a categorical variable both in the variable list being set to a specific value and as a `by` variable. This is helpful in examining the predictions for several groups as if they were set at a particular group's value (possibly also holding some other variables to certain values also).

▷ Example

Using the automobile dataset, let's understand automobile price as a function of whether the car was manufactured domestically. We first look at the average price for domestic and foreign cars.

```
. use http://www.stata-press.com/data/r8/auto
(1978 Automobile Data)

. table foreign, c(mean price sd price) format(%8.3f)
```

Car type	mean(price)	sd(price)
Domestic	6072.423	3097.104
Foreign	6384.682	2621.915

These average prices do not seem very far apart. However, we do not think that these averages are telling us the full story since there are other variables that have an impact on the price of automobiles. As an (admittedly fake) first attempt at modeling automobile price, we decide to perform a regression.

```
. regress price mpg weight turn foreign
```

Source	SS	df	MS
Model	334771309	4	83692827.3
Residual	300294087	69	4352088.22
Total	635065396	73	8699525.97

```
Number of obs =      74
F(  4,     69) =   19.23
Prob > F       =  0.0000
R-squared      =  0.5271
Adj R-squared  =  0.4997
Root MSE       =  2086.2
```

price	Coef.	Std. Err.	t	P>|t|	[95% Conf. Interval]
mpg	-.4660076	73.51407	-0.01	0.995	-147.1226 146.1905
weight	4.284532	.7404967	5.79	0.000	2.807282 5.761782
turn	-229.2059	114.2423	-2.01	0.049	-457.1131 -1.298679
foreign	3221.415	706.4847	4.56	0.000	1812.017 4630.813
_cons	1368.197	4887.597	0.28	0.780	-8382.292 11118.69

We now ask ourselves what the price of domestic and foreign cars would be if they were compared at identical values of the explanatory variables: mpg, `weight`, and `turn` under this regression model. We compare the prices predicted from the model with these three variables set at their respective mean values. The `adjust` command provides the answer.

(Continued on next page)

```
. adjust mpg weight turn, by(foreign) se ci center
```

```
          Dependent variable: price      Command: regress
          Covariates set to mean: mpg = 21.297297, weight = 3019.4595, turn = 39.648647
```

Car type	xb	stdp	lb	ub
Domestic	5207.54	(320.823)	[4567.52	5847.56]
Foreign	8428.95	(552.515)	[7326.72	9531.19]

```
Key:  xb       =  Linear Prediction
      stdp     =  Standard Error
      [lb , ub] =  [95% Confidence Interval]
```

We see that under this regression model, foreign cars are predicted to be more expensive than domestic cars when compared at the average values of mpg, weight, and turn. The standard errors and confidence intervals are also presented. What if instead of prediction standard errors and confidence intervals, we wanted to know the forecast standard errors and prediction intervals?

```
. adjust mpg weight turn, by(foreign) stdf ci center
```

```
          Dependent variable: price      Command: regress
          Covariates set to mean: mpg = 21.297297, weight = 3019.4595, turn = 39.648647
```

Car type	xb	stdf	lb	ub
Domestic	5207.54	(2110.69)	[996.826	9418.25]
Foreign	8428.95	(2158.09)	[4123.68	12734.2]

```
Key:  xb       =  Linear Prediction
      stdf     =  Standard Error (forecast)
      [lb , ub] =  [95% Prediction Interval]
```

Understand the difference between these two tables. The reported means are the same, but their reported standard errors differ. The first table uses the se option (stdp option of predict), the standard error of the linear prediction. This standard error measures uncertainty of the mean originating from the uncertainty of the estimated model coefficients. Were our model fitted on an infinite population, we would be certain as to the model's coefficients and hence the mean of each population. These standard errors would then be zero.

Even if we knew the mean with certainty—even if the stdp standard errors were zero—we would be uncertain as to the price of each individual car. This is because individual cars have individual prices drawn from a distribution whose mean we would know; $price_j = \mu_j + \epsilon_j$.

In the second table, the reported standard errors are noticeably larger than those in the first. These standard errors reflect our total uncertainty as to the price of individual cars, $\sqrt{\sigma_\mu^2 + \sigma_\epsilon^2}$. This uncertainty is based on our uncertainty of the mean itself, σ_μ—the prediction's standard error—and the inherent uncertainty because of the unmeasured characteristics of the individual cars themselves, σ_ϵ, the residual standard error. These two components, appropriately combined, are called the forecast standard error, and are obtained with the stdf option.

Also note that the first table presents confidence intervals based on the stdp standard error, and that the second table presents what are commonly called prediction intervals based on the larger stdf forecast standard errors. Confidence intervals are intervals on our prediction for the mean. Prediction intervals are intervals on our prediction for individual observations. ◁

▷ Example

We also want to know the predicted cost for domestic and foreign cars when some of the variables are set at particular values. For instance, if we want to compare the predicted price when mpg is 25, turn is 35.2, and weight is at its mean value, we do the following:

. adjust mpg=25 turn=35.2 weight, by(foreign)

```
        Dependent variable: price      Command: regress
    Covariate set to mean: weight = 3019.4595
Covariates set to value: mpg = 25, turn = 35.2
```

Car type	xb
Domestic	6225.47
Foreign	9446.88

Key: xb = Linear Prediction

Imagine that we now want to find the predicted average price of foreign and domestic cars under this regression model when mpg and weight are set to their overall means but the turn variable is left alone, meaning it takes on the values observed car by car.

. adjust mpg weight, by(foreign) se gen(pred err)

```
     Dependent variable: price      Command: regress
       Created variables: pred, err
      Variable left as is: turn
   Covariates set to mean: mpg = 21.297297, weight = 3019.4595
```

Car type	xb	stdp
Domestic	4796.42	(342.766)
Foreign	9400.69	(621.791)

Key: xb   = Linear Prediction
      stdp = Standard Error

Specifying gen(pred err) generates prediction and error variables that we can use. Let's take a look at a few observations and compare them with the actual price and the predicted price using predict without any constraints.

(Continued on next page)

```
. predict pred2 , xb
. list foreign turn price pred2 pred err in 47/58, sepby(foreign)
```

	foreign	turn	price	pred2	pred	err
47.	Domestic	42	5,798	7585.93	4668.595	373.002
48.	Domestic	42	4,934	6600.487	4668.595	373.002
49.	Domestic	45	5,222	4798.425	3980.978	628.3688
50.	Domestic	40	4,723	5901.609	5127.007	314.9057
51.	Domestic	43	4,424	6156.588	4439.389	445.2716
52.	Domestic	41	4,172	3484.962	4897.801	325.7249
53.	Foreign	37	9,690	8226.297	9036.04	548.7275
54.	Foreign	36	6,295	5196.463	9265.246	589.1915
55.	Foreign	34	9,735	8138.971	9723.657	719.4052
56.	Foreign	35	6,229	6711.028	9494.451	647.5291
57.	Foreign	32	4,589	5893.468	10182.07	890.1414
58.	Foreign	34	5,079	6554.16	9723.657	719.4052

Note the differences in the predictions from the `predict` command and those from `adjust`. `predict` uses each observation's individual values for the variables in the regression model. `adjust` substitutes certain values for some or all of the variables in the regression model depending on what was specified in the `adjust` command. The first produces predicted values for the cars. The second produces predicted values for the cars with certain characteristics changed.

◁

▷ Example

Say we wish to look at the predicted cost of domestic and foreign cars by repair record (`rep78`) under the current regression model, holding `mpg` and `weight` to their means and allowing `turn` to vary. `adjust` allows us to do this even though we did not include `rep78` in the regression model.

(Continued on next page)

```
. adjust mpg weight, by(rep78 foreign) se ci center format(%9.2f)
```

Dependent variable: price	Command: regress
Variable left as is: turn	
Covariates set to mean: mpg = 21.289856, weight = 3032.0291	

Repair Record 1978	Car type	
	Domestic	Foreign
1	4951.66 (322.08) [4309.13,5594.19]	
2	4407.30 (471.15) [3467.38,5347.21]	
3	4790.37 (351.31) [4089.51,5491.22]	9471.91 (632.09) [8210.93,10732.89]
4	4722.45 (368.21) [3987.90,5457.01]	9548.31 (653.36) [8244.89,10851.73]
5	6097.69 (579.71) [4941.19,7254.19]	9420.97 (618.80) [8186.50,10655.45]

```
Key:  Linear Prediction
      (Standard Error)
      [95% Confidence Interval]
```

This is an example of a two-way table produced by adjust. Up to seven-way tables are possible.

You may have noticed that the means of mpg and weight in this run of adjust are not the same as in the previous runs. This is due to the fact that the rep78 variable (which was not a part of the regression) has five missing values, and adjust does casewise deletion when confronted with missing values.

◁

▷ Example

What if we wanted to find the predicted cost of foreign and domestic cars under this regression model while setting weight to its mean, letting mpg and turn vary, and pretending for the moment that all the cars are domestic? adjust handles this since it allows variables to be set to a specific value for the prediction, and yet these variables may still differentiate subsets of the data in the by() option.

(Continued on next page)

```
. adjust weight foreign=0, by(foreign) se ci center
```

```
      Dependent variable: price      Command: regress
    Variables left as is: mpg, turn
    Covariate set to mean: weight = 3019.4595
   Covariate set to value: foreign = 0
```

Car type	xb	stdp	lb	ub
Domestic	4797.11	(363.698)	[4071.55	5522.66]
Foreign	6177.65	(637.952)	[4904.97	7450.33]

```
      Key: xb       = Linear Prediction
           stdp     = Standard Error
           [lb , ub] = [95% Confidence Interval]
```

In this table, we obtain the predicted prices of all cars as if they were domestic. The $6,178 prediction, for instance, is the average predicted price of our sample of foreign cars were they instead domestic and had average weight. The foreign-car sample has a different prediction than the domestic-car sample because the cars in the two samples have different mpg and turn, and we left these differences just as we observed them.

We now do the same thing, except that we treat all cars as if they were foreign by typing

```
. adjust weight foreign=1, by(foreign) se ci center
```

```
      Dependent variable: price      Command: regress
    Variables left as is: mpg, turn
    Covariate set to mean: weight = 3019.4595
   Covariate set to value: foreign = 1
```

Car type	xb	stdp	lb	ub
Domestic	8018.52	(627.607)	[6766.48	9270.56]
Foreign	9399.07	(685.01)	[8032.51	10765.6]

```
      Key: xb       = Linear Prediction
           stdp     = Standard Error
           [lb , ub] = [95% Confidence Interval]
```

Put either way, the tables report the same difference in prices due to mpg and turn between the domestic and foreign car samples: 9399.07 − 8018.52 or 6177.65 − 4797.11.

◁

▷ Example

What if we decide to include the rep78 variable in the regression model of our earlier examples? An easy way to do that is with xi; see [R] xi.

(Continued on next page)

```
. xi : regress price mpg weight turn I.rep78
I.rep78          _Irep78_1-5          (naturally coded; _Irep78_1 omitted)
```

Source	SS	df	MS		
Model	242819042	7	34688434.6	Number of obs =	69
Residual	333977917	61	5475047.82	F(7, 61) =	6.34
				Prob > F =	0.0000
				R-squared =	0.4210
Total	576796959	68	8482308.22	Adj R-squared =	0.3545
				Root MSE =	2339.9

price	Coef.	Std. Err.	t	P>|t|	[95% Conf. Interval]	
mpg	-86.24749	84.98694	-1.01	0.314	-256.1894	83.69441
weight	3.39851	.8279604	4.10	0.000	1.742901	5.05412
turn	-321.7209	136.6736	-2.35	0.022	-595.0167	-48.42515
_Irep78_2	1143.126	1860.47	0.61	0.541	-2577.113	4863.365
_Irep78_3	1074.757	1715.121	0.63	0.533	-2354.84	4504.354
_Irep78_4	1541.853	1759.521	0.88	0.384	-1976.527	5060.234
_Irep78_5	2813.323	1849.747	1.52	0.133	-885.4749	6512.121
_cons	9030.873	5599.464	1.61	0.112	-2165.946	20227.69

Now we wish to return to our two-way adjusted table presented in an earlier example and examine the adjusted predictions under this new regression model. We will set mpg and weight to their mean values and allow turn to vary, and obtain the predictions for domestic and foreign cars by repair record.

```
. adjust mpg weight, by(foreign rep78) se
```

```
Dependent variable: price      Command: regress
Variables left as is: turn, _Irep78_2, _Irep78_3, _Irep78_4, _Irep78_5
Covariates set to mean: mpg = 21.289856, weight = 3032.0291
```

Car type	Repair Record 1978				
	1	2	3	4	5
Domestic	4308.5	4687.54	5156.86	5528.63	8730.43
	(1655.28)	(861.486)	(509.245)	(677.039)	(880.691)
Foreign			7206.34	7780.68	8873.42
			(759.055)	(798.379)	(910.117)

```
Key:  Linear Prediction
      (Standard Error)
```

adjust can take advantage of the original rep78 variable in the by option. You will notice that the output says that the xi created variables are left as is along with the turn variable. This is true, but with the rep78 variable in the by option, adjust still produces the desired results.

If you have used xi in your estimation command, you can freely use in the by() option the original variables on which xi operated. The same is not true for setting these variables to specific values. In that case, you must use the names produced by xi. For example, let's say that we wish to create the same adjusted prediction table as before, but we now want to treat all the data as if the data had a repair record of 3. Here is how we would do it:

```
. adjust mpg weight _Irep78_2=0 _Irep78_3=1 _Irep78_4=0 _Irep78_5=0, by(for rep78) se
```

```
        Dependent variable: price      Command: regress
        Variable left as is: turn
  Covariates set to mean: mpg = 21.289856, weight = 3032.0291
 Covariates set to value: _Irep78_2 = 0, _Irep78_3 = 1, _Irep78_4 = 0,
                          _Irep78_5 = 0
```

Car type	Repair Record 1978				
	1	2	3	4	5
Domestic	5383.26	4619.17	5156.86	5061.54	6991.86
	(468.873)	(653.654)	(509.245)	(530.558)	(687.006)
Foreign			7206.34	7313.58	7134.85
			(759.055)	(796.544)	(734.568)

```
   Key:  Linear Prediction
         (Standard Error)
```

If you wanted to do the same thing except set the repair record to 1 (the level dropped by xi), then in the adjust command, set all the xi created variables to zero.

```
. adjust mpg weight _Irep78_2=0 _Irep78_3=0 _Irep78_4=0 _Irep78_5=0, by(for rep78) se
  (output omitted )
```

◁

▷ Example

The adjust command also works after multiple-equation models. Let us take our first example regression and replace it with a corresponding multivariate regression using mvreg:

(Continued on next page)

```
. mvreg gear_ratio price displ = mpg weight turn foreign
```

Equation	Obs	Parms	RMSE	"R-sq"	F	P
gear_ratio	74	5	.2632419	0.6854	37.58139	0.0000
price	74	5	2086.166	0.5271	19.2305	0.0000
displacement	74	5	40.98463	0.8118	74.38435	0.0000

	Coef.	Std. Err.	t	P>|t|	[95% Conf. Interval]	
gear_ratio						
mpg	.0098519	.0092763	1.06	0.292	-.0086538	.0283577
weight	-.0002951	.0000934	-3.16	0.002	-.0004815	-.0001087
turn	.012322	.0144156	0.85	0.396	-.0164364	.0410804
foreign	.4308748	.0891474	4.83	0.000	.2530305	.6087191
_cons	3.079496	.6167391	4.99	0.000	1.849135	4.309857
price						
mpg	-.4660076	73.51407	-0.01	0.995	-147.1226	146.1905
weight	4.284532	.7404967	5.79	0.000	2.807282	5.761782
turn	-229.2059	114.2423	-2.01	0.049	-457.1131	-1.298679
foreign	3221.415	706.4847	4.56	0.000	1812.017	4630.813
_cons	1368.197	4887.597	0.28	0.780	-8382.292	11118.69
displacement						
mpg	.2235286	1.444251	0.15	0.877	-2.657673	3.10473
weight	.1003079	.0145477	6.90	0.000	.071286	.1293298
turn	-.4931961	2.244395	-0.22	0.827	-4.970641	3.984249
foreign	-26.13646	13.87953	-1.88	0.064	-53.82537	1.552458
_cons	-83.01403	96.02129	-0.86	0.390	-274.5713	108.5432

We simply indicate which equation from the multiple-equation model is to be used by adjust. The equation may be specified by number or by name. We use equation(price) below, but could have specified equation(#2) instead.

```
. adjust mpg weight turn, by(foreign) se ci center equation(price)
```

Equation: price   Command: mvreg
Covariates set to mean: mpg = 21.297297, weight = 3019.4595, turn = 39.648647

Car type	xb	stdp	lb	ub
Domestic	5207.54	(320.823)	[4567.52	5847.56]
Foreign	8428.95	(552.515)	[7326.72	9531.19]

```
Key:  xb      =  Linear Prediction
      stdp    =  Standard Error
      [lb , ub]  =  [95% Confidence Interval]
```

As expected, this table is the same as produced in the first example.

◁

▷ Example

adjust following anova helps explore the underlying cause for significant terms in the ANOVA or ANOCOVA table. The sysage.dta dataset illustrating ANOCOVA in [R] **anova** provides an example.

```
. use http://www.stata-press.com/data/r8/sysage
(Systolic Blood Pressure Data)
. anova systolic drug disease drug*disease age, continuous(age)
```

| | Number of obs = | 58 | R-squared | = 0.6826 |
| | Root MSE | = 8.1164 | Adj R-squared = | 0.5980 |

Source	Partial SS	df	MS	F	Prob > F
Model	6375.73983	12	531.311652	8.07	0.0000
drug	2762.01519	3	920.671731	13.98	0.0000
disease	605.323109	2	302.661555	4.59	0.0153
drug*disease	608.728232	6	101.454705	1.54	0.1871
age	2116.40132	1	2116.40132	32.13	0.0000
Residual	2964.41534	45	65.8758965		
Total	9340.15517	57	163.862371		

We see that `age` is a significant covariate and that `drug` and `disease` are significant factors, while the interaction is not. However, the interaction does not look as if it can be completely ignored. To further explore this interaction, we use `adjust`:

```
. adjust age, by(disease drug) se f(%6.3f) replace label(Predicted Systolic)
```

```
Dependent variable: systolic    Command: anova
Covariate set to mean: age = 45.155174
```

Patient's Disease	Drug Used			
	1	2	3	4
1	28.641	26.972	15.184	19.164
	(3.316)	(3.634)	(4.690)	(3.760)
2	29.809	32.427	4.288	12.294
	(4.068)	(4.063)	(3.630)	(3.315)
3	17.999	19.153	7.427	13.630
	(3.654)	(3.318)	(4.063)	(3.631)

```
Key:  Predicted Systolic
      (Standard Error)
```

From this table, it appears that drug 3 gives the lowest predicted systolic measure. Also notice that the systolic measure for disease 2 appears to vary more widely across the different drugs (a low of 4.288 for drug 3 and a high of 32.427 for drug 2).

We specified the `replace` option so that at this point, the data from the adjusted table are now in memory. Remember to specify `replace` only if you have previously saved your original data.

(Continued on next page)

```
. list drug disease xb stdp, sepby(disease)
```

	drug	disease	xb	stdp
1.	1	1	28.64146	3.315753
2.	2	1	26.97245	3.634287
3.	3	1	15.18372	4.690391
4.	4	1	19.16392	3.760155
5.	1	2	29.80869	4.067505
6.	2	2	32.42668	4.062614
7.	3	2	4.287933	3.629817
8.	4	2	12.29404	3.314871
9.	1	3	17.99923	3.654392
10.	2	3	19.15318	3.318073
11.	3	3	7.426678	4.062614
12.	4	3	13.63019	3.631155

A graph of the interaction can be produced from these data.

```
. scatter xb drug, sort(disease drug) c(L) m(i) mlabel(disease) mlabp(0) mlabsiz(medium)
```

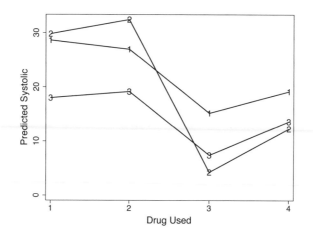

This simple example shows one of the many uses of the data after using the `replace` option.

◁

▷ Example

To illustrate the `pr` option of `adjust`, we turn to the low-birth-weight dataset illustrated in [R] **logistic** that was obtained from Hosmer and Lemeshow (2000). Below we show a `logistic` model (`probit`, `logit`, and several other commands are also allowed with the `pr` option of `adjust`).

```
. use http://www.stata-press.com/data/r8/lbw
(Hosmer & Lemeshow data)

. xi : logistic low age lwt i.race smoke , nolog
i.race            _Irace_1-3        (naturally coded; _Irace_1 omitted)
```

Logistic regression					Number of obs	=	189
					LR chi2(5)	=	20.08
					Prob > chi2	=	0.0012
Log likelihood = -107.29639					Pseudo R2	=	0.0856

low	Odds Ratio	Std. Err.	z	P>|z|	[95% Conf. Interval]	
age	.9777443	.0334083	-0.66	0.510	.9144097	1.045466
lwt	.9875761	.006305	-1.96	0.050	.9752956	1.000011
_Irace_2	3.425372	1.771281	2.38	0.017	1.243215	9.437768
_Irace_3	2.5692	1.069301	2.27	0.023	1.136391	5.808555
smoke	2.870346	1.09067	2.77	0.006	1.363	6.044672

In this case, we will ask for adjusted probability estimates under this model, setting lwt to its mean and age to 30. We will ask for these adjusted probability estimates by race and smoke.

```
. adjust age = 30 lwt , by(race smoke) pr ci format(%7.4f)
```

```
Dependent variable: low      Command: logistic
Variables left as is: _Irace_2, _Irace_3
Covariate set to mean: lwt = 129.8201
Covariate set to value: age = 30
```

	smoked during pregnancy	
race	0	1
white	0.1226	0.2863
	[0.0572,0.2434]	[0.1670,0.4452]
black	0.3237	0.5787
	[0.1412,0.5822]	[0.3110,0.8070]
other	0.2642	0.5075
	[0.1464,0.4291]	[0.2838,0.7283]

```
Key:  Probability
      [95% Confidence Interval]
```

The confidence interval is for the adjusted estimated probabilities. Both the probabilities and the confidence intervals are obtained by first computing the linear predictions and associated confidence intervals, and then transforming them to probabilities. If the pr option were not specified, we would have obtained the adjusted linear predictions.

(Continued on next page)

```
. adjust age = 30 lwt , by(race smoke) ci format(%7.4f) noheader
```

race	smoked during pregnancy	
	0	1
white	-1.9681	-0.9136
	[-2.8020,-1.1341]	[-1.6070,-0.2202]
black	-0.7368	0.3176
	[-1.8053,0.3317]	[-0.7954,1.4305]
other	-1.0245	0.0300
	[-1.7633,-0.2856]	[-0.9259,0.9859]

```
Key:  Linear Prediction
      [95% Confidence Interval]
```

It is easy to confirm that the entries in this table can be transformed to the probabilities in the previous table. For instance, $.1226 = \exp(-1.9681)/\{1 + \exp(-1.9681)\}$.

◁

▷ Example

In this example, we specify the exp option for adjust following a stcox regression on the drugtr.dta data introduced in the section *Cox regression with censored data* in [ST] **stcox**. To make the adjust table more meaningful, we generate a new age variable that has the minimum age in the data (47 in this case) subtracted from the age. This will produce hazard ratios in the adjust table relative to someone age 47 instead of to a newborn.

```
. use http://www.stata-press.com/data/r8/drugtr
(Patient Survival in Drug Trial)

. generate age0 = age-47

. stcox drug age0, nolog

        failure _d:  died
   analysis time _t:  studytime

Cox regression -- Breslow method for ties

No. of subjects =        48              Number of obs   =        48
No. of failures =        31
Time at risk    =       744
                                         LR chi2(2)      =     33.18
Log likelihood  =  -83.323546            Prob > chi2     =    0.0000
```

_t _d	Haz. Ratio	Std. Err.	z	P>|z|	[95% Conf. Interval]	
drug	.1048772	.0477017	-4.96	0.000	.0430057	.2557622
age0	1.120325	.0417711	3.05	0.002	1.041375	1.20526

Using either age0 or age with stcox produces identical results—the reported hazard ratios are relative to a one-unit change in the variable. If we wanted to see the hazard ratios for the placebo and treatment drug when age is 50 (age0 is 3) with age 47 (age0 is 0) as the base, we could use adjust:

```
. adjust age0=3, by(drug) exp stubwidth(11) label(Hazard Ratio)
```

```
        Dependent variable: _t      Command: stcox
   Covariate set to value: age0 = 3
```

Drug type (0=placebo)	exp(xb)
0	1.40615
1	.147473

```
     Key:  exp(xb)  =  Hazard Ratio
```

These hazard ratios are for 50 year olds with respect to 47 year olds on placebo. Without the `exp` option, we would have obtained a table of the linear predictions instead of the hazard ratios.

◁

Methods and Formulas

`adjust` is implemented as an ado-file.

Acknowledgment

The `adjust` command is based in part on the `adjmean` and `adjprop` commands (Garrett 1995, 1998) written by Joanne Garrett of the University of North Carolina at Chapel Hill.

References

Conroy, R. M. 2002. Choosing an appropriate real-life measure of effect size: the case of a continuous predictor and a binary outcome. *The Stata Journal* 2: 290–295.

Garrett, J. M. 1995. sg33: Calculation of adjusted means and adjusted proportions. *Stata Technical Bulletin* 24: 22–25. Reprinted in *Stata Technical Bulletin Reprints*, vol. 4, pp. 161–165.

——. 1998. sg33.1: Enhancements for calculation of adjusted means and adjusted proportions. *Stata Technical Bulletin* 43: 16–24. Reprinted in *Stata Technical Bulletin Reprints*, vol. 8, pp. 111–123.

Higbee, K. T. 1998. sg89: Adjusted predictions and probabilities after estimation. *Stata Technical Bulletin* 44: 30–37. Reprinted in *Stata Technical Bulletin Reprints*, vol. 8, pp. 165–173.

Hosmer, D. W., Jr., and S. Lemeshow. 2000. *Applied Logistic Regression*. 2d ed. New York: John Wiley & Sons.

Also See

Related:	[R] **table**,
	[ST] **epitab**,
	[SVY] **svytab**
Background:	[U] **23 Estimation and post-estimation commands**,
	[R] **predict**,
	[P] **tabdisp**

Title

alpha — Cronbach's alpha

Syntax

alpha *varlist* [if *exp*] [in *range*] [, <u>a</u>sis <u>c</u>asewise <u>d</u>etail generate(*newvar*)

    <u>i</u>tem <u>l</u>abel <u>m</u>in(#) <u>r</u>everse(*varlist*) <u>s</u>td]

by ... : may be used with alpha; see [R] **by**.

Description

alpha computes the interitem correlations or covariances for all pairs of variables in *varlist* and Cronbach's α statistic for the scale formed from them. At least two variables must be specified with alpha.

Options

asis indicates that the sense (sign) of each item should be taken as presented in the data. The default is to empirically determine the sense and reverse the scorings for any that enter negatively.

casewise specifies that cases with missing values should be deleted listwise. The default is pairwise computation of covariances/correlations.

detail lists the individual interitem correlations and covariances.

generate(*newvar*) specifies that the scale constructed from *varlist* is to be stored in *newvar*. Unless asis is specified, the sense of items entering negatively is automatically reversed. If std is also specified, the scale is constructed using standardized (mean 0, variance 1) values of the individual items. Unlike most Stata commands, generate() does not employ casewise deletion. A score is created for every observation for which there is a response to at least one item (one variable in *varlist* is not missing). The summative score is divided by the number of items over which the sum is calculated.

item specifies that item-test and item-rest correlations and the effects of removing an item from the scale are displayed. item is valid only when more than two variables are specified in *varlist*.

label requests that the detailed output table be displayed in a compact format that enables the inclusion of variable labels.

min(#) specifies that only cases with at least # observations be included in the computations. casewise is a shorthand for min(k), where k is the number of variables in *varlist*.

reverse(*varlist*) specifies that the signs (directions) of the variables (items) in *varlist* should be reversed. Any variables specified in reverse() that are not also included in alpha's *varlist* are ignored.

std specifies that the items in the scale are to be standardized (mean 0, variance 1) before summing.

Remarks

Cronbach's alpha (Cronbach 1951) assesses the reliability of a summative rating (Likert 1932) scale composed of the variables (called items) specified. The set of items is often called a test or battery. A scale is simply the sum of the individual item scores, reversing the scoring for statements that have negative correlations with the factor (e.g., attitude) being measured. Scales can be formed using the raw item scores or standardized item scores.

The reliability α is defined as the square of the correlation between the measured scale and the underlying factor. If one thinks of a test as being composed of a random sample of items from a hypothetical domain of items designed to measure the same thing, α represents the expected correlation of one test with an alternative form containing the same number of items. The square root of α is the estimated correlation of a test with errorless true scores (Nunnally and Bernstein 1994, 235). The value of α in the case of dichotomous items is often referred to as "Kuder–Richardson Formula 20" (KR-20); see Kuder and Richardson (1937), Allen and Yen (1979, 83–85), and Nunnally and Bernstein (1994, 235).

In addition to reporting α, `alpha` will generate the summative scale from the items (variables) specified and automatically reverse the sense of any when necessary. Stata's decision can be overridden by specifying the `reverse(`*varlist*`)` option.

Since α concerns reliability in measuring an unobserved factor, it is related to factor analysis. The test should be designed to measure a single factor, and, since the scale will be composed of an unweighted sum, the factor loadings should all contribute roughly equal information to the score. Both of these assumptions can be verified with `factor`; see [R] **factor**. Equality of factor loadings can also be assessed using the `item` option.

▷ Example

To illustrate `alpha`, we apply it, first without and then with the `item` option, to the automobile dataset after randomly introducing missing values:

```
. use http://www.stata-press.com/data/r8/automiss
(1978 Automobile Data)

. alpha price headroom rep78 trunk weight length turn displ, std

Test scale = mean(standardized items)
Reversed item: rep78

Average interitem correlation:      0.5251
Number of items in the scale:            8
Scale reliability coefficient:      0.8984
```

The scale derived from our somewhat arbitrarily chosen automobile items (variables) appears rather good since the estimated correlation between it and the underlying factor it measures is $\sqrt{.8984} \approx .9478$ and the estimated correlation between this battery of eight items and all other eight-item batteries from the same domain is .8984. Since the "items" are not on the same scale, it is important that `std` was specified so that the scale and its reliability were based on the sum of standardized variables. Note that we could obtain the scale in a new variable called `sc` with the option `gen(sc)`.

Though the scale appears good, to determine if all the items fit the scale, we include the `item` option:

```
. alpha price headroom rep78 trunk weight length turn displ, std item

Test scale = mean(standardized items)
```

			item-test	item-rest	average inter-item	
Item	Obs	Sign	correlation	correlation	correlation	alpha
price	70	+	0.5260	0.3719	0.5993	0.9128
headroom	66	+	0.6716	0.5497	0.5542	0.8969
rep78	61	−	0.4874	0.3398	0.6040	0.9143
trunk	69	+	0.7979	0.7144	0.5159	0.8818
weight	64	+	0.9404	0.9096	0.4747	0.8635
length	69	+	0.9382	0.9076	0.4725	0.8625
turn	66	+	0.8678	0.8071	0.4948	0.8727
displacement	63	+	0.8992	0.8496	0.4852	0.8684
Test scale					0.5251	0.8984

"Test" denotes the additive scale; in this case, .5251 is the average interitem correlation and .8984 is the alpha coefficient for a test scale based on all items.

"Obs" shows the number of nonmissing values of the items; "Sign" indicates the direction in which an item variable entered the scale; a "−" denotes that the item was reversed. The remaining four columns in the table provide information on the effect of a single item on the scale.

Column four gives the item-test correlations. Apart from the sign of the correlation for items that entered the scale in reversed order, these correlations are the same numbers as those computed by the commands

```
. alpha price headroom rep78 trunk weight length turn displ, std
. correlate price headroom rep78 trunk weight length turn displ
```

Typically, the item-test correlations should be roughly the same for all items. Item-test correlations may actually not be very adequate to detect items that fit poorly, because the poorly fitting items may distort the scale. Accordingly, it may be more useful to consider item-rest correlations (Nunnally and Bernstein 1994); i.e., the correlation between an item and the scale that is formed by all other items. The average interitem correlations (covariances if std is omitted) of all items, excluding one, are shown in column six. Finally, column seven gives Cronbach's α for the test scale, which consists of all but the one item.

In this example, neither the price item nor the rep78 item seem to fit well in the scale in all respects. The item-test and item-rest correlations of price and rep78 are much lower than for the other items. The average interitem correlation increases substantially by removing either price or rep78; apparently they do not correlate strongly with the other items. Finally, we see that Cronbach's α coefficient will increase from .8984 to .9128 if the item price is dropped, and it will increase from .8984 to .9143 if rep78 is dropped. For well-fitting items, we would, of course, expect that α decreases by shortening the test.

The variable names for the automobile data are reasonably informative. This may not always be true; items in batteries commonly used to measure personality traits, attitudes, or values, etc. are usually named with indexed names such as item12a, item12b, etc. The label option forces alpha to produce the same statistical information in a more compact format that leaves room to include variable (item) labels. In this compact format, alpha excludes the number of nonmissing values of the items, displays the statistics using fewer digits, and uses somewhat cryptic headers:

```
. alpha price headroom rep78 trunk weight length turn displ, std item label detail
Test scale = mean(standardized items)
```

Items	S	it-cor	ir-cor	ii-cor	alpha	label
price	+	0.526	0.372	0.599	0.913	Price
headroom	+	0.672	0.550	0.554	0.897	Headroom (in.)
rep78	−	0.487	0.340	0.604	0.914	Repair Record 1978
trunk	+	0.798	0.714	0.516	0.882	Trunk space (cu. ft.)
weight	+	0.940	0.910	0.475	0.863	Weight (lbs.)
length	+	0.938	0.908	0.473	0.862	Length (in.)
turn	+	0.868	0.807	0.495	0.873	Turn Circle (ft.)
displacement	+	0.899	0.850	0.485	0.868	Displacement (cu. in.)
Test scale				0.525	0.898	mean(standardized items)

Interitem correlations (reverse applied) (obs=pairwise, see below)

	price	headroom	rep78	trunk
price	1.0000			
headroom	0.1174	1.0000		
rep78	−0.0479	0.1955	1.0000	
trunk	0.2748	0.6841	0.2777	1.0000
weight	0.5093	0.5464	0.3624	0.6486
length	0.4511	0.5823	0.3162	0.7404
turn	0.3528	0.4067	0.4715	0.5900
displacement	0.5537	0.5166	0.3391	0.6471

	weight	length	turn	displacement
weight	1.0000			
length	0.9425	1.0000		
turn	0.8712	0.8589	1.0000	
displacement	0.8753	0.8422	0.7723	1.0000

Pairwise number of observations

	price	headroom	rep78	trunk
price	70			
headroom	62	66		
rep78	59	54	61	
trunk	65	61	59	69
weight	60	56	52	60
length	66	61	58	64
turn	62	58	56	62
displacement	59	58	51	58

	weight	length	turn	displacement
weight	64			
length	60	69		
turn	57	61	66	
displacement	54	58	56	63

Since the detail option was also specified, the interitem correlation matrix was printed, together with the number of observations used for each entry (since these varied across the matrix). Note the negative sign attached to rep78 in the output, indicating the sense in which it entered the scale.

Better looking output with less cryptic headers is produced if the linesize is set to a value of at least 100:

(Continued on next page)

```
. set linesize 100
. alpha price headroom rep78 trunk weight length turn displ, std item label
Test scale = mean(standardized items)
```

Item	Obs	Sign	item-test corr.	item-rest corr.	inter-item corr.	alpha	Label
price	70	+	0.5260	0.3719	0.5993	0.9128	Price
headroom	62	+	0.6716	0.5497	0.5542	0.8969	Headroom (in.)
rep78	59	–	0.4874	0.3398	0.6040	0.9143	Repair Record 1978
trunk	65	+	0.7979	0.7144	0.5159	0.8818	Trunk space (cu. ft.)
weight	60	+	0.9404	0.9096	0.4747	0.8635	Weight (lbs.)
length	66	+	0.9382	0.9076	0.4725	0.8625	Length (in.)
turn	62	+	0.8678	0.8071	0.4948	0.8727	Turn Circle (ft.)
displacement	59	+	0.8992	0.8496	0.4852	0.8684	Displacement (cu. in.)
Test scale					0.5251	0.8984	mean(standardized items)

◁

Users of `alpha` require some standard for judging values of α. We paraphrase Nunnally and Bernstein (1994, 265): In the early stages of research, modest reliability of 0.70 or higher will suffice; values in excess of 0.80 are often wasteful of time and funds. In contrast, where measurements on individuals are of interest, a reliability of 0.80 may not be nearly high enough. Even with a reliability of 0.90, the standard error of measurement is almost one-third as large as the standard deviation of test scores; a reliability of 0.90 is the minimum that should be tolerated, and a reliability of 0.95 should be considered the desirable standard.

Saved Results

`alpha` saves in `r()`:

Scalars

r(alpha)	scale reliability coefficient
r(k)	number of items in the scale
r(cov)	average interitem covariance
r(rho)	average interitem correlation if `std` is specified

Matrices

r(Alpha)	scale reliability coefficient
r(ItemTestCorr)	item test correlation
r(ItemRestCorr)	item rest correlation
r(MeanInterItemCov)	average interitem covariance
r(MeanInterItemCorr)	average interitem correlation if `std` is specified

Note that if the option `item` is specified, results are saved as row matrices for the k subscales when one variable is removed.

Methods and Formulas

`alpha` is implemented as an ado-file.

Let x_i, $i = 1, \ldots, k$, be the variables over which α is to be calculated. Let s_i be the sign with which x_i enters the scale. If `asis` is specified, $s_i = 1$ for all i. Otherwise, principal factor analysis is performed on x_i and the first factor's score predicted; see [R] **factor**. s_i is -1 if correlation of the x_i and the predicted score is negative and $+1$ otherwise.

Let r_{ij} be the correlation between x_i and x_j, c_{ij} the covariance, and n_{ij} the number of observations used in calculating the correlation or covariance. The average correlation is

$$\overline{r} = \frac{\sum\limits_{i=2}^{k}\sum\limits_{j=1}^{i-1} s_i s_j n_{ij} r_{ij}}{\sum\limits_{i=2}^{k}\sum\limits_{j=1}^{i-1} n_{ij}}$$

and the average covariance similarly is

$$\overline{c} = \frac{\sum\limits_{i=2}^{k}\sum\limits_{j=1}^{i-1} s_i s_j n_{ij} c_{ij}}{\sum\limits_{i=2}^{k}\sum\limits_{j=1}^{i-1} n_{ij}}$$

Let c_{ii} denote the variance of x_i, and define the average variance as

$$\overline{v} = \frac{\sum\limits_{i=1}^{k} n_{ii} c_{ii}}{\sum\limits_{i=1}^{k} n_{ii}}$$

If `std` is specified, the scale reliability α is calculated as defined by the general form of the Spearman–Brown Prophecy Formula (Nunnally and Bernstein 1994, 232; Allen and Yen 1979, 85–88):

$$\alpha = \frac{k\overline{r}}{1 + (k-1)\overline{r}}$$

This corresponds to α under the assumption that the summative rating is the sum of the standardized variables (Nunnally and Bernstein 1994, 234). If `std` is not specified, α is defined (Nunnally and Bernstein 1994, 232, 234) as

$$\alpha = \frac{k\overline{c}}{\overline{v} + (k-1)\overline{c}}$$

Let x_{ij} reflect the value of item i in the jth observation. If `std` is specified, the jth value of the scale computed from the k x_{ij} items is

$$S_j = \frac{1}{k_j}\sum_{i=1}^{k} s_i S(x_{ij})$$

where $S()$ is the function that returns the standardized (mean 0, variance 1) value if x_{ij} is not missing and zero if x_{ij} is missing. k_j is the number of nonmissing values in x_{ij}, $i = 1, \ldots, k$. If `std` is not specified, $S()$ is the function that returns x_{ij}, or missing if x_{ij} is missing.

Lee J. Cronbach (1916–2001) was an American psychometrician and educational psychologist who worked principally on measurement theory, program evaluation, and instruction. He taught and researched at the State College of Washington, the University of Chicago, the University of Illinois, and at Stanford. Cronbach's initial paper on alpha led to a theory of test reliability, "generalizability theory", a comprehensive statistical model for identifying sources of measurement error.

Acknowledgment

This improved version of `alpha` was written by Jeroen Weesie of Utrecht University, the Netherlands.

References

Allen, M. J. and W. M. Yen. 1979. *Introduction to Measurement Theory*. Monterey, CA: Brooks/Cole Publishing Company.

Bleda, M. J. and A. Tobias. 2000. sg143: Cronbach's alpha one-sided confidence interval. *Stata Technical Bulletin* 56: 26–27. Reprinted in *Stata Technical Bulletin Reprints*, vol. 10, pp. 187–189.

Cronbach, L. J. 1951. Coefficient alpha and the internal structure of tests. *Psychometrika* 16: 297–334.

Kuder, G. F. and M. W. Richardson. 1937. The theory of the estimation of test reliability. *Psychometrika* 2: 151–160.

Likert, R. A. 1932. A technique for the measurement of attitudes. *Archives of Psychology* 140: 5–55.

Nunnally, J. C. and I. H. Bernstein. 1994. *Psychometric Theory*. 3d ed. New York: McGraw–Hill.

Tarlov, A. R., J. E. Ware, Jr., S. Greenfield, E. C. Nelson, E. Perrin, and M. Zubkoff. 1989. The medical outcomes study. *Journal of the American Medical Association* 262: 925–930.

Weesie, J. 1997. sg66: Enhancements to the alpha command. *Stata Technical Bulletin* 35: 32–34. Reprinted in *Stata Technical Bulletin Reprints*, vol. 6, pp. 176–179.

Also See

Related: [R] **factor**

Title

anova — Analysis of variance and covariance

Syntax

<u>an</u>ova *varname* [*term* [/] [*term* [/] ...]] [*weight*] [if *exp*] [in *range*] [, [<u>no</u>]<u>an</u>ova

    <u>cat</u>egory(*varlist*) <u>cl</u>ass(*varlist*) <u>noconst</u>ant <u>cont</u>inuous(*varlist*)

    <u>repeated</u>(*varlist*) bse(*term*) bseunit(*varname*) <u>grouping</u>(*varname*) detail

    <u>partial</u> <u>sequential</u> <u>regress</u>]

where *term* is of the form   *varname*[{ * | | }*varname*[...]]

by ... : may be used with anova; see [R] **by**.

aweights and fweights are allowed; see [U] **14.1.6 weight**.

anova shares the features of all estimation commands; see [U] **23 Estimation and post-estimation commands**.

Syntax for predict

predict after anova follows the same syntax as predict after regress, and can provide predictions, residuals, standardized residuals, studentized residuals, the standard error of the residuals, the standard error of the prediction, the diagonal elements of the projection (hat) matrix, and Cook's D. See [R] **regress** for details.

Syntax for test following anova

<u>te</u>st [*exp* = *exp*] [, <u>a</u>ccumulate <u>no</u>test matvlc(*matname*)]

<u>te</u>st [*term* [*term* ...]] [/ *term* [*term* ...]] [, <u>s</u>ymbolic]

where *exp* must have references to coefficients enclosed in _coef[] (or synonym _b[]) and *term* is as defined for anova.

Description

The anova command fits analysis-of-variance (ANOVA) and analysis-of-covariance (ANOCOVA) models for balanced and unbalanced designs, including designs with missing cells; for repeated measures ANOVA; and for factorial, nested, or mixed designs. anova can also be used to produce regression estimates by those who have no interest in ANOVA and ANOCOVA output.

Users wanting to fit one-way ANOVA models may find the oneway or loneway commands more convenient; see [R] **oneway** and [R] **loneway**. For those interested in MANOVA or MANCOVA, see [R] **manova**.

Options

[no]anova indicates that the ANOVA table is or is not to be displayed. The anova command typically displays the ANOVA table, and in those cases, the noanova option suppresses the display. For instance, typing anova, detail noanova would show the detail-output for the last ANOVA model while suppressing the ANOVA table itself.

If you specify the regress option, the ANOVA table is automatically suppressed. In that case, also specifying the anova option would show both the regression output and the ANOVA table.

category(*varlist*) indicates the names of the variables in the *terms* that are categorical or class variables. Stata ordinarily assumes that all variables are categorical variables, so, in most cases, this option need not be specified. If you specify this option, however, the variables referenced in the *terms* that are not listed in the category() option are assumed to be continuous. Also see the class() and continuous() options.

class(*varlist*) is a synonym for category(*varlist*).

noconstant suppresses the constant term (intercept) from the ANOVA or regression model.

continuous(*varlist*) indicates the names of the variables in the *terms* that are continuous. Stata ordinarily assumes that all variables are categorical variables. Also see the category() and class() options.

repeated(*varlist*) indicates the names of the categorical variables in the *terms* that are to be treated as repeated measures variables in a repeated measures ANOVA or ANCOVA.

bse(*term*) indicates the between-subjects error term in a repeated measures ANOVA. This option is needed only in the rare case when the anova command cannot automatically determine the between-subjects error term.

bseunit(*varname*) indicates the variable representing the lowest unit in the between-subjects error term in a repeated measures ANOVA. This option is rarely needed since the anova command automatically selects the first variable listed in the between-subjects error term as the default for this option.

grouping(*varname*) indicates a variable that determines which observations are grouped together in computing the covariance matrices that will be pooled together and used in a repeated measures ANOVA. This option is rarely needed since the anova command automatically selects the combination of all variables except the first (or as specified in the bseunit option) in the between-subjects error term as the default for grouping observations.

detail presents a table showing the actual values of the categorical variables along with their mapping into level numbers. You do not have to specify this option at the time of estimation. You can obtain the output at any time by typing anova, detail.

partial presents the ANOVA table using partial (or marginal) sums of squares. This is the default. Also see the sequential option.

sequential presents the ANOVA table using sequential sums of squares.

regress presents the regression output corresponding to the specified model. Specifying regress implies the noanova option, so if you want both the regression output and the ANOVA table, you must also specify the anova option. You need not specify the regress option at the time of estimation. You can obtain the underlying regression estimates at any time by typing anova, regress.

Options for test after anova

accumulate allows a hypothesis to be tested jointly with the previously tested hypotheses.

notest suppresses the output. This option is useful when you are interested only in the joint test with additional hypotheses specified in a subsequent call of test, accumulate.

matvlc(*matname*), a programmer's option, saves the variance–covariance matrix of the linear combination(s) involved in the suite of tests. For the test $Lb = c$, what is returned in *matname* is LVL', where V is the estimated variance–covariance matrix of b.

symbolic requests the symbolic form of the test rather than the test statistic. When this option is specified without any terms (test, symbolic), the symbolic form of the estimable functions is displayed.

Remarks

Remarks are presented under the headings

Introduction
One-way analysis of variance
Two-way analysis of variance
N-way analysis of variance
Analysis of covariance
Nested designs
Mixed designs
Latin square designs
Repeated measures analysis of variance
Weighted data
Obtaining the covariance matrix
Testing effects
Obtaining symbolic forms
Testing coefficients
How Stata numbers levels
anova as an alternative to regress

Introduction

anova uses least squares to fit linear models, and can report both regression and ANOVA output. The command is designed to be most useful to persons wishing to fit analysis-of-variance or analysis-of-covariance models (henceforth referred to simply as ANOVA models), but is also useful for persons wishing to fit regression models with numerous categorical variables.

If your interest is in formal ANOVA, you should read this entire entry. If your interest is solely in regression, you may want to skip to *anova as an alternative to regress*.

Persons interested in regression should also see [R] **regress**.

If your interest is in one-way ANOVA, you may find the oneway command more convenient; see [R] **oneway**.

Analysis of variance was pioneered by Fisher in 1925. Fisher (1935) considered the design of factorial experiments. Many books discuss analysis of variance; see, for instance, Altman (1991), Cobb (1998), Snedecor and Cochran (1989), Steel and Torrie (1980), or Winer, Brown, and Michels (1991). For a classic source, see Scheffé (1959). Kennedy and Gentle (1980) discuss the computing problems of analysis of variance. Edwards (1985) is primarily concerned with the relationship between multiple regression and analysis of variance. Rabe-Hesketh and Everitt (2000, Chapters 4 and 5) illustrate their discussion with Stata output. Repeated measures analysis of variance is discussed in Winer, Brown, and Michels (1991), Kuehl (1994), and Milliken and Johnson (1984). Pioneering work in repeated measures analysis of variance can be found in Box (1954), Geisser and Greenhouse (1958), Huynh and Feldt (1976), and Huynh (1978).

One-way analysis of variance

anova, entered without options, performs and reports standard ANOVA. For instance, to perform a one-way layout of a variable called endog on exog, type anova endog exog.

▷ Example

You run an experiment varying the amount of fertilizer used in growing apple trees. You test four concentrations, using each concentration in three groves of twelve trees each. Later in the year, you measure the average weight of the fruit.

If all had gone well, you would have had three observations on the average weight for each of the four concentrations. Instead, two of the groves were mistakenly leveled by a confused man on a large bulldozer. You are left with the following data:

```
. use http://www.stata-press.com/data/r8/apple
(Apple trees)
. list, abbrev(10) sepby(treatment)
```

	treatment	weight
1.	1	117.5
2.	1	113.8
3.	1	104.4
4.	2	48.9
5.	2	50.4
6.	2	58.9
7.	3	70.4
8.	3	86.9
9.	4	87.7
10.	4	67.3

To obtain one-way analysis-of-variance results, you type

```
. anova weight treatment
```

| | | Number of obs = | 10 | R-squared | = 0.9147 |
| | | Root MSE | = 9.07002 | Adj R-squared = | 0.8721 |

Source	Partial SS	df	MS	F	Prob > F
Model	5295.54433	3	1765.18144	21.46	0.0013
treatment	5295.54433	3	1765.18144	21.46	0.0013
Residual	493.591667	6	82.2652778		
Total	5789.136	9	643.237333		

You find significant (at better than the 1% level) differences among the four concentrations.

Although the output is a usual analysis-of-variance table, let's run through it anyway. Above the table is a summary of the underlying regression. The model was fitted on 10 observations, and the root mean square error (Root MSE) is 9.07. The R^2 for the model is 0.9147, and the adjusted R^2 is 0.8721.

The first line of the table summarizes the model. The sum of squares (Partial SS) for the model is 5295.5 with 3 degrees of freedom (df). This results in a mean square (MS) of $5295.5/3 \approx 1765.2$. The corresponding F statistic is 21.46 and has a significance level of 0.0013. Thus, the model appears to be significant at the 0.13% level.

The next line summarizes the first (and only) term in the model, treatment. Since there is only one term, the line is identical to that for the overall model.

The third line summarizes the residual. The residual sum of squares is 493.59 with 6 degrees of freedom, resulting in a mean square error of 82.27. It is the square root of this latter number that is reported as the Root MSE.

The model plus the residual sum of squares equal the total sum of squares, which is reported as 5789.1 in the last line of the table. This is the total sum of squares of weight after removal of the mean. Similarly, the model plus the residual degrees of freedom sum to the total degrees of freedom, 9. Remember that there are 10 observations. Subtracting 1 for the mean, we are left with 9 total degrees of freedom.

◁

❑ Technical Note

Rather than using the anova command, we could have performed this analysis using the oneway command. The first example in [R] **oneway** repeats this same analysis. You may wish to compare the output.

❑

It is possible and even probable that you will want to see the underlying regression corresponding to a model after seeing the ANOVA table. After fitting an ANOVA model using the anova command, you can obtain the regression output by typing anova, regress.

▷ Example

Returning to the apple tree experiment, we found that the fertilizer concentration appears to affect the average weight of the fruit significantly. Although that is interesting, we next want to know which concentration appears to grow the heaviest fruit. To find out, we examine the underlying regression coefficients.

(Continued on next page)

```
. anova, regress
```

Source	SS	df	MS		
Model	5295.54433	3	1765.18144		
Residual	493.591667	6	82.2652778		
Total	5789.136	9	643.237333		

	Number of obs =	10
	F(3, 6) =	21.46
	Prob > F =	0.0013
	R-squared =	0.9147
	Adj R-squared =	0.8721
	Root MSE =	9.07

weight	Coef.	Std. Err.	t	P>|t|	[95% Conf. Interval]	
_cons	77.5	6.413473	12.08	0.000	61.8068	93.1932
treatment						
1	34.4	8.279758	4.15	0.006	14.14016	54.65984
2	-24.76667	8.279758	-2.99	0.024	-45.02651	-4.506828
3	1.15	9.070021	0.13	0.903	-21.04354	23.34354
4	(dropped)					

See [R] **regress** for an explanation of how to read this table. In summary, we find that concentration 1 produces significantly heavier fruits when compared with concentration 4, the omitted (dropped) group; concentration 2 produces significantly lighter fruits; and concentrations 3 and 4 appear to be roughly equivalent.

◁

❏ Technical Note

After fitting the model using anova, we could have simply typed regress rather than anova, regress to obtain the same output. regress typed without arguments reshows the last regression. Since anova defines a regression, typing regress after anova is another way of displaying the regression.

❏

If you type anova without any arguments, the ANOVA table will be redisplayed.

▷ Example

We previously typed anova weight treatment to produce and display the ANOVA table for our apple tree experiment. We typed anova, regress to obtain the regression coefficients. If we want to redisplay the ANOVA table, we can type anova without arguments:

```
. anova
```

	Number of obs =	10	R-squared =	0.9147
	Root MSE = 9.07002		Adj R-squared =	0.8721

Source	Partial SS	df	MS	F	Prob > F
Model	5295.54433	3	1765.18144	21.46	0.0013
treatment	5295.54433	3	1765.18144	21.46	0.0013
Residual	493.591667	6	82.2652778		
Total	5789.136	9	643.237333		

◁

Two-way analysis of variance

You can include multiple explanatory variables with the `anova` command, and you can specify interactions by placing '*' between the variable names. For instance, typing `anova y a b` performs a two-way layout of `y` on `a` and `b`. Typing `anova y a b a*b` performs a full two-way factorial layout.

Note: With the default partial sums of squares, when you specify interacted terms, the order of the terms does not matter. Typing `anova y a b a*b` is the same as typing `anova y b a b*a`.

▷ Example

The classic two-way factorial ANOVA problem, at least as far as computer manuals are concerned, is a two-way analysis-of-variance design from Afifi and Azen (1979).

Fifty-eight patients, each suffering from one of three different diseases, were randomly assigned to one of four different drug treatments, and the change in their systolic blood pressure was recorded. Here are the data:

	Disease 1	Disease 2	Disease 3
Drug 1	42, 44, 36 13, 19, 22	33, 26, 33 21	31, −3, 25 25, 24
Drug 2	28, 23, 34 42, 13	34, 33, 31 36	3, 26, 28 32, 4, 16
Drug 3	1, 29, 19	11, 9, 7 1, −6	21, 1, 9 3
Drug 4	24, 9, 22 −2, 15	27, 12, 12 −5, 16, 15	22, 7, 25 5, 12

Let's assume that we have entered these data into Stata and stored the data as `systolic.dta`. Below we use the data, `list` the first 10 observations, `summarize` the variables, and `tabulate` the control variables:

```
. use http://www.stata-press.com/data/r8/systolic
(Systolic Blood Pressure Data)
. list in 1/10
```

	drug	disease	systolic
1.	1	1	42
2.	1	1	44
3.	1	1	36
4.	1	1	13
5.	1	1	19
6.	1	1	22
7.	1	2	33
8.	1	2	26
9.	1	2	33
10.	1	2	21

```
. summarize
```

Variable	Obs	Mean	Std. Dev.	Min	Max
drug	58	2.5	1.158493	1	4
disease	58	2.017241	.8269873	1	3
systolic	58	18.87931	12.80087	−6	44

```
. tabulate drug disease
```

| | Patient's Disease | | | |
Drug Used	1	2	3	Total
1	6	4	5	15
2	5	4	6	15
3	3	5	4	12
4	5	6	5	16
Total	19	19	20	58

Each observation in our data corresponds to one patient, and for each patient we record drug, disease, and the increase in the systolic blood pressure, systolic. The tabulation reveals that the data are not balanced—there are not equal numbers of patients in each drug–disease cell. Stata does not require that the data be balanced. We can perform a two-way factorial analysis of variance by typing

```
. anova systolic drug disease drug*disease
```

| | | Number of obs = | 58 | R-squared | = | 0.4560 |
| | | Root MSE | = 10.5096 | Adj R-squared = | | 0.3259 |

Source	Partial SS	df	MS	F	Prob > F
Model	4259.33851	11	387.212591	3.51	0.0013
drug	2997.47186	3	999.157287	9.05	0.0001
disease	415.873046	2	207.936523	1.88	0.1637
drug*disease	707.266259	6	117.87771	1.07	0.3958
Residual	5080.81667	46	110.452536		
Total	9340.15517	57	163.862371		

You should also be familiar with Stata's table command; see [R] **table**. Although it will not perform analysis of variance, it can produce useful summary tables of your data:

```
. table drug disease, c(mean systolic) row col f(%8.2f)
```

| | Patient's Disease | | | |
Drug Used	1	2	3	Total
1	29.33	28.25	20.40	26.07
2	28.00	33.50	18.17	25.53
3	16.33	4.40	8.50	8.75
4	13.60	12.83	14.20	13.50
Total	22.79	18.21	15.80	18.88

◁

❑ Technical Note

A few words should be said about how to interpret the significance of terms like drug and disease in unbalanced data. If you are familiar with SAS, the sums of squares and the F statistic reported by Stata correspond to SAS type III sums of squares. (Stata can also calculate sequential sums of squares, but we will postpone that topic for now.)

Let's think in terms of the following tableau:

	Disease 1	Disease 2	Disease 3	
Drug 1	μ_{11}	μ_{12}	μ_{13}	$\mu_{1\cdot}$
Drug 2	μ_{21}	μ_{22}	μ_{23}	$\mu_{2\cdot}$
Drug 3	μ_{31}	μ_{32}	μ_{33}	$\mu_{3\cdot}$
Drug 4	μ_{41}	μ_{42}	μ_{43}	$\mu_{4\cdot}$
	$\mu_{\cdot 1}$	$\mu_{\cdot 2}$	$\mu_{\cdot 3}$	$\mu_{\cdot\cdot}$

In this diagram, μ_{ij} is the mean increase in systolic blood pressure associated with drug i and disease j, $\mu_{i\cdot}$ is the mean for drug i, $\mu_{\cdot j}$ is the mean for disease j, and $\mu_{\cdot\cdot}$ is the overall mean.

If the data are balanced, meaning that there are an equal number of observations going into the calculation of each mean μ_{ij}, then the row means $\mu_{i\cdot}$ are given by

$$\mu_{i\cdot} = \frac{\mu_{i1} + \mu_{i2} + \mu_{i3}}{3}$$

In our case, the data are not balanced, but we define the $\mu_{i\cdot}$ according to that formula anyway. The test for the main effect of drug amounts to the test that

$$\mu_{1\cdot} = \mu_{2\cdot} = \mu_{3\cdot} = \mu_{4\cdot}$$

To be absolutely clear, the F test of the term drug, called the *main effect* of drug, is formally equivalent to the test of the three constraints:

$$\frac{\mu_{11} + \mu_{12} + \mu_{13}}{3} = \frac{\mu_{21} + \mu_{22} + \mu_{23}}{3}$$

$$\frac{\mu_{11} + \mu_{12} + \mu_{13}}{3} = \frac{\mu_{31} + \mu_{32} + \mu_{33}}{3}$$

$$\frac{\mu_{11} + \mu_{12} + \mu_{13}}{3} = \frac{\mu_{41} + \mu_{42} + \mu_{43}}{3}$$

In our data, we obtain a significant F statistic of 9.05, and thus reject those constraints.

❏

❏ Technical Note

Stata can display the symbolic form underlying the test statistics it presents, as well as display other test statistics and their symbolic forms; see *Obtaining symbolic forms* below. Without explanation, here is the result of requesting the symbolic form for the main effect of drug in our data:

(Continued on next page)

```
. test drug, symbolic
_cons           0
drug
         1          r1
         2          r2
         3          r3
         4          -(r1+r2+r3)
disease
         1          0
         2          0
         3          0
drug*disease
      1  1          1/3 r1
      1  2          1/3 r1
      1  3          1/3 r1
      2  1          1/3 r2
      2  2          1/3 r2
      2  3          1/3 r2
      3  1          1/3 r3
      3  2          1/3 r3
      3  3          1/3 r3
      4  1          -1/3 (r1+r2+r3)
      4  2          -1/3 (r1+r2+r3)
      4  3          -1/3 (r1+r2+r3)
```

This says exactly what we said in the previous technical note.

❑

❑ Technical Note

As anyone familiar with ANOVA knows, the statement that there is no main effect of a variable is not the same as the statement that it has no effect at all, but it is still worth repeating. Stata's ability to perform ANOVA on unbalanced data can easily be put to ill use.

For example, consider the following table of the probability of surviving a bout with one of two diseases according to the drug administered to you:

	Disease 1	Disease 2
Drug 1	1	0
Drug 2	0	1

If you have disease 1 and are administered drug 1, you live. If you have disease 2 and are administered drug 2, you live. In all other cases, you die.

This table has no main effects of either drug or disease, although there is a large interaction effect. You might now be tempted to reason that since there is only an interaction effect, you would be indifferent between the two drugs in the absence of knowledge about which disease infects you. Given an equal chance of having either disease, you reason that it does not matter which drug is administered to you—either way, your chances of surviving are 0.5.

You may not, however, have an equal chance of having either disease. If you knew that disease 1 were 100 times more likely to occur in the population, and if you knew that you had one of the two diseases, you would express a strong preference for receiving drug 1.

When you calculate the significance of main effects on unbalanced data, you must ask yourself why the data are unbalanced. If the data are unbalanced for random reasons and you are making predictions for a balanced population, then the test of the main effect makes perfect sense. If, however, the data are unbalanced because the underlying populations are unbalanced, and you are making predictions for such unbalanced populations, the test of the main effect may be practically—if not statistically—meaningless.

❏

▷ Example

Stata not only has the ability to perform ANOVA on unbalanced populations, it can perform ANOVA on populations that are so unbalanced that entire cells are missing. For instance, using our systolic-blood-pressure data, let's refit the model eliminating the drug-1–disease-1 cell. Since anova follows the same syntax as all other Stata commands, we can explicitly specify the data to be used by typing the if qualifier at the end of the anova command. In this case, we want to use the data that are not drug 1 and disease 1:

```
. anova systolic drug disease drug*disease if !(drug==1 & disease==1)
```

	Number of obs =		52	R-squared	= 0.4545
	Root MSE	= 10.1615		Adj R-squared =	0.3215

Source	Partial SS	df	MS	F	Prob > F
Model	3527.95897	10	352.795897	3.42	0.0025
drug	2686.57832	3	895.526107	8.67	0.0001
disease	327.792598	2	163.896299	1.59	0.2168
drug*disease	703.007602	5	140.60152	1.36	0.2586
Residual	4233.48333	41	103.255691		
Total	7761.44231	51	152.185143		

◁

❏ Technical Note

The test of the main effect of drug in the presence of missing cells is more complicated than that for unbalanced data. Our underlying tableau is now of the following form:

	Disease 1	Disease 2	Disease 3	
Drug 1		μ_{12}	μ_{13}	
Drug 2	μ_{21}	μ_{22}	μ_{23}	$\mu_{2\cdot}$
Drug 3	μ_{31}	μ_{32}	μ_{33}	$\mu_{3\cdot}$
Drug 4	μ_{41}	μ_{42}	μ_{43}	$\mu_{4\cdot}$
		$\mu_{\cdot 2}$	$\mu_{\cdot 3}$	

The hole in the drug-1–disease-1 cell indicates that the mean is unobserved. Considering the main effect of drug, the test is unchanged for the rows in which all the cells are defined:

$$\mu_{2\cdot} = \mu_{3\cdot} = \mu_{4\cdot}$$

The first row, however, requires special attention. In this case, we want the average outcome for drug 1, which is averaged over just diseases 2 and 3, to be equal to the average values of all other drugs averaged over those same two diseases:

$$\frac{\mu_{12} + \mu_{13}}{2} = \frac{\left(\mu_{22} + \mu_{23}\right)/2 + \left(\mu_{32} + \mu_{33}\right)/2 + \left(\mu_{42} + \mu_{43}\right)/2}{3}$$

Thus, the test contains three constraints:

$$\frac{\mu_{21} + \mu_{22} + \mu_{23}}{3} = \frac{\mu_{31} + \mu_{32} + \mu_{33}}{3}$$

$$\frac{\mu_{21} + \mu_{22} + \mu_{23}}{3} = \frac{\mu_{41} + \mu_{42} + \mu_{43}}{3}$$

$$\frac{\mu_{12} + \mu_{13}}{2} = \frac{\mu_{22} + \mu_{23} + \mu_{32} + \mu_{33} + \mu_{42} + \mu_{43}}{6}$$

❏

Stata can calculate two types of sums of squares, *partial* and *sequential*. If you do not specify which sums of squares to calculate, Stata calculates partial sums of squares. The technical notes above have gone into great detail about the definition and use of partial sums of squares. Use the sequential option to obtain sequential sums of squares.

❏ Technical Note

Before illustrating sequential sums of squares, consider one more feature of the partial sums. If you know how such things are calculated, you may worry that the terms must be specified in some particular order, that Stata would balk or, even worse, produce different results if you typed, say, anova drug*disease drug disease rather than anova drug disease drug*disease. We assure you that is not the case.

When you type a model, Stata internally reorganizes the terms, forms the cross-product matrix, inverts it, converts the result to an upper-Hermite form, and then performs the hypothesis tests. As a final touch, Stata reports the results in the same order that you typed the terms.

❏

▷ Example

You wish to estimate the effects on systolic blood pressure of drug and disease using sequential sums of squares. You want to introduce disease first, then drug, and finally, the interaction of drug and disease:

```
. anova systolic disease drug disease*drug, sequential
```

	Number of obs =	58	R-squared	= 0.4560
	Root MSE = 10.5096		Adj R-squared = 0.3259

Source	Seq. SS	df	MS	F	Prob > F
Model	4259.33851	11	387.212591	3.51	0.0013
disease	488.639383	2	244.319691	2.21	0.1210
drug	3063.43286	3	1021.14429	9.25	0.0001
disease*drug	707.266259	6	117.87771	1.07	0.3958
Residual	5080.81667	46	110.452536		
Total	9340.15517	57	163.862371		

The F statistic on disease is now 2.21. When we fitted this same model using partial sums of squares, the statistic was 1.88.

◁

N-way analysis of variance

You may include high-order interaction terms, such as a third-order interaction between the variables A, B, and C, by typing A*B*C.

▷ Example

You wish to determine the operating conditions that maximize yield for a manufacturing process. There are three temperature settings, two chemical supply companies, and two mixing methods under investigation. Three observations are obtained for each combination of these three factors.

```
. use http://www.stata-press.com/data/r8/manuf
(manufacturing process data)

. describe

Contains data from http://www.stata-press.com/data/r8/manuf.dta
  obs:            36                        manufacturing process data
  vars:            4                        5 Jul 2002 17:24
  size:          288 (93.5% of memory free)
```

variable name	storage type	display format	value label	variable label
temperature	byte	%9.0g	temp	machine temperature setting
chemical	byte	%9.0g	supplier	chemical supplier
method	byte	%9.0g	meth	mixing method
yield	byte	%9.0g		product yield

```
Sorted by:
```

You wish to perform a three-way factorial analysis of variance.

```
. anova yield temp chem temp*chem meth temp*meth chem*meth temp*chem*meth
```

		Number of obs =	36	R-squared	= 0.5474
		Root MSE	= 2.62996	Adj R-squared =	0.3399

Source	Partial SS	df	MS	F	Prob > F
Model	200.75	11	18.25	2.64	0.0227
temperature	30.50	2	15.25	2.20	0.1321
chemical	12.25	1	12.25	1.77	0.1958
temperature*chemical	24.50	2	12.25	1.77	0.1917
method	42.25	1	42.25	6.11	0.0209
temperature*method	87.50	2	43.75	6.33	0.0062
chemical*method	.25	1	.25	0.04	0.8508
temperature*chemical*method	3.50	2	1.75	0.25	0.7785
Residual	166.00	24	6.91666667		
Total	366.75	35	10.4785714		

The interaction between temperature and method appears to be the important story in these data. A table of means for this interaction is given below.

```
. table method temp, c(mean yield) row col f(%8.2f)
```

mixing method	machine temperature setting low	medium	high	Total
stir	7.50	6.00	6.00	6.50
fold	5.50	9.00	11.50	8.67
Total	6.50	7.50	8.75	7.58

You decide to use the folding method of mixing and a high temperature in your manufacturing process.

◁

Analysis of covariance

You can include multiple explanatory variables with the anova command, but unless you explicitly state otherwise, all the variables are interpreted as *categorical variables.* Using the continuous (*varlist*) option, you can designate variables as *continuous* and thus perform analysis of covariance.

▷ Example

Let's now return to the systolic-blood-pressure example. Remember that the data contained three variables: systolic, the increase in systolic blood pressure; disease, which of four diseases the patient endured; and drug, which of three drugs were administered. We have another variant of this dataset that includes one more variable, the age of the patient, age. (This example, which was based on real data, now enters the fictional world. We concocted the age data based on nothing more than our own fanciful imagination.)

```
. use http://www.stata-press.com/data/r8/sysage
(Systolic Blood Pressure Data)
. summarize age
```

Variable	Obs	Mean	Std. Dev.	Min	Max
age	58	45.15517	13.9985	20	73

Let's now estimate systolic as a function of drug, disease, age, and disease interacted with age:

```
. anova systolic drug disease age disease*age, continuous(age)
```

		Number of obs =	58	R-squared	=	0.6221
		Root MSE	= 8.48737	Adj R-squared =		0.5604

Source	Partial SS	df	MS	F	Prob > F
Model	5810.41855	8	726.302318	10.08	0.0000
drug	2791.94475	3	930.648251	12.92	0.0000
disease	129.092158	2	64.5460789	0.90	0.4148
age	1817.80067	1	1817.80067	25.23	0.0000
disease*age	43.4069507	2	21.7034754	0.30	0.7412
Residual	3529.73663	49	72.0354414		
Total	9340.15517	57	163.862371		

◁

We typed `anova systolic drug disease age disease*age, continuous(age)` to obtain the above estimates. Rather than typing `continuous(age)`, we could have typed `category(drug disease)`.

In general, we can specify either the continuous variables or the categorical variables. If we do not specify either option, Stata assumes that all the variables are categorical. If we specify the `continuous(`*varlist*`)` option, Stata assumes that the remaining variables are categorical. If we specify the `category(`*varlist*`)` option, Stata assumes that the remaining variables are continuous. We suggest typing whichever list is shorter.

You can type `class(`*varlist*`)` rather than `category(`*varlist*`)` if the word `class` is more appealing. They are synonyms.

Remember that you can specify interactions by typing *varname*`*`*varname*. You have seen examples of interacting categorical variables with categorical variables and, directly above, a categorical variable (`disease`) with a continuous variable (`age`).

You can also interact continuous variables with continuous variables. To include an age^2 term in our model, we could type `age*age`. If we also wanted to interact the categorical variable `disease` with the age^2 term, we could type `disease*age*age` (or even `age*disease*age`).

Nested designs

In addition to specifying interaction terms, nested terms can also be specified in an analysis of variance. A vertical bar is used to indicate nesting: A|B is read as A nested within B. A|B|C is read as A nested within B, which is nested within C. A|B*C is read as A is nested within the interaction of B and C. A*B|C is read as the interaction of A and B, which is nested within C.

Different error terms can be specified for different parts of the model. The forward slash is used to indicate that the next term in the model is the error term for what precedes it. For instance, `anova y A / B|A` indicates that the F test for A is to be tested using the mean square from B|A in the denominator. Error terms (terms following the slash) are generally not tested unless they are themselves followed by a slash. Residual error is the default error term.

For example, consider *A / B / C*, where *A*, *B*, and *C* may be arbitrarily complex terms. Then `anova` will report *A* tested by *B* and *B* tested by *C*. If we add one more slash on the end to form *A / B / C /*, then `anova` would also report *C* tested by the residual error.

▷ Example

You have collected data from a manufacturer that is evaluating which of five different brands of machinery to buy to perform a particular function in an assembly line. Twenty assembly-line employees were selected at random for training on these machines with four employees assigned to learn a particular machine. The output from each employee (operator) on the brand of machine for which they were trained was measured during four trial periods. In this example, the operator is nested within machine. Due to sickness and employee resignations, the final data are not balanced. The following table gives the mean output and sample size for each machine and operator combination.

```
. use http://www.stata-press.com/data/r8/machine
(machine data)
```

```
. table machine operator, c(mean output n output) col f(%8.2f)
```

five brands of machine	operator nested in machine				
	1	2	3	4	Total
1	9.15 2	9.48 4	8.27 3	8.20 4	8.75 13
2	15.03 3	11.55 2	11.45 2	11.52 4	12.47 11
3	11.27 3	10.13 3	11.13 3		10.84 9
4	16.10 3	18.97 3	15.35 4	16.60 3	16.65 13
5	15.30 4	14.35 4	10.43 3		13.63 11

Assuming that `operator` is random (i.e., you wish to infer to the larger population of possible operators) and `machine` is fixed (i.e., only these five machines are of interest), the typical test for `machine` uses `operator` nested within `machine` as the error term. `operator` nested within `machine` can be tested by residual error. Our earlier warning concerning designs with unplanned missing cells and/or unbalanced cell sizes also applies to interpreting the ANOVA results from this unbalanced nested example.

```
. anova output machine / operator|machine /
```

| | | | Number of obs = | 57 | R-squared | = 0.8661 |
| | | | Root MSE | = 1.47089 | Adj R-squared = | 0.8077 |

Source	Partial SS	df	MS	F	Prob > F
Model	545.822288	17	32.1071934	14.84	0.0000
machine	430.980792	4	107.745198	13.82	0.0001
operator|machine	101.353804	13	7.79644648		
operator|machine	101.353804	13	7.79644648	3.60	0.0009
Residual	84.3766582	39	2.16350406		
Total	630.198947	56	11.2535526		

Notice that `operator|machine` is preceded by a slash, indicating that it is the error term for the term(s) before it (in this case, `machine`). `operator|machine` is also followed by a slash that indicates it should be tested with residual error. Notice that the output lists the `operator|machine` term twice, once as the error term for machine, and again as a term tested by residual error. A line is placed in the ANOVA table to separate the two. In general, a dividing line is placed in the output to separate the terms into groups that are tested with the same error term. The overall model is tested by residual error, and is separated from the remainder of the table by a blank line at the top of the table.

The results indicate that the machines are not all equal and that there are significant differences between operators.

◁

▷ Example

A medical researcher comes to you for help in analyzing some data he has collected. Two skin-rash treatment protocols were tested at eight clinics (four clinics for each protocol). Three doctors were selected at random from each of the clinics to administer the particular protocol to four of their patients. Each patient was treated for four separate rash patches and the response was measured. The data are described below.

```
. use http://www.stata-press.com/data/r8/rash
(skin rash data)

. describe

Contains data from http://www.stata-press.com/data/r8/rash.dta
  obs:            384                          skin rash data
  vars:             5                          21 Jun 2002 14:29
  size:         3,456 (93.0% of memory free)   (_dta has notes)
```

variable name	storage type	display format	value label	variable label
response	byte	%9.0g		
treatment	byte	%9.0g		2 treatment protocols
clinic	byte	%9.0g		4 clinics per treatment
doctor	byte	%9.0g		3 doctors per clinic
patient	byte	%9.0g		4 patients per doctor

```
Sorted by:
```

The researcher wants to determine if the treatment protocols are significantly different. He would also like to know if clinic, doctor, or patient are significant effects. In this analysis, treatment is a fixed factor, whereas clinic, doctor, and patient are random factors. Your first thought when presented with these data is that there are more powerful experimental designs that could have been used. For instance, a better design would be to test both treatments on each patient. However, the data have already been collected, so you proceed with the analysis of this fully nested ANOVA design.

Notice that in the following anova command, we use abbreviations for the variable names. This can sometimes make long ANOVA model statements easier to read. Also, with larger ANOVA models, matsize may need to be increased; see [R] **matsize**.

(Continued on next page)

```
. set matsize 140
. anova response t / c|t / d|c|t / p|d|c|t /
                         Number of obs =      384    R-squared      =  0.5040
                         Root MSE      = 11.6192    Adj R-squared  =  0.3404

              Source |   Partial SS     df       MS             F      Prob > F

               Model |  39505.9896      95   415.852522          3.08    0.0000

           treatment |  4240.04167       1   4240.04167          9.79    0.0204
    clinic|treatment |  2599.48958       6   433.248264

    clinic|treatment |  2599.48958       6   433.248264          0.93    0.4982
doctor|clinic|treatment |  7429.58333    16   464.348958

doctor|clinic|treatment |  7429.58333    16   464.348958          1.32    0.2065
patient|doctor|clinic|
           treatment |  25236.875       72   350.512153

patient|doctor|clinic|
           treatment |  25236.875       72   350.512153          2.60    0.0000

            Residual |  38882.00       288   135.006944

               Total |  78387.9896     383   204.66838
```

You conclude that the two treatment protocols are significantly different. You also see that `clinic` and `doctor` are not significant while `patient` is significant. The mean response for each of the two treatment protocols is shown below.

```
. table treatment , c(mean response) f(%8.2f) stubwidth(11)
```

2 treatment protocols	mean(response)
1	39.18
2	45.83

Treatment protocol 2 gives the largest response. We will return to this example when we explore the use of `test` after `anova`.

◁

Mixed designs

An analysis of variance can consist of both nested and crossed terms. A split-plot ANOVA design provides an example.

▷ Example

Two reading programs and three skill enhancement techniques are under investigation. Ten classes of first grade students were randomly assigned so that five classes were taught with one reading program and another five classes were taught with the other. The 30 students in each class were divided into six groups with five students each. Within each class, the six groups were divided randomly so that each of the three skill enhancement techniques was taught to two of the groups within each class. At the end of the school year, a reading assessment test was administered to all the students. In this split-plot ANOVA, the whole-plot treatment is the two reading programs and the split-plot treatment is the three skill enhancement techniques.

```
. use http://www.stata-press.com/data/r8/reading
(Reading experiment data)

. describe
Contains data from http://www.stata-press.com/data/r8/reading.dta
  obs:           300                          Reading experiment data
  vars:            5                          5 Jul 2002 17:32
  size:         2,700 (86.2% of memory free)  (_dta has notes)
```

variable name	storage type	display format	value label	variable label
score	byte	%9.0g		reading score
program	byte	%9.0g		reading program
class	byte	%9.0g		class nested in program
skill	byte	%9.0g		skill enhancement technique
group	byte	%9.0g		group nested in class and skill

```
Sorted by:
```

In this split-plot ANOVA, the error term for program is class nested within program. The error term for skill and the program by skill interaction is the class by skill interaction nested within program. Other terms are also involved in the model, and can be seen below.

Our anova command is longer than will fit on a single line of this manual. Where we have chosen to break the command into multiple lines is arbitrary. If you were typing this command into Stata, you would just type along, and let Stata automatically wrap across lines as necessary.

```
. anova score prog / class|prog skill prog*skill / class*skill|prog
> / group|class*skill|prog /
```

```
                        Number of obs =     300     R-squared     =  0.3738
                        Root MSE      = 14.6268     Adj R-squared =  0.2199
```

Source	Partial SS	df	MS	F	Prob > F
Model	30656.5167	59	519.601977	2.43	0.0000
program	4493.07	1	4493.07	8.73	0.0183
class|program	4116.61333	8	514.576667		
skill	1122.64667	2	561.323333	1.54	0.2450
program*skill	5694.62	2	2847.31	7.80	0.0043
class*skill|program	5841.46667	16	365.091667		
class*skill|program	5841.46667	16	365.091667	1.17	0.3463
group|class*skill|program	9388.1	30	312.936667		
group|class*skill|program	9388.1	30	312.936667	1.46	0.0636
Residual	51346.4	240	213.943333		
Total	82002.9167	299	274.257246		

The program*skill term is significant as is the program term for these particular data. Let us look at a table of mean scores by program and skill.

```
. table prog skill, c(mean score) row col f(%8.2f)
```

reading program	skill enhancement technique 1	2	3	Total
1	68.16	52.86	61.54	60.85
2	50.70	56.54	52.10	53.11
Total	59.43	54.70	56.82	56.98

It appears that the first reading program and the first skill enhancement technique perform best when combined. It is also clear that there is an interaction between the reading program and the skill enhancement technique.

◁

❑ Technical Note

There are several valid ways to write complicated anova terms. In the reading experiment example, we had a term group|class*skill|program. This can be read as group is nested within both class and skill and further nested within program. You can also write this term as group|class*skill*program or group|program*class*skill or group|skill*class|program etc. All variations will produce the same result. Some people prefer having only one '|' in a term and would use group|class*skill*program, which is read as group nested within class, skill, and program.

❑

Latin square designs

It is possible to use anova to analyze a Latin square design. Consider the following example, published in Snedecor and Cochran (1989).

▷ Example

Data from a Latin square design is as follows:

Row	Column 1	Column 2	Column 3	Column 4	Column 5
1	257(B)	230(E)	279(A)	287(C)	202(D)
2	245(D)	283(A)	245(E)	280(B)	260(C)
3	182(E)	252(B)	280(C)	246(D)	250(A)
4	203(A)	204(C)	227(D)	193(E)	259(B)
5	231(C)	271(D)	266(B)	334(A)	338(E)

In Stata, the data might appear as follows:

(Continued on next page)

```
. use http://www.stata-press.com/data/r8/latinsq
. list
```

	row	c1	c2	c3	c4	c5
1.	1	257	230	279	287	202
2.	2	245	283	245	280	260
3.	3	182	252	280	246	250
4.	4	203	204	227	193	259
5.	5	231	271	266	334	338

Before anova can be used on these data, the data must be organized so that the outcome measurement is in one column. reshape is not sufficient for this task because there is information about the treatments in the sequence of these observations. pkshape is designed to reshape this type of data; see [R] **pkshape**.

```
. pkshape row row c1-c5, order(beacd daebc ebcda acdeb cdbae)
. list
```

	sequence	outcome	treat	carry	period
1.	1	257	1	0	1
2.	2	245	5	0	1
3.	3	182	2	0	1
4.	4	203	3	0	1
5.	5	231	4	0	1
6.	1	230	2	1	2
7.	2	283	3	5	2
8.	3	252	1	2	2
9.	4	204	4	3	2
10.	5	271	5	4	2
11.	1	279	3	2	3
12.	2	245	2	3	3
13.	3	280	4	1	3
14.	4	227	5	4	3
15.	5	266	1	5	3
16.	1	287	4	3	4
17.	2	280	1	2	4
18.	3	246	5	4	4
19.	4	193	2	5	4
20.	5	334	3	1	4
21.	1	202	5	4	5
22.	2	260	4	1	5
23.	3	250	3	5	5
24.	4	259	1	2	5
25.	5	338	2	3	5

(*Continued on next page*)

```
. anova outcome sequence period treat
```

	Number of obs =	25	R-squared	= 0.6536
	Root MSE	= 32.4901	Adj R-squared =	0.3073

Source	Partial SS	df	MS	F	Prob > F
Model	23904.08	12	1992.00667	1.89	0.1426
sequence	13601.36	4	3400.34	3.22	0.0516
period	6146.16	4	1536.54	1.46	0.2758
treat	4156.56	4	1039.14	0.98	0.4523
Residual	12667.28	12	1055.60667		
Total	36571.36	24	1523.80667		

◁

These methods will work with any type of Latin square design, including those with replicated measurements. For more information, see [R] **pk**, [R] **pkcross**, and [R] **pkshape**.

Repeated measures analysis of variance

One approach for analyzing repeated measures data is to use MANOVA; see [R] **manova**. In this approach, the data are placed in wide form (see [R] **reshape**), and the repeated measures enter the MANOVA as dependent variables.

A second approach for analyzing repeated measures is to use anova. However, one of the underlying assumptions for the F tests in ANOVA is independence of the observations. In a repeated measures design, this assumption is almost certainly violated, or is at least suspect. In a repeated measures ANOVA, the subjects (or whatever the experimental units are called) are observed for each level of one or more of the other categorical variables in the model. These variables are called the repeated measure variables. Observations from the same subject are likely to be correlated.

The approach used in repeated measures ANOVA to correct for this lack of independence is to apply a correction to the degrees of freedom of the F test for terms in the model that involve repeated measures. This correction factor, ϵ, lies between the reciprocal of the degrees of freedom for the repeated term and 1. Box (1954) provided the pioneering work in this area. Milliken and Johnson (1984) refer to the lower bound of this correction factor as Box's conservative correction factor. Winer, Brown, and Michels (1991) simply call it the conservative correction factor.

Geisser and Greenhouse (1958) provide an estimate for the correction factor that is called the Greenhouse–Geisser ϵ. This value is estimated from the data. Huynh and Feldt (1976) show that the Greenhouse–Geisser ϵ tends to be conservatively biased. They provide a revised correction factor called the Huynh–Feldt ϵ. The Huynh–Feldt ϵ can exceed 1. When this happens, it is set to 1. Thus, there is a natural ordering for these correction factors:

$$\text{Box's conservative } \epsilon \leq \text{Greenhouse–Geisser } \epsilon \leq \text{Huynh–Feldt } \epsilon \leq 1$$

A correction factor of 1 is the same as no correction.

anova with the repeated() option computes these correction factors and displays the revised test results in a table that follows the standard ANOVA table. In the resulting table, H-F stands for Huynh–Feldt, G-G stands for Greenhouse–Geisser, and Box stands for Box's conservative ϵ.

▷ Example

This example is taken from Table 4.3 of Winer, Brown, and Michels (1991). The reaction time for five subjects each tested with four drugs was recorded in the variable score. Here is a table of the data (see [P] **tabdisp** if unfamiliar with tabdisp):

```
. use http://www.stata-press.com/data/r8/t43
(T4.3 -- Winer, Brown, Michels)
. tabdisp person drug, cellvar(score)
```

person	drug 1	2	3	4
1	30	28	16	34
2	14	18	10	22
3	24	20	18	30
4	38	34	20	44
5	26	28	14	30

drug is the repeated variable in this simple repeated measures ANOVA example. The ANOVA is specified as follows:

```
. anova score person drug, repeated(drug)
```

		Number of obs =	20	R-squared	= 0.9244
		Root MSE	= 3.06594	Adj R-squared =	0.8803

Source	Partial SS	df	MS	F	Prob > F
Model	1379	7	197	20.96	0.0000
person	680.8	4	170.2	18.11	0.0001
drug	698.2	3	232.733333	24.76	0.0000
Residual	112.8	12	9.4		
Total	1491.8	19	78.5157895		

```
Between-subjects error term:  person
                    Levels:  5          (4 df)
     Lowest b.s.e. variable:  person

Repeated variable: drug
                              Huynh-Feldt epsilon        = 1.0789
                             *Huynh-Feldt epsilon reset to 1.0000
                              Greenhouse-Geisser epsilon = 0.6049
                              Box's conservative epsilon = 0.3333
```

Source	df	F	Prob > F Regular	H-F	G-G	Box
drug	3	24.76	0.0000	0.0000	0.0006	0.0076
Residual	12					

Notice that in this case, the Huynh–Feldt ϵ is 1.0789, which is larger than 1. It is reset to 1, which is the same as making no adjustment to the standard test computed in the main ANOVA table. The Greenhouse–Geisser ϵ is 0.6049, and its associated p-value is computed from an F ratio of 24.76 using 1.8147 ($= 3\epsilon$) and 7.2588 ($= 12\epsilon$) degrees of freedom. Box's conservative ϵ is set equal to the reciprocal of the degrees of freedom for the repeated term. In this case, it is 1/3, so that Box's conservative test is computed using 1 and 4 degrees of freedom for the observed F ratio of 24.76.

Even using Box's conservative ϵ, drug is significant with a p-value of 0.0076. The following table gives the mean score (i.e., response time) for each of the four drugs:

```
. table drug, c(mean score) f(%8.2f)
```

drug	mean(score)
1	26.40
2	25.60
3	15.60
4	32.00

The ANOVA table for this example provides an F test for person. This F test should be ignored. An appropriate test for person would require replication (i.e., multiple measurements for person and drug combinations). Also, without replication there is no test available for investigating the interaction between person and drug.

◁

▷ Example

Table 7.7 of Winer, Brown, and Michels (1991) provides another repeated measures ANOVA example. There are four dial shapes and two methods for calibrating dials. Subjects are nested within calibration method, and an accuracy score is obtained. The data are shown below.

```
. use http://www.stata-press.com/data/r8/t77
(T7.7 -- Winer, Brown, Michels)
. tabdisp shape subject calib, cell(score)
```

4 dial shapes	2 methods for calibrating dials and subject nested in calib					
	——— 1 ———			——— 2 ———		
	1	2	3	1	2	3
1	0	3	4	4	5	7
2	0	1	3	2	4	5
3	5	5	6	7	6	8
4	3	4	2	8	6	9

The calibration method and dial shapes are fixed factors, whereas subjects are random. The appropriate test for calibration method uses the nested subject term as the error term. Both the dial shape and the interaction between dial shape and calibration method are tested with the dial shape by subject interaction nested within calibration method. In this case, we drop this term from the anova command, and it becomes residual error. The dial shape is the repeated variable, since each subject is tested with all four dial shapes. Here is the anova command that produces the desired results:

(Continued on next page)

```
. anova score calib / subject|calib shape calib*shape, repeated(shape)
```

| | Number of obs = | 24 | R-squared | = 0.8925 |
| | Root MSE | = 1.11181 | Adj R-squared | = 0.7939 |

Source	Partial SS	df	MS	F	Prob > F
Model	123.125	11	11.1931818	9.06	0.0003
calib	51.0416667	1	51.0416667	11.89	0.0261
subject|calib	17.1666667	4	4.29166667		
shape	47.4583333	3	15.8194444	12.80	0.0005
calib*shape	7.45833333	3	2.48611111	2.01	0.1662
Residual	14.8333333	12	1.23611111		
Total	137.958333	23	5.99818841		

```
Between-subjects error term:  subject|calib
                     Levels:  6          (4 df)
       Lowest b.s.e. variable:  subject
        Covariance pooled over:  calib     (for repeated variable)

Repeated variable: shape
                                 Huynh-Feldt epsilon      = 0.8483
                                 Greenhouse-Geisser epsilon = 0.4751
                                 Box's conservative epsilon = 0.3333
```

| | | | | ————— Prob > F ————— | | |
Source	df	F	Regular	H-F	G-G	Box
shape	3	12.80	0.0005	0.0011	0.0099	0.0232
calib*shape	3	2.01	0.1662	0.1791	0.2152	0.2291
Residual	12					

The repeated measure ϵ corrections are applied to any terms that are tested in the main ANOVA table and have the repeated variable in the term. These ϵ corrections are given in a table below the main ANOVA table. In this case, the repeated measures tests for shape and calib*shape are presented.

Calibration method is significant, as is dial shape. The interaction between calibration method and dial shape is not significant. The repeated measure ϵ corrections do not change these conclusions, but they do change the significance level for the tests on shape and calib*shape. Also notice that in this example, unlike the previous example, the Huynh–Feldt ϵ is less than 1.

The following table gives the mean score for dial shapes and calibration method. Since the interaction was not significant, we focus our attention on the row and the column labeled "Total".

```
. table shape calib, c(mean score) row col f(%8.2f)
```

4 dial shapes	2 methods for calibrating dials		
	1	2	Total
1	2.33	5.33	3.83
2	1.33	3.67	2.50
3	5.33	7.00	6.17
4	3.00	7.67	5.33
Total	3.00	5.92	4.46

◁

❑ Technical Note

The computation of the Greenhouse–Geisser and Huynh–Feldt epsilons in a repeated measures ANOVA requires the number of levels and degrees of freedom for the between-subjects error term. It also requires a value computed from a pooled covariance matrix. The observations are grouped based on all but the lowest level variable in the between-subjects error term. The covariance over the repeated variables is computed for each resulting group, and then these covariance matrices are pooled. The dimension of the pooled covariance matrix is the number of levels of the repeated variable (or combination of levels for multiple repeated variables). In the previous example, there are four levels of the repeated variable (shape), so the resulting covariance matrix is 4×4.

The anova command attempts automatically to determine the between-subjects error term and the lowest level variable in the between-subjects error term in order to group the observations for computation of the pooled covariance matrix. anova will issue an error message indicating that the bse() or bseunit() option is required when it is unable to determine them. The user may also override the default selections of anova by specifying the bse(), bseunit(), or grouping() options. The term specified in the bse() option must be a term in the ANOVA model.

The default selection for the between-subjects error term (the bse() option) is the interaction of the nonrepeated categorical variables in the ANOVA model. The first variable listed in the between-subjects error term is automatically selected as the lowest level variable in the between-subjects error term, but can be overridden with the bseunit() option. This is often a term such as subject or subsample within subject and is most often listed first in the term due to the nesting notation of ANOVA. This makes sense in most repeated measures ANOVA designs when the terms of the model are written in standard form. For instance, in the previous example, there are three categorical variables (subject, calib, and shape), with shape the repeated variable. In this case, anova looked for a term involving only subject and calib to determine the between-subjects error term. It found subject|calib as the term with 6 levels and 4 degrees of freedom. anova then picked subject as the default for the bseunit() option (the lowest variable in the between-subjects error term), since it was listed first in the term.

The grouping of observations proceeds based on the different combinations of values of the variables in the between-subjects error term excluding the lowest level variable (as found by default or as specified with the bseunit() option). The user may specify the grouping() option to change the default grouping used in computing the pooled covariance matrix.

The between-subjects error term, number of levels, degrees of freedom, lowest variable in the term, and grouping information are presented after the main ANOVA table and before the rest of the repeated measures output.

❑

▷ Example

Data with two repeated variables are given in Table 7.13 of Winer, Brown, and Michels (1991). The accuracy scores of subjects making adjustments to three dials during three different periods of time are recorded. Three subjects are exposed to a certain noise background level, while a different set of three subjects is exposed to a different noise background level. Here is a table of accuracy scores for the noise, subject, period, and dial variables:

(Continued on next page)

```
. use http://www.stata-press.com/data/r8/t713
(T7.13 -- Winer, Brown, Michels)
. tabdisp subject dial period, by(noise) cell(score) stubwidth(11)
```

noise background and subject nested in noise	10 minute time periods and dial								
	——— 1 ———			——— 2 ———			——— 3 ———		
	1	2	3	1	2	3	1	2	3
1									
1	45	53	60	40	52	57	28	37	46
2	35	41	50	30	37	47	25	32	41
3	60	65	75	58	54	70	40	47	50
2									
1	50	48	61	25	34	51	16	23	35
2	42	45	55	30	37	43	22	27	37
3	56	60	77	40	39	57	31	29	46

noise, period, and dial are fixed, whereas subject is random. Both period and dial are repeated variables. The ANOVA for this example is specified below.

```
. anova score noise / subject|noise period noise*period
> / period*subject|noise dial noise*dial
> / dial*subject|noise period*dial noise*period*dial, repeated(period dial)
```

	Number of obs =	54	R-squared	=	0.9872
	Root MSE = 2.81859		Adj R-squared =		0.9576

Source	Partial SS	df	MS	F	Prob > F
Model	9797.72222	37	264.803303	33.33	0.0000
noise	468.166667	1	468.166667	0.75	0.4348
subject|noise	2491.11111	4	622.777778		
period	3722.33333	2	1861.16667	63.39	0.0000
noise*period	333.00	2	166.50	5.67	0.0293
period*subject|noise	234.888889	8	29.3611111		
dial	2370.33333	2	1185.16667	89.82	0.0000
noise*dial	50.3333333	2	25.1666667	1.91	0.2102
dial*subject|noise	105.555556	8	13.1944444		
period*dial	10.6666667	4	2.66666667	0.34	0.8499
noise*period*dial	11.3333333	4	2.83333333	0.36	0.8357
Residual	127.111111	16	7.94444444		
Total	9924.83333	53	187.261006		

(Continued on next page)

```
Between-subjects error term:  subject|noise
                    Levels:  6           (4 df)
        Lowest b.s.e. variable:  subject
        Covariance pooled over:  noise       (for repeated variables)
Repeated variable: period
                                    Huynh-Feldt epsilon          =  1.0668
                                    *Huynh-Feldt epsilon reset to 1.0000
                                    Greenhouse-Geisser epsilon =  0.6476
                                    Box's conservative epsilon =  0.5000

                                            ————— Prob > F —————
              Source  |   df      F     Regular    H-F      G-G       Box
      ————————————————+————————————————————————————————————————————————————
              period  |    2    63.39   0.0000   0.0000   0.0003    0.0013
        noise*period  |    2     5.67   0.0293   0.0293   0.0569    0.0759
 period*subject|noise |    8


Repeated variable: dial
                                    Huynh-Feldt epsilon          =  2.0788
                                    *Huynh-Feldt epsilon reset to 1.0000
                                    Greenhouse-Geisser epsilon =  0.9171
                                    Box's conservative epsilon =  0.5000

                                            ————— Prob > F —————
              Source  |   df      F     Regular    H-F      G-G       Box
      ————————————————+————————————————————————————————————————————————————
                dial  |    2    89.82   0.0000   0.0000   0.0000    0.0007
          noise*dial  |    2     1.91   0.2102   0.2102   0.2152    0.2394
   dial*subject|noise |    8


Repeated variables: period*dial
                                    Huynh-Feldt epsilon          =  1.3258
                                    *Huynh-Feldt epsilon reset to 1.0000
                                    Greenhouse-Geisser epsilon =  0.5134
                                    Box's conservative epsilon =  0.2500

                                            ————— Prob > F —————
              Source  |   df      F     Regular    H-F      G-G       Box
      ————————————————+————————————————————————————————————————————————————
           period*dial|    4     0.34   0.8499   0.8499   0.7295    0.5934
     noise*period*dial|    4     0.36   0.8357   0.8357   0.7156    0.5825
             Residual |   16
```

For each repeated variable and for each combination of interactions of repeated variables, there are different ϵ correction values. The anova command produces tables for each applicable combination.

The two most significant factors in this model appear to be dial and period. The noise by period interaction also may be significant depending on which correction factor you use. Below are tables of the mean accuracy score for dial and for period by noise.

```
. table dial, c(mean score) f(%8.2f)
```

dial	mean(score)
1	37.39
2	42.22
3	53.22

```
. table noise period, c(mean score) f(%8.2f) row col stubwidth(10)
```

noise background	10 minute time periods 1	2	3	Total
1	53.78	49.44	38.44	47.22
2	54.89	39.56	29.56	41.33
Total	54.33	44.50	34.00	44.28

We see that dial shape 3 produces the highest score, and that the scores tend to decrease over the time periods.

◁

The previous example had two repeated measurement variables. Up to four repeated measurement variables may be specified in the anova command.

Weighted data

Like all estimation commands, anova can produce estimates on weighted data. See [U] **14.1.6 weight** for details on specifying the weight.

▷ Example

You wish to investigate the prevalence of byssinosis, a form of pneumoconiosis to which workers exposed to cotton dust are subject. You have data on 5,419 workers in a large cotton mill. You know whether each worker smokes, his or her race, and the dustiness of the work area. The variables are

smokes	Smoker or nonsmoker in the last five years.
race	White or other.
workplace	1 (most dusty), 2 (less dusty), 3 (least dusty).

You wish to fit an ANOVA model explaining the prevalence of byssinosis according to a full factorial model of smokes, race, and workplace.

The data are unbalanced. Moreover, although you have data on 5,419 workers, the data are grouped according to the explanatory variables along with some other variables, resulting in 72 observations. For each observation, you know the number of workers in the group (pop), the prevalence of byssinosis (prob), and the values of the three explanatory variables. Thus, you wish to fit a three-way factorial model on grouped data.

We begin by showing you a bit of the data. The data are from Higgins and Koch (1977).

(Continued on next page)

```
. use http://www.stata-press.com/data/r8/byssin
(Byssinosis incidence)

. describe

Contains data from http://www.stata-press.com/data/r8/byssin.dta
  obs:            72                          Byssinosis incidence
 vars:             5                          21 Jun 2002 14:25
 size:         1,152 (89.7% of memory free)
```

variable name	storage type	display format	value label	variable label
smokes	int	%8.0g	smokes	Smokes
race	int	%8.0g	race	Race
workplace	int	%8.0g	workplace	
				Dustiness of workplace
pop	int	%8.0g		Population size
prob	float	%9.0g		Prevalence of byssinosis

```
Sorted by:

. list in 1/5, abbrev(10) divider
```

	smokes	race	workplace	pop	prob
1.	yes	white	most	40	.075
2.	yes	white	less	74	0
3.	yes	white	least	260	.0076923
4.	yes	other	most	164	.152439
5.	yes	other	less	88	0

The first observation in the data represents a group of 40 white workers who smoke and work in a "most" dusty work area. Of those 40 workers, 7.5% have byssinosis. The second observation represents a group of 74 white workers who also smoke, but who work in a "less" dusty environment. None of those workers has byssinosis.

Almost every Stata command allows weights. In this case, we want to weight the data by pop. We can, for instance, make a table of the number of workers by their smoking status and race:

```
. tabulate smokes race [freq=pop]
```

	Race		
Smokes	other	white	Total
no	799	1,431	2,230
yes	1,104	2,085	3,189
Total	1,903	3,516	5,419

The [freq=pop] at the end of the tabulate command tells Stata to count each observation as representing pop persons. When making the tally, tabulate treats the first observation as representing 40 workers, the second as representing 74 workers, and so on.

Similarly, we can make a table of the dustiness of the workplace:

(Continued on next page)

```
. tabulate workplace [freq=pop]
```

Dustiness of workplace	Freq.	Percent	Cum.
least	3,450	63.66	63.66
less	1,300	23.99	87.65
most	669	12.35	100.00
Total	5,419	100.00	

We can discover the average incidence of byssinosis among these workers by typing

```
. summarize prob [freq=pop]
```

Variable	Obs	Mean	Std. Dev.	Min	Max
prob	5419	.0304484	.0567373	0	.287037

We discover that 3.04% of these workers have byssinosis. Across all cells, the byssinosis rates vary from 0 to 28.7%. Just to prove to you that there might be something here, let's obtain the average incidence rates according to the dustiness of the workplace:

```
. table workplace smokes race [freq=pop], c(mean prob)
```

Dustiness of workplace	Race and Smokes			
	—— other ——		—— white ——	
	no	yes	no	yes
least	.0107527	.0101523	.0081549	.0162774
less	.02	.0081633	.0136612	.0143149
most	.0820896	.1679105	.0833333	.2295082

Enough preliminary. Let's now fit the ANOVA model.

```
. anova prob workplace smokes race workplace*smokes workplace*race
> smokes*race workplace*smokes*race  [aweight=pop]
(sum of wgt is    5.4190e+03)
```

	Number of obs = 65		R-squared = 0.8300		
	Root MSE = .025902		Adj R-squared = 0.7948		
Source	Partial SS	df	MS	F	Prob > F
Model	.173646538	11	.015786049	23.53	0.0000
workplace	.097625175	2	.048812588	72.76	0.0000
smokes	.013030812	1	.013030812	19.42	0.0001
race	.001094723	1	.001094723	1.63	0.2070
workplace*smokes	.019690342	2	.009845171	14.67	0.0000
workplace*race	.001352516	2	.000676258	1.01	0.3718
smokes*race	.001662874	1	.001662874	2.48	0.1214
workplace*smokes*race	.000950841	2	.00047542	0.71	0.4969
Residual	.035557766	53	.000670901		
Total	.209204304	64	.003268817		

Of course, if we want to see the underlying regression, we could type anova, regress, or simply regress.

◁

Obtaining the covariance matrix

After estimating with `anova`, you can obtain the covariance matrix of the estimators in the same way as after `regress`. You can refer to e(V) as in `matrix list e(V)`. (Alternatively, you can use the `vce` command; see [R] **vce**.)

Testing effects

After fitting an ANOVA model using the `anova` command, you can test for the significance of effects in the ANOVA table as well as effects that are not reported in the ANOVA table by using the `test` command. You follow `test` by the list of effects that you wish to test. By default, `test` uses the residual mean square error in the denominator of the F ratio. You can specify other error terms using the slash notation, just as you would with `anova`.

▷ Example

Returning to our byssinosis data, we can easily obtain a test on a particular term from the ANOVA table. Here are two examples:

```
. test smokes
```

Source	Partial SS	df	MS	F	Prob > F
smokes	.013030812	1	.013030812	19.42	0.0001
Residual	.035557766	53	.000670901		

```
. test smokes*race
```

Source	Partial SS	df	MS	F	Prob > F
smokes*race	.001662874	1	.001662874	2.48	0.1214
Residual	.035557766	53	.000670901		

Both of these tests use residual error by default, and agree with the ANOVA table produced earlier.

◁

❏ Technical Note

After `anova`, you can use the '/' syntax in `test` to perform tests with a variety of non-$\sigma^2 I$ error structures. However, be warned that in most unbalanced models, the mean squares are not independent and do not have equal expectations under the null hypothesis. Also be warned that you assume responsibility for the validity of the test statistic.

❏

▷ Example

We return to the nested ANOVA example where five brands of machinery were compared in an assembly line. We can obtain appropriate tests for the nested terms using `test`, even if we had run the `anova` command without initially indicating the proper error terms.

```
. use http://www.stata-press.com/data/r8/machine
(machine data)
```

```
. anova output machine operator|machine
```

	Number of obs =	57	R-squared	= 0.8661
	Root MSE	= 1.47089	Adj R-squared =	0.8077

Source	Partial SS	df	MS	F	Prob > F
Model	545.822288	17	32.1071934	14.84	0.0000
machine	430.980792	4	107.745198	49.80	0.0000
operator|machine	101.353804	13	7.79644648	3.60	0.0009
Residual	84.3766582	39	2.16350406		
Total	630.198947	56	11.2535526		

In this ANOVA table, `machine` is tested with residual error. With this particular nested design, the appropriate error term for testing `machine` is `operator` nested within `machine`. This is easily obtained from `test`.

```
. test machine / operator|machine
```

Source	Partial SS	df	MS	F	Prob > F
machine	430.980792	4	107.745198	13.82	0.0001
operator|machine	101.353804	13	7.79644648		

This result from `test` matches what we obtained from our original `anova` command as presented in our discussion of nested designs.

◁

▷ Example

The other nested ANOVA example was based on the skin-rash data. The ANOVA table is presented here again. As before, we will use abbreviations of variable names in typing the commands.

```
. use http://www.stata-press.com/data/r8/rash
(skin rash data)
. anova response t / c|t / d|c|t / p|d|c|t /
```

	Number of obs =	384	R-squared	= 0.5040
	Root MSE	= 11.6192	Adj R-squared =	0.3404

Source	Partial SS	df	MS	F	Prob > F
Model	39505.9896	95	415.852522	3.08	0.0000
treatment	4240.04167	1	4240.04167	9.79	0.0204
clinic|treatment	2599.48958	6	433.248264		
clinic|treatment	2599.48958	6	433.248264	0.93	0.4982
doctor|clinic|treatment	7429.58333	16	464.348958		
doctor|clinic|treatment	7429.58333	16	464.348958	1.32	0.2065
patient|doctor|clinic| treatment	25236.875	72	350.512153		
patient|doctor|clinic| treatment	25236.875	72	350.512153	2.60	0.0000
Residual	38882.00	288	135.006944		
Total	78387.9896	383	204.66838		

In practice, it is often beneficial to pool nonsignificant nested terms to increase the power of tests on remaining terms. One rule of thumb is to allow the pooling of a term whose p-value is larger than 0.25. In this skin-rash example, the p-value for the test of clinic is 0.4982. This indicates that the clinic effect is negligible and might be ignored. Currently, treatment is tested by clinic|treatment, which has only 6 degrees of freedom. If we pool the clinic and doctor terms and use this pooled estimate as the error term for treatment, we would have a term with 22 degrees of freedom.

Below are two tests. The first is a test of treatment with the pooled clinic and doctor terms. The second is a test of this pooled term by patient.

```
. test t / c|t d|c|t
```

Source	Partial SS	df	MS	F	Prob > F
treatment	4240.04167	1	4240.04167	9.30	0.0059
clinic|treatment doctor| clinic|treatment	10029.0729	22	455.866951		

```
. test c|t d|c|t / p|d|c|t
```

Source	Partial SS	df	MS	F	Prob > F
clinic|treatment doctor| clinic|treatment patient|doctor|clinic|	10029.0729	22	455.866951	1.30	0.2014
treatment	25236.875	72	350.512153		

Notice that in the first example, we included two terms after the forward slash (c|t and d|c|t). test after anova allows multiple terms both before and after the slash. The terms before the slash are combined, and are then tested by the combined terms that follow the slash (or residual error if no slash is present).

The p-value for treatment using the pooled term is 0.0059. Originally, it was 0.0204. The increase in the power of the test is due to the increase in degrees of freedom for the pooled error term.

We can get identical results if we drop clinic from the anova model. (Realize that this dataset has unique numbers for each doctor so that there is no confusion of doctors when clinic is dropped.)

```
. anova response t / d|t / p|d|t /
```

	Number of obs =	384	R-squared	=	0.5040
	Root MSE	= 11.6192	Adj R-squared =		0.3404

Source	Partial SS	df	MS	F	Prob > F
Model	39505.9896	95	415.852522	3.08	0.0000
treatment	4240.04167	1	4240.04167	9.30	0.0059
doctor|treatment	10029.0729	22	455.866951		
doctor|treatment	10029.0729	22	455.866951	1.30	0.2014
patient|doctor| treatment	25236.875	72	350.512153		
patient|doctor| treatment	25236.875	72	350.512153	2.60	0.0000
Residual	38882.00	288	135.006944		
Total	78387.9896	383	204.66838		

This agrees with our earlier test results.

◁

Another example of `test` after `anova` is given as the last example in the section *anova as an alternative to regress*. In that example, two terms from the `anova` are jointly tested (pooled).

Obtaining symbolic forms

`test` can also produce the symbolic form of the estimable functions and symbolic forms for particular tests.

▷ Example

After fitting an ANOVA model, you type `test, symbolic` to obtain the symbolic form of the estimable functions. For instance, returning to our blood-pressure data, let's begin by re-estimating `systolic` on `drug`, `disease`, and `drug*disease`:

```
. use http://www.stata-press.com/data/r8/systolic
(Systolic Blood Pressure Data)
. anova systolic drug disease drug*disease
```

	Number of obs =	58	R-squared	=	0.4560
	Root MSE	= 10.5096	Adj R-squared =		0.3259

Source	Partial SS	df	MS	F	Prob > F
Model	4259.33851	11	387.212591	3.51	0.0013
drug	2997.47186	3	999.157287	9.05	0.0001
disease	415.873046	2	207.936523	1.88	0.1637
drug*disease	707.266259	6	117.87771	1.07	0.3958
Residual	5080.81667	46	110.452536		
Total	9340.15517	57	163.862371		

To obtain the symbolic form of the estimable functions, type

```
. test, symbolic
_cons           r0
drug
        1       r1
        2       r2
        3       r3
        4       r0 - (r1+r2+r3)
disease
        1       r5
        2       r6
        3       r0 - (r5+r6)
drug*disease
    1   1       r8
    1   2       r9
    1   3       r1 - (r8+r9)
    2   1       r11
    2   2       r12
    2   3       r2 - (r11+r12)
    3   1       r14
    3   2       r15
    3   3       r3 - (r14+r15)
    4   1       r5 - (r8+r11+r14)
    4   2       r6 - (r9+r12+r15)
    4   3       r0 - (r1+r2+r3+r5+r6-r8-r9-r11-r12-r14-r15)
```

◁

▷ Example

To obtain the symbolic form for a particular test, you type test *term* [*term* ...], symbolic. For instance, the symbolic form for the test of the main effect of drug is

```
. test drug, symbolic
_cons          0
drug
        1       r1
        2       r2
        3       r3
        4       -(r1+r2+r3)
disease
        1       0
        2       0
        3       0
drug*disease
    1   1       1/3 r1
    1   2       1/3 r1
    1   3       1/3 r1
    2   1       1/3 r2
    2   2       1/3 r2
    2   3       1/3 r2
    3   1       1/3 r3
    3   2       1/3 r3
    3   3       1/3 r3
    4   1       -1/3 (r1+r2+r3)
    4   2       -1/3 (r1+r2+r3)
    4   3       -1/3 (r1+r2+r3)
```

If we omit the symbolic option, we instead see the result of the test:

```
. test drug
```

Source	Partial SS	df	MS	F	Prob > F
drug	2997.47186	3	999.157287	9.05	0.0001
Residual	5080.81667	46	110.452536		

◁

Testing coefficients

The test command will allow you to perform tests directly on the coefficients of the underlying regression model. When you specify the expressions, you must enclose references to coefficients in _coef[]; see [U] **16.5 Accessing coefficients and standard errors**. For instance, the coefficient on the first level of drug and the second level of disease is referred to as _coef[drug[1]*disease[2]]. If you were to omit the _coef[], Stata would think that you are trying to multiply two things together rather than referring to the coefficient on the interaction of two terms.

▷ Example

Let's begin by testing whether the coefficient on the first drug is equal to the coefficient on the second in our blood-pressure data. We have already fitted the model anova systolic drug disease drug*disease, and you can see the results of that estimation in the opening example of *Obtaining symbolic forms*. Even though we have done quite a bit since we fitted the model, Stata still remembers and we can perform tests at any time.

```
. test _coef[drug[1]]=_coef[drug[2]]

 ( 1)   drug[1] - drug[2] = 0

          F(  1,    46) =     0.12
                 Prob > F =     0.7272
```

We find that the two coefficients are not significantly different, at least at any significance level smaller than 73%. Let's now add the constraint that the coefficient on the first drug interacted with the first disease is equal to the coefficient on the second drug again interacted with the first disease. We do that by typing the new constraint and adding the `accumulate` option:

```
. test _coef[drug[1]*disease[1]]=_coef[drug[2]*disease[1]], accumulate

 ( 1)   drug[1] - drug[2] = 0
 ( 2)   drug[1]*disease[1] - drug[2]*disease[1] = 0

          F(  2,    46) =     0.08
                 Prob > F =     0.9200
```

Let's continue. Our goal is to determine whether the first drug is significantly different from the second drug. So far, our test includes the equality of the two drug coefficients along with the equality of the two drug coefficients when interacted with the first disease. We must add two more equations, one for each of the remaining two diseases.

```
. test _coef[drug[1]*disease[2]]=_coef[drug[2]*disease[2]], accumulate

 ( 1)   drug[1] - drug[2] = 0
 ( 2)   drug[1]*disease[1] - drug[2]*disease[1] = 0
 ( 3)   drug[1]*disease[2] - drug[2]*disease[2] = 0

          F(  3,    46) =     0.22
                 Prob > F =     0.8806
. test _coef[drug[1]*disease[3]]=_coef[drug[2]*disease[3]], accumulate

 ( 1)   drug[1] - drug[2] = 0
 ( 2)   drug[1]*disease[1] - drug[2]*disease[1] = 0
 ( 3)   drug[1]*disease[2] - drug[2]*disease[2] = 0
 ( 4)   drug[1]*disease[3] - drug[2]*disease[3] = 0
        Constraint 4 dropped

          F(  3,    46) =     0.22
                 Prob > F =     0.8806
```

The overall F statistic is 0.22, which is hardly significant. We cannot reject the hypothesis that the first drug has the same effect as the second drug.

You may notice that we also got the message "Constraint 4 dropped". For the technically inclined, the last constraint was unnecessary given the normalization of the model. You need not worry about such problems because Stata handles them automatically.

◁

❑ Technical Note

You can use `test` to perform other, more complicated tests. In such cases, you will probably want to review the symbolic forms of particular tests, and you will certainly want to review the symbolic form of the estimable functions. We explained how to do that above.

Let's check that Stata gives the right answers by laboriously typing the gory details of the test for the main effect of drug. Stata already told us the symbolic form in the previous subsection. The obsessed among you have no doubt already worked through the algebra and established that Stata was correct. Our chances of typing all the constraints correctly, however, are so small that we typed them into a do-file:

```
. do mainef

. test _coef[drug[1]]+ ///
>          (_coef[drug[1]*disease[1]] + _coef[drug[1]*disease[2]] + ///
>          _coef[drug[1]*disease[3]] - _coef[drug[4]*disease[1]] - ///
>          _coef[drug[4]*disease[2]] - _coef[drug[4]*disease[3]])/3 = 0,  ///
>          notest

  (output omitted)

. test _coef[drug[2]]+ ///
>          (_coef[drug[2]*disease[1]] + _coef[drug[2]*disease[2]] + ///
>          _coef[drug[2]*disease[3]] - _coef[drug[4]*disease[1]] - ///
>          _coef[drug[4]*disease[2]] - _coef[drug[4]*disease[3]])/3 = 0,  ///
>          accumulate notest

  (output omitted)

. test _coef[drug[3]]+ ///
>          (_coef[drug[3]*disease[1]] + _coef[drug[3]*disease[2]] + ///
>          _coef[drug[3]*disease[3]] - _coef[drug[4]*disease[1]] - ///
>          _coef[drug[4]*disease[2]] - _coef[drug[4]*disease[3]])/3 = 0,  ///
>          accumulate

 ( 1)  drug[1] + .3333333 drug[1]*disease[1] + .3333333 drug[1]*disease[2] + .3
> 333333 drug[1]*disease[3] - .3333333 drug[4]*disease[1] - .3333333 drug[4]*di
> sease[2] - .3333333 drug[4]*disease[3] = 0
 ( 2)  drug[2] + .3333333 drug[2]*disease[1] + .3333333 drug[2]*disease[2] + .3
> 333333 drug[2]*disease[3] - .3333333 drug[4]*disease[1] - .3333333 drug[4]*di
> sease[2] - .3333333 drug[4]*disease[3] = 0
 ( 3)  drug[3] + .3333333 drug[3]*disease[1] + .3333333 drug[3]*disease[2] + .3
> 333333 drug[3]*disease[3] - .3333333 drug[4]*disease[1] - .3333333 drug[4]*di
> sease[2] - .3333333 drug[4]*disease[3] = 0

      F(  3,    46) =    9.05
           Prob > F =    0.0001

end of do-file
```

We have our result. The F statistic has 3 degrees of freedom and is 9.05. This is the same result we obtained when we typed `test drug`. Typing `test drug` was easier, however.

❏

How Stata numbers levels

We have covered all aspects of the `anova` command except one mechanical detail: the definition of a categorical variable. Throughout the above text, we have made statements like "Stata assumes that all the variables are categorical unless you explicitly state otherwise". Although the statement makes perfect sense, anyone familiar with statistical programs knows that it left something unsaid. Most programs place additional requirements on the definition of categorical variables, namely, that they be sequential integers.

Stata does not care whether your variables are integers, whether they are positive, or whether the numbering scheme is sequential or jumps around helter-skelter. Stata will figure it out.

▷ Example

Let's prove our claim. Below we have a small dataset containing three variables: `outcome`, `scheme1`, and `scheme2`.

```
. use http://www.stata-press.com/data/r8/levels
```

```
. list
```

	outcome	scheme1	scheme2
1.	28	2	-1.1
2.	23	2	-1.1
3.	34	2	-1.1
4.	42	2	-1.1
5.	13	2	-1.1
6.	29	3	2
7.	19	3	2
8.	9	5	2.1
9.	-2	5	2.1
10.	15	5	2.1

Let's think of an ANOVA model of outcome on scheme1 and outcome on scheme2. If you look closely, you will see that scheme1 and scheme2 are two different ways of labeling the same thing. In scheme1, the levels are labeled 2, 3, and 5; in scheme2, those same levels are labeled -1.1, 2, and 2.1.

anova produces the same output, no matter which labeling scheme we use:

```
. anova outcome scheme1
```

Number of obs =   10   R-squared   = 0.5474
Root MSE   = 9.86094   Adj R-squared = 0.4181

Source	Partial SS	df	MS	F	Prob > F
Model	823.333333	2	411.666667	4.23	0.0624
scheme1	823.333333	2	411.666667	4.23	0.0624
Residual	680.666667	7	97.2380952		
Total	1504	9	167.111111		

```
. anova outcome scheme2
```

Number of obs =   10   R-squared   = 0.5474
Root MSE   = 9.86094   Adj R-squared = 0.4181

Source	Partial SS	df	MS	F	Prob > F
Model	823.333333	2	411.666667	4.23	0.0624
scheme2	823.333333	2	411.666667	4.23	0.0624
Residual	680.666667	7	97.2380952		
Total	1504	9	167.111111		

◁

❑ Technical Note

Although statistical results are unaffected by the numbering scheme you use, there is a minor difference in how Stata presents regression results (as well as the results of test with the symbolic option). Below we use anova with the regress option to refit our model based on scheme1. The regress option tells Stata to present the regression table rather than the ANOVA output.

```
. anova outcome scheme1, regress
```

Source	SS	df	MS
Model	823.333333	2	411.666667
Residual	680.666667	7	97.2380952
Total	1504.00	9	167.111111

Number of obs =	10
F(2, 7) =	4.23
Prob > F =	0.0624
R-squared =	0.5474
Adj R-squared =	0.4181
Root MSE =	9.8609

outcome	Coef.	Std. Err.	t	P>|t|	[95% Conf. Interval]	
_cons	7.333333	5.693215	1.29	0.239	-6.128981	20.79565
scheme1						
2	20.66667	7.201411	2.87	0.024	3.638036	37.6953
3	16.66667	9.001763	1.85	0.107	-4.619122	37.95245
5	(dropped)					

Notice that in labeling the regression coefficients, Stata used our numbering scheme. The first level of scheme1 is labeled 2, the second level 3, and the third level 5, just as we numbered them.

Let's now repeat the experiment using the scheme2 numbering scheme:

```
. anova outcome scheme2, regress
```

Source	SS	df	MS
Model	823.333333	2	411.666667
Residual	680.666667	7	97.2380952
Total	1504.00	9	167.111111

Number of obs =	10
F(2, 7) =	4.23
Prob > F =	0.0624
R-squared =	0.5474
Adj R-squared =	0.4181
Root MSE =	9.8609

outcome	Coef.	Std. Err.	t	P>|t|	[95% Conf. Interval]	
_cons	7.333333	5.693215	1.29	0.239	-6.128981	20.79565
scheme2						
1	20.66667	7.201411	2.87	0.024	3.638036	37.6953
2	16.66667	9.001763	1.85	0.107	-4.619122	37.95245
3	(dropped)					

Remember that scheme2 labeled the first level -1.1, the second level 2, and the third level 2.1. This time, however, our regression results are labeled 1, 2, and 3.

Stata uses our numbering scheme to label results whenever all our numbers are positive integers less than 99. The first numbering scheme meets that criterion; the second numbering scheme does not. In the second case, Stata created a mapping of our values onto the set of sequential integers. Thus, level -1.1 is labeled 1, level 2 is labeled 2, and level 2.1 is labeled 3.

Stata will show us the mapping if we specify the detail option. We request that Stata show us only the mapping and not present the ANOVA table:

```
. anova, detail noanova
```

Factor	Value	Value	Value	Value
scheme2	1 -1.1	2 2	3 2.1	

Stata makes a small table. In each entry, the number to the left is how Stata labels the level in its regression output. The number to the right is the true value of the underlying variable.

❑

❑ Technical Note

Since the labeling affects only the output of regression and test with the symbolic option, it may not seem important. There is, however, a case when you need to know how Stata labels the levels. If you use the test command to construct your own tests that explicitly refer to individual coefficients of the underlying regression model, you need to refer to those levels as Stata refers to them. Before you panic, realize that you are unlikely to be performing tests of that type. Most tests can be performed without explicitly referring to the coefficients, and so the labeling is irrelevant.

Nevertheless, the coefficient on the "third" level of scheme2, which you crazily labeled 2.1, is referred to as _coef[scheme2[3]]; see [U] **16.5 Accessing coefficients and standard errors**. On the other hand, the "third" level of scheme1, which you more reasonably labeled 5, is referred to as _coef[scheme1[5]]. You can find out how Stata labeled the levels from the regression output or from the detail output.

If this seems confusing and you are planning on performing tests directly on the coefficients of the underlying regression, label your levels sequentially with integers starting at 1, as most other programs require. Or, if you decide to opt for the freedom of having arbitrary labeling schemes, adopt a labeling scheme that uses only positive integers less than 99. This way, your labeling scheme will be Stata's labeling scheme. If you use a truly arbitrary labeling scheme that contains floating-point numbers, however, Stata will create a mapping, and you will have to know that mapping to refer to the coefficients.

❑

Even with nested designs, the scheme you use in numbering the nested levels does not matter except as noted in the above technical note. If you have B|A (meaning B nested within A), you may choose to number the levels of B within each level of A

```
A   1   1   1   2   2   2
B   1   2   3   1   2   3
```

or you may number the levels of B disregarding A:

```
A   1   1   1   2   2   2
B   1   2   3   4   5   6
```

The numbering of the levels does not have to be sequential or composed of integer values.

▷ Example

The machine example used to describe the anova nesting notation provides an illustration. In this example, each operator was numbered sequentially, starting with 1, within each machine. We create op2 that numbers the operators in a strange way, and show the result of running anova, substituting op2 for operator.

```
. use http://www.stata-press.com/data/r8/machine
(machine data)
. generate op2 = 100.4*machine + 10.3*operator
```

```
. anova output machine / op2|machine / , detail
  Factor      Value          Value          Value          Value
  ───────────────────────────────────────────────────────────────────
  machine     1 1            2 2            3 3            4 4
              5 5
  op2         1 110.7        2 121          3 131.3        4 141.6
              5 211.1        6 221.4        7 231.7        8 242
              9 311.5        10 321.8       11 332.1       12 411.9
              13 422.2       14 432.5       15 442.8       16 512.3
              17 522.6       18 532.9
```

	Number of obs =	57	R-squared	=	0.8661
	Root MSE	= 1.47089	Adj R-squared	=	0.8077

Source	Partial SS	df	MS	F	Prob > F
Model	545.822288	17	32.1071934	14.84	0.0000
machine	430.980792	4	107.745198	13.82	0.0001
op2|machine	101.353804	13	7.79644648		
op2|machine	101.353804	13	7.79644648	3.60	0.0009
Residual	84.3766582	39	2.16350406		
Total	630.198947	56	11.2535526		

This agrees with our previous result.

◁

anova as an alternative to regress

Even if you have no interest in formal ANOVA, you may still find the anova command useful. It has the ability to construct dummy variables on the fly, and when you are fitting regressions containing many dummy variables, anova is quicker than regress in producing the estimates.

Read the first part of this entry (the part you probably skipped) just to become familiar with the anova syntax. Then remember the following rules-of-thumb:

1. Specify the regress option on the end of the anova command. This way, you will see only the regression table and not be bothered with the ANOVA table.

2. Specify the continuous(*varlist*) option so that Stata will know which variables in your model are continuous, or, if it is more convenient, specify the category(*varlist*) option so that Stata will know which variables are categorical.

3. Use the ANOVA table to obtain the overall significance of categorical variables (dummy sets) in certain circumstances, namely, when the categorical variable is not interacted with any other categorical variable in the model. For instance, if you type

   anova drate region age, continuous(age)

   the F statistic reported in the ANOVA table for region is the overall significance of the dummy set for region. The same is true if you type

   anova drate region age region*age, continuous(age)

   The same is *not* true if you type

   anova drate region age region*sex, continuous(age)

In this case, the F statistic on `region` is the effect of `region` after orthogonalization with the `region*sex` dummies. If you do not understand this rule, shy away from the ANOVA table.

▷ Example

You have Census data recording the death rate (`drate`) and median age (`age`) for each state. The dataset also includes the region of the country in which each state is located (`region`):

```
. use http://www.stata-press.com/data/r8/census2
(1980 Census data by state)
. summarize drate age region
```

Variable	Obs	Mean	Std. Dev.	Min	Max
drate	50	84.3	13.07318	40	107
age	50	29.5	1.752549	24	35
region	50	2.66	1.061574	1	4

`age` is coded in integral years from 24 to 35 and `region` is coded from 1 to 4, with 1 standing for the Northeast, 2 for the North Central, 3 for the South, and 4 for the West.

When you examine the data more closely, you discover large differences in the death rate across regions of the country:

```
. tabulate region, summarize(drate)
```

Census region	Summary of Death Rate Mean	Std. Dev.	Freq.
NE	93.444444	7.0553368	9
N Cntrl	88.916667	5.5833899	12
South	88.3125	8.5457104	16
West	68.769231	13.342625	13
Total	84.3	13.073185	50

Naturally, you wonder if these differences might not be explained by differences in the median ages of the populations. To find out, you fit a regression model of `drate` on `region` and `age`. In this case, you decide to start by looking at the ANOVA table because there are no interacted variables. The table will report exactly what you expect it to report—the significance of dummy sets.

```
. anova drate region age
```

		Number of obs =	50	R-squared	= 0.7927
		Root MSE =	6.7583	Adj R-squared =	0.7328

Source	Partial SS	df	MS	F	Prob > F
Model	6638.86529	11	603.533208	13.21	0.0000
region	1320.00973	3	440.003244	9.63	0.0001
age	2237.24937	8	279.656171	6.12	0.0000
Residual	1735.63471	38	45.6745977		
Total	8374.5	49	170.908163		

You have the answer to your question: Differences in median ages do not eliminate the differences in death rates across the four regions. The ANOVA table summarizes the two terms in the model, `region` and `age`. The `region` term contains 3 degrees of freedom, and the `age` term contains 8 degrees of freedom. Both are significant at better than the 1% level.

It is worth noting that the age term contains 8 degrees of freedom. Since you did not explicitly indicate that age was to be treated as a continuous variable, it was treated as *categorical*, meaning unique coefficients were estimated for each level of age. The only clue of this is that the number of degrees of freedom associated with the age term exceeds 1. This becomes more obvious if you review the regression coefficients:

```
. anova, regress
```

Source	SS	df	MS		
Model	6638.86529	11	603.533208		
Residual	1735.63471	38	45.6745977		
Total	8374.5	49	170.908163		

```
                                    Number of obs =      50
                                    F( 11,    38) =   13.21
                                    Prob > F      =  0.0000
                                    R-squared     =  0.7927
                                    Adj R-squared =  0.7328
                                    Root MSE      =  6.7583
```

drate	Coef.	Std. Err.	t	P>|t|	[95% Conf. Interval]
_cons	93.925	7.295544	12.87	0.000	79.15594 108.6941
region					
1	13.37147	4.195344	3.19	0.003	4.878439 21.8645
2	13.81431	2.974005	4.65	0.000	7.793748 19.83486
3	13.075	2.747792	4.76	0.000	7.512391 18.63762
4	(dropped)				
age					
24	-38.925	9.944825	-3.91	0.000	-59.05724 -18.79275
26	-53.925	9.944825	-5.42	0.000	-74.05724 -33.79275
27	-24.61666	8.015933	-3.07	0.004	-40.84407 -8.389257
28	-26.26488	7.393098	-3.55	0.001	-41.23143 -11.29834
29	-20.064	7.23115	-2.77	0.009	-34.7027 -5.425299
30	-18.05497	7.074489	-2.55	0.015	-32.37652 -3.733414
31	-9.011922	8.011676	-1.12	0.268	-25.23071 7.206869
32	-11.89646	8.384027	-1.42	0.164	-28.86904 5.07611
35	(dropped)				

If you want to treat age as a continuous variable, you must include the continuous(*varlist*) option. In the following case, only one variable, age, is continuous.

```
. anova drate region age, continuous(age)
```

```
                        Number of obs =      50    R-squared     =  0.7203
                        Root MSE      = 7.21483    Adj R-squared =  0.6954
```

Source	Partial SS	df	MS	F	Prob > F
Model	6032.08254	4	1508.02064	28.97	0.0000
region	1645.66228	3	548.554092	10.54	0.0000
age	1630.46662	1	1630.46662	31.32	0.0000
Residual	2342.41746	45	52.0537213		
Total	8374.5	49	170.908163		

The age term now has 1 degree of freedom. The regression coefficients are

(Continued on next page)

```
. anova, regress
      Source │      SS       df       MS              Number of obs =       50
─────────────┼─────────────────────────────           F(  4,    45) =    28.97
       Model │ 6032.08254     4  1508.02064            Prob > F      =   0.0000
    Residual │ 2342.41746    45  52.0537213            R-squared     =   0.7203
─────────────┼─────────────────────────────           Adj R-squared =   0.6954
       Total │    8374.5     49  170.908163            Root MSE      =   7.2148

─────────────┬───────────────────────────────────────────────────────────────
       drate │    Coef.   Std. Err.      t    P>|t|     [95% Conf. Interval]
─────────────┼───────────────────────────────────────────────────────────────
       _cons │ -41.97859   19.88906   -2.11   0.040    -82.03722   -1.919959
      region │
          1  │ 13.37578    3.723447    3.59   0.001     5.876378    20.87519
          2  │ 15.16831    3.022157    5.02   0.000     9.081374    21.25525
          3  │ 14.07378    2.865756    4.91   0.000     8.301846     19.8457
          4  │ (dropped)
         age │ 3.922947    .7009425    5.60   0.000     2.511177    5.334718
─────────────┴───────────────────────────────────────────────────────────────
```

Although we started analyzing these data in an attempt to explain the regional differences in death rate, let's focus on the effect of age for a moment. In our first model, each level of **age** had a unique death rate associated with it. For instance, the predicted death rate in a northeastern state with a median age of 24 was

$$93.93 + 13.37 - 38.93 \approx 68.37$$

whereas the predicted death rate from our current model is

$$-41.98 + 13.38 + 3.92 \cdot 24 \approx 65.48$$

Our previous model had an R^2 of 0.7927, whereas our current model has an R^2 of 0.7203. This "small" loss of predictive power accompanies a gain of 7 degrees of freedom, so we suspect that the continuous-age model is as good as the discrete-age model.

◁

❑ Technical Note

There is enough information in the two ANOVA tables to attach a statistical significance to our suspicion that the loss of predictive power is offset by the savings in degrees of freedom. To wit: Since the continuous-age model is nested within the discrete-age model, we can perform a standard Chow test. For those of us who know such formulas off the top of our heads, the F statistic is

$$\frac{(2342.41746 - 1735.63471)/7}{45.6745977} = 1.90$$

There is, however, a better way.

We can find out whether our continuous model is as good as our discrete model by putting **age** in the model twice, once as a continuous variable and once as a categorical variable. The categorical variable will then measure deviations around the straight line implied by the continuous variable, and the F test for the significance of the categorical variable will test whether those deviations are jointly zero.

There is no way to tell Stata that the variable **age** in a model is in one instance continuous and in another categorical. As far as Stata is concerned, every variable in the model is either continuous or categorical, so we must fool Stata by creating the same variable with two different names:

```
. generate cage=age
. anova drate region cage age, continuous(cage)
                              Number of obs =       50    R-squared       =  0.7927
                              Root MSE      =  6.7583    Adj R-squared =   0.7328

          Source |   Partial SS     df       MS              F     Prob > F

           Model |  6638.86529      11   603.533208          13.21    0.0000

          region |  1320.00973       3   440.003244           9.63    0.0001
            cage |  91.9613243       1   91.9613243           2.01    0.1641
             age |  606.782747       7   86.6832496           1.90    0.0970

        Residual |  1735.63471      38   45.6745977

           Total |      8374.5      49   170.908163
```

We first created a new variable called `cage` that is identical to the `age` variable. We then told Stata to fit an ANOVA model of `drate` on the variables `region`, `cage`, and `age`, where the variable `cage` is continuous. Since we did not specify otherwise, Stata assumes that the other two variables, `region` and `age`, and most importantly, `age`, are categorical.

We find that the F test for the significance of the (categorical) `age` variable is 1.90, just as we calculated above. It is significant at the 9.7% level. If we hold to a 5% significance level, we cannot reject the hypothesis that the effect of `age` is linear.

❏

> ## Example

In our Census data, we still find significant differences across the regions after controlling for the median age of the population. We might now wonder whether the regional differences are differences in level—independent of age—or are instead differences in the regional effects of age. Just as you can interact categorical variables with other categorical variables, you can interact categorical variables with continuous variables.

```
. anova drate region age region*age, continuous(age)
                              Number of obs =       50    R-squared       =  0.7365
                              Root MSE      = 7.24852    Adj R-squared =   0.6926

          Source |   Partial SS     df       MS              F     Prob > F

           Model |   6167.7737       7   881.110529          16.77    0.0000

          region |  188.713602       3   62.9045339           1.20    0.3225
             age |  873.425599       1   873.425599          16.62    0.0002
      region*age |  135.691162       3   45.2303874           0.86    0.4689

        Residual |   2206.7263      42   52.5411023

           Total |      8374.5      49   170.908163
```

The `region*age` term in our model measures the differences in slopes across the regions. We cannot reject the hypothesis that there are no such differences. We also note that the `region` effect is now "insignificant". This does not mean that there are no regional differences in death rates since each test is a *marginal* or *partial* test. In this example, with `region*age` included in the model, `region` is being tested at the point where `age` is zero. Apart from this value not existing in the dataset, it is also a long way from the mean value of `age`, so the test of `region` at this point is pretty meaningless (although quite valid if you acknowledge what is being tested).

To obtain a more sensible test of `region`, we can subtract the mean from the `age` variable and use this in the model.

```
. quietly summarize age
. generate mage = age - r(mean)
. anova drate region mage region*mage, continuous(mage)
```

| | | | | Number of obs = | 50 | R-squared | = | 0.7365 |
| | | | | Root MSE | = 7.24852 | Adj R-squared = | | 0.6926 |

Source	Partial SS	df	MS	F	Prob > F
Model	6167.7737	7	881.110529	16.77	0.0000
region	1166.14735	3	388.715783	7.40	0.0004
mage	873.425599	1	873.425599	16.62	0.0002
region*mage	135.691162	3	45.2303874	0.86	0.4689
Residual	2206.7263	42	52.5411023		
Total	8374.5	49	170.908163		

`region` is significant when tested at the mean of the `age` variable.

◁

▷ Example

We can `test` for the overall significance of `region` in the last model. See *Testing effects* earlier in this entry for an explanation of the use of the `test` command after `anova`. The simple form of the `test` syntax is

test $\left[\textit{term} \left[\textit{term} \left[\ldots\right]\right]\right]$

After running the model `anova drate region mage region*mage, continuous(mage)`, type

```
. test region region*mage
```

Source	Partial SS	df	MS	F	Prob > F
region region*mage	1781.35344	6	296.89224	5.65	0.0002
Residual	2206.7263	42	52.5411023		

The overall F statistic associated with the `region` and `region*mage` terms is 5.65, and it is significant at the 0.02% level.

If `test` works, typing `test` followed by a single term in our model should produce output that exactly matches that provided by the `anova` command. If you look back at the ANOVA output, you will see that the `region` term, by itself, had a sum of squares of 1166.15, which, based on 3 degrees of freedom, yielded an F statistic of 7.40 and a significance level of 0.0004.

```
. test region
```

Source	Partial SS	df	MS	F	Prob > F
region	1166.14735	3	388.715783	7.40	0.0004
Residual	2206.7263	42	52.5411023		

`test` yields the same result.

◁

Saved Results

anova saves in e():

Scalars

e(N)	number of observations
e(mss)	model sum of squares
e(df_m)	model degrees of freedom
e(rss)	residual sum of squares
e(df_r)	residual degrees of freedom
e(r2)	R-squared
e(r2_a)	adjusted R-squared
e(F)	F statistic
e(rmse)	root mean square error
e(ll)	log likelihood
e(ll_0)	log likelihood, constant-only model
e(N_bse)	number of levels of the between-subjects error term
e(df_bse)	degrees of freedom for the between-subjects error term
e(box#)	Box's conservative epsilon for a particular combination of repeated variable(s) (repeated() only)
e(gg#)	Greenhouse–Geisser epsilon for a particular combination of repeated variable(s) (repeated() only)
e(hf#)	Huynh–Feldt epsilon for a particular combination of repeated variable(s) (repeated() only)

Macros

e(cmd)	anova
e(depvar)	name of dependent variable
e(varnames)	name(s) of the right-hand-side variables
e(repvars)	name(s) of repeated variable(s) (repeated() only)
e(repvar#)	name(s) of repeated variable(s) for a particular combination (repeated() only)
e(model)	ols
e(wtype)	weight type
e(wexp)	weight expression
e(predict)	program used to implement predict

Matrices

e(b)	coefficient vector
e(V)	variance–covariance matrix of the estimators
e(Srep)	covariance matrix based on repeated measures (repeated() only)

Functions

e(sample)	marks estimation sample

References

Afifi, A. A. and S. P. Azen. 1979. *Statistical Analysis: A Computer-Oriented Approach*. 2d ed. New York: Academic Press.

Altman, D. G. 1991. *Practical Statistics for Medical Research*. London: Chapman & Hall.

Box, G. E. P. 1954. Some theorems on quadratic forms applied in the study of analysis of variance problems, I. Effect of inequality of variance in the one–way classification. *Annals of Mathematical Statistics* 25: 290–302.

Cobb, G. W. 1998. *Introduction to Design and Analysis of Experiments*. New York: Springer.

Edwards, A. L. 1985. *Multiple Regression and the Analysis of Variance and Covariance.* 2d ed. New York: W. H. Freeman and Company.

Fisher, R. A. 1925. *Statistical Methods for Research Workers.* Edinburgh: Oliver & Boyd.

——. 1935. *The Design of Experiments.* Edinburgh: Oliver & Boyd.

——. 1990. *Statistical Methods, Experimental Design, and Scientific Inference.* Oxford: Oxford University Press. Facsimile reprint of *Statistical Methods for Research Workers* (1925, 14/e 1970), *The Design of Experiments* (1935, 8/e 1966), and *Statistical Methods and Scientific Inference* (1956, 3/e 1973).

Geisser, S. and S. Greenhouse. 1958. An extension of Box's results on the use of the F distribution in multivariate analysis. *Annals of Mathematical Statistics* 29: 885–891.

Gleason, J. R. 1999. sg103: Within subjects (repeated measures) ANOVA, including between subjects factors. *Stata Technical Bulletin* 47: 40–45. Reprinted in *Stata Technical Bulletin Reprints*, vol. 8, pp. 236–243.

——. 2000. sg132: Analysis of variance from summary statistics. *Stata Technical Bulletin* 54: 42–46. Reprinted in *Stata Technical Bulletin Reprints*, vol. 9, pp. 328–332.

Higgins, J. E. and G. G. Koch. 1977. Variable selection and generalized chi-square analysis of categorical data applied to a large cross-sectional occupational health survey. *International Statistical Review* 45: 51–62. (Data reprinted in *Data*, ed. D. F. Andrews and A. M. Herzberg. New York: Springer, 1985.)

Huynh, H. 1978. Some approximate tests for repeated measurement designs. *Psychometrika* 43: 161–175.

Huynh, H. and L. S. Feldt. 1976. Estimation of the Box correction for degrees of freedom from sample data in randomized block and split-plot designs. *Journal of Educational Statistics* 1: 69–82.

Kennedy, W. J., Jr., and J. E. Gentle. 1980. *Statistical Computing.* New York: Macmillan.

Kuehl, R. O. 1994. *Statistical Principles of Research Design and Analysis.* Belmont, CA: Duxbury Press.

Milliken, G. A. and D. E. Johnson. 1984. *Analysis of Messy Data, Volume 1: Designed Experiments.* New York: Van Nostrand Reinhold.

Rabe-Hesketh, S. and B. Everitt. 2000. *A Handbook of Statistical Analysis using Stata.* 2d ed. Boca Raton, FL: Chapman & Hall/CRC.

Scheffé, H. 1959. *The Analysis of Variance.* New York: John Wiley & Sons.

Snedecor, G. W. and W. G. Cochran. 1989. *Statistical Methods.* 8th ed. Ames, IA: Iowa State University Press.

Steel, R. G. D. and J. H. Torrie. 1980. *Principles and Procedures of Statistics.* 2d ed. New York: McGraw–Hill.

Winer, B. J., D. R. Brown, and K. M. Michels. 1991. *Statistical Principles in Experimental Design.* 3d ed. New York: McGraw–Hill.

Also See

Complementary:	[R] **adjust**, [R] **encode**, [R] **lincom**, [R] **linktest**, [R] **predict**, [R] **regression diagnostics**, [R] **reshape**, [R] **test**, [R] **vce**, [R] **xi**
Related:	[R] **loneway**, [R] **manova**, [R] **oneway**, [R] **regress**
Background:	[U] **16.5 Accessing coefficients and standard errors**, [U] **23 Estimation and post-estimation commands**

Title

append — Append datasets

Syntax

<u>ap</u>pend using *filename* [, <u>nol</u>abel keep(*varlist*)]

Description

append appends a Stata-format dataset stored on disk to the end of the dataset in memory. If *filename* is specified without an extension, .dta is assumed.

Note that Stata also has the capability to join observations from two datasets into a single observation; see [R] **merge**. Also see [U] **25 Commands for combining data** for a comparison of append, merge, and joinby.

Options

nolabel prevents Stata from copying the value label definitions from the disk dataset into the dataset in memory. Even if you do not specify this option, label definitions from the disk dataset never replace definitions already in memory.

keep(*varlist*) specifies the variables to be kept from the using data. If keep() is not specified, all variables are kept.

The *varlist* in keep(*varlist*) differs from standard differs from standard Stata varlists in two ways: variable names in *varlist* may not be abbreviated, except by the use of wildcard characters; and you may not refer to a range of variables, such as price-weight.

Remarks

The disk dataset must be a Stata-format dataset; that is, it must have been created by save; see [R] **save**.

▷ Example

You have two datasets stored on disk that you want to combine into a single dataset. The first dataset, called even.dta, contains the sixth through eighth positive even numbers. The second dataset, called odd.dta, contains the first five positive odd numbers. The datasets are

```
. use even
(6th through 8th even numbers)
. list
```

	number	even
1.	6	12
2.	7	14
3.	8	16

```
. use odd
(First five odd numbers)
. list
```

	number	odd
1.	1	1
2.	2	3
3.	3	5
4.	4	7
5.	5	9

We will append the even data onto the end of the odd. Since the odd is already in memory (we just used it above), we type append using even. The result is

```
. append using even
. list
```

	number	odd	even
1.	1	1	.
2.	2	3	.
3.	3	5	.
4.	4	7	.
5.	5	9	.
6.	6	.	12
7.	7	.	14
8.	8	.	16

Since the variable number is in both datasets, the variable was extended with the new data from the file even.dta. Since there is no variable called odd in the new data, the additional observations on odd were forward-filled with *missing*. Since there is no variable called even in the original data, the first observations on even were back-filled with *missing*.

◁

▷ Example

The order of variables in the two datasets is irrelevant. Stata always appends variables by name:

```
. use odd1
(First five odd numbers)
. describe
Contains data
  obs:             5                    First five odd numbers
  vars:            2                    5 Jul 2002 17:00
  size:           60 (99.9% of memory free)   (_dta has notes)
```

variable name	storage type	display format	value label	variable label
odd	float	%9.0g		Odd numbers
number	float	%9.0g		

```
Sorted by: number
```

```
. describe using even
Contains data                                        6th through 8th even numbers
    obs:            3                                 5 Jul 2002 17:00
   vars:            2
   size:           30
```

variable name	storage type	display format	value label	variable label
number	int	%8.0g		
even	float	%9.0g		Even numbers

```
Sorted by:
. append using even
. list
```

	odd	number	even
1.	1	1	.
2.	3	2	.
3.	5	3	.
4.	7	4	.
5.	9	5	.
6.	.	6	12
7.	.	7	14
8.	.	8	16

The results are the same as in the first example.

◁

When Stata appends two datasets, the definitions of the dataset in memory, called the *master* dataset, override the definitions of the dataset on disk, called the *using* dataset. This extends to value labels, variable labels, characteristics, and date–time stamps. If there are conflicts in numeric storage types, the more precise storage type will be used regardless of whether this storage type was in the *master* dataset or the *using* dataset. If a variable is stored as a str# in one dataset and a numeric storage type in the other, the definition in the *master* dataset will prevail. If a variable is stored as a longer string in one dataset than in the other, the longer str# storage type will prevail.

❑ Technical Note

If a variable is a string in one dataset and numeric in the other, Stata issues a warning message and then appends the data. If the using dataset contains the string variable, the combined dataset will have numeric missing values for the appended data on this variable; the contents of the string variable in the using data are ignored. If the using dataset contains the numeric variable, the combined dataset will have null strings for the appended data on this variable; the contents of the numeric variable in the using data are ignored.

❑

▷ Example

Since Stata has five numeric variable types—byte, int, long, float, and double—it is possible that you may attempt to append datasets containing variables with the same name but of different numeric types; see [U] **15.2.2 Numeric storage types**.

Let's describe the datasets in the example above:

```
. describe using odd
Contains data                              First five odd numbers
  obs:           5                         5 Jul 2002 17:03
  vars:          2
  size:         60
```

variable name	storage type	display format	value label	variable label
number	float	%9.0g		
odd	float	%9.0g		Odd numbers

```
Sorted by:
. describe using even
Contains data                              6th through 8th even numbers
  obs:           3                         5 Jul 2002 17:00
  vars:          2
  size:         30
```

variable name	storage type	display format	value label	variable label
number	int	%8.0g		
even	float	%9.0g		Even numbers

```
Sorted by:
. describe using oddeven
Contains data                              First five odd numbers
  obs:           8                         5 Jul 2002 17:04
  vars:          3
  size:        128
```

variable name	storage type	display format	value label	variable label
number	float	%9.0g		
odd	float	%9.0g		Odd numbers
even	float	%9.0g		Even numbers

```
Sorted by:
```

The variable number was stored as a float in odd.dta but as an int in even.dta. Since float is the more precise storage type, the resulting dataset, oddeven.dta, had number stored as a float. Had we, instead, appended odd.dta to even.dta, number would still have been stored as a float:

```
. use even
(6th through 8th even numbers)
. append using odd
number was int now float
```

(Continued on next page)

```
. describe

Contains data from even.dta
  obs:              8                          6th through 8th even numbers
  vars:             3                          5 Jul 2002 17:00
  size:           128 (99.8% of memory free)  (_dta has notes)
```

variable name	storage type	display format	value label	variable label
number	float	%8.0g		
even	float	%9.0g		Even numbers
odd	float	%9.0g		Odd numbers

```
Sorted by:
    Note:  dataset has changed since last saved
```

◁

▷ Example

Suppose you have a dataset in memory containing the variable educ and you have previously given a label variable educ "Education Level" command so that the variable label associated with educ is "Education Level". You now append a dataset called newdata.dta that also contains a variable named educ, except that its variable label is "Ed. Lev". After appending the two datasets, the variable educ is still labeled "Education Level". See [U] **15.6.2 Variable labels**.

◁

▷ Example

Assume that the values of the variable educ are labeled with a value label named educlbl. Further assume that in newdata.dta, the values of educ are also labeled by a value label named educlbl. Thus, there is one definition of educlbl in memory and another (although perhaps equivalent) definition in newdata.dta. When you append the new data, you will see the following:

```
. append using newdata
label educlbl already defined
```

When append comes upon a situation where one label in memory and another on disk have the same name, it warns you of the problem and sticks with the definition currently in memory, ignoring the definition in the disk file.

◁

❑ Technical Note

When you append two datasets that both contain definitions of the same value label, there is a danger that the codings are not equivalent. That is why Stata warns you with a message like "label educlbl already defined". If you do not know that the two value labels are equivalent, you should convert the value labeled variables into string variables, append the data, and then construct a new coding. decode and encode make this easy:

```
. use newdata, clear

. decode educ, gen(edstr)

. drop educ
```

```
. save newdata, replace
. use basedata
. decode educ, gen(edstr)
. drop educ
. append using newdata
. encode edstr, gen(educ)
. drop edstr
```

See [R] **encode**.

You can specify the `nolabel` option to force `append` to ignore all the value label definitions in the incoming file, whether or not there is a conflict. In practice, you will probably never want to do this.

❏

Also See

Complementary:	[R] **save**
Related:	[R] **cross**, [R] **joinby**, [R] **merge**
Background:	[U] **25 Commands for combining data**

Title

---

areg — Linear regression with a large dummy-variable set

Syntax

areg *depvar* [*indepvars*] [*weight*] [if *exp*] [in *range*] , <u>a</u>bsorb(*varname₁*)

[<u>l</u>evel(*#*) <u>r</u>obust <u>cl</u>uster(*varname₂*)]

by ... : may be used with areg; see [R] **by**.

aweights, fweights, and pweights are allowed; see [U] **14.1.6 weight**.

areg shares the features of all estimation commands; see [U] **23 Estimation and post-estimation commands**.

Syntax for predict

predict [*type*] *newvarname* [if *exp*] [in *range*] [, *statistic*]

where $y_j = \mathbf{x}_j \mathbf{b} + d_{\text{absorbvar}} + e_j$ and *statistic* is

xb	$\mathbf{x}_j \mathbf{b}$, fitted values (the default)
stdp	standard error of the prediction
<u>dr</u>esiduals	$d_{\text{absorbvar}} + e_j = y_j - \mathbf{x}_j \mathbf{b}$
* xbd	$\mathbf{x}_j \mathbf{b} + d_{\text{absorbvar}}$
* d	$d_{\text{absorbvar}}$
* <u>r</u>esiduals	residual

Unstarred statistics are available both in and out of sample; type predict ... if e(sample) ... if wanted only for the estimation sample. Starred statistics are calculated only for the estimation sample even when if e(sample) is not specified.

Description

areg fits a linear regression absorbing one categorical factor; that is, it fits a fixed-effects model.

Note: See the command xtreg, fe in [XT] **xtreg** for an improved version of areg.

Options

absorb(*varname₁*) specifies the categorical variable, which is to be included in the regression as if it were specified by dummy variables. absorb() is not optional.

level(*#*) specifies the confidence level, in percent, for confidence intervals. The default is level(95) or as set by set level; see [U] **23.6 Specifying the width of confidence intervals**.

robust specifies that the Huber/White/sandwich estimator of variance is to be used in place of the traditional calculation. This alternative variance estimator produces consistent standard errors, even if the data are weighted or the residuals are not identically distributed. robust combined with cluster() further allows residuals that are not independent within cluster (although they must be independent between clusters).

If you specify pweights, robust is implied; see [U] **23.14 Obtaining robust variance estimates**.

cluster(*varname₂*) specifies that the observations are independent across groups (clusters), but not necessarily within groups. *varname₂* specifies to which group each observation belongs. cluster() affects the estimated standard errors and variance–covariance matrix of the estimators (VCE), but not the estimated coefficients. cluster() can be used with pweights to produce estimates for unstratified cluster-sampled data, but see [SVY] **svy estimators** for a command designed specifically for survey data.

cluster() implies robust; that is, specifying robust cluster() is equivalent to typing cluster() by itself.

Note: Exercise caution when using the cluster() option with areg. The effective number of degrees of freedom for the robust variance estimator is $n_g - 1$, where n_g is the number of clusters. Thus, the number of levels of the absorb() variable should not exceed the number of clusters.

Options for predict

xb, the default, calculates the prediction of $\mathbf{x}_j\mathbf{b}$, the fitted values, using the average effect of the absorbed variable. Also see xbd below.

stdp calculates the standard error of $\mathbf{x}_j\mathbf{b}$.

dresiduals calculates $y_j - \mathbf{x}_j\mathbf{b}$, which are the residuals plus the effect of the absorbed variable.

xbd calculates $\mathbf{x}_j\mathbf{b} + d_{\mathrm{absorbvar}}$, which are the fitted values including the individual effects of the absorbed variable.

d calculates $d_{\mathrm{absorbvar}}$, the individual coefficients for the absorbed variable.

residuals calculates the residuals; that is, $y_j - (\mathbf{x}_j\mathbf{b} + d_{\mathrm{absorbvar}})$.

Remarks

Suppose that you have a regression model that includes among the explanatory variables a large number k of mutually exclusive and exhaustive dummies:

$$\mathbf{y} = \mathbf{X}\boldsymbol{\beta} + \mathbf{d}_1\gamma_1 + \mathbf{d}_2\gamma_2 + \cdots + \mathbf{d}_k\gamma_k + \boldsymbol{\epsilon}$$

For instance, the dummy variables $\mathbf{d}_i$ might indicate countries in the world or states of the United States. One solution would be to fit the model using regress, but this solution is only possible if k is small enough so that the total number of variables (the number of columns of $\mathbf{X}$ plus the number of $\mathbf{d}_i$'s plus one for $\mathbf{y}$) is sufficiently small—meaning less than matsize (see [R] **matsize**). For problems with more variables than the largest possible value of matsize (40 for Small Stata and 800 for Intercooled Stata), regress will not work. areg provides a way of obtaining estimates of $\boldsymbol{\beta}$—but not the γ_i's—in these cases. The effects of the dummy variables are said to be absorbed.

▷ Example

So that we can compare the results produced by areg with Stata's other regression commands, we will fit a model where k is small. It should be understood, however, that areg's real use is when k is large.

In our automobile data, we have a variable called rep78 that is coded 1, 2, 3, 4, and 5, where 1 means poor and 5 excellent. Let us assume that we wish to fit a regression of mpg on weight, gear_ratio, and rep78 (parameterized as a set of dummies). Since rep78 assumes only 5 values, we can fit this model using regress. We first use tabulate to generate the dummies (see [R] **tabulate** and [U] **28.2 Using indicator variables in estimation**).

```
. use http://www.stata-press.com/data/r8/auto
(1978 Automobile Data)
. tabulate rep78, gen(r)
```

Repair Record 1978	Freq.	Percent	Cum.
1	2	2.90	2.90
2	8	11.59	14.49
3	30	43.48	57.97
4	18	26.09	84.06
5	11	15.94	100.00
Total	69	100.00	

```
. regress mpg weight gear_ratio r1-r4
```

Source	SS	df	MS
Model	1575.97621	6	262.662702
Residual	764.226686	62	12.3262369
Total	2340.2029	68	34.4147485

Number of obs = 69
F(6, 62) = 21.31
Prob > F = 0.0000
R-squared = 0.6734
Adj R-squared = 0.6418
Root MSE = 3.5109

mpg	Coef.	Std. Err.	t	P>|t|	[95% Conf. Interval]
weight	-.0051031	.0009206	-5.54	0.000	-.0069433 -.003263
gear_ratio	.901478	1.565552	0.58	0.567	-2.228015 4.030971
r1	-2.036937	2.740728	-0.74	0.460	-7.515574 3.4417
r2	-2.419822	1.764338	-1.37	0.175	-5.946682 1.107039
r3	-2.557432	1.370912	-1.87	0.067	-5.297846 .1829814
r4	-2.788389	1.395259	-2.00	0.050	-5.577472 .0006939
_cons	36.23782	7.01057	5.17	0.000	22.22389 50.25175

To estimate the **areg** equivalent, we type

```
. areg mpg weight gear_ratio, absorb(rep78)
```

Number of obs = 69
F(2, 62) = 41.64
Prob > F = 0.0000
R-squared = 0.6734
Adj R-squared = 0.6418
Root MSE = 3.5109

mpg	Coef.	Std. Err.	t	P>|t|	[95% Conf. Interval]
weight	-.0051031	.0009206	-5.54	0.000	-.0069433 -.003263
gear_ratio	.901478	1.565552	0.58	0.567	-2.228015 4.030971
_cons	34.05889	7.056383	4.83	0.000	19.95338 48.1644
rep78	F(4,62) =		1.117	0.356	(5 categories)

Note that both **regress** and **areg** display the same R^2 values, root mean square error, and, for **weight** and **gear_ratio**, the same parameter estimates, standard errors, t statistics, significance levels, and confidence intervals. **areg**, however, does not report the coefficients for **rep78**, and, in fact, they are not even calculated. It is this computational trick that makes the problem manageable when k is large. **areg** does report a test that the coefficients associated with **rep78** are jointly zero. In this case, this test has a significance level of 35.6%. This F test for **rep78** is the same as we would obtain after **regress** if we were to specify **test r1 r2 r3 r4** or, equivalently, **testparm r1-r4**; see [R] **test**.

The model F tests reported by regress and areg also differ. The regress command reports a test that all coefficients except that of the constant are equal to zero; thus, the dummies are included in this test. The areg output shows a test that all coefficients excluding the dummies and the constant are equal to zero. This is the same test that can be obtained after regress by typing test weight gear_ratio.

◁

❑ Technical Note

The intercept reported by areg deserves some explanation because, given k mutually exclusive and exhaustive dummies, it is arbitrary. areg identifies the model by choosing the intercept that makes the prediction calculated at the means of the independent variables equal to the mean of the dependent variable: $\overline{y} = \overline{x}\,\widehat{\beta}$.

```
. predict yhat
(option xb assumed; fitted values)

. summarize mpg yhat if rep78 < .
```

Variable	Obs	Mean	Std. Dev.	Min	Max
mpg	69	21.28986	5.866408	12	41
yhat	69	21.28986	4.383224	11.58643	28.07367

We had to include if rep78 < . in our summarize command because we have missing values in our data. areg automatically dropped those missing values (as it should) in forming the estimates, but predict with the xb option is quite willing to make predictions for cases with missing rep78 because it does not know that rep78 is really part of our model.

Note that these predicted values do not include the absorbed effects (i.e., the $\mathbf{d}_i\gamma_i$). For predicted values that include these effects, you could use the xbd option of predict or see [XT] **xtreg**.

❑

▷ Example

areg, robust is a Huberized version of areg; see [P] **_robust**. Just as areg is equivalent to using regress with dummies, areg, robust is equivalent to using regress, robust with dummies. You can use areg, robust when you expect heteroskedastic or nonnormal errors. areg, robust, like ordinary regression, does assume that the observations are independent unless the cluster() option is specified. If the cluster(*varname₂*) option is specified, this independence assumption is relaxed and only the clusters identified by equal values of *varname₂* are assumed to be independent.

Assume we were to collect data by randomly sampling 10,000 doctors (from 1,000 hospitals) and then sampling 10 of each of their patients, yielding a total dataset of 100,000 patients in a cluster sample. If, in some regression, we wished to include effects of the hospitals to which the doctors belonged, we would want to include a dummy variable for each hospital, adding 1,000 variables to our model. regress would not be able to fit such a model, but areg could.

```
. areg depvar patient_vars, absorb(hospital) cluster(doctor)
```

◁

Saved Results

areg saves in e():

Scalars

e(N)	number of observations	e(ar2)	adjusted R-squared
e(tss)	total sum of squares	e(F)	F statistic
e(df_m)	model degrees of freedom	e(F_absorb)	F statistic for absorbed effect
e(rss)	residual sum of squares		(only when robust is not specified)
e(df_r)	residual degrees of freedom	e(df_a)	degrees of freedom for absorbed effect
e(r2)	R-squared		

Macros

e(cmd)	areg	e(wexp)	weight expression
e(depvar)	name of dependent variable	e(absvar)	name of absorb variable
e(wtype)	weight type	e(predict)	program used to implement predict

Matrices

e(b)	coefficient vector	e(V)	variance–covariance matrix of the estimators

Functions

e(sample)	marks estimation sample

Methods and Formulas

areg is implemented as an ado-file.

areg begins by recalculating *depvar* and *indepvars* to have mean 0 within the groups specified by absorb(). The overall mean of each variable is then added back in. The adjusted *depvar* is then regressed on the adjusted *indepvars* using regress, yielding the coefficient estimates. The variance–covariance matrix of the coefficients is then adjusted to account for the absorbed variables—this calculation yields the same results (up to numerical round-off error) as if the matrix had been calculated directly by the formulas given in [R] **regress**.

areg works similarly, calling _robust after regress to produce the robust variance estimates; see [P] **_robust**. The model F test uses the robust variance estimates. There is, however, no simple computational means of obtaining a robust test of the absorbed dummies; thus, this test is not displayed when the robust option is specified.

Also See

Complementary:	[R] **lincom**, [R] **mfx**, [R] **nlcom**, [R] **predict**, [R] **predictnl**, [R] **test**, [R] **testnl**, [R] **vce**, [R] **xi**
Related:	[R] **regress**, [P] **_robust**, [XT] **xtreg**, [XT] **xtregar**
Background:	[U] **16.5 Accessing coefficients and standard errors**, [U] **23 Estimation and post-estimation commands**, [U] **23.14 Obtaining robust variance estimates**, [U] **28.2 Using indicator variables in estimation**

Title

> **assert** — Verify truth of claim

Syntax

<u>ass</u>ert *exp* [if *exp*] [in *range*] [, <u>r</u>c0 <u>n</u>ull]

by ... : may be used with assert; see [R] **by**.

Description

assert verifies that *exp* is true. If it is, the command produces no output. If it is not, assert informs you that the "assertion is false" and issues a return code of 9; see [U] **11 Error messages and return codes**.

Options

rc0 forces a return code of 0 even if the assertion is false.

null forces a return code of 8 on null assertions.

Remarks

assert is seldom used interactively since it is easier to use inspect, summarize, or tabulate to look for evidence of errors in the dataset. These commands, however, require that you review the output to spot the error. assert is useful because it tells Stata not only what to do, but what you can expect to find. Groups of assertions are often combined in a do-file to certify data. If the do-file runs all the way through without complaining, every assertion in the file is true.

```
. do myassert
. use trans, clear
(xplant data)
. assert sex=="m" | sex=="f"
. assert packs==0 if !smoker
. assert packs>0 if smoker
. sort patient date
. by patient: assert sex==sex[_n-1] if _n>1
. by patient: assert abs(bp-bp[_n-1]) < 20 if bp< . & bp[_n-1]< .
. by patient: assert died==0 if _n!=_N
. by patient: assert died==0 | died==1 if _n==_N
. by patient: assert n_xplant==0 | n_xplant==1 if _n==_N
. assert inval==int(inval)
.
.
end of do-file
```

▷ Example

You receive data from Bob, a co-worker. He has been working on the dataset for some time, and it has now been delivered to you for analysis. Before analyzing the data, you (smartly) verify that the data are as Bob claims. In Bob's memo, he claims that (1) the dataset reflects the earnings of 522 employees, (2) the earnings are only for full-time employees, (3) the variable female is coded 1 for female and 0 otherwise, and (4) the variable exp contains the number of years, or fraction thereof, on the job. You assemble the following do-file:

```
use frombob, clear
assert _N==522
assert sal>=6000 & sal<=125000
assert female==1 | female==0
gen work=sum(female==1)
assert work[_N]>0
replace work=sum(female==0)
assert work[_N]>0
drop work
assert exp>=0 & exp<=40
```

Let's go through these assertions one by one. After using the data, you assert that _N equals 522. Remember, _N reflects the total number of observations in the dataset; see [U] **16.4 System variables (_variables)**. Bob said it was 522, so you check it. Bob's second claim was that the data are for only full-time employees. You know that everybody in your company makes a salary between $6,000 and $125,000, so you check that the salary figures are within this range. Bob's third assertion was that the female variable was coded zero or one.

You add something more. You know your company employs both males and females, so you check that there are some of each. You create a variable called work equal to the running sum of female observations, and then verify that the last observation of this variable is greater than zero. You then repeat the process for males and discard the work variable. Finally, you verify that the exp variable is never negative and is never larger than 40.

You save the above file as check.do, and here is what happens when you run it:

```
. do check
. use frombob, clear
(5/21 data)
. assert _N==522
. assert sal>6000 & sal<=125000
14 contradictions in 522 observations
assertion is false
r(9);
end of do-file
r(9);
```

Everything went fine until you checked the salary variable, and then Stata told you that there were 14 contradictions to your assertion and stopped the do-file. Seeing this, you now interactively summarize the sal variable and discover that 14 people have missing salaries. You dash off a memo to Bob asking him why these data are missing.

◁

▷ Example

Bob responds quickly. There was a mistake in reading the salaries for the consumer relations division. He says it's fixed. You believe him, but check with your do-file again. This time you type run instead of do, suppressing all the output:

```
. run check
.
```

Even though you suppressed the output, if there had been any contradictions, the messages would have printed. check.do ran fine, so all its assertions are true.

◁

❏ Technical Note

assert is especially useful when you are processing large amounts of data in a do-file and wish to verify that all is going as expected. The error in this case may not be in the data but in the do-file itself. For instance, your do-file is rolling along and it has just merged two datasets that it created by subsetting some other data. If everything has gone right so far, then every observation should have merged. When you are performing merge interactively, we recommend that you tabulate _merge to verify that the expected happened. In a do-file, we recommend that you include the line

```
assert _merge==3
```

to verify the correctness of the merge. If all the observations did not merge, the assertion will be false and your do-file will stop.

As another example, you are combining data from numerous sources and you know that after the first two datasets are combined, every individual's sex should be defined. So, you include the line

```
assert sex< .
```

in your do-file. Experienced Stata users include lots of assertions in their do-files when they process data.

❏

❏ Technical Note

assert is smart in how it evaluates expressions. When you say something like assert _N==522 or assert work[_N]>0, assert knows that the expression need be evaluated only once. When you say assert female==1 | female==0, assert knows that the expression needs to be evaluated once for each observation in the dataset.

Here are some more examples demonstrating assert's intelligence.

```
by female:  assert _N==100
```

asserts that there should be 100 observations for every unique value of female. The expression is evaluated once per by-group.

```
by female:  assert work[_N]>0
```

asserts that the last observation on work in every by-group should be greater than zero. It is evaluated once per by-group.

```
by female:  assert work>0
```

is evaluated once for each observation in the dataset and, in that sense, is formally equivalent to `assert work>0`. It is different in that, if there are any contradictions, it will tell you in which by-group the contradiction occurs.

❏

Also See

Complementary:	[P] **capture**, [P] **confirm**
Background:	[U] **19 Do-files**

Title

binreg — Generalized linear models: extensions to the binomial family

Syntax

binreg *depvar* [*varlist*] [*weight*] [if *exp*] [in *range*] [, <u>nocon</u>stant ml

<u>scale</u>(x2|dev|#) [<u>ln</u>]<u>off</u>set(*varname*) disp(#) coeff [or|rr|hr|rd]

<u>level</u>(#) <u>iterate</u>(#) <u>ltol</u>erance(#) <u>init</u>(*varname*) n(*varname*|#) <u>nolog</u>

glm_options]

by ... : may be used with binreg; see [R] **by**.

fweights, aweights, iweights, and pweights are allowed; see [U] **14.1.6 weight**.

This command shares the features of all estimation commands; see [U] **23 Estimation and post-estimation commands**.

Syntax for predict

predict [*type*] *newvarname* [if *exp*] [in *range*] [, *statistic* <u>nooff</u>set <u>standard</u>ized

<u>stu</u>dentized <u>modified</u> <u>adj</u>usted]

where *statistic* is one of

<u>mu</u> | xb | <u>e</u>ta | stdp | <u>a</u>nscombe | <u>c</u>ooksd | <u>d</u>eviance | <u>h</u>at | <u>li</u>kelihood |

<u>p</u>earson | <u>r</u>esponse | <u>s</u>core | <u>w</u>orking

These statistics are available both in and out of sample; type predict ... if e(sample) ... if wanted only for the estimation sample.

Description

binreg fits generalized linear models for the binomial family. It estimates odds ratios, risk ratios, health ratios, and risk differences. The available links are

Option	Implied link	Parameter
or	logit	Odds ratios = $\exp(\beta)$
rr	log	Risk ratios = $\exp(\beta)$
hr	log complement	Health ratios = $\exp(\beta)$
rd	identity	Risk differences = β

Note that estimates of odds, risk, and health ratios are obtained by exponentiating the appropriate coefficients. The option or produces the same results as Stata's logistic command, and or coeff yields the same results as the logit command. When no link is specified/implied, or is assumed (the logit link is implied).

Options

noconstant specifies that the linear predictor has no intercept term, thus forcing it through the origin on the scale defined by the link function.

ml requests the ML Newton–Raphson optimization of the log likelihood instead of the MQL IRLS optimization of the deviance.

scale(x2|dev|#) overrides the default scale parameter. By default, scale(1) is assumed for discrete distributions (binomial, Poisson, and negative binomial), and scale(x2) for continuous distributions (Gaussian, gamma, and inverse Gaussian).

scale(x2) specifies that the scale parameter be set to the Pearson chi-squared (or generalized chi-squared) statistic divided by the residual degrees of freedom.

scale(dev) sets the scale parameter to the deviance divided by the residual degrees of freedom. This provides an alternative to scale(x2) for continuous distributions and over- or under-dispersed discrete distributions.

scale(#) sets the scale parameter to #.

[ln]offset(*varname*) specifies an offset to be added to the linear predictor. offset() speci-fies the values directly: $g(E(y)) = xB + varname$. lnoffset() specifies exponentiated values: $g(E(y)) = xB + \ln(varname)$.

disp(#) multiplies the variance of y by # and divides the deviance by #. The resulting distributions are members of the quasi-likelihood family.

coeff displays the nonexponentiated coefficients and corresponding standard errors and confidence in-tervals. This has no effect when the rd option is specified, as it always presents the nonexponentiated coefficients.

or requests the logit link and results in odds ratios if coeff is not specified.

rr requests the log link and results in risk ratios if coeff is not specified.

hr requests the log-complement link and results in health ratios if coeff is not specified.

rd requests the identity link and results in risk differences if coeff is not specified.

level(#) specifies the confidence level, in percent, for confidence intervals. The default is level(95) or as set by set level; see [U] 23.6 Specifying the width of confidence intervals.

iterate(#) specifies the maximum number of iterations allowed in fitting the model; iterate(50) is the default.

ltolerance(#) specifies the convergence criterion for the change in deviance between iterations; ltolerance(1e-6) is the default.

init(*varname*) specifies *varname* containing an initial estimate for the mean of *depvar*. This can be useful if you encounter convergence difficulties.

n(*varname*|#) specifies either a constant integer to use as the denominator for the binomial family, or a variable which holds the denominator for each observation.

nolog suppresses the iteration log.

glm_options are the options allowed with glm, family(binomial); see [R] **glm**.

Options for predict

mu, the default, specifies that predict is to calculate $g^{-1}(\mathbf{x}\widehat{\boldsymbol{\beta}})$, the inverse link of the linear prediction.

xb calculates the linear prediction $\eta = \mathbf{x}\widehat{\boldsymbol{\beta}}$.

eta is a synonym for xb.

stdp calculates the standard error of the linear prediction.

anscombe calculates the Anscombe (1972) residuals. The aim here is to produce residuals that closely follow a normal distribution.

cooksd calculates Cook's distance, which measures the aggregate change in the estimated coefficients when each observation is left out of the estimation.

deviance calculates the deviance residuals. Deviance residuals are recommended by McCullagh and Nelder (1989) and by others as having the best properties for examining goodness of fit of a GLM. They are approximately normally distributed if the model is correct. They may be plotted against the fitted values or against a covariate to inspect the model's fit. Also see the pearson option below.

hat calculates the diagonals of the "hat" matrix as an analog to simple linear regression.

likelihood calculates a weighted average of the standardized deviance and standardized Pearson (described below) residuals.

pearson calculates the Pearson residuals. Be aware that Pearson residuals often have markedly skewed distributions for non-normal family distributions. Also see the deviance option above.

response calculates the differences between the observed and fitted outcomes.

score calculates the scores used in calculating the sandwich estimate of variance.

working calculates the working residuals, which are response residuals weighted according to the derivative of the link function.

nooffset is relevant only if you specified offset(*varname*) for binreg. It modifies the calculations made by predict so that they ignore the offset variable; the linear prediction is treated as $\mathbf{x}_j\mathbf{b}$ rather than as $\mathbf{x}_j\mathbf{b} + \text{offset}_j$.

standardized requests that the residual be multiplied by the factor $(1-h)^{-1/2}$, where h is the diagonal of the hat matrix. This is done to take the correlation between *depvar* and its predicted value into account.

studentized requests that the residual be multiplied by one over the square root of the estimated scale parameter.

modified requests that the denominator of the residual be modified to be a reasonable estimate of the variance of *depvar*. The base residual is multiplied by the factor $(k/w)^{-1/2}$, where k is either one or the user-specified dispersion parameter, and w is the specified weight (or one if left unspecified).

adjusted adjusts the deviance residual to make the convergence to the limiting normal distribution faster. The adjustment deals with adding to the deviance residual a higher-order term which depends on the variance function family. This option is only allowed when deviance is specified.

Remarks

Wacholder (1986) suggests methods for estimating risks ratios and risk differences from prospective binomial data. These estimates are obtained by selecting the proper link functions in the generalized linear model framework. (See *Methods and Formulas* for details, also see [R] **glm**.)

▷ Example

Wacholder (1986) presents an example, utilizing data from Wright et al. (1983), of an investigation of the relationship between alcohol consumption and the risk of a low-birth-weight baby. Covariates examined included whether the mother smoked (yes or no), mother's social class (three levels), and drinking frequency (light, moderate, or heavy). The data for the 18 possible categories determined by the covariates are illustrated below.

Let's first describe the data and list a few observations.

```
. use http://www.stata-press.com/data/r8/binreg
. list
```

	cat	d	n	alc	smo	soc
1.	1	11	84	3	1	1
2.	2	5	79	2	1	1
3.	3	11	169	1	1	1
4.	4	6	28	3	2	1
5.	5	3	13	2	2	1
6.	6	1	26	1	2	1
7.	7	4	22	3	1	2
8.	8	3	25	2	1	2
9.	9	12	162	1	1	2
10.	10	4	17	3	2	2
11.	11	2	7	2	2	2
12.	12	6	38	1	2	2
13.	13	0	14	3	1	3
14.	14	1	18	2	1	3
15.	15	12	91	1	1	3
16.	16	7	19	3	2	3
17.	17	2	18	2	2	3
18.	18	8	70	1	2	3

Each observation corresponds to one of the 18 covariate structures. The number of low-birth-weight babies out of n in each category is given by the variable d.

We begin by estimating risk ratios:

(Continued on next page)

```
. xi: binreg d I.soc I.alc I.smo, n(n) rr
I.soc               _Isoc_1-3         (naturally coded; _Isoc_1 omitted)
I.alc               _Ialc_1-3         (naturally coded; _Ialc_1 omitted)
I.smo               _Ismo_1-2         (naturally coded; _Ismo_1 omitted)

Iteration 1 : deviance =   14.2879
Iteration 2 : deviance =    13.607
Iteration 3 : deviance =  13.60503
Iteration 4 : deviance =  13.60503

Residual df  =        12                    No. of obs =         18
Pearson X2   =  11.51517                    Deviance   =  13.60503
Dispersion   =  .9595976                    Dispersion =  1.133752

Binomial (N=n) distribution, log link
```

d	Risk Ratio	EIM Std. Err.	z	P>|z|	[95% Conf. Interval]	
_Isoc_2	1.340001	.3127382	1.25	0.210	.848098	2.11721
_Isoc_3	1.349487	.3291488	1.23	0.219	.8366715	2.176619
_Ialc_2	1.191157	.3265354	0.64	0.523	.6960276	2.038503
_Ialc_3	1.974078	.4261751	3.15	0.002	1.293011	3.013884
_Ismo_2	1.648444	.332875	2.48	0.013	1.109657	2.448836

By default, the program outputs the risk ratios (the exponentiated regression coefficients) estimated by the model. We can see that the risk ratio comparing heavy drinkers with light drinkers, after adjusting for smoking and social class, is $\exp(0.6801017) = 1.9740785$. That is, mothers who drink heavily during their pregnancy have approximately twice the risk of delivering low-weight babies than mothers who are light drinkers.

The nonexponentiated coefficients can be obtained via the `coeff` option.

```
. xi: binreg d I.smo I.soc I.alc, n(n) rr coeff
I.smo               _Ismo_1-2         (naturally coded; _Ismo_1 omitted)
I.soc               _Isoc_1-3         (naturally coded; _Isoc_1 omitted)
I.alc               _Ialc_1-3         (naturally coded; _Ialc_1 omitted)

Iteration 1 : deviance =   14.2879
Iteration 2 : deviance =    13.607
Iteration 3 : deviance =  13.60503
Iteration 4 : deviance =  13.60503

Residual df  =        12                    No. of obs =         18
Pearson X2   =  11.51517                    Deviance   =  13.60503
Dispersion   =  .9595976                    Dispersion =  1.133752

Binomial (N=n) distribution, log link
Risk ratio coefficients
```

d	Coef.	EIM Std. Err.	z	P>|z|	[95% Conf. Interval]	
_Ismo_2	.4998317	.2019329	2.48	0.013	.1040505	.8956129
_Isoc_2	.2926702	.2333866	1.25	0.210	-.1647591	.7500994
_Isoc_3	.2997244	.2439066	1.23	0.219	-.1783238	.7777726
_Ialc_2	.1749248	.274133	0.64	0.523	-.362366	.7122156
_Ialc_3	.6801017	.2158856	3.15	0.002	.2569737	1.10323
_cons	-2.764079	.2031606	-13.61	0.000	-3.162266	-2.365891

Risk differences are obtained using the `rd` option:

```
. xi: binreg d I.soc I.alc I.smo, n(n) rd
I.smo            _Ismo_1-2           (naturally coded; _Ismo_1 omitted)
I.soc            _Isoc_1-3           (naturally coded; _Isoc_1 omitted)
I.alc            _Ialc_1-3           (naturally coded; _Ialc_1 omitted)

Iteration 1 : deviance =  18.67277
Iteration 2 : deviance =  14.94364
Iteration 3 : deviance =   14.9185
Iteration 4 : deviance =  14.91762
Iteration 5 : deviance =  14.91758
Iteration 6 : deviance =  14.91758
Iteration 7 : deviance =  14.91758
```

Residual df	=	12		No. of obs	=	18
Pearson X2	=	12.60353		Deviance	=	14.91758
Dispersion	=	1.050294		Dispersion	=	1.243132

Binomial (N=n) distribution, identity link
Risk difference coefficients

d	Coef.	EIM Std. Err.	z	P>|z|	[95% Conf. Interval]	
_Ismo_2	.0542415	.0270838	2.00	0.045	.0011582	.1073248
_Isoc_2	.0263817	.0232124	1.14	0.256	-.0191137	.0718771
_Isoc_3	.0365553	.0268668	1.36	0.174	-.0161026	.0892132
_Ialc_2	.0122539	.0257713	0.48	0.634	-.0382569	.0627647
_Ialc_3	.0801291	.0302878	2.65	0.008	.020766	.1394921
_cons	.059028	.0160693	3.67	0.000	.0275327	.0905232

The risk difference between the heavy drinkers and the light drinkers is simply the value of the coefficient for _Ialc_3 = 0.0801291. Because the risk differences are obtained directly from the coefficients estimated using the identity link, the coeff option has no effect in this case.

Health ratios are obtained using the hr option. The health ratios (exponentiated coefficients for the log-complement link) are reported directly.

```
. xi: binreg d I.soc I.alc I.smo, n(n) hr
I.smo            _Ismo_1-2           (naturally coded; _Ismo_1 omitted)
I.soc            _Isoc_1-3           (naturally coded; _Isoc_1 omitted)
I.alc            _Ialc_1-3           (naturally coded; _Ialc_1 omitted)

Iteration 1 : deviance =  21.15233
Iteration 2 : deviance =  15.16467
Iteration 3 : deviance =  15.13205
Iteration 4 : deviance =  15.13114
Iteration 5 : deviance =  15.13111
Iteration 6 : deviance =  15.13111
Iteration 7 : deviance =  15.13111
```

Residual df	=	12		No. of obs	=	18
Pearson X2	=	12.84204		Deviance	=	15.13111
Dispersion	=	1.07017		Dispersion	=	1.260925

Binomial (N=n) distribution, log-complement link
Health ratio (HR)

d	HR	EIM Std. Err.	z	P>|z|	[95% Conf. Interval]	
_Isoc_2	.9720541	.024858	-1.11	0.268	.9245342	1.022017
_Isoc_3	.9597182	.0290412	-1.36	0.174	.9044535	1.01836
_Ialc_2	.9871517	.0278852	-0.46	0.647	.9339831	1.043347
_Ialc_3	.9134243	.0325726	-2.54	0.011	.8517631	.9795493
_Ismo_2	.9409983	.0296125	-1.93	0.053	.8847125	1.000865

To see the nonexponentiated coefficients, we can specify the `coeff` option.

◁

Saved Results

`binreg` saves in `e()`:

Scalars

e(N)	number of observations	e(N_clust)	number of clusters
e(k)	number of parameters	e(ll)	log likelihood, if ML
e(df)	residual degrees of freedom	e(deviance)	deviance
e(phi)	scale parameter	e(deviance_p)	Pearson deviance
e(disp)	dispersion parameter	e(dispers)	dispersion
e(rc)	return code	e(dispers_p)	Pearson dispersion
e(df_m)	model degrees of freedom	e(disp)	dispersion parameter
e(aic)	model AIC, if ML	e(vf)	factor set by vfactor(),
e(bic)	model BIC		1 if not set

Macros

e(cmd)	binreg	e(offset)	offset
e(depvar)	name of dependent variable	e(predict)	program used to implement
e(link)	name of link function used by glm		predict
e(m)	number of binomial trials	e(clustvar)	cluster variable
e(se1)	std. error header, line 1	e(cons)	set if noconstant specified
e(se2)	std. error header, line 2	e(linkt)	link title
e(wtype)	weight type	e(linkf)	link form
e(wexp)	weight expression	e(title_fl)	family–link title
e(crittype)	optimization criterion		

Matrices

e(b)	coefficient vector	e(V)	variance–covariance matrix of
e(ilog)	iteration log (up to 20 iterations)		the estimators

Functions

e(sample)	marks estimation sample

Methods and Formulas

`binreg` is implemented as an ado-file.

Let π_i be the probability of success for the ith observation, $i = 1, \ldots, N$, and let $X\beta$ be the linear predictor. Then the link function relates the covariates of each observation to its respective probability through the linear predictor.

In logistic regression, the logit link is used:

$$\ln\left(\frac{\pi}{1 - \pi}\right) = X\beta$$

The regression coefficient β_k represents the change in the logarithm of the odds associated with a one-unit change in the value of the X_k covariate; thus, $\exp(\beta_k)$ is the ratio of the odds associated with a change of one unit in X_k.

For risk differences, the identity link $\pi = X\beta$ is used. The regression coefficient β_k represents the risk difference associated with a change of one unit in X_k. When using the identity link, it is possible to obtain fitted probabilities outside of the interval $(0, 1)$. As suggested by Wacholder, at each iteration, fitted probabilities are checked for range conditions (and put back in range if necessary). For example, if the identity link results in a fitted probability that is smaller than $1e - 4$, the probability is replaced with $1e - 4$ before the link function is calculated.

A similar adjustment is made for the logarithmic link, which is used for estimating the risk ratio, $\ln(\pi) = X\beta$, where $\exp(\beta_k)$ is the risk ratio associated with a change of one unit in X_k, and for the log-complement link used to estimate the probability of no disease or health, where $\exp(\beta_k)$ represents the "health ratio" associated with a change of one unit in X_k.

References

Hardin, J. and M. Cleves. 1999. sbe29: Generalized linear models: extensions to the binomial family. *Stata Technical Bulletin* 50: 21–25. Reprinted in *Stata Technical Bulletin Reprints*, vol. 9, pp. 140–146.

Kleinbaum, D. G. and M. Klein. 2002. *Logistic Regression: A Self-Learning Text*. 2d ed. New York: Springer.

Wacholder, S. 1986. Binomial regression in GLIM: estimating risk ratios and risk differences. *American Journal of Epidemiology* 123: 174–184.

Wright, J. T., E. J. Waterson, I. G. Barrison, P. J. Toplis, I. G. Lewis, M. G. Gordon, K. D. MacRae, N. F. Morris, and I. M. Murray-Lyon. 1983. Alcohol consumption, pregnancy and low birthweight. *Lancet* 1: 663–665.

Also See

Complementary:	[R] **adjust**, [R] **lincom**, [R] **linktest**, [R] **mfx**, [R] **nlcom**,
	[R] **predict**, [R] **predictnl** [R] **test**, [R] **testnl**, [R] **vce**, [R] **xi**
Related:	[R] **glm**
Background:	[U] **16.5 Accessing coefficients and standard errors**,
	[U] **23 Estimation and post-estimation commands**,
	[U] **23.14 Obtaining robust variance estimates**

Title

---
biprobit — Bivariate probit models

Syntax

Bivariate probit model

> biprobit *depvar_1* *depvar_2* [*varlist*] [*weight*] [if *exp*] [in *range*] [, robust
>
> cluster(*varname*) score(*newvarlist* | *stub**) partial noconstant
>
> constraints(*numlist*) noskip level(#) offset1(*varname*) offset2(*varname*)
>
> *maximize_options*]

Seemingly unrelated bivariate probit model

> biprobit *equation1* *equation2* [*weight*] [if *exp*] [in *range*] [, robust
>
> cluster(*varname*) score(*newvarlist* | *stub**) partial constraints(*numlist*)
>
> noskip level(#) *maximize_options*]

where *equation1* and *equation2* are specified as

> ([*eqname*:] *depvar* [=] [*varlist*] [, offset(*varname*) noconstant])

by ... : may be used with biprobit; see [R] **by**.

pweights, fweights, and iweights are allowed; see [U] **14.1.6 weight**.

biprobit shares the features of all estimation commands; see [U] **23 Estimation and post-estimation commands**.

(Continued on next page)

Syntax for predict

predict [*type*] *newvarname* [if *exp*] [in *range*] [, *statistic* <u>nooff</u>set]

where *statistic* is

<u>p</u>11	$\Phi_2(\mathbf{x}_j\mathbf{b}, \mathbf{z}_j\mathbf{g}, \rho)$, predicted probability $\Pr(y_{1j} = 1, y_{2j} = 1)$ (the default)
p10	$\Phi_2(\mathbf{x}_j\mathbf{b}, -\mathbf{z}_j\mathbf{g}, -\rho)$, predicted probability $\Pr(y_{1j} = 1, y_{2j} = 0)$
p01	$\Phi_2(-\mathbf{x}_j\mathbf{b}, \mathbf{z}_j\mathbf{g}, -\rho)$, predicted probability $\Pr(y_{1j} = 0, y_{2j} = 1)$
p00	$\Phi_2(-\mathbf{x}_j\mathbf{b}, -\mathbf{z}_j\mathbf{g}, \rho)$, predicted probability $\Pr(y_{1j} = 0, y_{2j} = 0)$
pmarg1	$\Phi(\mathbf{x}_j\mathbf{b})$, marginal success probability for equation 1
pmarg2	$\Phi(\mathbf{z}_j\mathbf{g})$, marginal success probability for equation 2
pcond1	$\Phi_2(\mathbf{x}_j\mathbf{b}, \mathbf{z}_j\mathbf{g}, \rho)/\Phi(\mathbf{z}_j\mathbf{g})$, conditional probability of success for equation 1
pcond2	$\Phi_2(\mathbf{x}_j\mathbf{b}, \mathbf{z}_j\mathbf{g}, \rho)/\Phi(\mathbf{x}_j\mathbf{b})$, conditional probability of success for equation 2
xb1	$\mathbf{x}_j\mathbf{b}$, fitted values for equation 1
xb2	$\mathbf{z}_j\mathbf{g}$, fitted values for equation 2
stdp1	standard error of fitted values for equation 1
stdp2	standard error of fitted values for equation 2

where $\Phi()$ is the standard normal distribution function and $\Phi_2()$ is the bivariate standard normal distribution function.

These statistics are available both in and out of sample; type predict ... if e(sample) ... if wanted only for the estimation sample.

Description

biprobit fits maximum-likelihood two-equation probit models—either a bivariate probit or a seemingly unrelated probit (limited to two equations).

Options

robust specifies that the Huber/White/sandwich estimator of the variance is to be used in place of the conventional MLE variance estimator. robust combined with cluster() further allows observations that are not independent within cluster (although they must be independent between clusters).

If you specify pweights, robust is implied; see [U] **23.14 Obtaining robust variance estimates**.

cluster(*varname*) specifies that the observations are independent across groups (clusters), but not necessarily within groups. *varname* specifies to which group each observation belongs. cluster() affects the estimated standard errors and variance–covariance matrix of the estimators (VCE), but not the estimated coefficients. cluster() can be used with pweights to produce estimates for unstratified cluster-sampled data.

cluster() implies robust; that is, specifying robust cluster() is equivalent to typing cluster() by itself.

score(*newvarlist* | *stub*) creates a new variable for each equation in the model. Each new variable contains the observation's contribution to the score; see [U] **23.15 Obtaining scores**. There are three scores for a two-equation probit model, scores for the first equation, for the second equation, and for the ancillary parameter equation.

If score(*newvarlist*) is specified, the *newvarlist* must contain three new variables, one for each equation in the model. If score(*stub*) is specified, variables named *stub*1, *stub*2, and *stub*3 are created.

The first new variable specified will contain $u_{1j} = \partial \ln L_j / \partial (\mathbf{x}_j \boldsymbol{\beta})$ for each observation j in the sample, where $\ln L_j$ is the jth observation's contribution to the log likelihood.
The second new variable: $u_{2j} = \partial \ln L_j / \partial (\mathbf{z}_j \boldsymbol{\gamma})$
The third: $u_{3j} = \partial \ln L_j / \partial (\text{atanh } \rho)$

The jth observation's contribution to the score vector is

$$\left\{ \partial \ln L_j / \partial \boldsymbol{\beta} \ \ \partial \ln L_j / \partial \boldsymbol{\gamma} \ \ \partial \ln L_j / \partial (\text{atanh } \rho) \right\} = \left(u_{1j}\mathbf{x}_j \ \ u_{2j}\mathbf{z}_j \ \ u_{3j} \right)$$

The score vector can be obtained by summing over j.

partial specifies that the partial observability model should be fitted. Note that this particular model commonly has poor convergence properties, and we recommend that you use the difficult option if you want to fit the Poirier partial observability model; see [R] **ml**.

Note that this model computes the product of the two dependent variables such that you do not have to replace each with the product.

noconstant omits the constant term from the equation. This option may be specified on the regression equation, the selection equation, or both.

constraints(*numlist*) specifies by number the linear constraints to be applied during estimation. The default is to perform unconstrained estimation. Constraints are specified using the constraint command; see [R] **constraint**. See [R] **reg3** for the use of constraints in multiple-equation contexts.

noskip specifies that a full maximum-likelihood model with only a constant for the regression equation be fitted. This model is not displayed, but is used as the base model to compute a likelihood-ratio test for the model test statistic displayed in the estimation header. By default, the overall model test statistic is an asymptotically equivalent Wald test of all the parameters in the regression equation being zero (except the constant). For many models, this option can substantially increase estimation time.

level(*#*) specifies the confidence level, in percent, for confidence intervals. The default is level(95) or as set by set level; see [U] **23.6 Specifying the width of confidence intervals**.

offset(*varname*) is a rarely used option that specifies a variable to be added directly to $\mathbf{Xb}$. This option may be specified on either the regression or the selection equation (or both). In the seemingly unrelated model syntax, it is clear to which equation this option applies. In the bivariate probit syntax, use the offset1(*varname*) and offset2(*varname*) options to be clear.

maximize_options control the maximization process; see [R] **maximize**. With the possible exception of iterate(0) and trace, you should never have to specify them.

Options for predict

p11, the default, calculates the bivariate predicted probability $\Pr(y_{1j} = 1, y_{2j} = 1)$.

p10 calculates the bivariate predicted probability $\Pr(y_{1j} = 1, y_{2j} = 0)$.

p01 calculates the bivariate predicted probability $\Pr(y_{1j} = 0, y_{2j} = 1)$.

p00 calculates the bivariate predicted probability $\Pr(y_{1j} = 0, y_{2j} = 0)$.

pmarg1 calculates the univariate (marginal) predicted probability of success $\Pr(y_{1j} = 1)$.

pmarg2 calculates the univariate (marginal) predicted probability of success $\Pr(y_{2j} = 1)$.

pcond1 calculates the conditional (on success in equation 2) predicted probability of success
$\Pr(y_{1j} = 1, y_{2j} = 1)/\Pr(y_{2j} = 1)$.

pcond2 calculates the conditional (on success in equation 1) predicted probability of success
$\Pr(y_{1j} = 1, y_{2j} = 1)/\Pr(y_{1j} = 1)$.

xb1 calculates the probit linear prediction $\mathbf{x}_j\mathbf{b}$.

xb2 calculates the probit linear prediction $\mathbf{z}_j\mathbf{g}$.

stdp1 calculates the standard error of the linear prediction of equation 1.

stdp2 calculates the standard error of the linear prediction of equation 2.

nooffset is relevant only if you specified offset(*varname*) for biprobit. It modifies the calculations made by predict so that they ignore the offset variable; the linear prediction is treated as
$\mathbf{x}_j\mathbf{b}$ rather than as $\mathbf{x}_j\mathbf{b} + \text{offset}_j$.

Remarks

For a good introduction to the bivariate probit models, see Greene (2003, 710–714) and Pindyck
and Rubinfeld (1998). Poirier (1980) explains the partial observability model. Van de Ven and Van
Pragg (1981) explain the probit model with sample selection; see [R] **heckprob** for details.

▷ Example

We use the data from Pindyck and Rubinfeld (1998, 332). In this dataset, the variables are whether
children attend private school (private), number of years the family has been at the present residence
(years), log of property tax (logptax), log of income (loginc), and whether one voted for an
increase in property taxes (vote).

We wish to model the bivariate outcomes of whether children attend private school and whether
the head of the household voted for an increase in property tax based on the other covariates.

```
. use http://www.stata-press.com/data/r8/school
. biprobit private vote years logptax loginc
Fitting comparison equation 1:
Iteration 0:   log likelihood = -31.967097
Iteration 1:   log likelihood = -31.454068
Iteration 2:   log likelihood = -31.448959
Iteration 3:   log likelihood = -31.448958
Fitting comparison equation 2:
Iteration 0:   log likelihood = -63.036914
Iteration 1:   log likelihood = -58.581911
Iteration 2:   log likelihood = -58.497419
Iteration 3:   log likelihood = -58.497288
Comparison:    log likelihood = -89.946246
```

```
Fitting full model:
Iteration 0:   log likelihood = -89.946246
Iteration 1:   log likelihood = -89.258897
Iteration 2:   log likelihood = -89.254028
Iteration 3:   log likelihood = -89.254028
```

```
Bivariate probit regression                Number of obs   =        95
                                            Wald chi2(6)    =      9.59
Log likelihood = -89.254028                 Prob > chi2     =    0.1431
```

	Coef.	Std. Err.	z	P>|z|	[95% Conf.	Interval]
private						
years	-.0118884	.0256778	-0.46	0.643	-.0622159	.0384391
logptax	-.1066962	.6669782	-0.16	0.873	-1.413949	1.200557
loginc	.3762037	.5306484	0.71	0.478	-.663848	1.416255
_cons	-4.184694	4.837817	-0.86	0.387	-13.66664	5.297253
vote						
years	-.0168561	.0147834	-1.14	0.254	-.0458309	.0121188
logptax	-1.288707	.5752266	-2.24	0.025	-2.416131	-.1612839
loginc	.998286	.4403565	2.27	0.023	.1352031	1.861369
_cons	-.5360573	4.068509	-0.13	0.895	-8.510188	7.438073
/athrho	-.2764525	.2412099	-1.15	0.252	-.7492153	.1963102
rho	-.2696186	.2236753			-.6346806	.1938267

```
Likelihood-ratio test of rho=0:     chi2(1) =  1.38444    Prob > chi2 = 0.2393
```

The output shows several iteration logs. The first iteration log corresponds to running the univariate probit model for the first equation, and the second log corresponds to running the univariate probit for the second model. If $\rho = 0$, then the sum of the log likelihoods from these two models will equal the log likelihood of the bivariate probit model; this sum is printed in the iteration log as the comparison log likelihood.

The final iteration log is for fitting the full bivariate probit model. A likelihood-ratio test of the log likelihood for this model and the comparison log likelihood is presented at the end of the output. If we had specified the robust option, then this test would be presented as a Wald test instead of as a likelihood-ratio test.

Note that we could have fitted the same model using the seemingly unrelated syntax as

```
. biprobit (private=years logptax loginc) (vote=years logptax loginc)
```

◁

(Continued on next page)

Saved Results

biprobit saves in e():

Scalars

e(N)	number of observations	e(rc)	return code
e(k)	number of variables	e(chi2)	χ^2
e(k_eq)	number of equations	e(chi2_c)	χ^2 for comparison test
e(k_dv)	number of dependent variables	e(p)	significance
e(df_m)	model degrees of freedom	e(rho)	ρ
e(ll)	log likelihood	e(ic)	number of iterations
e(ll_0)	log likelihood, constant-only model	e(rank)	rank of e(V)
e(ll_c)	log likelihood, comparison model	e(rank0)	rank of e(V) for constant-only
e(N_clust)	number of clusters		model

Macros

e(cmd)	biprobit	e(opt)	type of optimization
e(depvar)	name(s) of dependent variable(s)	e(chi2type)	Wald or LR; type of model χ^2 test
e(title)	title in estimation output	e(chi2_ct)	Wald or LR; type of model χ^2 test
e(wtype)	weight type		corresponding to e(chi2_c)
e(wexp)	weight expression	e(offset1)	offset for first equation
e(clustvar)	name of cluster variable	e(offset2)	offset for second equation
e(vcetype)	covariance estimation method	e(scorevars)	variables containing scores
e(user)	name of likelihood-evaluator	e(crittype)	optimization criterion
	program	e(predict)	program used to implement predict

Matrices

e(b)	coefficient vector	e(V)	variance–covariance matrix of
e(ilog)	iteration log (up to 20 iterations)		the estimators

Functions

e(sample)	marks estimation sample

Methods and Formulas

biprobit is implemented as an ado-file.

The log likelihood, L, is given by

$$\xi_i^\beta = x_i\beta + \text{offset}_i^\beta$$

$$\xi_i^\gamma = z_i\gamma + \text{offset}_i^\gamma$$

$$q_{1i} = \begin{cases} 1 & \text{if } y_{1i} \neq 0 \\ -1 & \text{otherwise} \end{cases}$$

$$q_{2i} = \begin{cases} 1 & \text{if } y_{2i} \neq 0 \\ -1 & \text{otherwise} \end{cases}$$

$$\rho_i^* = q_{1i}q_{2i}\rho$$

$$L = \sum_{i=1}^{n} w_i \ln \Phi_2\left(q_{1i}\xi_i^\beta, q_{2i}\xi_i^\gamma, \rho_i^*\right)$$

where $\Phi_2()$ is the cumulative bivariate normal distribution function (with mean $\begin{bmatrix} 0 & 0 \end{bmatrix}'$) and w_i is an optional weight for observation i. This derivation assumes that

$$y_{1i}^* = x_i\beta + \epsilon_{1i} + \text{offset}_i^\beta$$
$$y_{2i}^* = z_i\gamma + \epsilon_{2i} + \text{offset}_i^\gamma$$
$$E(\epsilon_1) = E(\epsilon_2) = 0$$
$$\text{Var}(\epsilon_1) = \text{Var}(\epsilon_2) = 1$$
$$\text{Cov}(\epsilon_1, \epsilon_2) = \rho$$

where y_{1i}^* and y_{2i}^* are the unobserved latent variables; instead, we observe only $y_{ji} = 1$ if $y_{ji}^* > 0$ and $y_{ji} = 0$ otherwise (for $j = 1, 2$).

In the maximum likelihood estimation, ρ is not directly estimated. Directly estimated is atanh ρ:

$$\text{atanh}\,\rho = \frac{1}{2}\ln\left(\frac{1+\rho}{1-\rho}\right)$$

From the form of the likelihood, it is clear that if $\rho = 0$, then the log likelihood for the bivariate probit models is equal to the sum of the log likelihoods of the two univariate probit models. A likelihood-ratio test may therefore be performed by comparing the likelihood of the full bivariate model with the sum of the log likelihoods for the univariate probit models.

References

Greene, W. H. 2003. *Econometric Analysis*. 5th ed. Upper Saddle River, NJ: Prentice–Hall.

Hardin, J. W. 1996. sg61: Bivariate probit models. *Stata Technical Bulletin* 33: 15–20. Reprinted in *Stata Technical Bulletin Reprints*, vol. 6, pp. 152–158.

Heckman, J. 1979. Sample selection bias as a specification error. *Econometrica* 47: 153–161.

Pindyck, R. and D. Rubinfeld. 1998. *Econometric Models and Economic Forecasts*. 4th ed. New York: McGraw–Hill.

Poirier, D. 1981. Partial observability in bivariate probit models. *Journal of Econometrics* 12: 209–217.

Van de Ven, W. P. M. M. and B. M. S. Van Pragg. 1981. The demand for deductibles in private health insurance: A probit model with sample selection. *Journal of Econometrics* 17: 229–252.

Also See

Complementary:	[R] **adjust**, [R] **constraint**, [R] **lincom**, [R] **lrtest**, [R] **mfx**, [R] **nlcom**, [R] **predict**, [R] **predictnl**, [R] **suest**, [R] **test**, [R] **testnl**, [R] **vce**, [R] **xi**
Related:	[R] **heckman**, [R] **heckprob**, [R] **probit**
Background:	[U] **16.5 Accessing coefficients and standard errors**, [U] **23 Estimation and post-estimation commands**, [U] **23.14 Obtaining robust variance estimates**, [U] **23.15 Obtaining scores**

Title

> **bitest** — Binomial probability test

Syntax

> **bitest** *varname* == #*p* [*weight*] [if *exp*] [in *range*] [, detail]
>
> **bitesti** #*N* #*succ* #*p* [, detail]

by ... : may be used with **bitest** (but not with **bitesti**); see [R] **by**.
bitest allows fweights; see [U] **14.1.6 weight**.

Description

bitest performs exact hypothesis tests for binomial random variables. The null hypothesis is that the probability of a success on a single trial is #*p*. The total number of trials is the number of nonmissing values of *varname* (in **bitest**) or #*N* (in **bitesti**). The number of observed successes is the number of 1s in *varname* (in **bitest**) or #*succ* (in **bitesti**). *varname* must contain only 0s, 1s, and missing.

bitesti is the immediate form of **bitest**; see [U] **22 Immediate commands** for a general introduction to immediate commands.

Options

detail shows the probability of the observed number k_{obs} of successes, the probability of the number k_{opp} of successes on the opposite tail of the distribution that is used to compute the two-sided p-value, and the probability of the point next to k_{opp}. This information can be safely ignored. See the technical note below for details.

Remarks

▷ Example

You test 15 university students for high levels of one measure of visual quickness which, from other evidence, you believe is present in 30% of the nonuniversity population. Included in your data is quick, taking on the values 1 ("success") or 0 ("failure") depending on the outcome of the test.

```
. bitest quick == 0.3
```

Variable	N	Observed k	Expected k	Assumed p	Observed p
quick	15	7	4.5	0.30000	0.46667

```
Pr(k >= 7)          = 0.131143  (one-sided test)
Pr(k <= 7)          = 0.949987  (one-sided test)
Pr(k <= 1 or k >= 7) = 0.166410  (two-sided test)
```

The first part of the output reveals that, assuming a true probability of success of 0.3, the expected number of successes is 4.5, and you observed 7. Said differently, the assumed frequency under the null hypothesis H_0 is 0.3 and the observed frequency is 0.47.

The first line under the table is a one-sided test; it is the probability of observing 7 or more successes conditional on $p = 0.3$. It is a test of $H_0: p = 0.3$ versus the alternative hypothesis $H_A: p > 0.3$. Said in English, the alternative hypothesis is that more than 30% of university students score at high levels on this test of visual quickness. The p-value for this hypothesis test is 0.13.

The second line under the table is a one-sided test of H_0 versus the opposite alternative hypothesis $H_A: p < 0.3$.

The third line is the two-sided test. It is a test of H_0 versus the alternative hypothesis $H_A: p \neq 0.3$.

◁

❑ Technical Note

The p-value of a hypothesis test is the probability (calculated assuming H_0 is true) of observing any outcome as extreme or more extreme than the observed outcome. "Extreme" means in the direction of the alternative hypothesis. In the previous example, the outcomes $k = 8, 9, \ldots, 15$ are clearly "more extreme" than the observed outcome $k_{obs} = 7$ when considering the alternative hypothesis $H_A: p \neq 0.3$. However, outcomes with only a few successes are also in the direction of this alternative hypothesis. For two-sided hypotheses, outcomes with k successes are considered "as extreme or more extreme" than the observed outcome k_{obs} if $\Pr(k) \leq \Pr(k_{obs})$. Here, $\Pr(k = 0)$ and $\Pr(k = 1)$ are both less than $\Pr(k = 7)$, so they are included in the two-sided p-value.

The `detail` option allows you to see the probability (calculated assuming H_0 is true) of the observed successes ($k = 7$) and the probability of the boundary point ($k = 1$) of the opposite tail used for the two-sided p-value.

```
. bitest quick == 0.3, detail
         Variable |      N   Observed k   Expected k   Assumed p   Observed p
       -----------+--------------------------------------------------------
            quick |     15           7          4.5     0.30000     0.46667

  Pr(k >= 7)              = 0.131143  (one-sided test)
  Pr(k <= 7)              = 0.949987  (one-sided test)
  Pr(k <= 1 or k >= 7)    = 0.166410  (two-sided test)

  Pr(k == 7)              = 0.081130  (observed)
  Pr(k == 2)              = 0.091560
  Pr(k == 1)              = 0.030520  (opposite extreme)
```

Also shown is the probability of the point next to the boundary point. This probability, namely $\Pr(k = 2) = 0.092$, is certainly close to the probability of the observed outcome $\Pr(k = 7) = 0.081$, so some people might argue that $k = 2$ should be included in the two-sided p-value. Statisticians (at least some that we know) would reply that the p-value is a precisely defined concept, and that this is an arbitrary "fuzzification" of its definition. When you compute exact p-values according to the precise definition of a p-value, your Type I error is never more than what you say it is—so no one can criticize you for being anticonservative. Including the point $k = 2$ is being overly conservative since it makes the p-value larger yet. But it is your choice; being overly conservative, at least in statistics, is always safe. Know that `bitest` and `bitesti` always keep to the precise definition of a p-value, so if you wish to include this extra point, you must do so by hand or by using the `r()` saved results; see *Saved Results* below.

❑

Immediate form

▷ Example

The binomial test is a function of two statistics and one parameter: N the number of observations, k_{obs} the number of observed successes, and p the assumed probability of a success on a single trial. For instance, in a city of $N = 2,500,000$, you observe $k_{obs} = 36$ cases of a particular disease when the population rate for the disease is $p = 0.00001$.

```
. bitesti 2500000 36 .00001
          N    Observed k    Expected k    Assumed p    Observed p
    2500000          36            25         0.00001       0.00001
    Pr(k >= 36)                = 0.022458  (one-sided test)
    Pr(k <= 36)                = 0.985448  (one-sided test)
    Pr(k <= 14 or k >= 36)     = 0.034859  (two-sided test)
```

◁

▷ Example

Boice and Monson (1977) present data on breast cancer cases and person-years of observations for women with tuberculosis who were repeatedly exposed to multiple x-ray fluoroscopies, and women with tuberculosis who were not. The data are

	Exposed	Not Exposed	Total
Breast cancer	41	15	56
Person-years	28,010	19,017	47,027

We can thus test whether x-ray fluoroscopic examinations are associated with breast cancer; the assumed rate of exposure is $p = 28010/47027$.

```
. bitesti 56 41 28010/47027
          N    Observed k    Expected k    Assumed p    Observed p
         56          41       33.35446        0.59562       0.73214
    Pr(k >= 41)                = 0.023830  (one-sided test)
    Pr(k <= 41)                = 0.988373  (one-sided test)
    Pr(k <= 25 or k >= 41)     = 0.040852  (two-sided test)
```

◁

Saved Results

bitest and bitesti save in r():

Scalars

r(N)	number N of trials	r(k_opp)	opposite extreme k
r(P_p)	assumed probability p of success	r(P_k)	probability of observed k (detail only)
r(k)	observed number k of successes	r(P_oppk)	probability of opposite extreme k (detail only)
r(p_l)	lower one-sided p-value	r(k_nopp)	k next to opposite extreme (detail only)
r(p_u)	upper one-sided p-value	r(P_noppk)	probability of k next to opposite extreme
r(p)	two-sided p-value		(detail only)

Methods and Formulas

bitest and bitesti are implemented as ado-files.

Let N, k_{obs}, and p be, respectively, the number of observations, the observed number of successes, and the assumed probability of success on a single trial. The expected number of successes is Np, and the observed probability of success on a single trial is k_{obs}/N.

bitest and bitesti compute exact p-values based on the binomial distribution. The upper one-sided p-value is

$$\Pr(k \geq k_{\mathrm{obs}}) = \sum_{m=k_{\mathrm{obs}}}^{N} \binom{N}{m} p^m (1-p)^{N-m}$$

The lower one-sided p-value is

$$\Pr(k \leq k_{\mathrm{obs}}) = \sum_{m=0}^{k_{\mathrm{obs}}} \binom{N}{m} p^m (1-p)^{N-m}$$

If $k_{\mathrm{obs}} \geq Np$, the two-sided p-value is

$$\Pr(k \leq k_{\mathrm{opp}} \text{ or } k \geq k_{\mathrm{obs}})$$

where k_{opp} is the largest number $\leq Np$ such that $\Pr(k = k_{\mathrm{opp}}) \leq \Pr(k = k_{\mathrm{obs}})$. If $k_{\mathrm{obs}} < Np$, the two-sided p-value is

$$\Pr(k \leq k_{\mathrm{obs}} \text{ or } k \geq k_{\mathrm{opp}})$$

where k_{opp} is the smallest number $\geq Np$ such that $\Pr(k = k_{\mathrm{opp}}) \leq \Pr(k = k_{\mathrm{obs}})$.

References

Boice, J. D. and R. R. Monson. 1977. Breast cancer in women after repeated fluoroscopic examinations of the chest. *Journal of the National Cancer Institute* 59: 823–832.

Hoel, P. G. 1984. *Introduction to Mathematical Statistics.* 5th ed. New York: John Wiley & Sons.

Also See

Complementary:	[R] **ci**, [R] **prtest**
Background:	[U] **22 Immediate commands**

Title

bootstrap — Bootstrap sampling and estimation

Syntax

bootstrap "*command*" *exp_list* [, reps(#) size(#) dots saving(*filename*)

  double every(#) replace noesample noisily nowarn *bsample_options bstat_options*]

bstat [*varlist*] [using *filename*] [, accel(#|*matname*) stat(#|*matname*) n(#)

  bstat_options]

bsample [*exp*] [, weight(*varname*) *bsample_options*]

where *bsample_options* are

  cluster(*varlist*) idcluster(*newvarname*) strata(*varlist*)

and *bstat_options* are

  bca level(#) nobc nonormal nopercentile notable separate title(*text*)

exp_list contains
  newvarname = (*exp*)
  (*exp*)
  eexp

eexp is
  specname
  [*eqno*]*specname*

specname is
  _b
  _b[]
  _se
  _se[]

eqno is
  # #
  name

Distinguish between [ ], which are to be typed, and [ ], which indicate optional arguments.

bootstrap and bstat share the features of all estimation commands (except that predict is not allowed); see [U] **23 Estimation and post-estimation commands**.

Description

bootstrap runs *command* repeatedly, bootstrapping the statistics in *exp_list* by resampling from the data in memory. This is often referred to as the nonparametric bootstrap method. bs is a synonym for bootstrap.

command defines the statistical command to be executed. *command* must be bound in double quotes. Compound double quotes (`'"` and `"'`) are needed if the command itself contains double quotes. Most Stata commands and user-written programs can be used with bootstrap. If the bca option is supplied, then *command* must also work with jknife; see [R] **jknife**.

exp_list specifies the statistics to be collected from the execution of *command*.

bstat displays bootstrap estimates of standard error and bias, and calculates confidence intervals using up to four different methods: normal approximation, percentile, bias-corrected, and bias-corrected and accelerated. bootstrap automatically runs bstat after completing all the bootstrap replications. If the saving(*filename*) option is supplied to bootstrap, then bstat can be run on the data in *filename* to review the bootstrap results. If using *filename* is specified, bstat will use the data in *filename* to compute the bootstrap statistics while preserving the data in memory; otherwise, bstat will simply use the data in memory.

bsample is a low-level utility for do-it-yourselfers who prefer not to use bootstrap. bsample draws a sample with replacement from the existing data. By default, this bootstrap sample replaces the dataset in memory. However, if weight(*varname*) is specified, then the data in memory remain unchanged except for a set of frequency weights depicting the bootstrap sample, placed in *varname*. *exp* specifies the size of the sample and must be less than or equal to _N (within strata()). If *exp* is not specified, a sample of size _N is drawn (or size n_c when the cluster() option is specified, where n_c is the number of clusters).

Since bootstrapping is a random process, persons interested in reproducibility of results should first set the random number seed by typing set seed *#* before running bootstrap or bsample; see [R] **generate**.

Options

reps(*#*) specifies the number of bootstrap replications to be performed. The default is 50. How many replications should be specified? The conventional wisdom, summarized, for instance, in Mooney and Duval (1993, 11), is that 50–200 replications are generally adequate for estimates of standard error, and thus are adequate for normal-approximation confidence intervals. For estimates of confidence intervals using the percentile or bias-corrected methods, one typically requires 1,000 or more replications.

size(*#*) specifies the size of the samples to be drawn. The default is _N unless cluster() is specified. If cluster() is specified, the default is the number of clusters in the original dataset. When cluster sampling, the resulting sample sizes will differ between replications, unless all the clusters are of equal size. If size(*#*) is specified, *#* must be less than or equal to the number of observations, or, if clustered, the number of clusters (within strata()).

dots requests that a dot be placed on the screen at the beginning of each replication, thus providing entertainment if a large number of reps() are requested.

saving(*filename*) creates a Stata data file (.dta file) consisting of, for each statistic in *exp_list*, a variable containing the bootstrapped values of that statistic.

double specifies that the bootstrap results for each replication are to be stored as doubles, meaning 8-byte reals. By default, they are stored as floats, meaning 4-byte reals.

every(*#*) specifies that results are to be written to disk every #th replication. every() should only be specified in conjunction with saving() when performing bootstraps that take a long time. This will allow recovery of partial results should some other software crash your computer. See [P] **postfile**.

replace indicates that the file specified by saving() may already exist, and, if it does, it should be overwritten.

noesample is a rarely used option to keep from dropping out-of-sample observations before resampling the data.

noisily requests that any output from *command* be displayed.

nowarn suppresses the printing of a warning message when *command* does not set e(sample).

accel(*#* | *matname*) allows the user to specify the acceleration for each statistic to be summarized by bstat. The acceleration may be specified either as the value # when considering a single statistic, or as the $1 \times p$ matrix *matname*, containing the accelerations for the $p \geq 1$ statistics.

stat(*#* | *matname*) allows the user to specify the observed value of each statistic (that is, the value of the statistic computed using the original dataset) to be summarized by bstat. The observed value may be specified either as # when considering a single statistic, or as the $1 \times p$ matrix *matname*, containing the observed values of $p \geq 1$ statistics.

This option is not necessary when using a dataset created using the saving() option with bootstrap. In these cases, the observed value of the statistic is stored with the dataset as a characteristic (see [P] **char**), and is automatically retrieved by bstat as needed.

n(*#*) (bstat only) specifies the number of observations from which bootstrap samples were taken. This option only affects the output header of bstat.

weight(*varname*) identifies an existing variable where bsample can store the observation frequency of the bootstrap sample. This is an alternative to replacing the data in memory with the bootstrap sample.

cluster(*varlist*) specifies the variable(s) identifying resampling clusters. If specified, the sample drawn during each replication is a bootstrap sample of clusters.

idcluster(*newvarname*) creates a new variable containing a unique identifier for each resampled cluster.

strata(*varlist*) specifies the variable(s) identifying strata. If specified, bootstrap samples are taken independently within each stratum.

bca requests that bootstrap estimate the acceleration of each statistic in *exp_list*. This estimate is used to construct BC_a confidence intervals.

level(*#*) specifies the confidence level, in percent, for confidence intervals. The default is level(95) or as set by set level; see [U] **23.6 Specifying the width of confidence intervals**.

separate inserts a separator line between the *exp_list* statistics in the table generated by bstat.

title(*text*) specifies a title to be displayed above the table of bootstrap results; the default title is Bootstrap statistics.

Confidence interval options for bstat:

   bca requests displaying the BC_a confidence interval(s).

   nobc suppresses the displaying of bias-corrected confidence interval(s).

   nonormal suppresses the displaying of confidence interval(s) based on the normal approximation.

`nopercentile` suppresses the displaying of percentile confidence interval(s).

`notable` suppresses the displaying of all confidence intervals.

Remarks

With few assumptions, bootstrapping provides a way of estimating standard errors and other measures of statistical precision (Efron 1979, Efron and Stein 1981, Efron 1982, Efron and Tibshirani 1986, and Efron and Tibshirani 1993; also see Davison and Hinkley 1997, Mooney and Duval 1993, and Stine 1990). It provides a way to obtain such measures when no formula is otherwise available, or when available formulas make assumptions that are not tenable.

Mechanically, the procedure is this: One has a dataset containing N observations and an estimator that, when applied to the data, produces certain statistics. One draws, with replacement, N observations from the N observation dataset. In this random drawing, some of the original observations will appear once, some more than once, and some not at all. Using that dataset, one reapplies the estimator. One does this repeatedly, each time drawing a new random sample and re-estimating.

Thus, one builds a dataset of estimated statistics. From these data, one can calculate the standard deviation using the standard formula: $\{\sum(\theta_i^* - \bar{\theta}^*)^2/(k-1)\}^{1/2}$, where θ_i^* is the statistic calculated using the ith bootstrap sample and k is the number of replications. This formula gives an estimate of the standard error of the statistic, according to Hall and Wilson 1991. Note that although the average, $\bar{\theta}^*$, of the bootstrapped estimates is used in the calculation of the standard deviation, it is not used as the estimated value of the statistic itself. Instead, the point (called a replication). estimate used is the original observed statistic, θ_{obs}; that is, the value of the statistic computed using the original N observations.

Researchers new to bootstrapping may think that the $\bar{\theta}^*$ is somehow a better estimate of the parameter than θ_{obs}, but it is not. If the statistic is biased in some way, $\bar{\theta}^*$ exaggerates the bias. In fact, the bias can be estimated as $\bar{\theta}^* - \theta_{\text{obs}}$ (Efron 1982, 33). Knowing this, one might be tempted to subtract this estimate of bias from θ_{obs} to produce an unbiased statistic. The bootstrap bias estimate has, however, an indeterminate amount of random error. Thus, this unbiased estimator may have greater mean square error than the biased estimator (Mooney and Duval 1993, Hinkley 1978), so it is best to stick with θ_{obs} as the point estimate of the statistic.

The logic behind the bootstrap is this: All measures of precision come from a statistic's sampling distribution. When the statistic is estimated on a sample of size N from some population, the sampling distribution tells you the relative frequencies of the values of the statistic. The sampling distribution, in turn, is determined by the distribution of the population and the formula used to estimate the statistic.

In some cases, the sampling distribution can be derived analytically. For instance, if the underlying population is distributed normally and one calculates means, the sampling distribution for the mean is also normal, but with a smaller variance than the population. In other cases, deriving the sampling distribution is difficult, as in the case of means calculated from nonnormal populations. Sometimes, as in the case of means, it is not too difficult to derive the sampling distribution as $N \to \infty$. However, often it is poor judgment to trust this limiting distribution as an approximation to what occurs in finite samples.

As a mechanical matter, if we knew the population distribution, we could obtain the sampling distribution by simulation: we would draw random samples of size N, calculate the statistic, and make a tally. Bootstrapping does precisely this, but it uses the observed distribution of the sample in place of the true population distribution. Thus, the bootstrap procedure hinges on the assumption that the observed distribution is a good estimate of the underlying population distribution. In return, the bootstrap produces an estimate, called the bootstrap distribution, of the sampling distribution. From this, one can estimate the standard error of the statistic, produce confidence intervals, etc.

The accuracy with which the bootstrap distribution estimates the sampling distribution depends on the number of observations in the original sample and the number of replications in the bootstrap. A crudely estimated sampling distribution is quite adequate if one is only going to extract, say, a standard error. A better estimate is needed if one is going to use the 2.5th and 97.5th percentiles of the distribution to produce a 95% confidence interval. If one is going to extract many features simultaneously about the distribution, an even better estimate is needed. It is generally believed that replications on the order of 1,000 produce very good estimates, but that for estimates of standard errors, only 50–200 replications are needed.

▷ Example

Let's say that we wish to compute bootstrap estimates for the standard errors of the coefficients for the following regression:

```
. use http://www.stata-press.com/data/r8/auto
(1978 Automobile Data)

. regress mpg weight gear foreign
```

Source	SS	df	MS			
Model	1629.67805	3	543.226016			
Residual	813.781411	70	11.6254487			
Total	2443.45946	73	33.4720474			

Number of obs = 74
F(3, 70) = 46.73
Prob > F = 0.0000
R-squared = 0.6670
Adj R-squared = 0.6527
Root MSE = 3.4096

mpg	Coef.	Std. Err.	t	P>|t|	[95% Conf. Interval]	
weight	-.006139	.0007949	-7.72	0.000	-.0077245	-.0045536
gear_ratio	1.457113	1.541286	0.95	0.348	-1.616884	4.53111
foreign	-2.221682	1.234961	-1.80	0.076	-4.684734	.2413715
_cons	36.10135	6.285984	5.74	0.000	23.56435	48.63835

To run the bootstrap, we put the command in double quotes and give a list of the coefficients (see [U] **16.5 Accessing coefficients and standard errors** and [U] **16.6 Accessing results from Stata commands**) that we wish to bootstrap. Note that _b and _se are extended expressions that represent all of the coefficients in the model and their standard errors, respectively.

(Continued on next page)

```
. set seed 123456789
. bootstrap "regress mpg weight gear foreign" _b, reps(100) bca
command:      regress mpg weight gear foreign
statistics:   b_weight   = _b[weight]
              b_gear_r~o = _b[gear_ratio]
              b_foreign  = _b[foreign]
              b_cons     = _b[_cons]
```

Bootstrap statistics   Number of obs   =   74
                                              Replications   =   100

Variable	Reps	Observed	Bias	Std. Err.	[95% Conf. Interval]		
b_weight	100	-.006139	.0000414	.0005756	-.0072812	-.0049969	(N)
					-.007267	-.0049173	(P)
					-.007267	-.0049173	(BC)
					-.0073615	-.0050135	(BCa)
b_gear_ratio	100	1.457113	-.004336	1.407497	-1.335665	4.249892	(N)
					-1.240059	4.321906	(P)
					-1.883508	3.452275	(BC)
					-1.883508	3.452275	(BCa)
b_foreign	100	-2.221682	.1992346	1.330934	-4.862543	.41918	(N)
					-4.622502	.3200419	(P)
					-4.640817	.0877294	(BC)
					-4.640817	-.0230267	(BCa)
b_cons	100	36.10135	-.1026712	5.078842	26.02383	46.17888	(N)
					27.06266	46.05153	(P)
					27.83733	46.97556	(BC)
					27.83733	46.97556	(BCa)

```
Note:  N   = normal
       P   = percentile
       BC  = bias-corrected
       BCa = bias-corrected and accelerated
```

The table of bootstrap statistics is produced by the bstat command, which is automatically called by bootstrap upon completion of the replicated sampling.

The first confidence interval is based on the assumption of approximate normality of the sampling (and hence bootstrap) distribution (see *Methods and Formulas* below). Since it is based on the standard error, it is a reasonable estimate if normality is approximately true, even for a small number of replications. For the other confidence intervals, we should have many more replications, so let's run it again.

We will set the random number seed in case we wish to reproduce the results, and we also save the bootstrap distribution as a dataset called bsauto.dta.

(Continued on next page)

```
. set seed 1

. bootstrap "regress mpg weight gear foreign" _b, reps(1000) saving(bsauto) bca
command:       regress mpg weight gear foreign
statistics:    b_weight   = _b[weight]
               b_gear_r~o = _b[gear_ratio]
               b_foreign  = _b[foreign]
               b_cons     = _b[_cons]
```

Bootstrap statistics   Number of obs   =   74

                                               Replications   =   1000

Variable	Reps	Observed	Bias	Std. Err.	[95% Conf.	Interval]	
b_weight	1000	-.006139	.0000567	.000628	-.0073714	-.0049067	(N)
					-.0073044	-.0048548	(P)
					-.0074355	-.004928	(BC)
					-.0075282	-.0050258	(BCa)
b_gear_ratio	1000	1.457113	.1051695	1.455478	-1.399032	4.313259	(N)
					-1.262111	4.585372	(P)
					-1.523927	4.174376	(BC)
					-1.492223	4.231356	(BCa)
b_foreign	1000	-2.221682	-.019636	1.202329	-4.581061	.1376977	(N)
					-4.442199	.2677989	(P)
					-4.155504	.6170642	(BC)
					-4.216531	.5743973	(BCa)
b_cons	1000	36.10135	-.5022812	5.408944	25.48716	46.71555	(N)
					24.48569	46.07086	(P)
					25.59799	46.63227	(BC)
					25.85658	47.02108	(BCa)

```
Note:  N   = normal
       P   = percentile
       BC  = bias-corrected
       BCa = bias-corrected and accelerated
```

The estimated standard errors here differ from our previous estimates using only 100 replications by, respectively, 8%, 3%, 11%, and 6%. So much for our advice that 50–200 replications are good enough to estimate standard errors! Well, the more replications the better—that advice you should believe.

Note that the bias for the coefficient of foreign went from 15% of the standard error to 1% and flipped signs. Efron (1982, 8) comments that when the estimated bias is less than 25% of the standard error, bias should not be a serious concern. So, in this case, the estimated biases are nothing to note.

Which of the methods to compute confidence intervals should we use? If the statistic is unbiased, then the percentile (P) and bias-corrected (BC) methods should give similar results. From a computational standpoint, the bias-corrected confidence interval will be the same as the percentile confidence interval when the observed value of the statistic is equal to the median of the bootstrap distribution. Thus, for unbiased statistics, the two methods should give similar results as the number of replications becomes large. For biased statistics, the bias-corrected method should yield confidence intervals with better coverage probability (that is, closer to the nominal value of 95% or whatever was specified) than the percentile method. For statistics with variances that vary as a function of the parameter of interest, the "bias-corrected and accelerated method" (BC_a) will typically have better coverage probability that the others.

When the bootstrap distribution is approximately normal, all of these methods should give similar confidence intervals as the number of replications becomes large. If we examine the normality of these bootstrap distributions using, say, the pnorm command (see [R] **diagnostic plots**), we see that they very closely follow a normal distribution. Thus, in this case, the normal approximation would also be a valid choice. The chief advantage of the normal-approximation method is that it (supposedly) requires fewer replications than the other methods. Of course, it should only be used when the bootstrap distribution exhibits normality.

We can load `bsauto.dta` containing the bootstrap distributions for these coefficients:

```
. use http://www.stata-press.com/data/r8/bsauto, clear
(bootstrap: regress mpg weight gear foreign)
. describe
Contains data from http://www.stata-press.com/data/r8/bsauto.dta
  obs:          1,000                       bootstrap: regress mpg weight
                                              gear foreign
  vars:             4                       17 Oct 2002 15:37
  size:        20,000 (90.5% of memory free)

              storage  display    value
variable name   type   format     label      variable label

b_weight       float   %9.0g                 _b[weight]
b_gear_ratio   float   %9.0g                 _b[gear_ratio]
b_foreign      float   %9.0g                 _b[foreign]
b_cons         float   %9.0g                 _b[_cons]

Sorted by:
```

We can now run other commands, such as `pnorm`, on the bootstrap distributions. If we want to see the bootstrap statistics again, we can simply type

```
. bstat
```

The output will be the previously given table. To see a summary for `b_weight` only, we could type

```
. bstat b_weight
```

The default variable names assigned to the statistics in *exp_list* are `bs1`, `bs2`, ..., and each variable is labeled with the respective expression. The naming convention for the extended expressions `_b` (and `_b[]`) and `_se` (and `_se[]`) is to prepend `b_` and `se_`, respectively, onto the name of each element of the coefficient vector. In this example, the first coefficient is `_b[weight]`, so `bootstrap` named it `b_weight`. As an alternative, you can supply your own names when you run `bootstrap`. For example,

```
. bootstrap "regress mpg weight gear foreign" diff=(_b[weight]-_b[gear])
```

◁

❑ Technical Note

If you have two datasets from separate runs of `bootstrap`, you can combine them using `append` (see [R] **append**), and then get the bootstrap statistics for the combined datasets by running `bstat`. This all assumes that the runs were performed independently (different starting random number seeds), and that the original dataset, command, and bootstrap statistics are all the same.

❑

❑ Technical Note

When using `bootstrap`, do not forget to enclose the command in double quotes. Also, the list of statistics can contain complex expressions as long as each expression is enclosed in parentheses. For example, to bootstrap the range of a variable `x`, we could type

```
. bootstrap "summarize x" (r(max)-r(min)), reps(1000)
```

Of course, we could also bootstrap the minimum and maximum, and later compute the range.

```
. bootstrap "summarize x" r(max) r(min), reps(1000) saving(mybs)
(output omitted)
. use mybs, clear
(bootstrap: summarize x)
. generate range = bs1 - bs2
. bstat range, stat(19.5637501)
(output omitted)
```

The `stat()` option to `bstat` specifies the observed value of the statistic (`range`) to be summarized. This option is useful in cases such as the above, where the statistic of ultimate interest is not specified directly to `bootstrap`, but instead calculated by other means.

In the above example, the observed values of `r(max)` and `r(min)` are saved as characteristics of the dataset created by `bootstrap`, and are thus available for retrieval by `bstat`; see [P] **char**. The observed range, however, is unknown to `bstat`. Instead, it must be specified.

❑

❑ Technical Note

In the previous technical note, we executed the command

```
. bootstrap "summarize x" r(max) r(min), reps(1000) saving(mybs)
```

Note that we did not enclose `r(max)` and `r(min)` in single quotes as we would in most other contexts. The following would not produce what was intended:

```
. bootstrap "summarize x" 'r(max)' 'r(min)', reps(1000) saving(mybs)
```

To understand why, note that `'r(max)'`, like any reference to a local macro, will evaluate to a literal string containing the contents of `r(max)`, *before* `bootstrap` is even executed. As such, the above would appear to Stata as if we had typed, say,

```
. bootstrap "summarize x" 14.5441234 33.4393293, reps(1000) saving(mybs)
```

Even worse, the current contents of `r(min)` and `r(max)` could be empty, producing an even more confusing result!

The moral of this story is to refer to statistics by name; e.g., `r(max)`, and not by value, e.g., `'r(max)'`.

❑

▷ Example

Suppose we wish to estimate the *achieved significance level* (ASL) of a test statistic using the bootstrap. Here ASL is another name for p-value. An example is

$$\text{ASL} = \text{Prob}\left(\widehat{\theta}^* \geq \theta_{\text{obs}}|H_0\right)$$

for an upper tail alternative hypothesis, where H_0 denotes the null hypothesis, θ_{obs} is the observed value of the test statistic, and $\widehat{\theta}^*$ is the random variable corresponding to the test statistic, assuming H_0 is true.

For this example, we will compare the mean miles per gallon (mpg) between foreign and domestic cars using the two-sample t test with unequal variances. The following results indicate the p-value to be 0.0034 for the two-sided test using Satterthwaite's approximation. Thus, assuming that mean mpg is the same between foreign and domestic cars, we would expect to observe a t statistic to be more extreme (in absolute value) than 3.1797 in about 0.3% of all possible samples of the type that we observed. Thus, we have evidence to reject the null hypothesis that the means are equal. Note that we also placed the value of the test statistic in a scalar for later use.

```
. use http://www.stata-press.com/data/r8/auto
(1978 Automobile Data)
. ttest mpg, by(foreign) unequal
Two-sample t test with unequal variances
```

Group	Obs	Mean	Std. Err.	Std. Dev.	[95% Conf. Interval]	
Domestic	52	19.82692	.657777	4.743297	18.50638	21.14747
Foreign	22	24.77273	1.40951	6.611187	21.84149	27.70396
combined	74	21.2973	.6725511	5.785503	19.9569	22.63769
diff		-4.945804	1.555438		-8.120053	-1.771556

```
Satterthwaite's degrees of freedom:  30.5463
                 Ho: mean(Domestic) - mean(Foreign) = diff = 0
    Ha: diff < 0                  Ha: diff != 0                 Ha: diff > 0
      t =  -3.1797                  t =  -3.1797                  t =  -3.1797
  P < t =   0.0017            P > |t| =   0.0034            P > t =   0.9983
. scalar tobs = r(t)
```

Efron and Tibshirani (1993, 224), describe an alternative to Satterthwaite's approximation. Their method estimates the ASL by bootstrapping the statistic from the test of equal means. The thrust of the idea is to recenter the two samples to the combined sample mean so that the data now conform to the null hypothesis but the variances within the samples remain unchanged.

```
. summarize mpg, mean
. scalar omean = r(mean)
. summarize mpg if foreign==0, mean
. replace mpg = mpg - r(mean) + scalar(omean) if foreign==0
mpg was int now float
(52 real changes made)
. summarize mpg if foreign==1, mean
. replace mpg = mpg - r(mean) + scalar(omean) if foreign==1
(22 real changes made)
. sort foreign
. by foreign: summarize mpg
```

```
-> foreign = Domestic
```

Variable	Obs	Mean	Std. Dev.	Min	Max
mpg	52	21.2973	4.743297	13.47037	35.47038

```
-> foreign = Foreign
```

Variable	Obs	Mean	Std. Dev.	Min	Max
mpg	22	21.2973	6.611187	10.52457	37.52457

Each sample (foreign and domestic) is a stratum, so the bootstrapped samples must have the same number of foreign and domestic cars as the original dataset, respectively. This is facilitated by the `strata()` option to `bootstrap`. In the following, we bootstrap the test statistic using the modified dataset, and save the values in `bsauto2.dta`:

```
. keep mpg foreign

. set seed 1122344

. bootstrap "ttest mpg, by(foreign) unequal" t=r(t), rep(1000) strata(foreign)
> notable saving(bsauto2) nowarn dots
command:        ttest mpg , by(foreign) unequal
statistic:    t          = r(t)
  (output omitted)
```

We can use the data in `bsauto2.dta` to estimate ASL via the fraction of bootstrapped test statistics that are more extreme than 3.1797.

```
. use http://www.stata-press.com/data/r8/bsauto2, clear
(bootstrap: ttest mpg , by(foreign) unequal)

. generate indicator = abs(t)>=abs(scalar(tobs))

. summarize indicator, mean

. display "ASLboot = " r(mean)
ASLboot = .008
```

The result is $\text{ASL}_{\text{boot}} = 0.008$. Thus, assuming that the mean `mpg` is the same between foreign and domestic cars, we would expect to observe a t statistic to be more extreme (in absolute value) than 3.1797 in about 0.8% of all possible samples of the type we observed. This is still strong evidence to reject the hypothesis that the means are equal.

◁

▷ Example

Suppose that we wish to produce a bootstrap estimate of the ratio of two means. Since `summarize` only saves results for one variable, we must call `summarize` twice to compute the means. (Actually, we could use `collapse` to compute the means in a single call, but calling `summarize` twice is much faster.) Thus, we will have to write a small program that will return the results we want.

We write the program below and save it to a file called `ratio.ado` (see [U] **20 Ado-files**). Our program takes two variable names as input and saves them in the `local` macros `y` (first variable) and `x` (second variable). It then computes the single statistic mean of 'y' divided by mean of 'x'. This value is a returned as a scalar in `r(ratio)`.

```
program ratio, rclass
        version 8.0
        args y x
        confirm var 'y'
        confirm var 'x'
        tempname ymean yn
        summarize 'y', meanonly
        scalar 'ymean' = r(mean)
        scalar 'n_y' = r(n)
        summarize 'x', meanonly
        scalar 'n_x' = r(n)
        return scalar ratio = 'ymean'/r(mean)
end
```

It is important to remember to test any newly written commands before using them with `bootstrap`.

```
. use http://www.stata-press.com/data/r8/auto
(1978 Automobile Data)

. summarize price
```

Variable	Obs	Mean	Std. Dev.	Min	Max
price	74	6165.257	2949.496	3291	15906

```
. scalar mean1=r(mean)

. summarize weight
```

Variable	Obs	Mean	Std. Dev.	Min	Max
weight	74	3019.459	777.1936	1760	4840

```
. scalar mean2=r(mean)

. display scalar(mean1)/scalar(mean2)
2.0418412

. ratio price weight

. return list

scalars:
              r(ratio) =  2.041841210168278
           r(n_weight) =  74
            r(n_price) =  74
```

The results of running `bootstrap` on our program are

```
. use http://www.stata-press.com/data/r8/auto
(1978 Automobile Data)

. set seed 121

. bootstrap "ratio price weight" ratio=r(ratio), reps(1000) nowarn

command:       ratio price weight
statistic:     ratio     = r(ratio)
```

```
Bootstrap statistics                    Number of obs    =        74
                                        Replications     =      1000
```

Variable	Reps	Observed	Bias	Std. Err.	[95% Conf. Interval]	
ratio	1000	2.041841	-.0028549	.0940728	1.857238 2.226444	(N)
					1.867443 2.233249	(P)
					1.875737 2.240145	(BC)

```
Note:  N   = normal
       P   = percentile
       BC  = bias-corrected
```

As previously mentioned, we should specify the `saving()` option if we wish to save the bootstrap dataset.

◁

❑ Technical Note

`bootstrap` and `bsample` do not know which variables of the dataset in memory matter to the calculation at hand. You can speed their execution by dropping unnecessary variables because otherwise they are included in each bootstrap sample.

By the same token, you should drop observations with missing values. If you do not, this causes no problem in one sense because all Stata commands deal with missing values gracefully.

It does, however, cause a statistical problem. Bootstrap sampling is defined as drawing, with replacement, samples of size N from a set of N observations. `bootstrap` and `bsample` determine N by counting the number of observations in memory, not counting the number of nonmissing values on the relevant variables. The result is that too many observations are resampled and, moreover, the resulting bootstrap samples, since drawn from a population with missing values, are of unequal sizes.

If the number of missing values relative to sample size is small, this will make little difference. If you have a large number of missing values, however, you should first drop the observations that contain them.

To illustrate, we use the previous example, but replace some of the values of `price` with missing values. Notice that the number of values of `price` used to compute the mean for each bootstrap is not constant. This is the purpose of the `Warning` message.

```
. use http://www.stata-press.com/data/r8/auto
(1978 Automobile Data)
. replace price = . if inlist(_n,1,3,5,7)
(4 real changes made, 4 to missing)
. set seed 121
. bootstrap "ratio price weight" ratio=r(ratio) np=r(n_price) nw=r(n_weight), r
> eps(100)

command:       ratio price weight
statistics:    ratio     = r(ratio)
               np        = r(n_price)
               nw        = r(n_weight)

Warning:    Since ratio is not an estimation command or does not set e(sample),
            bootstrap has no way to determine which observations are used in
            calculating the statistics and so assumes that all observations are
            used.  This means no observations will be excluded from the
            resampling due to missing values or other reasons.

            If the assumption is not true, press Break, save the data, and drop
            the observations that are to be excluded.  Be sure the dataset in
            memory contains only the relevant data.
```

```
Bootstrap statistics                      Number of obs   =        74
                                          Replications    =       100
```

Variable	Reps	Observed	Bias	Std. Err.	[95% Conf. Interval]	
ratio	100	2.063051	-.0104267	.1126899	1.83945	2.286653	(N)
					1.853442	2.299524	(P)
					1.883254	2.310472	(BC)
np	100	70	.09	1.809598	66.40936	73.59064	(N)
					67	73	(P)
					67	74	(BC)
nw	100	74	0	0	74	74	(N)
					74	74	(P)
					.	.	(BC)

```
Note:  N   = normal
       P   = percentile
       BC  = bias-corrected
```

❑

❏ Technical Note

Although `bstat` allows users to specify the observed value and acceleration of each bootstrap statistic via the `stat()` and `accel()` options, programmers may be interested in what `bstat` requires when these options are not supplied.

The first thing `bstat` does is check the characteristics of the bootstrap dataset; for more information on characteristics of datasets, see [P] **char**.

`_dta[bs_version]`	bootstrap dataset version
`_dta[N]`	number of observations in the resampled dataset
`_dta[N_strata]`	number of strata in the resampled dataset
`_dta[N_cluster]`	number of clusters in the resampled dataset
varname`[observed]`	observed value of the statistic identified by *varname*
varname`[acceleration]`	estimate of acceleration of the statistic identified by *varname*

The bootstrap dataset version may be empty or equal to 2, otherwise `bstat` will display an error message then exit. If the bootstrap dataset version is 2, `_dta[N]` and *varname*`[observed]` are required, but `_dta[N_strata]`, `_dta[N_cluster]` and *varname*`[acceleration]` may be empty. Note that the variable characteristics are checked for each variable in the bootstrap dataset.

An empty bootstrap dataset version implies that the dataset was created by the pre–Stata 8 `bstrap` command. In this case, `bstat` will only check *varname*`[bstrap]` (which was replaced by *varname*`[observed]` in the version 2 bootstrap datasets) for each variable *varname* in the bootstrap dataset; all other characteristics are ignored.

❏

Saved Results

`bstat` saves in `e()`:

Scalars
`e(N)`	sample size	`e(N_clust)`	number of clusters
`e(N_strata)`	number of strata		

Macros
`e(cmd)`	bootstrap

Matrices
`e(b)`	observed statistic(s)	`e(V)`	bootstrap variance–covariance matrix
`e(reps)`	number of replications	`e(bs_b)`	bootstrap mean(s)
`e(bias)`	estimated bias(es)	`e(ci_normal)`	normal–approximation CI
`e(se)`	estimated standard error(s)	`e(ci_percent)`	percentile CI
`e(z0)`	median bias(es)	`e(ci_bc)`	bias-corrected CI
`e(accel)`	estimated acceleration(s)	`e(ci_bca)`	bias-corrected and accelerated CI

Methods and Formulas

`bootstrap`, `bstat`, and `bsample` are implemented as ado-files.

Let θ_{obs} be the observed value of the statistic; that is, the value of the statistic calculated using the original dataset. Let $i = 1, 2, \ldots, k$ denote the bootstrap samples, and let θ_i^* be the values of the statistic computed using each of these samples.

The standard error is estimated as

$$\widehat{se} = \left\{ \frac{1}{k-1} \sum_{i=1}^{k} (\theta_i^* - \bar{\theta}^*)^2 \right\}^{1/2}$$

where

$$\bar{\theta}^* = \frac{1}{k} \sum_{i=1}^{k} \theta_i^*$$

The bias is estimated as

$$\widehat{bias} = \bar{\theta}^* - \theta_{obs}$$

Confidence intervals with nominal coverage rates $1 - \alpha$ are calculated according to the following formulas. The normal-approximation method yields the confidence intervals

$$\left[\theta_{obs} - t_{1-\alpha/2,k-1}\,\widehat{se},\ \theta_{obs} + t_{1-\alpha/2,k-1}\,\widehat{se} \right]$$

where $t_{1-\alpha/2,k-1}$ is the $(1 - \alpha/2)$th quantile of the t distribution with $k-1$ degrees of freedom.

The percentile method yields the confidence intervals

$$\left[\theta_{\alpha/2}^*,\ \theta_{1-\alpha/2}^* \right]$$

where θ_p^* is the pth quantile (the $100p$th percentile) of the bootstrap distribution $(\theta_1^*, \ldots, \theta_k^*)$.

Let

$$z_0 = \Phi^{-1}\{\#(\theta_i^* \leq \theta_{obs})/k\}$$

where $\#(\theta_i^* \leq \theta_{obs})$ is the number of elements of the bootstrap distribution that are less than or equal to the observed statistic, and Φ is the standard cumulative normal. z_0 is known as the median bias of θ_{obs}. Let

$$a = \frac{\sum_{i=1}^{n} (\widehat{\theta}_{(\cdot)} - \widehat{\theta}_{(i)})^2}{6\{\sum_{i=1}^{n} (\widehat{\theta}_{(\cdot)} - \widehat{\theta}_{(i)})^2\}^{3/2}}$$

where $\widehat{\theta}_{(i)}$ are the leave-one-out (jackknife) estimates of $\widehat{\theta}$ and $\widehat{\theta}_{(\cdot)}$ is their mean. This is known as the jackknife estimate of acceleration for θ_{obs}. Let

$$p_1 = \Phi\left\{ z_0 + \frac{z_0 - z_{1-\alpha/2}}{1 - a(z_0 - z_{1-\alpha/2})} \right\}$$

$$p_2 = \Phi\left\{ z_0 + \frac{z_0 + z_{1-\alpha/2}}{1 - a(z_0 + z_{1-\alpha/2})} \right\}$$

where $z_{1-\alpha/2}$ is the $(1-\alpha/2)$th quantile of the normal distribution. The bias-corrected and accelerated (BC$_a$) method yields confidence intervals

$$\left[\theta_{p_1}^*,\ \theta_{p_2}^* \right]$$

where θ_p^* is the pth quantile of the bootstrap distribution as defined previously. The bias-corrected (but not accelerated) method is a special case of BC$_a$ with $a = 0$.

References

Davison, A. C. and D. V. Hinkley. 1997. *Bootstrap Methods and their Application.* Cambridge: Cambridge University Press.

Efron, B. 1979. Bootstrap methods: Another look at the jackknife. *Annals of Statistics* 7: 1–26.

——. 1982. *The Jackknife, the Bootstrap and Other Resampling Plans.* Philadelphia: Society for Industrial and Applied Mathematics.

Efron, B. and C. Stein. 1981. The jackknife estimate of variance. *Annals of Statistics* 9: 586–596.

Efron, B. and R. Tibshirani. 1986. Bootstrap measures for standard errors, confidence intervals, and other measures of statistical accuracy. *Statistical Science* 1: 54–77.

——. 1993. *An Introduction to the Bootstrap.* New York: Chapman & Hall.

Gleason, J. R. 1997. ip18: A command for randomly resampling a dataset. *Stata Technical Bulletin* 37: 17–22. Reprinted in *Stata Technical Bulletin Reprints*, vol. 7, pp. 77–83.

——. 1999. ip18.1: Update to resample. *Stata Technical Bulletin* 52: 9–10. Reprinted in *Stata Technical Bulletin Reprints*, vol. 9, p. 119.

Gould, W. W. 1994. ssi6.2: Faster and easier bootstrap estimation. *Stata Technical Bulletin* 21: 24–33. Reprinted in *Stata Technical Bulletin Reprints*, vol. 4, pp. 211–223.

Hall, P. and S. R. Wilson. 1991. Two guidelines for bootstrap hypothesis testing. *Biometrics.* 47: 757–762.

Hamilton, L. C. 1991. ssi2: Bootstrap programming. *Stata Technical Bulletin* 4: 18–27. Reprinted in *Stata Technical Bulletin Reprints*, vol. 1, pp. 208–220.

——. 1992. *Regression with Graphics.* Pacific Grove, CA: Brooks/Cole Publishing Company.

——. 2002. *Statistics with Stata.* Belmont, CA: Duxbury.

Hinkley, D. V. 1978. Improving the jackknife with special reference to correlation estimation. *Biometrika* 65: 13–22.

Mooney, C. Z. and R. D. Duval. 1993. *Bootstrapping: A Nonparametric Approach to Statistical Inference.* Newbury Park, CA: Sage Publications.

Stine, R. 1990. An introduction to bootstrap methods: examples and ideas. In *Modern Methods of Data Analysis*, ed. J. Fox and J. S. Long, 353–373. Newbury Park, CA: Sage Publications.

Also See

Complementary:	[P] **postfile**
Related:	[R] **jknife**, [R] **permute**, [R] **sample**, [R] **simulate**, [R] **statsby**
Background:	[U] **16.5 Accessing coefficients and standard errors**,
	[U] **16.6 Accessing results from Stata commands**,
	[U] **21 Programming Stata**

Title

> **boxcox** — Box–Cox regression models

Syntax

> boxcox *depvar* [*indepvars*] [*weight*] [if *exp*] [in *range*]
>
> [, model(<u>lhs</u>only | <u>rhs</u>only | <u>lam</u>bda | theta) <u>notrans</u>(*varlist*) lrtest
>
> from(*init_specs*) <u>nocons</u>tant <u>nolog</u> nologlr <u>iter</u>ate(*#*) <u>level</u>(*#*)]

by ... : may be used with boxcox; see [R] **by**.

fweights and iweights are allowed; see [U] **14.1.6 weight**.

boxcox shares the features of all estimation commands; see [U] **23 Estimation and post-estimation commands**.

boxcox, model(lhs) is the model that was fitted by boxcox in versions before Stata 7.

Syntax for predict

> predict [*type*] *newvarname* [if *exp*] [in *range*]
>
> [, [xbt | yhat | <u>resid</u>uals] <u>nooff</u>set]

These statistics are available both in and out of sample; type predict ... if e(sample) ... if wanted only for the estimation sample.

Description

boxcox finds the maximum likelihood estimates of the parameter(s) of the Box–Cox transform, the coefficients on the independent variables, and the standard deviation of the normally distributed errors for a model in which *depvar* is regressed on *indepvars*. The user has the option of fitting the following models:

Option	Estimates
lhsonly	$y_j^{(\theta)} = \beta_1 x_{1j} + \beta_2 x_{2j} + \cdots + \beta_k x_{kj} + \epsilon_j$
rhsonly	$y_j = \beta_1 x_{1j}^{(\lambda)} + \beta_2 x_{2j}^{(\lambda)} + \cdots + \beta_k x_{kj}^{(\lambda)} + \epsilon_j$
rhsonly notrans()	$y_j = \beta_1 x_{1j}^{(\lambda)} + \beta_2 x_{2j}^{(\lambda)} + \cdots + \beta_k x_{kj}^{(\lambda)} + \gamma_1 z_{1j} + \cdots + \gamma_l z_{lj} + \epsilon_j$
lambda	$y_j^{(\lambda)} = \beta_1 x_{1j}^{(\lambda)} + \beta_2 x_{2j}^{(\lambda)} + \cdots + \beta_k x_{kj}^{(\lambda)} + \epsilon_j$
lambda notrans()	$y_j^{(\lambda)} = \beta_1 x_{1j}^{(\lambda)} + \beta_2 x_{2j}^{(\lambda)} + \cdots + \beta_k x_{kj}^{(\lambda)} + \gamma_1 z_{1j} + \cdots + \gamma_l z_{lj} + \epsilon_j$
theta	$y_j^{(\theta)} = \beta_1 x_{1j}^{(\lambda)} + \beta_2 x_{2j}^{(\lambda)} + \cdots + \beta_k x_{kj}^{(\lambda)} + \epsilon_j$
theta notrans()	$y_j^{(\theta)} = \beta_1 x_{1j}^{(\lambda)} + \beta_2 x_{2j}^{(\lambda)} + \cdots + \beta_k x_{kj}^{(\lambda)} + \gamma_1 z_{1j} + \cdots + \gamma_l z_{lj} + \epsilon_j$

Any variable to be transformed must be strictly positive.

Options

model (lhsonly | rhsonly | lambda | theta) specifies which of the four models to fit.

   model(lhsonly) applies the Box–Cox transform to *depvar* only. model(lhsonly) is the default value.

   model(rhsonly) causes the transform to be applied to the *indepvars* only.

   model(lambda) causes the transform to be applied to both *depvar* and *indepvars*, and they are transformed by the same parameter.

   model(theta) causes the transform to be applied to both *depvar* and *indepvars*, but this time, each side is transformed by a separate parameter.

notrans(*varlist*) specifies that the variables in *varlist* are to be included as nontransformed independent variables.

lrtest specifies that a likelihood-ratio test of significance is to be performed and reported for each independent variable.

from(*init_specs*) allows the user to specify the initial values for Box–Cox transformation parameter(s); see [R] **maximize**.

Model	Initial value specification
lhsonly	from(θ_0, copy)
rhsonly	from(λ_0, copy)
lambda	from(λ_0, copy)
theta	from(λ_0 θ_0, copy)

noconstant suppresses the constant term (intercept) in the model.

nolog suppresses the iteration log when fitting the full model.

nologlr suppresses the iteration log when fitting the restricted models required by the lrtest option. If nologlr is specified when lrtest is not, then it is ignored.

iterate(#) specifies the maximum number of iterations that the maximum likelihood optimizer will undertake in search of a solution.

level(#) specifies the confidence level, in percent, for confidence intervals. The default is level(95) or as set by set level; see [U] **23.6 Specifying the width of confidence intervals**.

Options for predict

xbt, the default, calculates the "linear" prediction. For all the models except model(lhsonly), all the *indepvars* are transformed.

yhat calculates the predicted value of y.

residuals calculates the residuals after the predicted value of y has been subtracted from the actual value.

nooffset is relevant only if you specified offset(*varname*) for boxcox. It modifies the calculations made by predict so that they ignore the offset variable; the linear prediction is treated as $\mathbf{x}_j\mathbf{b}$ rather than as $\mathbf{x}_j\mathbf{b} + \text{offset}_j$.

Remarks

Remarks are presented under the headings

> *Introduction*
> *Theta model*
> *Lambda model*
> *Left-hand-side-only model*
> *Right-hand-side-only model*

Introduction

The Box–Cox transform

$$y^{(\lambda)} = \frac{y^\lambda - 1}{\lambda}$$

has been widely used in applied data analysis. Box and Cox (1964) developed the transformation and argued that the transformation could make the residuals more closely normal and less heteroskedastic. Cook and Weisberg (1982) discuss the transform in this light. Since the transform embeds several popular functional forms, it has received some attention as a method for testing functional forms, in particular,

$$y^{(\lambda)} = \begin{cases} y - 1 & \text{if } \lambda = 1 \\ \ln(y) & \text{if } \lambda = 0 \\ 1 - 1/y & \text{if } \lambda = -1 \end{cases}$$

Davidson and MacKinnon (1993) discuss this use of the transform. Atkinson (1985) also gives a good general treatment.

Theta model

boxcox obtains the maximum likelihood estimates of the parameters for four different models. The most general of the models, the theta model, is

$$y_j^{(\theta)} = \beta_0 + \beta_1 x_{1j}^{(\lambda)} + \beta_2 x_{2j}^{(\lambda)} + \cdots + \beta_k x_{kj}^{(\lambda)} + \gamma_1 z_{1j} + \gamma_2 z_{2j} + \cdots + \gamma_l z_{lj} + \epsilon_j$$

where $\epsilon \sim N(0, \sigma^2)$. Here the dependent variable y is subject to a Box–Cox transform with parameter θ. Each of the *indepvars* $x_1, x_2, \ldots, x_k$ is transformed by a Box–Cox transform with parameter λ. The $z_1, z_2, \ldots, z_l$ specified in the notrans() option are independent variables that are not transformed.

Box and Cox (1964) argued that this transformation would leave behind residuals that more closely follow a normal distribution than those produced by a simple linear regression model. Users should bear in mind that the normality of ϵ is assumed and that boxcox obtains maximum likelihood estimates of the $k + l + 4$ parameters under this assumption. boxcox does not choose λ and θ so that the residuals are approximately normally distributed. Users interested in this type of transformation to normality should see the official Stata commands lnskew0 and bcskew0 in [R] **lnskew0**. However, those commands work on a more restrictive model in which none of the independent variables are transformed.

▷ Example

Consider an example using the auto data.

```
. use http://stata-press.com/data/r8/auto
(1978 Automobile Data)
. boxcox mpg weight price, notrans(foreign) model(theta) lrtest
Fitting comparison model

Iteration 0:   log likelihood = -234.39434
Iteration 1:   log likelihood = -228.26891
Iteration 2:   log likelihood = -228.26777
Iteration 3:   log likelihood = -228.26777

Fitting full model

Iteration 0:   log likelihood = -194.13727
 (output omitted )
Iteration 5:   log likelihood = -175.67343

Fitting comparison models for LR tests

Iteration 0:   log likelihood = -179.58214
Iteration 1:   log likelihood = -177.59036
Iteration 2:   log likelihood = -177.58739
Iteration 3:   log likelihood = -177.58739

Iteration 0:   log likelihood = -203.92855
Iteration 1:   log likelihood = -201.30202
Iteration 2:   log likelihood = -201.18235
Iteration 3:   log likelihood = -201.18233

Iteration 0:   log likelihood = -178.83799
Iteration 1:   log likelihood = -175.98405
Iteration 2:   log likelihood = -175.97931
Iteration 3:   log likelihood = -175.97931
```

Number of obs	=	74
LR chi2(4)	=	105.19
Prob > chi2	=	0.000

Log likelihood = -175.67343

mpg	Coef.	Std. Err.	z	P>|z|	[95% Conf. Interval]
/lambda	.7601691	.6289991	1.21	0.227	-.4726465 1.992985
/theta	-.7189314	.3244439	-2.22	0.027	-1.35483 -.0830331

Estimates of scale-variant parameters

	Coef.	chi2(df)	P>chi2(df)	df of chi2
Notrans				
foreign	-.0114338	3.828	0.050	1
_cons	1.377399			
Trans				
weight	-.000239	51.018	0.000	1
price	-6.18e-06	0.612	0.434	1
/sigma	.0143509			

Test H0:	Restricted log likelihood	chi2	Prob > chi2
theta=lambda = -1	-181.64479	11.94	0.001
theta=lambda = 0	-178.2406	5.13	0.023
theta=lambda = 1	-194.13727	36.93	0.000

The output is composed of the iteration logs and three distinct tables. The first table contains a standard header for a maximum likelihood estimator and a standard output table for the Box–Cox transform parameters. The second table contains the estimates of the scale-variant parameters. The third table contains the output from likelihood-ratio tests on three standard functional form specifications.

If we were to interpret this output, the right-hand-side transformation would not significantly add to the regression, while the left-hand-side transformation would make the 5% but not the 1% cutoff. price is certainly not significant, and foreign lies right on the 5% cutoff. weight is clearly significant. The output also says that the linear and multiplicative inverse specifications are both strongly rejected. A natural log specification can be rejected at the 5% level, but not the 1% level.

◁

□ Technical Note

Spitzer (1984) showed that the Wald statistics of whether the coefficients of the right-hand-side variables, transformed or untransformed, are significantly different from zero are not invariant to changes in the scale of the transformed dependent variable. Davidson and MacKinnon (1993) also discuss this point. It is worth noting that this problem is an example of the manipulability of Wald statistics in nonlinear models. Lafontaine and White (1986) analyze this problem numerically, and Phillips and Park (1988) analyze it using Edgeworth expansions. See Drukker (2000b) for a more detailed discussion of this issue. Since the parameter estimates and their Wald tests are not scale invariant, no Wald tests or confidence intervals are reported for these parameters. However, when the lrtest option is specified, likelihood-ratio tests are performed and reported. Schlesselman (1971) showed that, if a constant is included in the model, then the parameter estimates of the Box–Cox transforms are scale invariant. For this reason, it is highly recommended that the noconstant option not be used.

The lrtest option does not perform a likelihood-ratio test on the constant. Hence, no value for this statistic is reported. Unless the data are properly scaled, the restricted model frequently does not converge. For this reason, no likelihood-ratio test on the constant is performed by the lrtest option. However, if a user has a special interest in performing this test, then it can be done by fitting the constrained model separately. If problems with convergence are encountered, rescaling the data by their means may help.

□

Lambda model

A less general model than the one above is called the lambda model. It specifies that the same parameter be used in both the left-hand side and right-hand side transformations. Specifically,

$$y_j^{(\lambda)} = \beta_0 + \beta_1 x_{1j}^{(\lambda)} + \beta_2 x_{2j}^{(\lambda)} + \cdots + \beta_k x_{kj}^{(\lambda)} + \gamma_1 z_{1j} + \gamma_2 z_{2j} + \cdots + \gamma_l z_{lj} + \epsilon_j$$

where $\epsilon \sim N(0, \sigma^2)$. Here, the *depvar* variable y and each of the *indepvars* $x_1, x_2, \ldots, x_k$ are transformed by a Box–Cox transform with the common parameter λ. Again, the $z_1, z_2, \ldots, z_l$ are independent variables that are not transformed.

Left-hand-side-only model

Even more restrictive than a common transformation parameter is transforming the dependent variable only. Since the dependent variable is on the left-hand side of the equation, this model is known as the lhsonly model. In this case, one is estimating the parameters of the model

$$y_j^{(\theta)} = \beta_0 + \beta_1 x_{1j} + \beta_2 x_{2j} + \cdots + \beta_k x_{kj} + \epsilon_j$$

where $\epsilon \sim N(0, \sigma^2)$. In this case, only the *depvar*, y, is transformed by a Box–Cox transform with the parameter θ.

This is the model that was fitted by Stata 6.0 and earlier versions. Even so, this implementation offers some advantages over the previous one. In particular, one can easily obtain likelihood-ratio tests of the significance of the independent variables. In contrast, the previous boxcox offers Wald statistics that use variance estimates of the coefficients that are conditional on θ. This difference is important. Spitzer (1984) shows that the variance estimates conditional on θ will underestimate the true variance.

▷ Example

In this example, mpg is again hypothesized to be a function of weight, price, and foreign in a Box–Cox model in which only mpg is subject to the transform.

```
. boxcox mpg weight price foreign, model(lhs) lrtest  nolog nologlr
Fitting comparison model
Fitting full model
Fitting comparison models for LR tests
```

		Number of obs	=	74
		LR chi2(3)	=	105.04
Log likelihood = -175.74705		Prob > chi2	=	0.000

mpg	Coef.	Std. Err.	z	P>|z|	[95% Conf. Interval]
/theta	-.7826999	.281954	-2.78	0.006	-1.33532 -.2300802

Estimates of scale-variant parameters

	Coef.	chi2(df)	P>chi2(df)	df of chi2
Notrans				
weight	-.0000294	58.056	0.000	1
price	-4.66e-07	0.469	0.493	1
foreign	-.0097564	4.644	0.031	1
_cons	1.249845			
/sigma	.0118454			

Test HO:	Restricted log likelihood	LR statistic chi2	P-Value Prob > chi2
theta = -1	-176.04312	0.59	0.442
theta = 0	-179.54104	7.59	0.006
theta = 1	-194.13727	36.78	0.000

It is worth noting that this model rejects both linear and log specifications of mpg, but fails to reject the hypothesis that 1/mpg is linear in the independent variables. These findings are in line with what an engineer would have expected. In engineering terms, gallons per mile represent actual energy consumption, and energy consumption should be approximately linear in weight.

◁

Right-hand-side-only model

The fourth model leaves the *depvar* alone and transforms a subset of the *indepvars* using the parameter λ. This is the rhsonly model. In this model, the *depvar*, y, is given by

$$y_j = \beta_0 + \beta_1 x_{1j}^{(\lambda)} + \beta_2 x_{2j}^{(\lambda)} + \cdots + \beta_k x_{kj}^{(\lambda)} + \gamma_1 z_{1j} + \gamma_2 z_{2j} + \cdots + \gamma_l z_{lj} + \epsilon_j$$

where $\epsilon \sim N(0, \sigma^2)$. Here, each of the *indepvars* $x_1, x_2, \ldots, x_k$ are transformed by a Box–Cox transform with the parameter λ. Again, the $z_1, z_2, \ldots, z_l$ are independent variables that are not transformed.

▷ Example

Here is an example with the rhsonly model. In this example, price and foreign are not included in the list of covariates. (You are invited to use the auto data and check that they fare no better here than above.)

```
. boxcox mpg weight, model(rhs) lrtest  nolog nologlr
Fitting full model
Fitting comparison models for LR tests
Comparison model for LR test on weight is a linear regression
Lambda is not identified in the restricted model
```

		Number of obs	=	74
		LR chi2(2)	=	82.90
Log likelihood = -192.94368		Prob > chi2	=	0.000

mpg	Coef.	Std. Err.	z	P>|z|	[95% Conf. Interval]
/lambda	-.4460916	.6551107	-0.68	0.496	-1.730085	.8379018

Estimates of scale-variant parameters

	Coef.	chi2(df)	P>chi2(df)	df of chi2
Notrans				
_cons	1359.092			
Trans				
weight	-614.3876	82.901	0.000	1
/sigma	3.281854			

Test HO:	Restricted log likelihood	LR statistic chi2	P-Value Prob > chi2
lambda = -1	-193.2893	0.69	0.406
lambda = 0	-193.17892	0.47	0.493
lambda = 1	-195.38869	4.89	0.027

The interpretation of the output is similar to all the cases above, except for one caveat. As requested, a likelihood-ratio test was performed on the lone independent variable. However, when it is dropped to form the constrained model, the comparison model is not a right-hand-side-only Box–Cox model, but rather a simple linear regression on a constant model. When weight is dropped, there are no longer any transformed variables. Hence, λ is not identified and it must also be dropped. This process leaves a linear regression on a constant as the "comparison model". It also implies that the test statistic has 2 degrees of freedom instead of 1. At the top of the output, a more concise warning informs the user of this point.

A similar identification issue can also arise in the lambda and theta models when only one independent variable is specified. In these cases, warnings also appear on the output.

◁

Saved Results

boxcox saves in e():

Scalars

e(N)	number of observations	e(ll_tm1)	log likelihood of model $\lambda=\theta=-1$
e(ll)	log likelihood	e(chi2_tm1)	LR of $\lambda=\theta=-1$ vs. full model
e(chi2)	LR statistic of full vs. comparison	e(p_tm1)	p-value of $\lambda=\theta=-1$ vs. full model
e(df_m)	full model degrees of freedom	e(ll_t0)	log likelihood of model $\lambda=\theta=0$
e(ll0)	log likelihood of the restricted model	e(chi2_t0)	LR of $\lambda=\theta=0$ vs. full model
e(df_r)	restricted model degrees of freedom	e(p_t0)	p-value of $\lambda=\theta=0$ vs. full model
e(ll_t1)	log likelihood of model $\lambda=\theta=1$	e(rc)	return code
e(chi2_t1)	LR of $\lambda=\theta=1$ vs. full model	e(ic)	number of iterations
e(p_t1)	p-value of $\lambda=\theta=1$ vs. full model		

Macros

e(cmd)	boxcox	e(wexp)	weight expression
e(depvar)	name of dependent variable	e(chi2type)	LR; type of model χ^2 test
e(model)	lhsonly, rhsonly, lambda, or theta	e(lrtest)	lrtest if requested
e(ntrans)	yes if nontransformed *indepvars*	e(predict)	program used to implement
e(wtype)	weight type		predict

Matrices

e(b)	coefficient vector	e(df)	degrees of freedom of LR tests on
e(V)	variance–covariance matrix of		*indepvars*
	the estimators (see note below)	e(chi2m)	LR statistics for tests on *indepvars*
e(pm)	p-values for LR tests on *indepvars*		

Functions

e(sample)	marks estimation sample

Note that e(V) contains all zeros, except for the element(s) that correspond to the parameter(s) of the Box–Cox transform.

Methods and Formulas

`boxcox` is implemented as an ado-file.

In the internal computations,

$$
y^{(\lambda)} = \begin{cases} \frac{y^{\lambda}-1}{\lambda} & \text{if } |\lambda| > 10^{-10} \\ \\ \ln(y) & \text{otherwise} \end{cases}
$$

The unconcentrated log likelihood for the `theta` model is

$$
\ln L = \left(\frac{-N}{2}\right) \{\ln(2\pi) + \ln(\sigma^2)\} + (\theta - 1)\sum_{i=1}^{N} \ln(y_i) - \left(\frac{1}{2\sigma^2}\right) \text{SSR}
$$

where

$$
\text{SSR} = \sum_{i=1}^{N}(y_i^{(\theta)} - \beta_0 + \beta_1 x_{i1}^{(\lambda)} + \beta_2 x_{i2}^{(\lambda)} + \cdots + \beta_k x_{ik}^{(\lambda)} + \gamma_1 z_{i1} + \gamma_2 z_{i2} + \cdots + \gamma_l z_{il})^2
$$

Writing the SSR in matrix form,

$$
\text{SSR} = (\mathbf{Y}^{(\theta)} - \mathbf{X}^{(\lambda)}\mathbf{b}' - \mathbf{Z}\mathbf{g}')'(\mathbf{Y}^{(\theta)} - \mathbf{X}^{(\lambda)}\mathbf{b}' - \mathbf{Z}\mathbf{g}')
$$

where $\mathbf{Y}^{(\theta)}$ is an $N \times 1$ vector of elementwise transformed data, $\mathbf{X}^{(\lambda)}$ is an $N \times k$ matrix of elementwise transformed data, $\mathbf{Z}$ is an $N \times l$ matrix of untransformed data, $\mathbf{b}$ is a $1 \times k$ vector of coefficients, and $\mathbf{g}$ is a $1 \times l$ vector of coefficients. Letting

$$
\mathbf{W}_\lambda = \left(\mathbf{X}^{(\lambda)} \ \mathbf{Z}\right)
$$

be the horizontal concatenation of $\mathbf{X}^{(\lambda)}$ and $\mathbf{Z}$ and

$$
\mathbf{d}' = \begin{pmatrix} \mathbf{b}' \\ \mathbf{g}' \end{pmatrix}
$$

be the vertical concatenation of the coefficients yields

$$
\text{SSR} = (\mathbf{Y}^{(\theta)} - \mathbf{W}_\lambda \mathbf{d}')'(\mathbf{Y}^{(\theta)} - \mathbf{W}_\lambda \mathbf{d}')
$$

For given values of λ and θ, the solutions for $\mathbf{d}'$ and σ^2 are

$$
\widehat{\mathbf{d}}' = (\mathbf{W}_\lambda' \mathbf{W}_\lambda)^{-1}\mathbf{W}_\lambda' \mathbf{Y}^{(\theta)}
$$

and

$$
\widehat{\sigma}^2 = \frac{1}{N}\left(\mathbf{Y}^{(\theta)} - \mathbf{W}_\lambda \widehat{\mathbf{d}}'\right)'\left(\mathbf{Y}^{(\theta)} - \mathbf{W}_\lambda \widehat{\mathbf{d}}'\right)
$$

Substituting these solutions into the log-likelihood function yields the concentrated log-likelihood function

$$
\ln L_c = \left(-\frac{N}{2}\right)\{\ln(2\pi) + 1 + \ln(\widehat{\sigma}^2)\} + (\theta - 1)\sum_{i=1}^{N}\ln(y_i)
$$

Similar calculations yield the concentrated log-likelihood function for the `lambda` model,

$$\ln L_c = \left(-\frac{N}{2}\right)\left\{\ln(2\pi) + 1 + \ln(\widehat{\sigma}^2)\right\} + (\lambda - 1)\sum_{i=1}^{N}\ln(y_i)$$

the `lhsonly` model,

$$\ln L_c = \left(-\frac{N}{2}\right)\left\{\ln(2\pi) + 1 + \ln(\widehat{\sigma}^2)\right\} + (\theta - 1)\sum_{i=1}^{N}\ln(y_i)$$

and the `rhsonly` model,

$$\ln L_c = \left(-\frac{N}{2}\right)\left\{\ln(2\pi) + 1 + \ln(\widehat{\sigma}^2)\right\}$$

where $\widehat{\sigma}^2$ is specific to each model and is defined analogously to that in the `theta` model.

References

Atkinson, A. C. 1985. *Plots, Transformations and Regression.* Oxford: Oxford University Press.

Box, G. E. P. and D. R. Cox. 1964. An analysis of transformations. *Journal of the Royal Statistical Society*, Series B 26: 211–243.

Carroll, R. J. and D. Ruppert. 1988. *Transformation and Weighting in Regression.* New York: Chapman & Hall.

Cook, R. D. and S. Weisberg. 1982. *Residuals and Influence in Regression.* New York: Chapman & Hall.

Davidson, R. and J. G. MacKinnon. 1993. *Estimation and Inference in Econometrics.* Oxford: Oxford University Press.

Drukker, D. M. 2000a. sg130: Box–Cox regression models. *Stata Technical Bulletin* 54: 27–36. Reprinted in *Stata Technical Bulletin Reprints*, vol. 9, pp. 307–319.

——. 2000b. sg131: On the manipulability of Wald statistics in Box–Cox regression models. *Stata Technical Bulletin* 54: 36–42. Reprinted in *Stata Technical Bulletin Reprints*, vol. 9, pp. 319–327.

Lafontaine, F. and K. J. White. 1986. Obtaining any Wald statistic you want. *Economics Letters* 21: 35–40.

Phillips, P. C. B. and J. Y. Park. 1988. On the formulation of Wald tests of nonlinear restrictions. *Econometrica* 56: 1065–1083.

Schlesselman, J. J. 1971. Power families: A note on the Box and Cox transformation. *Journal of the Royal Statistical Society*, Series B 33: 307–311.

Spitzer, J. J. 1984. Variance estimates in models with the Box–Cox transformation: Implications for estimation and hypothesis testing. *The Review of Economics and Statistics* 66: 645–652.

Also See

Complementary:	[R] **adjust**, [R] **lincom**, [R] **mfx**, [R] **nlcom**, [R] **predict**, [R] **regress**, [R] **test**, [R] **testnl**
Related:	[R] **lnskew0**
Background:	[U] **16.5 Accessing coefficients and standard errors**, [U] **23 Estimation and post-estimation commands**

Title

> **brier** — Brier score decomposition

Syntax

brier *outcome*$_{\text{var}}$ *forecast*$_{\text{var}}$ [if *exp*] [in *range*] [, group(*#*)]

by ... : may be used with brier; see [R] **by**.

Description

brier computes the Yates, Sanders, and Murphy decompositions of the Brier Mean Probability Score. *outcome*$_{\text{var}}$ contains 0/1 values reflecting the actual outcome of the experiment and *forecast*$_{\text{var}}$ contains the corresponding probabilities as predicted by, say, logit, probit, or a human forecaster.

Options

group(*#*) specifies the number of groups that will be used to compute the decomposition. group(10) is the default.

Remarks

You have a binary (0/1) response and a formula that predicts the corresponding probabilities of having observed a positive outcome (1). If the probabilities were obtained from logistic regression, there are numerous methods that assess goodness of fit (see, for instance, lfit in [R] **logistic**). However, the probabilities might be computed from a published formula or from a model fitted on another sample, both completely unrelated to the data at hand, or perhaps, the forecasts are not from a formula at all. In any case, you now have a *test dataset* consisting of the forecast probabilities and observed outcomes. Your test dataset might, for instance, record predictions made by a meteorologist on the probability of rain along with a variable recording whether it actually rained.

The Brier score is an aggregate measure of disagreement between the observed outcome and a prediction—the average squared error difference. The Brier score decomposition is a partition of the Brier score into components that suggest reasons for discrepancy. These reasons fall roughly into three groups: (1) lack of overall calibration between the average predicted probability and the actual probability of the event in your data; (2) misfit of the data in groups defined within your sample; and (3) inability to match actual 0 and 1 responses.

(1) refers to simply overstating or understating the probabilities.

(2) refers to what is standardly called a goodness-of-fit test: the data are grouped, and the predictions for the group are compared with the outcomes.

(3) refers to an individual-level measure of fit. Imagine that the grouped outcomes are predicted on average correctly, but that, within the group, the outcomes are poorly predicted.

Using logit or probit analysis to fit your data will guarantee that there is no lack of fit due to (1) and a good model fitter will be able to avoid problem (2). Problem (3) is inherent in any prediction exercise.

> ▷ Example

You have data on the outcomes of 20 basketball games (win) and the probability of victory predicted by a local pundit (for).

```
. use http://www.stata-press.com/data/r8/bball
. summarize win for
```

Variable	Obs	Mean	Std. Dev.	Min	Max
win	20	.65	.4893605	0	1
for	20	.4785	.2147526	.15	.9

```
. brier win for, group(5)
```

Mean probability of outcome	0.6500	
of forecast	0.4785	
Correlation	0.5907	
ROC area	0.8791	p = 0.0030
Brier score	0.1828	
Spiegelhalter's z-statistic	-0.6339	p = 0.7369
Sanders-modified Brier score	0.1861	
Sanders resolution	0.1400	
Outcome index variance	0.2275	
Murphy resolution	0.0875	
Reliability-in-the-small	0.0461	
Forecast variance	0.0438	
Excess forecast variance	0.0285	
Minimum forecast variance	0.0153	
Reliability-in-the-large	0.0294	
2*Forecast-Outcome-Covar	0.1179	

The mean probabilities of forecast and outcome are simply the mean of the predicted probabilities and the actual outcomes (win/losses). The correlation is the product-moment correlation between them.

The Brier score measures the total difference between the event (winning) and the forecast probability of that event as an average squared difference. As a benchmark, a perfect forecaster would have a Brier score of 0, a perfect misforecaster (predicts probability of win is 1 when loses and 0 when wins) would have a Brier score of 1; a fence-sitter (forecasts every game as 50/50) would have a Brier score of .25. Our pundit is doing reasonably well.

Spiegelhalter's Z statistic is a standard normal test statistic for testing whether an individual Brier score is extreme. The ROC area is the area under the receiver operating curve and the associated test is a test of whether it is greater than 0.5. The more accurate are the forecast probabilities, the larger is the ROC area.

The Sanders-modified Brier score measures the difference between a grouped forecast measure and the event, where the data are grouped by sorting the sample on the forecast and dividing it into approximately equally sized groups. The difference between the modified and the unmodified score is typically minimal. In order that this and the other statistics which require grouping, the Sanders and Murphy resolutions and Reliability-in-the-small, be well-defined, group boundaries are chosen so as not to allocate observations with the same forecast probability to different groups. This is done by grouping on the forecast using xtile, n(#), with # being the number of groups; see [R] **pctile**.

Sanders resolution measures error that arises from statistical considerations in evaluating the forecast for a group. A group with all positive or all negative outcomes would have a Sanders resolution of 0; it would most certainly be feasible to predict exactly what happened to each member of the group. If the group had 40% positive responses, on the other hand, a forecast that assigned $p = .4$ to each member of the group would be a good one, and yet, there would be "errors" in the squared difference sense. (The "error" would be $(1 - .4)^2$ or $(0 - .4)^2$ for each member.) The Sanders resolution is the average across groups of such "expected" errors. The .1400 value in our data out of an overall Brier score of .1828 or .1861 suggests that a substantial portion of the "error" in our data is inherent.

Outcome index variance is just the variance of the outcome variable. This is the expected value of the Brier score if all the forecast probabilities were merely the average observed outcome. Remember that a fence-sitter has an expected Brier score of .25; a smarter fence sitter (who would guess $p = .65$ for these data) would have a Brier score of .2275.

The Murphy resolution measures the variation in the average outcomes across groups. If all groups have the same frequency of positive outcomes, little information in any forecast is possible and the Murphy resolution is 0. If groups differ markedly, the Murphy resolution is as large as .25. The .0875 means there is some, but not a lot of variation, and .0875 is probably higher than in most real cases. If you had groups in your data that varied between 40% and 60% positive outcomes, the Murphy resolution would be .01; between 30% and 70%, .04.

Reliability-in-the-small measures the error that comes from the average forecast within group not measuring the average outcome within group—a classical goodness-of-fit measure, 0 meaning a perfect fit and 1 meaning a complete lack of fit. The calculated value of 0.0461 shows some amount of lack of fit. Remember, the number is squared, and we are saying that probabilities could be just more than $\sqrt{.0461} = .215$ or 21.5% off.

Forecast variance measures the amount of discrimination being attempted—that is, the variation in the forecasted probabilities. A small number indicates a fence-sitter making constant predictions. If the forecasts were from a logistic regression model, forecast variance would tend to increase with the amount of information available. Our pundit shows considerable forecast variance of .0438 (standard deviation $\sqrt{.0438} = .2093$), which is in line with the reliability-in-the-small, suggesting that the forecaster is attempting as much variation as is available in these data.

Excess forecast variance is the amount of actual forecast variance over a theoretical minimum. The theoretical minimum—called the minimum forecast variance—corresponds to forecasts of p_0 for observations ultimately observed to be negative responses and p_1 for observations ultimately observed to be positive outcomes. Moreover, p_0 and p_1 are set to the average forecasts made for the ultimate negative and positive outcomes. These predictions would be just as good as the predictions the forecaster did make, and any variation in the actual forecast probabilities above this is useless. If this number is large, above 1–2 percent, then the forecaster may be attempting more than is possible. The .0285 in our data suggests this possibility.

Reliability-in-the-large measures the discrepancy between the mean forecast and the observed fraction of positive outcomes. This will be 0 for forecasts made by most statistical models—at least when measured on the same sample used for estimation—since they, by design, reproduce sample means. For our human pundit, the .0294 says that there is a $\sqrt{.0294}$ or 17 percentage point difference. (This difference can also be found by calculating the difference in the averages of the observed outcomes and forecast probabilities: $.65 - .4785 = .17$.) That difference, however, is not significant, as we would see if we typed `ttest win=for`; see [R] **ttest**. If these data were larger and the bias persisted, this would be a critical shortcoming of the forecast.

Twice the forecast-outcome covariance is a measure of how accurately the forecast corresponds to the outcome. It is similar in concept to R-squared in linear regression.

◁

Methods and Formulas

`brier` is implemented as an ado-file.

See Wilks (1995, 259–263) or Schmidt and Griffith (1998) for a discussion of the Brier score.

Let d_j, $j = 1, \ldots, N$, be the observed outcomes, $d_j = 0$ or $d_j = 1$, and let f_j be the corresponding forecasted probabilities that d_j is 1, $0 \le f_j \le 1$. Assume the data are ordered so that $f_{j+1} \ge f_j$ (`brier` sorts the data to obtain this order). Divide the data into K nearly equally sized groups, group 1 containing observations 1 through $j_2 - 1$, group 2 observations j_2 through $j_3 - 1$, and so on.

Define

$$\overline{f}_0 = \text{average } f_j \text{ among } d_j = 0$$
$$\overline{f}_1 = \text{average } f_j \text{ among } d_j = 1$$
$$\overline{f} = \text{average } f_j$$
$$\overline{d} = \text{average } d_j$$
$$\widetilde{f}_k = \text{average } f_j \text{ in group } k$$
$$\widetilde{d}_k = \text{average } d_j \text{ in group } k$$
$$\widetilde{n}_k = \text{number of observations in group } k$$

The Brier score is $\sum_j (d_j - f_j)^2 / N$.

The Sanders-modified Brier score is $\sum_j (d_j - \widetilde{f}_{k(j)})^2 / N$.

Let p_j denote the true but unknown probability that $d_j = 1$. Under the null hypothesis that $p_j = f_j$ for all j, Spiegelhalter (1986) determined that the expectation and variance of the Brier score is given by the following:

$$E(\text{Brier}) = \frac{1}{N} \sum_{j=1}^{N} f_j (1 - f_j)$$

$$\text{Var}(\text{Brier}) = \frac{1}{N^2} \sum_{j=1}^{N} f_j (1 - f_j)(1 - 2f_j)^2$$

Denoting the observed value of the Brier score by O(Brier), Spiegelhalter's Z statistic is given by

$$Z = \frac{O(\text{Brier}) - E(\text{Brier})}{\sqrt{\text{Var}(\text{Brier})}}$$

The corresponding p-value is given by the upper-tail probability of Z under the standard normal distribution.

The area under the ROC curve is estimated by applying the trapezoidal rule to the empirical ROC curve. This area is Wilcoxon's test statistic, so the corresponding p-value is just that of a one-sided Wilcoxon test of the null hypothesis that the distribution of predictions is constant across the two outcomes.

The Sanders resolution is $\sum_k \widetilde{n}_k \{\widetilde{d}_k (1 - \widetilde{d}_k)\} / N$.

The outcome index variance is $\overline{d}(1 - \overline{d})$.

The Murphy resolution is $\sum_k \tilde{n}_k (\tilde{d}_k - \overline{d})^2 / N$.

Reliability-in-the-small is $\sum_k \tilde{n}_k (\tilde{d}_k - \tilde{f}_k)^2 / N$.

The forecast variance is $\sum_j (f_j - \overline{f})^2 / N$.

The minimum forecast variance is $\left\{ \sum_{j \in F} (f_j - \overline{f}_0)^2 + \sum_{j \in S} (f_j - \overline{f}_1)^2 \right\} / N$, where F is the set of observations for which $d_j = 0$ and S is the complement.

The excess forecast variance is the difference between the forecast variance and the minimum forecast variance.

Reliability-in-the-large is $(\overline{f} - \overline{d})^2$.

Twice the outcome covariance is $2(\overline{f}_1 - \overline{f}_0)\overline{d}(1 - \overline{d})$.

Glenn Wilson Brier (1913–1998) was an American meteorological statistician who, after taking degrees in physics and statistics, was for many years head of Meteorological Statistics at the U.S. Weather Bureau, Washington, DC. In the latter part of his career, he was associated with Colorado State University. Brier worked especially on verification and evaluation of predictions and forecasts, statistical decision-making, the statistical theory of turbulence, the analysis of weather modification experiments, and the application of permutation techniques.

Acknowledgment

We would like to thank Richard Goldstein for his contributions to this improved version of `brier`.

References

Brier, G. W. 1950. Verification of forecasts expressed in terms of probability. *Monthly Weather Review* 78: 1–3.

Goldstein, R. 1996. sg55: Extensions to the brier command. *Stata Technical Bulletin* 32: 21–22. Reprinted in *Stata Technical Bulletin Reprints*, vol. 6, pp. 133–134.

Hadorn, D., E. B. Keeler, W. H. Rogers, and R. Brook. 1993. *Assessing the Performance of Mortality Prediction Models*. N-3599-HCFA. Santa Monica, CA: The Rand Corporation.

Holloway, L. and P. Mielke. 1998. Glenn Wilson Brier 1913–1998. *Bulletin of the American Meteorological Society* 79: 1438–1439.

Murphy, A. H. 1973. A new vector partition of the probability score. *Journal of Applied Meteorology* 12: 595–600.

———. 1997. Forecast verification. In *Economic Value of Weather and Climate Forecasts*, ed. R. W. Katz and A. H. Murphy, 19–74. Cambridge: Cambridge University Press.

Redelmeier, D. A., D. A. Bloch, and D. H. Hickam. 1991. Assessing predictive accuracy: how to compare Brier scores. *Journal of Clinical Epidemiology* 44: 1141–1146.

Rogers, W. H. 1992. sbe9: Brier score decomposition. *Stata Technical Bulletin* 10: 20–22. Reprinted in *Stata Technical Bulletin Reprints*, vol. 2, pp. 92–94.

Sanders, F. 1963. On subjective probability forecasting. *Journal of Applied Meteorology* 2: 191–201.

Schmidt, C. H. and J. L. Griffith. 1998. Multivariate classification rules: calibration and discrimination. In *Encyclopedia of Biostatistics*, ed. P. Armitage and T. Colton, 2844–2850. New York: John Wiley & Sons.

Spiegelhalter, D. J. 1986. Probabilistic prediction in patient management and clinical trials. *Statistics in Medicine* 5: 421–433.

Von Storch, H. and F. W. Zwiers. 1999. *Statistical Analysis in Climate Research*. Cambridge: Cambridge University Press.

Wilks, D. S. 1995. *Statistical Methods in the Atmospheric Sciences*. San Diego: Academic Press.

Yates, J. F. 1982. External correspondence: Decompositions of the mean probability score. *Organizational Behavior and Human Performance* 30: 132–156.

Also See

Complementary: [R] **logistic**, [R] **logit**, [R] **predict**, [R] **probit**

Title

by — Repeat Stata command on subsets of the data

Syntax

by *varlist* : *stata_cmd*

by̲sort *varlist* : *stata_cmd*

The above diagrams show by and bysort as they are typically used.
The full syntax of the commands is

by *varlist*$_1$ $\left[(varlist_2)\right]$ $\left[\,,\ \text{s̲ort rc0}\ \right]$: *stata_cmd*

by̲sort *varlist*$_1$ $\left[(varlist_2)\right]$ $\left[\,,\ \text{rc0}\ \right]$: *stata_cmd*

Description

Most Stata commands allow the by prefix, which repeats the command for each group of observations for which the values of the variables in *varlist* are the same. by without the sort option requires that the data be sorted by *varlist*; see [R] **sort**.

Stata commands that work with the by prefix indicate this immediately following their syntax diagram by reporting, for example, "by ... : may be used with logistic; see [R] **by**".

by and bysort are really the same command; bysort is just by with the sort option.

The *varlist*$_1$ (*varlist*$_2$) syntax is of special use to programmers. It verifies that the data are sorted by *varlist*$_1$ *varlist*$_2$, and then performs a by as if only *varlist*$_1$ were specified. For instance,

```
by pid (time): gen growth = (bp - bp[_n-1])/bp
```

performs the generate by values of pid, but first verifies that the data are sorted by pid and time within pid.

Options

sort specifies that if the data are not already sorted by *varlist*, by is to sort them.

rc0 specifies that even if the *stata_cmd* produces an error in one of the by-groups, then by ... : is still to run the *stata_cmd* on the remaining by-groups. The default action is to stop when an error occurs. rc0 is especially useful when *stata_cmd* is an estimation command, and some by-groups have insufficient observations.

144

Remarks

▷ Example

```
. use http://www.stata-press.com/data/r8/auto5
(1978 Automobile Data)
. by foreign : regress mpg weight displ
not sorted
r(5);
. sort foreign
. by foreign : regress mpg weight displ
```

-> foreign = Domestic

Source	SS	df	MS		
Model	880.666134	2	440.333067	Number of obs =	52
Residual	266.776174	49	5.44441171	F(2, 49) =	80.88
				Prob > F =	0.0000
				R-squared =	0.7675
				Adj R-squared =	0.7580
Total	1147.44231	51	22.4988688	Root MSE =	2.3333

mpg	Coef.	Std. Err.	t	P>|t|	[95% Conf. Interval]	
weight	-.005813	.0008759	-6.64	0.000	-.0075732	-.0040528
displacement	-.0015662	.0071435	-0.22	0.827	-.0159216	.0127892
_cons	39.47539	1.773799	22.25	0.000	35.91081	43.03998

-> foreign = Foreign

Source	SS	df	MS		
Model	524.521708	2	262.260854	Number of obs =	22
Residual	393.341928	19	20.7022067	F(2, 19) =	12.67
				Prob > F =	0.0003
				R-squared =	0.5715
				Adj R-squared =	0.5263
Total	917.863636	21	43.7077922	Root MSE =	4.55

mpg	Coef.	Std. Err.	t	P>|t|	[95% Conf. Interval]	
weight	.0047562	.0073953	0.64	0.528	-.0107224	.0202348
displacement	-.2779164	.1287029	-2.16	0.044	-.5472947	-.0085382
_cons	44.6697	5.745669	7.77	0.000	32.64388	56.69552

Note that by requires that the data be sorted. In the above example, we could have typed 'by foreign, sort: regress mpg weight displ' or 'bysort foreign: regress mpg weight displ' rather than the separate sort; all would yield the same results.

◁

For more examples, see [U] **14.1.2 by varlist:**, [U] **14.5 by varlist: construct**, and [U] **31.2 The by construct**.

Also See

Related:	[R] sort,
	[P] **foreach**, [P] **forvalues**, [P] **while**
Background:	[U] **14.1.2 by varlist:** ,
	[U] **14.4 varlists**,
	[U] **14.5 by varlist: construct**,
	[U] **31.2 The by construct**

Title

> **canon** — Canonical correlations

Syntax

canon (*varlist₁*) (*varlist₂*) [*weight*] [if *exp*] [in *range*] [, lc(*#*) noconstant level(*#*)]

by ... : may be used with canon; see [R] **by**.

aweights and fweights are allowed; see [U] **14.1.6 weight**.

canon shares the features of all estimation commands; see [U] **23 Estimation and post-estimation commands**.

Syntax for predict

predict [*type*] *newvarname* [if *exp*] [in *range*] , { u | v | stdu | stdv }

Note that one of the statistics must be specified.

These statistics are available both in and out of sample; type predict ... if e(sample) ... if wanted only for the estimation sample.

Description

canon estimates canonical correlations and provides the loadings for calculating the appropriate linear combinations corresponding to those correlations.

canon typed without arguments redisplays previous estimation results.

Options

lc(*#*) specifies that linear combinations for the *#*th canonical correlation are to be displayed. lc(1) is the default.

noconstant specifies that means are not to be subtracted when calculating correlations.

level(*#*) specifies the confidence level, in percent, for confidence intervals for the coefficients in the reported linear combination. The default is level(95) or as set by set level; see [U] **23.6 Specifying the width of confidence intervals**. These "confidence intervals" are the result of an approximate and aggressive calculation; see the technical note below.

Options for predict

Note that there is not a default statistic for predict after canon; that is, you must specify one of the options.

u and v calculate the linear combinations of *varlist₁* and *varlist₂*, respectively. For the first canonical correlation (lc(1)), u and v are the linear combinations having maximal correlation. For the second canonical correlation (lc(2)), u and v have maximal correlation subject to the constraints that u is orthogonal to the lc(1) u, and v is orthogonal to the lc(1) v. The third and higher are defined similarly.

stdu and stdv calculate the standard errors of the respective linear combinations.

Remarks

Canonical correlations (Hotelling 1935, 1936) attempt to describe the relationships between two sets of variables. Given two sets of variables, $\mathbf{X} = (x_1, x_2, \ldots, x_K)$ and $\mathbf{Y} = (y_1, y_2, \ldots, y_L)$, the goal is to find linear combinations of $\mathbf{X}$ and $\mathbf{Y}$ so that the correlation between the linear combinations is as high as possible. That is, letting $\widehat{x}_1$ and $\widehat{y}_1$ be the linear combinations,

$$\widehat{x}_1 = \beta_{11}x_1 + \beta_{12}x_2 + \cdots + \beta_{1K}x_K$$

$$\widehat{y}_1 = \gamma_{11}y_1 + \gamma_{12}y_2 + \cdots + \gamma_{1L}y_L$$

we wish to find the maximum correlation between $\widehat{x}_1$ and $\widehat{y}_1$. The second canonical correlation coefficient is defined as the ordinary correlation between

$$\widehat{x}_2 = \beta_{21}x_1 + \beta_{22}x_2 + \cdots + \beta_{2K}x_K \quad \text{and}$$

$$\widehat{y}_2 = \gamma_{21}y_1 + \gamma_{22}y_2 + \cdots + \gamma_{2L}y_L$$

This correlation is maximized subject to the constraints that $\widehat{x}_1$ and $\widehat{x}_2$ along with $\widehat{y}_1$ and $\widehat{y}_2$ are orthogonal, and that $\widehat{x}_1$ and $\widehat{y}_2$ along with $\widehat{x}_2$ and $\widehat{y}_1$ are also orthogonal. The third, and so on, are defined similarly. There are $m = \min(K, L)$ such correlations.

▷ Example

Consider two scientists trying to describe how "big" a car is. The first scientist takes physical measurements—the length, weight, headroom, and trunk space—whereas the second takes mechanical measurements—the engine displacement, mileage rating, gear ratio, and turning circle. Can they agree on a conceptual framework?

```
. use http://www.stata-press.com/data/r8/auto
(1978 Automobile Data)
. canon (length weight headroom trunk) (displ mpg gear_ratio turn)
Linear combinations for canonical correlation 1        Number of obs =      74
```

	Coef.	Std. Err.	t	P>|t|	[95% Conf. Interval]	
u						
length	.0094779	.0060748	1.56	0.123	-.0026292	.021585
weight	.0010162	.0001615	6.29	0.000	.0006943	.0013381
headroom	.0351132	.0641755	0.55	0.586	-.0927884	.1630148
trunk	-.0022823	.0158555	-0.14	0.886	-.0338823	.0293176
v						
displacement	.0053704	.0009541	5.63	0.000	.0034688	.007272
mpg	-.0461481	.0107324	-4.30	0.000	-.0675377	-.0247585
gear_ratio	.0329583	.1598716	0.21	0.837	-.2856654	.3515821
turn	.0793927	.0158975	4.99	0.000	.0477091	.1110762

```
                              (Standard errors estimated conditionally)
Canonical correlations:
  0.9476   0.3400   0.0634   0.0447
```

canon reported the linear combinations corresponding to the first canonical correlation along with all four of the correlations. We find that the two views are closely related: the best linear combination of the physical measurements is correlated at almost 0.95 with the best linear combination of the mechanical measurements.

We can prove that the first canonical correlation is correct by calculating the reported linear combinations and then calculating the ordinary correlation:

```
. predict physical, u
. predict mechanical, v
. correlate mechanical physical
(obs=74)
```

	mechan~l	physical
mechanical	1.0000	
physical	0.9476	1.0000

◁

❑ Technical Note

canon reports standard errors for the coefficients in the linear combinations; most other software does not. You should view these standard errors as lower bounds for the true standard errors: the calculation is quite aggressive. It is based on the assumption that the coefficients for one set of measurements are correct for the purpose of calculating the coefficients and standard errors of the other relationship based on a linear regression.

❑

Saved Results

canon saves in e():

Scalars

e(N)	number of observations	e(df_r)	residual degrees of freedom
e(df)	degrees of freedom	e(n_lc)	number of linear combinations

Macros

e(cmd)	canon	e(wexp)	weight expression
e(wtype)	weight type	e(predict)	program used to implement predict

Matrices

e(b)	coefficient vector	e(V)	variance–covariance matrix of the estimators
e(ccorr)	canonical correlation coefficients		

Functions

e(sample)	marks estimation sample

Methods and Formulas

canon is implemented as an ado-file.

Let the correlation matrix between the two sets of variables be

$$\begin{pmatrix} \mathbf{A} & \mathbf{B} \\ \mathbf{B}' & \mathbf{C} \end{pmatrix}$$

That is, $\mathbf{A}$ is the correlation matrix of the first set of variables with themselves, $\mathbf{C}$ is the correlation matrix of the second set of variables with themselves, and $\mathbf{B}$ contains the cross-correlations.

The squared canonical correlations are then the eigenvalues of $\mathbf{V} = \mathbf{B'A}^{-1}\mathbf{BC}^{-1}$ or $\mathbf{W} = \mathbf{BC}^{-1}\mathbf{B'A}^{-1}$ (either will work), both nonsymmetric matrices (Wilks 1962, 587–592). The corresponding left eigenvectors are the linear combinations for the two sets of variables in standardized (variance 1) form.

To calculate standard errors in this form, assume that the left eigenvectors of $\mathbf{V}$ are fixed, and write $\mathbf{V} = (\mathbf{v}_1, \mathbf{v}_2, \ldots, \mathbf{v}_m)$. The left eigenvector of $\mathbf{W}$ corresponding to $\mathbf{v}_k$ is proportional to $\mathbf{v}_k\mathbf{B'C}^{-1}$, which has variance $(1 - r_k^2)\mathbf{C}^{-1}$, where r_k is the corresponding canonical correlation. These answers are then scaled to have mean 0 and variance 1, and are in terms of the original scale of the variables.

References

Hotelling, H. 1935. The most predictable criterion. *Journal of Educational Psychology* 26: 139–142.

——. 1936. Relations between two sets of variates. *Biometrika* 28: 321–377.

Wilks, S. S. 1962. *Mathematical Statistics.* New York: John Wiley & Sons.

Also See

Complementary:	[R] **adjust**, [R] **lincom**, [R] **nlcom**, [R] **predict**, [R] **predictnl**, [R] **test**, [R] **testnl**, [R] **vce**
Related:	[R] **correlate**, [R] **factor**, [R] **pca**, [R] **pcorr**, [R] **regress**
Background:	[U] **23 Estimation and post-estimation commands**

Title

cd — Change directory

Syntax

Stata for Windows:

cd

cd $\left[\,"\,\right]$ *directory_name* $\left[\,"\,\right]$

cd $\left[\,"\,\right]$ *drive* : $\left[\,"\,\right]$

cd $\left[\,"\,\right]$ *drive* : *directory_name* $\left[\,"\,\right]$

pwd

Stata for Macintosh:

cd

cd $\left[\,"\,\right]$ *directory_name* $\left[\,"\,\right]$

pwd

Stata for Unix:

cd $\left[\,\textit{directory\_name}\,\right]$

pwd

Note for Stata for Windows and Stata for Macintosh users: If your *directory_name* contains embedded spaces, remember to enclose it in double quotes.

Description

Stata for Windows: cd changes the working directory to the specified drive and directory. pwd is equivalent to typing cd without arguments; both display the name of the current working directory. Note: Users can shell out to a DOS window; see [R] **shell**. However, typing !cd *directory_name* will not change Stata's current directory; use the cd command to change directories.

Stata for Macintosh and Stata for Unix: cd (synonym chdir) changes the current working directory to *directory_name* or, if *directory_name* is not specified, the home directory. pwd displays the path of the current working directory.

(Continued on next page)

Remarks

Stata for Windows

When you start Stata for Windows, your working directory is set to the *Start in* directory specified in the **Properties**. You can change this; see [GSW] **A.4 The Windows Properties Sheet**. You can always see what your working directory is by looking at the status bar at the bottom of the Stata window.

Once you are in Stata, you can change your directory with the cd command.

```
. cd
c:\data
. cd city
c:\data\city
. cd d:
D:\
. cd kande
D:\kande
. cd "additional detail"
D:\kande\additional detail
. cd c:
C:\
. cd data\city
C:\data\city
. cd \a\b\c\d\e\f\g
C:\a\b\c\d\e\f\g
. cd ..
C:\a\b\c\d\e\f
. cd ...
C:\a\b\c\d
. cd ....
C:\a
```

When we typed 'cd d:', we changed to the current directory of the D drive. We navigated our way to d:\kande\additional detail with three commands: cd d:, then cd kande, then cd "additional detail". Note the double quotes around "additional detail"—they are necessary because of the space in the directory name. We could have changed to this directory in a single command: cd "d:\kande\additional detail".

Notice the last three cd commands in the example above. You are probably familiar with the cd .. syntax to move up one directory from where you are. The last two cd commands above let you take advantage of a feature of Windows to let you move up more than one directory. cd ... is shorthand for 'cd ..\..'. cd .... is shorthand for 'cd ..\..\..'. Note that these shorthand cd commands are not limited to Stata—they will work in your DOS windows under Windows as well.

❑ Technical Note

Note that when you type cd d: to change to the current directory of the D drive, Windows changes to the current directory of the process that started Stata.

A better way to understand this is to think about starting Stata from a DOS window under Windows. Pretend that in your DOS window, the current directory on the C drive is C:\WINDOWS, and the current directory on the D drive is D:\KANDE. Imagine starting Stata from the DOS prompt by typing c:\stata\wstata.exe. Inside Stata, you could type cd "d:\kande\additional detail" to change your current directory. You could then type cd c: to change to the current directory on the C drive—C:\WINDOWS. If you then typed 'cd d:', you would switch to what Windows remembers as the current directory on the D drive—D:\KANDE!

No matter where you cd to inside Stata, if you cd away from the D drive and then cd back to the D drive without specifying a path, your current directory will be the current directory of the D drive in DOS before you started Stata.

❑

Stata for Macintosh

Macintosh users should read [U] **14.6 File-naming conventions** for a description of how filenames are written in a command language before reading this entry.

Invoking an application and then changing folders is an action foreign to most Macintosh users. If it is foreign to you, you can ignore cd and pwd. However, they can be useful. You can see the current folder (where Stata saves files and looks for files) by typing pwd. You can change the current folder by using cd or by selecting **Set Current Folder...** from the **File** menu. Stata's cd understands '~' as an abbreviation for the home directory, so you can type things like cd ~/data.

```
. pwd
/Users/bill/proj
. cd "~/data/city"
/Users/bill/data/city

. _
```

If you now wanted to change to "/Users/bill/data/city/ny", you could type cd ny. If you wanted instead to change to "/Users/bill/data", you could type 'cd ..'.

Stata for Unix

cd and pwd are equivalent to Unix's cd and pwd commands. Like csh, Stata's cd understands '~' as an abbreviation for the home directory $HOME, so you can type things like cd ~/data; see [U] **14.6 File-naming conventions**.

```
. pwd
/usr/bill/proj
. cd ~/data/city
/usr/bill/data/city

. _
```

If you now wanted to change to /usr/bill/data/city/ny, you could type cd ny. If you wanted instead to change to /usr/bill/data, you could type 'cd ..'.

Also See

Complementary:	[R] **shell**
Related:	[R] **copy**, [R] **dir**, [R] **erase**, [R] **mkdir**, [R] **shell**, [R] **type**
Background:	[U] **14.6 File-naming conventions**

Title

centile — Report centile and confidence interval

Syntax

centile [*varlist*] [if *exp*] [in *range*] [, centile(*numlist*) cci normal meansd

level(*#*)]

by ... : may be used with centile; see [R] **by**.

Description

centile estimates specified centiles and calculates confidence intervals. If no *varlist* is specified, centile calculates centiles for all the variables in the dataset. If centile() is not specified, medians (centile(50)) are reported.

Options

centile(*numlist*) specifies the centiles to be reported. The default is to display the 50th centile. Specifying centile(5) requests that the 5th centile be reported. Specifying centile(5 50 95) requests that the 5th, 50th, and 95th centiles be reported. Specifying centile(10(10)90) requests that the 10th, 20th, ..., 90th centiles be reported; see [P] **numlist**.

cci (conservative confidence interval) forces the confidence limits to fall exactly on sample values. Confidence intervals displayed with the cci option are slightly wider than those with the default (nocci) option.

normal causes the confidence interval to be calculated using a formula for the standard error of a normal-distribution quantile given by Kendall and Stuart (1969, 237). The normal option is useful when you want empirical centiles—that is, centiles based on sample order statistics rather than on the mean and standard deviation—and are willing to assume normality.

meansd causes the centile and confidence interval to be calculated based on the sample mean and standard deviation, and assumes normality.

level(*#*) specifies the confidence level, in percent, for confidence intervals. The default is level(95) or as set by set level; see [R] **level**.

Remarks

The qth centile of a continuous random variable X is defined as the value of C_q, which fulfills the condition $\Pr(X \leq C_q) = q/100$. The value of q must be in the range $0 < q < 100$, though q is not necessarily an integer. By default, centile estimates C_q for the variables in *varlist* and for the value(s) of q given in centile(*numlist*). It makes no assumptions as to the distribution of X, and, if necessary, uses linear interpolation between neighboring sample values. Extreme centiles (for example, the 99th centile in samples smaller than 100) are fixed at the minimum or maximum sample value. An "exact" confidence interval for C_q is also given, using the binomial-based method described below in *Methods and Formulas*. The detailed theory is given by Conover (1999, 143–148). Again, linear interpolation is employed to improve the accuracy of the estimated confidence limits, but extremes are fixed at the minimum or maximum sample value.

You can prevent `centile` from interpolating when calculating binomial-based confidence intervals by specifying `cci`. The resulting intervals are generally wider than with the default; that is, the coverage (confidence level) tends to be greater than the nominal value (given as usual by `level(#)`, by default 95%).

If the data are believed to be normally distributed (a common case), there are two alternative methods for estimating centiles. If `normal` is specified, C_q is calculated as just described, but its confidence interval is based on a formula for the standard error (s.e.) of a normal-distribution quantile given by Kendall and Stuart (1969, 237). If `meansd` is alternatively specified, C_q is estimated as $\bar{x} + z_q \times s$, where $\bar{x}$ and s are the sample mean and standard deviation, and z_q is the qth centile of the standard normal distribution (e.g., $z_{95} = 1.645$). The confidence interval is derived from the s.e. of the estimate of C_q.

▷ Example

Using the `auto.dta`, we estimate the 5th, 50th, and 95th centiles of the variable `price`:

```
. use http://www.stata-press.com/data/r8/auto
(1978 Automobile Data)

. format price %8.2fc

. centile price, centile(5 50 95)
```

				— Binom. Interp. —	
Variable	Obs	Percentile	Centile	[95% Conf. Interval]	
price	74	5	3,727.75	3,291.23	3,914.16
		50	5,006.50	4,593.57	5,717.90
		95	13,498.00	11,061.53	15,865.30

`summarize` produces somewhat different results from `centile`; see *Methods and Formulas*.

```
. summarize price, detail
```

Price

	Percentiles	Smallest		
1%	3291	3291		
5%	3748	3299		
10%	3895	3667	Obs	74
25%	4195	3748	Sum of Wgt.	74
50%	5006.5		Mean	6165.257
		Largest	Std. Dev.	2949.496
75%	6342	13466		
90%	11385	13594	Variance	8699526
95%	13466	14500	Skewness	1.653434
99%	15906	15906	Kurtosis	4.819188

The confidence limits produced using the `cci` option are slightly wider than those produced without this option:

```
. centile price, c(5 50 95) cci
```

				— Binomial Exact —	
Variable	Obs	Percentile	Centile	[95% Conf. Interval]	
price	74	5	3,727.75	3,291.00	3,955.00
		50	5,006.50	4,589.00	5,719.00
		95	13,498.00	10,372.00	15,906.00

If we are willing to assume `price` is normally distributed, we could include either the `normal` or the `meansd` option:

```
. centile price, c(5 50 95) normal
```

			— Normal, based on observed centiles —		
Variable	Obs	Percentile	Centile	[95% Conf. Interval]	
price	74	5	3,727.75	3,211.19	4,244.31
		50	5,006.50	4,096.68	5,916.32
		95	13,498.00	5,426.81	21,569.19

```
. centile price, c(5 50 95) meansd
```

			— Normal, based on mean and std. dev.—		
Variable	Obs	Percentile	Centile	[95% Conf. Interval]	
price	74	5	1,313.77	278.93	2,348.61
		50	6,165.26	5,493.24	6,837.27
		95	11,016.75	9,981.90	12,051.59

With the `normal` option, the centile estimates are by definition the same as before. The confidence intervals for the 5th and 50th centiles are similar to the previous ones, but the interval for the 95th centile is very different. The results using the `meansd` option are also very different from both previous sets of estimates.

We can use `sktest` (see [R] **sktest**) to check the correctness of the normality assumption:

```
. sktest price
```

Skewness/Kurtosis tests for Normality

			—— joint ——	
Variable	Pr(Skewness)	Pr(Kurtosis)	adj chi2(2)	Prob>chi2
price	0.000	0.013	21.77	0.0000

`sktest` reveals that `price` is definitely not normally distributed, so the normal assumption is not reasonable and the `normal` and `meansd` options are not appropriate for these data. We should rely on the results from the default choice, which does not assume normality. If the data are normally distributed, however, the precision of the estimated centiles and their confidence intervals will be ordered (best) `meansd` > `normal` > [default] (worst). The `normal` option is useful when we really do want empirical centiles (that is, centiles based on sample order statistics rather than on the mean and standard deviation) but are willing to assume normality.

◁

Saved Results

`centile` saves in `r()`:

Scalars

r(N)	number of observations	r(lb_#)	#-requested centile lower confidence bound
r(n_cent)	number of centiles requested	r(ub_#)	#-requested centile upper confidence bound
r(c_#)	value of # centile		

Macros

r(centiles) centiles requested

Methods and Formulas

centile is implemented as an ado-file.

Default case

The calculation is based on the method of Mood and Graybill (1963, 408). Let $x_1 \leq x_2 \leq \cdots \leq x_n$ be a sample of size n arranged in ascending order. Denote the estimated qth centile of the x's as c_q. We require that $0 < q < 100$. Let $R = (n+1)q/100$ have integer part r and fractional part f; that is, $r = \text{int}(R)$ and $f = R - r$. (If R is itself an integer, then $r = R$ and $f = 0$.) Note that $0 \leq r \leq n$. For convenience, define $x_0 = x_1$ and $x_{n+1} = x_n$. C_q is estimated by

$$c_q = x_r + f \times (x_{r+1} - x_r)$$

that is, c_q is a weighted average of x_r and x_{r+1}. Loosely speaking, a (conservative) $p\%$ confidence interval for C_q involves finding the observations ranked t and u, which correspond, respectively, to the $\alpha = (100 - p)/200$ and $1 - \alpha$ quantiles of a binomial distribution with parameters n and $q/100$; i.e., $\text{B}(n, q/100)$. More precisely, define the ith value $(i = 0, \ldots, n)$ of the cumulative binomial distribution function as $F_i = \Pr(S \leq i)$, where S has distribution $\text{B}(n, q/100)$. For convenience, let $F_{-1} = 0$ and $F_{n+1} = 1$. t is found such that $F_t \leq \alpha$ and $F_{t+1} > \alpha$, and u is found such that $1 - F_u \leq \alpha$ and $1 - F_{u-1} > \alpha$.

With the cci option in force, the (conservative) confidence interval is (x_{t+1}, x_{u+1}) and its actual coverage probability is $F_u - F_t$.

The default case uses linear interpolation on the F_i as follows. Let

$$g = (\alpha - F_t)/(F_{t+1} - F_t)$$
$$h = \{\alpha - (1 - F_u)\}/\{(1 - F_{u-1}) - (1 - F_u)\}$$
$$= (\alpha - 1 + F_u)/(F_u - F_{u-1})$$

The interpolated lower and upper confidence limits (c_{qL}, c_{qU}) for C_q are

$$c_{qL} = x_{t+1} + g \times (x_{t+2} - x_{t+1})$$
$$c_{qU} = x_{u+1} - h \times (x_{u+1} - x_u)$$

For example, suppose we want a 95% confidence interval for the median of a sample of size 13. $n = 13$, $q = 50$, $p = 95$, $\alpha = .025$, $R = 14 \times 50/100 = 7$, and $f = 0$. Therefore, the median is the 7th observation. Some example data x_i and the values of F_i are as follows:

i	F_i	$1 - F_i$	x_i	i	F_i	$1 - F_i$	x_i
0	0.0001	0.9999	–	7	0.7095	0.2905	33
1	0.0017	0.9983	5	8	0.8666	0.1334	37
2	0.0112	0.9888	7	9	0.9539	0.0461	45
3	0.0461	0.9539	10	10	0.9888	0.0112	59
4	0.1334	0.8666	15	11	0.9983	0.0017	77
5	0.2905	0.7095	23	12	0.9999	0.0001	104
6	0.5000	0.5000	28	13	1.0000	0.0000	211

The median is $x_7 = 33$. Also, $F_2 \leq .025$ and $F_3 > .025$, so $t = 2$; $1 - F_{10} \leq .025$ and $1 - F_9 > .025$, so $u = 10$. The conservative confidence interval is therefore

$$(c_{50L}, c_{50U}) = (x_{t+1}, x_{u+1}) = (x_3, x_{11}) = (10, 77)$$

with actual coverage $F_{10} - F_2 = .9888 - .0112 = .9776$ (97.8% confidence). For the interpolation calculation, we have

$$g = (.025 - .0112)/(.0461 - .0112) = .395$$
$$h = (.025 - 1 + .9888)/(.9888 - .9539) = .395$$

So,

$$c_{50L} = x_3 + .395 \times (x_4 - x_3) = 10 + .395 \times 5 = 11.98$$
$$c_{50U} = x_{11} - .395 \times (x_{11} - x_{10}) = 77 - .395 \times 18 = 69.89$$

normal case

The value of c_q is as above. Its s.e. is given by the formula

$$s_q = \sqrt{q(100 - q)} \Big/ \Big\{ 100nZ(c_q; \bar{x}, s) \Big\}$$

where $\bar{x}$ and s are the mean and s.d. of the x_i, and

$$Z(Y; \mu, \sigma) = \left(1/\sqrt{2\pi\sigma^2} \right) e^{-(Y - \mu)^2/2\sigma^2}$$

is the density function of a normally distributed variable Y with mean μ and s.d. σ. The confidence interval for C_q is $(c_q - z_{100(1-\alpha)} s_q, c_q + z_{100(1-\alpha)} s_q)$.

meansd case

The value of c_q is $\bar{x} + z_q \times s$. Its s.e. is given by the formula

$$s_q^\star = s\sqrt{1/n + z_q^2/(2n - 2)}$$

The confidence interval for C_q is $(c_q - z_{100(1-\alpha)} \times s_q^\star, c_q + z_{100(1-\alpha)} \times s_q^\star)$.

Acknowledgment

centile was written by Patrick Royston of the MRC Clinical Trials Unit, London.

References

Conover, W. J. 1999. *Practical Nonparametric Statistics*. 3d ed. New York: John Wiley & Sons.

Kendall, M. G. and A. Stuart. 1969. *The Advanced Theory of Statistics, Vol. I*. 3d ed. London: Griffin.

Mood, A. M. and F. A. Graybill. 1963. *Introduction to the Theory of Statistics*. 2d ed. New York: McGraw–Hill.

Newson, R. 2000. snp16: Robust confidence intervals for median and other percentile differences between two groups. *Stata Technical Bulletin* 58: 30–35. Reprinted in *Stata Technical Bulletin Reprints*, vol. 10, pp. 324–331.

Royston, P. 1992. sg7: Centile estimation command. *Stata Technical Bulletin* 8: 12–15. Reprinted in *Stata Technical Bulletin Reprints*, vol. 2, pp. 122–125.

Also See

Related: [R] **ci**, [R] **pctile**, [R] **summarize**

Title

> **cf** — Compare two datasets

Syntax

cf *varlist* using *filename* [, verbose]

Description

cf compares *varlist* of the dataset in memory (master dataset) with the corresponding variables in *filename* (using dataset). cf returns nothing (i.e., a return code of 0) if the specified variables are identical and a return code of 9 if there are any differences.

Options

verbose mentions the result of the comparison variable-by-variable. Unless verbose is specified, only the differences are mentioned.

Remarks

The messages produced by cf are of the following form:

```
varname: does not exist in using
varname: ___ in master but ___ in using
varname: ___ mismatches
varname: match
```

An example of the second message is "str4 in master but float in using". Unless verbose is specified, the fourth message does not appear—silence indicates matches.

▷ Example

You think the dataset in memory is identical to mydata.dta, but you are unsure. If there are differences, you want to understand them before continuing:

```
. cf _all using mydata

. _
```

In this case, all of the variables that are in the master dataset are in mydata.dta, and these variables are the same in both datasets. Alternatively, you might see

```
. cf _all using mydata
         mpg:  2 mismatches
    headroom:  does not exist in using
displacement:  does not exist in using
   gear_ratio:  does not exist in using
r(9);
```

160

Two changes were made to the mpg variable, and the variables headroom, displacement, and gear_ratio do not exist in mydata.dta.

◁

Methods and Formulas

cf is implemented as an ado-file. If you are using Small Stata, you may get the error "too many variables" when you stipulate _all and have many variables in your dataset. (This will not happen if you are using Stata/SE or Intercooled Stata.) If this happens, you will have to perform the comparison with groups of variables.

References

Gleason, J. R. 1995. dm36: Comparing two Stata data sets. *Stata Technical Bulletin* 28: 10–13. Reprinted in *Stata Technical Bulletin Reprints*, vol. 5, pp. 39–43.

Also See

Related: [R] **compare**

Title

checksum — Calculate checksum of file

Syntax

checksum *filename* [, save replace <u>sa</u>ving(*filename2* [, replace])]

<u>se</u>t checksum { on | off } [<u>perma</u>nently]

Description

checksum creates *filename*.sum files for later use by Stata when it reads files over a network. These optional files are used to reduce the chances of corrupted files going undetected. Whenever Stata reads file *filename*.*suffix* over a network, whether it be by use, net, update, etc., it also looks for *filename*.sum. If Stata finds that file, Stata reads it, too, and then uses its contents to verify that the first file was received without error. If there are errors, Stata informs the user that the file could not be read.

set checksum on tells Stata to verify that files downloaded over a network have been received without error.

set checksum off, which is the default, tells Stata to bypass the file verification.

❏ Technical Note

checksum calculates a CRC checksum following the POSIX 1003.2 specification and displays the file size in bytes. checksum produces the same results as the Unix cksum command. Comparing the checksum of the original file with the received file guarantees the integrity of the received file.

When comparing Stata's checksum results with those of Unix, do not confuse Unix's sum and cksum commands. Unix's cksum and Stata's checksum use a more robust algorithm than that used by Unix's sum. On some Unixes, there is no cksum command, and the more robust algorithm is obtained by specifying an option with sum.

❏

Options

save saves the output of the checksum command to the ASCII file *filename*.sum. The default is to display a report but not create a file.

replace is for use with save; it permits Stata to overwrite an existing *filename*.sum file.

saving(*filename2* [, replace]) is an alternative to save. It saves the output in the specified filename. You must supply a file extension if you want one, as none is assumed.

permanently specifies that, in addition to making the change right now, the checksum setting should be remembered in the future, and will become the default setting for when you invoke Stata.

Remarks

Say you wish to put a dataset on your homepage so that colleagues can use it over the Internet by typing

```
. use http://www.myuni.edu/department/~joe/mydata
```

mydata.dta is important, and, even though the chances of the file mydata.dta being corrupted by the Internet are small, you wish to guard against that. The solution is to create the checksum file named mydata.sum and also place that on your homepage. Your colleagues will need type nothing different, but now Stata will verify that all goes well. When they use the file, they will see either

```
. use http://www.myuni.edu/department/~joe/mydata
(important data from joe)
```

or

```
. use http://www.myuni.edu/department/~joe/mydata
file transmission error (checksums do not match)
http://www.myuni.edu/department/~joe/mydata.dta not downloaded
r(639);
```

To make the checksum file, change to the directory where the file is located and type

```
. checksum mydata.dta, save
Checksum for mydata.dta = 263508742, size = 4052
file mydata.sum saved
```

Saved Results

checksum saves in r():

Scalars

r(version)	checksum version number
r(filelen)	length of file, in bytes
r(checksum)	checksum value

Also See

Complementary: [R] **net**, [R] **save**

Title

ci — Confidence intervals for means, proportions, and counts

Syntax

ci [*varlist*] [*weight*] [if *exp*] [in *range*] [, level(#) binomial poisson

   exposure(*varname*) total separator(#)]

cii #$_{\text{obs}}$ #$_{\text{mean}}$ #$_{\text{sd}}$ [, level(#)]   (normal variable)

cii #$_{\text{obs}}$ #$_{\text{succ}}$ [, level(#)]   (binomial variable)

cii #$_{\text{exposure}}$ #$_{\text{events}}$, poisson [level(#)]   (Poisson variable)

by ... : may be used with ci (but not with cii); see [R] **by**.
aweights and fweights are allowed; see [U] **14.1.6 weight**.

Description

ci computes standard errors and confidence intervals for each of the variables in *varlist*.

cii is the immediate form of ci; see [U] **22 Immediate commands** for a general discussion of immediate commands.

Options

level(#) specifies the confidence level, in percent, for confidence intervals. The default is level(95) or as set by set level; see [R] **level**.

binomial tells ci that the variables are 0/1 binomial variables and that exact binomial confidence intervals will be calculated. (cii produces binomial confidence intervals when only two numbers are specified.)

poisson specifies that the variables are Poisson-distributed counts; exact confidence intervals will be calculated.

exposure(*varname*) is used only with poisson. It is not necessary to also specify poisson if exposure() is specified; poisson is assumed. *varname* contains the total exposure (typically a time or an area) during which the number of events recorded in *varlist* were observed.

total is for use with the by ... : prefix. It requests that, in addition to output for each by-group, output be added for all groups combined.

separator(#) specifies how often separation lines should be inserted into the output. The default is separator(5), meaning that a line is drawn after every 5 variables. separator(10) would draw the line after every 10 variables. separator(0) suppresses the separation line.

Remarks

Remarks are presented under the headings

> *Ordinary confidence intervals*
> *Binomial confidence intervals*
> *Poisson confidence intervals*
> *Immediate form*

Ordinary confidence intervals

▷ Example

Without the `binomial` or `poisson` options, `ci` produces "ordinary" confidence intervals, which is to say, confidence intervals that are correct if the variable is distributed normally.

```
. use http://www.stata-press.com/data/r8/auto
(1978 Automobile Data)
. ci mpg price
```

Variable	Obs	Mean	Std. Err.	[95% Conf. Interval]	
mpg	74	21.2973	.6725511	19.9569	22.63769
price	74	6165.257	342.8719	5481.914	6848.6

The standard error of the mean of `mpg` is 0.67, and the 95% confidence interval is $[19.96, 22.64]$. We can obtain wider, 99% confidence intervals by typing

```
. ci mpg price, level(99)
```

Variable	Obs	Mean	Std. Err.	[99% Conf. Interval]	
mpg	74	21.2973	.6725511	19.51849	23.07611
price	74	6165.257	342.8719	5258.405	7072.108

◁

▷ Example

`by()` breaks out the confidence intervals according to by-group; `total` adds an overall summary. For instance,

```
. ci mpg, by(foreign) total
```

-> foreign = Domestic

Variable	Obs	Mean	Std. Err.	[95% Conf. Interval]	
mpg	52	19.82692	.657777	18.50638	21.14747

-> foreign = Foreign

Variable	Obs	Mean	Std. Err.	[95% Conf. Interval]	
mpg	22	24.77273	1.40951	21.84149	27.70396

-> Total

Variable	Obs	Mean	Std. Err.	[95% Conf. Interval]	
mpg	74	21.2973	.6725511	19.9569	22.63769

◁

❑ Technical Note

You can control the formatting of the numbers in the output by attaching a display format to the variable; see [U] **15.5 Formats: controlling how data are displayed**. For instance,

```
. format mpg %9.2f
. ci mpg
    Variable |      Obs        Mean    Std. Err.     [95% Conf. Interval]
    ---------+---------------------------------------------------------------
         mpg |       74       21.30         0.67        19.96       22.64
```

❑

Binomial confidence intervals

▷ Example

You have data on employees including a variable marking whether the employee was promoted last year.

```
. use http://www.stata-press.com/data/r8/promo
. ci promoted, binomial
                                              — Binomial Exact —
    Variable |      Obs        Mean    Std. Err.     [95% Conf. Interval]
    ---------+---------------------------------------------------------------
    promoted |       20          .1     .067082     .0123485     .3169827
```

The interpretation is as follows: If the true probability of being promoted were 0.012, the chances of observing a result as extreme or more extreme than the result observed ($20 \cdot 0.1 = 2$ or more promotions) would be 2.5%. If the true probability of being promoted were 0.317, the chances of observing a result as extreme or more extreme than observed (2 or fewer promotions) would be 2.5%.

◁

❑ Technical Note

Binomial confidence intervals can differ markedly from ordinary confidence intervals when sample sizes are small or when the probability of a positive outcome is extreme. In the above case, ci without the `binomial` option reports the confidence interval $[-.048, .248]$. As sample sizes increase, the binomial and ordinary confidence intervals become virtually identical, but it is always better to use the binomial calculation when the underlying variable follows the binomial distribution.

❑

❑ Technical Note

Let us repeat the promotion example, but this time with data in which there are no promotions over the observed period:

```
. use http://www.stata-press.com/data/r8/promonone
. ci promoted, binomial
                                              — Binomial Exact —
    Variable |      Obs        Mean    Std. Err.     [95% Conf. Interval]
    ---------+---------------------------------------------------------------
    promoted |       20           0           0            0    .1684335*
(*) one-sided, 97.5% confidence interval
```

The confidence interval is $[0, .168]$, and this is the confidence interval most books publish. It is not, however, a true 95% confidence interval because the lower tail has vanished. As Stata notes, it is a one-sided, 97.5% confidence interval. If you wanted to put 5% in the right tail, you could type ci promoted, binomial level(90).

❑

❑ Technical Note

ci with the binomial option ignores any variables that do not take on the values 0 and 1 exclusively. For instance, with our automobile dataset,

```
. use http://www.stata-press.com/data/r8/auto
(1978 Automobile Data)
. ci mpg foreign, binomial
```

Variable	Obs	Mean	Std. Err.	— Binomial Exact — [95% Conf. Interval]	
foreign	74	.2972973	.0531331	.196584	.4148353

Note that we also requested the confidence interval for mpg, but Stata ignored us. It does that so you can type ci, binomial and obtain correct confidence intervals for all the variables that are 0/1 in your data.

❑

Poisson confidence intervals

▷ Example

You have data on the number of bacterial colonies on a Petri dish. The dish has been divided into 36 small squares, and the number of colonies in each square has been counted. Each observation in your dataset represents a square on the dish. The variable count records the number of colonies in each square counted, which varies from 0 to 5.

```
. use http://www.stata-press.com/data/r8/petri
. ci count, poisson
```

Variable	Exposure	Mean	Std. Err.	— Poisson Exact — [95% Conf. Interval]	
count	36	2.333333	.2545875	1.861159	2.888813

ci reports the average number of colonies per square is 2.33. If the expected number of colonies per square were as low as 1.86, the probability of observing 2.33 or more colonies per square would be 2.5%. If the expected number were as large as 2.89, the probability of observing $36 \cdot 2.33 = 84$ or fewer colonies per square would be 2.5%.

◁

❑ Technical Note

The number of "observations"—how finely the Petri dish is divided—makes no difference. The Poisson distribution is a function only of the count. In our example above, we observed a total of $2.33 \cdot 36 = 84$ colonies and a confidence interval of $[1.86 \cdot 36, 2.89 \cdot 36] = [67, 104]$. We would obtain the same $[67, 104]$ confidence interval if our dish were divided into, say, 49 squares rather than 36.

In terms of the counts, it is not even important that all the squares be of the same size. In terms of *rates*, however, such differences do matter, but in an easy-to-calculate way. Rates are obtained from counts by dividing by exposure, which is typically a number multiplied by either time or an area. In the case of our Petri dishes, we divide by an area to obtain a rate, but if our example were cast in terms of being infected by a disease, we might divide by person-years to obtain the rate. Rates are convenient because they are easier to compare: we might have 2.3 colonies per square inch or .0005 infections per person-year.

So, let us assume that we wish to obtain the number of colonies per square inch, and, moreover, that not all the "squares" on our dish are of equal size. We have a variable called `area` that records the area of each "square":

```
. ci count, exposure(area)
```

Variable	Exposure	Mean	Std. Err.	— Poisson Exact — [95% Conf. Interval]	
count	3	28	3.055051	22.33391	34.66575

The rates are now in more familiar terms. In our sample, there are 28 colonies per square inch and the 95% confidence interval is $[22.3, 34.7]$. When we did not specify `exposure()`, ci assumed that each observation contributed 1 to exposure.

❑

❑ Technical Note

As with the `binomial` option, had there been no colonies on our dish, ci would calculate a one-sided confidence interval:

```
. use http://www.stata-press.com/data/r8/petrinone
. ci count, poisson
```

Variable	Exposure	Mean	Std. Err.	— Poisson Exact — [95% Conf. Interval]	
count	36	0	0	0	.102434*

(*) one-sided, 97.5% confidence interval

❑

Immediate form

▷ Example

You are reading a soon-to-be-published paper by a colleague. In it is a table showing the number of observations, mean, and standard deviation of 1980 median family income for the Northeast and West. You correctly feel that the paper would be much improved if it included the confidence intervals. The paper claims that for 166 cities in the Northeast, the average of median family income is $19,509 with a standard deviation of $4,379:

```
. cii 166 19509 4379
```

Variable	Obs	Mean	Std. Err.	[95% Conf. Interval]	
	166	19509	339.8763	18837.93	20180.07

For the West:

```
. cii 256 22557 5003
    Variable |    Obs       Mean   Std. Err.     [95% Conf. Interval]
             |    256      22557   312.6875        21941.22   23172.78
```

◁

▷ Example

You flip a coin 10 times and it comes up heads only once. You are shocked and decide to obtain a 99% confidence interval for this coin:

```
. cii 10 1, level(99)
                                             — Binomial Exact —
    Variable |    Obs       Mean   Std. Err.     [99% Conf. Interval]
             |     10         .1   .0948683        .0005011    .5442871
```

◁

▷ Example

The number of reported traffic accidents in Santa Monica over a 24-hour period is 27. You need know nothing else:

```
. cii 1 27, poisson
                                             — Poisson  Exact —
    Variable | Exposure     Mean   Std. Err.     [95% Conf. Interval]
             |      1         27   5.196152        17.79773    39.28305
```

◁

Saved Results

ci and cii saves in r():

Scalars

r(N)	number of observations or exposure	r(lb)	lower bound of confidence interval
r(mean)	mean	r(ub)	upper bound of confidence interval
r(se)	estimate of standard error		

Methods and Formulas

ci and cii are implemented as ado-files.

Ordinary

Define n, $\bar{x}$, and s^2 as the number of observations, (weighted) average, and (unbiased) estimated variance of the variable in question; see [R] **summarize**.

The standard error of the mean s_μ is defined as $\sqrt{s^2/n}$.

Let α be $1 - l/100$, where l is the significance level specified by the user. Define t_α as the two-sided t statistic corresponding to a significance level of α with $n - 1$ degrees of freedom; t_α is obtained from Stata as $\mathtt{invttail}(n\text{-}1,0.5\text{*}\alpha)$. The lower and upper confidence bounds are, respectively, $\overline{x} - s_\mu t_\alpha$ and $\overline{x} + s_\mu t_\alpha$.

Binomial

Given k successes out of n trials, the mean probability is $p = k/n$ with standard error $\sqrt{p(1-p)/n}$. ci calculates the exact confidence interval $[k_1, k_2]$ such that

$$\Pr(K \leq k_1) \leq \alpha/2$$

and

$$\Pr(K \geq k_2) \leq \alpha/2$$

Solution is by bisection. If $k = 0$ or $k = n$, the calculation of the appropriate tail is skipped.

Poisson

Given a count k, the expected count is k and the standard deviation is $\sqrt{k}$. ci calculates the exact confidence interval $[k_1, k_2]$ such that

$$\Pr(K \leq k_1) \leq \alpha/2$$

and

$$\Pr(K \geq k_2) \leq \alpha/2$$

Solution is by Newton's method. If $k = 0$, the calculation of k_1 is skipped. All values are reported as rates, which are the above numbers divided by the total exposure.

References

Feller, W. 1968. *An Introduction to Probability Theory and Its Applications*, vol. 1. 3d ed. New York: John Wiley & Sons.

Gleason, J. R. 1999. sg119: Improved confidence intervals for binomial proportions. *Stata Technical Bulletin* 52: 16–18. Reprinted in *Stata Technical Bulletin Reprints*, vol. 9, pp. 208–211.

Hamilton, L. C. 1996. *Data Analysis for Social Scientists*. Belmont, CA: Duxbury Press.

Hoel, P. G. 1984. *Introduction to Mathematical Statistics*. 5th ed. New York: John Wiley & Sons.

Rothman, K. J. and S. Greenland. 1998. *Modern Epidemiology*. 2d ed. Philadelphia: Lippincott–Raven.

Seed, P. T. 2001. sg159: Confidence intervals for correlations. *Stata Technical Bulletin* 59: 27–28. Reprinted in *Stata Technical Bulletin Reprints*, vol. 10, pp. 267–269.

Utts, J. M. 1999. *Seeing through Statistics*. 2d ed. Pacific Grove, CA: Duxbury Press.

Wang, D. 2000. sg154: Confidence intervals for the ratio of two binomial proportions by Koopman's method. *Stata Technical Bulletin* 58: 16–19. Reprinted in *Stata Technical Bulletin Reprints*, vol. 10, pp. 244–247.

Also See

Complementary:	[R] **bitest**, [R] **ttest**
Related:	[R] **centile**, [R] **means**, [R] **pctile**, [R] **summarize**, [ST] **stci**
Background:	[U] **22 Immediate commands**

Title

clogit — Conditional (fixed-effects) logistic regression

Syntax

clogit *depvar* [*indepvars*] [*weight*] [if *exp*] [in *range*] ,

group(*varname*) [level(#) or offset(*varname*) *maximize_options*]

by ... : may be used with clogit; see [R] **by**.

fweights and iweights are allowed (see [U] **14.1.6 weight**), but they are interpreted to apply to groups as a whole, not to individual observations. See *Use of weights* below.

clogit shares the features of all estimation commands; see [U] **23 Estimation and post-estimation commands**.

clogit may be used with sw to perform stepwise estimation; see [R] **sw**.

Syntax for predict

predict [*type*] *newvarname* [if *exp*] [in *range*] [, [pc1 | pu0 | xb | stdp]

nooffset]

These statistics are available both in and out of sample; type predict ... if e(sample) ... if wanted only for the estimation sample.

Description

clogit fits what biostatisticians and epidemiologists call conditional logistic regression for matched case–control groups (see, for example, Hosmer and Lemeshow 2000, chapter 7), and what economists and other social scientists call fixed-effects logit for panel data (see, for example, Chamberlain 1980). It also fits McFadden's choice model (McFadden 1974). Computationally, these models are exactly the same.

See [R] **logistic** for a list of related estimation commands.

Options

group(*varname*) is not optional; it specifies an identifier variable (numeric or string) for the matched groups. strata(*varname*) is a synonym for group().

level(#) specifies the confidence level, in percent, for confidence intervals. The default is level(95) or as set by set level; see [U] **23.6 Specifying the width of confidence intervals**.

or reports the estimated coefficients transformed to odds ratios; i.e., e^b rather than b. Standard errors and confidence intervals are similarly transformed. This option affects how results are displayed and not how they are estimated. or may be specified at estimation or when replaying previously estimated results.

offset(*varname*) specifies that *varname* is to be included in the model with coefficient constrained to be 1.

maximize_options control the maximization process; see [R] **maximize**. You should never have to specify them.

Options for predict

pc1, the default, calculates the probability of a positive outcome conditional on one positive outcome within group.

pu0 calculates the probability of a positive outcome, assuming that the fixed effect is zero.

xb calculates the linear prediction.

stdp calculates the standard error of the linear prediction.

nooffset is relevant only if you specified offset(*varname*) for clogit. It modifies the calculations made by predict so that they ignore the offset variable; the linear prediction is treated as $x_j b$ rather than as $x_j b + \text{offset}_j$.

Remarks

Remarks are presented under the headings

> *Matched case–control data*
> *Use of weights*
> *Fixed-effects logit*
> *McFadden's choice model*
> *Predictions*

clogit fits maximum likelihood models with a dichotomous dependent variable coded as 0/1 (more precisely, clogit interprets 0 and not 0 to indicate the dichotomy). Conditional logistic analysis differs from regular logistic regression in that the data are grouped and the likelihood is calculated relative to each group; i.e., a conditional likelihood is used; see *Methods and Formulas* at the end of this entry.

Biostatisticians and epidemiologists fit these models when analyzing matched case–control studies with 1 : 1 matching, 1 : k_{2i} matching, or $k_{1i} : k_{2i}$ matching, where i denotes the ith matched group for $i = 1, 2, \ldots, n$, where n is the total number of groups. clogit fits a model appropriate for all these matching schemes or for any mix of the schemes, since the matching $k_{1i} : k_{2i}$ can vary from group to group. Note that clogit always uses the true conditional likelihood, not an approximation. (Using the true likelihood for $k_{1i} : k_{2i}$ matching when $k_{1i} > 1$ was introduced in Stata version 5.) Biostatisticians and epidemiologists sometimes refer to the matched groups as "strata", but we will stick to the more generic term "group".

Economists and other social scientists fitting fixed-effects logit models have data that look exactly like the data biostatisticians and epidemiologists call $k_{1i} : k_{2i}$ matched case–control data. In terms of how the data are arranged, $k_{1i} : k_{2i}$ matching means that in the ith group the dependent variable is 1 a total of k_{1i} times and 0 a total of k_{2i} times. There are a total of $T_i = k_{1i} + k_{2i}$ observations for the ith group. This data arrangement is what economists and other social scientists call "panel data" or "cross-sectional time-series data".

McFadden's choice model (McFadden 1974) in its basic form is simply an application of conditional logistic regression with 1 : k_{2i} matching. The only new wrinkle here is how you set up the variables in your dataset. We discuss this in detail in the section *McFadden's choice model* below.

So, no matter what terminology you use, the computation and the use of the clogit command is the same. The following example shows how your data should be arranged to use clogit.

▷ Example

Suppose we have grouped data with the variable id containing a unique identifier for each group. Our outcome variable y contains 0s and 1s. If we were biostatisticians, y = 1 would indicate a case, y = 0 would be a control, and id would be an identifier variable that indicates the groups of matched case–controls.

If we were economists, $y = 1$ might indicate, for example, that a person was unemployed at any time during a year, $y = 0$ that a person was employed all year, and `id` would be an identifier variable for persons.

If we list the first few observations of this dataset, it looks like

```
. use http://www.stata-press.com/data/r8/clogitid
. list y x1 x2 id in 1/11
```

	y	x1	x2	id
1.	0	0	4	1014
2.	0	1	4	1014
3.	0	1	6	1014
4.	1	1	8	1014
5.	0	0	1	1017
6.	0	0	7	1017
7.	1	1	10	1017
8.	0	0	1	1019
9.	0	1	7	1019
10.	1	1	7	1019
11.	1	1	9	1019

Pretending we are biostatisticians, we describe our data as follows: The first group (id $= 1014$) consists of 4 matched persons: 1 case ($y = 1$) and 3 controls ($y = 0$); i.e., $1 : 3$ matching. The second group has $1 : 2$ matching, and the third $2 : 2$.

Pretending we are economists, we describe our data as follows: The first group consists of 4 observations (one per year) for person 1014. This person had a period of unemployment during 1 year out of 4. The second person had a period of unemployment during 1 year out of 3, and the third 2 years out of 4.

Our independent variables are `x1` and `x2`. To fit the conditional (fixed-effects) logistic model, we type

```
. clogit y x1 x2, group(id)
note: multiple positive outcomes within groups encountered.
Iteration 0:   log likelihood = -126.34772
Iteration 1:   log likelihood =  -123.4154
Iteration 2:   log likelihood = -123.41386
```

Conditional (fixed-effects) logistic regression		Number of obs	=	369
		LR chi2(2)	=	9.07
		Prob > chi2	=	0.0107
Log likelihood = -123.41386		Pseudo R2	=	0.0355

y	Coef.	Std. Err.	z	P>|z|	[95% Conf. Interval]	
x1	.653363	.2875214	2.27	0.023	.0898313	1.216895
x2	.0659169	.0449555	1.47	0.143	-.0221942	.154028

◁

❏ Technical Note

Note the message "note: multiple positive outcomes within groups encountered" at the top of the clogit output for the previous example. This is merely informing you that you have $k_{1i} : k_{2i}$ matching with $k_{1i} > 1$ for at least one group. If your data should be $1 : k_{2i}$ matched, then there is an error in the data somewhere.

We can see the distribution of k_{1i} and $T_i = k_{1i} + k_{2i}$ for the data of the previous example by using the following steps.

```
. by id, sort: gen k1 = sum(y)
. by id: replace k1 = . if _n < _N
(303 real changes made, 303 to missing)
. by id: gen T = sum(y < .)
. by id: replace T = . if _n < _N
(303 real changes made, 303 to missing)
. tab k1
```

k1	Freq.	Percent	Cum.
1	48	72.73	72.73
2	12	18.18	90.91
3	4	6.06	96.97
4	2	3.03	100.00
Total	66	100.00	

```
. tab T
```

T	Freq.	Percent	Cum.
2	5	7.58	7.58
3	5	7.58	15.15
4	12	18.18	33.33
5	11	16.67	50.00
6	13	19.70	69.70
7	8	12.12	81.82
8	3	4.55	86.36
9	7	10.61	96.97
10	2	3.03	100.00
Total	66	100.00	

So, we see that k_{1i} ranges from 1 to 4 and T_i ranges from 2 to 10 for these data.

❏

❏ Technical Note

In the case of $k_{1i} : k_{2i}$ matching (and hence in the general case of fixed-effects logit), clogit uses a recursive algorithm to compute the likelihood. This means that there are no limits on the size of T_i. However, computation time is proportional to $\sum T_i \min(k_{1i}, k_{2i})$, so clogit will take roughly 10 times longer to fit a model with 10 : 10 matching than one with 1 : 10. But clogit is very fast, so computation time only becomes an issue when $\min(k_{1i}, k_{2i})$ is around 100 or more. See *Methods and Formulas* at the end of this entry for details.

❏

Matched case–control data

Here, we give a more detailed example of matched case–control data.

▷ Example

Hosmer and Lemeshow (2000, 25) present data on matched pairs of infants, one with low birth weight and another with regular birth weight. The data are matched on age of the mother. Several possible maternal exposures are considered: race (three categories), smoking status, presence of hypertension, presence of uterine irritability, previous preterm delivery, and weight at the last menstrual period.

```
. use http://www.stata-press.com/data/r8/lowbirth
(Applied Logistic Regression, Hosmer & Lemeshow)

. describe

Contains data from http://www.stata-press.com/data/r8/lowbirth.dta
  obs:            112                          Applied Logistic Regression,
                                                 Hosmer & Lemeshow
  vars:            11                          24 Jul 2002 10:57
  size:         1,792 (99.5% of memory free)
```

variable name	storage type	display format	value label	variable label
pairid	byte	%8.0g		Case-control pair id
low	byte	%8.0g		Baby has low birth weight
age	byte	%8.0g		Age of mother
lwt	int	%8.0g		Mother's last menstrual weight
smoke	byte	%8.0g		Mother smoked during pregnancy
ptd	byte	%8.0g		Mother had previous preterm baby
ht	byte	%8.0g		Mother has hypertension
ui	byte	%8.0g		Uterine irritability
race1	byte	%8.0g		mother is white
race2	byte	%8.0g		mother is black
race3	byte	%8.0g		mother is other

```
Sorted by:
```

We list the case–control indicator variable low, the match identifier variable pairid, and two of the covariates, lwt and smoke, for the first 10 observations.

```
. list low lwt smoke pairid in 1/10
```

	low	lwt	smoke	pairid
1.	0	135	0	1
2.	1	101	1	1
3.	0	98	0	2
4.	1	115	0	2
5.	0	95	0	3
6.	1	130	0	3
7.	0	103	0	4
8.	1	130	1	4
9.	0	122	1	5
10.	1	110	1	5

We fit a conditional logistic model of low birth weight on mother's weight, race, smoking behavior, and history.

```
. clogit low lwt smoke ptd ht ui race2 race3, strata(pairid) nolog
Conditional (fixed-effects) logistic regression    Number of obs   =        112
                                                    LR chi2(7)      =      26.04
                                                    Prob > chi2     =     0.0005
Log likelihood = -25.794271                         Pseudo R2       =     0.3355
```

low	Coef.	Std. Err.	z	P>|z|	[95% Conf. Interval]	
lwt	-.0183757	.0100806	-1.82	0.068	-.0381333	.0013819
smoke	1.400656	.6278396	2.23	0.026	.1701131	2.631199
ptd	1.808009	.7886502	2.29	0.022	.2622829	3.353735
ht	2.361152	1.086128	2.17	0.030	.2323797	4.489924
ui	1.401929	.6961585	2.01	0.044	.0374836	2.766375
race2	.5713643	.6896449	0.83	0.407	-.7803149	1.923044
race3	-.0253148	.6992044	-0.04	0.971	-1.39573	1.345101

We might prefer to see results presented as odds ratios. We could have specified the or option when we first fitted the model, or we can now redisplay results and specify or:

```
. clogit, or
Conditional (fixed-effects) logistic regression    Number of obs   =        112
                                                    LR chi2(7)      =      26.04
                                                    Prob > chi2     =     0.0005
Log likelihood = -25.794271                         Pseudo R2       =     0.3355
```

low	Odds Ratio	Std. Err.	z	P>|z|	[95% Conf. Interval]	
lwt	.9817921	.009897	-1.82	0.068	.9625847	1.001383
smoke	4.057862	2.547686	2.23	0.026	1.185439	13.89042
ptd	6.098293	4.80942	2.29	0.022	1.299894	28.60938
ht	10.60316	11.51639	2.17	0.030	1.261599	89.11467
ui	4.06303	2.828513	2.01	0.044	1.038195	15.90088
race2	1.770681	1.221141	0.83	0.407	.4582617	6.84175
race3	.975003	.6817263	-0.04	0.971	.2476522	3.838573

Smoking, previous preterm delivery, hypertension, uterine irritability, and possibly the mother's weight all contribute to low birth weight. race2 (mother black) and race3 (mother other) are statistically insignificant when compared with the race1 (mother white) omitted group, although the race2 effect is large. We can test the joint statistical significance of race2 and race3 using test:

```
. test race2 race3
 ( 1)   race2 = 0
 ( 2)   race3 = 0
        chi2(  2) =     0.88
      Prob > chi2 =     0.6436
```

For a more complete description of test, see [R] **test**. Note that test presents results in terms of coefficients rather than odds ratios. Jointly testing that the coefficients on race2 and race3 are zero is equivalent to jointly testing that the odds ratios are 1.

In this example, one case was matched to one control, so-called 1 : 1 matching. From clogit's point-of-view, that was not important—k_1 cases could have been matched to k_2 controls ($k_1 : k_2$ matching), and we would have fitted the model in the same way. Furthermore, the matching can change from group to group, which we have denoted as $k_{1i} : k_{2i}$ matching, where i denotes the group. clogit does not care. To fit the conditional logistic regression model, we specified the group(*varname*) option, in our case, group(pairid). The case and control are stored in separate observations. clogit knew they were linked (in the same group) because the related observations share the same value of pairid.   ◁

❏ Technical Note

clogit provides a way to extend McNemar's test to multiple controls per case ($1 : k_{2i}$ matching) and to multiple controls matched with multiple cases ($k_{1i} : k_{2i}$ matching).

In Stata, McNemar's test is calculated by the mcc command; see [ST] **epitab**. The mcc command, however, requires that the matched case and control appear in a single observation, so the data will need to be manipulated from one to two observations per stratum before using clogit. Alternatively, if you begin with clogit's two-observations-per-group organization, you will have to change it to one observation per group if you wish to use mcc. In either case, reshape provides an easy way to change the organization of the data. We will demonstrate its use below, but we direct you to [R] **reshape** for a more thorough discussion.

In the above example, we used clogit to analyze the relationship between low birth weight and various characteristics of the mother. Assume we now want to assess the relationship between low birth weight and smoking ignoring the mother's other characteristics. Using clogit, we obtain the following results:

```
. clogit low smoke, strata(pairid) or
Iteration 0:   log likelihood = -37.257978
Iteration 1:   log likelihood = -35.431994
Iteration 2:   log likelihood = -35.419285
Iteration 3:   log likelihood = -35.419282
Conditional (fixed-effects) logistic regression    Number of obs   =        112
                                                    LR chi2(1)      =       6.79
                                                    Prob > chi2     =     0.0091
Log likelihood = -35.419282                         Pseudo R2       =     0.0875
```

low	Odds Ratio	Std. Err.	z	P>|z|	[95% Conf. Interval]
smoke	2.75	1.135369	2.45	0.014	1.224347 6.176763

Let us compare our estimated odds ratio and 95% confidence interval with that produced by mcc. We begin by reshaping the data:

```
. keep low smoke pairid
. reshape wide smoke, i(pairid) j(low 0 1)
Data                              long    ->    wide

Number of obs.                     112    ->      56
Number of variables                  3    ->       3
j variable (2 values)              low    ->    (dropped)
xij variables:
                                 smoke    ->    smoke0 smoke1
```

We now have the variables smoke0 (formed from smoke and low = 0), recording 1 if the control mother smoked and 0 otherwise; and smoke1 (formed from smoke and low = 1), recording 1 if the case mother smoked and 0 otherwise. We can now use mcc:

(Continued on next page)

```
. mcc smoke1 smoke0
```

| | Controls | | |
Cases	Exposed	Unexposed	Total
Exposed	8	22	30
Unexposed	8	18	26
Total	16	40	56

```
McNemar's chi2(1) =      6.53   Prob > chi2 = 0.0106
Exact McNemar significance probability      = 0.0161
```

Proportion with factor

Cases	.5357143
Controls	.2857143

		[95% Conf. Interval]		
difference	.25	.0519726	.4480274	
ratio	1.875	1.148685	3.060565	
rel. diff.	.35	.1336258	.5663742	
odds ratio	2.75	1.179154	7.143667	(exact)

Note that both methods estimated the same odds ratio and that the 95% confidence intervals are similar. clogit produced a confidence interval of $[1.22, 6.18]$, while mcc produced a confidence interval of $[1.18, 7.14]$.

❏

Use of weights

With clogit, weights apply to groups as a whole, not to individual observations. For example, if there is a group in your dataset with a frequency weight of 3, it means that there are a total of 3 groups in your sample with the same values of the dependent and independent variables as this one group. Weights must have the same value for all observations belonging to the same group; otherwise, an error message will be displayed.

▷ Example

We use the example from the above discussion of the mcc command. Here, we had a total of 56 matched case–control groups, each with one case matched to one control. We had 8 matched pairs in which both the case and the control are exposed, 22 pairs in which the case is exposed and the control is unexposed, 8 pairs in which the case is unexposed and the control is exposed, and 18 pairs in which they are both unexposed.

Using weights, it is easy to enter these data into Stata and run clogit.

```
. input id case exposed weight
           id      case    exposed     weight
1. 1 1 1 8
2. 1 0 1 8
3. 2 1 1 22
4. 2 0 0 22
5. 3 1 0 8
6. 3 0 1 8
7. 4 1 0 18
8. 4 0 0 18
9. end
```

```
. clogit case exposed [w=weight], strata(id) or
(frequency weights assumed)
Iteration 0:   log likelihood = -37.257978
Iteration 1:   log likelihood = -35.431994
Iteration 2:   log likelihood = -35.419285
Iteration 3:   log likelihood = -35.419282
Conditional (fixed-effects) logistic regression    Number of obs   =        112
                                                   LR chi2(1)      =       6.79
                                                   Prob > chi2     =     0.0091
Log likelihood = -35.419282                        Pseudo R2       =     0.0875
```

case	Odds Ratio	Std. Err.	z	P>|z|	[95% Conf. Interval]	
exposed	2.75	1.135369	2.45	0.014	1.224347	6.176763

◁

Fixed-effects logit

The fixed-effects logit model can be written as

$$\Pr(y_{it} = 1 \mid \mathbf{x}_{it}) = F(\alpha_i + \mathbf{x}_{it}\boldsymbol{\beta})$$

where F is the cumulative logistic distribution

$$F(z) = \frac{\exp(z)}{1 + \exp(z)}$$

$i = 1, 2, \ldots, n$ denotes the independent units (called "groups" by clogit), and $t = 1, 2, \ldots, T_i$ denotes the observations for the ith unit (group).

Fitting this model using a full maximum-likelihood approach leads to difficulties, however. When T_i is fixed, the maximum likelihood estimates for α_i and $\boldsymbol{\beta}$ are inconsistent (Andersen 1970 and Chamberlain 1980). This difficulty can be circumvented by looking at the probability of $\mathbf{y}_i = (y_{i1}, \ldots, y_{iT_i})$ conditional on $\sum_{t=1}^{T_i} y_{it}$. This conditional probability does not involve the α_i, so they are never estimated when the resulting conditional likelihood is used. See Hamerle and Ronning (1995) for a succinct and lucid development. See *Methods and Formulas* for the estimation equation.

To demonstrate fixed-effects logit, we use the same dataset that was used in [R] **probit** to illustrate probit, robust cluster() and in [XT] **xtprobit** to illustrate xtprobit.

▷ Example

We are studying unionization of women in the United States and are using the union dataset; see [XT] **xt**. We fit the fixed-effects logit model:

```
. use http://www.stata-press.com/data/r8/union
(NLS Women 14-24 in 1968)

. clogit union age grade not_smsa south black, group(idcode)
note: multiple positive outcomes within groups encountered.
note: 2744 groups (14165 obs) dropped due to all positive or
      all negative outcomes.
note: black omitted due to no within-group variance.
```

```
Iteration 0:   log likelihood = -4540.1394
Iteration 1:   log likelihood =   -4516.15
Iteration 2:   log likelihood = -4516.1385
```

Conditional (fixed-effects) logistic regression				Number of obs	=	12035
				LR chi2(4)	=	68.09
				Prob > chi2	=	0.0000
Log likelihood = -4516.1385				Pseudo R2	=	0.0075

union	Coef.	Std. Err.	z	P>|z|	[95% Conf. Interval]	
age	.0170301	.004146	4.11	0.000	.0089042	.0251561
grade	.0853572	.0418781	2.04	0.042	.0032777	.1674367
not_smsa	.0083678	.1127962	0.07	0.941	-.2127087	.2294444
south	-.748023	.1251749	-5.98	0.000	-.9933613	-.5026848

We received three messages at the top of the output. The first one, "multiple positive outcomes within groups encountered", we expected. Our data do indeed have multiple positive outcomes (union = 1) in many groups. (Here, of course, a group consists of all the observations for a particular individual.)

The second message tells us that 2744 groups were "dropped" by clogit. When either union = 0 or union = 1 for all observations for an individual, then this individual's contribution to the log-likelihood is zero. Although these are perfectly valid observations in every sense, they have no effect on the estimation, and so they are not included in the total "Number of obs". Hence, the reported "Number of obs" gives the effective sample size of the estimation. Here it is 12,035 observations—only 46% of the total 26,200.

It is easy to check that there are indeed 2,744 groups with union either all 0 or all 1. We will generate a variable that contains the fraction of observations for each individual that has union = 1.

```
. by idcode, sort: generate fraction = sum(union)/sum(union < .)

. by idcode: replace fraction = . if _n < _N
(21766 real changes made, 21766 to missing)

. tabulate fraction
```

fraction	Freq.	Percent	Cum.
0	2,481	55.95	55.95
.0833333	30	0.68	56.63
.0909091	33	0.74	57.37
.1	53	1.20	58.57
(output omitted)			
.9	10	0.23	93.59
.9090909	11	0.25	93.84
.9166667	10	0.23	94.07
1	263	5.93	100.00
Total	4,434	100.00	

Since $2481 + 263 = 2744$, we confirm what clogit did.

The third warning message from clogit said "black omitted due to no within-group variance". Obviously, race stays constant for an individual across time. Any such variables are collinear with the α_i (i.e., the fixed effects), and just as the α_i drop out of the conditional likelihood, so do all variables that are unchanging within groups. Thus, they cannot be estimated with the conditional fixed-effects model.

There are several alternative estimators implemented in Stata that you could conceivably use with these data:

```
cloglog ... ,  robust cluster(...)
logit ... ,  robust cluster(...)
probit ... ,  robust cluster(...)
scobit ... ,  robust cluster(...)
xtcloglog ... ,  i(...)
xtgee ... ,  i(...) family(binomial) link(logit) corr(exchangeable)
xtlogit ... ,  i(...)
xtprobit ... ,  i(...)
```

See [R] **cloglog**, [R] **logit**, [R] **probit**, [R] **scobit**, [XT] **xtcloglog**, [XT] **xtgee**, [XT] **xtlogit**, and [XT] **xtprobit** for details.

◁

McFadden's choice model

clogit can also be used to fit McFadden's choice model (McFadden 1974; for a brief introduction, see, for example, Greene 2003, Section 21.7).

For such models, we have a set of unordered choices, say, $1, 2, \ldots, T$. Let y_{it} be an indicator variable for the choice actually chosen by the ith individual. That is, $y_{it} = 1$ if individual i chose choice t, and $y_{it'} = 0$ for $t' \neq t$. We write the independent variables of the model as $\mathbf{z}_{it} = [\mathbf{x}_{it} \ \mathbf{w}_i]$, where $\mathbf{x}_{it}$ are attributes of the choices for the ith individual and $\mathbf{w}_i$ are attributes of the individual.

▷ Example

We have data on 295 consumers and their choice of automobile. We have a three-category choice car, which represents the nationality of the manufacturer of the consumer's car, whether American, Japanese, or European. We want to explore the relationship of the choice of car to dealer, the number of dealerships of each nationality in the consumer's city, and to the sex (variable sex) and income (variable income in 1000s of dollars) of the consumer. dealer is obviously an attribute of the choice ($\mathbf{x}_{it}$ in our previous notation), and sex and income attributes of the individual ($\mathbf{w}_i$). The consumer's choice of car is indicated by the variable choice (y_{it}).

Let's list some of the data.

```
. use http://www.stata-press.com/data/r8/choice
. list id car choice dealer sex income in 1/12
```

	id	car	choice	dealer	sex	income
1.	1	American	0	18	male	46.7
2.	1	Japan	0	8	male	46.7
3.	1	Europe	1	5	male	46.7
4.	2	American	1	17	male	26.1
5.	2	Japan	0	6	male	26.1
6.	2	Europe	0	2	male	26.1
7.	3	American	1	12	male	32.7
8.	3	Japan	0	6	male	32.7
9.	3	Europe	0	2	male	32.7
10.	4	American	0	18	female	49.2
11.	4	Japan	1	7	female	49.2
12.	4	Europe	0	4	female	49.2

Since we want to examine how the consumer's attributes apply to the choices, we must interact the attributes with dummy variables for the choices. Here's how we do it:

```
. gen japan  = (car==2)
. gen europe = (car==3)
. gen sexJap = sex*japan
. gen sexEur = sex*europe
. gen incJap = income*japan
. gen incEur = income*europe
```

We can now run our model.

```
. clogit choice japan europe sexJap sexEur incJap incEur dealer, group(id)
Iteration 0:  log likelihood = -284.51561
Iteration 1:  log likelihood = -251.47313
Iteration 2:  log likelihood = -250.78678
Iteration 3:  log likelihood =  -250.7794
Iteration 4:  log likelihood =  -250.7794
```

Conditional (fixed-effects) logistic regression

		Number of obs	=	885
		LR chi2(7)	=	146.62
		Prob > chi2	=	0.0000
Log likelihood = -250.7794		Pseudo R2	=	0.2262

choice	Coef.	Std. Err.	z	P>|z|	[95% Conf. Interval]	
japan	-1.352189	.6911829	-1.96	0.050	-2.706882	.0025049
europe	-2.355249	.8526681	-2.76	0.006	-4.026448	-.6840502
sexJap	-.5346039	.3141564	-1.70	0.089	-1.150339	.0811314
sexEur	.5704111	.4540247	1.26	0.209	-.319461	1.460283
incJap	.0325318	.012824	2.54	0.011	.0073973	.0576663
incEur	.032042	.0138676	2.31	0.021	.004862	.0592219
dealer	.0680938	.0344465	1.98	0.048	.00058	.1356076

Displaying the results as odds ratios makes them easier to interpret.

```
. clogit, or
```

Conditional (fixed-effects) logistic regression

		Number of obs	=	885
		LR chi2(7)	=	146.62
		Prob > chi2	=	0.0000
Log likelihood = -250.7794		Pseudo R2	=	0.2262

choice	Odds Ratio	Std. Err.	z	P>|z|	[95% Conf. Interval]	
japan	.2586735	.1787907	-1.96	0.050	.0667446	1.002508
europe	.0948699	.0808925	-2.76	0.006	.0178376	.5045692
sexJap	.5859013	.1840647	-1.70	0.089	.3165294	1.084513
sexEur	1.768994	.803167	1.26	0.209	.7265405	4.307179
incJap	1.033067	.013248	2.54	0.011	1.007425	1.059361
incEur	1.032561	.0143191	2.31	0.021	1.004874	1.061011
dealer	1.070466	.0368737	1.98	0.048	1.00058	1.145232

We see, for example, that in this sample men (sex = 1) are less likely to own Japanese cars than women (odds ratio 0.59), but that men are more likely to own European cars (odds ratio 1.77).

◁

❏ Technical Note

McFadden's choice model is closely related to multinomial logistic regression (mlogit). If all independent variables are attributes of the individual, then the model is exactly the same as multinomial logit. Let's try running the previous example with just the attributes of the individual, omitting dealer, the attribute of the choice.

```
. clogit choice sexJap incJap japan sexEur incEur europe, group(id)
Iteration 0:   log likelihood = -284.66485
Iteration 1:   log likelihood = -253.31044
Iteration 2:   log likelihood =  -252.7268
Iteration 3:   log likelihood = -252.72012
Iteration 4:   log likelihood = -252.72012
```

Conditional (fixed-effects) logistic regression

			Number of obs	=	885
			LR chi2(6)	=	142.74
			Prob > chi2	=	0.0000
Log likelihood = -252.72012			Pseudo R2	=	0.2202

choice	Coef.	Std. Err.	z	P>|z|	[95% Conf. Interval]
sexJap	-.4694799	.3114939	-1.51	0.132	-1.079997 .141037
incJap	.0276854	.0123666	2.24	0.025	.0034472 .0519236
japan	-1.962652	.6216804	-3.16	0.002	-3.181123 -.7441806
sexEur	.5388442	.4525278	1.19	0.234	-.348094 1.425782
incEur	.0273669	.013787	1.98	0.047	.000345 .0543889
europe	-3.180029	.7546837	-4.21	0.000	-4.659182 -1.700876

To run mlogit, we must rearrange the dataset. mlogit requires a dependent variable that indicates the choice—1, 2, or 3—for each individual. This is just our variable car for those observations that represent the choice actually chosen.

```
. keep if choice == 1
(590 observations deleted)

. mlogit car sex income
Iteration 0:   log likelihood =  -259.1712
Iteration 1:   log likelihood = -252.81165
Iteration 2:   log likelihood = -252.72014
Iteration 3:   log likelihood = -252.72012
```

Multinomial logistic regression

			Number of obs	=	295
			LR chi2(4)	=	12.90
			Prob > chi2	=	0.0118
Log likelihood = -252.72012			Pseudo R2	=	0.0249

car	Coef.	Std. Err.	z	P>|z|	[95% Conf. Interval]
Japan					
sex	-.4694799	.3114939	-1.51	0.132	-1.079997 .141037
income	.0276854	.0123666	2.24	0.025	.0034472 .0519236
_cons	-1.962652	.6216803	-3.16	0.002	-3.181123 -.7441807
Europe					
sex	.5388442	.4525278	1.19	0.234	-.3480941 1.425783
income	.0273669	.013787	1.98	0.047	.000345 .0543889
_cons	-3.180029	.7546837	-4.21	0.000	-4.659182 -1.700876

(Outcome car==American is the comparison group)

The results are exactly the same.

❏

Predictions

predict may be used after clogit to obtain predicted values of the index $\mathbf{x}_{it}\beta$. Predicted probabilities for conditional logistic regression must be interpreted carefully. Probabilities are estimated for each group as a whole, not for individual observations. Furthermore, the probabilities are conditional on the number of positive outcomes in the group (i.e., the number of cases and the number of controls), or it is assumed that the fixed effect is zero.

predict produces probabilities of a positive outcome within group conditional on there being one positive outcome,

$$\Pr(y_{it} = 1) = \frac{\exp(\mathbf{x}_{it}\beta)}{\sum_{t=1}^{T_i} \exp(\mathbf{x}_{it}\beta)}$$

or predict calculates pu0,

$$\Pr(y_{it} = 1) = \frac{\exp(\mathbf{x}_{it}\beta)}{1 + \exp(\mathbf{x}_{it}\beta)}$$

predict may be used for both within-sample and out-of-sample predictions.

▷ Example

Suppose that you have $1 : k_{2i}$ matched data and that you have previously fitted the following model:

```
. clogit y x1 x2 x3, group(id)
```

To obtain the predicted values of the index, you could type predict idx, xb to create a new variable called idx. From idx, you could then calculate the predicted probabilities. Easier, however, would be to type

```
. predict phat
(option pc1 assumed; conditional probability for single outcome within group)
```

phat would then contain the predicted probabilities.

It is important to say again that the predicted probabilities are really predicted probabilities for the group as a whole (i.e., they are the predicted probability of observing $y_{it} = 1$ *and* $y_{it'} = 0$ for all $t' \neq t$). Thus, if you want to obtain the predicted probabilities for the estimation sample, it is important that when you make the calculation, predictions be restricted to the same sample on which you estimated the data. You cannot predict the probabilities and then just keep the relevant ones, because the entire sample determines each probability. Thus, assuming that you are not attempting to make out-of-sample predictions, you type

```
. predict phat if e(sample)
(option pc1 assumed; conditional probability for single outcome within group)
```

◁

(*Continued on next page*)

Saved Results

clogit saves in e():

Scalars

e(N)	number of observations	e(ll)	log likelihood
e(df_m)	model degrees of freedom	e(ll_0)	log likelihood, constant-only model
e(r2_p)	pseudo R-squared	e(chi2)	χ^2

Macros

e(cmd)	clogit	e(chi2type)	LR; type of model χ^2 test
e(depvar)	name of dependent variable	e(offset)	offset
e(group)	name of group() variable	e(crittype)	optimization criterion
e(wtype)	weight type	e(predict)	program used to implement predict
e(wexp)	weight expression		

Matrices

e(b)	coefficient vector	e(V)	variance–covariance matrix of the estimators

Functions

e(sample)	marks estimation sample

Methods and Formulas

Breslow and Day (1980, 247–279), Collett (1991, 262–276), and Hosmer and Lemeshow (2000, 223–259) provide a biostatistical point of view on conditional logistic regression. Hamerle and Ronning (1995) give a succinct and lucid review of fixed-effects logit; Chamberlain (1980) is a standard reference for this model. Greene (2003, chapter 21) provides a straightforward textbook description of conditional logistic regression from an economist's point of view, as well as a brief description of choice models.

Let $i = 1, 2, \ldots, n$ denote the groups and let $t = 1, 2, \ldots, T_i$ denote the observations for the ith group. Let y_{it} be the dependent variable taking on values 0 or 1. Let $\mathbf{y}_i = (y_{i1}, \ldots, y_{iT_i})$ be the outcomes for the ith group as a whole. Let $\mathbf{x}_{it}$ be a row vector of covariates. Let

$$k_{1i} = \sum_{t=1}^{T_i} y_{it}$$

be the observed number of ones for the dependent variable in the ith group. Biostatisticians would say that there are k_{1i} cases matched to $k_{2i} = T_i - k_{1i}$ controls in the ith group.

We consider the probability of a possible value of $\mathbf{y}_i$ conditional on $\sum_{t=1}^{T_i} y_{it} = k_{1i}$ (Hamerle and Ronning 1995, equation 8.33; Hosmer and Lemeshow 2000, equation 7.4),

$$\Pr\left(\mathbf{y}_i \mid \sum_{t=1}^{T_i} y_{it} = k_{1i}\right) = \frac{\exp\left(\sum_{t=1}^{T_i} y_{it}\mathbf{x}_{it}\boldsymbol{\beta}\right)}{\sum_{\mathbf{d}_i \in S_i} \exp\left(\sum_{t=1}^{T_i} d_{it}\mathbf{x}_{it}\boldsymbol{\beta}\right)}$$

where d_{it} is equal to 0 or 1 with $\sum_{t=1}^{T_i} d_{it} = k_{1i}$, and S_i is the set of all possible combinations of k_{1i} ones and k_{2i} zeros. Clearly, there are $\binom{T_i}{k_{1i}}$ such combinations, but one does not have to enumerate all these combinations to compute the denominator of the above equation. It can be computed recursively.

Denote the denominator by

$$f_i(T_i, k_{1i}) = \sum_{\mathbf{d}_i \in S_i} \exp\left(\sum_{t=1}^{T_i} d_{it}\mathbf{x}_{it}\boldsymbol{\beta}\right)$$

Consider, computationally, how f_i changes as we go from a total of one observation in the group to two observations to three, etc. Doing this, we derive the recursive formula

$$f_i(T, k) = f_i(T-1, k) + f_i(T-1, k-1)\,\exp(\mathbf{x}_{iT}\boldsymbol{\beta})$$

where we define $f_i(T, k) = 0$ if $T < k$ and $f_i(T, 0) = 1$.

The conditional log-likelihood is

$$L = \sum_{i=1}^{n}\left\{\sum_{t=1}^{T_i} y_{it}\mathbf{x}_{it}\boldsymbol{\beta} - \log f_i(T_i, k_{1i})\right\}$$

The derivatives of the conditional log-likelihood can also be computed recursively by taking derivatives of the recursive formula for f_i.

Computation time is roughly proportional to

$$p^2 \sum_{i=1}^{n} T_i \, \min(k_{1i}, k_{2i})$$

where p is the number of independent variables in the model. If $\min(k_{1i}, k_{2i})$ is small, computation time is not an issue. But if it is large, say, 100 or more, patience may be required.

Note that if T_i is large for all groups, the bias of the unconditional fixed-effects estimator is not a concern, and one can confidently use logit with an indicator variable for each group (provided, of course, that the number of groups does not exceed matsize; see [R] **matsize**).

References

Andersen, E. B. 1970. Asymptotic properties of conditional maximum likelihood estimators. *Journal of the Royal Statistical Society* B 32: 283–301.

Breslow, N. E. and N. E. Day. 1980. *Statistical Methods in Cancer Research*, vol. 1. Lyon: International Agency for Research on Cancer.

Chamberlain, G. 1980. Analysis of covariance with qualitative data. *Review of Economic Studies* 47: 225–238.

Collett, D. 1991. *Modelling Binary Data*. London: Chapman & Hall.

Greene, W. H. 2003. *Econometric Analysis*. 5th ed. Upper Saddle River, NJ: Prentice–Hall.

Hamerle, A. and G. Ronning. 1995. Panel analysis for qualitative variables. In *Handbook of Statistical Modeling for the Social and Behavioral Sciences*, ed. G. Arminger, C. C. Clogg, and M. E. Sobel, 401–451. New York: Plenum Press.

Hosmer, D. W., Jr., and S. Lemeshow. 2000. *Applied Logistic Regression*. 2d ed. New York: John Wiley & Sons.

Kleinbaum, D. G. and M. Klein. 2002. *Logistic Regression: A Self-Learning Text*. 2d ed. New York: Springer.

Long, J. S. and J. Freese. 2001. *Regression Models for Categorical Dependent Variables using Stata*. College Station, TX: Stata Press.

McFadden, D. 1974. Conditional logit analysis of qualitative choice behavior. In *Frontiers in Econometrics*, ed. P. Zarembka, 105–142. New York: Academic Press.

Also See

Complementary:	[R] **lincom**, [R] **linktest**, [R] **lrtest**, [R] **nlcom**, [R] **predict**, [R] **predictnl**, [R] **suest**, [R] **sw**, [R] **test**, [R] **testnl**, [R] **vce**, [R] **xi**
Related:	[R] **cloglog**, [R] **logistic**, [R] **logit**, [R] **mlogit**, [R] **nlogit**, [R] **ologit**, [R] **oprobit**, [R] **probit**, [R] **scobit**, [XT] **xtcloglog**, [XT] **xtlogit**, [XT] **xtgee**, [XT] **xtprobit**
Background:	[U] **16.5 Accessing coefficients and standard errors**, [U] **23 Estimation and post-estimation commands**, [R] **maximize**

Title

> **cloglog** — Maximum-likelihood complementary log-log estimation

Syntax

> cloglog *depvar* [*indepvars*] [*weight*] [if *exp*] [in *range*] [, level(*#*)
>
> noconstant robust cluster(*varname*) score(*newvar*) offset(*varname*)
>
> constraints(*numlist*) asis nolog *maximize_options*]

by ... : may be used with cloglog; see [R] **by**.

fweights, iweights, and pweights are allowed; see [U] **14.1.6 weight**.

This command shares the features of all estimation commands; see [U] **23 Estimation and post-estimation commands**.

cloglog may be used with sw to perform stepwise estimation; see [R] **sw**.

Syntax for predict

> predict [*type*] *newvarname* [if *exp*] [in *range*] [, [p | xb | stdp] nooffset]

These statistics are available both in and out of sample; type predict ... if e(sample) ... if wanted only for the estimation sample.

Description

cloglog fits maximum-likelihood complementary log-log models.

See [R] **logistic** for a list of related estimation commands.

Options

level(*#*) specifies the confidence level, in percent, for confidence intervals. The default is level(95) or as set by set level; see [U] **23.6 Specifying the width of confidence intervals**.

noconstant suppresses the constant term (intercept) in the model.

robust specifies that the Huber/White/sandwich estimator of variance is to be used in place of the traditional calculation; see [U] **23.14 Obtaining robust variance estimates**. robust combined with cluster() allows observations that are not independent within cluster (although they must be independent between clusters).

If you specify pweights, robust is implied; see [U] **23.16 Weighted estimation**.

cluster(*varname*) specifies that the observations are independent across groups (clusters) but not necessarily within groups. *varname* specifies to which group each observation belongs; e.g., cluster(personid) in data with repeated observations on individuals. cluster() affects the estimated standard errors and variance–covariance matrix of the estimators (VCE), but not the estimated coefficients; see [U] **23.14 Obtaining robust variance estimates**. cluster() can be used with pweights to produce estimates for unstratified cluster-sampled data.

cluster() implies robust; specifying robust cluster() is equivalent to typing cluster() by itself.

score(*newvar*) creates a new variable for the scores from the equation in the model. The new variable contains each observation's contribution to the score; see [U] **23.15 Obtaining scores**.

The new variable will contain $u_j = \partial \ln L_j / \partial(\mathbf{x}_j \mathbf{b})$ for each observation j in the sample. The score vector is $\sum \partial \ln L_j / \partial \mathbf{b} = \sum u_j \mathbf{x}_j$; i.e., the product of *newvar* with each covariate summed over observations.

offset(*varname*) specifies that *varname* is to be included in the model with coefficient constrained to be 1.

constraints(*numlist*) specifies by number the linear constraints to be applied during estimation. The default is to perform unconstrained estimation. Constraints are specified using the constraint command; see [R] **constraint**.

asis forces retention of perfect predictor variables and their associated perfectly predicted observations, and may produce instabilities in maximization; see [R] **probit**.

nolog suppresses the iteration log.

maximize_options control the maximization process; see [R] **maximize**. You should never have to specify them.

Options for predict

p, the default, calculates the probability of a positive outcome.

xb calculates the linear prediction.

stdp calculates the standard error of the linear prediction.

nooffset is relevant only if you specified offset(*varname*) for cloglog. It modifies the calculations made by predict so that they ignore the offset variable; the linear prediction is treated as $\mathbf{x}_j \mathbf{b}$ rather than as $\mathbf{x}_j \mathbf{b} + \text{offset}_j$.

Remarks

cloglog fits maximum likelihood models with dichotomous dependent variables coded as 0/1 (or, more precisely, coded as 0 and not 0).

▷ Example

You have data on the make, weight, and mileage rating of 22 foreign and 52 domestic automobiles. You wish to fit a model explaining whether a car is foreign based on its weight and mileage. Here is an overview of your data:

```
. use http://www.stata-press.com/data/r8/auto
(1978 Automobile Data)

. keep make mpg weight foreign

. describe

Contains data from http://www.stata-press.com/data/r8/auto.dta
  obs:            74                          1978 Automobile Data
 vars:             4                          14 Oct 2002 09:02
 size:         1,998 (99.7% of memory free)   (_dta has notes)
```

variable name	storage type	display format	value label	variable label
make	str18	%-18s		Make and Model
mpg	int	%8.0g		Mileage (mpg)
weight	int	%8.0gc		Weight (lbs.)
foreign	byte	%8.0g	origin	Car type

```
Sorted by:  foreign
     Note:  dataset has changed since last saved

. inspect foreign
foreign:  Car type                              Number of Observations
```

<pre>
                                                          Non-
                                        Total   Integers Integers
     | #   Negative   -   -   -
     | #   Zero   52   52   -
     | #   Positive   22   22   -
     | #
     | #   #   Total   74   74   -
     | #   #   Missing   -
     +----------------------
     0   1   74
         (2 unique values)
</pre>

```
             foreign is labeled and all values are documented in the label.
```

The variable foreign takes on two unique values, 0 and 1. The value 0 denotes a domestic car and 1 denotes a foreign car.

The model that you wish to fit is

$$\Pr(\texttt{foreign} = 1) = F(\beta_0 + \beta_1 \texttt{weight} + \beta_2 \texttt{mpg})$$

where $F(z) = 1 - \exp\left\{-\exp(z)\right\}$.

To fit this model, you type

(Continued on next page)

```
. cloglog foreign weight mpg
Iteration 0:   log likelihood = -33.526894
Iteration 1:   log likelihood = -27.868343
Iteration 2:   log likelihood =  -27.74293
Iteration 3:   log likelihood = -27.742769
Iteration 4:   log likelihood = -27.742769
```

```
Complementary log-log regression              Number of obs   =         74
                                              Zero outcomes   =         52
                                              Nonzero outcomes =        22

                                              LR chi2(2)      =      34.58
Log likelihood = -27.742769                   Prob > chi2     =     0.0000
```

foreign	Coef.	Std. Err.	z	P>|z|	[95% Conf. Interval]
weight	-.0029153	.0006974	-4.18	0.000	-.0042823	-.0015483
mpg	-.1422911	.076387	-1.86	0.062	-.2920069	.0074247
_cons	10.09694	3.351841	3.01	0.003	3.527448	16.66642

You find that heavier cars are less likely to be foreign and that cars yielding better gas mileage are also less likely to be foreign, at least when holding the weight of the car constant.

See [R] **maximize** for an explanation of the output.

◁

❏ Technical Note

Stata interprets a value of 0 as a negative outcome (failure) and treats all other values (except missing) as positive outcomes (successes). Thus, if your dependent variable takes on the values 0 and 1, 0 is interpreted as failure and 1 as success. If your dependent variable takes on the values 0, 1, and 2, 0 is still interpreted as failure, but both 1 and 2 are treated as successes.

If you prefer a more formal mathematical statement, when you type cloglog y x, Stata fits the model

$$\Pr(y_j \neq 0 \mid \mathbf{x}_j) = 1 - \exp\left\{-\exp(\mathbf{x}_j\boldsymbol{\beta})\right\}$$

❏

Robust standard errors

If you specify the robust option, cloglog reports robust standard errors as described in [U] **23.14 Obtaining robust variance estimates**. In the case of the model of foreign on weight and mpg, the robust calculation increases the standard error of the coefficient on mpg by 44 percent:

(Continued on next page)

```
. cloglog foreign weight mpg, robust
Iteration 0:    log pseudo-likelihood = -33.526894
Iteration 1:    log pseudo-likelihood = -27.868343
Iteration 2:    log pseudo-likelihood =  -27.74293
Iteration 3:    log pseudo-likelihood = -27.742769
Iteration 4:    log pseudo-likelihood = -27.742769
```

Complementary log-log regression   Number of obs   =   74
                                                  Zero outcomes   =   52
                                                  Nonzero outcomes =   22

                                                  Wald chi2(2)   =   29.74
Log pseudo-likelihood = -27.742769   Prob > chi2   = 0.0000

foreign	Coef.	Robust Std. Err.	z	P>|z|	[95% Conf. Interval]	
weight	-.0029153	.0007484	-3.90	0.000	-.0043822	-.0014484
mpg	-.1422911	.1102466	-1.29	0.197	-.3583704	.0737882
_cons	10.09694	4.317305	2.34	0.019	1.635174	18.5587

Without `robust`, the standard error for the coefficient on `mpg` was reported to be .076, with a resulting confidence interval of $[-.29, .01]$.

`robust` with the `cluster()` option has the ability to relax the independence assumption required by the complementary log-log estimator to being just independence between clusters. To demonstrate this, we will switch to a different dataset.

You are studying unionization of women in the United States and are using the `union` dataset; see [XT] **xt**. You fit the following model ignoring that women are observed an average of 5.9 times each in this dataset:

```
. use http://www.stata-press.com/data/r8/union
(NLS Women 14-24 in 1968)

. cloglog union age grade not_smsa south southXt
Iteration 0:    log likelihood = -13609.987
Iteration 1:    log likelihood = -13544.321
Iteration 2:    log likelihood = -13544.202
Iteration 3:    log likelihood = -13544.202
```

Complementary log-log regression   Number of obs   =   26200
                                                  Zero outcomes   =   20389
                                                  Nonzero outcomes =   5811

                                                  LR chi2(5)   = 640.06
Log likelihood = -13544.202   Prob > chi2   = 0.0000

union	Coef.	Std. Err.	z	P>|z|	[95% Conf. Interval]	
age	.0085897	.0023034	3.73	0.000	.0040752	.0131043
grade	.0447187	.0057069	7.84	0.000	.0335334	.0559039
not_smsa	-.1906552	.0317663	-6.00	0.000	-.252916	-.1283943
south	-.6446647	.0557644	-11.56	0.000	-.7539609	-.5353684
southXt	.0068271	.0047297	1.44	0.149	-.0024428	.0160971
_cons	-1.966755	.0991779	-19.83	0.000	-2.16114	-1.77237

The reported standard errors in this model are probably meaningless. Women are observed repeatedly, and so the observations are not independent. Looking at the coefficients, you find a large southern effect against unionization and little time trend. The `robust` and `cluster()` options provide a way to fit this model and obtain correct standard errors:

```
. cloglog union age grade not_smsa south southXt, robust cluster(id) nolog
```

Complementary log-log regression

Number of obs	=	26200
Zero outcomes	=	20389
Nonzero outcomes	=	5811

Log pseudo-likelihood = -13544.202

Wald chi2(5)	=	160.78
Prob > chi2	=	0.0000

(standard errors adjusted for clustering on idcode)

union	Coef.	Robust Std. Err.	z	P>|z|	[95% Conf. Interval]	
age	.0085897	.0033831	2.54	0.011	.0019591	.0152204
grade	.0447187	.0125927	3.55	0.000	.0200375	.0693999
not_smsa	-.1906552	.064189	-2.97	0.003	-.3164632	-.0648471
south	-.6446647	.0833807	-7.73	0.000	-.8080878	-.4812415
southXt	.0068271	.0063038	1.08	0.279	-.0055282	.0191824
_cons	-1.966755	.186019	-10.57	0.000	-2.331346	-1.602165

These standard errors are roughly 50% larger than those reported by the inappropriate conventional calculation. By comparison, another way we could fit this model is with an equal-correlation population-averaged complementary log-log model:

```
. xtcloglog union age grade not_smsa south southXt, i(id) pa nolog
```

GEE population-averaged model			Number of obs	=	26200
Group variable:		idcode	Number of groups	=	4434
Link:		cloglog	Obs per group: min =	1
Family:		binomial	avg =	5.9
Correlation:		exchangeable	max =	12
			Wald chi2(5)	=	232.44
Scale parameter:		1	Prob > chi2	=	0.0000

union	Coef.	Std. Err.	z	P>|z|	[95% Conf. Interval]	
age	.0045777	.0021754	2.10	0.035	.0003139	.0088415
grade	.0544267	.0095097	5.72	0.000	.035788	.0730654
not_smsa	-.1051731	.0430512	-2.44	0.015	-.189552	-.0207943
south	-.6578891	.061857	-10.64	0.000	-.7791266	-.5366515
southXt	.0142329	.004133	3.44	0.001	.0061325	.0223334
_cons	-2.074687	.1358008	-15.28	0.000	-2.340851	-1.808522

The coefficient estimates are similar, but these standard errors are smaller than those produced by cloglog, robust cluster(). This is as we would expect. If the within-panel correlation assumptions are valid, the population-averaged estimator should be more efficient.

In addition to this estimator, we may use the xtgee command to fit a panel estimator (with complementary log-log link) and any number of assumptions on the within-idcode correlation.

What is important to understand is that cloglog, robust cluster() is robust to assumptions about within-cluster correlation. That is, it inefficiently sums within cluster for the standard error calculation rather than attempting to exploit what might be assumed about the within-cluster correlation (as do the xtgee population-averaged models).

Obtaining predicted values

Once you have fitted a model, you can obtain the predicted probabilities using the `predict` command for both the estimation sample and other samples; see [U] **23 Estimation and post-estimation commands** and [R] **predict**. Here, we will make only a few additional comments.

`predict` without arguments calculates the predicted probability of a positive outcome. With the `xb` option, it calculates the linear combination $x_j b$, where x_j are the independent variables in the jth observation and b is the estimated parameter vector.

With the `stdp` option, `predict` calculates the standard error of the prediction, which is *not* adjusted for replicated covariate patterns in the data.

▷ Example

In the first example, we fitted the complementary log-log model `cloglog foreign weight mpg`. To obtain predicted probabilities,

```
. use http://www.stata-press.com/data/r8/auto
(1978 Automobile Data)
. cloglog foreign weight mpg
  (output omitted)
. predict p
(option p assumed; Pr(foreign))
. summarize foreign p
```

Variable	Obs	Mean	Std. Dev.	Min	Max
foreign	74	.2972973	.4601885	0	1
p	74	.2928348	.29732	.0032726	.9446067

◁

(Continued on next page)

Saved Results

cloglog saves in e():

Scalars

e(N)	number of observations	e(ll_0)	log likelihood, constant-only model
e(k)	number of variables	e(N_clust)	number of clusters
e(k_eq)	number of equations	e(rc)	return code
e(k_dv)	number of dependent variables	e(chi2)	χ^2
e(N_f)	number of zero outcomes	e(p)	significance
e(N_s)	number of nonzero outcomes	e(ic)	number of iterations
e(df_m)	model degrees of freedom	e(rank)	rank of e(V)
e(ll)	log likelihood		

Macros

e(cmd)	cloglog	e(user)	name of likelihood-evaluator program
e(depvar)	name of dependent variable	e(opt)	type of optimization
e(title)	title in estimation output	e(chi2type)	Wald or LR; type of model χ^2 test
e(wtype)	weight type	e(offset)	offset
e(wexp)	weight expression	e(vcetype)	covariance estimation method
e(clustvar)	name of cluster variable	e(crittype)	optimization criterion
e(scorevars)	variable containing score	e(predict)	program used to implement predict

Matrices

e(b)	coefficient vector	e(V)	variance–covariance matrix of
e(ilog)	iteration log (up to 20 iterations)		the estimators

Functions

e(sample)	marks estimation sample

Methods and Formulas

Complementary log-log analysis (related to the gompit model, so-named due to its relationship to the Gompertz distribution) is an alternative to logit and probit analysis, but it is unlike these other estimators in that the transformation is not symmetric. Typically this model is used when the positive (or negative) outcome is rare.

The log-likelihood function for complementary log-log is

$$\ln L = \sum_{j \in S} w_j \ln F(\mathbf{x}_j \mathbf{b}) + \sum_{j \notin S} w_j \ln \left\{ 1 - F(\mathbf{x}_j \mathbf{b}) \right\}$$

where S is the set of all observations j such that $y_j \neq 0$, $F(z) = 1 - \exp\left\{ -\exp(z) \right\}$, and w_j denotes the optional weights. $\ln L$ is maximized as described in [R] **maximize**.

One can fit a gompit model by reversing the success–failure sense of the dependent variable and using cloglog.

If robust standard errors are requested, the calculation described in *Methods and Formulas* of [R] **regress** is carried forward with $\mathbf{u}_j = [\exp(\mathbf{x}_j \mathbf{b}) \exp\left\{ -\exp(\mathbf{x}_j \mathbf{b}) \right\} / F(\mathbf{x}_j \mathbf{b})]\mathbf{x}_j$ for the positive outcomes and $\{-\exp(\mathbf{x}_j \mathbf{b})\}\mathbf{x}_j$ for the negative outcomes.

Acknowledgment

We would like to thank Joseph Hilbe of Arizona State University for providing the inspiration for the `cloglog` command (Hilbe 1996, 1998).

References

Clayton, D. and M. Hills. 1993. *Statistical Models in Epidemiology*. Oxford: Oxford University Press.

Hilbe, J. 1996. sg53: Maximum-likelihood complementary log-log regression. *Stata Technical Bulletin* 32: 19–20. Reprinted in *Stata Technical Bulletin Reprints*, vol. 6, pp. 129–131.

——. 1998. sg53.2: Stata-like commands for complementary log-log regression. *Stata Technical Bulletin* 41: 23. Reprinted in *Stata Technical Bulletin Reprints*, vol. 7, pp. 166–167.

Long, J. S. 1997. *Regression Models for Categorical and Limited Dependent Variables*. Thousand Oaks, CA: Sage Publications.

Long, J. S. and J. Freese. 2001. *Regression Models for Categorical Dependent Variables using Stata*. College Station, TX: Stata Press.

Also See

Complementary:	[R] **adjust**, [R] **constraint**, [R] **lincom**, [R] **linktest**, [R] **lrtest**, [R] **mfx**, [R] **nlcom**, [R] **predict**, [R] **predictnl**, [R] **suest**, [R] **sw**, [R] **test**, [R] **testnl**, [R] **vce**, [R] **xi**
Related:	[R] **biprobit**, [R] **clogit**, [R] **cusum**, [R] **glm**, [R] **glogit**, [R] **hetprob**, [R] **logistic**, [R] **logit**, [R] **mlogit**, [R] **ologit**, [R] **probit**, [R] **scobit**, [XT] **xtcloglog**, [XT] **xtprobit**
Background:	[U] **16.5 Accessing coefficients and standard errors**, [U] **23 Estimation and post-estimation commands**, [U] **23.14 Obtaining robust variance estimates**, [U] **23.15 Obtaining scores**, [R] **maximize**

Title

> **cnsreg** — Constrained linear regression

Syntax

> cnsreg *depvar indepvars* [*weight*] [if *exp*] [in *range*] , <u>c</u>onstraints(*numlist* | *matname*)
>
> [<u>noconst</u>ant <u>level</u>(#)]

by ... : may be used with cnsreg; see [R] **by**.

aweights and fweights are allowed; see [U] **14.1.6 weight**.

cnsreg shares the features of all estimation commands; see [U] **23 Estimation and post-estimation commands**.

Syntax for predict

> predict [*type*] *newvarname* [if *exp*] [in *range*] [, *statistic*]

where *statistic* is

xb	$\mathbf{x}_j \mathbf{b}$, fitted values (the default)
<u>r</u>esiduals	residuals
<u>p</u>r(*a*,*b*)	$\Pr(a < y_j < b)$
e(*a*,*b*)	$E(y_j \mid a < y_j < b)$
<u>ystar</u>(*a*,*b*)	$E(y_j^*)$, $y_j^* = \max(a, \min(y_j, b))$
stdp	standard error of the prediction
stdf	standard error of the forecast

where *a* and *b* may be numbers or variables; *a* missing ($a \geq .$) means $-\infty$, and *b* missing ($b \geq .$) means $+\infty$; see [U] **15.2.1 Missing values**.

These statistics are available both in and out of sample; type predict ... if e(sample) ... if wanted only for the estimation sample.

Description

cnsreg fits constrained linear regression models. cnsreg typed without arguments redisplays the previous cnsreg results.

Options

constraints(*numlist* | *matname*) specifies the constraints to be applied and is not optional. constraints(*numlist*) specifies the constraints by number. constraints(*matname*) specifies a matrix that contains the constraints.

noconstant suppresses the constant term (intercept) in the model.

level(#) specifies the confidence level, in percent, for confidence intervals. The default is level(95) or as set by set level; see [U] **23.6 Specifying the width of confidence intervals**.

Options for predict

xb, the default, calculates the linear prediction.

residuals calculates the residuals; that is, $y_j - \mathbf{x}_j\mathbf{b}$.

pr(a,b) calculates $\Pr(a < \mathbf{x}_j\mathbf{b} + u_j < b)$, the probability that $y_j|\mathbf{x}_j$ would be observed in the interval (a,b).

a and b may be specified as numbers or variable names; lb and ub are variable names;
pr(20,30) calculates $\Pr(20 < \mathbf{x}_j\mathbf{b} + u_j < 30)$;
pr(lb,ub) calculates $\Pr(lb < \mathbf{x}_j\mathbf{b} + u_j < ub)$; and
pr(20,ub) calculates $\Pr(20 < \mathbf{x}_j\mathbf{b} + u_j < ub)$.

a missing ($a \geq .$) means $-\infty$; pr(.,30) calculates $\Pr(-\infty < \mathbf{x}_j\mathbf{b} + u_j < 30)$;
pr(lb,30) calculates $\Pr(-\infty < \mathbf{x}_j\mathbf{b} + u_j < 30)$ in observations for which $lb \geq .$
(and calculates $\Pr(lb < \mathbf{x}_j\mathbf{b} + u_j < 30)$ elsewhere).

b missing ($b \geq .$) means $+\infty$; pr(20,.) calculates $\Pr(+\infty > \mathbf{x}_j\mathbf{b} + u_j > 20)$;
pr(20,ub) calculates $\Pr(+\infty > \mathbf{x}_j\mathbf{b} + u_j > 20)$ in observations for which $ub \geq .$
(and calculates $\Pr(20 < \mathbf{x}_j\mathbf{b} + u_j < ub)$ elsewhere).

e(a,b) calculates $E(\mathbf{x}_j\mathbf{b} + u_j \,|\, a < \mathbf{x}_j\mathbf{b} + u_j < b)$, the expected value of $y_j|\mathbf{x}_j$ conditional on $y_j|\mathbf{x}_j$ being in the interval (a,b), which is to say, $y_j|\mathbf{x}_j$ is censored.
a and b are specified as they are for pr().

ystar(a,b) calculates $E(y_j^*)$, where $y_j^* = a$ if $\mathbf{x}_j\mathbf{b} + u_j \leq a$, $y_j^* = b$ if $\mathbf{x}_j\mathbf{b} + u_j \geq b$, and $y_j^* = \mathbf{x}_j\mathbf{b} + u_j$ otherwise, which is to say, y_j^* is truncated. a and b are specified as they are for pr().

stdp calculates the standard error of the prediction. It can be thought of as the standard error of the predicted expected value or mean for the observation's covariate pattern. This is also referred to as the standard error of the fitted value.

stdf calculates the standard error of the forecast. This is the standard error of the point prediction for a single observation. It is commonly referred to as the standard error of the future or forecast value. By construction, the standard errors produced by stdf are always larger than those by stdp; see [R] **regress** Methods and Formulas.

Remarks

▷ Example

In principle, constrained linear regression estimates can be obtained by modifying the list of independent variables. For instance, if you wanted to fit the model

$$\mathtt{mpg} = \beta_0 + \beta_1\,\mathtt{price} + \beta_2\,\mathtt{weight} + u$$

and constrain $\beta_1 = \beta_2$, you could write

$$\mathtt{mpg} = \beta_0 + \beta_1(\mathtt{price} + \mathtt{weight}) + u$$

and run a regression of mpg on price + weight. The estimated coefficient on the sum would be the constrained estimate of β_1 and β_2. Using cnsreg, however, is easier:

```
. use http://www.stata-press.com/data/r8/auto
(1978 Automobile Data)
. constraint define 1 price = weight
. cnsreg mpg price weight, constraint(1)
Constrained linear regression                          Number of obs =       74
                                                       F(  1,     72) =    37.59
                                                       Prob > F       =   0.0000
                                                       Root MSE       =    4.722

 ( 1)   price - weight = 0
```

mpg	Coef.	Std. Err.	t	P>|t|	[95% Conf. Interval]	
price	-.0009875	.0001611	-6.13	0.000	-.0013086	-.0006664
weight	-.0009875	.0001611	-6.13	0.000	-.0013086	-.0006664
_cons	30.36718	1.577958	19.24	0.000	27.22158	33.51278

You define constraints using the `constraint` command; see [R] **constraint**. You fit the model using `cnsreg` and specify the constraint number or numbers in the `constraints()` option.

Just to show that the results above are correct, here is the result of applying the constraint by hand:

```
. generate x = price + weight
. regress mpg x
```

Source	SS	df	MS		Number of obs = 74
Model	838.065767	1	838.065767		F(1, 72) = 37.59
Residual	1605.39369	72	22.2971346		Prob > F = 0.0000
					R-squared = 0.3430
					Adj R-squared = 0.3339
Total	2443.45946	73	33.4720474		Root MSE = 4.722

mpg	Coef.	Std. Err.	t	P>|t|	[95% Conf. Interval]	
x	-.0009875	.0001611	-6.13	0.000	-.0013086	-.0006664
_cons	30.36718	1.577958	19.24	0.000	27.22158	33.51278

◁

▷ Example

Models can be fitted subject to multiple simultaneous constraints. You simply define the constraints and then include the constraint numbers in the `constraints()` option. For instance, assume you wish to fit the model

$$\text{mpg} = \beta_0 + \beta_1 \text{price} + \beta_2 \text{weight} + \beta_3 \text{displ} + \beta_4 \text{gear\_ratio} + \beta_5 \text{foreign} +$$
$$\beta_6 \text{length} + u$$

subject to the constraints

$$\beta_1 = \beta_2 = \beta_3 = \beta_6$$
$$\beta_4 = -\beta_5 = \beta_0/20$$

(This model, like the one in the previous example, is admittedly senseless.) You fit the model by typing

```
. constraint def 1 price=weight
. constraint def 2 displ=weight
```

```
. constraint def 3 length=weight
. constraint def 5 gear_ratio = -foreign
. constraint def 6 gear_ratio = _cons/20
. cnsreg mpg price weight displ gear_ratio foreign length, c(1-3,5-6)
```

Constrained linear regression   Number of obs =   74
                                                        F(2,   72) = 785.20
                                                        Prob > F   = 0.0000
                                                        Root MSE   = 4.6823

```
( 1)  price - weight = 0
( 2)  - weight + displacement = 0
( 3)  - weight + length = 0
( 4)  gear_ratio + foreign = 0
( 5)  gear_ratio - .05 _cons = 0
```

mpg	Coef.	Std. Err.	t	P>|t|	[95% Conf. Interval]	
price	-.000923	.0001534	-6.02	0.000	-.0012288	-.0006172
weight	-.000923	.0001534	-6.02	0.000	-.0012288	-.0006172
displacement	-.000923	.0001534	-6.02	0.000	-.0012288	-.0006172
gear_ratio	1.326114	.0687589	19.29	0.000	1.189046	1.463183
foreign	-1.326114	.0687589	-19.29	0.000	-1.463183	-1.189046
length	-.000923	.0001534	-6.02	0.000	-.0012288	-.0006172
_cons	26.52229	1.375178	19.29	0.000	23.78092	29.26365

There are many ways we could have specified the constraints() option (which we abbreviated c() above). We typed c(1-3,5-6), meaning we want constraints 1 through 3 and 5 and 6; those numbers correspond to the constraints we defined. The only reason we did not use the number 4 was to emphasize that constraints do not have to be consecutively numbered. We typed c(1-3,5-6), but we could have typed c(1,2,3,5,6) or c(1-3,5,6) or c(1-2,3,5,6) or even c(1-6), which would have worked as long as constraint 4 is not defined. If we had previously defined a constraint 4, c(1-6) would have included it.

◁

Saved Results

cnsreg saves in e():

Scalars

e(N)	number of observations	e(F)	*F* statistic
e(df_m)	model degrees of freedom	e(rmse)	root mean square error
e(df_r)	residual degrees of freedom	e(ll)	log likelihood

Macros

e(cmd)	cnsreg	e(wexp)	weight expression
e(depvar)	name of dependent variable	e(predict)	program used to implement predict
e(wtype)	weight type		

Matrices

e(b)	coefficient vector	e(V)	variance–covariance matrix of the estimators

Functions

e(sample)	marks estimation sample

Methods and Formulas

cnsreg is implemented as an ado-file.

Let n be the number of observations, p the total number of parameters (prior to restrictions and including the constant), and c the number of constraints. The coefficients are calculated as $\mathbf{b}' = \mathbf{T}\{(\mathbf{T}'\mathbf{X}'\mathbf{W}\mathbf{X}\mathbf{T})^{-1}(\mathbf{T}'\mathbf{X}'\mathbf{W}\mathbf{y} - \mathbf{T}'\mathbf{X}'\mathbf{W}\mathbf{X}\mathbf{a}')\} + \mathbf{a}'$, where $\mathbf{T}$ and $\mathbf{a}$ are as defined in [P] **matrix constraint**. $\mathbf{W} = \mathbf{I}$ if no weights are specified. If weights are specified, let $\mathbf{v}$: $1 \times n$ be the specified weights. If fweight frequency weights are specified, $\mathbf{W} = \text{diag}(\mathbf{v})$. If aweight analytic weights are specified, then $\mathbf{W} = \text{diag}[\mathbf{v}/(\mathbf{1}'\mathbf{v})(\mathbf{1}'\mathbf{1})]$, which is to say, the weights are normalized to sum to the number of observations.

The mean square error is $s^2 = (\mathbf{y}'\mathbf{W}\mathbf{y} - 2\mathbf{b}'\mathbf{X}'\mathbf{W}\mathbf{y} + \mathbf{b}'\mathbf{X}'\mathbf{W}\mathbf{X}\mathbf{b})/(n - p + c)$. The variance–covariance matrix is $s^2\mathbf{T}(\mathbf{T}'\mathbf{X}'\mathbf{W}\mathbf{X}\mathbf{T})^{-1}\mathbf{T}'$.

Also See

Complementary:	[R] **adjust**, [R] **constraint**, [R] **lincom**, [R] **linktest**, [R] **mfx**, [R] **nlcom**, [R] **predict**, [R] **predictnl**, [R] **test**, [R] **testnl**, [R] **vce**, [R] **xi**
Related:	[R] **reg3**, [R] **regress**
Background:	[U] **16.5 Accessing coefficients and standard errors**, [U] **23 Estimation and post-estimation commands**

Title

codebook — Produce a codebook describing the contents of data

Syntax

codebook [*varlist*] [, all header notes mv tabulate(#) problems detail]

Description

codebook examines the variable names, labels, and data to produce a code book describing the dataset.

Options

all is equivalent to specifying options header and notes. It provides a complete report, which excludes only performing mv.

header adds a header to the top of the output, which lists the dataset name, the date that the dataset was last saved, etc.

notes list any notes attached to the variables; see [R] **notes**.

mv specifies that codebook is to search the data to determine the pattern of missing values. This is a cpu-intensive task.

tabulate(#) specifies the number of unique values of the variables to use to determine whether a variable is categorical or continuous. Missing values are not included in this count. The default is 9; when there are more than 9 unique values, the variable is classified as continuous. Extended missing values will be included in the tabulation.

problems specifies that a summary report is produced describing potential problems that were diagnosed.

- variables are value labeled with a nondefined value label
- incompletely value-labeled variables
- variables that are constant, including always missing
- trailing, trimming, and embedded spaces in string variables
- noninteger valued date variables

detail may only be specified with the problems option. It specifies that the detailed report on the variables is not suppressed.

Remarks

codebook, without arguments, is most usefully combined with log to produce a printed listing for enclosure in a notebook documenting the data; see [U] **18 Printing and preserving output**. codebook is, however, also useful interactively, since you can specify one or a few variables.

▷ Example

codebook examines the data in producing its results. For variables that codebook thinks are continuous, it presents the mean, the standard deviation, and the 10th, 25th, 50th, 75th, and 90th percentiles. For variables that it thinks are categorical, it presents a tabulation. In part, codebook makes this determination by counting the number of unique values of the variable. If the number is 9 or fewer, codebook reports a tabulation; otherwise, it reports summary statistics.

codebook distinguishes the standard missing values (.) and the extended missing values (.a/.z, denoted by .*). If extended missing values are found, codebook reports the number of distinct missing value codes that occurred in that variable. Missing values are ignored with the tabulate option when determining whether a variable is treated as continuous or categorical.

```
. use http://www.stata-press.com/data/r8/educ3
(ccdb46, 52-54)

. codebook fips division, all
                Dataset:  http://www.stata-press.com/data/r8/educ3.dta
             Last saved:  6 Sep 2002 09:26

                  Label:  ccdb46, 52-54
    Number of variables:  42
 Number of observations:  956
                   Size:  149,136 bytes ignoring labels, etc.

_dta:
  1.  confirmed data with steve on 7/22
```

```
fips                                                        state/place code
-------------------------------------------------------------------------------
                  type:  numeric (long)

                 range:  [10060,560050]              units:  1
         unique values:  956                      missing .:  0/956

                  mean:     256495
              std. dev:     156998

           percentiles:      10%       25%       50%       75%       90%
                           61462    120426    252848    391360    482530
```

```
division                                                      Census Division
-------------------------------------------------------------------------------
                  type:  numeric (int)
                 label:  division, but 1 value is not labeled

                 range:  [1,9]                        units:  0
         unique values:  9                        missing .:  4/956
        unique mv codes:  2                       missing .*:  2/956

            tabulation:  Freq.   Numeric  Label
                            69         1  N. Eng.
                            97         2  Mid Atl
                           202         3  E.N.C.
                            78         4  W.N.C.
                           115         5  S. Atl.
                            46         6  E.S.C.
                            89         7  W.S.C.
                            59         8  Mountain
                           195         9  Pacific
                             4         .
                             2        .a
```

Since division has 9 unique values, codebook reported a tabulation. If division had one more unique value, codebook would have switched to reporting summary statistics unless we had included the tabulate(#) option.

◁

▷ Example

The mv option is quite useful. It instructs codebook to search the data to determine the pattern of missing values. Different kinds of missing values are not distinguished in the patterns.

```
. use http://www.stata-press.com/data/r8/citytemp
(City Temperature Data)
. codebook cooldd heatdd tempjan tempjuly, mv
```

cooldd					Cooling degree days
type:	numeric (int)				
range:	[0,4389]			units:	1
unique values:	438			missing .:	3/956
mean:	1240.41				
std. dev:	937.668				
percentiles:	10%	25%	50%	75%	90%
	411	615	940	1566	2761
missing values:	heatdd==mv <-> cooldd==mv				
	tempjan==mv --> cooldd==mv				
	tempjuly==mv --> cooldd==mv				

heatdd					Heating degree days
type:	numeric (int)				
range:	[0,10816]			units:	1
unique values:	471			missing .:	3/956
mean:	4425.53				
std. dev:	2199.6				
percentiles:	10%	25%	50%	75%	90%
	1510	2460	4950	6232	6919
missing values:	cooldd==mv <-> heatdd==mv				
	tempjan==mv --> heatdd==mv				
	tempjuly==mv --> heatdd==mv				

tempjan					Average January temperature
type:	numeric (float)				
range:	[2.2,72.6]			units:	.1
unique values:	310			missing .:	2/956
mean:	35.749				
std. dev:	14.1881				
percentiles:	10%	25%	50%	75%	90%
	20.2	25.1	31.3	47.8	55.1
missing values:	tempjuly==mv <-> tempjan==mv				

```
 tempjuly                                               Average July temperature

            type:  numeric (float)
           range:  [58.099998,93.599998]        units:  0
   unique values:  196                      missing .:  0/956
 unique mv codes:  1                       missing .*:  2/956

            mean:  75.0538
        std. dev:  5.49504

     percentiles:        10%       25%       50%       75%       90%
                        68.8      71.8     74.25      78.7      82.3

  missing values:        tempjan==mv <-> tempjuly==mv
```

codebook reports that if `tempjan` is missing, `tempjuly` is missing, and vice versa. In the output for the `cooldd` variable, codebook also reports that the pattern of missing values is the same for `cooldd` and `heatdd`. In both cases, the correspondence is indicated with "`<->`".

For `cooldd`, codebook also states that "`tempjan==mv --> cooldd==mv`". The one-way arrow means that a missing `tempjan` value implies a missing `cooldd` value, but a missing `cooldd` value does not necessarily imply a missing `tempjan` value.

◁

Another feature of codebook—this one for numeric variables—is to determine the units of the variable. For instance, in the example above, `tempjan` and `tempjuly` both have units of .1, meaning that temperature is recorded to tenths of a degree. codebook handles precision considerations in making this determination (note that `tempjan` and `tempjuly` are `float`s and see [U] **16.10 Precision and problems therein**). If we had a variable in our dataset recorded in 100s (e.g., 21,500, 36,800, etc.), codebook would have reported the units as 100. If we had a variable that took on only values divisible by 5 (5, 10, 15, etc.), codebook would have reported the units as 5.

▷ Example

When codebook determines that neither a tabulation nor a listing of summary statistics is appropriate, for instance, in the case of a string variable or in the case of a numeric variable taking on many labeled values, it reports a few examples instead.

```
. codebook name

 name                                                         (unlabeled)

            type:  string (str5), but longest is str3
   unique values:  10                    missing "":  0/10

        examples:  "10 "
                   "3  "
                   "5  "
                   "7  "

         warning:  variable has trailing blanks
```

codebook is also on the lookout for common problems that might cause you to make errors when dealing with the data. In the case of string variables, this includes leading, embedded, and trailing blanks. codebook informed us that `name` includes embedded blanks. If `name` had leading or trailing blanks, it would have mentioned that, too.

In case variables are value labeled, codebook performs two checks. First, if a variable label *labname* is associated with a variable, codebook checks whether *labname* is actually defined. Second, it checks whether all values are value labeled. Partial labeling of a variable may mean that the label was defined incorrectly (for instance, the variable has values 0 and 1, the value label maps 1 to "man" and 2 to "female"), or that the variable was defined incorrectly (e.g., a variable gender with three values). codebook checks whether date variables are integer valued.

If the option problems is specified, codebook does not provide detailed descriptions on each of the variables, but reports on the potential problems in the data only.

```
. codebook, problems

    Potential problems in dataset   Some funny variables.dta
              potential problems    variables

            constant (or all missing)   human planet
           vars with nonexisting label   educ
           incompletely labeled vars    gender
        strvars that may be compressed   name address city country planet
          strvars with leading blanks   city country
         strvars with trailing blanks    name planet
         strvars with embedded blanks    address
         noninteger valued date vars    birthdate
```

◁

Saved Results

codebook saves in r() macros the lists of variables with potential problems:

r(cons)	constant (or missing)
r(labelnotfound)	undefined value labeled
r(notlabeled)	value labeled, but with unlabeled categories
r(str_type)	compressible
r(str_leading)	leading blanks
r(str_trailing)	trailing blanks
r(str_embedded)	embedded blanks
r(realdate)	noninteger dates

Methods and Formulas

codebook is implemented as an ado-file.

Also See

| Related: | [R] **describe**, [R] **inspect**, [R] **labelbook**, [R] **notes** |
| Background: | [U] **18 Printing and preserving output** |

Title

> **collapse** — Make dataset of means, medians, etc.

Syntax

collapse *clist* [*weight*] [if *exp*] [in *range*] [, by(*varlist*) cw fast]

where *clist* is either

[(*stat*)] *varlist* [[(*stat*)] ...]

[(*stat*)] *target_var=varname* [*target_var=varname* ...] [[(*stat*)] ...]

or any combination of the *varlist* and *target_var* forms, and *stat* is one of

mean	means (default)		median	medians
sd	standard deviations		p1	1st percentile
sum	sums		p2	2nd percentile
rawsum	sums ignoring optionally specified weight		...	3rd–49th percentiles
count	number of nonmissing observations		p50	50th percentile (same as median)
max	maximums		...	51st–97th percentiles
min	minimums		p98	98th percentile
iqr	interquartile range		p99	99th percentile

If *stat* is not specified, mean is assumed.

aweights, fweights, iweights, and pweights are allowed; see [U] **14.1.6 weight**, and see the *Weights* section below. pweights may not be used with statistic sd.

varlist and *varname* in *clist* may contain time-series operators; see [U] **14.4.3 Time-series varlists**.

Examples:

```
. collapse age educ income, by(state)

. collapse (mean) age educ (median) income, by(state)

. collapse (mean) age educ income (median) medinc=income, by(state)

. collapse (p25) gpa [fw=number], by(year)
```

Description

collapse converts the dataset in memory into a dataset of means, sums, medians, etc. *clist* must refer to numeric variables exclusively.

Note: See [R] **contract** if you want to collapse to a dataset of frequencies.

Options

by(*varlist*) specifies the groups over which the means, etc. are to be calculated. If not specified, the resulting dataset will contain one observation. If specified, *varlist* may refer to either string or numeric variables.

cw specifies casewise deletion. If not specified, all possible observations are used for each calculated statistic.

fast specifies that collapse not go to extra work so that it can restore the original dataset should the user press *Break*. fast is intended for use by programmers.

Remarks

collapse takes the dataset in memory and creates a new dataset containing summary statistics of the original data. Since the syntax diagram for collapse makes using it appear more complicated than it is, collapse is best explained with examples.

▷ Example

Consider the following artificial data on the grade-point average (gpa) of college students:

```
. use http://www.stata-press.com/data/r8/college
. describe
Contains data from http://www.stata-press.com/data/r8/college.dta
  obs:              12
  vars:              4                          6 Jul 2002 15:17
  size:            168 (99.9% of memory free)
```

variable name	storage type	display format	value label	variable label
gpa	float	%9.0g		gpa for this year
hour	int	%9.0g		Total academic hours
year	int	%9.0g		1 = freshman, 2 = sophomore, 3 = junior, 4 = senior
number	int	%9.0g		number of students

```
Sorted by:  year
. list, sep(4)
```

	gpa	hour	year	number
1.	3.2	30	1	3
2.	3.5	34	1	2
3.	2.8	28	1	9
4.	2.1	30	1	4
5.	3.8	29	2	3
6.	2.5	30	2	4
7.	2.9	35	2	5
8.	3.7	30	3	4
9.	2.2	35	3	2
10.	3.3	33	3	3
11.	3.4	32	4	5
12.	2.9	31	4	2

```
. collapse (p25) gpa [fw=number], by(year)
```

```
. list
```

	year	gpa
1.	1	2.8
2.	2	2.5
3.	3	3.3
4.	4	2.9

```
. use http://www.stata-press.com/data/r8/college, clear
. collapse gpa hour [fw=number], by(year)
. list
```

	year	gpa	hour
1.	1	2.788889	29.44444
2.	2	2.991667	31.83333
3.	3	3.233333	32.11111
4.	4	3.257143	31.71428

```
. use http://www.stata-press.com/data/r8/college, clear
. collapse (mean) gpa hour (median) medgpa=gpa medhour=hour [fw=num], by(year)
. list
```

	year	gpa	hour	medgpa	medhour
1.	1	2.788889	29.44444	2.8	29
2.	2	2.991667	31.83333	2.9	30
3.	3	3.233333	32.11111	3.3	33
4.	4	3.257143	31.71428	3.4	32

```
. use http://www.stata-press.com/data/r8/college, clear
. collapse (count) gpa hour (min) mingpa=gpa minhour=hour [fw=num], by(year)
. list
```

	year	gpa	hour	mingpa	minhour
1.	1	18	18	2.1	28
2.	2	12	12	2.5	29
3.	3	9	9	2.2	30
4.	4	7	7	2.9	31

```
. use http://www.stata-press.com/data/r8/college, clear
. replace gpa = . in 2/4
(3 real changes made, 3 to missing)
```

(Continued on next page)

```
. list, sep(4)
```

	gpa	hour	year	number
1.	3.2	30	1	3
2.	.	34	1	2
3.	.	28	1	9
4.	.	30	1	4
5.	3.8	29	2	3
6.	2.5	30	2	4
7.	2.9	35	2	5
8.	3.7	30	3	4
9.	2.2	35	3	2
10.	3.3	33	3	3
11.	3.4	32	4	5
12.	2.9	31	4	2

```
. collapse gpa hour [fw=num], by(year)
. list
```

	year	gpa	hour
1.	1	3.2	29.44444
2.	2	2.991667	31.83333
3.	3	3.233333	32.11111
4.	4	3.257143	31.71428

```
. use http://www.stata-press.com/data/r8/college, clear
. replace gpa = . in 2/4
(3 real changes made, 3 to missing)
. collapse (mean) gpa hour [fw=num], by(year) cw
. list
```

	year	gpa	hour
1.	1	3.2	30
2.	2	2.991667	31.83333
3.	3	3.233333	32.11111
4.	4	3.257143	31.71428

◁

▷ Example

We have individual-level data from the Census in which each observation is a person. Among other variables, the dataset contains the numeric variables age, educ, and income and the string variable state. We want to create a 50-observation dataset containing the means of age, education, and income for each state.

```
. collapse age educ income, by(state)
```

The resulting dataset contains means because collapse assumes that you want means if you do not specify otherwise. To make this explicit, we could have typed

```
. collapse (mean) age educ income, by(state)
```

Had we wanted the mean for age and educ, but the median for income, we could have typed

> . collapse (mean) age educ (median) income, by(state)

or, if we wanted the mean for age and educ, but both the mean and the median for income,

> . collapse (mean) age educ income (median) medinc=income, by(state)

This last dataset will contain three variables containing means—age, educ, and income—and one variable containing the median of income—medinc.

◁

Variable-wise or casewise deletion

▷ Example

Let us assume that in our Census data, we have 25,000 persons for whom age is recorded but only 15,000 for whom income is recorded; that is, income is missing for 10,000 observations. If you wanted summary statistics for age and income, by default, collapse will use all 25,000 observations when calculating the summary statistics for age. If you prefer that collapse use only the 15,000 observations for which income is not missing, specify the cw (casewise) option:

> . collapse (mean) age income (median) medinc=income, by(state) cw

◁

Weights

collapse allows all four weight types and defaults to aweights. Weight normalization only impacts the sum, count, and sd statistics.

Here are the definitions for count and sum with weights:

count:
    unweighted: _N, the number of physical observations
    aweight: _N, the number of physical observations
    fweight, iweight, pweight: $W = \sum w_j$, the sum of the user-specified weights
sum:
    unweighted: $\sum x_j$, the sum of the variable
    aweight: $\sum v_j x_j$; $v_j = (w_j$ normalized to sum to _N$)$
    fweight, iweight, pweight: $\sum w_j x_j$

The sd statistic with weights returns the bias-corrected standard deviation, which is based on the factor $\sqrt{N/(N-1)}$, where N is the number of observations. sd is not allowed with pweighted data. Otherwise, sd is changed by the weights through the computation of the count (N) as outlined above.

For instance, consider a case where there are 25 physical observations in the dataset and a weighting variable that sums to 57. In the unweighted case, the weight is not specified and $N = 25$. In the analytically weighted case, N is still 25; the scale of the weight is irrelevant. In the frequency-weighted case, however, $N = 57$, the sum of the weights.

▷ Example

Using our same Census data, suppose that instead of starting with individual-level data and aggregating to state level, we started with state-level data and wanted to aggregate to the region level. Also assume that our dataset contains pop, the population of each state.

To obtain unweighted means and medians of age and income, by region, along with total population,

```
. collapse (mean) age income (median) medage=age medinc=income (sum) pop, by(region)
```

To obtain weighted means and medians of age and income, by region, along with total population and using frequency weights:

```
. collapse (mean) age income (median) medage=age medinc=income (count) pop
>    [fweight=pop], by(region)
```

Note: Specifying (sum) pop would not have worked because that would have yielded the pop-weighted sum of pop. Specifying (count) age would have worked as well as (count) pop because count merely counts the number of nonmissing observations. The counts here, however, are frequency-weighted and equal the sum of pop.

Same as above, but using analytic weights:

```
. collapse (mean) age income (median) medage=age medinc=income (rawsum) pop
>    [aweight=pop], by(region)
```

Note: Specifying (count) pop would not have worked because, with analytic weights, count would count numbers of physical observations. Specifying (sum) pop would not have worked because sum would calculate weighted sums (with a normalized weight). The rawsum function, however, ignores the weights and just sums the specified variable. rawsum would have worked as the solution to all three cases.

◁

A final example

▷ Example

We have state data containing information on each state's median age, marriage rate, and divorce rate. We want to form a new dataset containing various summary statistics, by region, of the variables:

```
. use http://www.stata-press.com/data/r8/census5
(1980 Census data by state)
. describe
Contains data from http://www.stata-press.com/data/r8/census5.dta
  obs:            50                          1980 Census data by state
  vars:            6                          6 Jul 2002 15:22
  size:         1,800 (98.6% of memory free)
```

variable name	storage type	display format	value label	variable label
state	str14	%14s		State
region	int	%8.0g	cenreg	Census region
pop	long	%10.0g		Population
median_age	float	%9.2f		Median age
marriage_rate	float	%9.0g		
divorce_rate	float	%9.0g		

```
Sorted by: region
```

```
. collapse (median) median_age marriage divorce (mean) avgmrate=marriage
> avgdrate=divorce [aw=pop], by(region)
. list
```

	region	median~e	marria~e	divorc~e	avgmrate	avgdrate
1.	NE	31.90	.0080657	.0035295	.0081472	.0035359
2.	N Cntrl	29.90	.0093821	.0048636	.0096701	.004961
3.	South	29.60	.0112609	.0065792	.0117082	.0059439
4.	West	29.90	.0089093	.0056423	.0125199	.0063464

```
. describe
Contains data
  obs:             4                        1980 Census data by state
  vars:            6
  size:          104 (98.8% of memory free)
```

	storage	display	value	
variable name	type	format	label	variable label
region	int	%8.0g	cenreg	Census region
median_age	float	%9.2f		(p 50) median_age
marriage_rate	float	%9.0g		(p 50) marriage_rate
divorce_rate	float	%9.0g		(p 50) divorce_rate
avgmrate	float	%9.0g		(mean) marriage_rate
avgdrate	float	%9.0g		(mean) divorce_rate

```
Sorted by:  region
    Note:  dataset has changed since last saved
```

◁

Methods and Formulas

collapse is implemented as an ado-file.

Also See

Related: [R] **contract**, [R] **egen**, [R] **statsby**, [R] **summarize**

Title

> **compare** — Compare two variables

Syntax

> compare *varname*$_1$ *varname*$_2$ $[$if *exp*$]$ $[$in *range*$]$

by ... : may be used with compare; see [R] **by**.

Description

> compare reports the differences and similarities in *varname*$_1$ and *varname*$_2$.

Remarks

▷ Example

One of the more useful accountings made by compare is the pattern of missing values:

```
. use http://www.stata-press.com/data/r8/fullauto
(Automobile Models)
. compare rep77 rep78
```

	count	minimum	difference average	maximum
rep77<rep78	16	-3	-1.3125	-1
rep77=rep78	43			
rep77>rep78	7	1	1	1
jointly defined	66	-3	-.2121212	1
rep77 missing only	3			
jointly missing	5			
total	74			

We see that in 5 observations both rep77 and rep78 are missing and that in 3 more observations, rep77 is also missing.

◁

❑ Technical Note

compare may be used with numeric variables, string variables, or both. When used with string variables, the summary of the differences (minimum, average, maximum) is not reported. When used with string and numeric variables, the breakdown by <, =, and > is also suppressed.

For strings, both "" and "." are treated as missing values. Stata does not normally attach any special meaning to the string ".", but some Stata users use the string "." to mean missing value.

❑

Methods and Formulas

compare is implemented as an ado-file.

Also See

Related: [R] **codebook**, [R] **inspect**

Title

compress — Compress data in memory

Syntax

compress [*varlist*]

Description

compress attempts to reduce the amount of memory used by your data.

Remarks

compress reduces the size of your dataset by considering demoting

doubles	to	longs, ints, or bytes
floats	to	ints or bytes
longs	to	ints or bytes
ints	to	bytes
strings	to	shorter strings

compress leaves your data logically unchanged but (probably) appreciably smaller. compress never makes a mistake, results in loss of precision, or hacks off strings.

▷ Example

If you do not specify a *varlist*, compress considers all the variables in your dataset, so typing compress by itself is enough:

```
. compress
mpg was float now byte
price was long now int
yenprice was double now long
weight was double now int
make was str26 now str18

. _
```

If there are no compression possibilities, compress does nothing. For instance, typing compress again results in

```
. compress

. _
```

◁

Also See

Related: [R] **recast**

216

Title

constraint — Define and list constraints

Syntax

<u>cons</u>traint [<u>def</u>ine] # [*exp=exp* | *coefficientlist*]

<u>cons</u>traint <u>dir</u> [*numlist* | _all]

<u>cons</u>traint drop { *numlist* | _all }

<u>cons</u>traint <u>l</u>ist [*numlist* | _all]

<u>cons</u>traint get #

<u>cons</u>traint free

where *coefficientlist* is as defined in [R] **test**.

is restricted to the range 1 to 1,999, inclusive.

Description

constraint defines, lists, and drops linear constraints. Constraints are for use by models that allow constrained estimation.

Remarks

The use of constraints is discussed in [R] **cnsreg**, [R] **mlogit**, and [R] **reg3**; this entry is concerned only with practical aspects of defining and manipulating constraints.

Constraints are defined by the constraint command. The currently defined constraints can be listed by either constraint list or constraint dir; both do the same thing. Existing constraints can be eliminated by constraint drop.

constraint get and constraint free are programmer's commands. constraint get returns the contents of the specified constraint in macro r(contents) and returns in scalar r(defined) 0 or 1; 1 being returned if the constraint was defined. constraint free returns the number of a free (unused) constraint in macro r(free).

▷ Example

Constraints are numbered from 1 to 1,999, and you assign the number when you define the constraint:

```
. constraint 2 [Insured]site2 = 0
```

The currently defined constraints can be listed by constraint list:

```
. constraint list
     2:   [Insured]site2 = 0
```

`constraint drop` is used to drop constraints:

```
. constraint drop 2
. constraint list
```

The empty list after `constraint list` indicates that no constraints are defined. Below, we demonstrate the various syntaxes allowed by `constraint`:

```
. constraint 1 [Insured]
. constraint 10 [Insured]: site1 site2
. constraint 11 [Insured]: site3 site4
. constraint 20 [Prepay=Unins]: site1 site2 site3 site4
. constraint 21 [Prepay=Unins]: race
. constraint 30 [Prepay]
. constraint 31 [Insure]
. constraint list
     1:  [Insured]
    10:  [Insured]: site1 site2
    11:  [Insured]: site3 site4
    20:  [Prepay=Unins]: site1 site2 site3 site4
    21:  [Prepay=Unins]: race
    30:  [Prepay]
    31:  [Insure]
. constraint drop 20-25, 31
. constraint list
     1:  [Insured]
    10:  [Insured]: site1 site2
    11:  [Insured]: site3 site4
    30:  [Prepay]
. constraint drop _all
. constraint list
```

◁

❏ Technical Note

The syntax of the constraint itself is not checked by the `constraint` command because a constraint can only be interpreted in the context of a model. Thus, `constraint` is willing to define constraints that subsequently will not make sense. Any errors in the constraints will be detected, and mentioned, at the time of estimation.

❏

References

Weesie, J. 1999. sg100: Two-stage linear constrained estimation. *Stata Technical Bulletin* 47: 24–30. Reprinted in *Stata Technical Bulletin Reprints*, vol. 8, pp. 217–225.

Also See

Complementary: [R] **cnsreg**, [R] **ml**, [R] **mlogit**

Title

| contract — Make dataset of frequencies |

Syntax

contract *varlist* [*weight*] [if *exp*] [in *range*] [, freq(*varname*) zero nomiss]

fweights are allowed; see [U] **14.1.6 weight**.

Description

contract replaces the dataset in memory with a new dataset consisting of all combinations of *varlist* that exist in the data and a new variable that contains the frequency of each combination.

Options

freq(*varname*) specifies a name for the frequency variable. If not specified, _freq is used. The name must be new.

zero specifies that combinations with frequency zero are wanted.

nomiss specifies that observations with missing values on any of the variables in *varlist* will be dropped. If nomiss is not specified, all observations possible are used.

Remarks

contract takes the dataset in memory and creates a new dataset containing all combinations of *varlist* that exist in the data and a new variable that contains the frequency of each combination.

Sometimes it is desirable to collapse a dataset into frequency form. Several observations identical on one or more variables will be replaced by one such observation together with the frequency of the corresponding set of values. For example, in certain generalized linear models, the frequency of some combination of values is the response variable, so we need to produce that response variable. The set of covariate values associated with each frequency is sometimes called a covariate class or covariate pattern. Such collapsing is reversible for the variables concerned, as the original dataset could be reconstituted by using expand (see [R] **expand**) with the variable containing the frequencies of each covariate class.

▷ Example

Suppose that we wish to collapse the auto dataset to a set of frequencies of the two variables rep78, which takes values 1, 2, 3, 4, and 5, and foreign, which takes values labeled 'Domestic' and 'Foreign'.

(Continued on next page)

```
. use http://www.stata-press.com/data/r8/auto
(1978 Automobile Data)

. contract rep78 foreign

. list
```

	rep78	foreign	_freq
1.	1	Domestic	2
2.	2	Domestic	8
3.	3	Domestic	27
4.	3	Foreign	3
5.	4	Domestic	9
6.	4	Foreign	9
7.	5	Domestic	2
8.	5	Foreign	9
9.	.	Domestic	4
10.	.	Foreign	1

By default, contract uses the variable name _freq for the new variable that contains the frequencies. If _freq is in use, then the user is reminded to specify a new variable name via the freq( ) option.

Specifying the zero option requests that combinations with frequency zero also be listed.

```
. use http://www.stata-press.com/data/r8/auto
(1978 Automobile Data)

. contract rep78 foreign, zero

. list
```

	rep78	foreign	_freq
1.	1	Domestic	2
2.	1	Foreign	0
3.	2	Domestic	8
4.	2	Foreign	0
5.	3	Domestic	27
6.	3	Foreign	3
7.	4	Domestic	9
8.	4	Foreign	9
9.	5	Domestic	2
10.	5	Foreign	9
11.	.	Domestic	4
12.	.	Foreign	1

◁

Methods and Formulas

contract is implemented as an ado-file.

Acknowledgment

contract was written by Nicholas J. Cox of the University of Durham (Cox 1998).

References

Cox, N. J. 1998. dm59: Collapsing datasets to frequencies. *Stata Technical Bulletin* 44: 2–3. Reprinted in *Stata Technical Bulletin Reprints*, vol. 8, pp. 20–21.

Also See

Complementary:	[R] **expand**
Related:	[R] **collapse**

Title

> **copy** — Copy file from disk or URL

Syntax

> copy *filename_1* *filename_2* [, <u>pub</u>lic <u>t</u>ext replace]

filename_1 may be a filename or a URL. *filename_2* may *not* be a URL.

Double quotes may be used to enclose the filenames, and the quotes must be used if the filename contains embedded blanks.

Description

> copy copies *filename_1* to *filename_2*.

Options

> public specifies that *filename_2* is to be readable by everyone; otherwise, the file will be created according to the default permissions of your operating system.

> text specifies that *filename_1* is to be interpreted as a text file and is to be translated to the native form of text files on your computer. Computers differ on how end-of-line is recorded: Unix systems record a single linefeed character, Windows computers record a carriage-return/linefeed combination, and Macintosh computers record just a carriage return. text specifies that *filename_1* is to be examined to determine how it has end-of-line recorded, and then the line-end characters are to be switched to whatever is appropriate for your computer when the copy is made.

> There is no reason to specify text when copying a file already on your computer to a different location because the file would already be in your computer's format.

> Do not specify text unless you know the file is a text file; if the file is binary and you specify text, the copy will be useless. Be warned that most word processors produce binary, not text files. The term text, as it is used here, specifies a particular ASCII way of recording textual information.

> When other parts of Stata read text files, they do not care how lines are terminated, so there is no reason to translate end-line characters on that score. You specify text because you may want to look at the file using other software.

> replace specifies that *filename_2* may already exist and, if so, that it is to be replaced.

Remarks

Examples:

Windows:

```
. copy orig.dta newcopy.dta
. copy "my document" "copy of document"
. copy ..\mydir\doc.txt document\doc.tex
. copy http://www.stata.com/examples/simple.dta simple.dta
. copy http://www.stata.com/examples/simple.txt simple.txt, text
```

Unix:

    . copy orig.dta newcopy.dta

    . copy ../mydir/doc.txt document/doc.tex

    . copy http://www.stata.com/examples/simple.dta simple.dta

    . copy http://www.stata.com/examples/simple.txt simple.txt, text

Macintosh:

    . copy orig.dta newcopy.dta

    . copy "my document" "copy of document"

    . copy ../mydir/doc.txt document/doc.tex

    . copy http://www.stata.com/examples/simple.dta simple.dta

    . copy http://www.stata.com/examples/simple.txt simple.txt, text

Also See

Related: [R] **cd**, [R] **dir**, [R] **erase**, [R] **mkdir**, [R] **shell**, [R] **type**

Background: [U] **14.6 File-naming conventions**

Title

copyright — Display copyright information

Syntax

```
copyright
```

Description

`copyright` presents copyright notifications concerning tools, libraries, and the like used in the construction of Stata.

Remarks

The correct form for a copyright notice is

Copyright *dates* by *author/owner*

Note that the word "copyright" is spelled out. You can use the © symbol, but (C) has never been given legal recognition. The phrase "All Rights Reserved" was historically required, but is no longer needed.

Currently, most works are copyrighted from the moment they are written, and no copyright notice is required. Copyright concerns the protection of the expression and structure of facts and ideas, not the facts and ideas themselves. Also note that copyright concerns the ownership of the expression and not the name given to the expression, which is covered under trademark law.

Copyright law as it exists today began in England in 1710 with the Statute of Anne, *An Act for the Encouragement of Learning by Vesting the Copies of Printed Books in the Authors or Purchases of Such Copies, during the Times therein mentioned*. In 1672, Massachusetts introduced the first copyright law in what was to become the United States. After the Revolutionary War, copyright was introduced into the U.S. Constitution in 1787 and went into effect on 31may1790. On 9jun1790, the first copyright in the U.S. was registered for *The Philadelphia Spelling Book* by John Barry.

There are significant differences in the understanding of copyright in the English- and non-English-speaking world. The Napoleonic or Civil Code, the dominant legal system in the non-English-speaking world, splits the rights into two classes: the author's economic rights and the author's moral rights. Moral rights are available only to "natural persons". Legal persons (corporations) have economic rights, but not moral rights.

Also See

Related: Copyright page of this book

Title

> **corr2data** — Create a dataset with a specified correlation structure

Syntax

> corr2data *newvarlist* [, n(*#*) <u>mea</u>ns(*vector*) corr(*matname*) cov(*matname*)
>
> <u>sds</u>(*vector*) <u>d</u>ouble clear]

Description

corr2data can be used to add new variables with specified correlation structures to the existing dataset or to create a dataset with a specified correlation structure.

Options

n(*#*) specifies the number of observations to be generated. The default is the current number of observations. If n(*#*) is not specified or is the same as the current number of observations, corr2data will add the new variables to the existing dataset; otherwise, corr2data will replace the dataset in memory.

means(*vector*) specifies the means of the generated variables. The default is means(0).

corr(*matname*) specifies the correlation matrix. cov() and corr() may not be specified together. If neither corr() nor cov() is specified, the default is orthogonal data.

cov(*matname*) specifies the covariance matrix. cov() and corr() may not be specified together. If neither corr() nor cov() is specified, the default is orthogonal data.

sds(*vector*) specifies the standard deviations of the generated variables. sds() and cov() may not be specified together.

double specifies that the new variables are to be stored as Stata doubles, meaning 8-byte reals. If double is not specified, variables are stored as floats, meaning 4-byte reals. See [R] **data types**.

clear specifies that it is okay to replace the dataset in memory even though the current dataset has not been saved on disk.

Remarks

▷ Example

We first run a factor analysis using the auto dataset.

```
. use http://www.stata-press.com/data/r8/auto
(1978 Automobile Data)
. factor weight length trunk
(obs=74)
            (principal factors; 2 factors retained)
    Factor    Eigenvalue    Difference    Proportion    Cumulative
      1         2.37834       2.36209        1.0184        1.0184
      2         0.01625       0.07536        0.0070        1.0253
      3        -0.05911          .          -0.0253        1.0000
```

```
                Factor Loadings
   Variable  |     1          2       Uniqueness

     weight  |  0.95026    -0.07919     0.09073
     length  |  0.97237     0.00264     0.05448
      trunk  |  0.72789     0.09986     0.46020
```

Suppose that for some reason, we no longer have the `auto` dataset. Instead we know the covariance matrix of `weight`, `length` and `trunk`, and we want to do the same factor analysis again. The covariance matrix is

```
. mat list V

symmetric V[3,3]
            weight      length       trunk
weight   604029.84
length   16370.922   495.78989
 trunk   2234.6612   69.202518   18.296187
```

In order to do the factor analysis in Stata, we need to create a dataset that has the specified correlation structure.

```
. corr2data x y z, n(74) cov(V)
(obs 74)

. factor x y z
(obs=74)
```

```
              (principal factors; 2 factors retained)
   Factor     Eigenvalue    Difference    Proportion    Cumulative

      1         2.37834       2.36209        1.0184        1.0184
      2         0.01625       0.07536        0.0070        1.0253
      3        -0.05911          .          -0.0253        1.0000
```

```
                Factor Loadings
   Variable  |     1          2       Uniqueness

         x  |  0.95026    -0.07919     0.09073
         y  |  0.97237     0.00264     0.05448
         z  |  0.72789     0.09986     0.46020
```

Note that the results from the factor analysis based on the generated data are the same as those based on the real data.

◁

Methods and Formulas

`corr2data` is implemented as an ado-file. Two steps are involved in generating the desire dataset. The first step is to generate a zero-mean, zero-correlated dataset. The second step is to apply the desired correlation structure and the means to the zero-mean, zero-correlated dataset. In both steps, we take into account the fact that given any matrix $\mathbf{A}$ and any vector of variables $\mathbf{X}$, $\mathrm{Var}(\mathbf{A}'\mathbf{X}) = \mathbf{A}'\mathrm{Var}(\mathbf{X})\mathbf{A}$.

Also See

Related: [R] **drawnorm**

Background: [R] **data types**

Title

> **correlate** — Correlations (covariances) of variables or estimators

Syntax

<u>cor</u>relate [*varlist*] [*weight*] [if *exp*] [in *range*] [, <u>m</u>eans <u>nof</u>ormat <u>c</u>ovariance

_coef <u>w</u>rap]

pwcorr [*varlist*] [*weight*] [if *exp*] [in *range*] [, <u>o</u>bs sig <u>p</u>rint(#) <u>st</u>ar(#)

<u>b</u>onferroni <u>sid</u>ak]

by . . . : may be used with correlate and pwcorr; see [R] **by**.

aweights and fweights are allowed; see [U] **14.1.6 weight**.

The *varlist* following correlate may contain time-series operators; see [U] **14.4.3 Time-series varlists**.

Description

The correlate command displays the correlation matrix or covariance matrix for a group of variables or for the coefficients of the most recent estimation. Also see [R] **vce**.

pwcorr displays all the pairwise correlation coefficients between the variables in *varlist*, or, if *varlist* is not specified, all the variables in the dataset.

Options

means causes summary statistics (means, standard deviations, minimums, and maximums) to be displayed with the matrix.

noformat displays the summary statistics requested by the means option in g format regardless of the display formats associated with the variables.

covariance displays the covariances rather than the correlation coefficients.

_coef displays the correlations (or covariances if covariance is also specified) between the coefficients of the last estimation.

wrap requests that no action be taken on wide correlation matrices to make them readable. It prevents Stata from breaking wide matrices into pieces to enhance readability. You might want to specify this option if you are displaying results in a window wider than 80 characters. In that case, you may need to set linesize to however many characters you can display across a single line; see [R] **log**.

obs adds a line to each row of the matrix reporting the number of observations used to calculate the correlation coefficient.

sig adds a line to each row of the matrix reporting the significance level of each correlation coefficient.

print(#) specifies the significance level of correlation coefficients to be printed. Correlation coefficients with larger significance levels are left blank in the matrix. Typing pwcorr, print(.10) would list only correlation coefficients significant at the 10% level or better.

star(#) specifies the significance level of correlation coefficients to be starred. Typing pwcorr, star(.05) would star all correlation coefficients significant at the 5% level or better.

bonferroni makes the Bonferroni adjustment to calculated significance levels. This affects printed significance levels and the print() and star() options. Thus, pwcorr, print(.05) bonferroni prints coefficients with Bonferroni-adjusted significance levels of .05 or less.

sidak makes the Šidák adjustment to calculated significance levels. This affects printed significance levels and the print() and star() options. Thus, pwcorr, print(.05) sidak prints coefficients with Šidák-adjusted significance levels of .05 or less.

Remarks

correlate

Typing correlate by itself produces a correlation matrix for all the variables in the dataset. If you specify the *varlist*, a correlation matrix for just those variables is displayed.

▷ Example

You have state data on demographic characteristics of the population. To obtain a correlation matrix, type correlate:

```
. use http://www.stata-press.com/data/r8/census3
(1980 Census data by state)

. correlate
(obs=50)
```

	state	brate	pop	medage	division	region	mrgrate
state	1.0000						
brate	0.0208	1.0000					
pop	−0.0540	−0.2830	1.0000				
medage	−0.0624	−0.8800	0.3294	1.0000			
division	−0.1345	0.6356	−0.1081	−0.5207	1.0000		
region	−0.1339	0.6086	−0.1515	−0.5292	0.9688	1.0000	
mrgrate	0.0509	0.0677	−0.1502	−0.0177	0.2280	0.2490	1.0000
dvcrate	−0.0655	0.3508	−0.2064	−0.2229	0.5522	0.5682	0.7700
medage2	−0.0621	−0.8609	0.3324	0.9984	−0.5162	−0.5239	−0.0202

	dvcrate	medage2
dvcrate	1.0000	
medage2	−0.2192	1.0000

Since you did not specify the wrap option, Stata did its best to make the result readable by breaking the table into two parts.

To obtain the correlations between mrgrate, dvcrate, and medage, type correlate mrgrate dvcrate medage:

```
. correlate mrgrate dvcrate medage
(obs=50)
```

	mrgrate	dvcrate	medage
mrgrate	1.0000		
dvcrate	0.7700	1.0000	
medage	−0.0177	−0.2229	1.0000

◁

▷ Example

The variable pop in our previous example represents the total population of the state. Thus, to obtain population-weighted correlations between mrgrate, dvcrate, and medage, type

```
. correlate mrgrate dvcrate medage [w=pop]
(analytic weights assumed)
(sum of wgt is   2.2591e+08)
(obs=50)

                 mrgrate  dvcrate   medage

     mrgrate |    1.0000
     dvcrate |    0.5854   1.0000
      medage |   -0.1316  -0.2833   1.0000
```

◁

With the covariance option, correlate can be used to obtain covariance matrices, as well as correlation matrices. This can be done for both weighted and unweighted data.

▷ Example

To obtain the matrix of covariances between mrgrate, dvcrate, and medage, type correlate mrgrate dvcrate medage, covariance:

```
. correlate mrgrate dvcrate medage, covariance
(obs=50)

                 mrgrate  dvcrate   medage

     mrgrate |   .000662
     dvcrate |   .000063  1.0e-05
      medage |  -.000769 -.001191  2.86775
```

You could have obtained the pop-weighted covariance matrix by typing correlate mrgrate dvcrate medage [w=pop], covariance.

◁

By specifying the _coef option, you can use correlate to display the correlation or covariance matrix for the coefficients from the last fitted model. You may not specify a *varlist*, in *range*, or if *exp* since the sample was determined by the most recent estimation command. You may not specify a weight, either. If the most recent estimates were weighted, the correlation (covariance) matrix displayed is correctly weighted already.

▷ Example

The only possible forms of correlate with the _coef option are correlate, _coef and correlate, _coef covariance. Before you can use one of these two forms, you must fit a model—here we will use regression—but we emphasize that you can use correlate after any estimation procedure, even maximum likelihood procedures such as clogit, logistic, logit, ologit, and mlogit. We run a regression of mrgrate on medage and medage2, excluding Nevada from the data:

```
. use http://www.stata-press.com/data/r8/census6
(1980 Census data by state)

. regress mrgrate medage medage2 if state !="Nevada"
```

Source	SS	df	MS		Number of obs =	49
					F(2, 46) =	11.91
Model	.000179759	2	.00008988		Prob > F =	0.0001
Residual	.00034728	46	7.5496e-06		R-squared =	0.3411
					Adj R-squared =	0.3124
Total	.000527039	48	.00001098		Root MSE =	.00275

mrgrate	Coef.	Std. Err.	t	P>|t|	[95% Conf. Interval]	
medage	-.0041675	.0040848	-1.02	0.313	-.0123899	.0040548
medage2	.0000518	.0000692	0.75	0.459	-.0000876	.0001911
_cons	.0928522	.0602392	1.54	0.130	-.0284031	.2141075

To obtain the correlation matrix of the coefficients, we now type `correlate, _coef`:

```
. correlate, _coef
```

	medage	medage2	_cons
medage	1.0000		
medage2	-0.9984	1.0000	
_cons	-0.9983	0.9935	1.0000

The results show a large amount of collinearity among the explanatory variables.

We did not have to type the `correlate` command immediately after running the regression. We could have gone on to do other things—retrieving the residuals, plotting them, and so on—before requesting to see the correlation matrix. Stata never forgets the most recent estimates (unless you explicitly eliminate them by typing `discard`).

We can obtain the covariance matrix of the estimators by typing `correlate, _coef covariance`:

```
. correlate, _coef covariance
```

	medage	medage2	_cons
medage	.000017		
medage2	-2.8e-07	4.8e-09	
_cons	-.000246	4.1e-06	.003629

◁

pwcorr

`correlate` calculates correlation coefficients using casewise deletion: when you request correlations of variables $x_1, x_2, \ldots, x_k$, any observation for which any of $x_1, x_2, \ldots, x_k$ is missing is not used. Thus, if x_3 and x_4 have no missing values, but x_2 is missing for half the data, the correlation between x_3 and x_4 is calculated using only the half of the data for which x_2 is not missing. Of course, you can obtain the correlation between x_3 and x_4 using all the data by typing `correlate` x_3 x_4.

`pwcorr` makes obtaining such pairwise correlation coefficients easier.

▷ Example

Using the auto.dta, we investigate the correlation between several of the variables.

```
. use http://www.stata-press.com/data/r8/auto1
(Automobile Models)
. pwcorr mpg price rep78 foreign, obs sig
```

	mpg	price	rep78	foreign
mpg	1.0000			
	74			
price	-0.4594	1.0000		
	0.0000			
	74	74		
rep78	0.3739	0.0066	1.0000	
	0.0016	0.9574		
	69	69	69	
foreign	0.3613	0.0487	0.5922	1.0000
	0.0016	0.6802	0.0000	
	74	74	69	74

```
. pwcorr mpg price headroom rear_seat trunk rep78 foreign, print(.05) star(.01)
```

	mpg	price	headroom	rear_s~t	trunk	rep78	foreign
mpg	1.0000						
price	-0.4594*	1.0000					
headroom	-0.4220*		1.0000				
rear_seat	-0.5213*	0.4194*	0.5238*	1.0000			
trunk	-0.5703*	0.3143*	0.6620*	0.6480*	1.0000		
rep78	0.3739*					1.0000	
foreign	0.3613*		-0.2939	-0.2409	-0.3594*	0.5922*	1.0000

```
. pwcorr mpg price headroom rear_seat trunk rep78 foreign, print(.05) bon
```

	mpg	price	headroom	rear_s~t	trunk	rep78	foreign
mpg	1.0000						
price	-0.4594	1.0000					
headroom	-0.4220		1.0000				
rear_seat	-0.5213	0.4194	0.5238	1.0000			
trunk	-0.5703		0.6620	0.6480	1.0000		
rep78	0.3739					1.0000	
foreign	0.3613				-0.3594	0.5922	1.0000

◁

❑ Technical Note

The correlate command will report the correlation matrix of the data, but there are occasions when you need the matrix stored as a Stata matrix so you can further manipulate it. You can obtain it by typing

```
. matrix accum R = varlist, nocons dev
. matrix R = corr(R)
```

The first line places the cross-product matrix of the data in matrix R. The second line converts that to a correlation matrix. Also see [P] **matrix define** and [P] **matrix accum**.

❑

Saved Results

correlate saves in r():

Scalars

r(N)	number of observations	r(Var_1)	variance of first variable (covariance only)
r(rho)	ρ (first and second variables)	r(Var_2)	variance of second variable (covariance only)
r(cov_12)	covariance (covariance only)		

Note that pwcorr will leave in its wake only the results of the last call that it makes internally to correlate, for the correlation between the last variable and itself. Only rarely is this useful.

Methods and Formulas

pwcorr is implemented as an ado-file.

For a discussion of correlation, see, for instance, Snedecor and Cochran (1989, 177–195); for a more introductory explanation, see Edwards (1984).

According to Snedecor and Cochran (1989, 180), the term "co-relation" was first proposed by Galton (1888). The product-moment correlation coefficient is often called the Pearson product-moment correlation coefficient because Pearson (1896, 1898) was partially responsible for popularizing its use. See Stigler (1986) for information on the history of correlation.

The estimate of the product-moment correlation coefficient ρ is

$$\widehat{\rho} = \frac{\sum_{i=1}^{n} w_i (x_i - \overline{x})(y_i - \overline{y})}{\sqrt{\sum_{i=1}^{n} w_i (x_i - \overline{x})^2} \sqrt{\sum_{i=1}^{n} w_i (y_i - \overline{y})^2}}$$

where w_i are the weights if specified, or $w_i = 1$ if weights are not specified. $\overline{x} = (\sum w_i x_i)/(\sum w_i)$ is the mean of x, and $\overline{y}$ is similarly defined.

The unadjusted significance level is calculated by pwcorr as

$$p = 2 * \mathtt{ttail}(n - 2, \widehat{\rho}\sqrt{n-2}/\sqrt{1 - \widehat{\rho}^2})$$

Let v be the number of variables specified so that $k = v(v-1)/2$ correlation coefficients are to be estimated. If bonferroni is specified, the adjusted significance level is $p' = \min(1, kp)$. If sidak is specified, $p' = \min\left\{1, 1 - (1 - p)^n\right\}$. In both cases, see *Methods and Formulas* in [R] **oneway** for a more complete description of the logic behind these adjustments.

As for the correlation or covariance matrix of estimators, see the appropriate estimation command. When correlate is used after a maximum likelihood procedure, it obtains the covariance matrix from the inverse of the information matrix.

References

Edwards, A. L. 1984. *An Introduction to Linear Regression and Correlation.* 2d ed. New York: W. H. Freeman and Company.

Galton, F. 1888. Co-relations and their measurement, chiefly from anthropometric data. *Proceedings of the Royal Society of London* 45: 135–145.

Gleason, J. R. 1996. sg51: Inference about correlations using the Fisher z-transform. *Stata Technical Bulletin* 32: 13–18. Reprinted in *Stata Technical Bulletin Reprints*, vol. 6, pp. 121–128.

Goldstein, R. 1996. sg52: Testing dependent correlation coefficients. *Stata Technical Bulletin* 32: 18. Reprinted in *Stata Technical Bulletin Reprints*, vol. 6, pp. 128–129.

Pearson, K. 1896. Mathematical contributions to the theory of evolution.—III. Regression, heredity, and panmixia. *Philosophical Transactions of the Royal Society of London*, A, 187: 253–318.

Pearson, K. and L. N. G. Filon. 1898. Mathematical contributions to the theory of evolution.—IV. On the probable errors of frequency constants and on the influence of random selection on variation and correlation. *Philosophical Transactions of the Royal Society of London*, A, 191: 229–311.

Seed, P. T. 2001. sg159: Confidence intervals for correlations. *Stata Technical Bulletin* 59: 27–28. Reprinted in *Stata Technical Bulletin Reprints*, vol. 10, pp. 267–269.

Snedecor, G. W. and W. G. Cochran. 1989. *Statistical Methods*. 8th ed. Ames, IA: Iowa State University Press.

Stigler, S. M. 1986. *The History of Statistics*. Cambridge, MA: The Belknap Press of Harvard University Press.

Wolfe, F. 1997. sg64: pwcorrs: An enhanced correlation display. *Stata Technical Bulletin* 35: 22–25. Reprinted in *Stata Technical Bulletin Reprints*, vol. 6, pp. 163–167.

——. 1999. sg64.1: Update to pwcorrs. *Stata Technical Bulletin* 49: 17. Reprinted in *Stata Technical Bulletin Reprints*, vol. 9, p. 159.

Also See

Complementary:	[R] **matsize**, [R] **vce**
Related:	[R] **pcorr**, [R] **spearman**, [R] **summarize**

Title

count — Count observations satisfying specified condition

Syntax

<u>coun</u>t [if *exp*] [in *range*]

by . . . : may be used with count; see [R] **by**.

Description

count counts the number of observations that satisfy the specified conditions. If no conditions are specified, count displays the number of observations in the data.

Remarks

count may strike you as an almost useless command, but it can be one of Stata's handiest.

▷ Example

How many times have you obtained a statistical result and then asked yourself how it was possible? You think a moment, and then mutter aloud "Wait a minute. Is income ever *negative* in these data?" or "Is sex ever equal to *3*?" count can quickly answer those questions:

```
. count
    641
. count if income<0
      0
. count if sex==3
      1
. by division: count if sex==3
-> division=        1        1
-> division=        2        0
-> division=        3        0
```

We have 641 observations. income is never negative. sex, however, takes on the value 3 once. When we decompose the count by division, we see that it takes on that odd value in division 1.

◁

Saved Results

count saves in r():

Scalars

r(N)   number of observations

Also See

Related: [R] **tabulate**

Title

> **cross** — Form every pairwise combination of two datasets

Syntax

> cross using *filename*

Description

cross forms every pairwise combination of the data in memory with the data in *filename*. If *filename* is specified without a suffix, .dta is assumed.

Remarks

This is a rarely used command; also see [R] **joinby**, [R] **merge**, and [R] **append**.

Crossing refers to the operation of merging two datasets in every way possible. That is, the first observation of the data in memory is merged with every observation of *filename*, followed by the second, and so on. Thus, the result will have $N_1 N_2$ observations, where N_1 and N_2 are the number of observations in memory and in *filename*, respectively.

Typically, the datasets will have no common variables. If they do, such variables will take on only the values of the data in memory.

▷ Example

You wish to form a dataset containing all combinations of three age categories and two sexes to serve as a stub. The three age categories are 20, 30, and 40. The two sexes are male and female:

```
. input str6 sex

            sex
  1. male
  2. female
  3. end
. save sex
file sex.dta saved
. drop _all
. input agecat

         agecat
  1. 20
  2. 30
  3. 40
  4. end
. cross using sex
```

. list

	agecat	sex
1.	20	male
2.	30	male
3.	40	male
4.	20	female
5.	30	female
6.	40	female

◁

Methods and Formulas

cross is implemented as an ado-file.

Also See

Complementary:	[R] **save**
Related:	[R] **append**, [R] **fillin**, [R] **joinby**, [R] **merge**

Title

> **cumul** — Cumulative distribution

Syntax

> cumul *varname* [*weight*] [if *exp*] [in *range*] , generate(*newvar*) [freq]

by ... : may be used with cumul; see [R] **by**.

fweights and aweights are allowed; see [U] **14.1.6 weight**.

Description

> cumul creates *newvar* defined as the empirical cumulative distribution function (e.c.d.f.) of *varname*.

Options

> generate(*newvar*) is not optional. It specifies the name of the new variable to be created.

> freq specifies the cumulative be in frequency units; otherwise, it is normalized so that *newvar* is 1 for the largest value of *varname*.

Remarks

> ▷ Example

> cumul is most often used with graph to graph the empirical cumulative distribution. For instance, you have data on the median family income of 957 U.S. cities:

(Continued on next page)

238

```
. use http://www.stata-press.com/data/r8/hsng
(1980 Census housing data)

. cumul faminc, gen(cum)

. line cum faminc, sort ylab(, grid) ytitle("") xlab(, grid)
> title("Cumulative of median family income")
> subtitle("1980 Census, 957 U.S. Cities")
```

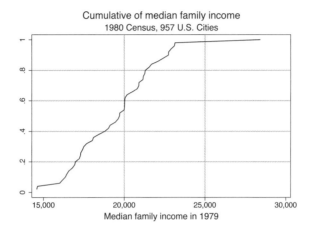

It would have been enough to type line cum faminc, sort, but we wanted to make the graph look better; see [G] **graph twoway line**.

If you had wanted a weighted cumulative, you would have typed cumul faminc [w=pop] at the first step.

◁

▷ Example

To graph two (or more) cumulatives on the same graph, use cumul and stack; see [R] **stack**. For instance, you have data on the average January and July temperature of 956 U.S. cities:

```
. use http://www.stata-press.com/data/r8/citytemp
(City Temperature Data)

. cumul tempjan, gen(cjan)

. cumul tempjuly, gen(cjuly)

. stack  cjan tempjan  cjuly tempjuly, into(c temp) wide clear

. line cjan cjuly temp, sort ylab(, grid) ytitle("") xlab(, grid)
> xtitle("Temperature (F)")
> title("Cumulatives:" "Average January and July Temperatures")
> subtitle("956 U.S. Cities") clstyle(. dot)
```

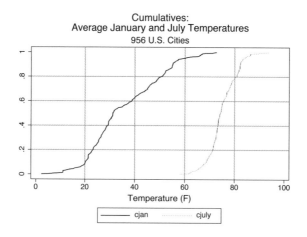

As before, it would have been enough to type `line cjan cjuly temp, sort`. See [R] **stack** for an explanation of how this works.

◁

□ Technical Note

According to Beniger and Robyn (1978), Fourier (1821) published the first graph of a cumulative frequency distribution, which was later given the name "ogive" by Galton (1875).

□

Methods and Formulas

`cumul` is implemented as an ado-file.

References

Beniger, J. R. and D. L. Robyn. 1978. Quantitative graphics in statistics: a brief history. *The American Statistician* 32: 1–11.

Clayton, D. and M. Hills. 1999. gr37: Cumulative distribution function plots. *Stata Technical Bulletin* 49: 10–12. Reprinted in *Stata Technical Bulletin Reprints*, vol. 9, pp. 96–98.

Cox, N. J. 1999. gr41: Distribution function plots. *Stata Technical Bulletin* 51: 12–16. Reprinted in *Stata Technical Bulletin Reprints*, vol. 9, pp. 108–112.

Fourier, J. B. J. 1821. Notions générales, sur la population. *Recherches Statistiques sur la Ville de Paris et le Département de la Seine* 1: 1–70.

Galton, F. 1875. Statistics by intercomparison, with remarks on the law of frequency of error. *Philosophical Magazine* 49: 33–46.

Wilk, M. B. and R. Gnanadesikan. 1968. Probability plotting methods for the analysis of data. *Biometrika* 55: 1–17.

Also See

Complementary:	[R] **stack**
Related:	[R] **diagnostic plots**, [R] **kdensity**
Background:	*Stata Graphics Reference Manual*

Title

cusum — Cusum plots and tests for binary variables

Syntax

cusum *yvar* *xvar* [if *exp*] [in *range*] [, yfit(*fitvar*) nograph nocalc

generate(*newvar*) plot(*plot*) *line_options* *twoway_options*]

Description

cusum graphs the cumulative sum (cusum) of a binary (0/1) variable *yvar* against a (usually) continuous variable *xvar*.

Options

yfit(*fitvar*) calculates a cusum against *fitvar*; that is, the running sums of the "residuals" *fitvar* minus *yvar*. Typically, *fitvar* is the predicted probability of a positive outcome obtained from a logistic regression analysis.

nograph suppresses the plot.

nocalc suppresses calculation of the cusum test statistics.

generate(*newvar*) saves the cusum in *newvar*.

plot(*plot*) provides a way to add other plots to the generated graph. See [G] *plot_option*.

line_options affect the rendition of the plotted line(s); see [G] **graph twoway line**.

twoway_options are any of the options documented in [G] *twoway_options*, excluding by(). These include options for titling the graph (see [G] *title_options*), and options for saving the graph to disk (see [G] *saving_option*).

Remarks

The cusum is the running sum of the proportion of ones in the sample, a constant number, minus *yvar*,

$$c_j = \sum_{k=1}^{j} f - yvar_{(k)}, \qquad 1 \le j \le N$$

where $f = (\sum yvar)/N$ and $yvar_{(k)}$ refers to the corresponding value of *yvar* when *xvar* is placed in ascending order: $xvar_{(k+1)} \ge xvar_{(k)}$. Tied values of *xvar* are broken at random. If you want them broken the same way in two runs, you must set the random number seed to the same value before giving the cusum command; see [R] **generate**.

A U-shaped or inverted U-shaped cusum indicates, respectively, a negative or a positive trend of *yvar* with *xvar*. A sinusoidal shape is evidence of a nonmonotonic (for example, quadratic) trend. cusum displays the maximum absolute cusum for monotonic and nonmonotonic trends of *yvar* on *xvar*. These are nonparametric tests of departure from randomness of *yvar* with respect to *xvar*. Approximate values for the tests are given.

242

▷ Example

For the automobile dataset, `auto.dta`, we wish to investigate the relationship between `foreign` (0 = domestic, 1 = foreign) and car weight as follows:

```
. use http://www.stata-press.com/data/r8/auto
(1978 Automobile Data)
. cusum foreign weight
```

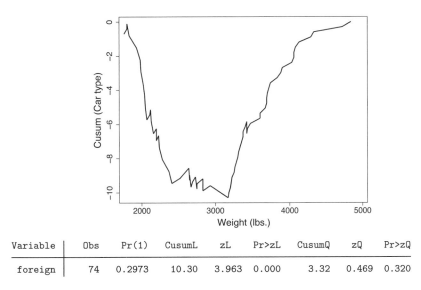

Variable	Obs	Pr(1)	CusumL	zL	Pr>zL	CusumQ	zQ	Pr>zQ
foreign	74	0.2973	10.30	3.963	0.000	3.32	0.469	0.320

The resulting plot, which is U-shaped, suggests a negative monotonic relationship. The trend is confirmed by a highly significant linear cusum statistic, labeled CusumL in the output above.

Some 29.73% of the cars are foreign (coded 1). The proportion of foreign cars diminishes with increasing weight. Stated crudely, the domestic cars are heavier than the foreign ones. We could have discovered that by typing `table foreign, stats(mean weight)`, but such an approach does not give the full picture of the relationship. The quadratic cusum (CusumQ) is not significant, so we do not suspect any tendency for the very heavy cars to be foreign rather than domestic. A slightly enhanced version of the plot shows the preponderance of domestic (coded 0) cars at the heavy end of the weight axis:

```
. label drop origin
. cusum foreign weight, c(none) mlabel(foreign) mlabp(0)
```

(Graph on next page)

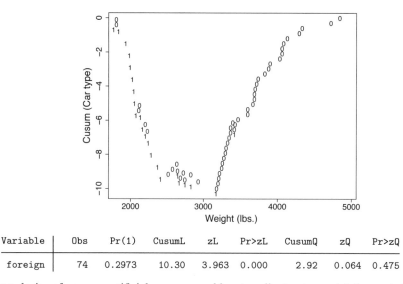

Variable	Obs	Pr(1)	CusumL	zL	Pr>zL	CusumQ	zQ	Pr>zQ
foreign	74	0.2973	10.30	3.963	0.000	2.92	0.064	0.475

The example is, of course, artificial, as we would not really try to model the probability of a car being foreign given its weight!

◁

Saved Results

cusum saves in r():

Scalars

r(N)	number of observations		r(P_zl)	*p*-value for test (linear)
r(prop1)	proportion of positive outcomes		r(cusumq)	quadratic cusum
r(cusuml)	cusum		r(zq)	test (quadratic)
r(zl)	test (linear)		r(P_zq)	*p*-value for test (quadratic)

Methods and Formulas

cusum is implemented as an ado-file.

Acknowledgment

cusum was written by Patrick Royston of the MRC Clinical Trials Unit, London.

References

Royston, P. 1992. The use of cusums and other techniques in modelling continuous covariates in logistic regression. *Statistics in Medicine* 11: 1115–1129.

——. 1993. sqv7: Cusum plots and tests for binary variables. *Stata Technical Bulletin* 12: 16–17. Reprinted in *Stata Technical Bulletin Reprints*, vol. 2, pp. 175–177.

Also See

Complementary: [R] **logistic**, [R] **logit**, [R] **probit**

Background: *Stata Graphics Reference Manual*

Title

> **data types** — Quick reference for data types

Description

This entry provides a quick reference for data types allowed by Stata. See [U] **15 Data** for details.

Remarks

Storage Type	Minimum	Maximum	Closest to 0 without being 0	bytes
byte	-127	100	± 1	1
int	$-32{,}767$	$32{,}740$	± 1	2
long	$-2{,}147{,}483{,}647$	$2{,}147{,}483{,}620$	± 1	4
float	$-1.70141173319 \times 10^{38}$	$1.70141173319 \times 10^{36}$	$\pm 10^{-36}$	4
double	$-8.9884656743 \times 10^{307}$	$8.9884656743 \times 10^{307}$	$\pm 10^{-323}$	8

Precision for float is 3.795×10^{-8}

Precision for double is 1.414×10^{-16}

String Storage Type	Maximum Length	Bytes	
str1	1	1	
str2	2	2	
...	.	.	
...	.	.	
...	.	.	
str80	80	80	*
...	.	.	
...	.	.	
...	.	.	
str244	244	244	

* strings larger than 80 are allowed only with Stata/SE.

Also See

Complementary:	[R] **compress**, [R] **destring**, [R] **encode**, [R] **format**, [R] **recast**
Background:	[U] **15.2.2 Numeric storage types**,
	[U] **15.4.4 String storage types**,
	[U] **15.5 Formats: controlling how data are displayed**,
	[U] **16.10 Precision and problems therein**

Title

db — Launch dialog

Syntax

db *commandname*

db *commandname* [, debug dryrun]

set maxdb # [, <u>permanently</u>]

where # must be between 5 and 1,000.

Description

db is the command-line way to launch a dialog for a Stata command.

The second syntax (which is the same but includes options) is for use by programmers.

If you wish to allow the launching of dialogs from a help file, see [P] **smcl** for information on the dialog SMCL directive.

set maxdb sets the maximum number of dialog boxes whose contents are remembered from one invocation to the next during a session. The default value of maxdb is 50.

Options

debug specifies that the underlying dialog box is to be loaded with debug messaging turned on.

dryrun specifies that, rather than launching the dialog, db is to show the commands it would issue to launch the dialog.

permanently specifies that, in addition to making the change right now, the maxdb setting will be remembered in the future and become the default setting for when you invoke Stata.

Remarks

The usual way to launch a dialog is to pull down Data, Graphics, or Statistics, and to make your selection from there. When you know the name of the command that you want to run, however, db provides a way to invoke the dialog from the command line.

db follows the same abbreviation rules that Stata's command-line interface follows. So, to launch the dialog for regress, you can type

    . db regress

or

    . db reg

Pretend that you use the dialog box for regress, either by pulling down **Statistics**, selecting *Linear regression and related*, and then selecting *Linear regression*; or by typing db regress. You fit a regression.

Much later during the session, you return to the regress dialog box. It will have the contents as you left them if (1) you have not typed clear between the first and second invocations; if (2) you have not typed discard between the two invocations; and if (3) you have used not more than 50 different dialog boxes—regardless of how many times you have used each—between the first and second invocations of regress. Use 51 or more and the contents of the regress dialog box will have been forgotten.

set maxdb determines how many different dialog boxes are remembered. A dialog box takes on average about 20k of memory, so the 50 default corresponds to allowing dialog boxes to consume about 1 megabyte of memory.

Also See

Related: [R] **which**

                      [P] **findfile**, [P] **smcl**

Complementary: [R] **set**

Title

> **describe** — Describe contents of data in memory or on disk

Syntax

> <u>d</u>escribe [*varlist*] [, <u>s</u>hort <u>d</u>etail <u>f</u>ullnames <u>n</u>umbers]
>
> <u>d</u>escribe [*varlist*] using *filename* [, <u>s</u>hort <u>d</u>etail <u>varl</u>ist]
>
> ds [*varlist*] [, <u>a</u>lpha <u>v</u>arwidth(*#*) <u>s</u>kip(*#*)]
>
> lookfor *string* [*string* [...]]

Description

describe produces a summary of the contents of the dataset in memory or of the data stored in a Stata-format dataset.

ds lists variable names in a compact format.

lookfor helps in finding variables by searching for *string* among all variable names and labels.

The *varlist* in the describe using syntax differs from standard Stata varlists in two ways. You cannot abbreviate variable names; that is, you have to type displacement rather than displ. Also, you may not refer to a range of variables; e.g., price-trunk.

Options

short suppresses the specific information for each variable. Only the general information (number of observations, number of variables, size, and sort order) is displayed.

detail includes information on the width of a single observation, the maximum number of observations holding the number of variables constant, the maximum number of variables holding the number of observations constant, the maximum width for a single observation, and the maximum size of the dataset.

fullnames specifies that describe is to display the full name of the variables. The default is to present an abbreviation when the variable name is longer than 15 characters. describe using always shows the full names of the variables, so fullnames may not be specified with describe using.

numbers specifies that describe is to present the variable number with the variable name. If numbers is specified, variable names are abbreviated when the name is longer than 8 characters. Options numbers and fullnames may not be specified together. numbers may not be specified with describe using.

(Continued on next page)

varlist (describe using only), an option for programmers, specifies that, in addition to the usual saved results, r(varlist) and r(sortlist) are to be saved, too. r(varlist) will contain the names of the variables in the dataset. r(sortlist) will contain the names of the variables by which the data are sorted.

With the possibility of truly large datasets that can be created by Stata/SE, it is possible that there might be too many variables in a dataset for their names to be stored in r(varlist), given the current maximum length of macros, as determined by set maxvar. Should that occur, describe using will issue the error message "too many variables", r(103).

alpha (ds only) specifies that the variables are listed in alphabetic order.

varwidth(#) (ds only) specifies the display width of the variable names. # defaults to 12.

skip(#) (ds only) specifies the number of spaces between variables. # defaults to 2.

Remarks

describe

If describe is typed without any operands, then the contents of the dataset currently in memory are described.

▷ Example

The basic description includes some general information on the number of variables and observations, along with a description of every variable in the dataset:

```
. use http://www.stata-press.com/data/r8/states
(State data)

. describe, numbers
Contains data from http://www.stata-press.com/data/r8/states.dta
  obs:            50                          State data
 vars:             5                          6 Jul 2002 17:39
 size:         1,300 (99.7% of memory free)   (_dta has notes)

              storage  display    value
variable name   type   format     label     variable label

1. state       str8    %9s
2. region      int     %8.0g      reg       Census Region
3. median~e    float   %9.0g                Median Age
4. marria~e    long    %12.0g               Marriages per 100,000
5. divorc~e    long    %12.0g               Divorces per 100,000

Sorted by:  region
```

In this example, the dataset in memory came from the file states.dta, and contains 50 observations on 5 variables. This dataset occupies only a small portion of the available memory, leaving 99.7% of memory free. The dataset is labeled "State data", and was last modified on July 6, 2002 at 17:39 (5:39 p.m.). The "_dta has notes" indicates that a note is attached to the dataset; see [U] **15.7 Notes attached to data**.

The first variable is named state. It is stored as a str8, and has a display format of %9s.

The next variable, region, is stored as an int and has a display format of %8.0g. This variable has associated with it a *value label* called reg, and the variable is labeled Census Region.

The third variable, which is abbreviated median~e, is stored as a float, has a display format of %9.0g, has no value label, and has a variable label of Median Age. The variables that are abbreviated marria~e and divorc~e are both stored as longs, and have display formats of %12.0g. These last two variables are labeled Marriages per 100,000 and Divorces per 100,000, respectively.

The data are sorted by region.

Since we specified the numbers option, the variables are numbered; e.g., region is variable 2 in this dataset.

◁

▷ Example

To view the full variable names, we could omit the numbers option and specify the fullnames option.

```
. describe, fullnames
Contains data from http://www.stata-press.com/data/r8/states.dta
    obs:          50                           State data
   vars:           5                           6 Jul 2002 17:39
   size:       1,300 (99.7% of memory free)    (_dta has notes)

                storage  display    value
variable name    type    format     label     variable label

state           str8    %9s
region          int     %8.0g       reg       Census Region
median_age      float   %9.0g                 Median Age
marriage_rate   long    %12.0g                Marriages per 100,000
divorce_rate    long    %12.0g                Divorces per 100,000

Sorted by:  region
```

In this case, we did not need to specify the fullnames option to see the unabbreviated variable names since the longest variable name is 13 characters. Omitting the numbers option results in 15-character variable names being displayed.

◁

❑ Technical Note

The above describe listing also shows that the size of the dataset is 1,300. In case you are curious,

$$\{(8 + 2 + 4 + 4 + 4) + 4\} \times 50 = 1300$$

The 8, 2, 4, 4, and 4 are the storage requirements for a str8, int, float, long, and long, respectively; see [U] **15.2.2 Numeric storage types**. The extra 4 is needed for pointers, etc. The 50 is the number of observations in the dataset.

❑

▷ Example

If you specify the `short` option, only general information about the data is presented:

```
. describe, short
Contains data from http://www.stata-press.com/data/r8/states.dta
  obs:            50                          State data
  vars:            5                          6 Jul 2002 17:39
  size:        1,300 (99.7% of memory free)
Sorted by:  region
```
◁

If you specify a *varlist*, only the variables in that *varlist* are described.

▷ Example

The `detail` option is useful for determining how many observations or variables you can add to your dataset:

```
. describe, detail
Contains data from http://www.stata-press.com/data/r8/states.dta
  obs:            50 (max=       34,869)      State data
  vars:            5 (max=        2,047)      6 Jul 2002 17:39
  width:          22 (max=        8,192)
  size:        1,300 (max=    1,046,728)          (_dta has notes)
```

variable name	storage type	display format	value label	variable label
state	str8	%9s		
region	int	%8.0g	reg	Census Region
median_age	float	%9.0g		Median Age
marriage_rate	long	%12.0g		Marriages per 100,000
divorce_rate	long	%12.0g		Divorces per 100,000

```
Sorted by:  region
```

If you did not increase the number of variables in this dataset, you could have a maximum of 34,869 observations. The maximum number of variables is 2,047, which is the maximum for Intercooled Stata. The 8,192 is the maximum width allowed by Intercooled Stata. The 1,046,728 is the maximum size for the dataset. The maximum dataset size could possibly be increased, since many operating systems allow you to change the size of memory; see [U] **7 Setting the size of memory** and [R] **memory**.
◁

▷ Example

Let's change datasets. The `describe` *varlist* command is particularly useful when combined with the '*' abbreviation character. For instance, we can describe all the variables whose names start with pop by typing `describe pop*`:

(Continued on next page)

```
. use http://www.stata-press.com/data/r8/census
(1980 Census data by state)
. describe pop*
```

variable name	storage type	display format	value label	variable label
pop	long	%12.0gc		Population
poplt5	long	%12.0gc		Pop, < 5 year
pop5_17	long	%12.0gc		Pop, 5 to 17 years
pop18p	long	%12.0gc		Pop, 18 and older
pop65p	long	%12.0gc		Pop, 65 and older
popurban	long	%12.0gc		Urban population

We can describe the variables state, region, and pop18p by specifying them:

```
. describe state region pop18p
```

variable name	storage type	display format	value label	variable label
state	str14	%-14s		State
region	int	%-8.0g	cenreg	Census region
pop18p	long	%12.0gc		Pop, 18 and older

◁

Typing describe using *filename* describes the data stored in *filename*. If an extension is not specified, .dta is assumed.

▷ Example

We can describe the contents of states.dta without disturbing the data we currently have in memory by typing

```
. describe using http://www.stata-press.com/data/r8/states
```

```
Contains data                         State data
    obs:            50                6 Jul 2002 17:39
   vars:             5
   size:         1,300
```

variable name	storage type	display format	value label	variable label
state	str8	%9s		
region	int	%8.0g	reg	Census Region
median_age	float	%9.0g		Median Age
marriage_rate	long	%12.0g		Marriages per 100,000
divorce_rate	long	%12.0g		Divorces per 100,000

```
Sorted by:  region
```

◁

ds

If ds is typed without any operands, then a compact list of the variable names for the data currently in memory is displayed.

▷ Example

ds can be especially useful if you have a dataset with over 1,000 variables, but you may find it convenient even if you have considerably fewer variables.

```
. ds
fips      hhsamp    hh10t19   hh20t29   hh30t39   hh40t49   hh50txx   medhhinc
medfinc   famsamp   femfam    rnkhhinc  mincpc    povfam    povfamf   povper
povperd   povchld   povchldd  genrev    igrev     igrevfs   cgtaxes   cgptaxes
cgstaxes
```

◁

▷ Example

You might wonder why you would ever specify a *varlist* with this command. Remember that a *varlist* understands the '*' abbreviation character and the '−' dash notation; see [U] **14.4 varlists**.

```
. ds p*
povfam    povfamf   povper    povperd   povchld   povchldd

. ds povfam-cgtaxes
povfam    povfamf   povper    povperd   povchld   povchldd  genrev    igrev
igrevfs   cgtaxes
```

◁

▷ Example

Since the primary use of ds is to inspect the names of variables, it is sometimes useful to let ds display the variable names in alphabetical order.

```
. ds, alpha
cgptaxes      cgstaxes      cgtaxes       famsamp       femsam
fips          genrev        hh10t19       hh20t29       hh30t39
hh40t49       hh50txx       hhsamp        igrev         igrevfs
medfinc       medhhinc      mincpc        povfam        povfamf
povper        povperd       pvchld        pvchldd       rnkhhinc
```

◁

lookfor

▷ Example

lookfor finds variables by searching for *string*, ignoring case, among the variable names and labels.

```
. lookfor tax
```

variable name	storage type	display format	value label	variable label
cgtaxes	long	%12.0gc		Taxes of city government
cgptaxes	long	%12.0gc		Property taxes of city government
cgstaxes	long	%12.0gc		Sales taxes of city government

```
. lookfor median
```

variable name	storage type	display format	value label	variable label
medhhinc	long	%12.0gc		Median household income 1979
medfinc	long	%12.0gc		Median family money income
rnkhhinc	int	%8.0g		Rank of median household income

lookfor median found rnkhhinc because the word median was in the variable label.

◁

▷ Example

If multiple strings are specified, variable names or labels containing any of the strings are listed.

```
. lookfor median tax
```

variable name	storage type	display format	value label	variable label
medhhinc	long	%12.0gc		Median household income 1979
medfinc	long	%12.0gc		Median family money income
rnkhhinc	int	%8.0g		Rank of median household income
cgtaxes	long	%12.0gc		Taxes of city government
cgptaxes	long	%12.0gc		Property taxes of city government
cgstaxes	long	%12.0gc		Sales taxes of city government

◁

Saved Results

describe saves in r():

Scalars

r(N)	number of observations	r(k_max)	maximum number of variables
r(k)	number of variables	r(widthmax)	maximum width of dataset
r(width)	width of dataset	r(changed)	data-have-changed-since-last-saved flag
r(N_max)	maximum number of observations		

Macros

r(varlist)	variables in dataset (describe using, varlist only)	r(sortlist)	variables by which data are sorted (describe using, varlist only)

ds saves in r():

Macros

r(varlist)   the varlist in the order displayed

lookfor saves in r():

Macros

r(varlist)   the varlist of found variables

Methods and Formulas

ds and lookfor are implemented as ado-files.

References

Cox, N. J. 1999. dm67: Numbers of missing and present values. *Stata Technical Bulletin* 49: 7–8. Reprinted in *Stata Technical Bulletin Reprints*, vol. 9, pp. 26–27.

——. 2000. dm78: Describing variables in memory. *Stata Technical Bulletin* 56: 2–4. Reprinted in *Stata Technical Bulletin Reprints*, vol. 10, pp. 15–17.

——. 2001a. dm67.1: Enhancements to numbers of missing and present values. *Stata Technical Bulletin* 60: 2–3. Reprinted in *Stata Technical Bulletin Reprints*, vol. 10, pp. 7–9.

——. 2001b. dm78.1: Describing variables in memory: update to Stata 7. *Stata Technical Bulletin* 60: 3. Reprinted in *Stata Technical Bulletin Reprints*, vol. 10, p. 17.

Gleason, J. R. 1998. dm61: A tool for exploring Stata datasets (Windows and Macintosh only). *Stata Technical Bulletin* 45: 2–5. Reprinted in *Stata Technical Bulletin Reprints*, vol. 8, pp. 22–27.

——. 1999. dm61.1: Update to varxplor. *Stata Technical Bulletin* 51: 2. Reprinted in *Stata Technical Bulletin Reprints*, vol. 9, p. 15.

Also See

Complementary:	[R] **compress**, [R] **format**, [R] **label**, [R] **notes**, [R] **order**, [R] **rename**
Related:	[R] **cf**, [R] **codebook**, [R] **compare**
Background:	[U] **7 Setting the size of memory**, [U] **15 Data**, [R] **memory**

Title

destring — Change string variables to numeric

Syntax

destring [*varlist*] , { g̲enerate(*newvarlist*) | replace } [i̲gnore("*chars*") force

float percent]

Description

destring converts variables in *varlist* from string to numeric. If *varlist* is not specified, destring will attempt to convert all variables in the dataset from string to numeric. Characters listed in ignore() are removed. Variables in *varlist* that are already numeric will not be changed. destring treats both empty strings "" and "." as indicating sysmiss (.), and interprets the strings ".a", ".b", ..., ".z" as the extended missing values .a, .b, ..., .z. Note that destring also ignores any leading or trailing spaces so that, for example, " " is equivalent to "" and " . " is equivalent to ".".

Options

Either generate() or replace must be specified. With either option, if any string variable contains nonnumeric values not specified with ignore(), then no corresponding variable will be generated, nor will that variable be replaced, unless force is specified.

generate(*newvarlist*) specifies that a new variable is to be created for each variable in *varlist*. *newvarlist* must contain the same number of new variable names as there are variables in *varlist*. If *varlist* is not specified, destring attempts to generate a numeric variable for each variable in the dataset; *newvarlist* must then contain the same number of new variable names as there are variables in the dataset.

Any variable labels or characteristics will be copied to the new variables created.

replace specifies that the variables in *varlist* should be converted to numeric variables. If *varlist* is not specified, destring attempts to convert all variables from string to numeric.

Any variable labels or characteristics will be retained.

ignore("*chars*") specifies nonnumeric characters to be removed. If any string variable contains any nonnumeric characters other than those specified with ignore(), no action will take place for that variable unless force is also specified.

force specifies that any string values containing nonnumeric characters, in addition to any specified with ignore(), are treated as indicating missing numeric values.

float specifies that any new numeric variables should be created initially as type float. The default is type double. destring attempts automatically to compress each new numeric variable after creation.

percent is to be used with percent variables. If any percent signs are found in the values of a variable, they are removed and all values of that variable are divided by 100 to convert it to fractional form. percent by itself implies that the percent sign "%" is an argument to ignore(), but the converse is not true.

257

Remarks

▷ Example

You read in a dataset, but somehow all variables were created as strings. The variables do not contain any nonnumeric characters, and you want to convert them all from string to numeric data types.

```
. use http://www.stata-press.com/data/r8/destring1
. describe id num code total income
```

variable name	storage type	display format	value label	variable label
id	str3	%9s		
num	str3	%9s		
code	str4	%9s		
total	str5	%9s		
income	str5	%9s		

```
. list
```

	id	num	code	total	income
1.	111	243	1234	543	23423
2.	111	123	2345	67854	12654
3.	111	234	3456	345	43658
4.	222	345	4567	57	23546
5.	333	456	5678	23	21432
6.	333	567	6789	23465	12987
7.	333	678	7890	65	9823
8.	444	789	8976	23	32980
9.	444	901	7654	23	18565
10.	555	890	6543	423	19234

```
. destring, replace
id has all characters numeric; replaced as int
num has all characters numeric; replaced as int
code has all characters numeric; replaced as int
total has all characters numeric; replaced as long
income has all characters numeric; replaced as long
. describe id num code total income
```

variable name	storage type	display format	value label	variable label
id	int	%10.0g		
num	int	%10.0g		
code	int	%10.0g		
total	long	%10.0g		
income	long	%10.0g		

(Continued on next page)

```
. list
```

	id	num	code	total	income
1.	111	243	1234	543	23423
2.	111	123	2345	67854	12654
3.	111	234	3456	345	43658
4.	222	345	4567	57	23546
5.	333	456	5678	23	21432
6.	333	567	6789	23465	12987
7.	333	678	7890	65	9823
8.	444	789	8976	23	32980
9.	444	901	7654	23	18565
10.	555	890	6543	423	19234

◁

▷ Example

Your dataset contains the variable `date`, which was accidentally recorded as a string because of spaces after the year and month. You want to remove the spaces. `destring` will convert it to numeric and remove the spaces.

```
. use http://www.stata-press.com/data/r8/destring2
. describe date
```

variable name	storage type	display format	value label	variable label
date	str14	%10s		

```
. list date
```

	date
1.	1999 12 10
2.	2000 07 08
3.	1997 03 02
4.	1999 09 00
5.	1998 10 04
6.	2000 03 28
7.	2000 08 08
8.	1997 10 20
9.	1998 01 16
10.	1999 11 12

```
. destring date, replace ignore(" ")
date: characters space removed; replaced as long
. describe date
```

variable name	storage type	display format	value label	variable label
date	long	%10.0g		

```
. list date
```

	date
1.	19991210
2.	20000708
3.	19970302
4.	19990900
5.	19981004
6.	20000328
7.	20000808
8.	19971020
9.	19980116
10.	19991112

◁

▷ Example

Your dataset contains the variables `date`, `price`, and `percent`. These variables were accidentally read into Stata as string variables because they contain spaces, dollar signs, commas, and percent signs. You want to remove all of these characters and create new variables for `date`, `price`, and `percent` containing numeric values. After removing the percent sign, you want to convert the variable `percent` to decimal form.

```
. use http://www.stata-press.com/data/r8/destring2, clear
. describe date price percent
```

variable name	storage type	display format	value label	variable label
date	str14	%10s		
price	str11	%11s		
percent	str3	%9s		

```
. list date price percent
```

	date	price	percent
1.	1999 12 10	$2,343.68	34%
2.	2000 07 08	$7,233.44	86%
3.	1997 03 02	$12,442.89	12%
4.	1999 09 00	$233,325.31	6%
5.	1998 10 04	$1,549.23	76%
6.	2000 03 28	$23,517.03	35%
7.	2000 08 08	$2.43	69%
8.	1997 10 20	$9,382.47	32%
9.	1998 01 16	$289,209.32	45%
10.	1999 11 12	$8,282.49	1%

```
. destring date price percent, generate(date2 price2 percent2) ignore("$ ,%") percent
date: characters space removed; date2 generated as long
price: characters $ , removed; price2 generated as double
percent: characters % removed; percent2 generated as double
```

```
. describe date date2 price price2 percent percent2
                  storage  display   value
    variable name   type   format    label      variable label

    date            str14   %10s
    date2           long    %10.0g
    price           str11   %11s
    price2          double  %10.0g
    percent         str3    %9s
    percent2        byte    %10.0g
. list date date2 price price2 percent percent2
```

	date	date2	price	price2	percent	percent2
1.	1999 12 10	19991210	$2,343.68	2343.68	34%	.34
2.	2000 07 08	20000708	$7,233.44	7233.44	86%	.86
3.	1997 03 02	19970302	$12,442.89	12442.89	12%	.12
4.	1999 09 00	19990900	$233,325.31	233325.31	6%	.06
5.	1998 10 04	19981004	$1,549.23	1549.23	76%	.76
6.	2000 03 28	20000328	$23,517.03	23517.03	35%	.35
7.	2000 08 08	20000808	$2.43	2.43	69%	.69
8.	1997 10 20	19971020	$9,382.47	9382.47	32%	.32
9.	1998 01 16	19980116	$289,209.32	289209.32	45%	.45
10.	1999 11 12	19991112	$8,282.49	8282.49	1%	.01

◁

Saved characteristics

Each time the destring command is issued, an entry will be made in the characteristics list of each converted variable. You can type char list to view these characteristics.

After the last example given above, we could use char list to find out what characters were removed by the destring command.

```
. char list
date2[destring]:      Characters removed were:  space
price2[destring]:     Characters removed were:  $ ,
percent2[destring]:   Characters removed were:  %
```

Acknowledgment

destring was originally written by Nicholas J. Cox of the University of Durham, U.K.

References

Cox, N. J. 1999a. dm45.1: Changing string variables to numeric: update. *Stata Technical Bulletin* 49: 2. Reprinted in *Stata Technical Bulletin Reprints*, vol. 9, p. 14.

——. 1999b. dm45.2: Changing string variables to numeric: correction. *Stata Technical Bulletin* 52: 2. Reprinted in *Stata Technical Bulletin Reprints*, vol. 9, p. 14.

Cox, N. J. and W. W. Gould. 1997. dm45: Changing string variables to numeric. *Stata Technical Bulletin* 37: 4–6. Reprinted in *Stata Technical Bulletin Reprints*, vol. 7, pp. 34–37.

Cox, N. J. and J. B. Wernow. 2000a. dm80: Changing numeric variables to string. *Stata Technical Bulletin* 56: 8. Reprinted in *Stata Technical Bulletin Reprints*, vol. 10, pp. 24–28.

——. 2000b. dm80.1: Update to changing numeric variables to string. *Stata Technical Bulletin* 57: 2. Reprinted in *Stata Technical Bulletin Reprints*, vol. 10, pp. 28–29.

Also See

Complementary: [R] **generate**

Related: [R] **egen**, [R] **encode**, [R] **functions**

Title

> **diagnostic plots** — Distributional diagnostic plots

Syntax

> symplot *varname* [if *exp*] [in *range*] [, *common_options*]
>
> quantile *varname* [if *exp*] [in *range*] [, *common_options*]
>
> qnorm *varname* [if *exp*] [in *range*] [, <u>g</u>rid *common_options*]
>
> pnorm *varname* [if *exp*] [in *range*] [, <u>g</u>rid *common_options*]
>
> qchi *varname* [if *exp*] [in *range*] [, df(*#*) <u>g</u>rid *common_options*]
>
> pchi *varname* [if *exp*] [in *range*] [, df(*#*) <u>g</u>rid *common_options*]
>
> qqplot *varname₁* *varname₂* [if *exp*] [in *range*] [, *common_options*]

where *common_options* are plot(*plot*), rlopts(*line_options*), *scatter_options*, and *twoway_options*.

Description

symplot graphs a symmetry plot of *varname*.

quantile plots the ordered values of *varname* against the quantiles of a uniform distribution.

qnorm plots the quantiles of *varname* against the quantiles of the normal distribution (Q–Q plot).

pnorm graphs a standardized normal probability plot (P–P plot).

qchi plots the quantiles of *varname* against the quantiles of a χ^2 distribution (Q–Q plot).

pchi graphs a χ^2 probability plot (P–P plot).

qqplot plots the quantiles of *varname₁* against the quantiles of *varname₂* (Q–Q plot).

See [R] **regression diagnostics** for regression diagnostic plots and [R] **logistic** for logistic regression diagnostic plots.

Options

grid adds grid lines at the .05, .10, .25, .50, .75, .90, and .95 quantiles when specified with qnorm or qchi. With pnorm and pchi, grid is equivalent to yline(.25,.5,.75) xline(.25,.5,.75).

df(*#*) specifies the degrees of freedom of the χ^2 distribution. The default is 1.

plot(*plot*) provides a way to add other plots to the generated graph. See [G] *plot_option*.

rlopts(*line_options*) affect the rendition of the reference line; see [G] **graph twoway line**.

scatter_options affect the rendition of the plotted points; see [G] **graph twoway scatter**.

twoway_options are any of the options documented in [G] *twoway_options*, excluding by(). These include options for titling the graph (see [G] *title_options*), and options for saving the graph to disk (see [G] *saving_option*).

Remarks

▷ Example

You have data on 74 automobiles. To make a symmetry plot of the variable price, type

```
. use http://www.stata-press.com/data/r8/auto
(1978 Automobile Data)

. symplot price
```

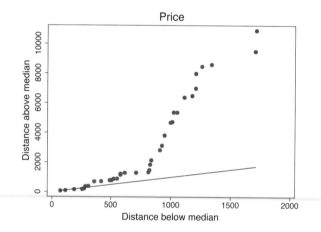

All points would lie along the reference line (defined as $y = x$) if car prices were symmetrically distributed. The points in this plot lie above the reference line, indicating that the distribution of car prices is skewed to the right—the most expensive cars are far more expensive than the least expensive cars are inexpensive.

The logic works as follows: A variable z is distributed symmetrically if

$$\text{median} - z_{(i)} = z_{(N+1-i)} - \text{median}$$

where $z_{(i)}$ indicates the ith order statistic of z. symplot graphs $y_i = \text{median} - z_{(i)}$ versus $x_i = z_{(N+1-i)} - \text{median}$.

For instance, consider the largest and smallest values of price in the example above. The most expensive car costs \$15,906, and the least expensive \$3,291. Let's compare these two cars with the typical car in the data, and see how much more it costs to buy the most expensive car, and compare that with how much less it costs to buy the least expensive car. If the automobile price distribution is symmetric, the price differences would be the same.

Before we can make this comparison, we must agree on a definition for the word "typical". Let's agree that "typical" means median. The price of the median car is \$5,006.50, so the most expensive car costs \$10,899.50 more than the median car, and the least expensive car costs \$1,715.50 less than the median car. We now have one piece of evidence that the car price distribution is not symmetric. We can repeat the experiment for the second most expensive car and the second least expensive car.

We find that the second most expensive car costs \$9,494.50 more than the median car, and the second least expensive car costs \$1,707.50 less than the median car. We now have more evidence. We can continue doing this with the third most expensive and the third least expensive, and so on.

Once we have all these numbers, we want to compare each pair and ask how similar, on average, they are. The easiest way to do that is to plot all the pairs.

◁

▷ Example

You have data on the prices of 74 automobiles. To make a quantile plot of `price`, type

```
. use http://www.stata-press.com/data/r8/auto
(1978 Automobile Data)

. quantile price, rlopts(clpattern(dash))
```

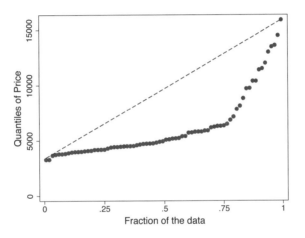

We changed the pattern of the reference line by specifying `rlopts(clpattern(dash))`.

In a quantile plot, each value of the variable is plotted against the fraction of the data that has values less than it. The diagonal line is a reference line. If automobile prices were rectangularly distributed, then all the data would be plotted along the line. Since all the points are below the reference line, we know that the price distribution is skewed right.

◁

▷ Example

Continuing with our price data on 74 automobiles, you now wish to compare the distribution of `price` with the normal distribution:

(Continued on next page)

```
. qnorm price, grid ylabel(, angle(horizontal) axis(1))
> ylabel(, angle(horizontal) axis(2))
```

Grid lines are 5, 10, 25, 50, 75, 90, and 95 percentiles

The result shows that the distributions are quite different.

◁

❏ Technical Note

The idea behind qnorm is recommended strongly by Miller (1997): he calls it probit plotting. His recommendations from much practical experience should interest many users. "My recommendation for detecting nonnormality is *probit plotting*" (Miller 1997, 10). "If a deviation from normality cannot be spotted by eye on probit paper, it is not worth worrying about. I never use the Kolmogorov–Smirnov test (or one of its cousins) or the χ^2 test as a preliminary test of normality. They do not tell you how the sample is differing from normality, and I have a feeling they are more likely to detect irregularities in the middle of the distribution than in the tails" (Miller 1997, 13–14).

❏

▷ Example

Quantile–normal plots emphasize the tails of the distribution. Normal probability plots put the focus on the center of the distribution:

(Continued on next page)

```
. pnorm price, grid
```

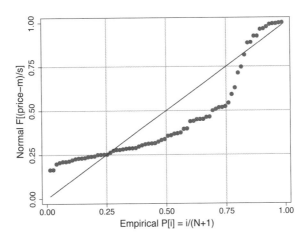

> Example

You have data on the weight and country of manufacture of 74 automobiles. You wish to compare the distributions of weights for domestic and foreign automobiles:

```
. use http://www.stata-press.com/data/r8/auto
(1978 Automobile Data)
. generate weightd=weight if !foreign
(22 missing values generated)
. generate weightf=weight if foreign
(52 missing values generated)
. qqplot weightd weightf
```

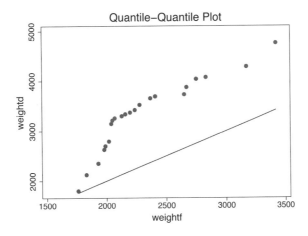

▷ Example

Suppose that we want to examine the distribution of the sum of squares of `price` and `mpg`, standardized for their variances.

```
. egen c1 = std(price)
. egen c2 = std(mpg)
. generate ch = c1^2 + c2^2
. qchi ch, df(2) grid ylabel(, alt axis(2)) xlabel(, alt axis(2))
```

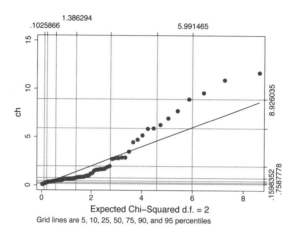

The quadratic form is clearly not χ^2 with 2 degrees of freedom.

◁

▷ Example

We can focus on the center of the distribution by doing a probability plot:

```
. pchi ch, df(2) grid
```

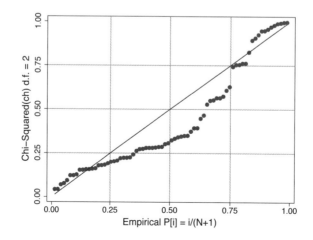

◁

Methods and Formulas

`symplot`, `quantile`, `qnorm`, `pnorm`, `qchi`, `pchi`, and `qqplot` are implemented as ado-files. Let $x_{(1)}$, $x_{(2)}$, ..., $x_{(N)}$ be the data sorted in ascending order.

If a continuous variable x has a cumulative distribution function $F(x) = P(X \leq x) = p$, the quantiles x_{p_i} are such that $F(x_{p_i}) = p_i$. For example, if $p_i = 0.5$, $x_{0.5}$ is the median. When plotting data, the probabilities p_i are often referred to as plotting positions. There are many different conventions for choice of plotting positions, given $x_{(1)} \leq \ldots \leq x_{(N)}$. Most belong to the family $(i-a)/(N-2a+1)$. $a = 0.5$ (suggested by Hazen) and $a = 0$ (suggested by Weibull) are popular choices.

`symplot` plots $\text{median} - x_{(i)}$ versus $x_{(N+1-i)} - \text{median}$.

`quantile` plots $x_{(i)}$ versus $(i-0.5)/N$ (the Hazen position).

`qnorm` plots $x_{(i)}$ against q_i, where $q_i = \Phi^{-1}(p_i)$, Φ is the cumulative normal distribution, and $p_i = i/(N+1)$ (the Weibull position).

`pnorm` plots $\Phi\{(x_i - \widehat{\mu})/\widehat{\sigma}\}$ versus $p_i = i/(N+1)$, where $\widehat{\mu}$ is the mean of the data and $\widehat{\sigma}$ is the standard deviation.

`qchi` and `pchi` are similar to `qnorm` and `pnorm`; the cumulative χ^2 distribution is used in place of the cumulative normal distribution.

`qqplot` is just a two-way scatterplot of one variable against the other after both variables have been sorted into ascending order, and both variables have the same number of nonmissing observations. If the variables have unequal numbers of nonmissing observations, interpolated values of the variable with more data are plotted against the variable with less.

Acknowledgments

We would like to thank Peter A. Lachenbruch of the Food and Drug Administration (FDA) for writing the original version of `qchi` and `pchi`. Patrick Royston of the MRC Clinical Trials Unit in London also published a very similar command in the *Stata Technical Bulletin* (Royston 1996).

References

Chambers, J. M., W. S. Cleveland, B. Kleiner, and P. A. Tukey. 1983. *Graphical Methods for Data Analysis*. Belmont, CA: Wadsworth International Group.

Cox, N. J. 1999. gr42: Quantile plots, generalized. *Stata Technical Bulletin* 51: 16–18. Reprinted in *Stata Technical Bulletin Reprints*, vol. 9, pp. 113–116.

——. 2001. gr42.1: Quantile plots, generalized: update to Stata 7. *Stata Technical Bulletin* 61: 10. Reprinted in *Stata Technical Bulletin Reprints*, vol. 10, pp. 55–56.

Daniel, C. and F. S. Wood. 1980. *Fitting Equations to Data*. 2d ed. New York: John Wiley & Sons.

Gan, F. F., K. J. Koehler, and J. C. Thompson. 1991. Probability plots and distribution curves for assessing the fit of probability models. *The American Statistician* 45: 14–21.

Hamilton, L. C. 1992. *Regression with Graphics*, 10–17. Pacific Grove, CA: Brooks/Cole Publishing Company.

——. 2002. *Statistics with Stata*. Belmont, CA: Duxbury.

Hoaglin, D. C. 1985. Using quantiles to study shape. In *Exploring Data Tables, Trends, and Shapes*, ed. D. C. Hoaglin, F. Mosteller, and J. W. Tukey, 417–460. New York: John Wiley & Sons.

Miller, R. G., Jr. 1997. *Beyond ANOVA: Basics of Applied Statistics*. London: Chapman & Hall.

Nolan, D. and T. Speed. 2000. *Stat Labs: Mathematical Statistics through Applications*. New York: Springer.

Royston, P. 1996. sg47: A plot and a test for the χ^2 distribution. *Stata Technical Bulletin* 29: 26–27. Reprinted in *Stata Technical Bulletin Reprints*, vol. 5, pp. 142–144.

Scotto, M. G. 2000. sg140: The Gumbel quantile plot and a test for choice of extreme models. *Stata Technical Bulletin* 55: 23–25. Reprinted in *Stata Technical Bulletin Reprints*, vol. 10, pp. 156–159.

Wilk, M. B. and R. Gnanadesikan. 1968. Probability plotting methods for the analysis of data. *Biometrika* 55: 1–17.

Also See

Related:	[R] **cumul**, [R] **logistic**, [R] **lv**, [R] **regression diagnostics**, [TS] **regression diagnostics**
Background:	*Stata Graphics Reference Manual*

Title

> **dir** — Display filenames

Syntax

$$\{\texttt{dir}\,|\,\texttt{ls}\}\ ["\,]\,[\textit{filespec}\,]\,["\,]\ [\ ,\ \underline{\texttt{w}}\texttt{ide}\ ]$$

Note: On Stata for Windows and Stata for Macintosh, double quotes must be used to enclose *filespec* if the name contains spaces.

Description

dir and ls—they mean the same thing—list the names of files in the specified directory; the names of the commands come from names popular on DOS and Unix computers. *filespec* may be any valid DOS, Unix, or Macintosh file path or file specification (see [U] **14.6 File-naming conventions**), and may include '*' to indicate any string of characters.

Options

wide under Windows and Macintosh produces an effect similar to specifying /W with the DOS DIR command—it compresses the resulting listing by placing more than one filename on a line. Under Unix, it produces the same effect as typing ls -F -C. Without the wide option, ls is equivalent to typing ls -F -l.

Remarks

Windows: Other than minor differences in presentation format, there is only one difference between the Stata and DOS dir commands. The DOS /P option is unnecessary, since Stata always pauses when the screen is full.

Unix: The only difference between the Stata and Unix ls commands is that piping through the more(1) or pg(1) filter is unnecessary—Stata always pauses when the screen is full.

Macintosh: Macintosh users will, in most cases, use the Finder to see the contents of folders. The DOS- and Unix-like dir command, however, can be useful because it can list only files with a specified suffix.

▷ Example

The only real difference between the Stata dir and DOS and Unix equivalent commands is that output never scrolls off the screen; Stata always pauses when the screen is full.

If you use Stata for Windows and wish to obtain a list of all your Stata-format data files, type

```
. dir *.dta
    3.9k   7/07/00 13:51   auto.dta
    0.6k   8/04/00 10:40   cancer.dta
    3.5k   7/06/98 17:06   census.dta
    3.4k   1/25/98  9:20   hsng.dta
    0.3k   1/26/98 16:54   kva.dta
    0.7k   4/27/00 11:39   sysage.dta
    0.5k   5/09/97  2:56   systolic.dta
   10.3k   7/13/98  8:37   Household Survey.dta
```

or, you could include the wide option:

```
. dir *.dta, wide
    3.9k auto.dta           0.6k cancer.dta          3.5k census.dta
    3.4k hsng.dta           0.3k kva.dta             0.7k sysage.dta
    0.5k systolic.dta      10.3k Household Survey.dta
```

Unix users will find it more natural to type

```
. ls *.dta
-rw-r----- 1 roger     2868 Mar  4 15:34 highway.dta
-rw-r----- 1 roger      941 Apr  5 09:43 hoyle.dta
-rw-r----- 1 roger    19312 May 14 10:36 p1.dta
-rw-r----- 1 roger    11838 Apr 11 13:26 p2.dta
```

but they could type dir if they preferred. Macintosh users may also type either command.

```
. dir *.dta
-rw-r----- 1 roger     2868 Mar  4 15:34 highway.dta
-rw-r----- 1 roger      941 Apr  5 09:43 hoyle.dta
-rw-r----- 1 roger    19312 May 14 10:36 p1.dta
-rw-r----- 1 roger    11838 Apr 11 13:26 p2.dta
```

◁

Also See

Related: [R] **cd**, [R] **copy**, [R] **erase**, [R] **mkdir**, [R] **shell**, [R] **type**

Background: [U] **14.6 File-naming conventions**

Title

---
display — Substitute for a hand calculator

Syntax

<u>di</u>splay *exp*

Description

display displays strings and values of scalar expressions.

display really has many more features and a more complex syntax diagram than the one shown above, but the diagram shown above is adequate for interactive use. For a full discussion of display's capabilities, see [P] **display**.

Remarks

display can be used as a substitute for a hand calculator.

▷ Example

display 2+2 produces the output 4. Stata variables may also appear in the expression, such as in display myvar/2. Since display works only with scalars, the resulting calculation is performed for only the first observation. You could type display myvar[10]/2 to display the calculation for the tenth observation. Here are some more examples:

```
. display sqrt(2)/2
.70710678
. display norm(-1.1)
.13566606
. di (57.2-3)/(12-2)
5.42
. display myvar/10
7
. display myvar[10]/2
3.5
```

◁

Also See

Related: [P] **display**

Background: [U] **16 Functions and expressions**

Title

do — Execute commands from a file

Syntax

{do | r̲u̲n̲} *filename* [*arguments*] [, nostop]

Description

do and run cause Stata to execute the commands stored in *filename* just as if they were entered from the keyboard. do echoes the commands as it executes them, whereas run is silent. If *filename* is specified without an extension, .do is assumed.

Options

nostop allows the do-file to continue executing even if an error occurs. Normally, Stata stops executing the do-file when it detects an error (nonzero return code).

Remarks

You can create *filename* (called a *do-file*) using Stata's do-file editor; see [R] **doedit**. This file will be a standard ASCII (text) file. A complete discussion of do-files can be found in [U] **19 Do-files**.

You can create *filename* using an editor outside of Stata; see [R] **shell** for a way to invoke your favorite editor from inside Stata. Make sure that you save the file in ASCII format.

Note that if the path or *filename* contains spaces, it should be enclosed in double quotes.

Also See

Complementary:	[R] **doedit**
Background:	[GSM] **15 Using the Do-file Editor**,
	[GSU] **15 Using the Do-file Editor**,
	[GSW] **15 Using the Do-file Editor**,
	[U] **18 Printing and preserving output**,
	[U] **19 Do-files**

Title

> **doedit** — Edit do-files and other text files

Syntax

<u>doed</u>it [*filename*]

Description

doedit opens a text editor that allows you to edit do-files and other text files.

The do-file editor lets you submit several commands to Stata at once.

Remarks

Pressing Stata's **Do-file Editor** button is equivalent to typing doedit.

doedit, typed by itself, invokes the editor with an empty document. If you specify *filename*, that file is displayed in the editor.

A tutorial discussion of doedit is found in the *Getting Started with Stata* manual. Read [U] **19 Do-files** for an explanation of do-files, and then read [GS] **15 Using the Do-file Editor** to learn how to use the do-file editor to create and execute do-files.

Also See

Background:	[GSM] **15 Using the Do-file Editor**,
	[GSU] **15 Using the Do-file Editor**,
	[GSW] **15 Using the Do-file Editor**,
	[U] **19 Do-files**

Title

dotplot — Comparative scatterplots

Syntax

dotplot *varname* [if *exp*] [in *range*] [, by(*groupvar*) nx(*#*) ny(*#*) center

[mean | median] bar nogroup bounded incr(*#*) *scatter_options*

twoway_options]

dotplot *varlist* [if *exp*] [in *range*] [, nx(*#*) ny(*#*) center [mean | median]

bar nogroup bounded incr(*#*) *scatter_options* *twoway_options*]

Description

A dotplot is a scatterplot with a grouping of values in the vertical direction ("binning", as in a histogram) and with separation between plotted points in the horizontal direction. The aim is to display all the data for several variables or groups in a single, compact graphic.

In the first syntax, dotplot produces a columnar dotplot of *varname*, with one column per value of *groupvar*. In the second syntax, dotplot produces a columnar dotplot for each variable in *varlist*, with one column per variable; by(*groupvar*) is not allowed. In each case, the "dots" are plotted as small circles to increase readability.

Options

by(*groupvar*) identifies the variable for which dotplot will display one columnar dotplot for each value of *groupvar*.

nx(*#*) sets the horizontal dot density. A larger value of # will increase the dot density, reducing the horizontal separation between dots. This will increase the separation between columns if two or more groups or variables are used.

ny(*#*) sets the vertical dot density (number of "bins" on the *y*-axis). A larger value of # will result in more bins and a plot that is less spread-out in the horizontal direction. # should be determined in conjunction with nx() to give the most pleasing appearance.

center centers the dots for each column on a hidden vertical line.

[mean | median] plots a horizontal line of pluses at the mean or median of each group.

bar plots horizontal dashed lines at the "shoulders" of each group. The "shoulders" are taken to be the upper and lower quartiles unless mean has been specified, in which case, they will be the mean plus or minus the standard deviation.

nogroup uses the actual values of *yvar* rather than grouping them (the default). This may be useful if *yvar* only takes on a few values.

bounded forces the minimum and maximum of the variable to be used as boundaries of the smallest and largest bins. It is intended for use with a single variable whose support is not the whole of the real line and whose density does not tend to zero at the ends of its support; e.g., a uniform random variable or an exponential random variable.

incr(#) specifies how the x-axis is to be labeled. incr(1), the default, labels all groups. incr(2) labels every second group.

scatter_options affect the rendition of the plotted points; see [G] **graph twoway scatter**.

twoway_options are any of the options documented in [G] *twoway_options*, excluding by(). These include options for titling the graph (see [G] *title_options*) and options for saving the graph to disk (see [G] *saving_option*).

Remarks

dotplot produces a figure that is a cross between a boxplot, a histogram, and a scatterplot. Like a boxplot, it is most useful for comparing the distributions of several variables or the distribution of a single variable in several groups. Like a histogram, the figure provides a crude estimate of the density, and, as with a scatterplot, each symbol (dot) represents a single observation.

▷ Example

dotplot may be used as an alternative to Stata's histogram graph for displaying the distribution of a single variable.

```
. set obs 1000
. generate norm = invnorm(uniform())
. dotplot norm, title("Normal distribution, sample size 1000")
```

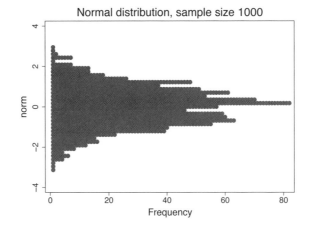

◁

(Continued on next page)

▷ Example

The by option enables dotplot to be used to compare the distribution of a single variable within different levels of a grouping variable. The options center, median, and bar create a graph that may be compared with Stata's boxplot; see [G] **graph box**. The next graph illustrates this using Stata's automobile dataset.

```
. use http://www.stata-press.com/data/r8/auto
(1978 Automobile Data)
. dotplot mpg, by(foreign) nx(25) ny(10) center median bar
```

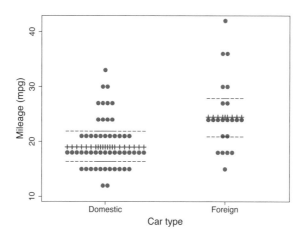

◁

▷ Example

The second version of dotplot enables one to compare the distribution of several variables. In the next graph, all ten variables contain measurements on tumor volume.

```
. dotplot g1r1-g1r10, ytitle("Tumor volume, cu mm")
```

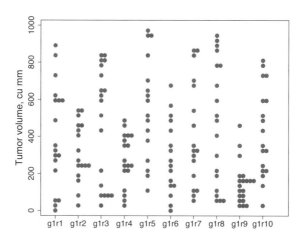

◁

▷ Example

When using the first form with the by option, it is possible to encode a third dimension in a dotplot by using a different plotting symbol for different groups. This will not work with a *varlist*. The example is of a hypothetical matched case–control study. The next graph shows the exposure of each individual in each matched stratum. Cases are marked by the letter 'x', and controls by the letter 'o'.

```
. label define symbol 0 "o" 1 "x"
. label values case symbol
. dotplot dose, by(strata) m(none) mlabel(case) mlabp(0) center
```

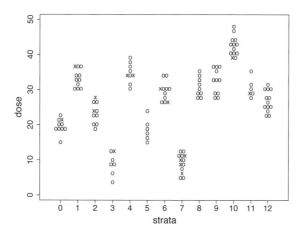

◁

▷ Example

dotplot can also be used with two virtually continuous variables as an alternative to jittering the data to distinguish ties. In this case, one must use the xlab option, since otherwise, dotplot will attempt to label too many points on the x-axis. It is often useful in such instances to use a value of nx that is smaller than the default. That was not necessary in this example, partly because of our choice of symbols.

```
. generate byte hi_price = (price>10000) if price < .
. label define symbol 0 "|" 1 "o"
. label values hi_price symbol
```

(Continued on next page)

```
. dotplot weight, by(gear_ratio) m(none) mlabel(hi_price) mlabp(0) center xlabel(#5)
```

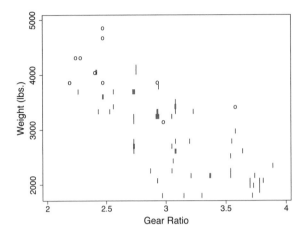

◁

▷ Example

The following figure is included mostly for aesthetic reasons. It also demonstrates dotplot's ability to cope with even very large datasets. The sample size for each variable is 10,000. This may take a long time to print!

```
. set obs 10000
. gen norm0 = invnorm(uniform())
. gen norm1 = invnorm(uniform()) + 1
. gen norm2 = invnorm(uniform()) + 2
. label variable norm0 "N(0,1)"
. label variable norm1 "N(1,1)"
. label variable norm2 "N(2,1)"

. dotplot norm0 norm1 norm2
```

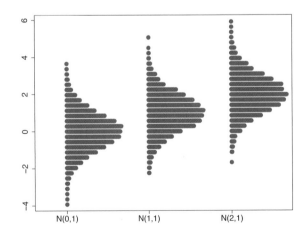

◁

Saved Results

dotplot saves in r():

Scalars

r(nx)	horizontal dot density
r(ny)	vertical dot density

Methods and Formulas

dotplot is implemented as an ado-file.

Acknowledgments

dotplot was written by Peter Sasieni of the Imperial Cancer Research Fund, London, and Patrick Royston of the MRC Clinical Trials Unit, London.

References

Sasieni. P. and P. Royston. 1994. gr14: dotplot: comparative scatterplots. *Stata Technical Bulletin* 19: 8–10. Reprinted in *Stata Technical Bulletin Reprints*, vol. 4, pp. 50–54.

——. 1996. Dotplots. *Applied Statistics* 45: 219–234.

Also See

Background: *Stata Graphics Reference Manual*

Title

---
drawnorm — Draw a sample from a normal distribution

Syntax

>   drawnorm *newvarlist* $\left[\right.$, n(#) seed(#) <u>means</u>(*row_vector*) corr(*matname*)
>
>   cov(*matname*) <u>sds</u>(*row_vector*) <u>d</u>ouble clear $\left.\right]$

Description

>   drawnorm draws a sample from a multivariate normal distribution with desired means and covariance matrix. The default is orthogonal data, mean 0, variance 1. The values generated are a function of the current random number seed or the number specified with set seed(); see [R] **generate**.

Options

>   n(#) specifies the number of observations to be generated. The default is the current number of observations. If n(#) is not specified or is the same as the current number of observations, drawnorm will add the new variables to the existing dataset; otherwise, drawnorm will replace the data in memory.

>   seed(#) specifies the initial value of the random number seed used by the uniform() function. The default is the current random number seed. Specifying seed(#) is the same as typing set seed # before issuing the drawnorm command.

>   means(*vector*) specifies the means of the generated variables. The default is means(0).

>   corr(*matname*) specifies the correlation matrix. cov() and corr() may not be specified together. If neither corr() nor cov() is specified, the default is orthogonal data.

>   cov(*matname*) specifies the covariance matrix. cov() and corr() may not be specified together. If neither corr() nor cov() is specified, the default is orthogonal data.

>   sds(*vector*) specifies the standard deviations of the generated variables. sds() and cov() may not be specified together.

>   double specifies that the new variables are to be stored as Stata doubles, meaning 8-byte reals. If double is not specified, variables are stored as floats, meaning 4-byte reals. See [R] **data types**.

>   clear specifies that it is okay to replace the dataset in memory even though the current dataset has not been saved on disk.

Remarks

▷ Example

>   Suppose that we want to draw a sample of 1,000 observations from a normal distribution $N(\mathbf{M}, \mathbf{V})$, where $\mathbf{M}$ is the mean matrix and $\mathbf{V}$ is the covariance matrix:

```
. mat list M
M[1,3]
     c1  c2  c3
r1    5  -6  .5
```

```
. mat list V

symmetric V[3,3]
     c1  c2  c3
r1   9
r2   5   4
r3   2   1   1

. drawnorm x y z, n(1000) cov(V) means(M)
(obs 1000)

. summarize
```

Variable	Obs	Mean	Std. Dev.	Min	Max
x	1000	5.001715	3.00608	-4.572042	13.66046
y	1000	-5.980279	2.004755	-12.08166	-.0963039
z	1000	.5271135	1.011095	-2.636946	4.102734

```
. correlate, cov
(obs=1000)
```

	x	y	z
x	9.03652		
y	5.04462	4.01904	
z	2.10142	1.08773	1.02231

◁

❏ Technical Note

The values generated by drawnorm are a function of the current random number seed. To reproduce the same dataset each time drawnorm is run with the same setup, specify the same seed number in the seed() option.

❏

Methods and Formulas

drawnorm is implemented as an ado-file.

Results are asymptotic. The more observations generated, the closer the correlation matrix of the dataset is to the desired correlation structure.

Let $\mathbf{V} = \mathbf{A}'\mathbf{A}$ be the desired covariance matrix and $\mathbf{M}$ be the desired mean matrix. We first generate $\mathbf{X}$, such that $\mathbf{X} \sim N(\mathbf{0}, \mathbf{I})$. Let $\mathbf{Y} = \mathbf{A}'\mathbf{X} + \mathbf{M}$, then $\mathbf{Y} \sim N(\mathbf{M}, \mathbf{V})$.

Also See

Related:	[R] **corr2data**, [R] **generate**
Background:	[R] **data types**

Title

> **drop** — Eliminate variables or observations

Syntax

> drop *varlist*
>
> drop if *exp*
>
> drop in *range* [if *exp*]
>
> keep *varlist*
>
> keep if *exp*
>
> keep in *range* [if *exp*]
>
> clear

by ... : may be used with the second syntax of drop and the second syntax of keep; see [R] **by**.

Description

drop eliminates variables or observations from the data in memory. drop may not be abbreviated.

keep works the same way as drop except that you specify the variables or observations to be kept rather than the variables or observations to be deleted. keep may not be abbreviated.

clear is equivalent to typing

```
. version 8
. drop _all
. label drop _all
. matrix drop _all
. scalar drop _all
. constraint drop _all
. eq drop _all
. file close _all
. postutil clear
. _return drop _all
. discard
```

Remarks

The entire dataset can be cleared by typing drop _all. Value labels, macros, and programs are unaffected by this. (Also see [U] **15.6 Dataset, variable, and value labels**, [U] **21.3 Macros**, and [P] **program**.) Alternatively, you can type clear. This does the same as drop _all, but also clears value labels, matrices, scalars, constraints, and equations, closes all open files and postfiles, and clears saved results. (See [U] **15.6 Dataset, variable, and value labels**, [P] **matrix utility**, [P] **scalar**, [R] **constraint**, [P] **file**, [P] **postfile**, and [P] **return**.)

▷ Example

We will systematically eliminate data until, at the very end, no data are left in memory. We begin by describing the data:

```
. use http://www.stata-press.com/data/r8/census11
(1980 Census data by state)
. describe
Contains data from http://www.stata-press.com/data/r8/census11.dta
  obs:           50                          1980 Census data by state
  vars:          14                          6 Sep 2002 10:08
  size:       3,400  (99.5% of memory free)
```

variable name	storage type	display format	value label	variable label
state	str14	%-14s		State
region	int	%-8.0g	cenreg	Census region
pop	long	%12.0gc		Population
poplt5	long	%12.0gc		Pop, < 5 year
pop5_17	long	%12.0gc		Pop, 5 to 17 years
pop18p	long	%12.0gc		Pop, 18 and older
pop65p	long	%12.0gc		Pop, 65 and older
popurban	long	%12.0gc		Urban population
medage	float	%9.2f		Median age
death	long	%12.0gc		Number of deaths
marriage	long	%12.0gc		Number of marriages
divorce	long	%12.0gc		Number of divorces
mrgrate	float	%9.0g		
dvcrate	float	%9.0g		

```
Sorted by:  region
     Note:  dataset has changed since last saved
```

We can eliminate all the variables whose names begin with pop by typing drop pop*:

```
. drop pop*
. describe
Contains data from http://www.stata-press.com/data/r8/census11.dta
  obs:           50                          1980 Census data by state
  vars:           8                          6 Sep 2002 10:08
  size:       2,200  (99.6% of memory free)
```

variable name	storage type	display format	value label	variable label
state	str14	%-14s		State
region	int	%-8.0g	cenreg	Census region
medage	float	%9.2f		Median age
death	long	%12.0gc		Number of deaths
marriage	long	%12.0gc		Number of marriages
divorce	long	%12.0gc		Number of divorces
mrgrate	float	%9.0g		
dvcrate	float	%9.0g		

```
Sorted by:  region
     Note:  dataset has changed since last saved
```

Let's eliminate more variables and then eliminate observations:

```
. drop marriage divorce mrgrate dvcrate
```

```
. describe
Contains data from http://www.stata-press.com/data/r8/census11.dta
  obs:            50                          1980 Census data by state
  vars:            4                          6 Sep 2002 10:08
  size:         1,400 (99.7% of memory free)
```

variable name	storage type	display format	value label	variable label
state	str14	%-14s		State
region	int	%-8.0g	cenreg	Census region
medage	float	%9.2f		Median age
death	long	%12.0gc		Number of deaths

```
Sorted by:  region
    Note:  dataset has changed since last saved
```

Next, we will `drop` any observation for which `medage` is greater than 32.

```
. drop if medage>32
(3 observations deleted)
```

Let's drop the first observation in each region:

```
. by region: drop if _n==1
(4 observations deleted)
```

Now we drop all but the last observation in each region:

```
. by region: drop if _n !=_N
(39 observations deleted)
```

Let's now drop the first 2 observations in our dataset:

```
. drop in 1/2
(2 observations deleted)
```

Finally, let's get rid of everything:

```
. drop _all
. describe
Contains data
  obs:            0
  vars:           0
  size:           0 (100.0% of memory free)
Sorted by:
```

◁

Typing `keep in 10/1` is the same as typing `drop in 1/9`.

Typing `keep if x==3` is the same as typing `drop if x !=3`.

`keep` is especially useful for keeping a few variables from a large dataset. Typing `keep myvar1 myvar2` is the same as typing `drop` followed by all the variables in the dataset *except* `myvar1` and `myvar2`.

Methods and Formulas

`clear` is implemented as an ado-file.

References

Cox, N. J. 2001. dm89: Dropping variables or observations with missing values. *Stata Technical Bulletin* 60: 7–8. Reprinted in *Stata Technical Bulletin Reprints*, vol. 10, pp. 44–46.

Also See

Background: [U] **14 Language syntax**,
            [U] **16 Functions and expressions**

Title

> **dstdize** — Direct and indirect standardization

Syntax

dstdize *charvar popvar stratavars* [if *exp*] [in *range*] , by(*groupvars*) [using(*filename*)

    base(# | *string*) saving(*filename*) print format(*%fmt*) level(#) nores]

istdize *casevar_s popvar_s stratavars* [if *exp*] [in *range*] using(*filename*) ,

    { popvars(*casevar_p popvar_p*) | rate(*ratevar_p* # | *ratevar_p crudevar_p*) }

    [by(*groupvars*) print format(*%fmt*) level(#)]

Description

dstdize produces standardized rates for *charvar*, which are defined as a weighted average of the stratum-specific rates. These rates can be used to compare the characteristic *charvar* across different populations identified by *groupvars*. Weights used in the standardization are given by *popvar*; the strata across which to average are defined by *stratavars*.

istdize produces indirectly standardized rates for a study population based on a standard population. This standardization method is appropriate when stratum-specific rates for the population being studied either are unavailable or are based on small samples and thus unreliable. The standardization uses the stratum-specific rates of a standard population to calculate the expected number of cases in the study population(s), sums them, and then compares them with the actual number of cases observed. The standard population is specified in another Stata data file named in the using option.

In addition to rates, the indirect standardization command produces point estimates and exact confidence intervals of the study population's standardized mortality ratio (SMR), if death is the event of interest, or the standardized incidence ratio (SIR) for studies of incidence. Here, we refer to both ratios as SMR.

casevar_s is the variable name for the study population's number of cases (usually deaths). It must contain integers, and each subpopulation identified by *groupvar* must have the same values or missing.

popvar_s identifies the number of subjects represented by each observation in the study population.

stratavars define the strata.

Options

by(*groupvars*) is not optional for the dstdize command; it specifies the variables identifying the study populations. If base() is also specified, there must be only one variable in the by() group. If you do not have a variable for this option, you can generate one using something like gen newvar=1 and then using newvar as the argument to this option.

For the istdize command, by(*groupvars*) specifies variables identifying study populations when more than one exists in the data. If this option is not specified, the entire study population is treated as one group.

using(*filename*) or base(# | *string*) may be used to specify the standard population for the dstdize command. You may not specify both options. using(*filename*) supplies the name of a .dta file containing the standard population. The standard population must contain the *popvar* and the *stratavars*. If using() is not specified, the standard population distribution will be obtained from the data. base(# | *string*) allows you to specify one of the values of *groupvar*—either a numeric value or a string—to be used as the standard population. If neither base() nor using() is specified, the entire dataset is used to determine an estimate of the standard population.

saving(*filename*) saves the computed standard population distribution as a Stata dataset that can be used in further analyses.

print outputs a table summary of the standard population before displaying the study population results.

format(%*fmt*) specifies the format in which to display the final summary table. The default is %10.0g.

level(#) specifies the confidence level, in percent, for a confidence interval of the adjusted rate; see [R] **level**.

nores suppresses saving results in r(). This option is seldom specified. Some saved results are stored in matrices. If there are more groups than matsize, dstdize will report "matsize too small". In that case, you can either increase matsize or specify nores. The nores option does not change how results are calculated. nores just specifies that results need not be left behind for use by other programs.

popvars(*casevar$_p$* *popvar$_p$*) or rate(*ratevar$_p$* # | *ratevar$_p$* *crudevar$_p$*) must be specified with istdize. Only one of these two options is allowed. These options are used to describe the standard population's data.

With popvars(*casevar$_p$* *popvar$_p$*), *casevar$_p$* records the number of cases (deaths) for each stratum in the standard population, and *popvar$_p$* records the total number of individuals in each stratum (individuals at risk).

With rate(*ratevar$_p$* # | *ratevar$_p$* *crudevar$_p$*), *ratevar$_p$* contains the stratum-specific rates. # | *crudevar$_p$* is used to specify the crude case rate either by a variable name or optionally by the crude case rate value. If a crude rate variable is used, it must be the same for all observations, although it could be missing for some.

Remarks

A frequently recurring problem in epidemiology and other fields is the comparison of rates for some characteristic across different populations. These populations often differ with respect to factors associated with the characteristic under study; thus, the direct comparison of overall rates may be quite misleading.

Direct standardization

The direct method of adjusting for differences among populations involves computing the overall rates that would result if, instead of having different distributions, all populations were to have the same standard distribution. The standardized rate is defined as a weighted average of the stratum-specific rates, with the weights taken from the standard distribution. Direct standardization may be applied only when the specific rates for a given population are available.

dstdize generates adjusted summary measures of occurrence, which can be used to compare prevalence, incidence, or mortality rates between populations that may differ with respect to certain characteristics (e.g., age, gender, race). These underlying differences may affect the crude prevalence, mortality, or incidence rates.

▷ Example

We have data (Rothman 1986, 42) on mortality rates for Sweden and Panama for the year 1962, and we wish to compare mortality in these two countries:

```
. use http://www.stata-press.com/data/r8/mortality
(1962 Mortality, Sweden & Panama)

. describe

Contains data from http://www.stata-press.com/data/r8/mortality.dta
  obs:              6                          1962 Mortality, Sweden & Panama
  vars:             4                          15 Oct 2002 22:35
  size:           114 (99.8% of memory free)
```

variable name	storage type	display format	value label	variable label
nation	str6	%9s		Nation
age_category	byte	%9.0g	age_lbl	Age Category
population	float	%10.0gc		Population in Age Category
deaths	float	%9.0gc		Deaths in Age Category

```
Sorted by:
. list, sepby(nation) abbrev(12) divider
```

	nation	age_category	population	deaths
1.	Sweden	0 - 29	3145000	3,523
2.	Sweden	30 - 59	3057000	10,928
3.	Sweden	60+	1294000	59,104
4.	Panama	0 - 29	741,000	3,904
5.	Panama	30 - 59	275,000	1,421
6.	Panama	60+	59,000	2,456

We divide the total number of cases in the population by the population to obtain the *crude rate*:

```
. collapse (sum) pop deaths, by(nation)
. list, abbrev(10) divider
```

	nation	population	deaths
1.	Panama	1075000	7,781
2.	Sweden	7496000	73,555

```
. generate crude = deaths/pop
. list, abbrev(10) divider
```

	nation	population	deaths	crude
1.	Panama	1075000	7,781	.0072381
2.	Sweden	7496000	73,555	.0098126

If we examine the total number of deaths in the two nations, it is striking that the total crude mortality rate in Sweden is higher than that of Panama. From the original data, we see one possible explanation: Swedes are older than Panamanians. This makes it difficult to directly compare the mortality rates.

Direct standardization gives us a means of removing the distortion caused by the differing age distributions. The adjusted rate is defined as the weighted sum of the crude rates, where the weights are given by the standard distribution. Suppose we wish to standardize these mortality rates to the following age distribution:

```
. use http://www.stata-press.com/data/r8/1962, clear
(Standard Population Distribution)
. list, abbrev(12) divider
```

	age_category	population
1.	0 - 29	.35
2.	30 - 59	.35
3.	60+	.3

```
. sort age_cat
. save 1962
file 1962.dta saved
```

If we multiply the above weights for the age strata by the crude rate for the corresponding age category, the sum gives us the standardized rate.

```
. use http://www.stata-press.com/data/r8/mortality, clear
(1962 Mortality, Sweden & Panama)
. gen crude=deaths/pop
. drop pop
. sort age_cat
. merge age_cat using 1962
age_category was byte now float
. list, sepby(age_category) abbrev(12)
```

	nation	age_category	deaths	crude	population	_merge
1.	Sweden	0 - 29	3,523	.0011202	.35	3
2.	Panama	0 - 29	3,904	.0052686	.35	3
3.	Sweden	30 - 59	10,928	.0035747	.35	3
4.	Panama	30 - 59	1,421	.0051673	.35	3
5.	Sweden	60+	59,104	.0456754	.3	3
6.	Panama	60+	2,456	.0416271	.3	3

```
. generate product = crude*pop
. by nation, sort: egen adj_rate = sum(product)
. drop _merge
. sort nation age_category
. list, sepby(nation)
```

	nation	age_ca~y	deaths	crude	popula~n	product	adj_rate
1.	Panama	0 - 29	3,904	.0052686	.35	.001844	.0161407
2.	Panama	30 - 59	1,421	.0051673	.35	.0018085	.0161407
3.	Panama	60+	2,456	.0416271	.3	.0124881	.0161407
4.	Sweden	0 - 29	3,523	.0011202	.35	.0003921	.0153459
5.	Sweden	30 - 59	10,928	.0035747	.35	.0012512	.0153459
6.	Sweden	60+	59,104	.0456754	.3	.0137026	.0153459

A comparison of the standardized rates indicates that the Swedes have a slightly lower mortality rate.

To perform the above analysis with dstdize,

```
. use http://www.stata-press.com/data/r8/mortality, clear
(1962 Mortality, Sweden & Panama)
. dstdize deaths pop age_cat, by(nation) using(1962)
```

```
-> nation= Panama
                        ─────Unadjusted─────   Std.
                          Pop.   Stratum  Pop.
    Stratum       Pop.   Cases  Dist.  Rate[s] Dst[P]   s*P

     0 - 29     741000    3904  0.689  0.0053  0.350 0.0018
    30 - 59     275000    1421  0.256  0.0052  0.350 0.0018
        60+      59000    2456  0.055  0.0416  0.300 0.0125

    Totals:    1075000    7781      Adjusted Cases:   17351.2
                                       Crude Rate:     0.0072
                                    Adjusted Rate:     0.0161
                         95% Conf. Interval: [0.0156, 0.0166]


-> nation= Sweden
                        ─────Unadjusted─────   Std.
                          Pop.   Stratum  Pop.
    Stratum       Pop.   Cases  Dist.  Rate[s] Dst[P]   s*P

     0 - 29    3145000    3523  0.420  0.0011  0.350 0.0004
    30 - 59    3057000   10928  0.408  0.0036  0.350 0.0013
        60+    1294000   59104  0.173  0.0457  0.300 0.0137

    Totals:    7496000   73555      Adjusted Cases: 115032.5
                                       Crude Rate:     0.0098
                                    Adjusted Rate:     0.0153
                         95% Conf. Interval: [0.0152, 0.0155]

Summary of Study Populations:
    nation            N     Crude      Adj_Rate      Confidence Interval

    Panama      1075000  0.007238     0.016141    [  0.015645,    0.016637]
    Sweden      7496000  0.009813     0.015346    [  0.015235,    0.015457]
```

The summary table above allows us to make a quick inspection of the results within the study populations, and the detail tables give the behavior among the strata within the study populations.
                                                                                     ◁

▷ Example

We have individual-level data on persons in four cities over a number of years. Included in the data is a variable indicating whether the person has high blood pressure together with information on the person's age, sex, and race. We wish to obtain standardized high blood pressure rates for each city in the years 1990 and 1992, using, as the standard, the age, sex, and race distribution of the four cities and two years combined.

Our dataset contains

```
. use http://www.stata-press.com/data/r8/hbp
```

```
. describe
Contains data from http://www.stata-press.com/data/r8/hbp.dta
  obs:         1,130
  vars:            7                            24 Aug 2002 16:20
  size:       23,730 (96.2% of memory free)
```

variable name	storage type	display format	value label	variable label
id	str10	%10s		Record identification number
city	byte	%8.0g		
year	int	%8.0g		
sex	byte	%8.0g	sexfmt	
age_group	byte	%8.0g	agefmt	
race	byte	%8.0g	racefmt	
hbp	byte	%8.0g	yn	high blood pressure

```
Sorted by:
```

The dstdize command is designed to work with aggregate data, but will work with individual-level data only if we create a variable recording the population represented by each observation. For individual-level data, this is one:

```
. gen pop = 1
```

Below, we specify print to obtain a listing of the standard population and level(90) to request 90% rather than 95% confidence intervals. The if year==1990 | year==1992 restricts the data to the two years for both summary tables and the standard population.

```
. dstdize hbp pop age race sex if year==1990 | year==1992, by(city year) print level(90)
```

————————Standard Population————————			
Stratum		Pop.	Dist.
15 - 19 Black Female		35	0.077
15 - 19 Black Male		44	0.097
15 - 19 Hispanic Female		5	0.011
15 - 19 Hispanic Male		10	0.022
15 - 19 White Female		7	0.015
15 - 19 White Male		5	0.011
20 - 24 Black Female		43	0.095
20 - 24 Black Male		67	0.147
20 - 24 Hispanic Female		14	0.031
20 - 24 Hispanic Male		13	0.029
20 - 24 White Female		4	0.009
20 - 24 White Male		21	0.046
25 - 29 Black Female		17	0.037
25 - 29 Black Male		44	0.097
25 - 29 Hispanic Female		7	0.015
25 - 29 Hispanic Male		13	0.029
25 - 29 White Female		9	0.020
25 - 29 White Male		16	0.035
30 - 34 Black Female		16	0.035
30 - 34 Black Male		32	0.070
30 - 34 Hispanic Female		2	0.004
30 - 34 Hispanic Male		3	0.007
30 - 34 White Female		5	0.011
30 - 34 White Male		23	0.051

```
Total:                       455
(6 observations excluded due to missing values)
```

-> city year= 1 1990

	Stratum		Pop.	Cases	Unadjusted Pop. Dist.	Stratum Rate[s]	Std. Pop. Dst[P]	s*P
15 - 19	Black	Female	6	2	0.128	0.3333	0.077	0.0256
15 - 19	Black	Male	6	0	0.128	0.0000	0.097	0.0000
15 - 19	Hispanic	Male	1	0	0.021	0.0000	0.022	0.0000
20 - 24	Black	Female	3	0	0.064	0.0000	0.095	0.0000
20 - 24	Black	Male	11	0	0.234	0.0000	0.147	0.0000
25 - 29	Black	Female	4	0	0.085	0.0000	0.037	0.0000
25 - 29	Black	Male	6	1	0.128	0.1667	0.097	0.0161
25 - 29	Hispanic	Female	2	0	0.043	0.0000	0.015	0.0000
25 - 29	White	Female	1	0	0.021	0.0000	0.020	0.0000
30 - 34	Black	Female	1	0	0.021	0.0000	0.035	0.0000
30 - 34	Black	Male	6	0	0.128	0.0000	0.070	0.0000

Totals: 47   3   Adjusted Cases: 2.0
                                                Crude Rate: 0.0638
                                             Adjusted Rate: 0.0418
                          90% Conf. Interval: [0.0074, 0.0761]

(output omitted)

-> city year= 5 1992

	Stratum		Pop.	Cases	Unadjusted Pop. Dist.	Stratum Rate[s]	Std. Pop. Dst[P]	s*P
15 - 19	Black	Female	6	0	0.087	0.0000	0.077	0.0000
15 - 19	Black	Male	9	0	0.130	0.0000	0.097	0.0000
15 - 19	Hispanic	Female	1	0	0.014	0.0000	0.011	0.0000
15 - 19	Hispanic	Male	2	0	0.029	0.0000	0.022	0.0000
15 - 19	White	Female	2	0	0.029	0.0000	0.015	0.0000
15 - 19	White	Male	1	0	0.014	0.0000	0.011	0.0000
20 - 24	Black	Female	13	0	0.188	0.0000	0.095	0.0000
20 - 24	Black	Male	10	0	0.145	0.0000	0.147	0.0000
20 - 24	Hispanic	Male	1	0	0.014	0.0000	0.029	0.0000
20 - 24	White	Male	3	0	0.043	0.0000	0.046	0.0000
25 - 29	Black	Female	2	0	0.029	0.0000	0.037	0.0000
25 - 29	Black	Male	2	0	0.029	0.0000	0.097	0.0000
25 - 29	Hispanic	Male	3	0	0.043	0.0000	0.029	0.0000
25 - 29	White	Male	1	0	0.014	0.0000	0.035	0.0000
30 - 34	Black	Female	4	0	0.058	0.0000	0.035	0.0000
30 - 34	Black	Male	5	0	0.072	0.0000	0.070	0.0000
30 - 34	Hispanic	Male	2	0	0.029	0.0000	0.007	0.0000
30 - 34	White	Female	1	0	0.014	0.0000	0.011	0.0000
30 - 34	White	Male	1	1	0.014	1.0000	0.051	0.0505

Totals: 69   1   Adjusted Cases: 3.5
                                                Crude Rate: 0.0145
                                             Adjusted Rate: 0.0505
                          90% Conf. Interval: [0.0505, 0.0505]

(Continued on next page)

```
Summary of Study Populations:
    city
    year              N      Crude     Adj_Rate       Confidence Interval

      1
    1990              47   0.063830    0.041758    [  0.007427,    0.076089]
      1
    1992              56   0.017857    0.008791    [  0.000000,    0.022579]
      2
    1990              64   0.046875    0.044898    [  0.009072,    0.080724]
      2
    1992              67   0.029851    0.014286    [  0.002537,    0.026035]
      3
    1990              69   0.159420    0.088453    [  0.050093,    0.126813]
      3
    1992              37   0.189189    0.046319    [  0.025271,    0.067366]
      5
    1990              46   0.043478    0.022344    [  0.002044,    0.042644]
      5
    1992              69   0.014493    0.050549    [  0.050549,    0.050549]
```
◁

Indirect standardization

Standardization of rates can be performed via the indirect method whenever the stratum-specific rates are either unknown or unreliable. If the stratum-specific rates are known, the direct standardization method is preferred.

In order to apply the indirect method, the following must be available:

1. The observed number of cases in each population to be standardized, O. For example, if death rates in two states are being standardized using the US death rate for the same time period, then you must know the total number of deaths in each state.

2. The distribution across the various strata for the population being studied, $n_1, \ldots, n_k$. If you are standardizing the death rate in the two states adjusting for age, then you must know the number of individuals in each of the k age groups.

3. The stratum-specific rates for the standard population, $p_1, \ldots, p_k$. For the example, you must have the US death rate for each stratum (age group).

4. The crude rate of the standard population, C. For the example, you must have the mortality rate for all the US for the year.

The indirect adjusted rate is then

$$R_{\text{indirect}} = C\frac{O}{E}$$

where E is the expected number of cases (deaths) in each population. See the *Methods and Formulas* section for a more detailed description of calculations.

▷ Example

This example is borrowed from Kahn and Sempos (1989, 95–105). We want to compare 1970 mortality rates in California and Maine, adjusting for age. Although we have age-specific population counts for the two states, we lack age-specific death rates. In this situation, direct standardization is not feasible. We can use the US population census data for the same year to produce indirectly standardized rates for these two states.

From the United States census, the standard population for this example was entered into Stata and saved in popkahn.dta.

```
. use http://www.stata-press.com/data/r8/popkahn
. list age pop deaths rate, sep(4)
```

	age	population	deaths	rate
1.	<15	57,900,000	103,062	.00178
2.	15-24	35,441,000	45,261	.00128
3.	25-34	24,907,000	39,193	.00157
4.	35-44	23,088,000	72,617	.00315
5.	45-54	23,220,000	169,517	.0073
6.	55-64	18,590,000	308,373	.01659
7.	65-74	12,436,000	445,531	.03583
8.	75+	7,630,000	736,758	.09656

Note that the standard population contains for each age stratum the total number of individuals (pop) and both the age-specific mortality rate (rate) and the number of deaths. It is not necessary that the standard population contain all three. If you only have the age-specific mortality rate, you can use the rate($ratevar_p$ $crudevar_p$) or rate($ratevar_p$ #) options, where $crudevar_p$ refers to the variable containing the total population's crude death rate or # is the total population's crude death rate.

Now let's look at the states' data (study population):

```
. use http://www.stata-press.com/data/r8/kahn, clear
. list, sep(4)
```

	state	age	populat~n	death	st	death_~e
1.	California	<15	5,524,000	166,285	1	.0016
2.	California	15-24	3,558,000	166,285	1	.0013
3.	California	25-34	2,677,000	166,285	1	.0015
4.	California	35-44	2,359,000	166,285	1	.0028
5.	California	45-54	2,330,000	166,285	1	.0067
6.	California	55-64	1,704,000	166,285	1	.0154
7.	California	65-74	1,105,000	166,285	1	.0328
8.	California	75+	696,000	166,285	1	.0917
9.	Maine	<15	286,000	11,051	2	.0019
10.	Maine	15-24	168,000	.	2	.0011
11.	Maine	25-34	110,000	.	2	.0014
12.	Maine	35-44	109,000	.	2	.0029
13.	Maine	45-54	110,000	.	2	.0069
14.	Maine	55-64	94,000	.	2	.0173
15.	Maine	65-74	69,000	.	2	.039
16.	Maine	75+	46,000	.	2	.1041

Note that for each state the number of individuals in each stratum (age group) is contained in the variable pop. The death variable is the total number of deaths observed in the state during the year. It must have the same value for all observations in the group, as for California, or it could be missing in all but one observation per group, as for Maine.

For matching these two datasets, it is important that the strata variables have the same name in both datasets, and ideally the same levels. If a level is missing from either dataset, that level will not be included in the standardization.

With the kahn.dta dataset in memory, we now execute the command. We will use the print option to obtain the standard population's summary table, and since we have both the standard population's age-specific count and deaths, we will specify the popvars($casevar_p$ $popvar_p$) option. Alternatively, we could specify the rate(rate 0.00945) option since we know that 0.00945 is the US crude death rate for 1970.

```
. istdize death pop age using http://www.stata-press.com/data/r8/popkahn,
> by(state) pop(deaths pop) print
```

```
————Standard Population————
 Stratum                Rate

     <15             0.00178
   15-24             0.00128
   25-34             0.00157
   35-44             0.00315
   45-54             0.00730
   55-64             0.01659
   65-74             0.03583
     75+             0.09656


Standard population's crude rate:       0.00945
```

```
-> state= California
                  Indirect Standardization
                  Standard
                  Population      Observed        Cases
 Stratum            Rate         Population      Expected

     <15           0.0018         5524000        9832.72
   15-24           0.0013         3558000        4543.85
   25-34           0.0016         2677000        4212.46
   35-44           0.0031         2359000        7419.59
   45-54           0.0073         2330000       17010.10
   55-64           0.0166         1704000       28266.14
   65-74           0.0358         1105000       39587.63
     75+           0.0966          696000       67206.23

Totals:                         19953000      178078.73

                                  Observed Cases:    166285
                                   SMR (Obs/Exp):      0.93
          SMR exact 95% Conf. Interval: [0.9293, 0.9383]
                                     Crude Rate:    0.0083
                                  Adjusted Rate:    0.0088
                   95% Conf. Interval: [0.0088, 0.0089]
```

(*Continued on next page*)

```
-> state= Maine
                    Indirect Standardization

                    Standard
                    Population     Observed        Cases
      Stratum          Rate       Population      Expected

        <15           0.0018        286000         509.08
       15-24          0.0013        168000         214.55
       25-34          0.0016        110000         173.09
       35-44          0.0031        109000         342.83
       45-54          0.0073        110000         803.05
       55-64          0.0166         94000        1559.28
       65-74          0.0358         69000        2471.99
        75+           0.0966         46000        4441.79

Totals:                             992000       10515.67

                                    Observed Cases:     11051
                                    SMR (Obs/Exp):       1.05
                    SMR exact 95% Conf. Interval: [1.0314, 1.0707]
                                    Crude Rate:        0.0111
                                    Adjusted Rate:     0.0099
                        95% Conf. Interval: [0.0097, 0.0101]
```

Summary of Study Populations (Rates):

| | Cases | | | |
state	Observed	Crude	Adj_Rate	Confidence Interval
California	166285	0.008334	0.008824	[0.008782, 0.008866]
Maine	11051	0.011140	0.009931	[0.009747, 0.010118]

Summary of Study Populations (SMR):

| | Cases | Cases | | Exact |
state	Observed	Expected	SMR	Confidence Interval
California	166285	178078.73	0.934	[0.929290, 0.938271]
Maine	11051	10515.67	1.051	[1.031405, 1.070687]

◁

Saved Results

dstdize saves in r():

Scalars
    r(k)   number of variables

Macros
    r(by)   variable names specified in by()
    r(c#)   values of r(by) for #th group

Matrices
    r(Nobs)   1 x k vector of number of observations
    r(crude)   1 x k vector of crude rates (*)
    r(adj)   1 x k vector of adjusted rates (*)
                (*) If, in a group, the number of observations is 0, then 9
                    is stored for the corresponding crude and adjusted rates.

Methods and Formulas

dstdize and istdize are implemented as ado-files.

The directly standardized rate S_R is defined by

$$S_R = \frac{\sum\limits_{i=1}^{k} w_i R_i}{\sum\limits_{i=1}^{k} w_i}$$

(Rothman 1986, 44), where R_i is the stratum-specific rate in stratum i, and w_i is the weight for stratum i derived from the standard population.

If n_i is the population of stratum i, the standard error $\mathrm{se}(S_R)$ in stratified sampling for proportions (ignoring the finite population correction) is

$$\mathrm{se}(S_R) = \frac{1}{\sum w_i} \sqrt{\sum_{i=1}^{k} \frac{w_i{}^2 R_i (1 - R_i)}{n_i}}$$

(Cochran 1977, 108), from which the confidence intervals are calculated.

For indirect standardization, define O as the observed number of cases in each population to be standardized; $n_1, \ldots, n_k$, the distribution across the various strata for the population being studied; $R_1, \ldots, R_k$, the stratum-specific rates for the standard population; and C, the crude rate of the standard population. Then the expected number of cases (deaths), E, in each population is obtained by applying the standard population stratum-specific rates, $R_1, \ldots, R_k$, to the study populations:

$$E = \sum_{i=1}^{k} n_i R_i$$

The indirectly adjusted rate is then

$$R_{\mathrm{indirect}} = C \frac{O}{E}$$

and O/E is the study population's standardized mortality ratio (SMR) if death is the event of interest or the standardized incidence ratio (SIR) for studies of disease (or other) incidence.

The exact confidence interval is calculated for each estimated SMR by assuming a Poisson process as described in Breslow and Day (1987, 69–71). These are obtained by first calculating the upper and lower bounds for the confidence interval of the Poisson-distributed observed events, O, say, L and U, respectively, and then computing $\mathrm{SMR}_L = L/E$ and $\mathrm{SMR}_U = U/E$.

Acknowledgments

We gratefully acknowledge the collaboration of Dr Joel A. Harrison, Cigna Healthcare of Texas; Dr José Maria Pacheco from the Departamento de Epidemiologia, Faculdade de Saúde Pública/USP, Sao Paulo, Brazil; and Dr John L. Moran from The Queen Elizabeth Hospital, Woodville, Australia.

References

Breslow, N. E. and N. E. Day. 1987. *Statistical Methods in Cancer Research*, vol. II. Lyon: International Agency for Research on Cancer.

Cleves, M. A. 1998. sg80: Indirect standardization. *Stata Technical Bulletin* 42: 43–47. Reprinted in *Stata Technical Bulletin Reprints*, vol. 7, pp. 224–228.

Cochran, W. G. 1977. *Sampling Techniques*. 3d ed. New York: John Wiley & Sons.

Fisher, L. D. and G. van Belle. 1993. *Biostatistics: A Methodology for the Health Sciences*. New York: John Wiley & Sons.

Fleiss, J. L. 1981. *Statistical Methods for Rates and Proportions*. 2d ed. New York: John Wiley & Sons.

Forthofer, R. and E. S. Lee. 1995. *Introduction to Biostatistics: A Guide to Design, Analysis, and Discovery*. New York: Academic Press.

Kahn, H. A. and C. T. Sempos. 1989. *Statistical Methods in Epidemiology*. New York: Oxford University Press.

McGuire, T. J. and J. A. Harrison. 1994. sbe11: Direct standardization. *Stata Technical Bulletin* 21: 5–9. Reprinted in *Stata Technical Bulletin Reprints*, vol. 4, pp. 88–94.

Pagano, M. and K. Gauvreau. 2000. *Principles of Biostatistics*. 2d ed. Pacific Grove, CA: Brooks/Cole.

Rothman, K. J. 1986. *Modern Epidemiology*. Boston: Little, Brown, and Company.

Wang, D. 2000. sbe40: Modeling mortality data using the Lee–Carter model. *Stata Technical Bulletin* 57: 15–17. Reprinted in *Stata Technical Bulletin Reprints*, vol. 10, pp. 118–121.

Also See

Related: [ST] **epitab**

Title

> **duplicates** — Inform on, tag, or drop duplicate observations

Syntax

> duplicates r̲eport [*varlist*] [if *exp*] [in *range*]
>
> duplicates e̲xamples [*varlist*] [if *exp*] [in *range*] [, *list_options*]
>
> duplicates l̲ist [*varlist*] [if *exp*] [in *range*] [, *list_options*]
>
> duplicates b̲rowse [*varlist*] [if *exp*] [in *range*] [, no̲label]
>
> duplicates t̲ag [*varlist*] [if *exp*] [in *range*] , g̲enerate(*newvar*)
>
> duplicates drop [if *exp*] [in *range*]
>
> duplicates drop *varlist* [if *exp*] [in *range*] , force

Description

duplicates reports on, gives examples of, lists, browses, tags, or drops duplicate observations, depending on the subcommand specified. Duplicates are those with identical values, either on all variables if no *varlist* is specified, or on a specified *varlist*.

duplicates report produces a table of whether observations occur as one or more copies and of how many are 'surplus' in the sense that they are the second (third, ...) copy of the first of each group of duplicates.

duplicates examples lists one example for each group of duplicated observations. Each example will be the first occurrence of each group in the dataset.

duplicates list lists all duplicated observations.

duplicates browse opens the Data Editor on the duplicated observations. You may not change the data while in the Editor.

duplicates tag generates a variable that is the number of duplicates for each observation. In particular, this will be 0 for all unique observations.

duplicates drop drops all but the first occurrence of each group of duplicated observations. The word drop may not be abbreviated.

Any observations not satisfying specified if and/or in conditions are ignored when executing report, examples, list, browse, or drop. The variable created by tag will have missing values for such observations.

(Continued on next page)

301

Options

Options for duplicates examples and duplicates list

list_options are options of list other than noobs and subvarname. See [R] **list**.

Options for duplicates browse

nolabel causes the underlying numeric values rather than the label values to be displayed in the Editor for variables with value labels. This is a rarely specified option.

Options for duplicates tag

generate(*newvar*) is a required option specifying the name of a new variable that will tag duplicates.

Options for duplicates drop

force specifies that observations duplicated with respect to a named *varlist* are to be dropped. The force option is required whenever such a *varlist* is given, as a reminder that information may be lost by dropping observations, given that those observations may differ on any of the variables not included in *varlist*.

Remarks

Several questions in data management and analysis hinge on the detection (and, in some cases, dropping) of duplicate observations. In Stata terms, *duplicate observations* are those with identical values, either on all variables if no *varlist* is specified, or on a specified *varlist*. That is, two or more observations that are identical on all variables concerned form a group of duplicates. (When the variables concerned are a set of explanatory variables, such a group is often called a *covariate pattern* or a *covariate class*.)

Linguistic purists will point out that duplicate observations are strictly only those that occur in pairs, and they might prefer a more literal term, although the most obvious replacement, "replicates", already has another statistical meaning. However, the looser term appears in practice to be much more frequently used for this purpose and to be as easy to understand.

Observations may occur as duplicates through some error; for example, somehow the same observations have been entered more than once into your dataset. A variant on this is the practice of deliberately entering a dataset twice. Each entry is a check on the other, and we hope to see that all observations occur as identical pairs, assuming that one or more variables serve as identifiers of unique records. If we see just one copy, or more than two copies, we guess that there was an error in data entry.

Alternatively, duplicate observations may also arise simply because some observations just happen to be identical, which is especially likely with categorical variables and/or very large datasets. In this second situation, consider whether contract, which automatically produces a count of each distinct set of observations, is more appropriate for your problem. See [R] **contract**.

Observations unique on all variables in *varlist* occur as single copies. Thus, there are no surplus observations in the sense that no observation may be dropped without loss of information on the contents of observations. (Information will inevitably be lost on the frequency of such observations. Please note again that if recording frequency is important to you, then `contract` is the better command to use.) Observations that are duplicated twice or more occur as that many copies, and, in each case, all but one copy may be considered surplus.

Phrased differently, the problem may be posed of producing a dataset, usually smaller than the original, in which each observation is *unique* (literally, each occurs once only) and *distinct* (each differs from all the others). If you are familiar with Unix systems, or with sets of Unix utilities ported to other platforms, you will know their `uniq` command, which removes duplicate adjacent lines from a file, usually as part of a pipe.

Suppose you are given a dataset in which some observations are unique (no other observation is identical on all variables) and other observations are duplicates (in each case, at least one other observation exists that is identical). Imagine dropping all but one observation from each group of duplicates (that is, dropping the surplus observations). The result is now that all observations are unique. This example helps to make clear the difference between (1) identifying unique observations before dropping surplus copies and (2) identifying unique observations after dropping surplus copies (whether in truth, or merely in imagination). Only if all observations are unique at the outset is there no difference between these two situations. Note, in passing, that `codebook` (see [R] **codebook**) reports the number of unique values for each variable in this second sense.

Suppose you have typed in a dataset for 200 individuals. However, a simple `describe` or `count` shows that you have 202 observations in your dataset. You guess that you may have typed in two observations twice. `duplicates report` gives a quick check on the occurrence of duplicates:

```
. duplicates report
Duplicates in terms of all variables
```

copies	observations	surplus
1	198	0
2	4	2

Your hypothesis is supported: 198 observations are unique (just 1 copy of each), while 4 occur as duplicates (2 copies of each; in each case, 1 may be dubbed surplus). You now wish to see which observations are duplicates, so the next step is to ask for a `duplicates list`.

```
. duplicates list
Duplicates in terms of all variables
```

group:	obs:	id	x	y
1	42	42	0	2
1	43	42	0	2
2	145	144	4	4
2	146	144	4	4

The records for `id` 42 and `id` 144 were evidently entered twice. Satisfied, you now issue `duplicates drop`.

```
. duplicates drop
Duplicates in terms of all variables
(2 observations deleted)
```

The report, list, and drop subcommands of duplicates are perhaps the most useful, especially for a relatively small dataset. For a larger dataset with many duplicates, a full listing may be too lengthy to be manageable, especially as you are necessarily seeing repetitions of the same data. duplicates examples gives you a more compact listing in which each group of duplicates is represented by just one observation (precisely, the first to occur).

On the same or other grounds, you may prefer duplicates browse, in which you open the Data Editor on the duplicate observations, and can move around inspecting those observations at will. Specifying browse rather than edit means that you cannot modify data while in the Data Editor. In particular, you cannot delete any of the duplicate observations (see [R] **edit**). This is our way of encouraging you to adopt what we regard as better style. If you drop observations, you should drop them directly, so that any changes you make to the data are easier to understand and to reproduce from a log of your session.

A subcommand that is occasionally useful is duplicates tag, which generates a new variable containing the number of duplicates for each observation. Thus, unique observations are tagged with value 0, and all duplicate observations are tagged with values greater than 0. For checking double data entry, in which we expect just 1 surplus copy for each individual record, we should generate a tag variable and then look at observations with tag not equal to 1, because both unique observations and groups with 2 or more surplus copies need inspection.

```
. duplicates tag, gen(tag)
Duplicates in terms of all variables
```

Acknowledgments

duplicates was written by Nicholas J. Cox, University of Durham, who in turn thanks Thomas Steichen, RJRT, for ideas contributed to an earlier jointly written program (Steichen and Cox 1998).

References

Jacobs, M. 1991. dm4: A duplicate value identification program. *Stata Technical Bulletin* 4: 5. Reprinted in *Stata Technical Bulletin Reprints*, vol. 1, p. 30.

Steichen, T. J. and N. J. Cox. 1998. dm53: Detection and deletion of duplicate observations. *Stata Technical Bulletin* 41: 2–4. Reprinted in *Stata Technical Bulletin Reprints*, pp. 52–55.

Wang, D. 2000. dm77: Removing duplicate observations in a dataset. *Stata Technical Bulletin* 54: 16–17. Reprinted in *Stata Technical Bulletin Reprints*, vol. 9, pp. 87–88.

Also See

| **Complementary:** | [R] **edit**, [R] **list** |
| **Related:** | [R] **codebook**, [R] **contract**, [R] **isid** |

Title

---

edit — Edit and list data using Data Editor

Syntax

<u>ed</u>it [*varlist*] [if *exp*] [in *range*] [, <u>nol</u>abel]

<u>b</u>rowse [*varlist*] [if *exp*] [in *range*] [, <u>nol</u>abel]

Description

edit brings up a spreadsheet-style data editor for entering new data and editing existing data. edit is a better alternative to input; see [R] **input**.

browse is like edit, except that it will not allow you to change the data. browse is a convenient alternative to list; see [R] **list**.

Options

nolabel causes the underlying numeric values rather than the label values (equivalent strings) to be displayed for variables with value labels; see [R] **label**.

Remarks

Remarks are presented under the headings

> *Modes*
> *The current observation and current variable*
> *Double-clicking action*
> *Buttons*
> *Changing values of existing cells*
> *Adding new variables*
> *Adding new observations*
> *Copying and pasting*
> *Exiting*
> *Logging changes*
> *Advice*

A tutorial discussion of edit and browse is found in the *Getting Started with Stata* manual. This entry provides technical details.

Pressing Stata's **Data Editor** button is equivalent to typing edit by itself. Pressing Stata's **Data Browser** button is equivalent to typing browse by itself.

edit, typed by itself, enters the editor with all observations on all variables. If you specify *varlist*, only those variables are displayed in the editor. If you specify one or both of in *range* and if *exp*, only the observations specified are displayed.

Modes

We will refer to the editor in the singular and have it understood that `edit` and `browse` are two aspects of the same thing. In fact, the editor has three modes.

Full-edit mode. This is the editor's mode that you enter when you type `edit` or type `edit` followed by a list of variables. All features of the editor are turned on.

Restricted-edit mode. This is the editor's mode that you enter when you use `edit`, with or without a list of variables, but include `in` *range*, `if` *exp*, or both. A few of the editor's features are turned off, most notably, the ability to sort data, the ability to delete observations on a data-wide basis, and the ability to paste data into the editor.

Browse mode. This is the editor's mode that you enter when you use `browse`. All the editing features are turned off, ensuring that the data cannot be changed. One feature that is left on may surprise you: the ability to sort data. Sorting, in Stata's mind, is not really a change to the dataset. On the other hand, if you enter using `browse` and specify `in` *range* or `if` *exp*, sorting will not be allowed. You can think of this as restricted-browse mode.

Actually, the editor does not set its mode to restricted just because you specify an `in` *range* or `if` *exp*. It sets its mode to restricted if you specify `in` or `if` and if this restriction is effective; that is, if the `in` or `if` actually causes some data to be omitted. For instance, typing `edit if x>0` would result in unrestricted full-edit mode if `x` were greater than zero for all observations.

The current observation and current variable

The bulk of the editor looks like a spreadsheet, with rows corresponding to observations and columns to variables. At all times, one of the cells is highlighted. This is called the current cell. The observation (row) of the current cell is called the current observation. The variable (column) of the current cell is called the current variable.

You change the current cell in the natural way—click with the mouse on another cell, use the arrow keys, or move the scroll bars.

Double-clicking action

When you double-click on a cell, the Variable Information dialog box appears. In edit mode, this allows you to change the variable's name, variable label, and format; see [U] **14.3 Naming conventions**, [U] **15.6.2 Variable labels**, and [U] **15.5 Formats: controlling how data are displayed**.

Buttons

Seven buttons appear at the top of the window.

Preserve updates the backup copy of the data. By default, when you enter the editor, a backup copy is made so that you can abort your changes. (There is a way to vary this; see the technical note below.) If you get to a point where you are satisfied with your changes, but still wish to continue, you do not have to exit and re-enter the editor. Press **Preserve**. **Preserve** is grayed out in browse mode.

Restore undoes your changes by restoring the backup copy of your data. Pressing **Restore** does not change the backup copy, so you can press **Restore**, try again, change your mind yet again, and re-press **Restore**. **Restore** is grayed out in browse mode. If you turn off the automatic backup feature (see technical note below), **Restore** is also grayed out in edit mode until you press **Preserve**.

Sort reorders the observations in ascending sequence of the current variable. **Sort** is grayed out in restricted-edit and restricted-browse modes.

≪ shifts the current variable to be the first variable in the dataset. In edit mode, the shift is real. When you exit the editor, the variables will remain in the order that you have specified. In browse mode, the shift is cosmetic. While in the editor, it appears as if the variable has been moved, but, when you exit, the variables remain in the same order as they were originally.

≫ shifts the current variable to be the last variable in the dataset. In edit mode, the shift is real. When you exit the editor, the variables will remain in the order that you have specified. In browse mode, the shift is cosmetic. While in the editor, it appears as if the variable has been moved, but, when you exit, the variables remain in the same order as they were originally.

Hide eliminates the variable from the editor. The effect is cosmetic. The variable is not dropped from the dataset; the editor merely stops displaying it.

Delete... brings up a popup window to either (1) delete the current variable, (2) delete the current observation, or (3) delete all observations, data-wide, whose current variable's value is equal to that of the current observation. The third option is not presented in restricted-edit mode. **Delete...** is grayed out in browse mode.

❏ Technical Note

By default, when you enter the editor, a backup copy of your data is made on disk. For large datasets, making this copy takes time. If you do not want the backup copy made automatically, pull down **Prefs–General Preferences...** from the Stata menu bar, select **Editor Prefs**, and turn off (uncheck) *Auto-Preserve*. When you enter the editor, **Restore** will now be grayed out until you press **Preserve**, if ever.

❏

Changing values of existing cells

Make the cell you wish to change the current cell. Type the new value and press *Enter*. When updating string variables, do not type double quotes around the string.

❏ Technical Note

Stata experts will wonder about storage types. Say variable mpg is stored as an int and you want to change the fourth observation to contain 22.5. Just do it. The editor will change the storage type of the variable. Similarly, if the variable is a str4 and you type alpha, it will be promoted to str5.

The editor will not, however, change numeric variable types to strings (unless the numeric variable contains only missing values). This is intentional—such a change could result in a loss of data, and you probably made a mistake.

❏

Adding new variables

Go to the first empty column and begin entering your data. The first entry that you make will create the variable, and it will determine whether that variable is numeric or string. It will be given a name like var1, but you can rename it by double-clicking on any cell in the column.

❑ Technical Note

Stata experts: the storage type will be determined automatically. If you type a number, the created variable will be numeric; if you type a string, it will be a string. Thus, if you want a string variable, be sure that your first entry cannot be interpreted as a number. A way to achieve this is to use surrounding quotes, so that "123" will be taken as the string "123", not the number 123. If you want a numeric variable, do not worry about whether it is byte, int, float, etc. If a byte will hold your first number, but, to hold your second number, you will need a float, the editor will recast the variable later.

❑

❑ Technical Note

If you do not type in the first empty column, but instead type in one to the right of it, the editor will create variables for all the intervening columns.

❑

Adding new observations

Go to the first empty row and begin entering your data. As soon as you add one cell below the last row of the dataset, the observation will be created.

❑ Technical Note

If you do not enter data in the first empty row, but instead enter data in a row below it, the editor will create observations for all the intervening rows.

❑

Copying and pasting

You can copy and paste data between Stata's editor and other spreadsheets.

First, select the data you wish to copy. In Stata, click on a cell and drag the mouse across other cells to select a range of cells. If you want to select an entire column, click once on the variable name at the top of that column. If you want to select an entire row, click once on the observation number at the left of that row. You can hold down the mouse button after clicking and drag to select multiple columns or rows.

Once you have selected the data, copy the data to the clipboard. In Stata, pull down **Edit** and choose **Copy**.

You can copy data to the clipboard from Stata with or without the variable names at the top of each column. You can access this option by pulling down **Prefs–General Preferences...**, choosing **Editor Prefs**, and checking or unchecking *Include variable names on copy to clipboard*.

If the data you have selected contain any values that have been labeled, you can choose to copy either the value labels or the underlying numeric values. You can access this option by pulling down **Prefs–General Preferences...**, choosing **Editor Prefs**, and checking or unchecking *Copy value labels instead of numbers*. For more information on value labels, see [U] **15.6.3 Value labels** and [R] **label**.

After you have copied data to the clipboard from Stata's editor or another spreadsheet, you can paste the data into Stata's editor. First, select the top left cell of the area to which you wish to paste by clicking on it once. Then, pull down **Edit** and choose **Paste**. If you entered Stata's editor in restricted-edit or in browse mode, **Paste** will be grayed out, and you will not be able to paste into Stata's editor.

Stata will paste the data from the clipboard into the editor, overwriting any data below and to the right of the cell you selected as the top left of the paste area.

❏ Technical Note

If you attempt to paste one or more string values into numeric variables, the original numeric values will be left unchanged for those cells. Stata will display a message box to let you know this has happened: "You attempted to paste one or more string values into numeric variables. The contents of these cells, if any, are unchanged."

If you see this message, you should look carefully at the data that you pasted into Stata's editor to make sure that you pasted into the area that you intended. We recommend that you press **Preserve** before pasting into Stata's editor so that you can **Restore** the data in case there is a mistake when you paste.

❏

Exiting

If you are using a Macintosh, click on the editor's close box.

If you are using Windows, click on the editor's close box (the box with an **X** at the right of the editor's title bar). You can also hold down *Alt* and press *F4* to exit the editor.

Logging changes

When you use `edit` to change existing data (as opposed to entering new data), you will find output in the Stata Results window documenting the changes that you made. A line of this output might be

```
- replace mpg=22.5 in 5
```

The syntax is that of a Stata command—the Stata command that could have been typed to achieve the same result as what you did in the editor. The dash in front of the command indicates that the change was done in the editor. If you are logging your results, you will have a permanent record of what you did.

Advice

1. People who care about data integrity know that editors are dangerous—it is too easy to accidentally make changes. Never use `edit` when you mean `browse`.

2. Protect yourself when you edit existing data by limiting exposure. If you need to change mpg, and need to see model to know which value of mpg to change, do not press the **Data Editor** button. Instead, type `edit model mpg`. It is now impossible for you to change (damage) variables other than model and mpg. Furthermore, if you know that you need to change mpg only if it is missing, then you can reduce your exposure even more by typing 'edit model mpg if mpg>=.'.

3. All of this said, Stata's editor is safer than most because it logs changes to the Results window. Use this feature—look at the log afterward and verify that the changes you made are the changes you wanted to make.

References

Brady, T. 1998. dm63: Dialog box window for browsing, editing, and entering observations. *Stata Technical Bulletin* 46: 2–6. Reprinted in *Stata Technical Bulletin Reprints*, vol. 8, pp. 28–34.

——. 2000. dm63.1: A new version of winshow for Stata 6. *Stata Technical Bulletin* 53: 3–5. Reprinted in *Stata Technical Bulletin Reprints*, vol. 9, pp. 15–19.

Also See

Related: [R] **input**, [R] **list**,
                 [GSM] **Getting started with Stata for Macintosh**,
                 [GSU] **Getting started with Stata for Unix**,
                 [GSW] **Getting started with Stata for Windows**

Title

> **egen** — Extensions to generate

Syntax

egen $[type]$ *newvar* = *fcn(arguments)* $[if\ exp]$ $[in\ range]$ $[,\ options]$

by ... : may be used with egen unless otherwise noted; see [R] **by**.

Description

egen creates *newvar* of the optionally specified storage type equal to *fcn(arguments)*. Depending on the *fcn*, *arguments* refers to an expression, *varlist*, or *numlist*, and the *options* are also *fcn* dependent. Note that explicit subscripting (using _N and _n), which is commonly used with generate, should not be used with egen; see [U] **16.7 Explicit subscripting**.

The *fcn*s are

any(*varname*) , values(*integer numlist*)
  may not be combined with by. It takes the value of *varname* if *varname* is equal to any of the integer values in a supplied *numlist*, and missing otherwise. Also see eqany(*varlist*) and neqany(*varlist*).

count(*exp*)   (allows by *varlist*:)
  creates a constant (within *varlist*) containing the number of nonmissing observations of *exp*. Also see robs() and rmiss().

concat(*varlist*) $[$, format(*%fmt*) decode maxlength(*#*) punct(*pchars*) $]$
  may not be combined with by. It concatenates *varlist* to produce a string variable. Values of string variables are unchanged. Values of numeric variables are converted to string as is, or are converted using a format under option format(*%fmt*), or decoded under option decode, in which case, maxlength() may also be used to control the maximum label length used. By default, variables are added end-to-end: punct(*pchars*) may be used to specify punctuation, such as a space, punct(" "), or a comma, punct(,).

cut(*varname*), { at(*#,#,...,#*) | group(*#*) } $[$ icodes label $]$
  may not be combined with by. It creates a new categorical variable coded with the left-hand ends of the grouping intervals specified in the at() option, which expects an ascending numlist.

  at(*#,#,...,#*) supplies the breaks for the groups, in ascending order. The list of break points may be simply a list of numbers separated by commas, but can also include the syntax a(b)c, meaning from a to c in steps of size b. If no breaks are specified, the command expects the option group().

  group(*#*) specifies the number of equal frequency grouping intervals to be used in the absence of breaks. Specifying this option automatically invokes icodes.

  icodes requests that the codes 0, 1, 2, etc. be used in place of the left-hand ends of the intervals.

  label requests that the integer-coded values of the grouped variable be labeled with the left-hand ends of the grouping intervals. Specifying this option automatically invokes icodes.

311

diff (*varlist*)

may not be combined with by. It creates an indicator variable equal to 1 if the variables in *varlist* are not equal, and 0 otherwise.

eqany (*varlist*), <u>v</u>alues (*integer numlist*)

may not be combined with by. It is 1 if any of the variables in *varlist* are equal to any of the integer values in a supplied *numlist*, and 0 otherwise. Values for any observations excluded by either ⌈if *exp*⌉ or ⌈in *range*⌉ are set to 0 (not missing). Also see any (*varname*) and neqany (*varlist*).

ends (*strvar*) ⌈, <u>p</u>unct (*pchars*) <u>tri</u>m { <u>h</u>ead | <u>l</u>ast | <u>t</u>ail } ⌉

may not be combined with by. It gives the first "word" or head (with the head option), the last "word" (with the last option), or the remainder or tail (with the tail option) from string variable *strvar*.

head, last and tail are determined by the occurrence of pchars, which is by default a single space " ".

The head is whatever precedes the first occurrence of *pchars*, or the whole of the string if it does not occur. The head of "frog toad" is "frog" and of "frog" is "frog". With punct (,), the head of "frog,toad" is "frog".

The last word is whatever follows the last occurrence of *pchars*, or the whole of the string if it does not occur. The last word of "frog toad newt" is "newt" and of "frog" is "frog". With punct (,), the last word of "frog,toad" is "toad".

The remainder or tail is whatever follows the first occurrence of *pchars*, which will be the empty string "" if it does not occur. The tail of "frog toad newt" is "toad newt" and of "frog" is "". With punct (,), the tail of "frog,toad" is "toad".

The trim option trims any leading or trailing spaces.

fill (*numlist*)

may not be combined with by. It creates a variable of ascending or descending numbers or complex repeating patterns. *numlist* must contain at least two numbers, and may be specified using standard *numlist* notation; see [U] **14.1.8 numlist**. ⌈if *exp*⌉ and ⌈in *range*⌉ are not allowed with fill ().

group (*varlist*) ⌈, <u>m</u>issing <u>l</u>abel <u>t</u>runcate (*num*) ⌉

may not be combined with by. It creates a single variable taking on values 1, 2, ... for the groups formed by *varlist*. *varlist* may contain numeric variables, string variables, or a combination of the two. missing indicates that missing values in *varlist* are to be treated like any other number when assigning groups, instead of missing values being assigned to the group missing. The label option returns integers from 1 up according to the distinct groups of *varlist* in sorted order. The integers will be labeled with the values of *varlist*, or the value labels if they exist. The truncate () option will truncate the values contributed to the label from each variable in *varlist* to the length specified by the integer argument *num*. The truncate option cannot be used without specifying the label option. The truncate option does not change the groups that are formed; it only changes their labels.

iqr (*exp*)   (allows by *varlist*:)

creates a constant (within *varlist*) containing the interquartile range of *exp*. Also see pctile ().

kurt (*varname*)   (allows by *varlist*:)

returns the kurtosis (within *varlist*) of *varname*.

ma(*exp*) [, t(*#*) <u>nomiss</u>]

may not be combined with by. It creates a *#*-period moving average of *exp*. If t() is not specified, t(3) is assumed, producing 3-period moving averages. *#* must be odd and *exp* must not produce missing values. Since moving averages are functions of lags and leads, ma() produces missing where the lags and leads do not exist—at the beginning and end of the series. nomiss forces the calculation of shorter, uncentered moving averages for the tails. [if *exp*] is not allowed with ma().

mad(*exp*)   (allows by *varlist*:)

returns the median absolute deviation from the median (within *varlist*) of *exp*.

max(*exp*)   (allows by *varlist*:)

creates a constant (within *varlist*) containing the maximum value of *exp*.

mdev(*exp*)   (allows by *varlist*:)

returns the mean absolute deviation from the mean (within *varlist*) of *exp*.

mean(*exp*)   (allows by *varlist*:)

creates a constant (within *varlist*) containing the mean of *exp*.

median(*exp*)   (allows by *varlist*:)

creates a constant (within *varlist*) containing the median of *exp*. Also see pctile().

min(*exp*)   (allows by *varlist*:)

creates a constant (within *varlist*) containing the minimum value of *exp*.

mode(*varname*) [, <u>min</u>mode <u>max</u>mode <u>num</u>mode(*integer*) <u>missing</u>]   (allows by *varlist*:)

produces the mode (within *varlist*) for *varname*, which may be numeric or string. The mode is the value occurring most frequently. If two or more modes exist, the mode produced will be a missing value. To avoid this, the minmode, maxmode, or nummode() options may be used to specify choices for selecting among the multiple modes. minmode returns the lowest value, and maxmode returns the highest value. nummode(*#*) will return the *#*th mode, counting from the lowest up. Missing values are excluded from determination of the mode unless missing is specified. Even so, the value of the mode is recorded for observations for which the values of *varname* are missing unless explicitly excluded, that is, by if *varname* < . or if *varname* != "".

mtr(*year income*)

may not be combined with by. It returns the U.S. marginal income tax rate for a married couple with taxable income *income* in year *year*, where $1930 \leq year \leq 2001$. *year* and *income* may be specified as variable names or constants; e.g., mtr(1993 faminc), mtr(surveyyr 28000), or mtr(surveyyr faminc). A blank or comma may be used to separate *income* from *year*.

neqany(*varlist*), <u>v</u>alues(*integer numlist*)

may not be combined with by. It returns the number of variables in *varlist* for which values are equal to any of the integer values in a supplied *numlist*. Values for any observations excluded by either [if *exp*] or [in *range*] are set to 0 (not missing). Also see any(*varname*) and eqany(*varlist*).

pc(*exp*) [, prop]   (allows by *varlist*:)

returns *exp* (within *varlist*) scaled to be a percent of total, between 0 and 100. The prop option returns *exp* scaled to be a proportion of total, between 0 and 1.

pctile(*exp*) [, p(*#*)]   (allows by *varlist*:)

creates a constant (within *varlist*) containing the *#*-th percentile of *exp*. If p(*#*) is not specified, 50 is assumed, meaning medians. Also see median().

rank(*exp*) $\big[$, $\big[$ f̲ield | t̲rack | u̲nique $\big]$ $\big]$ (allows by *varlist*:)
   creates ranks (within *varlist*) of *exp*; by default, equal observations are assigned the average rank.
   The field option calculates the field rank of *exp*: the highest value is ranked 1, and there is no
   correction for ties. Two values that are tied for 2nd remain rank 2. The track option calculates
   the track rank of *exp*: the lowest value is ranked 1, and there is no correction for ties. Two values
   that are tied for 2nd remain rank 2. The unique option calculates the unique rank of *exp*: values
   are ranked 1, ..., #, and values and ties are broken arbitrarily. Two values that are tied for 2nd
   are ranked 2 and 3.

rfirst(*varlist*)
   may not be combined with by. It gives the first nonmissing value in *varlist* for each observation
   (row). If all values in *varlist* are missing for an observation, *newvar* is set to missing.

rlast(*varlist*)
   may not be combined with by. It gives the last nonmissing value in *varlist* for each observation
   (row). If all values in *varlist* are missing for an observation, *newvar* is set to missing.

rmax(*varlist*)
   may not be combined with by. It gives the maximum value (ignoring missing values) in *varlist*
   for each observation (row). If all values in *varlist* are missing for an observation, *newvar* is set
   to missing.

rmean(*varlist*)
   may not be combined with by. It creates the (row) means of the variables in *varlist*, ignoring
   missing values; for example, if three variables are specified and, in some observations, one of
   the variables is missing, in those observations *newvar* will contain the mean of the two variables
   that do exist. Other observations will contain the mean of all three variables. Where none of the
   variables exist, *newvar* is set to missing.

rmin(*varlist*)
   may not be combined with by. It gives the minimum value in *varlist* for each observation (row).
   If all values in *varlist* are missing for an observation, *newvar* is set to missing.

rmiss(*varlist*)
   may not be combined with by. It gives the number of missing values in *varlist* for each observation
   (row).

robs(*varlist*) $\big[$, s̲trok $\big]$
   may not be combined with by. It gives the number of nonmissing values in *varlist* for each
   observation (row)—this is the value used by rmean() for the denominator in the mean calculation.

   String variables may not be specified unless option strok is also specified. If strok is specified,
   string variables will be counted as containing missing values when they contain "". Numeric
   variables will be counted as containing missing when their value is '$\geq$.' .

rsd(*varlist*)
   may not be combined with by. It creates the (row) standard deviations of the variables in *varlist*,
   ignoring missing values.

rsum(*varlist*)
   may not be combined with by. It creates the (row) sum of the variables in *varlist*, treating missing
   as 0.

sd(*exp*) (allows by *varlist*:)
   creates a constant (within *varlist*) containing the standard deviation of *exp*. Also see mean().

seq() $\left[\right.$, <u>f</u>rom(#) <u>to</u>(#) <u>b</u>lock(#) $\left. \right]$ (allows by *varlist*:)
   returns integer sequences. Values start from `from` (default 1) and increase to `to` (the default is the maximum number of values) in `blocks` (default size 1). If `to` is less than the maximum number, sequences restart at `from`. Numbering may also be separate within groups defined by *varlist*, or decreasing if `to` is less than `from`. Sequences depend on the sort order of observations, following three rules: (1) observations excluded by `if` or `in` are not counted, (2) observations are sorted by *varlist*, if specified, and (3) otherwise, the order is that when called. Note that no *arguments* are specified.

skew(*varname*)   (allows by *varlist*:)
   returns the skewness (within *varlist*) of *varname*.

std(*exp*) $\left[\right.$, <u>m</u>ean(#) <u>s</u>td(#) $\left. \right]$
   may not be combined with `by`. It creates the standardized values of *exp*. The options specify the desired mean and standard deviation. The default is `mean(0)` and `std(1)`, producing a variable with mean 0, standard deviation 1.

sum(*exp*)   (allows by *varlist*:)
   creates a constant (within *varlist*) containing the sum of *exp*. Also see `mean()`.

tag(*varlist*) $\left[\right.$, <u>m</u>issing $\left. \right]$
   may not be combined with `by`. It tags just one observation in each distinct group defined by *varlist*. When all observations in a group have the same value for a summary variable calculated for the group, it will be sufficient to use just one such value for many purposes. The result will be 1 or 0, according to whether the observation is tagged, and never missing. Values for any observations excluded by either $\left[\text{if } exp \right]$ or $\left[\text{in } range \right]$ are set to 0 (not missing). Hence, if `tag` is the variable produced by egen `tag = tag(`*varlist*`)`, the idiom `if tag` is always safe. `missing` specifies that missing values of *varlist* may be included.

Remarks

Remarks are presented under the headings

   Summary statistics
   Generating patterns
   Marking differences among variables
   Moving averages
   Ranks
   Standardized variables
   Row functions
   Categorical and integer variables
   String variables
   U.S. marginal income tax rate

Summary statistics

The functions `count()`, `iqr()`, `kurt()`, `mad()`, `max()`, `mdev()`, `mean()`, `median()`, `min()`, `mode()`, `pc()`, `pctile()`, `sd()`, `skew()`, and `sum()` create variables containing summary statistics. All functions take a `by ... :` prefix and, if specified, calculate the summary statistics within each by-group.

▷ Example

Without the `by ... :` prefix, the result produced by these functions is a constant for every observation in the data. For instance, you have data on cholesterol levels (`chol`) and wish to have a variable that, for each patient, records the deviation from the average across all patients:

```
. egen avg = mean(chol)
. generate dev = chol - avg
```

◁

▷ Example

These functions are most useful when the `by ... :` prefix is specified. For instance, assume that our dataset includes `dcode`, a hospital–patient diagnostic code, and `los`, the number of days that the patient remained in the hospital. We wish to obtain the deviation in length of stay from the median for all patients within the same diagnostic code:

```
. by dcode, sort: egen medstay = median(los)
. generate deltalos = los - medstay
```

◁

❏ Technical Note

Distinguish carefully between Stata's and `egen`'s `sum()` functions. Stata's creates the running sum, whereas `egen`'s creates a constant equal to the overall sum; for example,

```
. generate sum1=sum(a)
. egen sum2=sum(a)
. list
```

	a	sum1	sum2
1.	1	1	15
2.	2	3	15
3.	3	6	15
4.	4	10	15
5.	5	15	15

`sum()`, like the other `egen` summary statistic functions, can be usefully combined with the `by` prefix. A common problem in data management is the identification of duplicate (strictly, repeated) values. For example, these may arise from unintentional repetition in data entry or from the combination of datasets known to overlap.

Duplicates with respect to values of a list of variables, *varlist*, can be identified and counted like this:

```
. by varlist: egen dups = sum(_N > 1)
```

This adds up _N > 1 within each distinct group defined by *varlist*. This is because under by, _N is the number of observations in each group (not the total number of observations). With unique observations, _N == 1, and so _N > 1 is false and is numerically equal to 0. With repeated observations, _N > 1 is true and is numerically equal to 1, and adding up those 1s within each group is, naturally, the same as counting them. (See [U] **16.7 Explicit subscripting** for a discussion of the use of _n and _N with by.)

So, you can use

```
. tabulate dups
. list if dups
. drop if dups
```

and so forth. You can vary this idea with

```
. by varlist: egen unique = sum(_N == 1)
```

or

```
. by varlist: egen twos = sum(_N == 2)
```

if necessary.

❏

❏ Technical Note

The definitions and formulas used by these functions are the same as those used by summarize; see [R] **summarize**. For comparison with summarize, mean() and sd() correspond to the mean and standard deviation. sum() is the numerator of the mean and count() is its denominator. min() and max() correspond to the minimum and maximum. median() or, equally well, pctile() with p(50), is the median. pctile() with p(5) refers to the fifth percentile, and so on. iqr() is the difference between the 75th and 25th percentiles.

❏

▷ Example

The mode is the most common value of a dataset. This idea can be applied to numeric and string variables alike. It is perhaps most useful for categorical variables (whether defined by integers or strings) or for other integer-valued values, but mode() can be applied to variables of any type. Nevertheless, the modes of continuous (or nearly continuous) variables are perhaps better estimated either from inspection of a graph of a frequency distribution or from the results of some density estimation (see [R] **kdensity**).

Missing values need special attention. It is very possible that missing (whether the period (.) or extended missing values (.a, .b, ..., .z) for numeric variables or the empty string ("") for string variables) is the most common value in a variable. However, missing values are by default excluded from determination of modes. If you wish to include them, use the missing option.

In contrast, egen mode = mode(*varname*) allows the generation of nonmissing modes for observations for which *varname* is missing. This allows use of the mode as one simple means of imputation for categorical variables. If it is desired that the mode is missing whenever *varname* is missing, that is readily achieved by specifying if *varname* < . or if *varname* != "" or, most generally, if !missing(*varname*).

◁

mad() and mdev() produce alternative measures of spread. The median absolute deviation from the median and even the mean deviation will both be more resistant than the standard deviation to heavy tails or outliers, in particular from distributions with heavier tails than the normal or Gaussian. The first measure was named the MAD by Andrews et al. in 1972, but was already known to K. F. Gauss in 1816, according to Hampel et al. (1986). For further historical and statistical details, see David (1998).

Generating patterns

To create a sequence of numbers, simply "show" the `fill()` function how the sequence should look. It must be a linear progression to produce the expected results. Geometric progressions are not understood. To produce repeating patterns, you present `fill()` with the pattern twice in the *numlist*.

▷ Example

Here are some examples of ascending and descending sequences produced by `fill()`:

```
. set obs 12
obs was 0, now 12

. egen i=fill(1 2)

. egen w=fill(100 99)

. egen x=fill(22 17)

. egen y=fill(1 1 2 2)

. egen z=fill(8 8 8 7 7 7)

. list , sep(4)
```

	i	w	x	y	z
1.	1	100	22	1	8
2.	2	99	17	1	8
3.	3	98	12	2	8
4.	4	97	7	2	7
5.	5	96	2	3	7
6.	6	95	-3	3	7
7.	7	94	-8	4	6
8.	8	93	-13	4	6
9.	9	92	-18	5	6
10.	10	91	-23	5	5
11.	11	90	-28	6	5
12.	12	89	-33	6	5

◁

▷ Example

Here are examples of patterns produced by `fill()`:

```
. clear

. set obs 12
obs was 0, now 12

. egen a=fill(0 0 1 0 0 1)

. egen b=fill(1 3 8 1 3 8)

. egen c=fill(-3(3)6 -3(3)6)

. egen d=fill(10 20 to 50    10 20 to 50)
```

. list , sep(4)

	a	b	c	d
1.	0	1	-3	10
2.	0	3	0	20
3.	1	8	3	30
4.	0	1	6	40
5.	0	3	-3	50
6.	1	8	0	10
7.	0	1	3	20
8.	0	3	6	30
9.	1	8	-3	40
10.	0	1	0	50
11.	0	3	3	10
12.	1	8	6	20

◁

▷ Example

seq() creates a new variable containing one or more sequences of integers. It is mainly useful for the quick creation of observation identifiers or automatic numbering of levels of factors or categorical variables. seq() is based on the separate command seq (Cox 1997), but one notable detail has been changed, as noted at the end of this section.

In the simplest case,

. egen a = seq()

is just equivalent to the common idiom

. generate a = _n

a may also be obtained from

. range a 1 _N

(the actual value of _N may also be used).

In more complicated cases, seq() with option calls is equivalent to calls to those versatile functions int and mod.

. egen b = seq(), b(2)

produces integers in blocks of 2, while

. egen c = seq(), t(6)

restarts the sequence after 6 is reached.

. egen d = seq(), f(10) t(12)

shows that sequences may start with integers other than 1, and

. egen e = seq(), f(3) t(1)

shows that they may decrease.

Suppose that we have 12 observations in memory. The results of these commands are shown by

```
. list, sep(4)
```

	a	b	c	d	e
1.	1	1	1	10	3
2.	2	1	2	11	2
3.	3	2	3	12	1
4.	4	2	4	10	3
5.	5	3	5	11	2
6.	6	3	6	12	1
7.	7	4	1	10	3
8.	8	4	2	11	2
9.	9	5	3	12	1
10.	10	5	4	10	3
11.	11	6	5	11	2
12.	12	6	6	12	1

All these sequences could have been generated in one line with `generate` and with the use of the `int` and `mod` functions. The variables b through e are obtained with

```
. gen b = 1 + int((_n - 1)/2)
. gen c = 1 + mod(_n - 1, 6)
. gen d = 10 + mod(_n - 1, 3)
. gen e = 3 - mod(_n - 1, 3)
```

Nevertheless, `seq()` may save users from puzzling out such solutions or from typing in the needed values.

In general, the sequences produced depend on the sort order of observations, following three rules:

1. observations excluded by `if` or `in` are not counted;

2. observations are sorted by *varlist*, if specified; and

3. otherwise, the order is that when called.

Note that `seq` (Cox 1997) did not use Rule 3. The consequence was that the result of applying `seq` was not guaranteed to be identical from application to application whenever sorting was required, even with identical data, because of the indeterminacy of sorting. That is, if we sort (say) integer values, it is sufficient that all the 1s are together and are followed by all the 2s. But, there is no guarantee that the order of the 1s, as defined by any other variables, will be identical from sort to sort.

◁

The functions `fill()` and `seq()` are alternatives. In essence, `fill()` requires a minimal example that indicates the kind of sequence required, whereas `seq()` requires that the rule be specified through options. There are sequences that `fill()` can produce that `seq()` cannot, and vice versa. `fill()` cannot be combined with `if` or `in`, in contrast to `seq()`.

(Continued on next page)

Marking differences among variables

▷ Example

You have three measures of respondents' income obtained from different sources. You wish to create the variable `differ` equal to 1 in the case of disagreements:

```
. egen byte differ = diff(inc*)
. list
```

	inc1	inc2	inc3	differ
1.	12000	12000	12000	0
2.	14500	14500	.	1
3.	17500	17500	18000	1

Rather than typing `diff(inc*)`, you could have typed `diff(inc1 inc2 inc3)`.

◁

Moving averages

▷ Example

You have a time-series dataset and want to obtain moving averages. If you do not specify the `t()` option with `ma()`, you will obtain 3-period averages. Below, you obtain 3- and 5-period averages:

```
. egen y3 = ma(y)
(2 missing values generated)
. egen y5 = ma(y), t(5)
(4 missing values generated)
. list , sep(0)
```

	time	y	y3	y5
1.	1980	47.2	.	.
2.	1981	33.9	35.43333	.
3.	1982	25.2	29.73334	34.32
4.	1983	30.1	30.16667	31.52
5.	1984	35.2	32.83333	.
6.	1985	33.2	.	.

`ma()` assumes that the data are in chronological order. If you had specified the `nomiss` option, the missing values would have been filled in with shorter, uncentered averages.

◁

Ranks

▷ Example

You have a dataset containing eight observations on a variable named x, and these eight observations are divided into two groups of four observations. The eight values are 5, 4, −2, −3, 0, 0, *missing*, and 47. You wish to obtain the rank of the observations both overall and by group.

```
. egen rankx = rank(x)
(1 missing value generated)
. by grp, sort: egen rankx2 = rank(x)
(1 missing value generated)
. list , sep(4)
```

	x	grp	rankx	rankx2
1.	5	1	6	4
2.	4	1	5	3
3.	-2	1	2	2
4.	-3	1	1	1
5.	0	2	3.5	1.5
6.	0	2	3.5	1.5
7.	.	2	.	.
8.	47	2	7	3

◁

Standardized variables

▷ Example

You have a variable called age recording the median age in the 50 states. You wish to create the standardized value of age and verify the calculation:

```
. use http://www.stata-press.com/data/r8/states1
(State data)
. egen stdage = std(age)
. summarize age stdage
```

Variable	Obs	Mean	Std. Dev.	Min	Max
age	50	29.54	1.693445	24.2	34.7
stdage	50	6.41e-09	1	-3.153336	3.047044

```
. correlate age stdage
(obs=50)
```

	age	stdage
age	1.0000	
stdage	1.0000	1.0000

summarize shows that the new variable has a mean of approximately 0; 10^{-9} is the precision of a float and is close enough to zero for all practical purposes. If we wanted, we could have typed egen double stdage = std(age), making stdage a double-precision variable, and the mean would have been 10^{-16}. In any case, summarize also shows that the standard deviation is 1. correlate shows that the new variable and the original variable are perfectly correlated.

You may optionally specify the mean and standard deviation for the new variable. For instance,

```
. egen newage1 = std(age), std(2)
. egen newage2 = std(age), mean(2) std(4)
. egen newage3 = std(age), mean(2)
. summarize age newage1-newage3
```

Variable	Obs	Mean	Std. Dev.	Min	Max
age	50	29.54	1.693445	24.2	34.7
newage1	50	1.28e-08	2	-6.306671	6.094089
newage2	50	2	4	-10.61334	14.18818
newage3	50	2	1	-1.153336	5.047044

```
. correlate age newage1-newage3
(obs=50)
```

	age	newage1	newage2	newage3
age	1.0000			
newage1	1.0000	1.0000		
newage2	1.0000	1.0000	1.0000	
newage3	1.0000	1.0000	1.0000	1.0000

◁

Row functions

▷ Example

rsum(). generate's sum() function creates the vertical, running sum of its argument, while egen's sum() function creates a constant equal to the overall sum. egen's rsum() function, however, creates the horizontal sum of its arguments. They all treat missing as zero:

```
. egen hsum = rsum(a b c)
. generate vsum = sum(hsum)
. egen sum = sum(hsum)
. list
```

	a	b	c	hsum	vsum	sum
1.	.	2	3	5	5	63
2.	4	.	6	10	15	63
3.	7	8	.	15	30	63
4.	10	11	12	33	63	63

◁

▷ Example

rmean(), rsd(), and robs(). summarize displays the mean and standard deviation of a variable across observations; program writers can access the mean in r(mean) and the standard deviation in r(sd) (see [R] summarize). egen's rmean() function creates the means of observations across variables. rsd() creates the standard deviations of observations across variables. robs() creates a count of the number of nonmissing observations, the denominator of the rmean() calculation:

```
. egen avg = rmean(a b c)
. egen std = rsd(a b c)
. egen n = robs(a b c)
. list
```

	a	b	c	avg	std	n
1.	.	2	3	2.5	.7071068	2
2.	4	.	6	5	1.414214	2
3.	7	8	.	7.5	.7071068	2
4.	10	11	12	11	1	3

◁

▷ Example

rmiss(). rmiss() returns $k - \text{robs}()$, where k is the number of variables specified. rmiss() can be especially useful for finding casewise-deleted observations due to missing values.

```
. use http://www.stata-press.com/data/r8/auto3
(1978 Automobile Data)
. correlate price weight mpg
(obs=70)
```

	price	weight	mpg
price	1.0000		
weight	0.5309	1.0000	
mpg	-0.4478	-0.7985	1.0000

```
. egen excluded = rmiss(price weight mpg)
. list make price weight mpg if excluded !=0
```

	make	price	weight	mpg
5.	Buick Electra	.	4,080	15
12.	Cad. Eldorado	14,500	3,900	.
40.	Olds Starfire	4,195	.	24
51.	Pont. Phoenix	.	3,420	.

◁

▷ Example

rmin(), rmax(), rfirst(), and rlast(). These return the minimum, maximum, first, or last nonmissing value for the specified variables within an observation (row).

```
. egen min = rmin(x y z)
(1 missing value generated)
. egen max = rmax(x y z)
(1 missing value generated)
. egen first = rfirst(x y z)
(1 missing value generated)
. egen last = rlast(x y z)
(1 missing value generated)
```

```
. list, sep(4)
```

	x	y	z	min	max	first	last
1.	-1	2	3	-1	3	-1	3
2.	.	-6	.	-6	-6	-6	-6
3.	7	.	-5	-5	7	7	-5
4.	.	.	.	.	.	.	.
5.	4	.	.	4	4	4	4
6.	.	.	8	8	8	8	8
7.	.	3	7	3	7	3	7
8.	5	-1	6	-1	6	5	6

◁

Categorical and integer variables

▷ Example

any(), eqany(), and neqany() are for categorical or other variables taking integer values. If we define a subset of values specified by an integer *numlist* (see [U] **14.1.8 numlist**), then any() extracts the subset, leaving every other value missing, eqany() defines an indicator variable (1 if in subset, 0 otherwise), and neqany() counts occurrences of the subset across a set of variables. Therefore, with just one variable, eqany(*varname*) and neqany(*varname*) are equivalent.

With the auto dataset, we can generate a variable containing the high values of rep78 and a variable indicating whether rep78 has a high value:

```
. use http://www.stata-press.com/data/r8/auto
(1978 Automobile Data)
. egen hirep = any(rep78), v(3/5)
(15 missing values generated)
. egen ishirep = eqany(rep78), v(3/5)
```

In this case, it is easy to produce the same results with official Stata commands:

```
. generate hirep = rep78 if rep78 == 3 | rep78 == 4 | rep78 == 5
. generate byte ishirep = rep78 == 3 | rep78 == 4 | rep78 == 5
```

However, as the specification becomes more complicated, or involves several variables, the egen functions may be more convenient.

◁

▷ Example

group() maps the distinct groups of a *varlist* to a categorical variable that takes on integer values from 1 to the number of groups. The order of the groups is that of the sort order of *varlist*. The *varlist* may be of numeric variables, string variables, or a mixture of the two. The resulting variable can be useful for many purposes, including stepping through the distinct groups in an easy and systematic manner and tidying up an untidy ordering. Suppose the actual (and arbitrary) codes present in the data are 1, 2, 4, and 7, but we desire equally spaced numbers, as when the codes will be values on one axis of a graph. group() will map these to 1, 2, 3, and 4.

You have a variable `agegrp` that takes on the values 24, 40, 50, and 65, corresponding to age groups 18–24, 25–40, 41–50, and 51 and above. Perhaps you created this coding using the `recode()` function (see [U] **16.3 Functions** and [U] **28 Commands for dealing with categorical variables**) from another age-in-years variable:

```
. generate agegrp=recode(age,24,40,50,65)
```

You now wish the codes were 1, 2, 3, and 4:

```
. egen agegrp2 = group(agegrp)
```

◁

▷ Example

You have two categorical variables, `race` and `sex`, which may be string or numeric. You want to use `ir` (see [ST] **epitab**) to create a Mantel–Haenszel weighted estimate of the incidence rate. `ir`, however, will allow only one variable to be specified in its `by()` option. You type

```
. egen racesex = group(race sex)
. ir deaths smokes pyears, by(racesex)
(output omitted)
```

The new numeric variable `racesex` will be missing wherever `race` or `sex` is missing (meaning `.` for numeric variables and `""` for string variables), so missing values will be handled correctly. When we list some of the data, we see

```
. list race sex racesex, sep(0)
```

	race	sex	racesex
1.	black	female	1
2.	black	male	2
3.	white	female	3
4.	white	male	4
5.	white	male	4
6.		female	.
7.	white		.

`group()` began by putting the data in the order of the grouping variables, and then assigned the numeric codes. Note that observations 6 and 7 were assigned to `racesex==.` because, in one case, `race`, and in the other, `sex`, were not known. (These observations were then not used by the `ir` command.)

Had we wanted to treat the unknown groups just as we would any other category, we could have typed

```
. egen rs2=group(race sex), missing
. list race sex rs2, sep(0)
```

	race	sex	rs2
1.	black	female	2
2.	black	male	3
3.	white	female	5
4.	white	male	6
5.	white	male	6
6.		female	1
7.	white		4

◁

The resulting variable from `group` does not have value labels. Therefore, the values from 1 upward carry no indication of meaning. Interpretation requires comparison with the original *varlist*.

The `label` option produces a categorical variable with value labels. These value labels are either the actual values of *varname*, or any value labels of *varname*, if they exist. The values of *varname* could be as long as those of a single `str244` variable (with Stata/SE), but value labels may be no longer than 80 characters.

String variables

Concatenation of string variables is already provided in Stata. In context, Stata understands the addition symbol + as specifying concatenation, or adding strings end to end. `"soft"` + `"ware"` produces `"software"` and, given string variables `s1` and `s2`, `s1` + `s2` indicates their concatenation.

The complications that may arise in practice include (1) wanting to concatenate the string versions of numeric variables, and (2) wanting to concatenate variables, together with some separator such as a space or a comma. Given numeric variables `n1` and `n2`,

```
. generate str1 newstr = ""
. replace newstr = s1 + string(n1) + string(n2) + s2
```

shows how numeric values may be converted to their string equivalents before concatenation, and

```
. replace newstr = s1 + " " + s2 + " " + s3
```

shows how spaces may be added in between variables. Here, as often happens, it is assumed that we would rather let Stata work out the particular string data type required. That is, we first `generate` a variable of type `str1`, the most compact string type, and then the `replace` command automatically leads to promotion of the variable to the appropriate data type.

▷ Example

`concat()` allows you to do everything in one line in a very concise manner.

```
. egen newstr = concat(s1 n1 n2 s2)
```

carries with it an implicit instruction to convert numeric values to their string equivalents, and the appropriate string data type is worked out within `concat()` by Stata's automatic promotion. Moreover,

```
. egen newstr = concat(s1 s2 s3), p(" ")
```

specifies that spaces are to be used as separators. (The default is no separation of concatenated strings.)

As an example of punctuation other than a space, consider

```
. egen fullname = concat(surname forename), p(", ")
```

Noninteger numerical values can cause difficulties, but

```
. egen newstr = concat(n1 n2), format(%9.3f) p(" ")
```

specifies the use of format `%9.3f`. In other words, this is equivalent to

```
. generate str1 newstr = ""
. replace newstr = string(n1,"%9.3f") + " " + string(n2,"%9.3f")
```

See [R] **functions** for more on `string()`.

◁

As a final flourish, the decode option instructs concat() to use value labels. With that option, the maxlength() option may also be used. For further details on decode, see [R] **encode**. Unlike the decode command, however, concat() uses string(*varname*), not "", whenever values of *varname* are not associated with value labels, and the format() option, whenever specified, applies to this use of string().

▷ Example

The function ends(*strvar*) is for subdividing strings. The approach is to find specified separators using the index() string function and then to extract what is desired, which either precedes or follows the separators, using the substr() string function (see [U] **16.3.5 String functions**).

By default, substrings are considered to be separated by individual spaces, so we will give definitions in those terms and then generalize.

The *head* of the string is whatever precedes the first space, or the whole of the string if no space occurs. This could also be called the first 'word'. The *tail* of the string is whatever follows the first space. This could be nothing or one or more words. The *last word* in the string is whatever follows the last space, or the whole of the string if no space occurs.

To make this clear, let us look at some examples. The quotation marks here just mark the limits of each string, and are not part of the strings.

	head	tail	last
"frog"	"frog"	""	"frog"
"frog toad"	"frog"	"toad"	"toad"
"frog toad newt"	"frog"	"toad newt"	"newt"
"frog toad newt"	"frog"	" toad newt"	"newt"
"frog toad newt"	"frog"	"toad newt"	"newt"

The main subtlety is that these functions are literal, so the tail of "frog toad newt", in which two spaces follow "frog", includes the second of those spaces, and is thus " toad newt". Therefore, you may prefer to use the trim() option to trim the result of any leading and/or trailing spaces, producing "toad newt" in this instance.

The punct(*pchars*) option may be used to specify separators other than spaces. The general definitions of the head, tail, and last options are therefore in terms of whatever separator has been specified; that is, relative to the first or last occurrence of the separator in the string value. Thus, with punct(,) and the string "Darwin, Charles Robert", the head is "Darwin" and the tail and the last are both " Charles Robert". Note again the leading space in this example, which may be trimmed with trim(). The punctuation (here the comma ,) is discarded, just as it is with a single space.

pchars, the argument of punct(), will usually, but not always, be a single character. If two or more characters are specified, then these must occur together; punct(:;) would mean that words are separated by a colon followed by a semi-colon (that is :;). It is not implied, in particular, that the colon and semi-colon are alternatives. For that, the user must modify the programs presented here or resort to first principles using tokenize; see [P] **tokenize**.

With personal names, the options head or last might be applied to extract surnames if strings were like "Darwin, Charles Robert" or "Charles Robert Darwin", with the surname coming first or last. What then happens with surnames like "von Neumann" or "de la Mare"? "von Neumann, John" is no problem, if the comma is specified as a separator, but the option last is not intelligent enough to handle "Walter de la Mare" properly. For that, the best advice is to use programs specially written for person name extraction, such as extrname (Gould 1993).

◁

U.S. marginal income tax rate

mtr(*year income*) (Schmidt 1993, 1994) returns the U.S. marginal income tax rate for a married couple with taxable income *income* in year *year*, where $1930 \leq year \leq 2001$.

▷ Example

Schmidt (1993) examines the change in the progressivity of the U.S. tax schedule over the period from 1930 to 1990. As a measure of progressivity, he calculates the difference in the marginal tax rates at the 75th and 25th percentiles of income, using a dataset of percentiles of taxable income developed by Hakkio, Rush, and Schmidt (1993). (Certain aspects of the income distribution were imputed in these data.) A subset of the data contains

```
. describe
Contains data from income.dta
  obs:          61
  vars:          4                               30 May 2002 15:40
  size:      1,220 (99.8% of memory free)

             storage  display    value
variable name  type   format     label    variable label

year          float   %9.0g               Year
inc25         float   %9.0g               25th percentile
inc50         float   %9.0g               50th percentile
inc75         float   %9.0g               75th percentile

Sorted by:
. summarize
    Variable |     Obs        Mean    Std. Dev.       Min        Max

        year |      61        1960    17.75293       1930       1990
       inc25 |      61    6948.272    6891.921      819.4   27227.35
       inc50 |      61    11645.15    11550.71    1373.29   45632.43
       inc75 |      61    18166.43     18019.1    2142.33   71186.58
```

Given the series for income and the (four digit) year, we can generate the marginal tax rates corresponding to the 25th and 75th percentiles of income:

```
. egen mtr25 = mtr(year inc25)
. egen mtr75 = mtr(year inc75)
. summarize mtr25 mtr75
    Variable |     Obs        Mean    Std. Dev.       Min        Max

       mtr25 |      61    .1664898    .0677949     .01125        .23
       mtr75 |      61    .2442053    .1148427     .01125    .424625
```

◁

Methods and Formulas

egen is implemented as an ado-file.

Stata users have written many extra functions for egen. Type net search egen to locate Internet sources of programs.

Acknowledgments

The mtr() *fcn* of egen was written by Timothy J. Schmidt of the Federal Reserve Bank of Kansas City.

The cut *fcn* was written by David Clayton and Michael Hills (1999a, 1999b, 1999c).

Many of the other egen *fcn*s were written by Nicholas J. Cox of the University of Durham.

References

Andrews, D. F., P. J. Bickel, F. R. Hampel, P. J. Huber, W. H. Rogers, and J. W. Tukey. 1972. *Robust estimates of location: survey and advances.* Princeton: Princeton University Press.

Clayton, D. and M. Hills. 1999a. dm66: Recoding variables using grouped values. *Stata Technical Bulletin* 49: 6–7. Reprinted in *Stata Technical Bulletin Reprints*, vol. 9, pp. 23–25.

——. 1999b. dm66.1: Stata 6 version of recoding variables using grouped values. *Stata Technical Bulletin* 50: 3. Reprinted in *Stata Technical Bulletin Reprints*, vol. 9, p. 25.

——. 1999c. dm66.2: Update of cut to Stata 6. *Stata Technical Bulletin* 51: 2–3. Reprinted in *Stata Technical Bulletin Reprints*, vol. 9, pp. 25–26.

Cox, N. J. 1997. dm44: Sequences of integers. *Stata Technical Bulletin* 37: 2–4. Reprinted in *Stata Technical Bulletin Reprints*, vol. 7, pp. 32–33.

——. 1999. dm70: Extensions to generate, extended. *Stata Technical Bulletin* 50: 9–17. Reprinted in *Stata Technical Bulletin Reprints*, vol. 9, pp. 34–45.

——. 2000. dm70.1: Extensions to generate, extended: corrections. *Stata Technical Bulletin* 57: 2. Reprinted in *Stata Technical Bulletin Reprints*, vol. 10, p. 9.

——. 2001. dm90: Listing distinct values of a variable. *Stata Technical Bulletin* 60: 8–11. Reprinted in *Stata Technical Bulletin Reprints*, vol. 10, pp. 46–49.

Cox, N. J. and R. Goldstein. 1999a. dm72: Alternative ranking procedures. *Stata Technical Bulletin* 51: 5–7. Reprinted in *Stata Technical Bulletin Reprints*, vol. 9, pp. 48–51.

——. 1999b. dm72.1: Alternative ranking procedures: update. *Stata Technical Bulletin* 52: 2. Reprinted in *Stata Technical Bulletin Reprints*, vol. 9, p. 51.

David, H. A. 1998. Early sample measures of variability. *Statistical Science* 13: 368–377.

Esman, R. M. 1998. dm55: Generating sequences and patterns of numeric data: an extension to egen. *Stata Technical Bulletin* 43: 2–3. Reprinted in *Stata Technical Bulletin Reprints*, vol. 8, pp. 4–5.

Gould, W. W. 1993. dm13: Person name extraction. *Stata Technical Bulletin* 13: 6–11. Reprinted in *Stata Technical Bulletin Reprints*, vol. 3, pp. 25–31.

Hakkio, C. S., M. Rush, and T. J. Schmidt. 1993. The marginal income tax rate schedule from 1930 to 1990. Research Working Paper, Federal Reserve Bank of Kansas City.

Hampel, F. R., E. M. Ronchetti, P. J. Rousseeuw, and W. A. Stahel. 1986. *Robust statistics: the approach based on influence functions.* New York: John Wiley & Sons.

Ryan, P. 1999. dm71: Calculating the product of observations. *Stata Technical Bulletin* 51: 3–4. Reprinted in *Stata Technical Bulletin Reprints*, vol. 9, pp. 45–48.

——. 2001. dm87: Calculating the row product of observations. *Stata Technical Bulletin* 60: 3–4. Reprinted in *Stata Technical Bulletin Reprints*, vol. 10, pp. 39–41.

Schmidt, T. J. 1993. sss1: Calculating U.S. marginal income tax rates. *Stata Technical Bulletin* 15: 17–19. Reprinted in *Stata Technical Bulletin Reprints*, vol. 3, pp. 197–200.

——. 1994. sss1.1: Updated U.S. marginal income tax rate function. *Stata Technical Bulletin* 22: 29. Reprinted in *Stata Technical Bulletin Reprints*, vol. 4, p. 224.

Also See

Related: [R] **collapse**, [R] **generate**

Background: [U] **16.3 Functions**

Title

eivreg — Errors-in-variables regression

Syntax

eivreg *depvar* [*indepvars*] [*weight*] [if *exp*] [in *range*] [,

    <u>r</u>eliab(*indepvar #* [*indepvar #* [...]]) <u>l</u>evel(*#*)]

by ... : may be used with eivreg; see [R] **by**.

aweights and fweights are allowed; see [U] **14.1.6 weight**.

eivreg shares the features of all estimation commands; see [U] **23 Estimation and post-estimation commands**.

Syntax for predict

predict [*type*] *newvarname* [if *exp*] [in *range*] [, *statistic*]

where *statistic* is

xb	$\mathbf{x}_j\mathbf{b}$, fitted values (the default)
<u>r</u>esiduals	residuals
<u>p</u>r(*a,b*)	$\Pr(a < y_j < b)$
e(*a,b*)	$E(y_j \mid a < y_j < b)$
<u>y</u>star(*a,b*)	$E(y_j^*)$, $y_j^* = \max(a, \min(y_j, b))$
stdp	standard error of the prediction
stdf	standard error of the forecast

where *a* and *b* may be numbers or variables; *a* missing ($a \geq .$) means $-\infty$, and *b* missing ($b \geq .$) means $+\infty$; see [U] **15.2.1 Missing values**.

These statistics are available both in and out of sample; type predict ... if e(sample) ... if wanted only for the estimation sample.

Description

eivreg fits errors-in-variables regression models.

Options

reliab(*indepvar #* [*indepvar #* [...]]) specifies the measurement reliability for each independent variable measured with error. Reliabilities are specified as a pair consisting of an independent variable name (a name that appears in *indepvars*) and the corresponding reliability r, $0 < r \leq 1$. Independent variables for which no reliability is specified are assumed to have reliability 1. If the option is not specified, all variables are assumed to have reliability 1, and the result is thus the same as that produced by regress (which is to say, the ordinary least squares results).

level(*#*) specifies the confidence level, in percent, for confidence intervals. The default is level(95) or as set by set level; see [U] **23.6 Specifying the width of confidence intervals**.

Options for predict

xb, the default, calculates the linear prediction.

residuals calculates the residuals; that is, $y_j - \mathbf{x}_j \mathbf{b}$.

pr(a,b) calculates $\Pr(a < \mathbf{x}_j \mathbf{b} + u_j < b)$, the probability that $y_j | \mathbf{x}_j$ would be observed in the interval (a, b).

a and b may be specified as numbers or variable names; *lb* and *ub* are variable names;
pr(20,30) calculates $\Pr(20 < \mathbf{x}_j \mathbf{b} + u_j < 30)$;
pr(*lb*,*ub*) calculates $\Pr(lb < \mathbf{x}_j \mathbf{b} + u_j < ub)$;
and pr(20,*ub*) calculates $\Pr(20 < \mathbf{x}_j \mathbf{b} + u_j < ub)$.

a missing ($a \geq .$) means $-\infty$; pr(.,30) calculates $\Pr(-\infty < \mathbf{x}_j \mathbf{b} + u_j < 30)$;
pr(*lb*,30) calculates $\Pr(-\infty < \mathbf{x}_j \mathbf{b} + u_j < 30)$ in observations for which $lb \geq .$
(and calculates $\Pr(lb < \mathbf{x}_j \mathbf{b} + u_j < 30)$ elsewhere).

b missing ($b \geq .$) means $+\infty$; pr(20,.) calculates $\Pr(+\infty > \mathbf{x}_j \mathbf{b} + u_j > 20)$;
pr(20,*ub*) calculates $\Pr(+\infty > \mathbf{x}_j \mathbf{b} + u_j > 20)$ in observations for which $ub \geq .$
(and calculates $\Pr(20 < \mathbf{x}_j \mathbf{b} + u_j < ub)$ elsewhere).

e(a,b) calculates $E(\mathbf{x}_j \mathbf{b} + u_j \mid a < \mathbf{x}_j \mathbf{b} + u_j < b)$, the expected value of $y_j | \mathbf{x}_j$ conditional on $y_j | \mathbf{x}_j$ being in the interval (a, b), which is to say, $y_j | \mathbf{x}_j$ is censored.
a and b are specified as they are for pr().

ystar(a,b) calculates $E(y_j^*)$, where $y_j^* = a$ if $\mathbf{x}_j \mathbf{b} + u_j \leq a$, $y_j^* = b$ if $\mathbf{x}_j \mathbf{b} + u_j \geq b$, and $y_j^* = \mathbf{x}_j \mathbf{b} + u_j$ otherwise, which is to say, y_j^* is truncated. a and b are specified as they are for pr().

stdp calculates the standard error of the prediction. It can be thought of as the standard error of the predicted expected value or mean for the observation's covariate pattern. This is also referred to as the standard error of the fitted value.

stdf calculates the standard error of the forecast. This is the standard error of the point prediction for a single observation. It is commonly referred to as the standard error of the future or forecast value. By construction, the standard errors produced by stdf are always larger than those by stdp; see [R] **regress** *Methods and Formulas*.

Description

Errors-in-variables regression models are useful when one or more of the independent variables is measured with additive noise. Standard regression (as performed by regress) would underestimate the effect of the variable, and the other coefficients in the model can be biased to the extent they are correlated with the poorly measured variable. One can adjust for the biases if one knows the reliability:

$$r = 1 - \frac{\text{noise variance}}{\text{total variance}}$$

That is, given the model $\mathbf{y} = \mathbf{X}\mathcal{B} + \mathbf{u}$, for some variable $\mathbf{x}_i$ in $\mathbf{X}$, the $\mathbf{x}_i$ is observed with error, $\mathbf{x}_i = \mathbf{x}_i^* + \mathbf{e}$, and the noise variance is the variance of $\mathbf{e}$. The total variance is the variance of $\mathbf{x}_i$.

▷ Example

Pretend that in our automobile data, the weight of cars was measured with error, and pretend that the reliability of our measured weight is 0.85. The result of this would be to underestimate the effect of weight in a regression of, say, price on weight and foreign, and it would also bias the estimate of the coefficient on foreign (because being of foreign manufacture is correlated with the weight of cars). We would ignore all of this if we fitted the model with `regress`:

```
. use http://www.stata-press.com/data/r8/auto
(1978 Automobile Data)

. regress price weight foreign
```

Source	SS	df	MS
Model	316859273	2	158429637
Residual	318206123	71	4481776.38
Total	635065396	73	8699525.97

```
Number of obs =      74
F( 2,   71) =   35.35
Prob > F     =  0.0000
R-squared    =  0.4989
Adj R-squared =  0.4848
Root MSE     =    2117
```

price	Coef.	Std. Err.	t	P>|t|	[95% Conf. Interval]	
weight	3.320737	.3958784	8.39	0.000	2.531378	4.110096
foreign	3637.001	668.583	5.44	0.000	2303.885	4970.118
_cons	-4942.844	1345.591	-3.67	0.000	-7625.876	-2259.812

With `eivreg`, we can take account of our measurement error:

```
. eivreg price weight foreign, r(weight .85)
```

variable	assumed reliability
weight	0.8500
*	1.0000

```
errors-in-variables regression

Number of obs =      74
F( 2,   71) =   50.37
Prob > F     =  0.0000
R-squared    =  0.6483
Root MSE     = 1773.54
```

price	Coef.	Std. Err.	t	P>|t|	[95% Conf. Interval]	
weight	4.31985	.431431	10.01	0.000	3.459601	5.180099
foreign	4637.32	624.5362	7.43	0.000	3392.03	5882.609
_cons	-8257.017	1452.086	-5.69	0.000	-11152.39	-5361.64

The effect of weight is increased—as we knew it would be—and in this case, the effect of foreign manufacture is also increased. *A priori*, we only knew that the estimate of `foreign` might be biased; we did not know the direction.

◁

❏ Technical Note

Swept under the rug in our example is how one determines the reliability, r. It is not difficult to know that a variable is measured with error, but it is difficult to know the reliability since the ingredients for calculating r depend on the unobserved noise.

For the purposes of our example, we made up a value for r, and, in fact, we do not believe that weight is measured with error at all, so the reported `eivreg` results have no validity. The `regress` results were the statistically correct results in this case.

But let's pretend that we do suspect that weight is measured with error and that we do not know r. We could, in that case, experiment with various values of r as a way of describing the sensitivity of our estimates to possible error levels. We may not know r, but r does have a simple interpretation, and we could probably produce a sensible range for r by thinking about how the data were collected.

If the reliability r is less than the R^2 from a regression of the poorly measured variable on all the other variables, including the dependent variable, the information might as well not have been collected; no adjustment to the final results is possible. In the case of our automobile data, running a regression of weight on foreign and price would result in an R^2 of .6743. Thus, the reliability must be at least .6743 in this case. If you specify a reliability that is too small, eivreg will inform you of this and refuse to fit the model:

```
. eivreg price weight foreign, r(weight .6742)
reliability r() too small
r(399);
```

Returning to our problem of how to estimate r, too small or not, if the measurements are summaries of scaled items, the reliability may be estimated using the alpha command; see [R] **alpha**. If the score is computed from factor analysis and the data are scored using score's default options (see [R] **factor**), the square of the standard deviation of the score is an estimate of the reliability.   ❑

❑ Technical Note

Consider a model with more than one variable measured with error. For instance, say our model is that price is a function of weight, foreign, and mileage rating, and that both weight and mileage rating are measured with error.

```
. eivreg price weight foreign mpg, r(weight .85 mpg .9)
```

variable	assumed reliability		errors-in-variables regression	
			Number of obs =	74
weight	0.8500		F(3, 70) =	429.14
mpg	0.9000		Prob > F =	0.0000
*	1.0000		R-squared =	0.9728
			Root MSE =	496.41

price	Coef.	Std. Err.	t	P>|t|	[95% Conf. Interval]	
weight	12.88302	.6820532	18.89	0.000	11.52271	14.24333
foreign	8268.951	352.8719	23.43	0.000	7565.17	8972.732
mpg	999.2043	73.60037	13.58	0.000	852.413	1145.996
_cons	-56473.19	3710.015	-15.22	0.000	-63872.58	-49073.8

❑

(Continued on next page)

Saved Results

eivreg saves in e():

Scalars

e(N)	number of observations	e(r2)	R-squared
e(df_m)	model degrees of freedom	e(F)	F statistic
e(df_r)	residual degrees of freedom	e(rmse)	root mean square error

Macros

e(cmd)	eivreg	e(rellist)	*indepvars* and associated reliabilities
e(depvar)	name of dependent variable	e(predict)	program used to implement predict

Matrices

e(b)	coefficient vector	e(V)	variance–covariance matrix of the estimators

Functions

e(sample)	marks estimation sample

Methods and Formulas

eivreg is implemented as an ado-file.

Let the model to be fitted be

$$\mathbf{y} = \mathbf{X}^* \mathcal{B} + \mathbf{e}$$
$$\mathbf{X} = \mathbf{X}^* + \mathbf{U}$$

where $\mathbf{X}^*$ are the true values and $\mathbf{X}$ the observed values. Let $\mathbf{W}$ be the user-specified weights. If no weights are specified, $\mathbf{W} = \mathbf{I}$. If weights are specified, let $\mathbf{v}$ be the specified weights. If fweight frequency weights are specified, then $\mathbf{W} = \text{diag}(\mathbf{v})$. If aweight analytic weights are specified, then $\mathbf{W} = \text{diag}\{\mathbf{v}/(\mathbf{1}'\mathbf{v})(\mathbf{1}'\mathbf{1})\}$, which is to say, the weights are normalized to sum to the number of observations.

The estimates $\mathbf{b}$ of $\mathcal{B}$ are obtained as $\mathbf{A}^{-1}\mathbf{X}'\mathbf{W}\mathbf{y}$, where $\mathbf{A} = \mathbf{X}'\mathbf{W}\mathbf{X} - \mathbf{S}$. $\mathbf{S}$ is a diagonal matrix with elements $N(1 - r_i)s_i^2$. N is the number of observations, r_i is the user-specified reliability coefficient for the ith explanatory variable or 1 if not specified, and s_i^2 is the (appropriately weighted) variance of the variable.

The variance–covariance matrix of the estimators is obtained as $s^2 \mathbf{A}^{-1}\mathbf{X}'\mathbf{W}\mathbf{X}\mathbf{A}^{-1}$, where the root mean square error $s^2 = (\mathbf{y}'\mathbf{W}\mathbf{y} - \mathbf{b}\mathbf{A}\mathbf{b}')/(N - p)$, where p is the number of estimated parameters.

Also See

Complementary:	[R] **adjust**, [R] **lincom**, [R] **linktest**, [R] **mfx**, [R] **nlcom**, [R] **predict**, [R] **predictnl**, [R] **test**, [R] **testnl**, [R] **vce**, [R] **xi**
Related:	[R] **regress**
Background:	[U] **16.5 Accessing coefficients and standard errors**, [U] **23 Estimation and post-estimation commands**

Title

> **encode** — Encode string into numeric and vice versa

Syntax

> <u>en</u>code *varname* [if *exp*] [in *range*] , <u>g</u>enerate(*newvar*) [<u>l</u>abel(*name*)]

> <u>de</u>code *varname* [if *exp*] [in *range*] , <u>g</u>enerate(*newvar*) [<u>max</u>length(#)]

Description

encode creates a new variable named *newvar* based on the string variable *varname*, creating, adding to, or just using (as necessary) the value label *newvar* or, if specified, *name*. *Do not* use encode if *varname* contains numbers that merely happen to be stored as strings; instead use generate *newvar* =real(*varname*) or destring; see [U] **26.2 Categorical string variables**, [U] **16.3 Functions**, and [R] **destring**.

decode creates a new string variable named *newvar* based on the "encoded" numeric variable *varname* and its value label.

Options

generate(*newvar*) is not optional. It specifies the name of the variable to be created.

label(*name*) is optional. It specifies the name of the value label to be created, or, if the named value label already exists, used and added to as necessary. If label() is not specified, encode uses the same name for the label as it does for the new variable.

maxlength(#) specifies how many characters of the value label to retain; # must be between 1 and 80. The default is 80.

Remarks

encode is most useful in making string variables accessible to Stata's statistical routines, most of which can work with only numeric variables. encode is also useful in reducing the size of a dataset. If you are not familiar with value labels, read [U] **15.6.3 Value labels**.

The maximum number of associations within each value label is 65,536 (1,000 for Small Stata). Each association in a value label maps a string of up to 80 characters to a number. If your string has entries longer than that, only the first 80 characters are retained and are significant.

▷ Example

You have a dataset on high blood pressure, and among the variables is sex, a string variable containing either "male" or "female". You wish to run a regression of high blood pressure on race, sex, and age group. You type regress hbp race sex age_grp, and get the message "no observations".

```
. regress hbp sex race age_grp
no observations
r(2000);
```

337

Stata's statistical procedures cannot directly deal with string variables; as far as they are concerned, all observations on sex are missing. encode provides the solution:

```
. use http://www.stata-press.com/data/r8/hbp2
. encode sex, gen(gender)
. regress hbp gender race age_grp
```

Source	SS	df	MS		
Model	2.01013476	3	.67004492		
Residual	49.3886164	1117	.044215413		
Total	51.3987511	1120	.045891742		

```
Number of obs =     1121
F(  3,  1117) =    15.15
Prob > F      =   0.0000
R-squared     =   0.0391
Adj R-squared =   0.0365
Root MSE      =   .21027
```

hbp	Coef.	Std. Err.	t	P>|t|	[95% Conf. Interval]
gender	.0394747	.0130022	3.04	0.002	.0139633 .0649861
race	-.0409453	.0113721	-3.60	0.000	-.0632583 -.0186322
age_grp	.0241484	.00624	3.87	0.000	.0119049 .0363919
_cons	-.016815	.0389167	-0.43	0.666	-.093173 .059543

encode looks at a string variable and makes an internal table of all the values it takes on, in our case, "male" and "female". It then alphabetizes that list and assigns numeric codes to each entry. Thus, 1 becomes "female" and 2 becomes "male". It creates a new int variable (gender) and substitutes a 1 where sex is "female", a 2 where sex is "male", and a *missing* (.) where sex is *null* (""). It creates a value label (also named gender) that records the mapping 1 ↔ female and 2 ↔ male. Finally, encode labels the values of the new variable with the value label.

◁

▷ Example

It is difficult to distinguish the result of encode from the original string variable. For instance, in our last two examples, we typed encode sex, gen(gender). Let's compare the two variables:

```
. list sex gender in 1/4
```

	sex	gender
1.	female	female
2.		.
3.	male	male
4.	male	male

They look almost identical, although you should notice the missing value for gender in the second observation.

The difference does show, however, if we tell list to ignore the value labels and show how the data really appear:

```
. list sex gender in 1/4, nolabel
```

	sex	gender
1.	female	1
2.		.
3.	male	2
4.	male	2

We could also ask to see the underlying value label:

```
. label list gender
gender:
              1 female
              2 male
```

gender really is a numeric variable, but since *all* Stata commands understand value labels, the variable displays as "male" and "female" just as would the underlying string variable sex.

◁

▷ Example

You can drastically reduce the size of your dataset by encoding strings and then discarding the underlying string variable. Say you have a string variable that records each person's sex as "male" and "female". "female" has six characters, so at the least you have the variable stored as a str6.

The variable created by encode is an int, which takes only two bytes. Thus, if your dataset contained 1,000 people, the string variable takes (at least) 6,000 bytes, whereas the encoded variable takes only 2,000 bytes. Thus, you might

```
. encode sex, gen(gender)
. drop sex
. rename gender sex
```

See decode below for instructions on how to convert an encoded variable back to string form. See [R] **compress** for more ways to compress datasets.

◁

❑ Technical Note

In the examples given above, the value label did not exist before encode created it. That is not required. If the value label does exist, encode will use your encoding as far as it can and add new mappings for anything not found in your value label. For instance, if you wanted "female" to be encoded as 0 rather than 1 (possibly for use in linear regression), you could

```
. label define gender 0 "female"
. encode sex, gen(gender)
```

You can also specify the name of the value label. If you do not, the value label is assumed to have the same name as the newly created variable. For instance,

```
. label define sexlbl 0 "female"
. encode sex, gen(gender) label(sexlbl)
```

❑

decode

decode is used to convert numeric variables with associated value labels into true string variables.

▷ Example

You have a numeric variable named `female` that records the values 0 and 1. `female` is associated to a value label named `sexlbl` that says 0 means male and 1 means female:

```
. describe female

              storage  display    value
variable name   type   format     label        variable label

female          int    %9.0g      sexlbl
. label list sexlbl
sexlbl:
          0 male
          1 female
```

We see that `female` is stored as an `int`. It is a numeric variable. Nevertheless, it has an associated value label describing what the numeric codes mean, so if we `tabulate` the variable, for instance, it appears as if it contains the strings "male" and "female":

```
. tabulate female
     female |      Freq.     Percent        Cum.

       male |         85       55.92       55.92
     female |         67       44.08      100.00

      Total |        152      100.00
```

We can create a real string variable from this numerically encoded variable using `decode`:

```
. decode female, gen(sex)
. describe sex

              storage  display    value
variable name   type   format     label        variable label

sex             str6   %9s
```

We have a new variable called `sex`. It is a string, and Stata automatically created the shortest possible string. "female" has six characters, so our new variable is a `str6`. `female` and `sex` appear indistinguishable:

```
. list female sex in 1/4

        female        sex

  1.      male       male
  2.    female     female
  3.    female     female
  4.    female     female
```

But when we add `nolabel`, the difference is apparent:

```
. list female sex in 1/4, nolabel

        female        sex

  1.         0       male
  2.         1     female
  3.         1     female
  4.         1     female
```

◁

▷ Example

decode is most useful in instances where you wish to match merge two datasets on a variable that has been encoded inconsistently.

For instance, you have two datasets on individual states where one of the variables (state) takes on values like "CA" and "NY". The state variable was originally a string, but along the way the variable was encoded into an integer with corresponding value label in one or both datasets.

You wish to merge these two datasets, but either (1) one of the datasets has a string variable for state and the other an encoded variable, or (2) although both are numeric, you are not certain that the codings are consistent. Perhaps "CA" has been coded 5 in one dataset and 6 in another.

Since decode will take an encoded variable and turn it back into a string, decode provides the solution:

```
use first                 (load the first dataset)
decode state, gen(st)     (make a string state variable)
drop state                (discard the encoded variable)
sort st                   (sort on string)
save first, replace       (and save it)
use second                (load the second dataset)
decode state, gen(st)     (make a string variable)
drop state                (discard the encoded variable)
sort st                   (sort on string)
merge st using first      (merge the data)
```

Of course, now you should tabulate _merge to make sure that the merge went as expected; see [R] **merge**.

◁

References

Cox, N. J. and J. B. Wernow. 2000a. dm80: Changing numeric variables to string. *Stata Technical Bulletin* 56: 8–12. Reprinted in *Stata Technical Bulletin Reprints*, vol. 10, pp. 24–28.

——. 2000b. dm80.1: Update to changing numeric variables to string. *Stata Technical Bulletin* 57: 2. Reprinted in *Stata Technical Bulletin Reprints*, vol. 10, pp. 28–29.

Also See

Complementary: [R] **compress**

Background: [U] **15.6.3 Value labels**,
    [U] **26.2 Categorical string variables**

Title

erase — Erase a disk file

Syntax

$\{\,\texttt{erase}\,|\,\texttt{rm}\,\}\ \left[\,\texttt{"}\,\right]\textit{filename}\left[\,\texttt{"}\,\right]$

Note: Double quotes must be used to enclose *filename* if the name contains spaces.

Description

The `erase` command erases files stored on disk. Unix users may type `erase`, but they will probably prefer to type `rm`. Under Unix, `erase` is a synonym for `rm`.

Stata for Macintosh users: Be warned that `erase` is permanent; the file is not moved to the Trash, but is immediately removed from the disk.

Stata for Windows users: Be warned that `erase` is permanent; the file is not moved to the Recycle Bin, but is immediately removed from the disk.

Remarks

The only difference between Stata's `erase` (`rm`) and the DOS DEL or Unix `rm(1)` is that you may not specify groups of files. Stata requires that you erase files one at a time.

Macintosh users may prefer to discard files by dragging them to the Trash.

Windows users may prefer to discard files by dragging them to the Recycle Bin.

▷ Example

Stata provides six operating-system equivalent commands: `cd`, `copy`, `dir`, `erase`, `mkdir`, and `type`, or, from the Unix perspective, `cd`, `copy`, `ls`, `rm`, `mkdir`, and `cat`. These commands are provided for Macintosh users, too. In addition, Stata for Unix users can issue any operating system command using Stata's `shell` command, so you should never have to exit Stata to perform some housekeeping detail.

Suppose you have the file `mydata.dta` stored on disk and you wish to permanently eliminate it:

```
. erase mydata
file mydata not found
r(601);
. erase mydata.dta
.
```

Our first attempt, `erase mydata`, was unsuccessful. Although Stata ordinarily supplies the file extension for you, it does not do so when you type `erase`. You must be explicit. Our second attempt eliminated the file. Unix users could have typed `rm mydata.dta` if they preferred.

◁

Also See

Related: [R] **cd**, [R] **copy**, [R] **dir**, [R] **mkdir**, [R] **shell**, [R] **type**

Background: [U] **14.6 File-naming conventions**

Title

error messages — Error messages and return codes

Description

Whenever Stata detects that something is wrong—that what you typed is uninterpretable, that you are trying to do something you should not be trying to do, or that you requested the impossible—Stata responds by typing a message describing the problem together with a *return code*. For instance,

```
. lsit
unrecognized command:  lsit
r(199);
. list myvar
variable myvar not found
r(111);
. test a=b
last estimates not found
r(301);
```

In each case, the message is probably sufficient to guide you to a solution. When we typed `lsit`, Stata responded with "unrecognized command". We meant to type `list`. When we typed `list myvar`, Stata responded with "variable myvar not found". There is no variable named `myvar` in our data. When we typed `test a=b`, Stata responded with "last estimates not found". `test` tests hypotheses about previously fitted models, and we have not yet fitted a model.

The numbers in parentheses in the `r(199)`, `r(111)`, and `r(301)` messages are called the *return codes*. To find out more about these messages, type `search rc #`.

▷ Example

```
. search rc 301

[R]     error messages . . . . . . . . . . . . . . . . . . . . Return code 301
        last estimates not found;
        You typed an estimation command such as regress without arguments
        or attempted to perform a test or typed predict, but there were no
        previous estimation results.
```
                                                                            ◁

Programmers should see [P] **error** for details on programming error messages.

Also See

Complementary: [R] **search**

Title

> **estimates** — Estimation results

Syntax

estimates <u>st</u>ore *name* $\left[\,,\ \underline{t}itle(str)\ nocopy\,\right]$

estimates <u>ch</u>ange *name* $\left[\,,\ \underline{t}itle(str)\ \underline{sc}orevars(varlist)\,\right]$

estimates <u>res</u>tore *name* $\left[\,,\ drop\,\right]$

estimates <u>f</u>or *namelist* $\left[\,,\ \underline{noh}eader\ \underline{nos}top\,\right]:$ *any_cmd*

estimates <u>r</u>eplay $\left[namelist\right]$ $\left[\,,\ \underline{noh}eader\,\right]$

estimates <u>st</u>ats $\left[namelist\right]$

estimates <u>d</u>ir $\left[namelist\right]$

estimates <u>t</u>able $\left[namelist\right]$ $\left[\,,\ stats(scalarlist)\ star\left[(\#1\ \#2\ \#3)\right]\ keep(keeplist)\right.$

    <u>d</u>rop(*droplist*) b$\left[(fmt)\right]$ se$\left[(fmt)\right]$ t$\left[(fmt)\right]$ p$\left[(fmt)\right]$ <u>stf</u>mt(*fmt*) eform

    <u>var</u>width(#) <u>l</u>abel <u>sty</u>le(*style_spec*) <u>new</u>panel $\left.\right]$

estimates <u>q</u>uery

estimates drop *namelist*

estimates clear

where

name is	*identifier* | .
namelist is	_all | * | *name* $\left[name\ \dots\right]$
style_spec is	<u>one</u>line | <u>c</u>olumn | <u>no</u>lines

estimates may be abbreviated to est and to esti.

Description

    estimates provides the preferred method to store and restore sets of estimation results. When we say "set of estimation results", we mean the collection of scalars, macros, matrices, and functions saved in e() after any given Stata estimation (eclass) command. For brevity, in what follows we refer to a set of estimation results as an "estimation set" or just a "set". Estimation sets are identified by name. In a *namelist*, you may use the * and ? wildcards. _all or * refers to all estimation sets. A period . refers to the most recent ("active") estimation set, even if the set has not (yet) been stored.

estimates store stores the active estimation set under *name*. The results from this set remain active. A set already stored under *name* is silently overwritten.

estimates change sets or modifies the descriptive title of an already stored estimation set or adds information about score variables.

estimates restore restores a stored estimation set, making it the active one so that all post-estimation commands will act on it.

estimates for evaluates a post-estimation command for one or more stored estimation sets. The post-estimation command can access the names under which the sets were stored via e(_estimates_name).

estimates replay replays results from stored estimation sets. If no *namelist* is specified, results from all stored sets are replayed.

estimates table displays a table with coefficients and statistics for one or more estimation sets in parallel columns. In addition, standard errors, t statistics, p-values, and scalar statistics may be listed.

estimates stats lists model statistics, including the AIC and BIC model selection indices, for the specified estimation set(s). If no *namelist* is specified, statistics for all stored sets are listed.

estimates dir lists the names, commands, dependent variables, and descriptions of stored sets. If no *namelist* is specified, all stored sets are described.

estimates query displays identifying information on the active set of estimation results.

estimates drop permanently drops stored estimation sets. Dropping the active estimation set clears the stored information (if stored), not the results from active memory.

estimates clear permanently drops all stored estimation sets.

Typing estimates without a subcommand replays results from the active estimation set.

You may store up to 20 estimation sets. Sets with large numbers of parameters use a considerable amount of memory. Thus, you are advised to drop sets when they are no longer needed.

The following post-estimation commands refer to estimation sets via the names under which they were stored via estimates:

hausman	Hausman specification test
lrtest	Likelihood-ratio test
suest	Testing cross-model hypotheses

With the obvious exception of estimates restore, all subcommands of estimates and the post-estimation commands do not change the active estimation results.

Options

Options for subcommands except for estimates table

title(*str*) (with subcommands store and change) specifies a title documenting a stored set. The title is displayed by the subcommands dir, replay, and for. You may also set or change the title later by the estimates change subcommand.

nocopy (with subcommand store) specifies that after storing the results for set *name*, these results are no longer available as the active estimation results.

scorevars(*varlist*) (with subcommand change) is a technical option. It records in the stored estimation set the names of the score variables associated with the set's results in e(scorevars). Many post-estimation commands require score variables, and obtain their varnames from this eclass macro. Most estimation commands that have a score() option will automatically set the macro for you. If you use an estimation command that does not store the names or you computed the score variables yourself, you can store their names so that post-estimation commands can find them.

drop (with subcommand restore) specifies that after restoring the set *name*, this set is no longer stored for later restoration.

noheader (with subcommands for and replay) suppresses the display of a header describing the name and title of stored set.

nostop (with subcommand for) does not stop repeating the command for other stored sets if one of them results in an error.

Options for estimates table

stats(*scalarlist*) specifies one or more scalars to be displayed in the table. *scalarlist* may contain e() scalars and the following statistics:

aic	Akaike's information criterion
bic	Schwarz's information criterion
rank	rank of e(V) – number of free parameters in model

scalarlist may be separated by white space or commas. Analogous to coefficients, requested scalars not saved by a particular estimation command (i.e., not contained in e()) are displayed as blanks. If a period "." is displayed, it indicates that the e() scalar is stored with a missing value ".".

Example: stats(N ll chi2 aic) specifies that the number of observations N, the log-likelihood ll, the chi2 test (test that the coefficients in the first equation of the model are 0), and the AIC information criterion are to be displayed.

star[(*#1 #2 #3*)] specifies that the significance of coefficients is denoted by stars: *: $p < .05$, **: $p < .01$, and ***: $p < .001$. The optional argument may override these thresholds ($1 > \#1 > \#2 > \#3 > 0$). star may not be combined with se, t, or p.

keep(*keeplist*) specifies the coefficients (and their order!) to be included in the table. A *keeplist* comprises one or more specifications, separated by white space: a variable name (e.g., price), an equation name (e.g., mean:), or a full name (e.g., mean:price).

drop(*droplist*) specifies the coefficients to be dropped from the table. A *droplist* comprises one or more specifications, separated by white space: a variable name (e.g., price), an equation name (e.g., mean:), or a full name (e.g., mean:price). All coefficients that match a specification are dropped. drop(_cons) drops _cons from all equations.

b[(*fmt*)] specified without an argument is allowed only for consistency with the options se, t, and p, and has no effect. Coefficients are always displayed. However, the optional argument may be used to specify the display format for the coefficients (e.g., b(%9.3f)). It defaults to %10.0g.

se[(*fmt*)] specifies that the standard errors of the coefficients are displayed below the coefficients. A display format may be specified as an optional argument (e.g., se(%9.2f)). By default, the display format of the coefficients is used.

t[(*fmt*)] specifies that the *t*- or *z*-values (coef/se(coef)) are displayed below the coefficients. A display format may be specified as an optional argument (e.g., t(%9.2f)). It defaults to %7.2f.

p[(*fmt*)] specifies that the (two-sided) *p*-values of the coefficients are displayed below the coefficients. As is standard in Stata, the reference distribution is the *t* if the estimation command saved the residual degrees of freedom in e(df_r), and the normal distribution otherwise. A display format may be specified as an optional argument (e.g., t(%7.2f)). It defaults to %7.4f.

stfmt(*fmt*) specifies the display format for the scalar statistics. It defaults to the display format of the coefficients.

eform displays the coefficient table in exponentiated form: for each coefficient, $\exp(b)$ rather than b is displayed and standard errors are transformed. Display of the intercept, if any, is suppressed.

varwidth(*#*) specifies the number of characters used to display the names of variables and statistics. It defaults to 12.

label specifies that variable labels are displayed instead of variable names.

style(*style_spec*) specifies the "style" of the coefficients table. The following values are allowed:

style(oneline)   specifies that a vertical line is displayed after the variables, but not between the models

style(columns)   specifies that vertical lines are displayed after each column (variable names, models)

style(noline)   suppresses all vertical lines

The default style is style(oneline).

newpanel specifies that the statistics are displayed in a table separated by a blank line from the table with coefficients, rather than in the style of another equation in the table of coefficients.

Remarks

We illustrate estimates, or est as we usually type it, with data from the General Social Survey 1991 (GSS1991), and ask the all-pervasive question as to the determinants of happiness. GSS91 contains a variable named happy.

```
. use http://www.stata-press.com/data/r8/gss1991
. tabulate happy
```

general happiness	Freq.	Percent	Cum.
very happy	467	31.05	31.05
pretty happy	872	57.98	89.03
not too happy	165	10.97	100.00
Total	1,504	100.00	

```
. label list happy
happy:
           0 nap
           1 very happy
           2 pretty happy
           3 not too happy
           8 dk
           9 na
```

Note that the variable happy is coded so that a higher value means less happiness. This is an unfortunate (unhappy?) coding scheme that invites trouble later on. We should either rename the variable happy to unhappy, or recode happy to a new variable Happy with a less confusing coding. We choose the latter so that we may illustrate the recode command in the process.

```
. recode happy (1 = 3 "very happy") (2 = 2 "pretty happy")
> (3 = 1 "not very happy"), into (Happy)
(632 differences between happy and Happy)

. tabulate Happy
```

RECODE of happy (general happiness)	Freq.	Percent	Cum.
not very happy	165	10.97	10.97
pretty happy	872	57.98	68.95
very happy	467	31.05	100.00
Total	1,504	100.00	

So, that looks much better. To "explain" individual differences in happiness, we want to confront a socioeconomic model with a psychological model. The socioeconomic model reflects the theoretical notion that happiness originates from the resources obtained from one's economic position. In the GSS data, a series of indicators are available. We use the variables sex, age, years of education, unemployment status (indicator), race, and region. Region and race are specified as indicator variables, with Western US and Other (than white and black) as reference categories.

Since Happy is an ordinal variable, we chose to analyze the data using an ordinal probit regression model—if you never had the opportunity to learn about this model, think of the coefficients as if you are looking at an ordinary regression model, and you are hardly missing a thing.

```
. oprobit Happy age edu unemploy female white black RegionNE RegionSE

Iteration 0:   log likelihood = -1378.4417
Iteration 1:   log likelihood = -1346.6646
Iteration 2:   log likelihood = -1346.6342
```

Ordered probit estimates				Number of obs	=	1496
				LR chi2(8)	=	63.61
				Prob > chi2	=	0.0000
Log likelihood = -1346.6342				Pseudo R2	=	0.0231

Happy	Coef.	Std. Err.	z	P>|z|	[95% Conf. Interval]	
age	.0035074	.0017519	2.00	0.045	.0000737	.0069411
educ	.0489342	.0105765	4.63	0.000	.0282046	.0696638
unemploy	-.4315152	.1548332	-2.79	0.005	-.7349828	-.1280477
female	-.113792	.0608997	-1.87	0.062	-.2331532	.0055692
white	.2884495	.1702879	1.69	0.090	-.0453087	.6222078
black	-.0210907	.1862567	-0.11	0.910	-.3861471	.3439658
RegionNE	-.0974579	.0717395	-1.36	0.174	-.2380649	.043149
RegionSE	.1366342	.0817859	1.67	0.095	-.0236633	.2969317
_cut1	-.3261708	.2418437	(Ancillary parameters)			
_cut2	1.443842	.2435946				

After fitting the model, we use the subcommand store of estimates to store the estimation results under a name. We use the name ecosocio, and also specify a title to facilitate our recollection of the model when we want to refer to it later.

```
. est store ecosocio, title(Socio-economic model of happiness)
```

We conclude that people with more years of education (educ) and older people tend to be (or at least, say that they are) happier, while unemployed people and women are less happy. Differences between regions are not significant. Whites and blacks do not differ from the others. This does not, of course, mean that there are no differences between whites and black: whites are .30 happier, and the difference is highly significant (see `lincom` on estimating contrasts). After fitting a model, we can display the coefficients with `est table`—nothing spectacular—the real use of `est table` will become clear after we fit addition models. The option `star` specifies that p-values of coefficients are marked with the standard star symbols, reflecting (two-sided) p-values. These are based on the Gaussian or t distribution, depending on whether or not the estimating command has defined the residual degrees of freedom `e(df_r)`.

```
. est table, star
```

Variable	ecosocio
age	.0035074*
educ	.0489342***
unemploy	-.43151525**
female	-.11379196
white	.28844951
black	-.02109066
RegionNE	-.09745792
RegionSE	.13663421
_cut1	-.32617082
_cut2	1.4438416***

legend: * p<0.05; ** p<0.01; *** p<0.001

On occasion, you may like to use different cut-points. An optional argument to `star` allows you to specify three values between 0 and 1 in decreasing order. Readers who do not like the star convention may use the option `p`, which displays p-values below the coefficients.

```
. est table, star(0.10 0.05 0.01) var(15)
```

Variable	ecosocio
age	.0035074**
educ	.0489342***
unemploy	-.43151525***
female	-.11379196*
white	.28844951*
black	-.02109066
RegionNE	-.09745792
RegionSE	.13663421*
_cut1	-.32617082
_cut2	1.4438416***

legend: * p<0.10; ** p<0.05; *** p<0.01

We now turn to the psychological thesis that attributes (lack of) happiness to stressful life events. From the GSS data, we use indications for three types of events: having serious psychological problems or infertility `unhealthy`, having children in serious trouble (being in hospital, addicted, etc.), and a recent death of a family member or good friend. Again, we fit an ordinal probit model and time store the estimation set under the name `psychological`.

(Continued on next page)

```
. oprobit Happy childs unhealthy childprob deathfriend

Iteration 0:    log likelihood = -1380.6557
Iteration 1:    log likelihood = -1375.6426
Iteration 2:    log likelihood = -1375.6419

Ordered probit estimates                        Number of obs   =        1497
                                                LR chi2(4)      =       10.03
                                                Prob > chi2     =      0.0400
Log likelihood = -1375.6419                     Pseudo R2       =      0.0036
```

Happy	Coef.	Std. Err.	z	P>|z|	[95% Conf. Interval]	
childs	-.0037312	.0170324	-0.22	0.827	-.037114	.0296517
unhealthy	-.2480445	.1212681	-2.05	0.041	-.4857257	-.0103633
childprob	-.2320317	.1099764	-2.11	0.035	-.4475814	-.016482
deathfriend	.0746206	.0831478	0.90	0.369	-.088346	.2375873
_cut1	-1.261743	.0557112	(Ancillary parameters)			
_cut2	.465453	.0480391				

```
. est store psychological, title(the psychological model of happiness)
```

We see that the number of children (childs) does not affect one's happiness. Being unhealthy—possibly due to infertility—or having a troubled child, however, seems to have sizable effect on one's happiness. Surprisingly, recently losing a family member or friend does not affect happiness.

After fitting the "psychological model", we can reinspect the economic-sociological model with the replay command. The query subcommand after the replay demonstrates that running a subcommand such as replay, stats, or for does not affect the active estimation results. This would even be true if the psychological model had not been stored.

```
. est replay ecosocio
```

Model **ecosocio** (*Socio-economic model of happiness*)

```
Ordered probit estimates                        Number of obs   =        1496
                                                LR chi2(8)      =       63.61
                                                Prob > chi2     =      0.0000
Log likelihood = -1346.6342                     Pseudo R2       =      0.0231
```

Happy	Coef.	Std. Err.	z	P>|z|	[95% Conf. Interval]	
age	.0035074	.0017519	2.00	0.045	.0000737	.0069411
educ	.0489342	.0105765	4.63	0.000	.0282046	.0696638
unemploy	-.4315152	.1548332	-2.79	0.005	-.7349828	-.1280477
female	-.113792	.0608997	-1.87	0.062	-.2331532	.0055692
white	.2884495	.1702879	1.69	0.090	-.0453087	.6222078
black	-.0210907	.1862567	-0.11	0.910	-.3861471	.3439658
RegionNE	-.0974579	.0717395	-1.36	0.174	-.2380649	.043149
RegionSE	.1366342	.0817859	1.67	0.095	-.0236633	.2969317
_cut1	-.3261708	.2418437	(Ancillary parameters)			
_cut2	1.443842	.2435946				

```
. est query
(the active estimation result is psychological)
description: the psychological model of happiness
```

While the socioeconomic and psychological fields hardly seem to be in serious interdisciplinary discourse, it is easy to let Stata join in. We fit a model that "integrates" both perspectives, and store the model under the name `integrated`. Of course, a *theoretical* integration of the perspectives would require more serious thought.

```
. oprobit Happy age edu unemploy female white black RegionNE RegionSE childs
> unhealthy childprob deathfriend
Iteration 0:   log likelihood = -1375.1292
Iteration 1:   log likelihood =  -1338.205
Iteration 2:   log likelihood = -1338.1603
Iteration 3:   log likelihood = -1338.1603
Ordered probit estimates                    Number of obs   =       1493
                                            LR chi2(12)     =      73.94
                                            Prob > chi2     =     0.0000
Log likelihood = -1338.1603                 Pseudo R2       =     0.0269
```

Happy	Coef.	Std. Err.	z	P>|z|	[95% Conf. Interval]	
age	.002638	.0018638	1.42	0.157	-.001015	.006291
educ	.0512621	.0107943	4.75	0.000	.0301056	.0724185
unemploy	-.4093239	.1565738	-2.61	0.009	-.7162029	-.1024449
female	-.0985707	.0615925	-1.60	0.110	-.2192899	.0221484
white	.2975818	.1708873	1.74	0.082	-.0373512	.6325147
black	-.0349449	.1866724	-0.19	0.852	-.4008161	.3309262
RegionNE	-.0936445	.0718386	-1.30	0.192	-.2344456	.0471566
RegionSE	.1412788	.082098	1.72	0.085	-.0196304	.3021879
childs	.018439	.0189549	0.97	0.331	-.0187119	.0555899
unhealthy	-.2152097	.1237867	-1.74	0.082	-.4578272	.0274078
childprob	-.2593824	.1111938	-2.33	0.020	-.4773183	-.0414465
deathfriend	.0937752	.0851064	1.10	0.271	-.0730303	.2605807
_cut1	-.308504	.2453978	(Ancillary parameters)			
_cut2	1.470739	.247196				

```
. est store integrated
```

We have now fitted and stored three models. It is easy to lose track. The subcommands `stats` and `dir` list the stored models in different ways. Note that many subcommands support abbreviation rules for a *namelist* similar to *varlists*. Thus, `all` or `*` are shorthands for all stored models, and `int*d` matches all names that start with `int` and end in `d`.

```
. est stats *
```

Model	nobs	ll(null)	ll(model)	df	AIC	BIC
ecosocio	1496	-1378.442	-1346.634	10	2713.268	2766.374
psychologi~l	1497	-1380.656	-1375.642	6	2763.284	2795.151
integrated	1493	-1375.129	-1338.16	14	2704.321	2778.64

```
. est dir _all
```

model	command	depvar	npar	title
ecosocio	oprobit	Happy	10	*Socio-economic model of happiness*
psychologi~l	oprobit	Happy	6	*the psychological model of happiness*
integrated	oprobit	Happy	14	

est stats displays the model selection indices AIC and BIC (see Akaike 1974, Raftery 1996, Sakamoto et al. 1986, Schwarz 1978). AIC and BIC are defined as

```
AIC = -2*log(likelihood) + 2*df
BIC = -2*log(likelihood) + log(nobs)*df
```

The log likelihood of a model is denoted ll(model) in the table. AIC and BIC can be seen as measures that combine the fit and the complexity of a model. Here, complexity is seen in terms of the number of free parameters estimated (column df). df is determined as the rank of the (co)variance matrix of the parameters, e(V). The measures are such that "smaller is better". In this case, the AIC criterion selects the integrated model and BIC selects the ecosocio model. One should be cautious here, however, as the models were fitted on slightly different samples due to missing values.

In the est dir output, we observe that we "forgot" to specify a title for the integrated model. est change can be used to add a title after the fact.

```
. est change integrated, title(a happy social science model)
```

Note that est dir lists the number of parameters, npar, namely the dimension of the square matrix e(V). While in these three examples, the number of parameters npar are identical to the degrees of freedom df listed by est stats, this need not be true; e.g., if models have been fitted with constraints (see [R] **constraint**).

To interpret the integrated model, it is useful to jointly look at the other models. est table allows us to look at the three models in parallel, with blanks showing up in models that did not include the respective variables.

```
. est table integrated ecosocio psychological
```

Variable	integrated	ecosocio	psycholo~l
age	.00263799	.0035074	
educ	.05126206	.0489342	
unemploy	-.40932391	-.43151525	
female	-.09857074	-.11379196	
white	.29758178	.28844951	
black	-.03494495	-.02109066	
RegionNE	-.09364452	-.09745792	
RegionSE	.14127876	.13663421	
childs	.01843901		-.00373118
unhealthy	-.21520973		-.24804452
childprob	-.25938241		-.23203168
deathfriend	.0937752		.07462062
_cut1	-.30850401	-.32617082	-1.2617434
_cut2	1.4707386	1.4438416	.46545295

A disadvantage of this table is that it is not easy to compare the fit of models since statistics are missing. est table has the option stats() which may be used to specify one or more scalars (statistics) that are stored by estimators in e(). Multiple scalar statistics should be separated by blanks or commas. Just like with coefficients, est table displays blanks for a statistic that was not saved by an estimation command, while est table displays missing . if it was saved as a missing value. After fitting a model, you can type ereturn list to list the objects that were stored in e(). The *Saved Results* section from the manual entry for that command lists and describes these scalars.

Most estimators store e(N) (number of observations), e(ll) (log-likelihood value), and e(chi2) (the Wald or likelihood-ratio test statistics for, in this case, the hypotheses that all coefficients but the intercept are 0). regress and related commands store e(F), the model F statistic, and e(r2) e(r2_a), the unadjusted and adjusted fractions of explained variance, respectively.

In addition to stored results, `estimates table` can include the information criteria AIC and BIC (keywords `aic` and `bic` in lowercase) and the degrees of freedom of the model (keyword `rank`) in the table.

```
. est table integrated ecosocio psychological, stats(N ll chi2 aic bic) star
```

Variable	integrated	ecosocio	psychological
age	.00263799	.0035074*	
educ	.05126206***	.0489342***	
unemploy	-.40932391**	-.43151525**	
female	-.09857074	-.11379196	
white	.29758178	.28844951	
black	-.03494495	-.02109066	
RegionNE	-.09364452	-.09745792	
RegionSE	.14127876	.13663421	
childs	.01843901		-.00373118
unhealthy	-.21520973		-.24804452*
childprob	-.25938241*		-.23203168*
deathfriend	.0937752		.07462062
_cut1	-.30850401	-.32617082	-1.2617434***
_cut2	1.4707386***	1.4438416***	.46545295***
N	1493	1496	1497
ll	-1338.1603	-1346.6342	-1375.6419
chi2	73.937732	63.614951	10.027707
aic	2704.3206	2713.2684	2763.2838
bic	2778.6402	2766.3739	2795.1511

legend: * p<0.05; ** p<0.01; *** p<0.001

At this point, you likely observed that the estimation samples differ between the models—a point easily overlooked otherwise. This is due to missing values in the covariates. In a serious analysis, one would probably ensure that the models were fit on precisely the same data. For now, the simultaneous display of the coefficients of the three models has made it clear that the coefficients of the two "disciplinary" models were hardly affected by integrating the perspectives. Only the cut-points were affected. Note, however, that the differences between the cut-points are similar over all three modes. A formal test that these differences are the same can be conducted using `suest`; see [R] **suest**.

❑ Technical Note

In the above call to `est table`, you may have been tempted to put the model `integrated` last. There is a catch here. Suppose that you list model `ecosocio` and model `psychological`. What happens? `est table` scans through all variables in `psychological`, adding a new row for variables in `psychological` that are not in `ecosocio`. `est table` places these new rows after the rows for `ecosocio`, or, more precisely, after the variables in the same equation. Since `oprobit` puts the cut-points in the same equation as the regression coefficients, the variables in `psychological` that do not occur in `ecosocio` appear *after* the cut-points. This looks pretty odd. By putting the model `integrated` first, we ensured that the cut-points show up last since the "later" models `ecosocio` and `psychological` contain no new variables.

You can always find out how what names are used for the coefficients in the model by typing `vce` or `matrix list e(b)` after fitting the model.

❑

So, what could we do if we insist on including `integrated` last? The easiest thing to do is to drop the cut-points in the table via the drop() option. To illustrate another feature of est table, we specify vertical lines after each column via the option style(columns).

```
. est table ecosocio psychological integrated, stats(N ll rank aic bic)
> drop(_cut1 _cut2) style(columns)
```

Variable	ecosocio	psycholo~l	integrated
age	.0035074		.00263799
educ	.0489342		.05126206
unemploy	-.43151525		-.40932391
female	-.11379196		-.09857074
white	.28844951		.29758178
black	-.02109066		-.03494495
RegionNE	-.09745792		-.09364452
RegionSE	.13663421		.14127876
childs		-.00373118	.01843901
unhealthy		-.24804452	-.21520973
childprob		-.23203168	-.25938241
deathfriend		.07462062	.0937752
N	1496	1497	1493
ll	-1346.6342	-1375.6419	-1338.1603
rank	10	6	14
aic	2713.2684	2763.2838	2704.3206
bic	2766.3739	2795.1511	2778.6402

If you insist on having the cut-points in the table, there is a solution that is admittedly somewhat laborious. The option keep() allows the specification of the coefficients to be displayed. The coefficients appear in the order as specified in keep(). Thus, typing all coefficients followed by _cut1 and _cut2 would do the job.

We would rather illustrate the option keep() along with other features of est table. In addition to the coefficients (parameter estimates), est table can also display standard errors (option se), t statistics (estimate divided by its standard error, option t), and the p-value of the statistic (option p). An optional argument to these options specifies the display format. Thus, t(%8.2f) specifies that t statistics are displayed in display format %8.2f. The options b(*fmt*) and stfmt(*fmt*) specify the display format of the coefficients and of the model statistics, respectively.

```
. est table ecosocio psychological integrated,
> t(%8.2f) keep(age educ unemploy childprob unhealthy)
```

Variable	ecosocio	psycholo~l	integrated
age	.0035074		.00263799
	2.00		1.42
educ	.0489342		.05126206
	4.63		4.75
unemploy	-.43151525		-.40932391
	-2.79		-2.61
childprob		-.23203168	-.25938241
		-2.11	-2.33
unhealthy		-.24804452	-.21520973
		-2.05	-1.74

legend: b/t

The subcommand for provides the opportunity to run post-estimation commands such as adjust, mfx, predict, and test on one or more stored estimation sets. For instance, one can use est for to use adjust on some stored estimation set rather than on the active estimation results.

```
. est for ecosocio : adjust, by(childs female)
```

Model **ecosocio** (*Socio-economic model of happiness*)

```
        Dependent variable: Happy      Command: oprobit
        Variables left as is: age, educ, RegionNE, RegionSE, white, black, unemploy
```

number of children		female 0	1
	0	1.01192	.921221
	1	1.01321	.894226
	2	1.0521	.895689
	3	1.03476	.842401
	4	1.00115	.837161
	5	.909963	.883316
	6	.96747	.863325
	7	.943577	.798705
eight or more		1.01359	.757081

```
        Key:  Linear Prediction
. est q
(the active estimation set is integrated)
description: a happy social science model
```

Note that est query shows that integrated is still the active set; est for temporarily made ecosocio active, ran adjust, then switched the active set back to integrated. It is also possible to invoke a post-estimation command on a series of stored estimation results. For instance, we will test that having a troubled child childprob affects happiness in all models. Note that childprob does not occur in ecosocio. Thus, invoking test command for this model produces an error. The option nostop specifies that est for should continue processing after the error.

```
. est for *, nostop : test childprob
```

Model **ecosocio** (*Socio-economic model of happiness*)

childprob not found

Model **psychological** (*the psychological model of happiness*)

```
 ( 1)  childprob = 0
          chi2( 1) =    4.45
        Prob > chi2 =    0.0349
```

Model **integrated** (*a happy social science model*)

```
 ( 1)  childprob = 0
          chi2( 1) =    5.44
        Prob > chi2 =    0.0197
```

estimates has a series of other subcommands that are largely self-explaining. estimates drop drops a set. If you drop the set that is currently active, the stored results are no longer available.

Hence, these can no longer be `estimates restored`, but the active results themselves are not removed. `estimates clear` drops all stored sets.

```
. est drop integrated
. est dir
```

model	command	depvar	npar	title
ecosocio	oprobit	Happy	10	*Socio-economic model of happiness*
psychologi~l	oprobit	Happy	6	*the psychological model of happiness*

```
. est clear
```

Remark on time series operators

`estimates table` understands time-series operators and groups variables defined via time-series operators. Consider two models. Model A contains variables x and L.x, possibly preceded or followed by other variables, and model B contains x, D.x, and D2.x, also preceded or followed by other variables. Now, `estimates table A B` will group the variables defined on the basis of x in the order encountered; that is, as x, L.x, D.x, and D2.x. Similarly, `estimates table B A` lists the same variables in the order x, D.x, D2.x, L.x.

Saved Results

`estimates dir` saves in `r()`:

Macros
  r(names)   names of described models

`estimates stats` saves in `r()`:

Matrices
  r(S)   matrix with 6 columns N ll0 ll df AIC BIC
         rows correspond to models in the table

`estimates table` saves in `r()`:

Matrices
  r(coefs) $n \times 2m$ matrix M

   $M[i,2j-1] = i$th parameter estimate for model j; $i=1...,n$, $j=1...,m$
   $M[i,2j] = $ variance of $M[i,2j-1]$

  r(stats) $k \times m$ matrix S (if `stats()` was specified)

   $S[i,j] = i$th statistic for model j; $i=1...,k$, $j=1...,m$

In these matrices, coefficients and statistics that did not occur in the respective model are coded with `.z`.

Methods and Formulas

estimates is implemented as an ado-file.

estimates manages estimation results via the internal command _estimates. The estimates store command saves the name and title in the e-class object itself, namely as macros e(_estimate_name) and e(_estimate_title).

estimates store interfaces to _estimates hold, estimates restore to _estimates unhold, etc. Results stored (held) via _estimates are not visible in estimates. Thus, estimates clear only clears (drops from memory) the results that have been saved via estimates store, not those saved by _estimates hold. Thus, it is safe to use _estimates for your own purposes. On the other hand, _estimates drop may be used to drop models stored by estimate store.

estimates stats and estimates table display the information indices,

$$\text{AIC} = -2\text{log-likelihood} + 2p; \qquad \text{BIC} = -2\text{log-likelihood} + \log(N)p$$

where p is the number of parameters of the model (determined as the rank of e(V)), and N is the number of observations. Generally, "smaller is better". We point out that glm uses somewhat different definitions. If you are comparing models fitted on the same data, however, the same models will be selected under both definitions.

Acknowledgment

estimates was written by Jeroen Weesie, Department of Sociology, Utrecht University, the Netherlands.

References

Akaike, H. 1974. A new look at the statistical model identification. *IEEE Transactions on Automatic Control* 19: 716–723.

Gallup, J. L. 1998. sg97: Formatting regression output for published tables. *Stata Technical Bulletin* 46: 28–30. Reprinted in *Stata Technical Bulletin Reprints*, vol. 8, pp. 200–202.

——. 1999. sg97.1: Revision of outreg. *Stata Technical Bulletin* 49: 23. Reprinted in *Stata Technical Bulletin Reprints*, vol. 9, pp. 170–171.

——. 2000. sg97.2: Update to formatting regression output. *Stata Technical Bulletin* 58: 9–13. Reprinted in *Stata Technical Bulletin Reprints*, vol. 10, pp. 137–143.

——. 2001. sg97.3: Update to formatting regression output. *Stata Technical Bulletin* 59: 23. Reprinted in *Stata Technical Bulletin Reprints*, vol. 10, pp. 143.

Goldstein, R. 1992. srd12: Some model selection statistics. *Stata Technical Bulletin* 6: 22–26. Reprinted in *Stata Technical Bulletin Reprints*, vol. 1, pp. 194–199.

Long, J. S. and J. Freese. 2000. sg145: Scalar measures of fit for regression models. *Stata Technical Bulletin* 56: 34–40. Reprinted in *Stata Technical Bulletin Reprints*, vol. 10, pp. 197–205.

Raftery, A. 1996. Bayesian model selection in social research. In *Sociological methodology*, ed. P.V. Marsden, 111–163. Oxford: Basil Blackwell.

Sakamoto, Y., M. Ishiguro, and G. Kitagawa. 1986. *Akaike Information Criterion Statistics*. Dordrecht, Netherlands: Reidel.

Schwarz, G. 1978. Estimating the dimension of a model. *The Annals of Statistics* 6: 461–464.

Tobias, A. and M. J. Campbell. 1998. sg90: Akaike's information criterion and Schwarz's criterion. *Stata Technical Bulletin* 45: 23–25. Reprinted in *Stata Technical Bulletin Reprints*, vol. 8, pp. 174–177.

Tyler, J. H. 1997. sg73: Table making programs. *Stata Technical Bulletin* 40: 18–23. Reprinted in *Stata Technical Bulletin Reprints*, vol. 7, pp. 186–192.

Also See

Complementary: [P] **ereturn**

Title

---
estimation commands — Quick reference for estimation commands
---

Description

This entry provides a quick reference for Stata's estimation commands. Since enhancements to Stata are continually being added, type `search estimation commands` for possible additions to this list; see [R] **search**.

Remarks

Index to estimation commands

Command	Description	See
anova	Analysis of variance and covariance	[R] **anova**
arch	ARCH family of estimators	[TS] **arch**
areg	Linear regression with a large dummy-variable set	[R] **areg**
arima	Autoregressive integrated moving average models	[TS] **arima**
binreg	Generalized linear models: extensions to the binomial family	[R] **binreg**
biprobit	Bivariate probit models	[R] **biprobit**
blogit	Maximum likelihood logit on blocked data	[R] **glogit**
boxcox	Box–Cox regression models	[R] **boxcox**
bprobit	Maximum likelihood probit on blocked data	[R] **glogit**
bsqreg	Quantile regression with bootstrapped standard errors	[R] **qreg**
canon	Canonical correlations	[R] **canon**
clogit	Conditional (fixed-effects) logistic regression	[R] **clogit**
cloglog	Maximum-likelihood complementary log-log regression models	[R] **cloglog**
cnreg	Censored-normal regression	[R] **tobit**
cnsreg	Constrained linear regression	[R] **cnsreg**
dprobit	Maximum likelihood probit with reported coefficients transformed to the change in probability	[R] **probit**
eivreg	Errors-in-variables regression	[R] **eivreg**
fracpoly	Fractional polynomial regression	[R] **fracpoly**
frontier	Cross-sectional stochastic frontier models	[R] **frontier**
glm	Generalized linear models	[R] **glm**
glogit	Weighted least-squares logit estimates on grouped data	[R] **glogit**
gnbreg	Maximum-likelihood generalized negative binomial regression	[R] **nbreg**
gprobit	Weighted least-squares probit estimates on grouped data	[R] **glogit**
heckman	Heckman selection model	[R] **heckman**
heckprob	Probit models with sample selection	[R] **heckprob**
hetprob	Probit models with multiplicative heteroskedasticity	[R] **hetprob**

Command	Description	See
intreg	Interval regression	[R] **tobit**
iqreg	Interquantile regression	[R] **qreg**
ivreg	Instrumental variables and two-stage least-squares regression	[R] **ivreg**
logistic	Logistic regression	[R] **logistic**
logit	Maximum-likelihood logit estimation	[R] **logit**
manova	Multivariate analysis of variance and covariance	[R] **manova**
mfp	Multivariable fractional polynomial models	[R] **mfp**
mlogit	Maximum-likelihood multinomial logit models (polytomous logistic regression)	[R] **mlogit**
mvreg	Multivariate regression	[R] **mvreg**
nbreg	Maximum-likelihood negative binomial regression	[R] **nbreg**
newey	Regression with Newey–West standard errors	[TS] **newey**
nl	Nonlinear least squares	[R] **nl**
nlogit	Nested logit	[R] **nlogit**
ologit	Maximum-likelihood ordered logit	[R] **ologit**
oprobit	Maximum-likelihood ordered probit	[R] **oprobit**
poisson	Maximum-likelihood Poisson regression	[R] **poisson**
prais	Prais–Winsten and Cochrane–Orcutt regression	[TS] **prais**
probit	Maximum-likelihood probit estimation	[R] **probit**
qreg	Quantile (including median) regression (least absolute-value models—LAV or MAD—or minimum L1-norm models)	[R] **qreg**
reg3	Three-stage least-squares regression	[R] **reg3**
regress	Linear regression	[R] **regress**
rologit	Rank-ordered logistic regression	[R] **rologit**
rreg	Robust regression	[R] **rreg**
scobit	Skewed logit regression	[R] **scobit**
sqreg	Simultaneous quantile regression	[R] **qreg**
stcox	Maximum-likelihood proportional hazards models	[ST] **stcox**
streg	Maximum-likelihood parametric survival models (exponential, Weibull, Gompertz, lognormal, log-logistic, and generalized log-gamma)	[ST] **streg**
sureg	Zellner's seemingly unrelated regression	[R] **sureg**
svar	Structural vector autoregression models	[TS] **svar**
svygnbreg	Negative binomial regression for survey data	[SVY] **svy estimators**
svyheckman	Heckman selection model for survey data	[SVY] **svy estimators**
svyheckprob	Probit estimation with selection for survey data	[SVY] **svy estimators**
svyintreg	Pseudo-maximum-likelihood interval regression for complex survey data	[SVY] **svy estimators**
svyivreg	Instrumental variables regression for complex survey data	[SVY] **svy estimators**
svylogit	Pseudo-maximum-likelihood logistic regression for complex survey data	[SVY] **svy estimators**

Command	Description	See
svymlogit	Pseudo-maximum-likelihood multinomial logistic regression for complex survey data	[SVY] **svy estimators**
svynbreg	Negative binomial regression for survey data	[SVY] **svy estimators**
svyologit	Pseudo-maximum-likelihood ordered logit regression for complex survey data	[SVY] **svy estimators**
svyoprobit	Pseudo-maximum-likelihood ordered probit regression for complex survey data	[SVY] **svy estimators**
svypoisson	Pseudo-maximum-likelihood Poisson regression for complex survey data	[SVY] **svy estimators**
svyprobit	Pseudo-maximum-likelihood probit estimation for complex survey data	[SVY] **svy estimators**
svyregress	Linear regression for complex survey data	[SVY] **svy estimators**
sw *cmd*	Stepwise estimation (used with other est. commands)	[R] **sw**
tobit	Tobit regression	[R] **tobit**
treatreg	Treatment-effects model	[R] **treatreg**
truncreg	Truncated regression	[R] **truncreg**
var	Vector autoregression models	[TS] **var**
vwls	Linear regression using variance-weighted least squares	[R] **vwls**
xtabond	Arellano–Bond linear, dynamic panel-data estimator	[XT] **xtabond**
xtcloglog	Random-effects and population-averaged cloglog models	[XT] **xtcloglog**
xtfrontier	Stochastic frontier for panel-data models	[XT] **xtfrontier**
xtgee	Generalized estimating equations for population-averaged panel data models	[XT] **xtgee**
xtgls	Generalized least squares for panel data	[XT] **xtgls**
xthtaylor	Hausman–Taylor estimator for error component models	[XT] **xthtaylor**
xtintreg	Random-effects interval data regression models	[XT] **xtintreg**
xtivreg	Instrumental variables and two-stage least squares for panel-data models	[XT] **xtivreg**
xtlogit	Fixed-effects, random-effects, and population-averaged logit models	[XT] **xtlogit**
xtnbreg	Fixed-effects, random-effects, and population-averaged negative binomial models	[XT] **xtnbreg**
xtpoisson	Fixed-effects, random-effects, and population-averaged Poisson models	[XT] **xtpoisson**
xtprobit	Random-effects and population-averaged probit models	[XT] **xtprobit**
xtrchh	Hildreth–Houck random coefficients regression models	[XT] **xtrchh**
xtreg	Cross-sectional time-series regression models (between-, fixed- GLS random-, and ML random-effects, and population-averaged models)	[XT] **xtreg**
xtregar	Fixed- and random-effects linear models with an AR(1) disturbance	[XT] **xtregar**
xttobit	Random-effects tobit models	[XT] **xttobit**
zinb	Zero-inflated negative binomial models	[R] **zip**
zip	Zero-inflated Poisson models	[R] **zip**

Summary of estimation commands

Guide to Table

Weights: Allowed weights are listed with the default weight listed first. Possibilities are analytic weights (`aweigh`), frequency weights (`fweight`), importance weights (`iweight`), and probability weights (`pweight`).

robust: Does the command allow the `robust` option? Note that if the `robust` option is specified, `aweights` are treated as `pweights`. If the table contains an '(R)' in the `robust` column, this means that although the command does not take the `robust` option, the command gives robust estimates of the variance.

sw: Can the command be used with `sw` to perform stepwise estimation?

Command	Weights	robust	sw
anova	aweight, fweight	no	no
arch	iweight	yes	no
areg	aweight, fweight, pweight	yes	no
arima	iweight	yes	no
binreg	fweight, aweight, iweight, pweight	no	no
biprobit	pweight, fweight, iweight	yes	no
blogit	none	yes	no
boxcox	fweight, iweight	no	no
bprobit	none	yes	no
bsqreg	none	no	no
canon	aweight, fweight	no	no
clogit	fweight, iweight	no	yes
cloglog	fweight, iweight, pweight	yes	yes
cnreg	aweight, fweight	no	yes
cnsreg	aweight, fweight	no	no
dprobit	fweight, aweight, pweight	yes	no
eivreg	aweight, fweight	no	no
fracpoly	(1)	no	no
frontier	iweight, fweight, pweight	no	no
glm	fweight, aweight, iweight, pweight	yes	yes
glogit	none	no	no
gnbreg	fweight, aweight, iweight, pweight	yes	no
gprobit	none	no	no
heckman	pweight, aweight, fweight, iweight (2)	yes	no
heckprob	pweight, fweight, iweight	yes	no
hetprob	fweight, iweight, pweight	yes	no
intreg	aweight, fweight, iweight, pweight	yes	no
iqreg	none	no	no
ivreg	aweight, fweight, iweight, pweight	yes	no
logistic	fweight, pweight	yes	yes
logit	fweight, iweight, pweight	yes	yes
manova	aweight, fweight	no	no
mfp	(1)	no	no
mlogit	fweight, iweight, pweight	yes	no
mvreg	aweight, fweight	no	no

(1) This depends on the command.

(2) No weights are allowed if the `twostep` option is specified.

Command	Weights	robust	sw
nbreg	fweight, iweight, pweight	yes	yes
newey	aweight	(R)	no
nl	aweight, fweight	no	no
nlogit	fweight, iweight	yes	no
ologit	fweight, iweight, pweight	yes	yes
oprobit	fweight, iweight, pweight	yes	yes
poisson	fweight, iweight, pweight	yes	yes
prais	none	yes	no
probit	fweight, iweight, pweight	yes	yes
qreg	aweight, fweight	no	yes
reg3	aweight, fweight	no	no
regress	aweight, fweight, iweight, pweight	yes	yes
rologit	fweight, pweight, iweight	yes	no
rreg	none	no	no
scobit	fweight, iweight, pweight	yes	no
sqreg	none	no	no
stcox	fweight, iweight, pweight (3)	yes	no
streg	fweight, iweight, pweight (3)	yes	no
sureg	aweight, fweight	no	no
svar	none	no	no
svygnbreg	none	(R)	no
svyheckman	none	(R)	no
svyheckprob	none	(R)	no
svyintreg	none	(R)	no
svyivreg	none	(R)	no
svylogit	none	(R)	no
svymlogit	none	(R)	no
svynbreg	none	(R)	no
svyologit	none	(R)	no
svyoprobit	none	(R)	no
svypoisson	none	(R)	no
svyprobit	none	(R)	no
svyregress	none	(R)	no
tobit	aweight, fweight	no	yes
treatreg	pweight, aweight, fweight, iweight (2)	yes	no
truncreg	aweight, fweight, pweight	yes	no
var	none	no	no
vwls	fweight	no	no
xtabond	none	yes	no
xtcloglog	iweight, fweight, pweight (4)	(5)	no
xtfrontier	fweight, iweight	no	no
xtgee	iweight, fweight, pweight	yes	no
xtgls	aweight	(R)	no
xthtaylor	iweight, fweight	no	no
xtintreg	iweight	no	no
xtivreg	none	no	no
xtlogit	iweight, fweight, pweight (4)	(5)	no

(R) The command does not take the robust option, but does give robust variance estimates.

(2) No weights are allowed with the twostep estimates.

(3) Use stset to specify the weights; see [ST] **stset**.

(4) Random-effects and fixed-effects models only allow iweights.

(5) The command allows the robust option only with the pa option.

Command	Weights	robust	sw
xtnbreg	iweight, fweight, pweight (4)	(5)	no
xtpoisson	iweight, fweight, pweight (4)	(5)	no
xtprobit	iweight, fweight, pweight (4)	(5)	no
xtrchh	none	no	no
xtreg	iweight, fweight, pweight (6)	(5)	no
xtregar	fweight, aweight (7)	no	no
xttobit	iweight	no	no
zinb	fweight, iweight, pweight	yes	no
zip	fweight, iweight, pweight	yes	no

(4) Random-effects and fixed-effects models only allow iweight.

(5) The command allows the robust option only with the pa option.

(6) Only for the population-averaged model. iweights are allowed for the maximum likelihood (ML) random-effects model.

(7) Only for the fixed-effects model.

Summary of post-estimation commands

A number of post estimation commands are available.

adjust   **Tables of adjusted means and proportions**
is available after all estimation commands except areg, clogit, nl, and nlogit. adjust after fracpoly and mfp depends on the command.

lincom   **Linear combinations of estimators**
is available after all estimation commands except nl.

linktest   **Specification link test for single-equation models**
is available after the following estimation commands:

anova	eivreg	nbreg	rreg
binreg	glm	newey	scobit
bsqreg	hetprob	ologit	sqreg
clogit	intreg	oprobit	stcox
cloglog	iqreg	poisson	streg
cnreg	ivreg	probit	tobit
cnsreg	logistic	qreg	var
dprobit	logit	regress	vwls

lrtest   **Likelihood-ratio test after model estimation**
is available after the following estimation commands:

arch	cnreg	heckprob	nbreg	regress	tobit
arima	dprobit	hetprob	nlogit	rologit	treatreg
biprobit	frontier	intreg	ologit	scobit	truncreg
blogit	glm	logistic	oprobit	stcox	var
bprobit	gnbreg	logit	poisson	streg	zinb
clogit	heckman	mlogit	probit	svar	zip
cloglog					

lrtest after fracpoly and mfp depends on the command. lrtest after xt commands can be used only when a model is fit via maximum likelihood; e.g., xtpoisson, fe or xtreg, mle.

`mfx` **Obtain marginal effects or elasticities after estimation**
is available after all estimation commands except `anova`, `canon`, `clogit`, `manova`, `nl`, `nlogit`, and `svar`. `mfx` after `fracpoly` and `mfp` depends on the command.

`nlcom` **Nonlinear combinations of estimators**
is available after all estimation commands except `anova` and `manova`.

`predict` **Obtain predictions, residuals, etc., after estimation**
is available after all estimation commands.

`predictnl` **Nonlinear predictions after estimation**
is available after all estimation commands except `anova`, `boxcox`, and `manova`.

`suest` **Seemingly unrelated estimation**
is available if the estimation command takes a `score` option. An exception to this is `clogit`, which does not have a `score` option, but `suest` may still be used after it.

`test` **Test linear hypotheses after model estimation**
is available after all estimation commands.

`testnl` **Test nonlinear hypotheses after model estimation**
is available after all estimation commands except `anova` and `manova`.

Also See

Complementary: [R] **adjust**, [R] **lincom**, [R] **linktest**, [R] **lrtest**, [R] **mfx**, [R] **nlcom**,
[R] **predict**, [R] **predictnl**, [R] **suest**, [R] **sw**, [R] **test**, [R] **testnl**

Background: [U] **14.1.6 weight**,
[U] **23 Estimation and post-estimation commands**,
[U] **23.14 Obtaining robust variance estimates**

Title

---
exit — Exit Stata

Syntax

e̲xit [, clear]

Description

Typing `exit` causes Stata to stop processing and return control to the operating system. If the dataset in memory has changed since the last `save` command, you must specify the `clear` option before Stata will let you leave.

`exit` may also be used for exiting do-files or programs; see [P] **exit**.

Stata for Windows users may also exit Stata by clicking on the close box, double-clicking on the system menu box, or by holding down *Alt* and pressing *F4*.

Stata for Macintosh users may also exit Stata by clicking on the close box.

Options

`clear` permits you to `exit` even if the current dataset has not been `saved`.

Remarks

Type `exit` to leave Stata and return to the operating system. If the dataset in memory has changed since the last time it was saved, however, Stata will refuse. At that point, you can either `save` the dataset and then type `exit` or type `exit, clear`:

```
. exit
no; data in memory would be lost
r(4);
. exit, clear
```

Also See

Related: [P] **exit**

Title

expand — Duplicate observations

Syntax

expand $\left[=\right] exp$ $\left[\text{if } exp\right]$ $\left[\text{in } range\right]$

Description

expand replaces each observation in the current dataset with n copies of the observation, where n is equal to the integer part of the required expression. If the expression is less than 1 or equal to *missing*, it is interpreted as if it were 1, and the observation is retained but not duplicated.

Remarks

▷ Example

expand is, admittedly, a strange command. It can, however, be useful in tricky programs or for reformatting data for survival analysis (see examples in [ST] **epitab**). Here is a silly use of expand:

```
. list
```

	n	x
1.	-1	1
2.	0	2
3.	1	3
4.	2	4
5.	3	5

```
. expand n
(1 negative count ignored; observation not deleted)
(1 zero count ignored; observation not deleted)
(3 observations created)
. list
```

	n	x
1.	-1	1
2.	0	2
3.	1	3
4.	2	4
5.	3	5
6.	2	4
7.	3	5
8.	3	5

The new observations are added to the end of the dataset. expand informed us that it created 3 observations. The first 3 observations were not replicated since n was less than or equal to 1. n is 2 in the fourth observation, so expand created 1 replication of this observation, bringing the total number of observations of this type to 2. expand created 2 replications of observation 5 since n is 3.

Since there were 5 observations in the original dataset, and since expand adds new observations onto the end of the dataset, you could now undo the expansion by typing drop in 6/1.

◁

Also See

Complementary: [R] **contract**

Related: [R] **fillin**

Title

factor — Factor analysis

Syntax

<u>factor</u> [*varlist*] [*weight*] [if *exp*] [in *range*] [, [pcf | pf | ipf | ml]

      <u>factors</u>(#) <u>mineigen</u>(#) <u>means</u> <u>protect</u>(#) <u>random</u> *maximize_options*]

    <u>rotate</u> [, [<u>varimax</u> | <u>promax</u>[(#)]] <u>horst</u> <u>factors</u>(#)]

    <u>score</u> *newvarlist* [if *exp*] [in *range*] [, <u>bartlett</u> <u>norotate</u>]

by ... : may be used with factor; see [R] **by**.
aweights and fweights are allowed; see [U] **14.1.6 weight**.

Description

factor performs factor analysis of the variables in the *varlist*. factor can produce principal factor, iterated principal factor, principal-components factor, and maximum-likelihood factor analysis. factor displays the eigenvalues and the factor loadings or eigenvectors.

rotate modifies the results of the last factor command to create a set of loadings that are more interpretable than those produced by factor. Varimax and promax rotations are available.

score creates a set of new variables that are estimates of the factors produced by factor or rotate (i.e., unrotated or rotated factors). (score may also be used after the pca command; see [R] **pca**). In the case of factor analysis, both regression and Bartlett scoring are available.

For information about the greigen command, which displays a graph of the eigenvalues obtained by factor or pca, see [R] **pca**.

Options

pcf, pf, ipf, and ml indicate the type of estimation to be performed. The default is pf, meaning principal factors; pcf estimates principal-component factors; ipf estimates iterated principal components; and ml estimates maximum likelihood factors. Details follow:

pcf specifies that factor analysis be performed using the principal-components factor method. The communalities are assumed to be 1.

pf specifies that the principal factor method be used to analyze the correlation matrix of the variables. The factor loadings, sometimes called the factor patterns, are computed using the squared multiple correlations as estimates of the communality. pf is the default.

ipf specifies that the iterated principal factor method be used to analyze the correlation matrix of the variables. This re-estimates the communalities iteratively.

ml specifies the maximum-likelihood factor method.

370

factors(#) and mineigen(#) specify the maximum number of factors to be retained. factors() specifies the number directly, and mineigen() specifies it indirectly, saying to keep all factors with eigenvalues greater than the indicated value. The options can be specified individually, together, or not at all. Details follow:

factors(#) sets the maximum number of factors to be retained, which means saved for subsequent use by rotate and score. factor always prints the full set of eigenvalues, but prints the corresponding eigenvectors only for retained factors. Specifying a number larger than the number of variables in the *varlist* is equivalent to specifying the number of variables in the *varlist*, and is the default. factors(#) may also be specified with the rotate command. This requests that, even if more factors were previously retained, the rotation should be performed using only the first # factors.

mineigen(#) sets the minimum value of eigenvalues to be retained. The default is zero, meaning that factors associated with negative eigenvalues will not be printed or retained. Many sources also recommend mineigen(1), although the justification is complex and uncertain.

means requests that a table of means be presented before factorization.

protect(#) is used only with ml, and requests that # optimizations with random starting values be performed along with squared multiple-correlation coefficient starting values, and that the best of the solutions be reported. The output also indicates whether all starting values converged to the same solution. When specified with a large number, such as protect(50), this ensures that the solution found is global, and is not just a local maximum. If trace is also specified (see [R] **maximize**), the parameters and likelihoods of each maximization will be printed.

random is used only with ml, and requests that random starting values be used. This option is rarely used, and should only be used after protect() has shown the presence of multiple maxima.

varimax and promax⌈(#)⌉ specify the type of rotation to be performed. The default is the orthogonal varimax rotation. promax requests an oblique rotation. The optional argument specifies the promax power. Not specifying the argument is equivalent to specifying promax(3). Values less than 4 are recommended, but the choice is yours. Larger promax powers simplify the loading (generate more zeros and ones) at the cost of more correlation between factors. Choosing a value is a matter of trial-and-error, but most sources find values in excess of 4 undesirable in practice. The power must be greater than 1, but is not restricted to integers.

horst requests that the Horst (1965) modification to varimax and promax rotation be made. This modification standardizes the initial factor loadings for each variable to have length 1 before applying the varimax or promax optimizations; see *Methods and Formulas* below.

bartlett produces factors scored by the method suggested by Bartlett (1938). This method produces unbiased factors, but they may be less accurate than those produced by the default regression method suggested by Thomson (1951). Regression-scored factors have the smallest mean-square error from the true factors, but may be biased.

norotate specifies that unrotated factors be scored even when you have previously issued a rotate command. The default is to use rotated factors from rotate if available and unrotated factors otherwise.

maximize_options control the maximization process; see [R] **maximize**. You should never have to specify them. In addition, rotate allows the ltolerance(#) option to specify its convergence criterion. Its default value is 0.0001.

Remarks

Remarks are presented under the headings

> *Factor analysis*
> *Rotation*
> *Scoring*

Factor analysis is a statistical technique for data reduction. It helps you reduce the number of variables in an analysis by describing linear combinations of the variables that contain most of the information.

Factor analysis

Factor analysis originated with the work of Spearman (1904). Factor analysis is concerned with finding a small number of common factors (say q of them) that linearly reconstruct the p original variables

$$y_{ij} = z_{i1}b_{1j} + z_{i2}b_{2j} + \cdots + z_{iq}b_{qj} + e_{ij}$$

where y_{ij} is the value of the ith observation on the jth variable, z_{ik} is the ith observation on the kth common factor, b_{kj} is the set of linear coefficients called the factor loadings, and e_{ij} is similar to a residual, but is known as the jth variable's unique factor. Note that everything except the left-hand-side variable is to be estimated, so the model has an infinite number of solutions. Various constraints are introduced along with a definition of "reconstruct" to make the model determinate.

"Reconstruction" is typically defined in terms of prediction of the covariance matrix of the original variables, unlike principal components (see [R] **pca**), where reconstruction means minimum residual variance summed across all equations.

Once the factors and their loadings have been estimated, they are interpreted—an admittedly subjective process. Interpretation typically means examining the b_{kj}'s and assigning names to each factor. Due to the indeterminacy of the factor solution, one is not limited to examining solely the b_{kj}'s. The loadings could be rotated—that is, one could look at another set of b_{kj}'s that, while appearing different, are every bit as good as (and no better than) the original loadings. Such "rotations" come in two flavors—orthogonal and oblique rotations. Since there are an infinite number of potential rotations, different rotations could lead to different interpretations of the same data. These are not to be viewed as conflicting, but instead as two different ways of looking at the same thing.

▷ Example

We wish to analyze physicians' attitudes toward cost, and have a dataset of responses to six questions about cost asked of 568 physicians in the Medical Outcomes Study from Tarlov et al. (1989). Factor analysis is often used to validate a combination of questions that looks attractive at first glance. In this case, we wish to create a variable that summarizes the information on each physician's attitude toward cost.

Each of the responses is coded on a 5-point scale, where 1 means agree and 5 means disagree:

(Continued on next page)

```
. describe

Contains data from bg.dta
  obs:           568                          Physician-Cost Data
  vars:            7                          7 Aug 2002 12:42
  size:        7,952 (99.1% of memory free)
```

variable name	storage type	display format	value label	variable label
clinid	float	%9.0g		Physician Identifier
bg2cost1	byte	%8.0g		Best health care is expensive
bg2cost2	byte	%8.0g		Cost is a major consideration
bg2cost3	byte	%8.0g		Determine cost of tests first
bg2cost4	byte	%8.0g		Monitor likely complications only
bg2cost5	byte	%8.0g		Use all means regardless of cost
bg2cost6	byte	%8.0g		Prefer unnecessary tests to missing tests

```
Sorted by:  clinid
```

We can perform the factorization on bg2cost1, bg2cost2, ..., bg2cost6 by typing factor bg2cost*, using Stata's shorthand for "all variables that begin with ...":

```
. factor bg2cost*
(obs=527)
```

	(principal factors; 3 factors retained)			
Factor	Eigenvalue	Difference	Proportion	Cumulative
1	0.85395	0.31282	1.0309	1.0309
2	0.54113	0.51787	0.6533	1.6842
3	0.02326	0.17290	0.0281	1.7123
4	-0.14964	0.03949	-0.1807	1.5316
5	-0.18913	0.06211	-0.2283	1.3033
6	-0.25124	.	-0.3033	1.0000

	Factor Loadings			
Variable	1	2	3	Uniqueness
bg2cost1	0.24703	0.36704	-0.04462	0.80227
bg2cost2	-0.33745	0.33214	-0.07730	0.76983
bg2cost3	-0.37644	0.37557	0.02039	0.71682
bg2cost4	-0.32207	0.19416	0.10352	0.84786
bg2cost5	0.45504	0.24789	0.06415	0.72737
bg2cost6	0.47598	0.23641	-0.00680	0.71751

factor retained only the first three factors because the eigenvalues associated with the remaining factors are negative. According to the default mineigen(0) criterion, the factor has to have an eigenvalue greater than 0 to be retained. You can set this threshold higher by specifying mineigen(#) for yourself, causing factor to retain fewer factors automatically. You might want to do this: Although the program elected to retain three factors, only the first two appear to be meaningful.

The first factor seems to describe the physician's average position on cost since it affects the responses to all the questions "positively", as shown by the signs in the first column of the factor-loading table. We say "positively" because, obviously, the signs on three of the loadings are negative. When we look back at the results of describe, however, we find that the sense of the responses on bg2cost2, bg2cost3, and bg2cost4 are reversed. If the physician feels that cost should not be a major influence on medical treatment, he or she is likely to disagree with these three items and to agree with the other three.

The second factor loads positively (absolutely, not logically) on all six items, and could be interpreted as describing the physician's tendency to agree with any good-sounding idea put forth. Psychologists refer to this as the "positive response set". On statistical grounds, we would probably keep this second factor, although on substantive grounds, we would be tempted to dump it. We will keep it, though, to illustrate the `rotate` command.

◁

❏ Technical Note

Before turning to `rotate`, let us mention the alternative estimation strategies available for the factor model. We specified no options on the `factor` command when we fitted the above model, so we obtained the principal factor solution. The *communalities* (defined as $1 - uniqueness$) were estimated using the squared-multiple correlation coefficients.

We could have instead obtained the estimates from "principal-component factors", treating the communalities as all 1—meaning that there are no unique factors—by specifying the `pcf` option:

```
. factor bg2cost*, pcf
(obs=527)
```

(principal-component factors; 2 factors retained)

Factor	Eigenvalue	Difference	Proportion	Cumulative
1	1.70625	0.30334	0.2844	0.2844
2	1.40291	0.49423	0.2338	0.5182
3	0.90867	0.18568	0.1514	0.6696
4	0.72299	0.05604	0.1205	0.7901
5	0.66695	0.07471	0.1112	0.9013
6	0.59224	.	0.0987	1.0000

Variable	Factor Loadings 1	2	Uniqueness
bg2cost1	0.35804	0.62794	0.47750
bg2cost2	-0.48503	0.52443	0.48972
bg2cost3	-0.53262	0.57249	0.38856
bg2cost4	-0.49188	0.32540	0.65217
bg2cost5	0.62380	0.39624	0.45387
bg2cost6	0.65424	0.37806	0.42903

In this case, we find that the principal-component factor model is inappropriate. We started by assuming that the uniquenesses were 0, and now find that there is considerable uniqueness—there is considerable variance left over after our two factors. We should use some other method.

❏

❏ Technical Note

We could have fitted our model using iterated principal factors by specifying the `ipf` option. In this case, the initial estimates of the communalities would be the squared multiple-correlation coefficients, but the solution would then be iterated to obtain different (better) estimates:

(Continued on next page)

```
. factor bg2cost*, ipf
(obs=527)
```

(iterated principal factors; 5 factors retained)

Factor	Eigenvalue	Difference	Proportion	Cumulative
1	1.08374	0.31752	0.5103	0.5103
2	0.76622	0.53817	0.3608	0.8712
3	0.22805	0.19476	0.1074	0.9786
4	0.03328	0.02086	0.0157	0.9942
5	0.01243	0.01260	0.0059	1.0001
6	-0.00017	.	-0.0001	1.0000

Factor Loadings

Variable	1	2	3	4	5	Uniqueness
bg2cost1	0.24710	0.40594	-0.13494	-0.13041	0.02887	0.73810
bg2cost2	-0.40415	0.39592	-0.26370	0.03489	0.00398	0.60914
bg2cost3	-0.44801	0.45696	0.12920	0.01364	-0.05645	0.57041
bg2cost4	-0.33266	0.19427	0.26545	0.00912	0.08115	0.77446
bg2cost5	0.52944	0.33390	0.21614	-0.01336	-0.03319	0.56021
bg2cost6	0.51736	0.29434	-0.08016	0.12088	0.02657	0.62396

In this case, we retained too many factors. Unlike principal factors or principal-component factors, we cannot simply ignore the unnecessary factors because the uniquenesses are re-estimated from the data. We need to re-estimate:

```
. factor bg2cost*, ipf factors(2)
(obs=527)
```

(iterated principal factors; 2 factors retained)

Factor	Eigenvalue	Difference	Proportion	Cumulative
1	1.03960	0.30810	0.5870	0.5870
2	0.73150	0.60784	0.4130	1.0000
3	0.12366	0.11578	0.0698	1.0698
4	0.00787	0.03654	0.0044	1.0743
5	-0.02867	0.07425	-0.0162	1.0581
6	-0.10291	.	-0.0581	1.0000

Factor Loadings

Variable	1	2	Uniqueness
bg2cost1	0.22591	0.39406	0.79368
bg2cost2	-0.35900	0.29732	0.78272
bg2cost3	-0.51895	0.49345	0.48719
bg2cost4	-0.32299	0.16041	0.86994
bg2cost5	0.46677	0.32864	0.67412
bg2cost6	0.51785	0.33254	0.62125

It is instructive to compare the reported uniquenesses for this model and the previous one, where five factors were retained. Also note that as compared with the results we obtained from principal factors, these results do not differ much.

❑

❑ Technical Note

Finally, we could have fitted our model using the maximum likelihood method by specifying the `ml` option. As with `ipf`, if we do not specify the number of factors, it just so happens that Stata decides to retain more than two factors (it retained three), and, as with `ipf`, it is necessary to re-estimate with the number of factors that we really want. To save paper, we will start by retaining two factors:

```
. factor bg2cost*, ml factors(2)
(obs=527)
Iteration 0:  Log Likelihood =-26.638456
Iteration 1:  Log Likelihood =-6.5089835
Iteration 2:  Log Likelihood =-6.3648616
Iteration 3:  Log Likelihood =-6.3570128
Iteration 4:  Log Likelihood =-6.3565691
Iteration 5:  Log Likelihood =-6.3565452
Iteration 6:  Log Likelihood =-6.3565439
```

```
                (maximum-likelihood factors; 2 factors retained)
     Factor      Variance       Difference      Proportion      Cumulative

        1         1.02772         0.28110          0.5792          0.5792
        2         0.74662            .             0.4208          1.0000

Test:  2 vs. no    factors.  chi2( 12) =  238.23, Prob > chi2 =  0.0000
Test:  2 vs. more factors.  chi2(  4) =   12.61, Prob > chi2 =  0.0133
```

```
                   Factor Loadings
     Variable  |      1            2        Uniqueness

    bg2cost1   |  -0.13697      0.42354      0.80185
    bg2cost2   |   0.41413      0.19924      0.78879
    bg2cost3   |   0.62011      0.36904      0.47927
    bg2cost4   |   0.35771      0.09071      0.86382
    bg2cost5   |  -0.37507      0.43574      0.66945
    bg2cost6   |  -0.42929      0.43960      0.62246
```

In addition to the "standard" output, when you use the `ml` option, Stata reports likelihood-ratio tests of the number of factors in the model versus (1) no factors and (2) more factors. The second test is, in reality, a test against a model sufficiently rich to fit the observed correlation matrix perfectly. This test is only approximately chi-squared, and we have used the correction recommended by Bartlett (1951). Be aware that there are many variations on this test in use by different statistical packages.

The following comments were made by the analyst looking at these results: "There is, in my opinion, weak evidence of more than two factors. The χ^2 test for more than two factors is really a test of how well you are fitting the correlation matrix. It is not surprising that the model does not fit it perfectly. The significance of 1%, however, suggests to me that there might be a third factor. As for the loadings, they yield a similar interpretation to other factor models we fitted, although there are some noteworthy differences." When we challenged the analyst on this last statement, he added that he would want to rotate the resulting factors before committing himself further.

❏

❏ Technical Note

Going back to the two tests, Stata will sometimes comment, "Note: above tests may not apply; see manual". The approximations used in computing the χ^2 value and degrees of freedom are mathematically justified on the assumption that an *interior* solution to the factor maximum likelihood was found. This is the case in our example above, but that will not always be so.

Another possibility: boundary solutions, called Heywood solutions, often produce uniquenesses of 0, and in that case, at least at a formal level, the test cannot be justified. Nevertheless, we believe that the reported tests are useful even in such circumstances, provided they are interpreted cautiously.

This message is also printed when, in principle, there are enough free parameters to completely fit the correlation matrix, another sort of boundary solution. We say "in principle" because the correlation matrix frequently cannot be fit perfectly, so you will see a positive χ^2 with zero degrees of freedom. This warning note is printed because the geometric assumptions underlying the likelihood-ratio test break down.

❏

❑ Technical Note

In maximum likelihood analysis, there is a possibility of more than one local maximum, and you may want assurances that the maximum reported is the global maximum. Multiple maxima are especially likely when there is more than one group of variables, the groups are reasonably uncorrelated, and you attempt to fit a model with too few factors.

When you specify the `protect(#)` option, Stata performs # optimizations of the likelihood function, beginning each with random starting values, before continuing with the squared-multiple-correlations initialized solution. Stata then selects the maximum of the maxima and reports it, along with a note informing you if other local maxima were found. `protect(50)` provides considerable assurance.

If you then wish to explore any of the nonglobal maxima, include the `random` option. This option, which is never specified with `protect()`, uses random starting values, and reports the solution to which those random values converge. In the case of multiple maxima, giving the command repeatedly will eventually report all local maxima.

❑

Rotation

Rotation is an attempt to describe the information in several factors by re-expressing them so that loadings on a few initial variables are as large as possible. We have this freedom to re-express because of the indeterminate nature of the factors. For example, if you find that z_1 and z_2 are two factors, then $z_1 + z_2$ and $z_1 - z_2$ are equally valid solutions. It comes down to which set is more meaningful and interpretable.

❑ Technical Note

Said more technically: We are trying to find a set of q factor variables such that the observed variables can be explained by regressing them on the q factor variables. Usually, q is a small number such as 1 or 2. If $q \geq 2$, there is an inherent indeterminacy in the construction of the factors because any linear combination of the calculated factors serves equally well as a set of regressors. Rotation capitalizes on this indeterminacy to create a set of variables that looks as much like the original variables as possible.

❑

The `rotate` command modifies the results of the last `factor` command to create a set of loadings that are more interpretable than those produced by `factor`.

You may perform a single factor analysis followed by several `rotate` commands, thus experimenting with, say, retaining different numbers of factors and possibly with using different types of rotation. Please remember: If you retain too few factors, the variables for several distinct concepts may be merged, as happens in our example below. If you retain too many factors, several factors may attempt to measure the same concept, causing the factors to get in each other's way, and suggest too many distinct concepts after rotation.

▷ Example

Let us rotate the results from our previous analysis, starting with the default principal factor solution reported in the first example of the section *Factor analysis* above. If you look back at the example, you will note that `factor` retained three factors, although we made the argument that only two are worth retaining. We commented that you could refit the model specifying the `mineigen()` option, and we could also have mentioned the `factors()` option. It is not necessary to re-estimate, because we can tell `rotate` how many factors to retain for the rotation:

```
. rotate, factors(2)
                (varimax rotation)
              Rotated Factor Loadings
    Variable |     1          2      Uniqueness

    bg2cost1 | -0.09446    0.43223    0.80426
    bg2cost2 | -0.47327   -0.01425    0.77581
    bg2cost3 | -0.53161   -0.01239    0.71723
    bg2cost4 | -0.36294   -0.09851    0.85857
    bg2cost5 |  0.13543    0.50017    0.73149
    bg2cost6 |  0.15820    0.50736    0.71756
```

In this example, the factors are rotated so that the three "negative" items are grouped together, and the three "positive" items are grouped. This is not necessarily a step forward.

We should take note of the uniqueness column. *Uniqueness* is the percentage of variance for the variable that is not explained by the factors. It could be pure measurement error, or it could represent something that is measured reliably in that particular variable, but not by any of the others. The greater the uniqueness, the more likely that it is more than just measurement error. Values over 0.6 are definitely high; all the variables in this problem are even higher—over 0.71.

If the uniqueness is high, then the variable is not well explained by the factor(s). The quantity "1 − *uniqueness*" is called *communality*.

◁

> ## Example

In this example, we examine 19 variables describing various aspects of health. These variables were collected from a random half of 22,462 visitors to doctors' offices by Tarlov et al. (1989). Factor analysis yields three clear factors. We then examine several rotations of these three factors.

(Continued on next page)

```
. describe
Contains data from sp.dta
   obs:        11,231                          MOS SP Screener Raw Data
   vars:          20                           14 Jul 2002 12:29
   size:      303,237 (70.8% of memory free)
```

variable name	storage type	display format	value label	variable label
patid	float	%9.0g		Case ID
sp1ghp31	byte	%8.0g		Health excellent, very good, good, fair, poor
sp2pf01	byte	%8.0g		How long limit vigorous activity
sp2pf02	byte	%8.0g		How long limit moderate activity
sp2pf03	byte	%8.0g		How long limit walk/climb
sp2pf04	byte	%8.0g		How long limit bend/stoop
sp2pf05	byte	%8.0g		How long limit walk 1 block
sp2pf06	byte	%8.0g		How long limit eat/dress/bath
sp2rkeep	byte	%8.0g		does health keep work-job-hse
sp2rkind	byte	%8.0g		Can't do kind/amount of work
sp2sact0	byte	%8.0g		Last month limit activities
sp2mha01	byte	%8.0g		Last month very nervous
sp2mhp03	byte	%8.0g		Last month calm/peaceful
sp2mhd02	byte	%8.0g		Last month downhearted/blue
sp2mhp01	byte	%8.0g		Last month a happy person
sp2mhc01	byte	%8.0g		Last month down in the dumps
sp2ghp01	byte	%8.0g		somewhat ill
sp2ghp04	byte	%8.0g		Healthy as anybody I know
sp2ghp02	byte	%8.0g		Health is excellent
sp2ghp05	byte	%8.0g		Feel bad lately

```
Sorted by:  patid
```

We now perform our factorization, requesting that factors with eigenvalues less than or equal to 1 not be retained. Our dataset contains many missing values, a fact you can discover by comparing the number of observations in the dataset (shown by describe as 11,231) with the number of observations used by factor, 8,329. factor uses only complete observations.

```
. factor sp1ghp31-sp2ghp05, mineigen(1)
(obs=8329)
                   (principal factors; 3 factors retained)
```

Factor	Eigenvalue	Difference	Proportion	Cumulative
1	7.32506	4.88726	0.6873	0.6873
2	2.43779	1.38641	0.2287	0.9160
3	1.05138	0.68662	0.0986	1.0147
4	0.36476	0.07552	0.0342	1.0489
5	0.28924	0.13377	0.0271	1.0760
6	0.15547	0.02951	0.0146	1.0906
7	0.12596	0.10441	0.0118	1.1024
8	0.02155	0.02148	0.0020	1.1045
9	0.00007	0.03729	0.0000	1.1045
10	-0.03722	0.00450	-0.0035	1.1010
11	-0.04172	0.03271	-0.0039	1.0971
12	-0.07443	0.01751	-0.0070	1.0901
13	-0.09194	0.02319	-0.0086	1.0814
14	-0.11513	0.01561	-0.0108	1.0706
15	-0.13074	0.00624	-0.0123	1.0584
16	-0.13698	0.01258	-0.0129	1.0455
17	-0.14956	0.01608	-0.0140	1.0315
18	-0.16564	0.00431	-0.0155	1.0159
19	-0.16995	.	-0.0159	1.0000

Variable	Factor Loadings 1	2	3	Uniqueness
sp1ghp31	-0.65429	-0.05861	0.34895	0.44670
sp2pf01	0.61518	0.32407	-0.00419	0.51652
sp2pf02	0.69049	0.38099	0.22926	0.32551
sp2pf03	0.67373	0.38284	0.16968	0.37074
sp2pf04	0.65131	0.36714	0.23888	0.38394
sp2pf05	0.62350	0.33091	0.27403	0.42665
sp2pf06	0.43672	0.18049	0.22468	0.72622
sp2rkeep	0.68695	0.18325	0.08939	0.48653
sp2rkind	0.72533	0.24854	0.08135	0.40550
sp2sact0	0.65514	-0.07027	0.04680	0.56366
sp2mha01	0.53206	-0.48094	0.12855	0.46909
sp2mhp03	-0.48434	0.57765	-0.12693	0.41562
sp2mhd02	0.52591	-0.60933	0.17036	0.32311
sp2mhp01	-0.50216	0.60714	-0.12672	0.36316
sp2mhc01	0.49556	-0.52768	0.15652	0.45148
sp2ghp01	0.67159	0.02165	-0.36978	0.41176
sp2ghp04	-0.68815	-0.02208	0.42539	0.34500
sp2ghp02	-0.74789	-0.02575	0.44989	0.23759
sp2ghp05	0.61725	-0.27478	-0.16278	0.51700

The first factor is a general health factor. (To understand that claim, compare the factor loadings with the description of the variables as shown by describe above. Also note that, just as with the Physician-Cost data, the sense of some of the coded responses is reversed.) The second factor loads most highly on the five "mental health" items (with names sp2mha01 — sp2mhc01). The third factor loads most highly on "general health perception" items—their names have the letters ghp in them. The other items describe "physical health". These designations are based primarily on the wording of the questions, which is summarized in the variable labels.

```
. rotate
```
(varimax rotation)

Variable	Rotated Factor Loadings 1	2	3	Uniqueness
sp1ghp31	-0.28993	0.16325	0.66527	0.44670
sp2pf01	0.58577	-0.02818	-0.37358	0.51652
sp2pf02	0.78374	-0.08700	-0.22950	0.32551
sp2pf03	0.74408	-0.05968	-0.26841	0.37074
sp2pf04	0.75493	-0.08240	-0.19839	0.38394
sp2pf05	0.73367	-0.10930	-0.15206	0.42665
sp2pf06	0.50123	-0.12857	-0.07757	0.72622
sp2rkeep	0.60010	-0.20666	-0.33263	0.48653
sp2rkind	0.65823	-0.16896	-0.36426	0.40550
sp2sact0	0.41481	-0.38759	-0.33770	0.56366
sp2mha01	0.14263	-0.69104	-0.18174	0.46909
sp2mhp03	-0.05581	0.74727	0.15118	0.41562
sp2mhd02	0.08692	-0.80633	-0.13845	0.32311
sp2mhp01	-0.05079	0.78009	0.16035	0.36316
sp2mhc01	0.10614	-0.72029	-0.13578	0.45148
sp2ghp01	0.27007	-0.19585	-0.69061	0.41176
sp2ghp04	-0.25352	0.18694	0.74551	0.34500
sp2ghp02	-0.28271	0.20542	0.80018	0.23759
sp2ghp05	0.17002	-0.47554	-0.47744	0.51700

With rotation, the structure of the data becomes much clearer. The first rotated factor is physical health, the second is mental health, and the third is general health perception. The a priori designation of the items is confirmed.

Do not place much emphasis on physical health being the first factor. After rotation, the ordering of the factors is no longer meaningful. Moreover, the importance of any factor must be gauged against the number of variables that purportedly measure it. Here, we included nine variables that measured physical health, five that measured mental health, and five that measured general health perception. Had we started with only one mental health item, it would have had a high uniqueness, but we would not want to conclude that it was, therefore, largely noise.

Let us now consider retaining only two factors:

```
. rotate, factors(2)
```

(varimax rotation)

Variable	Rotated Factor Loadings 1	2	Uniqueness
sp1ghp31	-0.42847	-0.49794	0.44670
sp2pf01	0.21545	0.66110	0.51652
sp2pf02	0.22980	0.75440	0.32551
sp2pf03	0.21649	0.74404	0.37074
sp2pf04	0.21135	0.71717	0.38394
sp2pf05	0.21665	0.67180	0.42665
sp2pf06	0.18749	0.43376	0.72622
sp2rkeep	0.36505	0.61010	0.48653
sp2rkind	0.34708	0.68368	0.40550
sp2sact0	0.51888	0.40610	0.56366
sp2mha01	0.71674	0.02577	0.46909
sp2mhp03	-0.74991	0.07686	0.41562
sp2mhd02	0.80180	-0.07061	0.32311
sp2mhp01	-0.78323	0.08559	0.36316
sp2mhc01	0.72314	-0.03320	0.45148
sp2ghp01	0.46663	0.48348	0.41176
sp2ghp04	-0.47821	-0.49534	0.34500
sp2ghp02	-0.51850	-0.53960	0.23759
sp2ghp05	0.63420	0.23300	0.51700

This rotation does not seem nearly as satisfying. The second factor looks like physical health and general health perception, but some contrast with mental health is included. The first factor is mostly a combination of mental health and general health perception, but has some physical health in it.

◁

▷ Example

The literature suggests that physical health and mental health are not orthogonal to each other. In addition, general health perception may be largely a combination of the two. For these reasons, a promax rotation with two factors is worth trying:

```
. rotate, factors(2) promax
```

(promax rotation)

Variable	Rotated Factor Loadings 1	2	Uniqueness
sp1ghp31	-0.24522	-0.51453	0.44670
sp2pf01	-0.03863	0.71076	0.51652
sp2pf02	-0.06063	0.81234	0.32551
sp2pf03	-0.07026	0.80198	0.37074
sp2pf04	-0.06496	0.77280	0.38394
sp2pf05	-0.04162	0.72245	0.42665
sp2pf06	0.02219	0.46274	0.72622
sp2rkeep	0.13564	0.64293	0.48653

sp2rkind	0.08812	0.72532	0.40550
sp2sact0	0.37461	0.40637	0.56366
sp2mha01	0.72848	-0.02771	0.46909
sp2mhp03	-0.80312	0.14325	0.41562
sp2mhd02	0.85413	-0.14044	0.32311
sp2mhp01	-0.84091	0.15547	0.36316
sp2mhc01	0.75831	-0.09311	0.45148
sp2ghp01	0.29025	0.49563	0.41176
sp2ghp04	-0.29752	-0.50777	0.34500
sp2ghp02	-0.32159	-0.55333	0.23759
sp2ghp05	0.56171	0.20683	0.51700

The first factor is defined predominantly by mental health and the second by physical health. General health perception loads on both, but more on physical health than mental health. We think promax rotation was a success here.

◁

Scoring

The `score` command creates a set of new variables that are estimates of the first k factors produced by `factor` or `rotate`, or the first k principal components produced by `pca` (see [R] **pca**).

For factor models, two types of scoring are available: regression and Bartlett scoring.

The number of variables may be less than the number of factors created or rotated. If so, the first such factors will be used. If the number of variables is greater than the number of factors created or rotated, the unused factors will be filled with missing values.

▷ Example

The use of `score` is demonstrated after principal-component extraction in [R] **pca**. Here, we demonstrate its use with factor models. Using our automobile data, we wish to develop an index of roominess based on a car's headroom, rear-seat leg room, and trunk space. We begin by extracting the factors of the three variables:

```
. use http://www.stata-press.com/data/r8/auto1
(Automobile Models)

. factor headroom rear_seat trunk
(obs=74)
```

	(principal factors; 1 factor retained)			
Factor	Eigenvalue	Difference	Proportion	Cumulative
1	1.71426	1.79327	1.1799	1.1799
2	-0.07901	0.10329	-0.0544	1.1255
3	-0.18231	.	-0.1255	1.0000

	Factor Loadings	
Variable	1	Uniqueness
headroom	0.72800	0.47002
rear_seat	0.71439	0.48965
trunk	0.82093	0.32607

All the factor loadings are positive, so we have indeed obtained a "roominess" factor. The `score` command will now create the one retained factor, which we will call `f1`:

```
. score f1
              (based on unrotated factors)
                Scoring Coefficients
        Variable |      1
```
Variable	1
headroom	0.28323
rear_seat	0.26820
trunk	0.45964

If factor had retained more than one factor, typing score f1 would still have added only the first factor to our data. Typing score f1 f2, however, would have added the first two factors to our data. f1 is now our "roominess" index, so we might compare the roominess of domestic and foreign cars:

`. table foreign, c(mean f1 sd f1) row`

Foreign	mean(f1)	sd(f1)
Domestic	.2022442	.9031404
Foreign	-.4780318	.6106609
Total	4.51e-09	.8804116

We find that domestic cars are, on average, roomier than foreign cars, at least in our data.

◁

❑ Technical Note

Wait! Are factors not supposed to be normalized to have mean 0 and standard deviation 1? In our example above, the mean is $4.5 \cdot 10^{-9}$ and the standard deviation is .88. Why is that?

Let's take the mean first: The mean is supposed to be zero and $4.5 \cdot 10^{-9}$ is awfully close to zero, and, in fact, is zero to the accuracy of a float variable. If we had typed score double f1, so that f1 was stored as a double, we would have found the mean is $-9.5 \cdot 10^{-17}$, which is also zero to the accuracy of a double. The deviation from zero is due to numerical roundoff.

The explanation for the standard deviation of .88, on the other hand, is not numerical roundoff. At a theoretical level, the factor is supposed to have standard deviation 1, but the estimation routines almost never yield that result unless an exact solution to the factor model is found. This happens for the same reason that when you regress y on x, you do not get the same equation as if you regress x on y, unless x and y are perfectly collinear.

By the way, if we had two factors, one would expect the correlation between the two factors to be zero since that is how they are theoretically defined. The matrix algebra, however, does not usually work out for that to be so. It is somewhat analogous to the fact that if you regress y on x and the regression assumption about the errors being uncorrelated with the dependent variable is satisfied, then it automatically cannot be satisfied if you regress x on y.

The covariance matrix of the estimated factors is

$$E(\widehat{f}\widehat{f'}) = \mathrm{I} - (\mathrm{I} + \Gamma)^{-1}$$

where

$$\Gamma = \Lambda' \Psi^{-1} \Lambda$$

The columns of Λ are orthogonal to each other, but the inclusion of Ψ in the middle of the equation destroys that relationship unless all the elements of Ψ are equal.

❑

▷ Example

Let's pretend that we work for the K. E. Watt Company, a fictional industry group that generates statistics on automobiles. Our "roominess" index has mean 0 and standard deviation .88, but indexes we present to the public generally have mean 100 and standard deviation 10. First, we wish to rescale our index:

```
. generate roomidx = (f1/.88041161)*10 + 100
. table foreign, c(mean roomidx sd roomidx freq) row format(%9.2f)
```

Foreign	mean(roomidx)	sd(roomidx)	Freq.
Domestic	102.30	10.26	52
Foreign	94.57	6.94	22
Total	100.00	10.00	74

Now when we release our results, we can write, "The K. E. Watt index of roominess shows that domestic cars are, on average, roomier, with an index of 102 versus only 95 for foreign cars."

Now let's find the "roomiest" car in our data:

```
. sort roomidx
. list make model roomidx in 1
```

	make	model	roomidx
74.	Merc.	Marquis	116.7469

We can also write, "K. E. Watt finds that the Mercury Marquis is the roomiest automobile among those surveyed, with a roominess index of 117 versus an average of 100."

◁

❏ Technical Note

`score` provides two methods of scoring, the default regression scoring, which we have used above, and the optional Bartlett method. An artificial example will best illustrate the use and meaning of the methods. We begin by creating a known-to-be-correct factor model in which the true loadings are 0.4, 0.6, and 0.8. We make the sample size n sufficiently large so that statistical fluctuation due to sample size is not important.

```
. set seed 123456789
. set obs 10000
obs was 0, now 10000
. gen f = invnorm(uniform())
. gen x1 = .4*f + sqrt(.84)*invnorm(uniform())
. gen x2 = .6*f + sqrt(.64)*invnorm(uniform())
. gen x3 = .8*f + sqrt(.36)*invnorm(uniform())
. summarize x1 x2 x3
```

Variable	Obs	Mean	Std. Dev.	Min	Max
x1	10000	-.0016167	.9944344	-3.749768	3.89626
x2	10000	-.0060847	.9996945	-3.391357	4.160651
x3	10000	.0024834	.9983335	-3.206443	3.674309

Having concocted our data, the iterated principal factor method reproduces the true loadings most faithfully:

```
. factor x1 x2 x3, ipf factors(1)
(obs=10000)
                 (iterated principal factors; 1 factor retained)
    Factor     Eigenvalue     Difference     Proportion     Cumulative

       1         1.17863        1.17845         1.0000         1.0000
       2         0.00018        0.00041         0.0002         1.0002
       3        -0.00023            .          -0.0002         1.0000

                 Factor Loadings
    Variable  |      1       Uniqueness

          x1  |   0.39535      0.84369
          x2  |   0.57682      0.66727
          x3  |   0.83042      0.31040
```

Let us now compare regression and Bartlett scoring:

```
. score f1
              (based on unrotated factors)
              Scoring Coefficients
    Variable  |      1

          x1  |   0.11995
          x2  |   0.22134
          x3  |   0.68499

. score f1b, bartlett
              (based on unrotated factors)
              Scoring Coefficients
    Variable  |      1

          x1  |   0.50329
          x2  |   0.52925
          x3  |   0.59698
```

Comparing the two scoring vectors, we see that Bartlett scoring yields larger coefficients and that it weights x3 less relative to x1. The regression method is biased insofar as $E(f1)$ is not f, something we can reveal by regressing $f1$ on f:

```
. regress f1 f
     Source  |       SS          df        MS              Number of obs =    10000
-------------+----------------------------------           F( 1,  9998) =25132.99
      Model  |  5321.5801        1     5321.5801           Prob > F      =   0.0000
   Residual  |  2116.9448     9998    .211736827           R-squared     =   0.7154
-------------+----------------------------------           Adj R-squared =   0.7154
      Total  |  7438.52489    9999    .743926882           Root MSE      =   .46015

-------------+----------------------------------------------------------------
         f1  |     Coef.   Std. Err.      t     P>|t|     [95% Conf. Interval]
-------------+----------------------------------------------------------------
          f  |   .729048   .0045987    158.53   0.000     .7200336    .7380623
      _cons  |  .0004368   .0046015      0.09   0.924     -.008583    .0094567
-------------+----------------------------------------------------------------
```

Note the coefficient on f of $.73 < 1$. The Bartlett method, on the other hand, is unbiased:

```
. regress f1b f

      Source |       SS       df       MS              Number of obs =    10000
-------------+------------------------------           F(  1,  9998) =18986.25
       Model | 9898.47671        1 9898.47671          Prob > F      =   0.0000
    Residual | 5212.45427     9998 .521349697          R-squared     =   0.6551
-------------+------------------------------           Adj R-squared =   0.6550
       Total |  15110.931     9999 1.51124422          Root MSE      =   .72205

-------------+------------------------------------------------------------------
         f1b |      Coef.   Std. Err.       t    P>|t|     [95% Conf. Interval]
-------------+------------------------------------------------------------------
           f |   .9943058   .0072161   137.79   0.000     .9801609    1.008451
       _cons |   .0005958   .0072205     0.08   0.934    -.0135578    .0147493
-------------------------------------------------------------------------------
```

This difference is not as important as it might seem since the bias in the regression method is only a matter of scaling. We tested for deviations from regression assumptions in both of the above regression models, and found nothing (no nonlinearity or heteroskedasticity). This is to be expected since the data have a joint normal distribution and both f1 and f1b are linear combinations of the data.

The regression method is attempting to estimate $f1 = E(f|\text{data})$, not to compute f1 so that $E(f1b|f) = f$. However, the two methods do not produce identical estimators. When the factors are not well determined, the differences can be notable. Here the factor is well determined, so the difference is minimal. The regression estimator, rescaled, is slightly better:

```
. correlate f1 f1b f, means
(obs=10000)

    Variable |       Mean    Std. Dev.          Min          Max
-------------+--------------------------------------------------
          f1 |    2.77e-11      .862512    -3.084572     3.351701
         f1b |    2.16e-10     1.229327    -4.667728     4.665413
           f |   -.0005992     1.000659    -3.918931     3.641588


             |       f1      f1b        f
-------------+---------------------------
          f1 |   1.0000
         f1b |   0.9431   1.0000
           f |   0.8458   0.8094   1.0000
```

Notice that neither estimator follows the assumption that the scaled factor has unit variance. The regression estimator has a variance less than 1, and the Bartlett estimator has a variance greater than 1.

❑

Saved Results

factor saves in r():

Scalars

r(N)	number of observations	r(chi2_1)	χ^2 test against more factors
r(k_f)	number of retained factors	r(df_1)	degrees of freedom for r(chi2_1)
r(chi2_0)	χ^2 test against no factors	r(lambda#)	#th eigenvalue
r(df_0)	degrees of freedom for r(chi2_0)		

Methods and Formulas

The following is the statistical factor model. Suppose there are p variables and q factors. Let Ψ represent the $p \times p$ diagonal matrix of uniquenesses, and let Λ represent the $p \times q$ factor loading matrix. Let f be a $1 \times q$ matrix of factors. Then, the standardized (mean 0, variance 1) vector of observed variables x ($1 \times p$) is given by the system of regression equations,

$$x = f\Lambda' + e,$$

where e is a $1 \times p$ vector of uncorrelated errors with covariance equal to the uniqueness matrix Ψ.

Under the factor model, the correlation matrix of x, called Σ, is decomposed by factor analysis as

$$\Sigma = \Lambda\Lambda' + \Psi$$

Stata does this by an eigenvector calculation. An estimate is found for Ψ, and then the columns of Λ are computed as the eigenvectors, scaled by the square root of the appropriate eigenvalue.

See Lawley and Maxwell (1971), Harman (1976), and Clarke (1970).

Rotation

Varimax rotation (Kaiser 1958) retains the original factor assumption that the factors are orthogonal to each other and have unit variance. Promax rotation (Hendrickson and White 1964) allows the factors to be correlated with each other, but they still have unit variance. Because of the correlation, promax loadings can exceed 1.

Varimax attempts to find an orthogonal rotation matrix $\mathbf{M}$ such that

$$\Lambda = \Lambda_0 \mathbf{M}$$

achieves a maximum of

$$\sum_{r=1}^{k} \sum_{i=1}^{p} (\Lambda_{ir}^2 - d_r)^2$$

where

$$d_r = \sum_{i=1}^{p} \Lambda_{ir}^2 / p$$

This expression has multiple maxima because any exchange of columns of Λ yields an equally good maximum. However, it is known that there is a unique maximum (subject to exchange) for the two-factor problem, and, in testing our routines, we did not observe any alternative maxima in our tests for more than two factors.

You should note that there is some disagreement in the literature on what a varimax rotation is. Horst (1965), for example, suggests that the loadings be scaled so that their sum of squares adds to 1 for each variable. This can lead to a different solution if some variables have to be scaled much more than others. Some computer packages (such as SAS) have adopted the Horst scaling as the only option; Stata allows you to select it explicitly with the `horst` option. If you do not select this option, you do not obtain Horst scaling.

This disagreement among software implementations on the varimax solution also leads to disagreements on the promax solution, since the promax rotation is a function of varimax rotation. Let Λ be the varimax loading matrix. Then, the promax transform U has columns that minimize

$$\text{trace}(Q - \Lambda U)'(Q - \Lambda U)$$

where the elements of Q are formed by taking the corresponding elements of Λ to the promax index power (which Stata defaults to 3), with the sign of Λ. U is then scaled to be consistent with the assumption that the factors have unit variances. The transformed loadings are ΛU.

Scoring

The formula for regression scoring (Thomson 1951) in the orthogonal case is

$$\widehat{f} = \Lambda' \Sigma^{-1} x$$

where Λ is the varimax rotated or unrotated loading matrix. For the oblique case, it is

$$\widehat{f} = \Phi \Lambda' \Sigma^{-1} x$$

where $\Phi = (U'U)^{-1}$ using the scaled U matrix from the promax rotation step.

The formula for Bartlett scoring (Bartlett 1937, 1938) is

$$\Gamma^{-1} \Lambda' \Psi^{-1} x$$

where

$$\Gamma = \Lambda' \Psi^{-1} \Lambda$$

See Harman (1976) and Lawley and Maxwell (1971).

References

Bartlett, M. S. 1937. The statistical conception of mental factors. *British Journal of Psychology* 28: 97–104.

——. 1938. Methods of estimating mental factors. *Nature, London* 141: 609–610.

——. 1951. The effect of standardization on a χ^2 approximation in factor analysis. *Biometrika* 38: 337–344.

Clarke, M. R. B. 1970. A rapidly convergent method for maximum-likelihood factor analysis. *British Journal of Mathematical and Statistical Psychology* 23: 43–52.

Hamilton, L. C. 1992. *Regression with Graphics*, 249–288. Pacific Grove, CA: Brooks/Cole Publishing Company.

——. 2002. *Statistics with Stata*, Chapter 12. Belmont, CA: Duxbury.

Harman, H. H. 1976. *Modern Factor Analysis*. 3d ed. Chicago: University of Chicago Press.

Hendrickson, A. E. and P. O. White. 1964. Promax: A quick method for rotation to oblique simple structure. *British Journal of Statistical Psychology* 17: 65–70.

Horst, P. 1965. *Factor Analysis of Data Matrices*. New York: Holt, Rinehart, and Winston.

Kaiser, H. F. 1958. The varimax criterion for analytic rotation in factor analysis. *Psychometrika* 23: 187–200.

Lawley, D. N. and A. E. Maxwell. 1971. *Factor Analysis as a Statistical Method*. London: Butterworth & Company.

Rencher, A. C. 1998. *Multivariate Statistical Inference and Applications*. New York: John Wiley & Sons.

Spearman, C. 1904. General intelligence objectively determined and measured. *American Journal of Psychology* 15: 201–293.

Tarlov, A. R., J. E. Ware, Jr., S. Greenfield, E. C. Nelson, E. Perrin, and M. Zubkoff. 1989. The medical outcomes study. *Journal of the American Medical Association* 262: 925–930.

Thomson, G. H. 1951. *The Factorial Analysis of Human Ability*. London: University of London Press.

Also See

Complementary:	[R] **impute**,
	[P] **matrix get**
Related:	[R] **alpha**, [R] **canon**, [R] **corr2data**, [R] **pca**
Background:	*Stata Graphics Reference Manual*,
	[R] **maximize**

Title

> **fillin** — Rectangularize dataset

Syntax

fillin *varlist*

Description

fillin adds observations with missing data so that all interactions of *varlist* exist, thus making a complete rectangularization of *varlist*. fillin also adds the variable _fillin to the dataset. _fillin is 1 for created observations and 0 for previously existing observations.

Remarks

▷ Example

You have data on something by sex, race, and age group. You suspect that some of the combinations of sex, race, and age do not exist, but if so, you want them to exist with whatever remaining variables there are in the dataset, set to missing. That is, rather than having a missing observation for black females ages 20–24, you want to create an observation that contains missing values:

```
. use http://www.stata-press.com/data/r8/fillin1
. list
```

	sex	race	age_gr~p	x1	x2
1.	female	white	20-24	20393	14.5
2.	male	white	25-29	32750	12.7
3.	female	black	30-34	39399	14.2

```
. fillin sex race age_group
. list, sepby(sex)
```

	sex	race	age_gr~p	x1	x2	_fillin
1.	female	white	20-24	20393	14.5	0
2.	female	white	25-29	.	.	1
3.	female	white	30-34	.	.	1
4.	female	black	20-24	.	.	1
5.	female	black	25-29	.	.	1
6.	female	black	30-34	39399	14.2	0
7.	male	white	20-24	.	.	1
8.	male	white	25-29	32750	12.7	0
9.	male	white	30-34	.	.	1
10.	male	black	20-24	.	.	1
11.	male	black	25-29	.	.	1
12.	male	black	30-34	.	.	1

◁

Methods and Formulas

fillin is implemented as an ado-file.

Also See

Complementary: [R] **save**

Related: [R] **cross**, [R] **expand**, [R] **joinby**

Title

> **format** — Specify variable display format

Syntax

> format *varlist* %*fmt*

or

> format %*fmt* *varlist*

> <u>set</u> dp { <u>comma</u> | <u>period</u> } [, <u>perman</u>ently]

Description

> format allows you to specify the display format for variables. The internal precision of the variables is unaffected.

> set dp lets you globally set the symbol Stata uses to represent the decimal symbol. The default is period, meaning one and a half is displayed as 1.5; comma specifies that it be displayed as 1,5.

Options

> permanently specifies that, in addition to making the change right now, the dp setting should be remembered in the future, and will become the default setting for when you invoke Stata.

Remarks

> See [U] **15.5 Formats: controlling how data are displayed** for an explanation of %*fmt*. As a brief review, Stata's three numeric formats are denoted by a leading percent sign % followed by the string *w.d* (or *w,d* if you want European format), where *w* and *d* stand for two integers. The first integer, *w*, specifies the width of the format. The second integer, *d*, specifies the number of digits that are to follow the decimal point. Logic requires that *d* be less than *w*. Finally, a character denoting the format type (e, f, or g) is appended. For example, %9.2f specifies the f format that is nine characters wide and has two digits following the decimal point. In the case of f and g, a c may additionally be suffixed to indicate comma formats. Two more "numeric" formats, %d and %t, are used to display elapsed dates and various time-series formats; see [U] **27 Commands for dealing with dates** and [U] **15.5.4 Time-series formats**. String formats are denoted by %*w*s, where *w* indicates the width of the format.

▷ Example

> We have Census data by region and state on median age and population in 1980.

> ```
> . use http://www.stata-press.com/data/r8/census10
> (1980 Census data by state)
> ```

```
. describe
Contains data from http://www.stata-press.com/data/r8/census10.dta
  obs:            50                          1980 Census data by state
 vars:             4                          13 Jun 2002 10:24
 size:         1,400 (99.8% of memory free)
```

variable name	storage type	display format	value label	variable label
state	str14	%14s		State
region	int	%8.0g	cenreg	Census region
pop	long	%11.0g		Population
medage	float	%9.0g		Median age

```
Sorted by:
. list in 1/8
```

	state	region	pop	medage
1.	Alabama	South	3893888	29.3
2.	Alaska	West	401851	26.1
3.	Arizona	West	2718215	29.2
4.	Arkansas	South	2286435	30.6
5.	California	West	23667902	29.9
6.	Colorado	West	2889964	28.6
7.	Connecticut	NE	3107576	32
8.	Delaware	South	594338	29.8

The state variable has a display format of %14s. To left-align the state data, we type

```
. format state %-14s
. list in 1/8
```

	state	region	pop	medage
1.	Alabama	South	3893888	29.3
2.	Alaska	West	401851	26.1
3.	Arizona	West	2718215	29.2
4.	Arkansas	South	2286435	30.6
5.	California	West	23667902	29.9
6.	Colorado	West	2889964	28.6
7.	Connecticut	NE	3107576	32
8.	Delaware	South	594338	29.8

Although it seems like region is a string variable, it is really a numeric variable with an attached value label. You do the same thing to left-align a numeric variable as you do a string variable: insert a negative sign.

(Continued on next page)

```
. format region %-8.0g
. list in 1/8
```

	state	region	pop	medage
1.	Alabama	South	3893888	29.3
2.	Alaska	West	401851	26.1
3.	Arizona	West	2718215	29.2
4.	Arkansas	South	2286435	30.6
5.	California	West	23667902	29.9
6.	Colorado	West	2889964	28.6
7.	Connecticut	NE	3107576	32
8.	Delaware	South	594338	29.8

The pop variable would probably be easier to read if we inserted commas. You specify the comma format by appending a 'c':

```
. format pop %11.0gc
. list in 1/8
```

	state	region	pop	medage
1.	Alabama	South	3,893,888	29.3
2.	Alaska	West	401,851	26.1
3.	Arizona	West	2,718,215	29.2
4.	Arkansas	South	2,286,435	30.6
5.	California	West	23667902	29.9
6.	Colorado	West	2,889,964	28.6
7.	Connecticut	NE	3,107,576	32
8.	Delaware	South	594,338	29.8

Look at the value of pop for observation 5. There are no commas. This number was too large for Stata to insert commas and also respect the current width of 10. Let us try again:

```
. format pop %12.0gc
. list in 1/8
```

	state	region	pop	medage
1.	Alabama	South	3,893,888	29.3
2.	Alaska	West	401,851	26.1
3.	Arizona	West	2,718,215	29.2
4.	Arkansas	South	2,286,435	30.6
5.	California	West	23,667,902	29.9
6.	Colorado	West	2,889,964	28.6
7.	Connecticut	NE	3,107,576	32
8.	Delaware	South	594,338	29.8

Finally, medage would look better if the decimal points were vertically aligned.

```
. format medage %8.1f
. list in 1/8
```

	state	region	pop	medage
1.	Alabama	South	3,893,888	29.3
2.	Alaska	West	401,851	26.1
3.	Arizona	West	2,718,215	29.2
4.	Arkansas	South	2,286,435	30.6
5.	California	West	23,667,902	29.9
6.	Colorado	West	2,889,964	28.6
7.	Connecticut	NE	3,107,576	32.0
8.	Delaware	South	594,338	29.8

Display formats are permanently attached to variables by the `format` command. If you `save` the data, the next time you `use` it, `state` will still be formatted as `%-14s`, `region` will still be formatted as `%-8.0g`, etc.

◁

▷ Example

Suppose that you have an employee identification variable `empid` and that you want to have the leading zeros retained when you list your data. `format` has a leading zero option that allows this.

```
. describe empid
```

variable name	storage type	display format	value label	variable label
empid	float	%9.0g		

```
. list in 83/87
```

	empid
83.	98
84.	99
85.	100
86.	101
87.	102

```
. format empid %05.0f
. list in 83/87
```

	empid
83.	00098
84.	00099
85.	00100
86.	00101
87.	00102

◁

❑ Technical Note

The syntax of the `format` command allows a *varlist* and not just a *varname*. Thus, you can attach the %9.2f format to the variables `myvar`, `thisvar`, and `thatvar` by typing

. format myvar thisvar thatvar %9.2f

❑

European formats

Do you prefer that one and one half be written as 1,5 and that one thousand one and a half be written as 1.001,5? Stata will present numbers in that format if, when you set the format, you specify ',' rather than '.' in the following format:

. format pop %12,0gc

. format medage %9,2f

. list in 1/8

	state	region	pop	medage
1.	Alabama	South	3.893.888	29,30
2.	Alaska	West	401.851	26,10
3.	Arizona	West	2.718.215	29,20
4.	Arkansas	South	2.286.435	30,60
5.	California	West	23.667.902	29,90
6.	Colorado	West	2.889.964	28,60
7.	Connecticut	NE	3.107.576	32,00
8.	Delaware	South	594.338	29,80

Alternatively, you can leave the formats just as they were and instead type `set dp comma`. That tells Stata to interpret all formats as if you had typed the comma instead of the period:

. format pop %12.0gc   *(put the formats back as they were)*

. format medage %9.2f

. set dp comma   *(tell Stata to use European format)*

. list in 1/8
(same output appears as above)

`set dp comma` affects all of Stata's output, so if you run a regression, display summary statistics, or make a table, commas will be used instead of periods in the output:

. tabulate region [fw=pop]

Census region	Freq.	Percent	Cum.
NE	49135283	21,75	21,75
N Cntrl	58865670	26,06	47,81
South	74734029	33,08	80,89
West	43172490	19,11	100,00
Total	225907472	100,00	

You can return to using period by typing

```
. set dp period
```

Understand the difference: setting a variable's display format to be in European format will affect how the variable's values are displayed by list and in a few other places. Setting dp to comma will affect every bit of Stata.

Also understand that set dp comma affects only how Stata displays output, not how it gets input. When you need to type one and a half, you must type 1.5 regardless of context.

❑ Technical Note

set dp comma makes drastic changes inside Stata, and we mention this because some older, user-written programs may not be up to dealing with those changes. If you are using an older, user-written program, you might set dp comma, only to find that the program does not work and instead presents some sort of syntax error.

If, using any program, you do get an unanticipated error, try setting dp back to period.

Even with set dp comma, you might still see some output with the decimal symbol shown as period rather than comma. There are two places in Stata where Stata ignores set dp comma because the features are generally used to produce what will be treated as input, and set dp comma does not affect how Stata inputs numbers. First,

```
local x = sqrt(2)
```

stores the string "1.414213562373095" in x and not "1,414213562373095", so if some program were to display 'x' as a string in the output, the period would show. Most programs, however, would use 'x' in subsequent calculations, or, at the least, when the time came to display what was in 'x', would display it as a number. They would code

```
display ... 'x' ...
```

and not

```
display ... "'x'" ...
```

so the output would be

```
... 1,4142136 ...
```

The other place where Stata ignores set dp comma is the string() function. If you type

```
. gen str8 res = string(numvar)
```

new variable res will contain the string representation of numeric variable numvar, with the decimal symbol being period regardless of whether you have previously set dp comma. Of course, if you explicitly ask that string() use European format,

```
. gen str8 res = string(numvar,"%9,0g")
```

then string() honors your request; string() merely ignores the global set dp comma.

❑

Other effects of display formats, European and non-European

❑ Technical Note

You have data on the age of employees, and you type `summarize age` to obtain the mean and standard deviation. By default, Stata uses its default g format to provide as much precision as possible:

```
. summarize age
    Variable |     Obs       Mean   Std. Dev.       Min        Max
-------------+--------------------------------------------------------
         age |     204   29.64706    8.914091        18         66
```

If you attach a `%9.2f` format to the variable and specify the `format` option, Stata uses that specification to format the results:

```
. format age %9.2f
. summarize age, format
    Variable |     Obs       Mean   Std. Dev.       Min        Max
-------------+--------------------------------------------------------
         age |     204      29.65        8.91     18.00      66.00
```

❑

Also See

Related: [P] **display**

Background: [U] **15.5 Formats: controlling how data are displayed**,
[U] **15.5.4 Time-series formats**,
[U] **15.6 Dataset, variable, and value labels**,
[U] **27 Commands for dealing with dates**

Title

fracpoly — Fractional polynomial regression

Syntax

fracpoly *regression_cmd* *yvar* *xvar*$_1$ $\big[$*#* $\big[$*#...$\big]\big]$ $\big[$*xvar*$_2$ $\big[$*#* $\big[$*#...$\big]\big]\big]$ $\big[$...$\big]$ $\big[$*xvarlist*$\big]$

　　　$\big[$*weight*$\big]$ $\big[$if *exp*$\big]$ $\big[$in *range*$\big]$ $\big[$, adjust(*adj_list*) compare degree(*#*) log

　　　noconstant noscaling powers(*numlist*) *regression_cmd_options* $\big]$

fracpoly $\big[$, compare $\big]$

fracplot $\big[$*varname*$\big]$ $\big[$, ciopts(*rarea_options*) plot(*plot*)

　　　rlopts(*line_options*) *scatter_options* *twoway_options* $\big]$

fracpred *newvarname* $\big[$*varname*$\big]$ $\big[$, dresid for(*varname*) stdp $\big]$

fracgen *varname* *#* $\big[$*#* ...$\big]$ $\big[$if *exp*$\big]$ $\big[$in *range*$\big]$ $\big[$, adjust(no | mean | *#*)

　　　noscaling replace $\big]$

where *regression_cmd* may be clogit, glm, logistic, logit, poisson, probit, regress, stcox, or streg

and where *adj_list* is a comma-separated list with elements *varlist*: {mean | *#* | no}, except that the first element may optionally be of the form {mean | *#* | no} to specify the default for all variables.

Note that fracplot and fracpred, dresid are not allowed after fracpoly with clogit or probit.

fracpoly shares the features of all estimation commands; see [U] **23 Estimation and post-estimation commands**. All weight types supported by *regression_cmd* are allowed; see [U] **14.1.6 weight**.

Description

　　fracpoly fits fractional polynomials in *xvar*$_1$ to *yvar*. After execution, fracpoly leaves variables in the dataset named I*xvar*__1, I*xvar*__2, ..., where *xvar* represents the first four letters of the name of *xvar*$_1$. The new variables contain the best-fitting fractional polynomial powers of *xvar*$_1$.

　　Covariates other than *xvar*$_1$, which are optional, are specified in *xvar*$_2$, ... and *xvarlist*. They may be modeled linearly and/or with specified fractional polynomial transformations. Fractional polynomial powers are specified by typing numbers following the variable's name. A variable name typed without numbers following it is entered linearly.

　　fracplot plots the data and fit, with 95% confidence limits, from the most recently fitted fractional polynomial model. The data and fit are plotted against *varname*, which may be *xvar*$_1$ or another of the covariates (*xvar*$_2$, ..., or a variable from *xvarlist*). If *varname* is not specified, *xvar*$_1$ is assumed.

　　fracpred creates *newvarname* containing the fitted index or deviance residuals for the whole model, or the fitted index or its standard error for *varname*, which may be *xvar*$_1$ or another covariate.

fracgen creates new variables named *varname_1*, *varname_2*, ... containing fractional polynomial powers of *varname* using the power(s) (# [#...]) specified.

See [R] **mfp** for multivariable fractional polynomial model fitting.

Options

Options for use with fracpoly

adjust(*adj_list*) defines the adjustments for the covariates *xvar*$_1$, *xvar*$_2$, ..., *xvarlist*. The default is adjust(mean). A typical item in *adj_list* is *varlist*: {mean | # | no}. Items are separated by commas. The first item is special in that *varlist*: is optional, and if omitted, the default is (re)set to the specified value (mean or # or no). For example, adjust(no, age:mean) sets the default to no and sets the adjustment for age to mean.

compare reports significance tests between the best fractional polynomial models of increasing degree.

degree(#) determines the degree of fractional polynomial to be fitted. The default is degree(2); i.e., a model with two power terms.

log displays deviances and (for regress) residual standard deviations for each fractional polynomial model fitted.

noconstant suppresses the regression constant if this is permitted by *regression_cmd*.

noscaling suppresses scaling of *xvar*$_1$ and its powers.

powers(*numlist*) is the set of fractional polynomial powers from which models are to be chosen. The default is powers(-2,-1,-.5,0,.5,1,2,3) (0 means log).

regression_cmd_options are options appropriate to the regression command in use. For example, for stcox, *regression_cmd_options* may include efron or some other alternate method for handling tied failures.

Options for use with fracplot

ciopts(*rarea_options*) affect the rendition of the confidence bands; see [G] **graph twoway rarea**.

plot(*plot*) provides a way to add other plots to the generated graph. See [G] *plot_option*.

rlopts(*line_options*) affect the rendition of the reference line; see [G] **graph twoway line**.

scatter_options affect the rendition of the plotted points; see [G] **graph twoway scatter**.

twoway_options are any of the options documented in [G] *twoway_options*, excluding by(). These include options for titling the graph (see [G] *title_options*), and options for saving the graph to disk (see [G] *saving_option*).

Options for use with fracpred

dresid is for use with fracpred; it specifies that deviance residuals be calculated.

for(*varname*) is for use with fracpred; it specifies (partial) prediction for variable *varname*. The fitted values are adjusted to the value specified by the adjust() option in fracpoly.

stdp is for use with fracpred; it specifies calculation of the standard errors of the fitted values *varname*, adjusted for all the other predictors at the values specified by adjust().

Options for use with fracgen

adjust(no|mean|#) specifies whether *varname* is to be adjusted; the default is adjust(no).

noscaling suppresses scaling of *varname*.

replace specifies that variables named *varname_1*, named *varname_2*, ... may already exist, and, if so, that they may be replaced.

Remarks

Remarks are presented under the headings

       Introduction
       fracpoly
       Adjustment
       Output with the compare option
       fracplot
       fracgen
       Models with several continuous covariates
       Examples

Introduction

Regression models based on fractional polynomial (FP) functions of a continuous covariate are described by Royston and Altman (1994a). Detailed examples using an earlier and rather more complex version of the present set of commands are presented by Royston and Altman (1994b).

The purpose of FPs is to increase the flexibility afforded by the family of conventional polynomial models. Although polynomials are popular in data analysis, linear and quadratic functions are severely limited in their range of curve shapes, whereas cubic and higher order curves often produce undesirable artifacts, such as "edge effects" and "waves".

A polynomial of degree m may be written as

$$\beta_0 + \beta_1 x + \beta_2 x^2 + \cdots + \beta_m x^m$$

whereas a fractional polynomial (FP) of degree m has m integer and/or fractional powers $p_1 < \cdots < p_m$,

$$\beta_0 + \beta_1 x^{(p_1)} + \beta_2 x^{(p_2)} + \cdots + \beta_m x^{(p_m)}$$

where for a power p

$$x^{(p)} = \begin{cases} x^p & \text{if } p \neq 0 \\ \log x & \text{if } p = 0 \end{cases}$$

Note that x must be positive. An FP of first degree ($m = 1$) involves a single power or log transformation of x.

This family of FP functions may be extended in a mathematically natural way to include "repeated powers". An FP of degree m with exactly m repeated powers of p is defined as

$$\beta_0 + \beta_1 x^{(p)} + \beta_2 x^{(p)} \log x + \cdots + \beta_m x^{(p)} (\log x)^{m-1}$$

For example, an FP of second degree ($m = 2$) with repeated powers of 0.5 is

$$\beta_0 + \beta_1 x^{0.5} + \beta_2 x^{0.5} \log x$$

A general FP may include some unique and some repeated powers. For example, one with powers $(-1, 1, 3, 3)$ is

$$\beta_0 + \beta_1 x^{-1} + \beta_2 x + \beta_3 x^3 + \beta_4 x^3 \log x$$

The permitted powers are restricted to the set $\{-2, -1, -0.5, 0, 0.5, 1, 2, 3\}$. While such a limitation is not intrinsic to the approach, the experience of using FPs in data analysis indicates that it is not often worthwhile to include extra powers in the set.

Consider now the use of FPs in regression modeling. If the values of the powers $p_1, \ldots, p_m$ were known, the FP would resemble a conventional multiple linear regression model with coefficients $\beta_0, \beta_1, \ldots, \beta_m$. However, the powers are not (usually) known and must be estimated, together with the coefficients, from the data. Estimation involves a systematic search for the best power or combination of powers from the permitted set. For each possible combination, a linear regression model as just described is fit and the corresponding deviance (defined as minus twice the log likelihood) is noted. The model with the lowest deviance is deemed to have the best fit, and the corresponding powers and regression coefficients constitute the final FP model.

fracpoly

fracpoly finds and reports a multiple regression model comprising the best-fitting powers of $xvar_1$ together with other covariates specified by $xvar_2, \ldots, xvarlist$. The model that is fit depends on the type of *regression_cmd* used.

The regression output for the best-fitting model may be reproduced by typing *regression_cmd* without variables or options. predict, test, etc. may be used after fracpoly; the results will depend on *regression_cmd*.

Note that the standard errors of the fitted values (as estimated following use of fracpoly by using predict or fracpred with the stdp option) are somewhat too low, since no allowance has been made for the estimation of the powers.

If $xvar_1$ has any negative or zero values, fracpoly subtracts the minimum of *xvar* from *xvar* and then adds the rounding (or counting) interval. The interval is defined as the smallest positive difference between the ordered values of *xvar*. After this change of origin, the minimum value of $xvar_1$ is positive, so fractional polynomials (which require $xvar_1 > 0$) can be used. Unless the noscaling option is used, fracpoly scales the resulting variable by a power of 10 calculated from the data. The scaling is designed to improve numerical stability when fitting fractional polynomial models.

After execution, fracpoly leaves in the dataset variables named Ixvar__1, Ixvar__2, ..., which are the best-fitting fractional polynomial powers of $xvar_1$ (calculated, if necessary, following a change in origin and scale as just described, and if adjustment is specified, with a constant added or subtracted to the values following fractional polynomial transformation). Additional variables, whose names follow the same convention, are left in the dataset if $xvar_2$ has been specified.

Adjustment

As discussed by Garrett (1995, 1998), covariate adjustment is a sensible, indeed often essential, step when reporting and interpreting the results of multiple regression models. For this and other reasons, adjustment has been introduced as the default option in fracpoly. As written, the familiar straight-line regression function $E(y|x) = \beta_0 + \beta_1 x$ is 'adjusted' to 0 in that $\beta_0 = E(y|0)$. This is fine if $x = 0$ is a sensible base point. However, the sample values of x may not even encompass 0 (usually the case when FP models are contemplated). Then, β_0 is a meaningless intercept, and the standard error of its estimate $\widehat{\beta}_0$ will be large. For an FP model $E(y|x) = \beta_0 + \beta_1 x^{(p)}$, the point

$x^{(p)} = 0$ may even correspond to $x = \infty$ (consider $p < 0$). The scheme adopted by `fracpoly` is to adjust to the mean of x. For example, for the FP $E(y|x) = \beta_0 + \beta_1 x^{(p)} + \beta_1 x^{(q)}$, `fracpoly` actually fits the model

$$E(y|x) = \beta_0 + \beta_1 \left(x^{(p)} - \overline{x}^{(p)} \right) + \beta_2 \left(x^{(q)} - \overline{x}^{(q)} \right)$$

where $\overline{x}$ is the sample mean of the x values, and $E(y|\overline{x}) = \beta_0$, giving β_0 a respectable interpretation as the predicted value of y at the mean of x. This approach has the advantage that plots of the fitted values and 95% confidence intervals for $E(y|x)$ as a function of x, even within a multiple regression model, are always sensible (provided, of course, that the other predictors are suitably adjusted—otherwise, the confidence limits can be alarmingly wide).

Sometimes adjustment to the mean is not appropriate, an example being a binary covariate where often you will want to adjust to the lower value, usually 0 (i.e., not adjust). You should then use the `adjust()` option to override the default. An example is `adjust(x1:mean,x2-x5:no,x6:1)`.

Output with the compare option

If the `compare` option is used, `fracpoly` displays a table showing the best FP model for each degree $\leq m$. A p-value is given for comparing each pair of models whose degrees differ by 1. (The corresponding difference in model degrees of freedom is 2, as one extra power and one extra coefficient are estimated.) As with conventional polynomial regression, the preferred model is normally taken to be the one which is a significantly better fit than that of next lower degree, but not a significantly worse fit than that of next higher degree. The table also presents the *gain* for each FP model. The gain is defined as the deviance of a straight-line model minus the deviance of the FP model in question (Royston and Altman 1994a). In general, the larger the gain, the greater the nonlinearity of the relation between *yvar* and *xvar*$_1$ (conditional on the other covariates, if any), and the greater the benefit of choosing an FP model as opposed to a straight line. As with p-values, however, gain depends directly on sample size, and is *not*, therefore, an absolute measure of nonlinearity or of model fit.

fracplot

`fracplot` actually produces a component-plus-residual plot. For normal-error models with constant weights and a single covariate, this amounts to a plot of the observations with the fitted line inscribed. For other normal-error models, weighted residuals are calculated and added to the fitted values.

For models with additional covariates, the line is the partial linear predictor for the variable in question (*xvar*$_1$ or a covariate), and includes the intercept β_0.

For generalized linear and Cox models, the fitted values are plotted on the scale of the 'index' (linear predictor). Deviance residuals are added to the (partial) linear predictor to give component-plus-residual values. These are plotted as small circles.

fracgen

The basic syntax of `fracgen` is

> `fracgen` *varname* # $\left[\# \ldots \right]$

Each power (represented by # in the syntax diagram) should be separated by a space. `fracgen` creates new variable(s) called *varname*_1, *varname*_2, etc. Each variable is labeled according to its power, preliminary linear transformation, and adjustment, if applied.

Positive or negative powers of *varname* are defined in the usual way. A power of zero is interpreted as log.

Models with several continuous covariates

fracpoly estimates powers for FP models in just one continuous covariate ($xvar_1$), though other covariates of any kind ($xvar_2, \ldots, xvarlist$) may be included as linear or predefined fractional polynomial terms. An algorithm was suggested by Royston and Altman (1994a) for the joint estimation of FP models in several continuous covariates. It was later refined by Sauerbrei and Royston (1999) and is implemented in mfracpol (see also Royston and Ambler (1998)).

Examples

▷ Example

Consider the serum immunoglobulin-G (IgG) dataset from Isaacs et al. (1983), which consists of 298 independent observations in young children. The dependent variable sqrtigg is the square root of the IgG concentration, and the independent variable age is the age of each child. (Preliminary Box–Cox analysis shows that a square root transformation removes the skewness in IgG.) The aim is to find a model that accurately predicts the mean of sqrtigg given age. We use fracpoly to find the best FP model of degree 2 (the default option) and graph the resulting fit and 95% confidence interval:

```
. use http://www.stata-press.com/data/r8/igg
(Immunoglobulin in children)

. fracpoly regress sqrtigg age
........
-> gen double Iage__1 = age^-2-.1299 if e(sample)
-> gen double Iage__2 = age^2-7.695 if e(sample)
```

Source	SS	df	MS		Number of obs =	298
					F(2, 295) =	64.49
Model	22.2846976	2	11.1423488		Prob > F =	0.0000
Residual	50.9676492	295	.172771692		R-squared =	0.3042
					Adj R-squared =	0.2995
Total	73.2523469	297	.246640898		Root MSE =	.41566

sqrtigg	Coef.	Std. Err.	t	P>|t|	[95% Conf. Interval]	
Iage__1	-.1562156	.027416	-5.70	0.000	-.2101713	-.10226
Iage__2	.0148405	.0027767	5.34	0.000	.0093757	.0203052
_cons	2.283145	.0305739	74.68	0.000	2.222974	2.343315

Deviance: 319.45. Best powers of age among 44 models fit: -2 2.

(Continued on next page)

```
. fracplot age
```

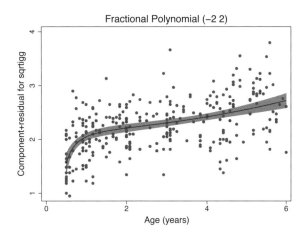

The fitted curve has an asymmetric S-shape. This model has powers $(-2, 2)$ and deviance 319.45. As many as 44 models have been quietly fit in the search for the best powers. Now, let us look at models of degree ≤ 4:

```
. fracpoly regress sqrtigg age, degree(4) compare
.................................................................
> .................................................................
> ........
-> gen double Iage__1 = ln(age)-1.02 if e(sample)
-> gen double Iage__2 = age^3-21.35 if e(sample)
-> gen double Iage__3 = age^3*ln(age)-21.78 if e(sample)
-> gen double Iage__4 = age^3*ln(age)^2-22.22 if e(sample)
```

Source	SS	df	MS		
Model	22.5754541	4	5.64386353	Number of obs =	298
Residual	50.6768927	293	.172958678	F(4, 293) =	32.63
				Prob > F =	0.0000
				R-squared =	0.3082
Total	73.2523469	297	.246640898	Adj R-squared =	0.2987
				Root MSE =	.41588

sqrtigg	Coef.	Std. Err.	t	P>|t|	[95% Conf. Interval]
Iage__1	.8761824	.1898721	4.61	0.000	.5024963 1.249868
Iage__2	-.1922029	.0684934	-2.81	0.005	-.3270044 -.0574015
Iage__3	.2043794	.074947	2.73	0.007	.0568767 .3518821
Iage__4	-.0560067	.0212969	-2.63	0.009	-.097921 -.0140924
_cons	2.238735	.0482705	46.38	0.000	2.143734 2.333736

```
Deviance:   317.74. Best powers of age among 494 models fit: 0 3 3 3.
Fractional polynomial model comparisons:
```

age	df	Deviance	Res. SD	Gain	P(term)	Powers
Not in model	0	427.539	.49663	—	—	
Linear	1	337.561	.42776	0.000	0.000	1
m = 1	2	327.436	.420554	10.125	0.002	0
m = 2	4	319.448	.415658	18.113	0.020	-2 2
m = 3	6	319.275	.416243	18.286	0.919	-2 1 1
m = 4	8	317.744	.415883	19.818	0.476	0 3 3 3

There is little to be gained by increasing the degree above 2, since the p-values indicate no significant improvement in fit.

Let us compare the curve shape from the $m = 2$ model with that from a conventional quartic polynomial, whose fit turns out to be significantly better than a cubic (not shown). We use the ability of `fracpoly` both to generate the required powers of `age`, namely $(1, 2, 3, 4)$ for the quartic and $(-2, 2)$ for the second degree FP, and to fit the model. We fit both models and graph the resulting curves:

```
. fracpoly regress sqrtigg age 1 2 3 4
-> gen double Iage__1 = age-2.774 if e(sample)
-> gen double Iage__2 = age^2-7.695 if e(sample)
-> gen double Iage__3 = age^3-21.35 if e(sample)
-> gen double Iage__4 = age^4-59.22 if e(sample)
```

Source	SS	df	MS		
Model	22.5835458	4	5.64588646		
Residual	50.668801	293	.172931061		
Total	73.2523469	297	.246640898		

Number of obs = 298
F(4, 293) = 32.65
Prob > F   = 0.0000
R-squared   = 0.3083
Adj R-squared = 0.2989
Root MSE   = .41585

sqrtigg	Coef.	Std. Err.	t	P>|t|	[95% Conf. Interval]	
Iage__1	2.047831	.4595962	4.46	0.000	1.143302	2.952359
Iage__2	-1.058902	.2822803	-3.75	0.000	-1.614456	-.5033479
Iage__3	.2284917	.0667591	3.42	0.001	.0971037	.3598798
Iage__4	-.0168534	.0053321	-3.16	0.002	-.0273475	-.0063594
_cons	2.240012	.0480157	46.65	0.000	2.145512	2.334511

```
Deviance:  317.70.

. predict fit1
(option xb assumed; fitted values)

. fracpoly regress sqrtigg age -2 2
-> gen double Iage__1 = age^-2-.1299 if e(sample)
-> gen double Iage__2 = age^2-7.695 if e(sample)
```

Source	SS	df	MS		
Model	22.2846976	2	11.1423488		
Residual	50.9676492	295	.172771692		
Total	73.2523469	297	.246640898		

Number of obs = 298
F(2, 295) = 64.49
Prob > F   = 0.0000
R-squared   = 0.3042
Adj R-squared = 0.2995
Root MSE   = .41566

sqrtigg	Coef.	Std. Err.	t	P>|t|	[95% Conf. Interval]	
Iage__1	-.1562156	.027416	-5.70	0.000	-.2101713	-.10226
Iage__2	.0148405	.0027767	5.34	0.000	.0093757	.0203052
_cons	2.283145	.0305739	74.68	0.000	2.222974	2.343315

```
Deviance:  319.45.

. predict fit2
(option xb assumed; fitted values)
```

(*Continued on next page*)

```
. scatter sqrtigg fit1 fit2 age, c(. l l) m(o i i) msize(small)
                                 ytitle("Square root of IgG")
                                 xtitle("Age, years")
```

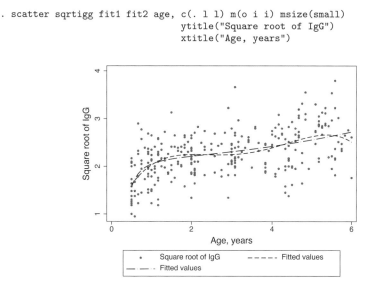

The quartic curve has an unsatisfactory "wavy" appearance that is implausible in the light of the known behavior of IgG, which increases throughout early life. The FP curve increases monotonically, and is therefore biologically the more plausible curve. The two models have approximately the same deviance.

◁

▷ Example

Data from Smith et al. (1992) contain times to complete healing of leg ulcers in a randomized controlled clinical trial of two treatments in 192 elderly patients. A number of covariates were available, of which an important one is mthson, the number of months since the recorded onset of the ulcer. Since the response variable is time to an event of interest and some (in fact, about one half) of the times are censored, it is appropriate to use Cox regression to analyze the data. We consider FPs in mthson, adjusting for 4 other covariates: age; ulcarea, the area of tissue initially affected by the ulcer; deepppg, a binary variable indicating the presence or absence of deep vein involvement; and treat, a binary variable indicating treatment type. We fit FPs of degree 1 and 2:

```
. use http://www.stata-press.com/data/r8/legulcer
(Leg ulcer clinical trial)

. stset ttevent, fail(cens)

  (output omitted )

. fracpoly stcox mthson age ulcarea deepppg treat, compare nohr
-> gen double Iage__1 = age-73.45 if e(sample)
-> gen double Iulca__1 = ulcarea-1326 if e(sample)
-> gen double Itrea__1 = treat-1 if e(sample)
........
-> gen double Imths__1 = X^.5-.493 if e(sample)
-> gen double Imths__2 = X^.5*ln(X)+.6973 if e(sample)
   (where: X = (mthson+1)/100)

         failure _d:  censored
   analysis time _t:  ttevent
```

```
Iteration 0:   log likelihood = -422.65089
Iteration 1:   log likelihood = -390.49313
Iteration 2:   log likelihood = -383.44258
Iteration 3:   log likelihood = -374.28707
Iteration 4:   log likelihood = -369.31417
Iteration 5:   log likelihood = -368.38104
Iteration 6:   log likelihood = -368.35448
Iteration 7:   log likelihood = -368.35446
Refining estimates:
Iteration 0:   log likelihood = -368.35446

Cox regression -- Breslow method for ties

No. of subjects =          192              Number of obs   =         192
No. of failures =           92
Time at risk    =        13825
                                            LR chi2(6)      =      108.59
Log likelihood  =   -368.35446             Prob > chi2     =      0.0000
```

_t _d	Coef.	Std. Err.	z	P>|z|	[95% Conf. Interval]
Imths__1	-2.81425	.6996385	-4.02	0.000	-4.185516 -1.442984
Imths__2	1.541451	.4703143	3.28	0.001	.6196521 2.46325
Iage__1	-.0261111	.0087983	-2.97	0.003	-.0433556 -.0088667
Iulca__1	-.0017491	.000359	-4.87	0.000	-.0024527 -.0010455
deepppg	-.5850499	.2163173	-2.70	0.007	-1.009024 -.1610758
Itrea__1	-.1624663	.2171048	-0.75	0.454	-.5879838 .2630513

Deviance: 736.71. Best powers of mthson among 44 models fit: .5 .5.

Fractional polynomial model comparisons:

mthson	df	Deviance	Gain	P(term)	Powers
Not in model	0	754.345	—	—	
Linear	1	751.680	0.000	0.103	1
m = 1	2	738.969	12.712	0.000	-.5
m = 2	4	736.709	14.971	0.323	.5 .5

The best-fit FP of degree 2 has powers $(0.5, 0.5)$ and deviance 736.71. However, this model does not fit significantly better than the FP of degree 1, which has power -0.5 and deviance 738.97. The latter model has gain 12.71, showing it to be a significantly better fit than a straight line ($p < 0.001$). We prefer the model with $m = 1$, for which the partial linear predictor is shown below.

(Continued on next page)

```
. quietly fracpoly stcox mthson age ulcarea deepppg treat, degree(1) nohr
. fracplot, ytitle(Partial linear predictor) m(i) ciopts(c(i i))
```

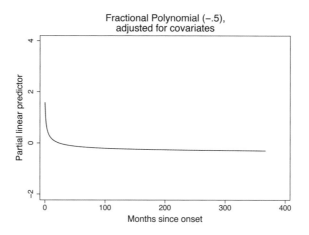

The "hazard" for healing is much higher for patients whose ulcer is of recent onset than for those who have had an ulcer for many months.

Notice that `fracpoly` has automatically adjusted the predictors to their mean values, but since in Cox regression there is no constant term, we cannot see the effects of adjustment in the table of regression estimates. The effects would be present if we were to graph the baseline hazard or survival function, since these functions are defined with all predictors set equal to 0.

◁

(*Continued on next page*)

Saved Results

In addition to what *regression_cmd* saves, `fracpoly` saves

Scalars	
`e(fp_N)`	number of nonmissing observations
`e(fp_dev)`	deviance for FP model of degree m
`e(fp_df)`	FP model degrees of freedom
`e(fp_d0)`	deviance for model without $xvar_1$
`e(fp_s0)`	residual SD for model without $xvar_1$
`e(fp_dlin)`	deviance for model linear in $xvar_1$
`e(fp_slin)`	residual SD for model linear in $xvar_1$
`e(fp_d1)`, `e(fp_d2)`, ...	deviances for FP models of degree 1,2,...,m
`e(fp_s1)`, `e(fp_s2)`, ...	residual SDs for FP models of degree 1,2,...,m
Macros	
`e(fp_cmd)`	`fracpoly`
`e(fp_depv)`	*yvar*
`e(fp_rhs)`	$xvar_1$
`e(fp_base)`	variables in $xvar_2$, ..., *xvarlist* after adjustment and FP transformation
`e(fp_xp)`	`I`*xvar*`__1`, `I`*xvar*`__2` etc.
`e(fp_fvl)`	variables in model finally estimated
`e(fp_wgt)`	weight type or `""`
`e(fp_wexp)`	weight expression if `` `e(fp_wgt)' != "" ``
`e(fp_pwrs)`	powers for FP model of degree m
`e(fp_x1)`, `e(fp_x2)`, ...	$xvar_1$ and variables in model
`e(fp_k1)`, `e(fp_k2)`, ...	powers for FP models of degree 1,2,...,m

Note that residual SDs are only stored when *regression_cmd* is `regress`.

Methods and Formulas

`fracpoly`, `fracplot`, `fracpred`, and `fracgen` are implemented as ado-files.

The general definition of an FP, accommodating possible "repeated powers", may be written in terms of functions $H_1(x), \dots, H_m(x)$ as

$$\beta_0 + \sum_{j=1}^{m} \beta_j H_j(x)$$

where $H_1(x) = x^{(p_1)}$ and for $j = 2, \dots, m$,

$$H_j(x) = \begin{cases} x^{(p_j)} & \text{if } p_j \neq p_{j-1} \\ H_{j-1}(x)\log x & \text{if } p_j = p_{j-1} \end{cases}$$

For example, an FP of degree 3 with powers $(1, 3, 3)$ has $H_1(x) = x$, $H_2(x) = x^3$, and $H_3(x) = x^3 \log x$, and equals $\beta_0 + \beta_1 x + \beta_2 x^3 + \beta_3 x^3 \log x$.

An FP model of degree m is taken to have $2m + 1$ degrees of freedom (df): one for β_0 and one for each β_j and its associated power. Since the powers in an FP are chosen from a finite set rather than from the entire real line, the df defined in this way are approximate.

The deviance D of a model is defined as -2 times its maximized log likelihood. For normal-errors models, we use the formula

$$D = n\left(1 - \bar{l} + \log \frac{2\pi\text{RSS}}{n}\right)$$

where n is the sample size, $\bar{l}$ is the mean of the log normalized weights ($\bar{l} = 0$ if the weights are all equal), and RSS is the residual sum of squares as fitted by `regress`.

The gain, G, for an FP model is defined as the deviance for a straight line (i.e., for the model $\beta_0 + \beta x$) minus the deviance for the FP model. The covariates in $xvar_2, \ldots, xvarlist$, if any, are assumed to have been fit in each model. The larger the gain, the greater the nonlinearity in the relationship between the outcome variable and x.

The fits of pairs of nested FP regression models with degrees k and $k-1$ for $k = 2, \ldots, m$ are compared by the `compare` option of `fracpoly`. The p-values reported by `compare` are calculated differently for normal and nonnormal regressions. Let D_k and D_{k-1} be the deviances of the models with degrees k and $k-1$, respectively. For normal-errors models such as `regress`, a variance ratio F is calculated as

$$F = \frac{n_2}{n_1}\left\{\exp\left(\frac{D_{k-1} - D_k}{n}\right) - 1\right\}$$

where n_1 is the numerator df (here, 2), n_2 is the denominator df (equal to $rdf - 2k$, where rdf is the residual df for the regression model involving only the covariates in $xvar_2$, if any, but not x). The p-value is obtained by referring F to an F distribution on $(2, rdf)$ df.

For nonnormal models (`stcox`, `glm`, `logistic`, `logit` or `poisson`), the p value is obtained by referring $D_{k-1} - D_k$ to a χ^2 distribution on 2 df. These p values for comparing models are approximate and are typically somewhat conservative (Royston and Altman 1994a).

The component-plus-residual values graphed by `fracplot` are calculated as follows: Let the data consist of triplets $(y_i, x_i, \mathbf{z}_i)$, $i = 1, \ldots, n$, where $\mathbf{z}_i$ is the vector of covariates for the ith observation, after applying possible fractional polynomial transformation and adjustment as described earlier. Let $\widehat{\eta}_i = \widehat{\beta}_0 + \{\mathbf{H}(x_i) - \mathbf{H}(x_0)\}'\widehat{\beta} + \mathbf{z}_i'\widehat{\gamma}$ be the linear predictor from the FP model, as given by the `fracpred` command, or equivalently, by the `predict` command with the `xb` option, following the use of `fracpoly`. Here, $\mathbf{H}(x_i) = \{H_1(x_i), \ldots, H_m(x_i)\}'$ is the vector of FP functions described above, $\mathbf{H}(x_0) = \{H_1(x_0), \ldots, H_m(x_0)\}'$ is the vector of adjustments to x_0 (often, x_0 is chosen to be the mean of the x_i), $\widehat{\beta}$ is the estimated parameter vector, and $\widehat{\gamma}$ is the estimated parameter vector for the covariates. The values $\widehat{\eta}_i^* = \widehat{\beta}_0 + \{\mathbf{H}(x_i) - \mathbf{H}(x_0)\}'\widehat{\beta}$ represent the behavior of the FP model for x at fixed values $\mathbf{z} = \mathbf{0}$ of the (adjusted) covariates. The ith component-plus-residual is defined as $\widehat{\eta}_i^* + d_i$, where d_i is the deviance residual for the ith observation. For normal-errors models, $d_i = \sqrt{w_i}(y_i - \widehat{\eta}_i)$, where w_i is the case weight (or 1, if *weight* is not specified). For logistic, Cox, and generalized linear regression models, see [R] **logistic**, [ST] **stcox**, and [R] **glm**, respectively, for the formula for d_i. The formula for `poisson` models is the same as that for `glm` with `family(poisson)`. For `stcox`, d_i is the partial martingale residual (see [ST] **stcox**).

`fracplot` plots the values of d_i and the curve represented by $\widehat{\eta}_i^*$ against x_i. The confidence interval for $\widehat{\eta}_i^*$ is obtained from the variance–covariance matrix of the entire model and takes into account the uncertainty in estimating β_0, β, and γ (but not in estimating the FP powers for x).

`fracpred` with the `for(`*varname*`)` option calculates the predicted index at $x_i = x_0$ and $\mathbf{z}_i = \mathbf{0}$; that is $\widehat{\eta}_i = \widehat{\beta}_0 + \{\mathbf{H}(x_i) - \mathbf{H}(x_0)\}'\widehat{\beta}$. The standard error is calculated from the variance–covariance matrix of $(\widehat{\beta}_0, \widehat{\beta})$, again ignoring estimation of the powers.

Acknowledgment

fracpoly, fracplot, fracpred, and fracgen were written by Patrick Royston of the MRC Clinical Trials Unit, London.

References

Becketti, S. 1995. sg26.2: Calculating and graphing fractional polynomials. *Stata Technical Bulletin* 24: 14–16. Reprinted in *Stata Technical Bulletin Reprints*, vol. 4, pp. 129–132.

Garrett, J. M. 1995. sg33: Calculation of adjusted means and adjusted proportions. *Stata Technical Bulletin* 24: 22–25. Reprinted in *Stata Technical Bulletin Reprints*, vol. 4, pp. 161–165.

——. 1998. sg33.1: Enhancements for calculation of adjusted means and adjusted proportions. *Stata Technical Bulletin* 43: 16–24. Reprinted in *Stata Technical Bulletin Reprints*, vol. 8, pp. 111–123.

Isaacs, D., D. G. Altman, C. E. Tidmarsh, H. B. Valman, and A. D. B. Webster. 1983. Serum immunoglobulin concentrations in preschool children measured by laser nephelometry: reference ranges for IgG, IgA, IgM. *Journal of Clinical Pathology* 36: 1193–1196.

Royston, P. 1995. sg26.3: Fractional polynomial utilities. *Stata Technical Bulletin* 25: 9–13. Reprinted in *Stata Technical Bulletin Reprints*, vol. 5, pp. 82–87.

Royston, P. and D. G. Altman. 1994a. Regression using fractional polynomials of continuous covariates: parsimonious parametric modelling (with discussion). *Applied Statistics* 43: 429–467.

——. 1994b. sg26: Using fractional polynomials to model curved regression relationships. *Stata Technical Bulletin* 21: 11–23. Reprinted in *Stata Technical Bulletin Reprints*, vol. 4, pp. 110–128.

Royston, P. and G. Ambler. 1998. sg81: Multivariable fractional polynomials. *Stata Technical Bulletin* 43: 24–32. Reprinted in *Stata Technical Bulletin Reprints*, vol. 8, pp. 123–132.

——. 1999a. sg81.1: Multivariable fractional polynomials: update. *Stata Technical Bulletin* 49: 17–23. Reprinted in *Stata Technical Bulletin Reprints*, vol. 9, pp. 161–168.

——. 1999b. sg81.2: Multivariable fractional polynomials: update. *Stata Technical Bulletin* 50: 25. Reprinted in *Stata Technical Bulletin Reprints*, vol. 9, p. 168.

——. 1999c. sg112: Nonlinear regression models involving power or exponential functions of covariates. *Stata Technical Bulletin* 49: 25–30. Reprinted in *Stata Technical Bulletin Reprints*, vol. 9, pp. 173–179.

——. 1999d. sg112.1: Nonlinear regression models involving power or exponential functions of covariates: update. *Stata Technical Bulletin* 50: 26. Reprinted in *Stata Technical Bulletin Reprints*, vol. 9, p. 180.

Sauerbrei, W. and P. Royston. 1999. Building multivariable prognostic and diagnostic models: transformation of the predictors by using fractional polynomials. *Journal of the Royal Statistical Society*, Series A 162: 71–94.

Smith, J. M., C. J. Dore, A. Charlett, and J. D. Lewis. 1992. A randomized trial of Biofilm dressing for venous leg ulcers. *Phlebology* 7: 108–113.

Also See

Complementary:	[R] **adjust**, [R] **lincom**, [R] **lrtest**, [R] **mfx**, [R] **nlcom**, [R] **predict**, [R] **predictnl**, [R] **test**, [R] **testnl**, [R] **vce**, [R] **xi**
Related:	[R] **mfp**
Background:	[U] **16.5 Accessing coefficients and standard errors**, [U] **23 Estimation and post-estimation commands**

Title

> **frontier** — Stochastic frontier models

Syntax

> frontier *depvar* [*varlist*] [*weight*] [if *exp*] [in *range*] [, $\underline{d}$istribution(*distname*)
>
> $\underline{u}$het(*varlist$_u$* [, $\underline{noconst}$ant]) $\underline{v}$het(*varlist$_v$* [, $\underline{noconst}$ant])
>
> cm(*varlist$_{cm}$* [, $\underline{noconst}$ant]) cost $\underline{noconst}$ant $\underline{constr}$aints(*numlist*)
>
> $\underline{uf}$rom(*matrix*) $\underline{level}$(#) $\underline{nolog}$ $\underline{nodiff}$icult *maximize_options*]

where *distname* is one of

> $\underline{h}$normal | $\underline{e}$xponential | $\underline{t}$normal

by ... : may be used with frontier; see [R] **by**.

fweights, iweights, and pweights are allowed; see [U] **14.1.6 weight**.

frontier shares the features of all estimation commands; see [U] **23 Estimation and post-estimation commands**.

Syntax for predict

> predict [*type*] *newvarname* [if *exp*] [in *range*] [, *statistic*]

where *statistic* is

xb	$x_i b$, fitted value (the default)
stdp	standard error of the prediction
u	estimates of minus the natural log of the technical efficiency via $E(u_i \mid \epsilon_i)$
m	estimates of minus the natural log of the technical efficiency via $M(u_i \mid \epsilon_i)$
te	estimates of the technical efficiency via $E\{\exp(-su_i) \mid \epsilon_i\}$

$$s = \begin{cases} 1, & \text{for production functions} \\ -1, & \text{for cost functions} \end{cases}$$

(Continued on next page)

Description

frontier fits stochastic production or cost frontier models. More precisely, frontier provides estimators for the parameters of a linear model with a disturbance generated by one of three possible mixture distributions. The disturbance is assumed to be a mixture of two components, one component having a strictly non-negative distribution and the other component having a symmetric distribution. frontier can fit models in which the nonnegative disturbance component is assumed to be from either a half-normal, exponential, or truncated-normal distribution. In addition, when the non-negative component of the disturbance is assumed to be either half-normal or exponential, frontier can fit models in which the error components are heteroskedastic conditional on a set of covariates. When the non-negative component of the disturbance is assumed to be from a truncated-normal distribution, frontier can also fit a conditional mean model, where the mean of the truncated normal distribution is modeled as a linear function of a set of covariates. These estimators have been used almost exclusively to estimate stochastic production and cost frontiers. In the econometrics literature, the non-negative component of the error term is typically referred to as a measure of inefficiency, and we use this terminology in much of the discussion that follows.

See Kumbhakar and Lovell (2000) for a detailed introduction to frontier analysis.

Options

distribution(*distname*) specifies the distribution of the inefficiency term. By default, the technical inefficiency component u_i is specified as having a half-normal distribution. Specifying distribution(exponential) or distribution(tnormal) causes the inefficiency component to be modeled as having an exponential or a truncated-normal distribution, respectively.

uhet(*varlist$_u$* [, noconstant]) specifies that the technical inefficiency component is heteroskedastic, with the variance function depending on a linear combination of *varlist$_u$*. Specifying noconstant suppresses the constant term from the variance function. This option may not be specified with distribution(tnormal).

vhet(*varlist$_v$* [, noconstant]) specifies that the idiosyncratic error component is heteroskedastic, with the variance function depending on a linear combination of *varlist$_v$*. Specifying noconstant suppresses the constant term from the variance function. This option may not be specified with distribution(tnormal).

cm(*varlist$_{cm}$*) may only be used if distribution(tnormal) is also specified. Having specified both options, frontier will fit a conditional mean model in which the mean of the truncated-normal distribution is modeled as a linear function of the set of covariates specified in *varlist$_{cm}$*. Specifying noconstant suppresses the constant in the mean function.

cost specifies that the frontier model will be fitted in terms of a cost function instead of a production function. By default, frontier fits the production frontier model.

noconstant suppresses the constant term in the frontier model.

constraints(*numlist*) specifies, by number, the linear constraints to be applied during estimation. The default is to perform unconstrained estimation. Constraints are specified using the constraint command; see [R] **constraint**. By default, when fitting the truncated-normal model or the conditional mean model, frontier maximizes a transformed log-likelihood; the models tend to be more convergent when the maximization is performed in the transformed parameter space (see *Methods and Formulas*). However, when constraints are applied, frontier will maximize the untransformed log-likelihood, and constraints are to be defined in the untransformed metric. To do otherwise would require that constraints be defined in the transformed metric.

ufrom(*matrix*) specifies a $1 \times K$ matrix of untransformed starting values when fitting a model in which the inefficiency term is specified as having a truncated-normal distribution; i.e., you must also specify distribution(tnormal). frontier can estimate the parameters of the truncated-normal model by maximizing either the log likelihood or a transformed log-likelihood (see *Methods and Formulas*). By default, when fitting the truncated-normal model or the conditional mean model, frontier maximizes the transformed log-likelihood; the models tend to be more convergent when the maximization is performed in the transformed parameter space (see *Methods and Formulas*). When maximizing the transformed log-likelihood, starting values must be specified in the same parameter space as the transformed log-likelihood. The matrix specified in ufrom() contains untransformed starting values, which frontier automatically transforms before passing them on to the transformed log likelihood. The specified matrix must have exactly the same number of columns as there are parameters to estimate.

level(#) specifies the confidence level, in percent, for confidence intervals of the coefficients. The default is level(95) or as set by set level; see [U] **23.6 Specifying the width of confidence intervals**.

nodifficult specifies that the maximization option difficult should not be specified. By default, difficult is specified since these models often have problems converging. If your model is taking many iterations to converge, try specifying nodifficult because changing this specification will sometimes help.

nolog suppresses the iteration log.

maximize_options control the maximization process; see [R] **maximize**. You will seldom need to specify any of the maximize options, except for iterate(0), and possibly from(). If the iteration log shows many "not concave" messages and it is taking many iterations to converge, try specifying better starting values by using the from() option. If you have specified distribution(tnormal) and you specify from() as well, then frontier will maximize the untransformed log likelihood rather than the default transformed log likelihood (see *Methods and Formulas*). If you want to specify starting values and want the more convergent transformed log likelihood to be maximized, then use the ufrom() option rather than from().

Options for predict

xb, the default, calculates the linear prediction.

stdp calculates the standard error of the linear prediction.

u produces estimates of minus the natural log of the technical efficiency via $E\left(u_i \mid \epsilon_i\right)$.

m produces estimates of minus the natural log of the technical efficiency via $M\left(u_i \mid \epsilon_i\right)$.

te produces estimates of the technical efficiency via $E\left\{\exp(-su_i) \mid \epsilon_i\right\}$.

Remarks

Stochastic production frontier models were introduced by Aigner, Lovell, and Schmidt (1977) and Meeusen van den Broeck (1977). Since then, stochastic frontier models have become a popular sub-field in econometrics. Kumbhakar and Lovell (2000) provide a good introduction to this area.

frontier fits three stochastic frontier models with distinct parameterizations of the inefficiency term. frontier can fit stochastic production or cost frontier models.

Let's review the nature of the stochastic frontier problem. Suppose that a producer has a production function $f(\mathbf{z}_i, \beta)$. In a world without error or inefficiency, the ith firm would produce

$$q_i = f(\mathbf{z}_i, \beta)$$

A fundamental element of stochastic frontier analysis is that each firm potentially produces less than it might due to a degree of inefficiency. Specifically,

$$q_i = f(\mathbf{z}_i, \beta)\xi_i$$

where ξ_i is the level of efficiency for firm i; ξ_i must be in the interval $(0, 1]$. If $\xi_i = 1$, then the firm is achieving the optimal output with the technology embodied in the production function $f(\mathbf{z}_i, \beta)$. When $\xi_i < 1$, the firm is not making the most of the inputs $\mathbf{z}_i$ given the technology embodied in the production function $f(\mathbf{z}_i, \beta)$. Since the output is assumed to be strictly positive (i.e., $q_i > 0$), the degree of technical efficiency is assumed to be strictly positive (i.e., $\xi_i > 0$).

Output is also assumed to be subject to random shocks, implying that

$$q_i = f(\mathbf{z}_i, \beta)\xi_i \exp(v_i)$$

Taking the natural log of both sides yields

$$\ln(q_i) = \ln\{f(\mathbf{z}_i, \beta)\} + \ln(\xi_i) + v_i$$

Assuming that there are k inputs and that the production function is linear in logs, defining $u_i = -\ln(\xi_i)$ yields

$$\ln(q_i) = \beta_0 + \sum_{j=1}^{k} \beta_j \ln(z_{ji}) + v_i - u_i \tag{1}$$

Since u_i is subtracted from $\ln(q_i)$, restricting $u_i \geq 0$ implies that $0 < \xi_i \leq 1$ as specified above.

Kumbhakar and Lovell (2000) provide a detailed version of the above derivation, and they show that performing an analogous derivation in the dual-cost function problem allows one to specify the problem as

$$\ln(c_i) = \beta_0 + \beta_q \ln(q_i) + \sum_{j=1}^{k} \beta_j \ln(p_{ji}) + v_i + u_i \tag{2}$$

where q_i is output, z_{ji} are input quantities, c_i is cost, and the p_{ji} are input prices.

Intuitively, the inefficiency effect is required to lower output or raise expenditure, depending on the specification.

❏ Technical Note

The model that `frontier` actually fits is of the form

$$y_i = \beta_0 + \sum_{j=1}^{k} \beta_j x_{ji} + v_i - su_i$$

where

$$s = \begin{cases} 1, & \text{for production functions} \\ -1, & \text{for cost functions} \end{cases}$$

so, in the context of the discussion above, $y_i = \ln(q_i)$ and $x_{ji} = \ln(z_{ji})$ for a production function, and for a cost function, $y_i = \ln(c_i)$ and the x_{ji} are the $\ln(p_{ji})$ and $\ln(q_i)$. It is incumbent upon the user to perform the natural logarithm transformation of the data prior to estimation if the estimation results are to be correctly interpreted in the context of a stochastic frontier production or cost model. frontier does not perform any transformations on the data.

❏

Different specifications of the u_i and the v_i terms give rise to distinct models. frontier provides estimators for the parameters of three basic models. In all three models, the idiosyncratic component v_i is assumed to be independently $N(0, \sigma_v)$ distributed over the observations. The basic models differ in their specification of the inefficiency term, u_i. The three basic models assume that

(1) exponential: the u_i are independently exponentially distributed with variance σ_u^2;

(2) hnormal: the u_i are independently half-normally $N^+(0, \sigma_u^2)$ distributed;

(3) tnormal: the $u_i \overset{\text{iid}}{\sim} N^+(\mu, \sigma_u^2)$ distributed with truncation point at 0.

Since frontier has estimators for the parameters of models (1) and (2) when the error components are conditionally heteroskedastic, these models only assume independence. In contrast, frontier does not model conditional heteroskedasticity in the truncated-normal model. frontier can, however, fit a conditional mean model in which the mean of the truncated-normal distribution is modeled as a linear function of a set of covariates. Such a model affords one the opportunity to avoid an assumption that the data are identically distributed. However, in contrast to the conditional heteroskedastic models, the differences in the way the data are distributed is attributed to the first moment of the distribution rather than the second moment.

▷ Example

For our first example we demonstrate the half-normal and exponential models by reproducing a study found in Greene (2003), which uses data that was originally published in Zellner and Revankar (1970). In this study of the transportation equipment manufacturing industry, observations on value added, capital, and labor are used to estimate a Cobb–Douglas production function. The variable lnv is the log-transformed value added, lnk is the log-transformed capital, and lnl is the log-transformed labor. OLS estimates are compared to those from stochastic frontier models using both the half-normal and exponential distribution for the inefficiency term.

(*Continued on next page*)

```
. use http://www.stata-press.com/data/r8/greene9, clear
. regress lnv lnk lnl
```

Source	SS	df	MS		Number of obs =	25
					F(2, 22) =	397.54
Model	44.1727741	2	22.086387		Prob > F =	0.0000
Residual	1.22225984	22	.055557265		R-squared =	0.9731
					Adj R-squared =	0.9706
Total	45.3950339	24	1.89145975		Root MSE =	.23571

lnv	Coef.	Std. Err.	t	P>|t|	[95% Conf. Interval]	
lnk	.2454281	.1068574	2.30	0.032	.0238193	.4670368
lnl	.805183	.1263336	6.37	0.000	.5431831	1.067183
_cons	1.844416	.2335928	7.90	0.000	1.359974	2.328858

```
. frontier lnv lnk lnl
Iteration 0:   log likelihood =  2.3357572
Iteration 1:   log likelihood =  2.4673009
Iteration 2:   log likelihood =  2.4695125
Iteration 3:   log likelihood =  2.4695222
Iteration 4:   log likelihood =  2.4695222
```

```
Stoc. frontier normal/half-normal model        Number of obs   =         25
                                                Wald chi2(2)    =     743.71
Log likelihood =  2.4695222                     Prob > chi2     =     0.0000
```

lnv	Coef.	Std. Err.	z	P>|z|	[95% Conf. Interval]	
lnk	.2585478	.098764	2.62	0.009	.0649738	.4521218
lnl	.7802451	.1199399	6.51	0.000	.5451672	1.015323
_cons	2.081135	.281641	7.39	0.000	1.529128	2.633141
/lnsig2v	-3.48401	.6195353	-5.62	0.000	-4.698277	-2.269743
/lnsig2u	-3.014599	1.11694	-2.70	0.007	-5.203761	-.8254368
sigma_v	.1751688	.0542616			.0954514	.3214633
sigma_u	.2215073	.1237052			.074134	.6618486
sigma2	.0797496	.0426989			-.0039388	.163438
lambda	1.264536	.1678684			.9355204	1.593552

```
Likelihood-ratio test of sigma_u=0: chibar2(01) = 0.43   Prob>=chibar2 = 0.256
. predict double u_h, u
```

(Continued on next page)

```
. frontier lnv lnk lnl, distribution(exponential)

Iteration 0:   log likelihood =  2.7270659
Iteration 1:   log likelihood =  2.8551532
Iteration 2:   log likelihood =  2.8604815
Iteration 3:   log likelihood =  2.8604897
Iteration 4:   log likelihood =  2.8604897

Stoc. frontier normal/exponential model        Number of obs   =         25
                                                Wald chi2(2)    =     845.68
Log likelihood =  2.8604897                     Prob > chi2     =     0.0000
```

lnv	Coef.	Std. Err.	z	P>|z|	[95% Conf. Interval]	
lnk	.2624859	.0919988	2.85	0.004	.0821717	.4428002
lnl	.7703795	.1109569	6.94	0.000	.5529079	.9878511
_cons	2.069242	.2356159	8.78	0.000	1.607444	2.531041
/lnsig2v	-3.527598	.4486176	-7.86	0.000	-4.406873	-2.648324
/lnsig2u	-4.002457	.9274575	-4.32	0.000	-5.820241	-2.184674
sigma_v	.1713925	.0384448			.1104231	.2660258
sigma_u	.1351691	.0626818			.0544692	.3354317
sigma2	.0476461	.0157921			.016694	.0785981
lambda	.7886525	.087684			.616795	.9605101

```
Likelihood-ratio test of sigma_u=0: chibar2(01) = 1.21   Prob>=chibar2 = 0.135

. predict double u_e, u

. list state u_h u_e
```

	state	u_h	u_e
1.	Alabama	.2011338	.14592865
2.	California	.14480966	.0972165
3.	Connecticut	.1903485	.13478797
4.	Florida	.51753139	.5903303
5.	Georgia	.10397912	.07140994
6.	Illinois	.12126696	.0830415
7.	Indiana	.21128212	.15450664
8.	Iowa	.24933153	.20073081
9.	Kansas	.10099517	.06857629
10.	Kentucky	.05626919	.04152443
11.	Louisiana	.20332731	.15066405
12.	Maine	.22263164	.17245793
13.	Maryland	.13534062	.09245501
14.	Massachusetts	.15636999	.10932923
15.	Michigan	.15809566	.10756915
16.	Missouri	.10288047	.0704146
17.	NewJersey	.09584337	.06587986
18.	NewYork	.27787793	.22249416
19.	Ohio	.22914231	.16981857
20.	Pennsylvania	.1500667	.10302905
21.	Texas	.20297875	.14552218
22.	Virginia	.14000132	.09676078
23.	Washington	.11047581	.07533251
24.	WestVirginia	.15561392	.11236153
25.	Wisconsin	.14067066	.0970861

The parameter estimates and the estimates of the inefficiency terms closely match those published in Greene (2003), but the standard errors of the parameter estimates are estimated differently (see the *Technical Note* below).

The output from `frontier` includes estimates of the standard deviations of the two error components, σ_v and σ_u, which are labeled `sigma_v` and `sigma_u`, respectively. In the log likelihood, they are parameterized as $\ln\sigma_v^2$ and $\ln\sigma_u^2$, and these estimates are labeled `lnsig2v` and `lnsig2u` in the output. `frontier` also reports two other useful parameterizations. The estimate of the total error variance, $\sigma_S^2 = \sigma_v^2 + \sigma_u^2$, is labeled `sigma2`, and the estimate of the ratio of the standard deviation of the inefficiency component to the standard deviation of the idiosyncratic component, $\lambda = \sigma_u/\sigma_v$, is labeled `lambda`.

At the bottom of the output, `frontier` reports the results of a test that there is no technical inefficiency component in the model. This is a test of the null hypothesis $H_0 : \sigma_u^2 = 0$ against the alternative hypotheses $H_1 : \sigma_u^2 > 0$. If the null hypothesis is true, then the stochastic frontier model reduces to an OLS model with normal errors. However, since the test lies on the boundary of the parameter space of σ_u^2, the standard likelihood-ratio test is not valid, and a one-sided generalized likelihood-ratio test must be constructed; see Gutierrez et al. (2001). For this example, the output shows LR = .43 with a p-value 0.256 for the half-normal model and a LR = 1.21 with a p-value 0.135 for the exponential model. There are a number of possible reasons for the failure to reject the null hypothesis, but the fact that the test is based upon an asymptotic distribution and the sample size was 25 is certainly a leading candidate among those possibilities.

◁

❑ Technical Note

`frontier` maximizes the log-likelihood function of a stochastic frontier model using the Newton–Raphson method, and the estimated variance–covariance matrix is calculated as the inverse of the negative Hessian (matrix of second partial derivatives); see [R] **ml**. When comparing the results to those published using other software, users should be aware of the difference in the optimization methods, which may result in different, yet asymptotically equivalent, variance estimates.

❑

▷ Example

In many cases, the error terms may not have constant variance. `frontier` allows the user to model heteroskedasticity in either error term as a linear function of a set of covariates. The variance of either the technical inefficiency or the idiosyncratic component may be modeled as

$$\sigma_i^2 = \exp(\mathbf{w}_i\boldsymbol{\delta})$$

The default constant included in $\mathbf{w}_i$ may be suppressed by appending a `noconstant` option to the list of covariates. Also, it is possible to simultaneously specify covariates for both σ_{u_i} and σ_{v_i}.

In the example below, we use a sample of 756 observations of fictional firms producing a manufactured good using capital and labor. The firms are hypothesized to employ a constant returns-to-scale technology, but the size of the firms differ. Believing that this variation in the size of the firms will induce heteroskedasticity into the idiosyncratic error term, we estimate the parameters of a Cobb–Douglas production function, employing a conditional heteroskedastic half-normal model, using the size of the firm as an explanatory variable in the variance function for the idiosyncratic error. We will also perform a test of the hypothesis that the firms employ a constant returns-to-scale technology.

```
. use http://www.stata-press.com/data/r8/frontier1, clear

. frontier lnoutput lnlabor lncapital, vhet(size)
Iteration 0:   log likelihood = -1508.3692
Iteration 1:   log likelihood =  -1501.583
Iteration 2:   log likelihood = -1500.3942
Iteration 3:   log likelihood = -1500.3794
Iteration 4:   log likelihood = -1500.3794
```

Stoc. frontier normal/half-normal model				Number of obs	=	756
				Wald chi2(2)	=	9.68
Log likelihood = -1500.3794				Prob > chi2	=	0.0079

lnoutput	Coef.	Std. Err.	z	P>|z|	[95% Conf. Interval]	
lnoutput						
lnlabor	.7090933	.2349374	3.02	0.003	.2486244	1.169562
lncapital	.3931345	.5422173	0.73	0.468	-.6695919	1.455861
_cons	1.252199	3.14656	0.40	0.691	-4.914946	7.419344
lnsig2v						
size	-.0016951	.0004748	-3.57	0.000	-.0026256	-.0007645
_cons	3.156091	.9265826	3.41	0.001	1.340023	4.97216
lnsig2u						
_cons	1.947487	.1017653	19.14	0.000	1.748031	2.146943
sigma_u	2.647838	.134729			2.396514	2.925518

```
. test _b[lnlabor] + _b[lncapital] = 1
 ( 1)  [lnoutput]lnlabor + [lnoutput]lncapital = 1
           chi2( 1) =    0.03
         Prob > chi2 =    0.8622
```

From the output above, it does appear that the variance of the idiosyncratic error term is a function of the size of the firm. Also, we failed to reject the hypothesis that the firms employ a constant returns to scale technology.

◁

❑ Technical Note

In small samples, the conditional heteroskedastic estimators will lack precision for the variance parameters, and may fail to converge altogether.

❏

▷ Example

Let's turn our attention to the truncated-normal model. Once again, we will use fictional data. For this example, we have 1,231 observations on the quantity of output, the total cost of production for each firm, the prices that each firm paid for labor and capital services, and a categorical variable measuring the quality of each firm's management. After taking the natural logarithm of the costs (lncost), prices (lnp_k and lnp_l), and output (lnout), we fit a stochastic cost frontier model and specify the distribution of the inefficiency term to be a truncated-normal.

```
. use http://www.stata-press.com/data/r8/frontier2, clear

. frontier lncost lnp_k lnp_l lnout, distribution(tnormal) cost
Iteration 0:   log likelihood = -2386.9523
Iteration 1:   log likelihood = -2386.5146
Iteration 2:   log likelihood = -2386.2704
Iteration 3:   log likelihood = -2386.2504
Iteration 4:   log likelihood = -2386.2493
Iteration 5:   log likelihood = -2386.2493
```

Stoc. frontier normal/truncated-normal model		Number of obs	=	1231
		Wald chi2(3)	=	8.82
Log likelihood = -2386.2493		Prob > chi2	=	0.0318

lncost	Coef.	Std. Err.	z	P>|z|	[95% Conf. Interval]	
lnp_k	.3410717	.2363861	1.44	0.149	-.1222366	.80438
lnp_l	.6608628	.4951499	1.33	0.182	-.3096131	1.631339
lnout	.7528653	.3468968	2.17	0.030	.0729601	1.432771
_cons	2.602609	1.083004	2.40	0.016	.4799595	4.725259
/mu	1.095705	.881517	1.24	0.214	-.632037	2.823446
/lnsigma2	1.5534	.1873464	8.29	0.000	1.186208	1.920592
/ilgtgamma	1.257862	.2589522	4.86	0.000	.7503255	1.765399
sigma2	4.727518	.8856833			3.274641	6.825001
gamma	.7786579	.0446303			.6792496	.8538846
sigma_u2	3.681119	.7503408			2.210478	5.15176
sigma_v2	1.046399	.2660035			.5250413	1.567756

```
HO: No inefficiency component:           z =   5.595           Prob>=z = 0.000
```

In addition to the coefficients, the output reports estimates for the parameters sigma_v2, sigma_u2, gamma, sigma2, ilgtgamma, lnsigma2, and mu. sigma_v2 is the estimate of σ_v^2. sigma_u2 is the estimate of σ_u^2. gamma is the estimate of $\gamma = \sigma_u^2/\sigma_S^2$. sigma2 is the estimate of $\sigma_S^2 = \sigma_v^2 + \sigma_u^2$. Since γ must be between 0 and 1, the optimization is parameterized in terms of the inverse logit of γ, and this estimate is reported as ilgtgamma. Since σ_S^2 must be positive, the optimization is parameterized in terms of $\ln(\sigma_S^2)$, whose estimate is reported as lnsigma2. Finally, mu is the estimate of μ, the mean of the truncated-normal distribution.

In the above output, the generalized log-likelihood test for the presence of the inefficiency term has been replaced with a test based on the third moment of the OLS residuals. Intuitively, when $\mu = 0$ and $\sigma_u = 0$, the truncated-normal model reduces to a linear regression model with normally distributed errors. However, the distribution of the test statistic under the null hypothesis is not well established, as it becomes impossible to reliably evaluate the log likelihood as σ_u approaches zero. This prohibits the use of the likelihood-ratio test in this case.

However, Coelli (1995) noted that the presence of an inefficiency term would cause the residuals from an OLS regression to be negatively skewed. By identifying negative skewness in the residuals with the presence of an inefficiency term, Coelli (1995) derived a one-sided test for the presence of the inefficiency term. The results of this test are given at the bottom of the output. For this example, the null hypothesis of no inefficiency component is rejected.

Having fit a truncated model on the data in the example below and detected a statistically significant inefficiency term in the model, we might question whether the inefficiency term is identically distributed over all firms or whether there might be heterogeneity across firms. frontier provides an extension to the truncated normal model by allowing the mean of the inefficiency term to be modeled as a linear function of a set of covariates. In our dataset, we have an additional categorical variable that provides a measurement of the quality of a firm's management. We refit the model, including the cm() option, specifying a set of binary indicator variables representing the different categories of the quality measurement variable as covariates.

```
. use http://www.stata-press.com/data/r8/frontier2, clear

. xi: frontier lncost lnp_k lnp_l lnout, distribution(tnormal) cm(i.quality) cost
i.quality        _Iquality_1-5     (naturally coded; _Iquality_1 omitted)
Iteration 0:   log likelihood = -2386.9523
Iteration 1:   log likelihood =  -2384.936
Iteration 2:   log likelihood = -2382.3942
Iteration 3:   log likelihood =  -2382.324
Iteration 4:   log likelihood = -2382.3233
Iteration 5:   log likelihood = -2382.3233
```

Stoc. frontier normal/truncated-normal model

			Number of obs	=	1231
			Wald chi2(3)	=	9.31
Log likelihood = -2382.3233			Prob > chi2	=	0.0254

lncost	Coef.	Std. Err.	z	P>|z|	[95% Conf. Interval]	
lncost						
lnp_k	.3611204	.2359749	1.53	0.126	-.1013819	.8236227
lnp_l	.680446	.4934935	1.38	0.168	-.2867835	1.647675
lnout	.7605533	.3466102	2.19	0.028	.0812098	1.439897
_cons	2.550769	1.078911	2.36	0.018	.4361417	4.665396
mu						
_Iquality_2	.5056067	.3382907	1.49	0.135	-.1574309	1.168644
_Iquality_3	.783223	.376807	2.08	0.038	.0446947	1.521751
_Iquality_4	.5577511	.3355061	1.66	0.096	-.0998288	1.215331
_Iquality_5	.6792882	.3428073	1.98	0.048	.0073981	1.351178
_cons	.6014025	.990167	0.61	0.544	-1.339289	2.542094
/lnsigma2	1.541784	.1790926	8.61	0.000	1.190769	1.892799
/ilgtgamma	1.242302	.2588968	4.80	0.000	.734874	1.749731
sigma2	4.67292	.8368852			3.289611	6.637923
gamma	.7759645	.0450075			.6758739	.8519189
sigma_u2	3.62602	.7139576			2.226689	5.025351
sigma_v2	1.0469	.2583469			.5405491	1.553251

In the econometrics literature, the conditional mean model was developed in the context of panel-data estimators. You can, in fact, apply frontier's conditional mean model to panel data.

◁

(Continued on next page)

Saved Results

frontier saves in e():

Scalars

e(N)	number of observations	e(ll)	log likelihood
e(df_m)	model degrees of freedom	e(sigma_u)	standard deviation of
e(k)	number of estimated parameters		technical inefficiency
e(k_eq)	number of equations	e(sigma_v)	standard deviation of v_i
e(k_dv)	number of dependent variables	e(rank)	rank of VCE
e(chi2)	χ^2	e(p)	model significance
e(ll_c)	log likelihood for H_0: $\sigma_u=0$	e(chi2_c)	LR test statistic
e(ic)	number of iterations	e(rc)	return code
e(z)	test for negative skewness of OLS residuals	e(p_z)	p-value for z

Macros

e(cmd)	frontier	e(model)	production or cost
e(depvar)	name of dependent variable	e(title)	name of model
e(chi2type)	Wald; type of model χ^2 test	e(het)	heteroskedastic component(s)
e(opt)	ml	e(user)	program used to implement ml
e(wtype)	weight type	e(wexp)	weight expression
e(predict)	program used to implement predict	e(dist)	distribution assumption for u_i

Matrices

e(b)	coefficient vector	e(V)	variance–covariance matrix
e(ilog)	iteration log (up to 20 iterations)		of the estimators

Functions

e(sample)	marks estimation sample

Methods and Formulas

Consider an equation of the form

$$y_i = \mathbf{x}_i\boldsymbol{\beta} + v_i - su_i$$

where

y_i is the dependent variable,

$\mathbf{x}_i$ is an $1 \times k$ vector of observations on the independent variables included as covariates,

$\boldsymbol{\beta}$ is a $k \times 1$ vector of coefficients, and

$$s = \begin{cases} 1, & \text{for production functions} \\ -1, & \text{for cost functions} \end{cases}$$

The log-likelihood functions are

Normal-half normal model:

$$\ln L = \sum_{i=1}^{N} \left\{ \frac{1}{2} \ln \left(\frac{2}{\pi} \right) - \ln \sigma_S + \ln \Phi \left(-\frac{s \epsilon_i \lambda}{\sigma_S} \right) - \frac{\epsilon_i^2}{2 \sigma_S^2} \right\}$$

Normal-exponential model:

$$\ln L = \sum_{i=1}^{N} \left\{ -\ln \sigma_u + \frac{\sigma_v^2}{2 \sigma_u^2} + \ln \Phi \left(\frac{-s \epsilon_i - \frac{\sigma_v^2}{\sigma_u}}{\sigma_v} \right) + \frac{s \epsilon_i}{\sigma_u} \right\}$$

Normal-truncated normal model:

$$\ln L = \sum_{i=1}^{N} \left\{ -\frac{1}{2} \ln (2\pi) - \ln \sigma_S - \ln \Phi \left(\frac{\mu}{\sigma_S \sqrt{\gamma}} \right) \right.$$
$$\left. + \ln \Phi \left[\frac{(1-\gamma)\mu - s\gamma\epsilon_i}{\{\sigma_S^2 \gamma (1-\gamma)\}^{1/2}} \right] - \frac{1}{2} \left(\frac{\epsilon_i + s\mu}{\sigma_S} \right)^2 \right\}$$

where $\sigma_S = (\sigma_u^2 + \sigma_v^2)^{1/2}$, $\lambda = \sigma_u / \sigma_v$, $\gamma = \sigma_u^2 / \sigma_S^2$, $\epsilon_i = y_i - \mathbf{x}_i \boldsymbol{\beta}$, and $\Phi()$ is the cumulative distribution function of the standard normal distribution.

To obtain estimation for u_i, either the mean or the mode of the conditional distribution $f(u|\epsilon)$ can be used.

$$E(u_i \mid \epsilon_i) = \mu_{*i} + \sigma_* \left\{ \frac{\phi(-\mu_{*i}/\sigma_*)}{\Phi(\mu_{*i}/\sigma_*)} \right\}$$

$$M(u_i \mid \epsilon_i) = \begin{cases} \mu_{*i}, & \text{if } \mu_{*i} >= 0 \\ 0, & \text{otherwise} \end{cases}$$

Then, estimates of the technical efficiency ($s = 1$) or cost efficiency ($s = -1$) will be estimated by

$$E_i = E \{ \exp(-s u_i) \mid \epsilon_i \}$$
$$= \left\{ \frac{1 - \Phi(s\sigma_* - \mu_{*i}/\sigma_*)}{1 - \Phi(-\mu_{*i}/\sigma_*)} \right\} \exp \left(-s\mu_{*i} + \frac{1}{2} \sigma_*^2 \right)$$

where μ_{*i} and σ_* are defined for the normal/half-normal model as

$$\mu_{*i} = -s \epsilon_i \sigma_u^2 / \sigma_S^2$$
$$\sigma_* = \sigma_u \sigma_v / \sigma_S$$

for the normal/exponential model as

$$\mu_{*i} = -s \epsilon_i - \sigma_v^2 / \sigma_u$$
$$\sigma_* = \sigma_v$$

and for the normal/truncated-normal model as

$$\mu_{*i} = \frac{-s\epsilon_i \sigma_u^2 + \mu \sigma_v^2}{\sigma_S^2}$$

$$\sigma_* = \sigma_u \sigma_v / \sigma_S$$

In the half-normal and exponential models, when heteroskedasticity is assumed, the standard deviations, σ_u or σ_v, will be replaced in the above equations by

$$\sigma_i^2 = \exp(\mathbf{w}_i \boldsymbol{\delta})$$

where $\mathbf{w}$ is the vector of explanatory variables in the variance function.

In the conditional-mean model, the mean parameter of the truncated normal distribution, μ, is modeled as a linear combination of the set of covariates $\mathbf{w}$.

$$\mu = \mathbf{w}_i \boldsymbol{\delta}$$

Therefore, the log-likelihood function can be rewritten as

$$\ln L = \sum_{i=1}^{N} \left\{ -\frac{1}{2} \ln (2\pi) - \ln \sigma_S - \ln \Phi \left(\frac{\mathbf{w}_i \boldsymbol{\delta}}{\sqrt{\sigma_S^2 \gamma}} \right) \right.$$
$$\left. + \ln \Phi \left(\frac{(1 - \gamma) \mathbf{w}_i \boldsymbol{\delta} - s\gamma \epsilon_i}{\sqrt{\sigma_S^2 \gamma (1 - \gamma)}} \right) - \frac{1}{2} \left(\frac{\epsilon_i + s\mathbf{w}_i \boldsymbol{\delta}}{\sigma_S} \right)^2 \right\}$$

The z-test reported in the output of the truncated-normal model is a third moment test developed by Coelli (1995) as an extension of a test previously developed by Pagan and Hall (1983). Coelli shows that under the null of normally distributed errors, the statistic

$$z = \frac{m_3}{\left(\frac{6m_2^3}{N} \right)^{1/2}}$$

has a standard normal distribution, where m_3 is the third moment from the OLS regression. Since the residuals are either negatively skewed (production function) or positively skewed (cost function), a one-sided p-value is used.

References

Aigner, D. J., C. A. K. Lovell, and P. Schmidt. 1977. Formulation and estimation of stochastic frontier production function models. *Journal of Econometrics* 6: 21–37.

Caudill, S. B., J. M. Ford, and D. M. Gropper. 1995. Frontier estimation and firm-specific inefficiency measures in the presence of heteroskedasticity. *Journal of Business and Economic Statistics* 13(1): 105–111.

Coelli, T. J. 1995. Estimators and hypothesis tests for a stochastic frontier function: A Monte Carlo analysis. *Journal of Productivity Analysis* 6(4): 247–268.

Gould, W. W. and W. M. Sribney. 1999. *Maximum Likelihood Estimation with Stata*. College Station, TX: Stata Press.

Greene, W. H. 2003. *Econometric Analysis*. 5th ed. Upper Saddle River, NJ: Prentice–Hall.

Gutierrez, R. G., S. L. Carter, and D. M. Drukker. 2001. sg160:On boundary-value likelihood-ratio tests. *Stata Technical Bulletin* 60: 15–18. Reprinted in *Stata Technical Bulletin Reprints*, vol. 10, pp. 269–273.

Kumbhakar, S. C. and C. A. K. Lovell. 2000. *Stochastic frontier analysis.* Cambridge: Cambridge University Press.

Pagan, A. R. and A. D. Hall. 1983. Diagnostic tests as residual analysis. *Econometric Reviews* 2: 159–218.

Stevenson, R. E. 1980. Likelihood functions for generalized stochastic frontier estimation. *Journal of Econometrics* 13(1): 57–66.

Zellner, A. and N. Revankar. 1970. Generalized production functions. *Review of Economic Studies* 37: 241–250.

Also See

Complementary:	[R] **adjust**, [R] **constraint**, [R] **lincom**, [R] **lrtest**, [R] **mfx**, [R] **nlcom**, [R] **predict**, [R] **predictnl**, [R] **test**, [R] **testnl**, [R] **vce**
Related:	[R] **regress**, [XT] **xtfrontier**
Background:	[U] **16.5 Accessing coefficients and standard errors**, [U] **23 Estimation and post-estimation commands**, [U] **23.14 Obtaining robust variance estimates**, [R] **maximize**

Title

functions — Functions

Description

This entry provides a complete reference for functions allowed by Stata.

A quick note on missing values: Stata denotes a numeric missing value by '.', '.a', '.b', ..., or '.z'. A string missing value is denoted by '""' (the empty string). Here, any one of these may be referred to by *missing*. If a numeric value x is missing, then $x \geq .$ will be true. If a numeric value x is not missing, then $x < .$ will be true.

Mathematical functions

abs(x)
Domain: −8e+307 to 8e+307
Range: 0 to 8e+307
Description: returns the absolute value of x

acos(x)
Domain: −1 to 1
Range: 0 to π
Description: returns the radian value of the arc-cosine of x

asin(x)
Domain: −1 to 1
Range: $-\pi/2$ to $\pi/2$
Description: returns the radian value of the arc-sine of x

atan(x)
Domain: −8e+307 to 8e+307
Range: $-\pi/2$ to $\pi/2$
Description: returns the radian value of the arc-tangent of x

atanh(x)
Domain: −1 to 1
Range: −8e+307 to 8e+307
Description: returns the arc-hyperbolic tangent of x, $\mathtt{atanh}(x) = \frac{1}{2}\{\ln(1+x) - \ln(1-x)\}$

ceil(x)
Domain :   −8e+307 to 8e+307
Range: integers in −8e+307 to 8e+307
Description: returns the unique integer n such that $n - 1 < x \leq n$; note, returns x (not '.') if x is missing, meaning $\mathtt{ceil}(.a) = .a$. Also see floor(x), int(x), and round(x).

cloglog(x)
Domain: 0 to 1
Range: −8e+307 to 8e+307
Description: returns the complementary log-log of x, $\mathtt{cloglog}(x) = \ln\{-\ln(1-x)\}$

comb(n,k)
   Domain n: integers 1 to 1e+305
   Domain k: integers 0 to n
   Range: 0 to 8e+307 and *missing*
   Description: returns the combinatorial function $n!/\{k!(n-k)!\}$

cos(x)
   Domain: $-$1e+18 to 1e+18
   Range: -1 to 1
   Description: returns the cosine of x, where x is in radians

digamma(x)
   Domain: $-$1e+15 to 8e+307
   Range: $-$8e+307 to 8e+307 and *missing*
   Description: returns the digamma function, $d\ln\Gamma(x)/dx$. This is the derivative of lngamma(x).

   The digamma function is also sometimes called the psi function, $\psi(x)$.

exp(x)
   Domain: $-$8e+307 to 709
   Range: 0 to 8e+307
   Description: returns the exponential function e^x. This function is the inverse of ln(x).

floor(x)
   Domain: $-$8e+307 to 8e+307
   Range: integers in $-$8e+307 to 8e+307
   Description: returns the unique integer n such that $n-1 \le x < n$;
                  note, returns x (not '.') if x is missing, meaning floor(.a) $=$ .a.
                  Also see ceil(x), int(x), and round(x).

int(x)
   Domain: $-$8e+307 to 8e+307
   Range: integers $-$8e+307 to 8e+307
   Description: the integer obtained by truncating x toward 0;
                  note, returns x (not '.') if x is missing, meaning int(.a) $=$ .a.
                  int(5.2) $= 5$
                  int(5.8) $= 5$
                  int(-5.8) $= -5$

   One way to obtain the closest integer to x is int$(x+$sign$(x)/2)$, which simplifies to int$(x+0.5)$ for $x \ge 0$. However, use of the round() function is preferred. Also see round(x), ceil(x),and floor(x).

invcloglog(x)
   Domain: $-$8e+307 to 8e+307
   Range: 0 to 1 and *missing*
   Description: returns the inverse of the complementary log-log function of x,
                  $\text{cloglog}^{-1}(x) = 1 - \exp\{-\exp(x)\}$

invlogit(x)
   Domain: $-$8e+307 to 8e+307
   Range: 0 to 1 and *missing*
   Description: returns the inverse of the logit function of x, $\text{logit}^{-1}(x) = e^x/(1+e^x)$

ln(x)

Domain: 1e–323 to 8e+307
Range: −744 to 709
Description: returns the natural logarithm ln(x). This function is the inverse of exp(x).

The logarithm of x in base b can be calculated via $\log_b(x) = \log_a(x)/\log_a(b)$. Hence,
$$\log_5(x) = \ln(x)/\ln(5) = \log(x)/\log(5) = \log10(x)/\log10(5)$$
$$\log_2(x) = \ln(x)/\ln(2) = \log(x)/\log(2) = \log10(x)/\log10(2)$$

You can calculate $\log_b(x)$ using whichever formula best suits your needs.

lnfact(n)

Domain: integers 0 to 1e+305
Range: 0 to 8e+307
Description: returns the natural log of factorial = ln($n!$)

If you wish to calculate $n!$, use round(exp(lnfact(n)),1) to ensure that the result is an integer. Logs of factorials are generally more useful than the factorials themselves because of overflow problems.

lngamma(x)

Domain: –2,147,483,648 to 1e+305 (excluding negative integers)
Range: –8e+307 to 8e+307
Description: returns $\ln\{\Gamma(x)\}$. Here, the gamma function $\Gamma(x)$ is defined by
$\Gamma(x) = \int_0^\infty t^{x-1}e^{-t}dt$. For integer values of $x > 0$, this is
ln(($x - 1$)!).

lngamma(x) for $x < 0$ returns a number such that exp(lngamma(x)) is equal to the absolute value of the correct answer. That is, lngamma(x) always returns a real (as opposed to complex) result.

log(x)

Domain: 1e–323 to 8e+307
Range: −744 to 709
Description: returns the natural logarithm ln(x). This is a synonym for ln(x). Also see ln(x)
            for more information.

log10(x)

Domain: 1e–323 to 8e+307
Range: −323 to 308
Description: returns the base 10 logarithm of x

logit(x)

Domain: 0 to 1
Range: –8e+307 to 8e+307 and *missing*
Description: returns the log of the odds ratio of x, $\mathtt{logit}(x) = \ln\left(\frac{x}{1-x}\right)$

(Continued on next page)

max(x_1,x_2,...,x_n)
   Domain x_1:   −8e+307 to 8e+307 and *missing*
   Domain x_2:   −8e+307 to 8e+307 and *missing*
   . . .
   Domain x_k: −8e+307 to 8e+307; *missing*
   Range: −8e+307 to 8e+307; *missing*
   Description: returns the maximum value of $x_1, x_2, \ldots, x_n$. Unless all arguments are *missing*, missing values are ignored.
             max(2,10,.,7) = 10
             max(.,.,.) = .

min(x_1,x_2,...,x_n)
   Domain x_1:   −8e+307 to 8e+307 and *missing*
   Domain x_2:   −8e+307 to 8e+307 and *missing*
   . . .
   Domain x_k: −8e+307 to 8e+307 and *missing*
   Range: −8e+307 to 8e+307; *missing*
   Description: returns the minimum value of $x_1, x_2, \ldots, x_n$. Unless all arguments are *missing*, missing values are ignored.
             min(2,10,.,7) = 2
             min(.,.,.) = .

mod(x,y)
   Domain x: −8e+307 to 8e+307
   Domain y: 0 to 8e+307
   Range: 0 to 8e+307
   Description: returns the modulus of x with respect to y: $\mathtt{mod}(x, y) = x - \bigl(y\ \mathtt{int}(x/y)\bigr)$

reldif(x,y)
   Domain x: −8e+307 to 8e+307 and *missing*
   Domain y: −8e+307 to 8e+307 and *missing*
   Range: −8e+307 to 8e+307 and *missing*
   Description: returns the "relative" difference $|x - y|/(|y| + 1)$
             If both arguments are the same time of extended missing value, this function will return 0. If only one argument is missing, or the two arguments are two different types of missing, the function will return *missing*.

round(x,y) or round(x)
   Domain x: −8e+307 to 8e+307
   Domain y: −8e+307 to 8e+307
   Range: −8e+307 to 8e+307
   Description: returns x rounded in units of y, or x rounded to the nearest integer if the argument y is omitted. Note: returns x (not '.') if x is missing, meaning round(.a) = .a and round(.a,y) = .a if y is not missing; if y is missing, '.' is returned.

For $y = 1$, or with y omitted, this amounts to the closest integer to x; round(5.2,1) is 5, as is round(4.8,1); round(-5.2,1) is −5, as is round(-4.8,1).

The rounding definition is generalized for $y \neq 1$. With $y = .01$, for instance, x is rounded to two decimal places; round(sqrt(2),.01) is 1.41. y may also be larger than 1; round(28,5) is 30, which is 28 rounded to the closest multiple of 5. For $y = 0$, the function is defined as returning x unmodified.

Also see int(x), ceil(x), and floor(x).

sign(x)
   Domain: –8e+307 to 8e+307; *missing*
   Range: –1, 0, 1; *missing*
   Description: returns the sign of x: –1 if $x < 0$, 0 if $x = 0$, 1 if $x > 0$, and *missing*
                 if $x = missing$

sin(x)
   Domain: –1e+18 to 1e+18
   Range: –1 to 1
   Description: returns sine of x, where x is in radians

sqrt(x)
   Domain: 0 to 8e+307
   Range: 0 to 1e+154
   Description: returns the square root of x

sum(x)
   Domain: –8e+307 to 8e+307; *missing*
   Range: –8e+307 to 8e+307 (and excluding *missing*)
   Description: returns the running sum of x treating missing values as zero

For example, following the command generate y=sum(x), the jth observation on y contains
the sum of the first through jth observations on x. See [R] **egen** for an alternative sum function
that produces a constant equal to the overall sum.

tan(x)
   Domain: –1e+18 to 1e+18
   Range: –1e+17 to 1e+17; *missing*
   Description: returns the tangent of x, where x is in radians

tanh(x)
   Domain: –8e+307 to 8e+307
   Range: –1 to 1; *missing*
   Description: returns the hyperbolic tangent of x, $\tanh(x) = (e^x - e^{-x})/(e^x + e^{-x})$

trigamma(x)
   Domain: –1e+15 to 8e+307
   Range: 0 to 8e+307; *missing*
   Description: returns the second derivative of lngamma(x) = $d^2 \ln\Gamma(x)/dx^2$. The trigamma
                 function is the derivative of digammma(x).

❏ Technical Note

The trigonometric functions are defined in terms of *radians*. There are 2π radians in a circle. If
you prefer to think in terms of *degrees*, since there are also 360 degrees in a circle, you may convert
degrees into radians using the formula $r = d\pi/180$, where d represents degrees and r represents
radians. Stata includes the built-in constant _pi, equal to π to machine precision. Thus, to calculate
the sine of theta, where theta is measured in degrees, you could type

```
sin(theta*_pi/180)
```

atan() similarly returns radians, not degrees. The arc-cotangent can be obtained as

```
acot(x) =_pi/2 - atan(x)
```

❏

Probability distributions and density functions

betaden(a,b,x)
      Domain a: 1e–323 to 8e+307
      Domain b: 1e–323 to 8e+307
      Domain x: 1e–323 to 8e+307
                      Interesting domain is $0 \le x \le 1$
      Range: 0 to 8e+307
      Description: returns the probability density of the Beta distribution,

$$\text{betaden}(a,b,x) = \frac{x^{a-1}(1-x)^{b-1}}{\int_0^\infty t^{a-1}(1-t)^{b-1}dt} = \frac{\Gamma(a+b)}{\Gamma(a)\Gamma(b)}x^{a-1}(1-x)^{b-1}$$

              where a and b are the shape parameters.

Binomial(n,k,θ)
      Domain n: 0 to 8e+307
      Domain k: 0 to n
      Domain θ: 0 to 1
      Range: 0 to 1
      Description: returns the probability of observing floor(k) or more successes in floor(n) trials
              when the probability of a success on a single trial is θ.

binorm(h,k,ρ)
      Domain h: –8e+307 to 8e+307
      Domain k: –8e+307 to 8e+307
      Domain ρ: -1 to 1
      Range: 0 to 1
      Description: returns the joint cumulative distribution $\Phi(h,k,\rho)$ of bivariate normal
              with correlation ρ; cumulative over $(-\infty, h] \times (-\infty, k]$:

$$\Phi(h,k,p) = \frac{1}{2\pi\sqrt{1-\rho^2}} \int_{-\infty}^{h} \int_{-\infty}^{k} \exp\left\{-\frac{1}{2(1-\rho^2)}\left(x_1^2 - 2\rho x_1 x_2 + x_2^2\right)\right\} dx_1\, dx_2$$

chi2(n,x)
      Domain n: 1e–323 to 8e+307 (may be nonintegral)
      Domain x: –8e+307 to 8e+307
                      Interesting domain is $x \ge 0$
      Range: 0 to 1
      Description: returns the cumulative χ^2 distribution with n degrees of freedom:
              chi2(n,x) = gammap($n/2, x/2$)

chi2tail(n,x)
      Domain n: 1e–323 to 8e+307 (may be nonintegral)
      Domain x: –8e+307 to 8e+307
                      Interesting domain is $x \ge 0$
      Range: 0 to 1
      Description: returns the reverse cumulative (upper-tail, survival) χ^2 distribution with n degrees
              of freedom: chi2tail(n,x) = $1 - $ chi2(n,x)

dgammapda(a,x)
> Domain a: 1e−7 to 1e+307
> Domain x: −8e+307 to 8e+307
>   Interesting domain is $x \geq 0$
> Range: −16 to 0 and *missing*
> Description: returns $\frac{\partial P(a,x)}{\partial a}$, where $P(a,x) = \texttt{gammap}(a,x)$

dgammapdada(a,x)
> Domain a: 1e−7 to 1e+307
> Domain x: −8e+307 to 8e+307
>   Interesting domain is $x \geq 0$
> Range: −0.02 to 4.77e+5 and *missing*
> Description: returns $\frac{\partial^2 P(a,x)}{\partial a^2}$, where $P(a,x) = \texttt{gammap}(a,x)$

dgammapdadx(a,x)
> Domain a: 1e−7 to 1e+305
> Domain x: −8e+307 to 8e+307
>   Interesting domain is $x \geq 0$
> Range: −0.04 to 8e+307 and *missing*
> Description: returns $\frac{\partial^2 P(a,x)}{\partial a \partial x}$, where $P(a,x) = \texttt{gammap}(a,x)$

dgammapdx(a,x)
> Domain a: 1e–323 to 8e+307
> Domain x: −8e+307 to 8e+307
>   Interesting domain is $x \geq 0$
> Range: 0 to 8e+307 and *missing*
> Description: returns $\frac{\partial P(a,x)}{\partial x}$, where $P(a,x) = \texttt{gammap}(a,x)$

dgammapdxdx(a,x)
> Domain a: 1e–323 to 8e+307
> Domain x: −8e+307 to 8e+307
>   Interesting domain is $x \geq 0$
> Range: 0 to 1e+40 and *missing*
> Description: returns $\frac{\partial^2 P(a,x)}{\partial x^2}$, where $P(a,x) = \texttt{gammap}(a,x)$

F(n_1,n_2,f)
> Domain n_1:   1e–323 to 8e+307 (may be nonintegral)
> Domain n_2:   1e–323 to 8e+307 (may be nonintegral)
> Domain f: −8e+307 to 8e+307
>   Interesting domain is $f \geq 0$
> Range: 0 to 1
> Description: returns the cumulative F distribution with n_1 numerator and n_2 denominator
>   degrees of freedom: $\text{F}(n_1, n_2, f) = \int_0^f \texttt{Fden}(n_1, n_2, t)\ dt$

(*Continued on next page*)

`Fden(`n_1`,`n_2`,`f`)`

    Domain n_1: 1e–323 to 8e+307 (may be nonintegral)
    Domain n_2: 1e–323 to 8e+307 (may be nonintegral)
    Domain f: –8e+307 to 8e+307
                 Interesting domain is $f \geq 0$
    Range: 0 to 8e+307
    Description: returns the probability density function of the F distribution with n_1 numerator and n_2 denominator degrees of freedom:

$$\texttt{Fden}(n_1, n_2, f) = \frac{\Gamma(\frac{n_1 + n_2}{2})}{\Gamma(\frac{n_1}{2})\Gamma(\frac{n_2}{2})} \left(\frac{n_1}{n_2}\right)^{\frac{n_1}{2}} \cdot f^{\frac{n_1}{2} - 1} \left(1 + \frac{n_1}{n_2} f\right)^{-\frac{1}{2}(n_1 + n_2)}$$

`Ftail(`n_1`,`n_2`,`f`)`

    Domain n_1: 1e–323 to 8e+307 (may be nonintegral)
    Domain n_2: 1e–323 to 8e+307 (may be nonintegral)
    Domain f: –8e+307 to 8e+307
                 Interesting domain is $f \geq 0$
    Range: 0 to 1
    Description: returns the reverse cumulative (upper-tail) F distribution with n_1 numerator and n_2 denominator degrees of freedom:
                 $\texttt{Ftail}(n_1, n_2, f) = 1 - \texttt{F}(n_1, n_2, f) = \int_f^\infty \texttt{Fden}(n_1, n_2, t)\,dt$

`gammaden(`a`,`b`,`g`,`x`)`

    Domain a: 1e–323 to 8e+307
    Domain b: 1e–323 to 8e+307
    Domain g: –8e+307 to 8e+307
    Domain x: –8e+307 to 8e+307
                 Interesting domain is $x \geq g$
    Range: 0 to 8e+307
    Description: returns the probability density function of the Gamma distribution defined by

$$\frac{1}{\Gamma(a) b^a} (x - g)^{a-1} e^{-(x-g)/b}$$

    where a is the shape parameter, b is the scale parameter b, and g is the location parameter.

(Continued on next page)

`gammap(a,x)`
    Domain a: 1e–323 to 8e+307
    Domain x: –8e+307 to 8e+307
                Interesting domain is $x \geq 0$
    Range: 0 to 1
    Description: returns the cumulative Gamma distribution with shape parameter a defined by

$$\frac{1}{\Gamma(a)} \int_0^x e^{-t} t^{a-1}\, dt$$

Note that the cumulative Poisson (the probability of observing k or fewer events if the expected is x) can be evaluated as `1-gammap(k+1,x)`. The reverse cumulative (the probability of observing k or more events) can be evaluated as `gammap(k,x)`. See Press et al. (1992, 216–221) for a more complete description and for suggested uses for this function.

`gammap()` is also known as the incomplete gamma function (ratio).

Probabilities for the three parameter Gamma distribution, see `gammaden()`, can be calculated by shifting and scaling x; i.e., `gammap(`$a,(x-g)/b$`)`

`ibeta(a,b,x)`
    Domain a: 1e–323 to 8e+307
    Domain b: 1e–323 to 8e+307
    Domain x: –8e+307 to 8e+307
                Interesting domain is $0 \leq x \leq 1$
    Range: 0 to 1
    Description: returns the cumulative Beta distribution with shape parameters a and b defined by

$$I_x(a,b) = \frac{\Gamma(a+b)}{\Gamma(a)\Gamma(b)} \int_0^x t^{a-1}(1-t)^{b-1}\, dt$$

Although Stata has a cumulative binomial function, see `Binomial()`, the probability that an event occurs k or fewer times in n trials, when the probability of a single event is p, can be evaluated as `cond(k==n,1,1-ibeta(k+1,n-k,p))`. The reverse cumulative binomial (the probability that an event occurs k or more times) can be evaluated as `cond(k==0,1,ibeta(k,n-k+1,p))`. See Press et al. (1992, 226–229) for a more complete description and for suggested uses for this function.

`ibeta()` is also known as the incomplete beta function (ratio).

`invbinomial(n,k,p)`
    Domain n: 1 to 8e+307
    Domain k: 1 to n
    Domain p: 0 to 1 (exclusive)
    Range: 0 to 1
    Description: returns the inverse binomial, but with a twist:

For $p \leq 0.5$, returns θ, θ = probability of success on a single trial, such that the probability of observing `floor(`k`)` or more successes in `floor(`n`)` trials is p; for $p > 0.5$, returns θ such that the probability of observing `floor(`k`)` or fewer successes in `floor(`n`)` trials is $1 - p$.

`invchi2(n,p)`
    Domain n: 1e–323 to 8e+307 (may be nonintegral)
    Domain p: 0 to 1
    Range: 0 to 8e+307
    Description: returns the inverse of `chi2()`:
                if `chi2(`n,x`)` $= p$, then `invchi2(`n,p`)` $= x$

invchi2tail(n,p)
    Domain n: 1e–323 to 8e+307 (may be nonintegral)
    Domain p: 0 to 1
    Range: 0 to 8e+307
    Description: returns the inverse of chi2tail():
                 if chi2tail(n,x) $= p$, then invchi2tail(n,p) $= x$

invF(n_1,n_2,p)
    Domain n_1: 1e–323 to 8e+307 (may be nonintegral)
    Domain n_2: 1e–323 to 8e+307 (may be nonintegral)
    Domain p: 0 to 1
    Range: 0 to 8e+307
    Description: returns the inverse cumulative F distribution:
                 if F(n_1,n_2,f) $= p$, then invF(n_1,n_2,p) $= f$

invFtail(n_1,n_2,p)
    Domain n_1: 1e–323 to 8e+307 (may be nonintegral)
    Domain n_2: 1e–323 to 8e+307 (may be nonintegral)
    Domain p: 0 to 1
    Range: 0 to 8e+307
    Description: returns the inverse reverse cumulative F distribution:
                 if Ftail(n_1,n_2,f) $= p$, then invFtail(n_1,n_2,p) $= f$

invgammap(a,p)
    Domain a: 1e–323 to 8e+307
    Domain p: 0 to 1
    Range: 0 to 8e+307
    Description: returns the inverse cumulative gamma distribution:
                 if gammap(a,x) $= p$, then invgammap(a,p) $= x$

invibeta(a,b,p)
    Domain a: 1e–323 to 8e+307
    Domain b: 1e–323 to 8e+307
    Domain p: 0 to 1
    Range: 0 to 1
    Description: returns the inverse cumulative Beta distribution:
                 if ibeta(a,b,x) $= p$, then invibeta(a,b,p) $= x$

invnchi2(n,λ,p)
    Domain n: integers 1 to 200
    Domain λ: 0 to 1,000
    Domain p: 0 to 1
    Range: 0 to 8e+307
    Description: returns the inverse cumulative noncentral χ^2 distribution:
                 if nchi2(n,λ,x) $= p$, then invnchi2(n,λ,p) $= x$;
                 n must be an integer

invnFtail(n_1,n_2,λ,p)
    Domain n_1: 1e–323 to 8e+307 (may be nonintegral)
    Domain n_2: 1e–323 to 8e+307 (may be nonintegral)
    Domain λ: 0 to 1,000
    Domain p: 0 to 1
    Range: 0 to 8e+307
    Description: returns the inverse reverse cumulative noncentral F distribution:
                 if nFtail(n_1,n_2,λ,x) $= p$, then invnFtail(n_1, n_2, λ, p) $= x$

`invnibeta(`a`,`b`,`λ`,`p`)`

> Domain a: 1e–323 to 8e+307
> Domain b: 1e–323 to 8e+307
> Domain λ: 0 to 1,000
> Domain p: 0 to 1
> Range: 0 to 1
> Description: returns the inverse cumulative noncentral Beta distribution:
>   if $\mathtt{nibeta}(a,b,\lambda,x) = p$, then $\mathtt{invibeta}(a,b,\lambda,p) = x$

`invnorm(`p`)`

> Domain p: 1e–323 to $1 - 2^{-53}$
> Range: -39 to 8.2095362
> Description: returns the inverse cumulative normal:
>   if $\mathtt{norm}(z) = p$, then $\mathtt{invnorm}(p) = z$

`invttail(`n`,`p`)`

> Domain n: 1e–323 to 1e+12 (may be nonintegral)
> Domain p: 0 to $1 - 2^{-52}$
> Range: 0 to 1e+10
> Description: returns the inverse reverse cumulative t distribution:
>   if $\mathtt{ttail}(n,t) = p$, then $\mathtt{invttail}(n,p) = t$

`nbetaden(`a`,`b`,`λ`,`x`)`

> Domain a: 1e–323 to 8e+307
> Domain b: 1e–323 to 8e+307
> Domain λ: 0 to 1,000
> Domain x: –8e+307 to 8e+307
>   Interesting domain is $0 \leq x \leq 1$
> Range: 0 to 8e+307
> Description: returns the probability density function of the noncentral Beta distribution,

$$\sum_{j=0}^{\infty} \frac{e^{-\lambda/2}(\lambda/2)^j}{\Gamma(j+1)} \left\{ \frac{\Gamma(a+b+j)}{\Gamma(a+j)\Gamma(b)} x^{a+j-1}(1-x)^{b-1} \right\}$$

> where a and b are shape parameters, λ is the noncentrality parameter, and x is the
> value of a Beta random variable. Note that
> $\mathtt{nbetaden}(a,b,0,x) = \mathtt{betaden}(a,b,x)$, but $\mathtt{betaden()}$ is the preferred
> function to use for the central Beta distribution. $\mathtt{nbetaden()}$ is computed using an
> algorithm described in Johnson et al. (1995).

(Continued on next page)

`nchi2(n,λ,x)`

    Domain n: integers 1 to 200

    Domain λ: 0 to 1,000

    Domain x: −8e+307 to 8e+307

                    Interesting domain is $x \geq 0$

    Range: 0 to 1

    Description: returns the cumulative noncentral χ^2 distribution,

$$\int_0^x \frac{e^{-t/2}\,e^{-\lambda/2}}{2^{n/2}} \sum_{j=0}^{\infty} \frac{t^{n/2+j-1}\,\lambda^j}{\Gamma(n/2+j)\,2^{2j}\,j!}\,dt$$

                where n denotes the degrees of freedom, λ is the noncentrality parameter, and x is the value of χ^2.

Note that $\texttt{nchi2}(n,0,x) = \texttt{chi2}(n,x)$, but `chi2()` is the preferred function to use for the central χ^2 distribution. `nchi2()` is computed using the algorithm of Haynam et al. (1970).

`nFden(n₁,n₂,λ,f)`

    Domain n_1: 1e–323 to 8e+307 (may be nonintegral)

    Domain n_2: 1e–323 to 8e+307 (may be nonintegral)

    Domain λ: 0 to 1,000

    Domain f: −8e+307 to 8e+307

                    Interesting domain is $f \geq 0$

    Range: 0 to 8e+307

    Description: returns the probability density function of the noncentral F distribution with n_1 numerator and n_2 denominator degrees of freedom and noncentrality parameter λ.

Note that $\texttt{nFden}(n_1,n_2,0,F) = \texttt{Fden}(n_1,n_2,F)$, but `Fden()` is the preferred function to use for the central F distribution.

Also note that if F follows the noncentral F distribution with n_1 and n_2 degrees of freedom and noncentrality parameter λ, then

$$\frac{n_1 F}{n_2 + n_1 F}$$

follows a noncentral Beta distribution with shape parameters $a = \nu_1/2$ and $b = \nu_2/2$ and noncentrality parameter λ as given in `nbetaden()`. `nFden()` is computed based on this relationship.

`nFtail(n₁,n₂,λ,f)`

    Domain n_1: 1e–323 to 8e+307 (may be nonintegral)

    Domain n_2: 1e–323 to 8e+307 (may be nonintegral)

    Domain λ: 0 to 1,000

    Domain f: −8e+307 to 8e+307

                    Interesting domain is $f \geq 0$

    Range: 0 to 1

    Description: returns the reverse cumulative (upper-tail) noncentral F distribution with n_1 numerator and n_2 denominator degrees of freedom and noncentrality parameter λ.

Note that `nFtail()` is computed using `nibeta()` based on the relationship between the noncentral Beta and F distributions. See Johnson et al. (1995) for more details.

`nibeta(`a`,`b`,`λ`,`x`)`

    Domain a: 1e–323 to 8e+307

    Domain b: 1e–323 to 8e+307

    Domain λ: 0 to 1,000

    Domain x: –8e+307 to 8e+307

                      Interesting domain is $0 \le x \le 1$

    Range: 0 to 1

    Description: returns the cumulative noncentral Beta distribution,

$$I_x(a, b, \lambda) = \sum_{j=0}^{\infty} \frac{e^{-\lambda/2}(\lambda/2)^j}{\Gamma(j + 1)} I_x(a + j, b)$$

                    where a and b are shape parameters, λ is the noncentrality parameter, x is the value of a Beta random variable, and $I_x(a, b)$ is the cumulative beta distribution, `ibeta()`. Note that `nibeta(`a`,`b`,0,`x`)` = `ibeta(`a`,`b`,`x`)`, but `ibeta()` is the preferred function to use for the central Beta distribution. `nibeta()` is computed using an algorithm described in Johnson et al. (1995).

`norm(`z`)`

    Domain z: –8e+307 to 8e+307

    Range: 0 to 1

    Description: returns the cumulative standard normal distribution:

                    `norm(`z`)` $= \int_{-\infty}^{z} \frac{1}{\sqrt{2\pi}} e^{-x^2/2} dx$

`normden(`z`)`

    Domain z: –8e+307 to 8e+307

    Range: 0 to .39894 . . .

    Description: returns the standard normal density, $N(0, 1)$

`normden(`z`,`σ`)`

    Domain z: –8e+307 to 8e+307

    Domain σ: 1e–308 to 8e+307

    Range: 0 to 8e+307

    Description: returns the rescaled standard normal density, $N(0, \sigma^2)$:

                    `normden(`z`,1)` = `normden(`z`)` and `normden(`z`,`σ`)` = `normden(`z`)`$/\sigma$

`normden(`x`,`μ`,`σ`)`

    Domain x: –8e+307 to 8e+307

    Domain μ: –8e+307 to 8e+307

    Domain σ: 1e–308 to 8e+307

    Range: 0 to 8e+307

    Description: returns the normal density with mean μ and standard deviation σ, $N(\mu, \sigma^2)$:

                    `normden(`x`,0,1)` = `normden(`x`)` and

                    `normden(`x`,`μ`,`σ`)` = `normden((`$x - \mu$`)`$/\sigma$`)`$/\sigma$

                    In general,

$$\text{normden}(z, \mu, \sigma) = \frac{1}{\sigma\sqrt{2\pi}} e^{-\frac{1}{2}\left(\frac{(z-\mu)}{\sigma}\right)^2}$$

`npnchi2(`n`,`x`,`p`)`

Domain n: integers 1 to 200

Domain x: 0 to 8e+307

Domain p: 1e–138 to $1 - 2^{-52}$

Range: 0 to 1,000

Description: returns the noncentrality parameter λ for noncentral χ^2:
if `nchi2(`n`,`λ`,`x`)` $= p$, then `npnchi2(`n`,`x`,`p`)` $= \lambda$

`tden(`n`,`t`)`

Domain n: 1e–323 to 8e+307

Domain t: 0 to 8e+307

Range: 0 to .39894 ...

Description: returns the probability density function of Student's t distribution

$$\texttt{tden}(n, t) = \frac{\Gamma((n+1)/2)}{\sqrt{\pi n}\,\Gamma(n/2)} \cdot \left(1 + t^2/n\right)^{-(n+1)/2}$$

`ttail(`n`,`t`)`

Domain n: 1e–323 to 8e+307

Domain t: 0 to 8e+307

Range: 0 to 1

Description: returns the reverse cumulative (upper-tail) Student's t distribution; it returns the
probability $T > t$:

$$\texttt{ttail}(n, t) = \int_{t}^{\infty} \frac{\Gamma((n+1)/2)}{\sqrt{\pi n}\,\Gamma(n/2)} \cdot \left(1 + x^2/n\right)^{-(n+1)/2} \, dx$$

`uniform()`

Range: 0 to nearly 1 (0 to $1 - 2^{-32}$)

Description: returns uniform pseudo-random numbers

`uniform()` returns uniformly distributed pseudo-random numbers on the interval $[0, 1)$. `uniform()` takes no arguments, but the parentheses must be typed. `uniform()` can be seeded with the `set seed` command; see the technical note at the end of this subsection.

To generate pseudo-random numbers over the interval $[a, b)$, use `a+(`b`-`a`)*uniform()`.

To generate pseudo-random integers over $[a, b]$, use `a+int((`b`-`a`+1)*uniform())`.

To generate normally distributed random numbers with mean 0 and standard deviation 1, use `invnorm(uniform())`.

To generate normally distributed random numbers with mean μ and standard deviation σ, use `μ+σ*invnorm(uniform())`.

❏ Technical Note

The uniform pseudo-random number function `uniform()` is based on George Marsaglia's (1994) 32-bit pseudo-random number generator KISS (Keep It Simple Stupid). The KISS generator is composed of two 32-bit pseudo-random number generators and two 16-bit generators (combined to make one 32-bit generator). The four generators are defined by the recursions

$$x_n = 69069\, x_{n-1} + 1234567 \quad \mathrm{mod}\ 2^{32} \tag{1}$$

$$y_n = y_{n-1}(I + L^{13})(I + R^{17})(I + L^{5}) \tag{2}$$

$$z_n = 65184\left(z_{n-1}\ \mathrm{mod}\ 2^{16}\right) + \mathrm{int}\left(z_{n-1}/2^{16}\right) \tag{3}$$

$$w_n = 63663\left(w_{n-1}\ \mathrm{mod}\ 2^{16}\right) + \mathrm{int}\left(w_{n-1}/2^{16}\right) \tag{4}$$

In recursion (2), the 32-bit word y_n is viewed as a 1×32 binary vector; L is the 32×32 matrix that produces a left shift of one (L has 1s on the first left subdiagonal, 0s elsewhere); and R is L transpose, affecting a right shift by one. In recursions (3) and (4), $\text{int}(x)$ is the integer part of x.

The KISS generator produces the 32-bit random number

$$R_n = x_n + y_n + z_n + 2^{16}w_n \quad \mod 2^{32}$$

uniform() takes the output from the KISS generator and divides it by 2^{32} to produce a real number on the interval $[0, 1)$.

The recursions (1)–(4) have, respectively, the periods

$$2^{32} \tag{1}$$
$$2^{32} - 1 \tag{2}$$
$$(65184 \cdot 2^{16} - 2)/2 \approx 2^{31} \tag{3}$$
$$(63663 \cdot 2^{16} - 2)/2 \approx 2^{31} \tag{4}$$

Thus, the overall period for the KISS generator is

$$2^{32} \cdot (2^{32} - 1) \cdot (65184 \cdot 2^{15} - 1) \cdot (63663 \cdot 2^{15} - 1) \approx 2^{126}$$

When Stata first comes up, it initializes the four recursions in KISS using the seeds

$$x_0 = 123456789 \tag{1}$$
$$y_0 = 521288629 \tag{2}$$
$$z_0 = 362436069 \tag{3}$$
$$w_0 = 2262615 \tag{4}$$

Successive calls to uniform() will then produce the sequence

$$\frac{R_1}{2^{32}}, \frac{R_2}{2^{32}}, \frac{R_3}{2^{32}}, \cdots$$

Hence, uniform() gives the same sequence of random numbers in every Stata session (measured from the start of the session) unless you reinitialize the seed. The full seed is the set of four numbers (x, y, z, w), but you can reinitialize the seed by simply issuing the command

```
. set seed #
```

where # is any integer between 0 and $2^{31} - 1$ inclusive. When this command is issued, the initial value x_0 is set equal to #, and the other three recursions are restarted at the seeds y_0, z_0, and w_0 given above. Then the first 100 random numbers are discarded, and successive calls to uniform() give the sequence

$$\frac{R'_{101}}{2^{32}}, \frac{R'_{102}}{2^{32}}, \frac{R'_{103}}{2^{32}}, \cdots$$

However, if the command

```
. set seed 123456789
```

is given, in this case only, the first 100 random numbers are not discarded, and you get exactly the same sequence of random numbers that uniform() produces by default; also see [R] **generate**.

❏

❏ Technical Note

The formula used by uniform() to produce pseudo-random numbers changed between releases 3.1 and 4.0. If you set version to 3.1 or earlier (see [P] **version**), set seed and uniform() refer to the prior generator, and so previously produced results are still reproducible. When version is set to 4.0 or higher, set seed and uniform() refer to the new function, but you can access the prior function using set seed0 and uniform0(). The only reason to use the prior function, however, is for the reproduction of previous results; the new function is better.

❏

❏ Technical Note

You may "capture" the current seed (x, y, z, w) by coding:

```
. local curseed = "'c(seed)'"
```

and, at a later point in your code, reestablish that seed by coding:

```
. set seed 'curseed'
```

When the seed is set this way, the first 100 random numbers are not discarded.

The contents of c(seed) is a 30-plus long character string containing something like "X075bcd151f123bb5159a55e50022865746ad". The string contains an encoding of the four numbers (x, y, z, w) along with checksums and redundancy to ensure that, at set seed time, it is valid.

❏

Matrix functions returning matrices

In addition to the functions listed below, see [P] **matrix svd** for singular value decomposition, [P] **matrix symeigen** for eigenvalues and eigenvectors of symmetric matrices, and [P] **matrix eigenvalues** for eigenvalues of nonsymmetric matrices.

cholesky(M)
    Domain: $n \times n$, positive definite, symmetric matrices
    Range: $n \times n$ lower-triangular matrices
    Description: returns the Cholesky decomposition of the matrix:
                  if $R = $ cholesky(S), then $RR^T = S$
                  R^T indicates the transpose of R
                  Row and column names are obtained from M

corr(M)
    Domain: $n \times n$ symmetric variance matrices
    Range: $n \times n$ symmetric correlation matrices
    Description: returns the correlation matrix of the variance matrix
                  Row and column names are obtained from M

diag(v)
> Domain: $1 \times n$ and $n \times 1$ vectors
> Range: $n \times n$ diagonal matrices
> Description: returns the square, diagonal matrix created from the row or column vector
> Row and column names are obtained from the column names of M if M is
> a row vector, or the row names of M if M is a column vector.

e(*name*)
> Domain: names
> Range: strings, scalars, matrices, and missing
> Description: returns the value of saved result e(*name*);
> see [U] **21.8 Accessing results calculated by other programs**
> e(*name*) = scalar missing if the saved result does not exist
> e(*name*) = specified matrix if the saved result is a matrix
> e(*name*) = scalar numeric value if the saved result is a scalar
> e(*name*) = scalar numeric value if the saved result is a string (macro)
> that can be interpreted as a number
> e(*name*) = a string containing the first 80 characters of the saved result otherwise

get(*systemname*)
> Domain: existing names of system matrices
> Range: matrices
> Description: returns copy of Stata internal system matrix *systemname*
> (this function is included for backwards compatibility with previous versions
> of Stata)

hadamard(M, N)
> Domain M: $m \times n$ matrices
> Domain N: $m \times n$ matrices
> Range: $m \times n$ matrices
> Description: returns a matrix whose i, j element is $M[i,j] \cdot N[i,j]$
> (if M and N are not the same size, this function reports a conformability error)

I(n)
> Domain: real scalars 1 to matsize
> Range: identity matrices
> Description: returns $n \times n$ identity matrix if n is an integer; otherwise, this function returns
> the round(n)×round(n) identity matrix.

inv(M)
> Domain: $n \times n$ nonsingular matrices
> Range: $n \times n$ matrices
> Description: returns the inverse of the matrix M. If M is singular, this will result in an error.
> The function syminv() should be used in preference to inv(), because syminv()
> is more accurate. The row names of the result are obtained from the column
> names of M, and the column names of the result are obtained from the row names
> of M.

J(r,c,z)
> Domain r: integer scalars 1 to matsize
> Domain c: integer scalars 1 to matsize
> Domain z: scalars −8e+307 to 8e+307
> Range: $r \times c$ matrices
> Description: returns the $r \times c$ matrix containing elements z

matuniform(r, c)
>   Domain r: integer scalars 1 to matsize
>   Domain c: integer scalars 1 to matsize
>   Range: $r \times c$ matrices
>   Description: returns the $r \times c$ matrices containing uniformly distributed pseudo-random numbers
>   on the interval $[0, 1)$.

nullmat(*matname*)
>   Domain: matrix names, existing and nonexisting
>   Range: matrices including null if *matname* does not exist

nullmat() is for use with the row-join (,) and column-join (\) operators in programming situations. Consider the following code fragment, which is an attempt to create the vector $(1, 2, 3, 4)$:

```
forvalues i = 1/4 {
        mat v = (v, 'i')
}
```

The above program will not work because, the first time through the loop, v will not yet exist, and thus, forming (v, 'i') makes no sense. nullmat() relaxes that restriction:

```
forvalues i = 1/4 {
        mat v = (nullmat(v), 'i')
}
```

The nullmat() function informs Stata that you know v might not exist, and, in that case, the function row-join is to be generalized. Joining nothing with 'i' results in ('i'). Thus, the first time through the loop, $v = (1)$ is formed. The second time through, v does exist and $v = (1, 2)$ is formed, and so on.

nullmat() can be used only with the , and \ operators.

r(*name*)
>   Domain: names
>   Range: strings, scalars, matrices, and missing
>   Description: returns the value of the saved result r(*name*);
>   see [U] **21.8 Accessing results calculated by other programs**
>   r(*name*) = scalar missing if the saved result does not exist
>   r(*name*) = specified matrix if the saved result is a matrix
>   r(*name*) = scalar numeric value if the saved result is a scalar
>   r(*name*) = scalar numeric value if the saved result is a string (macro)
>   that can be interpreted as a number
>   r(*name*) = a string containing the first 80 characters of the saved result otherwise

return(*name*)
>   Domain: names
>   Range: strings, scalars, matrices, and missing
>   Description: returns the value of the to-be-saved result return(*name*);
>   see [U] **21.8 Accessing results calculated by other programs** and
>   [U] **21.10 Saving results**
>   return(*name*) = scalar missing if the result does not exist
>   return(*name*) = specified matrix if the result is a matrix
>   return(*name*) = scalar numeric value if the result is a scalar
>   return(*name*) = scalar numeric value if the result is a string (macro)
>   that can be interpreted as a number
>   return(*name*) = a string containing the first 80 characters of the result otherwise

`sweep(M,i)`

> Domain M: $n \times n$ matrices
> Domain i: integer scalars 1 to n
> Range: $n \times n$ matrices
> Description: returns matrix M with ith row/column swept. The names of the resultant matrix are
>   obtained from M, except that the nth row and column names are interchanged.
>   If $B = \mathtt{sweep}(A, k)$, then

$$B_{kk} = \frac{1}{A_{kk}}$$

$$B_{ik} = -\frac{A_{ik}}{A_{kk}}, \qquad i \neq k$$

$$B_{kj} = \frac{A_{kj}}{A_{kk}}, \qquad j \neq k$$

$$B_{ij} = A_{ij} - \frac{A_{ik}A_{kj}}{A_{kk}}, \qquad i \neq k, j \neq k$$

`syminv(M)`

> Domain: $n \times n$ symmetric matrices
> Range: $n \times n$ symmetric matrices
> Description: if M is positive definite, this returns the inverse of M. If M is not positive definite,
>   rows will be inverted until the diagonal terms are zero or negative; the rows and
>   columns corresponding to these terms will be set to 0, producing a g2 inverse.
>   The row names of the result are obtained from the column names of M,
>   and the column names of the result are obtained from the row names of M.

`vec(M)`

> Domain M: matrices
> Range: column vectors ($n \times 1$ matrices)
> Description: returns a column vector formed by listing the elements of M, starting
>   with the first column and proceeding column by column.

`vecdiag(M)`

> Domain: $n \times n$ matrices
> Range: $1 \times n$ vectors
> Description: returns the row vector containing diagonal of matrix M
>   Note that `vecdiag()` is the opposite of `diag()`. The row name is
>   set to `r1`; the column names are obtained from the column names of M.

Matrix functions returning scalars

`colnumb(M,s)`

> Domain M: matrices
> Domain s: strings
> Range: integer scalars 1 to `matsize` and missing
> Description: returns the column number of M associated with row name s, or
>   returns missing if the column cannot be found.

`colsof(M)`

> Domain: matrices
> Range: integer scalars 1 to `matsize`
> Description: returns the number of columns of M

det(M)
   Domain M: $n \times n$ (square) matrices
   Range: scalars −8e+307 to 8e+307
   Description: returns the determinant of matrix M

diag0cnt(M)
   Domain M: $n \times n$ (square) matrices
   Range: integer scalars 0 to n
   Description: returns the number of zeros on the diagonal of M

el(s,i,j)
   Domain s: strings containing matrix name
   Domain i: scalars 1 to `matsize`
   Domain j: scalars 1 to `matsize`
   Range: scalars −8e+307 to 8e+307 and missing
   Description: returns s[`floor`(i),`floor`(j)], the i,j element of the matrix named s
                   returns missing if i or j are out of range or if matrix s does not exist.

issym(M)
   Domain M: matrices
   Range: integers 0 and 1
   Description: returns 1 if the matrix is symmetric, 0 otherwise.

matmissing(M)
   Domain M: matrices
   Range: integers 0 and 1
   Description: returns 1 if any elements of the matrix are missing, 0 otherwise.

mreldif(X,Y)
   Domain X: matrices
   Domain Y: matrices with same number of rows and columns as X
   Range: scalars −8e+307 to 8e+307
   Description: returns the maximum relative difference $\max_{i,j}\left(|x_{ij} - y_{ij}|/(|y_{ij}| + 1)\right)$

rownumb(M,s)
   Domain M: matrices
   Domain s: strings
   Range: integer scalars 1 to `matsize` and missing
   Description: returns the row number of M associated with row name s, or
                   returns missing if the row cannot be found.

rowsof(M)
   Domain: matrices
   Range: integer scalars 1 to `matsize`
   Description: returns the number of rows of M

trace(M)
   Domain M: $n \times n$ (square) matrices
   Range: scalars −8e+307 to 8e+307
   Description: returns the trace of matrix M

String functions

Stata includes the following *string functions*. In the display below, s is used to indicate a string subexpression—a string literal, a string variable, or another string expression—and n is used to indicate a numeric subexpression—a number, a numeric variable, or another numeric expression.

abbrev(s,n)

Domain s:	strings
Domain n:	5 to 32
Range:	strings
Description:	returns s, abbreviated to n characters.

If any of the characters of s are ".", and $n < 8$, then the value of n defaults to a value of 8. Otherwise, if $n < 5$, then n defaults to a value of 5. If $n = missing$, abbrev() will return the entire string s. abbrev() is typically used with variable names and variable names with time-series operators (the period case). abbrev("displacement",8) is displa~t

char(n)

Domain n:	integers 1 to 255
Range:	ASCII characters
Description:	returns the character corresponding to ASCII code n; returns "" if n is not in the domain.

index(s_1,s_2)

Domain s_1:	strings (to be searched)
Domain s_2:	strings (to search for)
Range:	integers 0 to 80
Description:	returns the position in s_1 at which s_2 is first found or else returns 0: index("this","is") $= 3$ and index("this","it") $= 0$

length(s)

Domain s:	strings
Range:	integers 0 to 80
Description:	returns the length of string s; length("ab") $= 2$

lower(s)

Domain s:	strings
Range:	strings with lowercased characters
Description:	returns the lowercase string: lower("THIS") $=$ "this"

ltrim(s)

Domain s:	strings
Range:	strings without leading blanks
Description:	returns the string without leading blanks: ltrim(" this") $=$ "this"

match(s_1,s_2)

Domain s:	strings
Range:	0 or 1
Description:	returns 1 if s_1 matches the pattern s_2; otherwise, it returns 0. match("17.4","1??4") returns 1. In s_2, "?" means 1 character goes here, and "*" means 0 or more characters goes here.

proper(s)
   Domain s: strings
   Range: strings
   Description: returns a string with the first letter capitalized and any other letters
      immediately following characters that are not letters capitalized, and all other
      letters converted to lowercase.
      proper("mR. joHn a. sMitH") = "Mr. John A. Smith"
      proper("jack o'reilly") = "Jack O'Reilly"
      proper("2-cent's worth") = "2-Cent'S Worth"

plural(n,s) or plural(n,s_1, s_2)
   Domain s: strings
   Domain s_1:   strings
   Domain s_2:   strings
   Range: strings
   Description: returns the plural of the first argument if $n \neq \pm 1$.
      The plural is formed by adding "s" to s if you called plural(n,s).
      If you called plural(n,s_1,s_2) and s_2 begins with the character "+", then the
      plural is formed by adding the remainder of s_2 to s_1. If s_2 begins with the character
      "-", then the plural is formed by subtracting the remainder of s_2 from s_1. If s_2
      begins with neither "+" nor "-", then the plural is formed by returning s_2.
      plural(1, "horse") = "horse"
      plural(2, "horse") = "horses"
      plural(2, "glass", "+es") = "glasses"
      plural(1, "mouse", "mice") = "mouse"
      plural(2, "mouse", "mice") = "mice"
      plural(2, "abcdefg", "-efg") = "abcd"

real(s)
   Domain s: strings
   Range: −8e+307 to 8e+307; *missing*
   Description: returns s converted to numeric or returns *missing*:
      real("5.2")+1 = 6.2 and real("hello") = .

reverse(s)
   Domain s: strings
   Range: reversed strings
   Description: returns the reversed string: reverse("hello") = "olleh"

rtrim(s)
   Domain s: strings
   Range: strings without trailing blanks
   Description: returns the string without trailing blanks: rtrim("this ") = "this"

string(n)
   Domain n: −8e+307 to 8e+307; *missing*
   Range: strings
   Description: returns n converted to a string:
      string(4)+"F" = "4F"
      string(1234567)="1234567"
      string(12345678) = "1.23e+07"
      string(.)="."

`string(n,s)`

Domain n: −8e+307 to 8e+307; *missing*

Domain s: strings containing *%fmt*

Range: strings

Description: returns n converted to a string:
```
string(4,"%9.2f") = "4.00"
string(123456789,"%11.0g") = "123456789"
string(123456789,"%13.0gc") = "123,456,789"
string(0,"%d") = "01jan1960"
string(225,"%tq") = "2016q2"
string(225,"not a format") = ""
```

`subinstr(s₁,s₂,s₃,n)`

Domain s_1:   strings (to be substituted into)

Domain s_2:   strings (to be substituted from)

Domain s_3:   strings (to be substituted with)

Domain n: integers 0 to 80; *missing*

Range: strings

Description: returns s_1, where the first n occurrences of s_2 have been replaced
                 with s_3. If $n = .$ (*missing*), then all occurrences are replaced.
```
subinstr("this is this","is","X",1) = "thX is this"
subinstr("this is this","is","X",2) = "thX X this"
subinstr("this is this","is","X",.) = "thX X thX"
```

`subinword(s₁,s₂,s₃,n)`

Domain s_1:   strings (to be substituted for)

Domain s_2:   strings (to be substituted from)

Domain s_3:   strings (to be substituted with)

Domain n: integers 0 to 80; *missing*

Range: strings

Description: returns s_1 where the first n occurrences of s_2 as a word have
                 been replaced with s_3. A word is defined as a space-separated token.
                 A token at the beginning or end of s_1 is considered space-separated.
                 If $n = .$ (*missing*), then all occurrences are replaced.
```
subinword("this is this","is","X",1) = "this X this"
subinword("this is this","is","X",.) = "this X this"
subinword("this is this","th","X",.) = "this is this"
```

`substr(s,n₁,n₂)`

Domain s: strings

Domain n_1:   integers 1 to 80 and −1 to −80

Domain n_2:   integers 0 to 80 and *missing*

Range: strings

Description: returns the substring of s starting at column n_1 for a length of n_2;
                 if $n_1 < 0$, n_1 is interpreted as distance from the end of the string;
                 if $n_2 = .$ (*missing*), the remaining portion of the string is returned:
```
substr("abcdef",2,3) = "bcd"
substr("abcdef",-3,2) = "de"
substr("abcdef",2,.) = "bcdef"
substr("abcdef",-3,.) = "def"
substr("abcdef",2,0) = ""
substr("abcdef",15,2) = ""
```

trim(s)
  Domain s: strings
  Range: strings without leading or trailing blanks
  Description: returns the string without leading and trailing blanks; equivalent to
                ()ltrim(rtrim(s)):
                trim(" this ") = "this"

upper(s)
  Domain s: strings
  Range: strings with uppercased characters
  Description: returns the uppercase string: upper("this") = "THIS"

word(s, n)
  Domain s: strings
  Domain n: integers $\ldots, -2, -1, 0, 1, 2, \ldots$
  Range: strings
  Description: returns the nth word in s. Positive numbers count words from the beginning of s,
                and negative numbers count words from the end of s. (1 is the first word in s,
                and -1 is the last word in s.) Returns *missing* ("") if n is *missing*.

wordcount(s)
  Domain s: strings
  Range: nonnegative integers $0, 1, 2, \ldots$
  Description: returns the number of words in s. A word is a set of characters that start
                and terminate with spaces, or that start with the beginning of the string,
                or that terminate with the end of the string.

Programming functions

autocode(x,n,x_0,x_1)
  Domain x: −8e+307 to 8e+307
  Domain n: integers 1 to 8e+307
  Domain x_0: −8e+307 to 8e+307
  Domain x_1: x_0 to 8e+307
  Range: x_0 to x_1
  Description: partitions the interval from x_0 to x_1 into n equal-length intervals and
                 returns the upper bound of the interval that contains x. This function is an
                 automated version of recode() (see below).
                 See [U] **28 Commands for dealing with categorical variables** for an example.

  The algorithm for autocode() is

$$
\begin{aligned}
&\text{if } (n\text{>=}.\mid\ x_0\text{>=}.\mid\ x_1\text{>=}.\mid\ n \le 0 \mid\ x_0 \ge x_1)\\
&\quad \text{then return } \textit{missing}\\
&\quad\quad \text{if } x \ge .,\ \text{then return } x\\
&\quad \text{otherwise}\\
&\quad\quad \text{for } i = 1 \text{ to } n - 1\\
&\quad\quad\quad xmap = x_0 + i * (x_1 - x_0)/n\\
&\quad\quad\quad \text{if } x \le xmap \text{ then return } xmap\\
&\quad\quad \text{end}\\
&\quad \text{otherwise}\\
&\quad\quad \text{return } x_1
\end{aligned}
$$

byteorder()

> Range: 0 and 1
>
> Description: returns 1 if your computer stores numbers using a hilo byte order, and evaluates to 2 if your computer stores numbers using a lohi byte order. Consider the number 1 written as a 2-byte integer. On some computers (called hilo), it is written as "00 01", and on other computers (called lohi), it is written as "01 00" (with the least significant byte written first). There are similar issues for 4-byte integers, 4-byte floats, and 8-byte floats. Stata automatically handles byte order differences for Stata created files. Users need not be concerned about this issue. Programmers producing customary binary files can use `byteorder()` to determine the native byte ordering.

c(*name*)

> Domain :   names
>
> Range: real values, strings and *missing*
>
> Description: returns the value of the system or constant result c(*name*); see [P] **creturn**. Referencing c(*name*) will give an error if the result does not exist
>
> c(*name*) will give a scalar if the result is scalar.
>
> c(*name*) will give a string containing the first 80 (or 244 for Stata/SE) characters of the result otherwise.

_caller()

> Range: 1.0 to 8
>
> Description: function for use by programmers; returns `version` of the program or session that invoked the currently running program; see [P] **version**. The current version at the time of this writing is 8, so 8 is the upper end of this range.
>
> If Stata 8.1 was the current version, 8.1 would be the upper end of this range, and likewise if Stata 9.0 was the current version, 9.0 would be the upper end of this range.

chop(x, ϵ)

> Domain x: −8e+307 to 8e+307
>
> Domain ϵ: −8e+307 to 8e+307
>
> Range: −8e+307 to 8e+307
>
> Description: returns `round(`x`)` if `abs`$\{x - $`round`$(x)\} < \epsilon$, otherwise returns x; returns x if x is missing.

clip(x,a,b)

> Domain x: −8e+307 to 8e+307
>
> Domain a: −8e+307 to 8e+307
>
> Domain b: −8e+307 to 8e+307
>
> Range: −8e+307 to 8e+307
>
> Description: returns x if $a < x < b$, b if $x \geq b$, a if $x \leq a$, and *missing* if x is missing or if $a > b$. If a and/or b is *missing*, this is interpreted as $a = -\infty$ and/or $b = +\infty$, respectively; returns x if x is missing.

(Continued on next page)

cond(x,a,b,c) or cond(x,a,b)
- Domain x: −8e+307 to 8e+307 and *missing*; $0 \Rightarrow$ *false*, otherwise interpreted as *true*
- Domain a: numbers and strings
- Domain b: numbers if a is a number; strings if a is a string
- Domain c: numbers if a is a number; strings if a is a string
- Range: a and b and c
- Description: returns a if x is *true*, b if x is *false*, and c if x is *missing*.

  If c is not specified and x evaluates to *missing*, then a is returned.

  cond(a>2,50,70) = 50 if a > 2 or a ≥ .

  cond(a>2,"this","that") = "that" if a ≤ 2

  cond(a>2,"this","that","missing") = "missing" if a ≥ .

  cond(a>2,"this","that","missing") = "this" if a ≥ 2 and a < .

e(*name*)
- Domain: names
- Range: strings, scalars, matrices, and missing
- Description: returns the value of saved result e(*name*);

  see [U] **21.8 Accessing results calculated by other programs**

  e(*name*) = scalar missing if the saved result does not exist

  e(*name*) = specified matrix if the saved result is a matrix

  e(*name*) = scalar numeric value if the saved result is a scalar

  e(*name*) = a string containing the first 80 characters (240 for Stata/SE) of the saved result otherwise

e(sample)
- Range: 0 and 1
- Description: returns 1 if observation is in estimation subsample and 0 otherwise.

epsdouble()
- Range: a double precision number close to 0
- Description: returns the machine precision of a double precision number. If $d <$ epsdouble() and (double) $x = 1$, then $x + d =$ (double) 1.

epsfloat()
- Range: a floating point number close to 0
- Description: returns the machine precision of a floating point number. If $d <$ epsfloat(), and (float) $x = 1$, then $x + d =$ (float) 1.

float(x)
- Domain: −1e+38 to 1e+38
- Range: −1e+38 to 1e+38
- Description: x rounded to float precision

Although you may store your numeric variables as byte, int, long, float, or double, Stata converts all numbers to double before performing any calculations. As a consequence, difficulties can arise when numbers that have no finite binary representation are compared.

For example, if the variable x is stored as a float and contains the value 1.1 (a repeating "decimal" in binary), the expression x==1.1 will evaluate to *false* because the literal 1.1 is the double representation of 1.1, which is different from the float representation stored in x. (They differ by 2.384×10^{-8}.) The expression x==float(1.1) will evaluate to *true* because the float function converts the literal 1.1 to its float representation before it is compared with x. (See [U] **16.10 Precision and problems therein** for more information.)

group(n)
:   Domain: 1 to 8e+307
:   Range: integers 1 to ceil(n)
:   Description: creates a categorical variable that divides the data into n nearly equal-sized subsamples, numbering the first group 1, the second 2, and so on.

inlist($z,a,b,\ldots$)
:   Domain :   all reals or all strings
:   Range: 0 or 1
:   Description: returns 1 if z is a member of the remaining arguments; otherwise, returns 0. All arguments must be reals or all must be strings. The number of arguments is between 2 and 255 for reals and between 2 and 10 for strings.

inrange(z,a,b)
:   Domain :   all reals or all strings
:   Range: 0 or 1
:   Description: returns 1 if it is known that $a \le z \le b$; otherwise, returns 0
                    The following ordered rules apply:
                    $z \ge$. returns 0.
                    $a \ge$. and $b =$. returns 1.
                    $a \ge$. returns 1 if $z \le b$; otherwise, it returns 0.
                    $b \ge$. returns 1 if $a \le z$; otherwise, it returns 0.
                    Otherwise, 1 is returned if $a \le z \le b$
                    In the above, if the arguments are strings, '.' is interpreted as "".

irecode($x,x_1,x_2,x_3,\ldots,\ x_n$)
:   Domain x: –8e+307 to 8e+307
:   Domain x_i: –8e+307 to 8e+307
:   Range: Nonnegative integers
:   Description: returns *missing* if x is *missing* or $x_1,\ldots,x_n$ is not weakly increasing; returns 0 if $x \le x_1$; returns 1 if $x_1 < x \le x_2$; returns 2 if $x_2 < x \le x_3$, ...; returns n if $x > x_n$. Also see autocode() and recode() for other styles of recode functions.
                    irecode(3, -10, -5, -3, -3, 0, 15, .) = 5.

matrix(*exp*)
:   Domain: any valid expression
:   Range: evaluation of *exp*
:   Description: restricts name interpretation to scalars and matrices; see scalar() function below.

maxbyte()
:   Range: a single integer number
:   Description: returns the largest value that can be stored in storage type byte. This function takes no arguments, but the parentheses must be included.

maxdouble()
:   Range: a single double-precision number
:   Description: returns the largest value that can be stored in storage type double. This function takes no arguments, but the parentheses must be included.

maxfloat()
:   Range: a single floating-point number
:   Description: returns the largest value that can be stored in storage type float. This function takes no arguments, but the parentheses must be included.

`maxint()`

Range: a single integer number

Description: returns the largest value that can be stored in storage type int. This function takes no arguments, but the parentheses must be included.

`maxlong()`

Range: a single integer number

Description: returns the largest value that can be stored in storage type long. This function takes no arguments, but the parentheses must be included.

$\mathtt{mi}(x_1, x_2, \ldots, x_n)$

Domain x_i: any string or numeric expression

Range: 0 and 1

Description: returns 1 if any x_i evaluates to *missing*. This is a synonym for $\mathtt{missing}(x_1, x_2, \ldots, x_n)$.

`minbyte()`

Range: a single integer number

Description: returns the smallest value that can be stored in storage type byte. This function takes no arguments, but the parentheses must be included.

`mindouble()`

Range: a single double precision number

Description: returns the smallest value that can be stored in storage type double. This function takes no arguments, but the parentheses must be included.

`minfloat()`

Range: a single floating-point number

Description: returns the smallest value that can be stored in storage type float. This function takes no arguments, but the parentheses must be included.

`minint()`

Range: a single integer number

Description: returns the smallest value that can be stored in storage type int. This function takes no arguments, but the parentheses must be included.

`minlong()`

Range: a single integer number

Description: returns the smallest value that can be stored in storage type long. This function takes no arguments, but the parentheses must be included.

$\mathtt{missing}(x_1, x_2, \ldots, x_n)$

Domain x_i: any string or numeric expression

Range: 0 and 1

Description: returns 1 if any x_i evaluates to *missing*

Stata has two concepts of missing values: numeric missing value (., .a, .b, ..., .z) and string missing value (""). `missing()` returns 1 (meaning true) if any expression x_i evaluates to *missing*. If x is numeric, $\mathtt{missing}(x)$ is equivalent to '$x \geq .$'. If x is string, $\mathtt{missing}(x)$ is equivalent to '$x==$""'.

(Continued on next page)

r(*name*)
    Domain: names
    Range: strings, scalars, matrices, and missing
    Description: returns the value of the saved result r(*name*);
                see [U] **21.8 Accessing results calculated by other programs**
                r(*name*) = scalar missing if the saved result does not exist
                r(*name*) = specified matrix if the saved result is a matrix
                r(*name*) = scalar numeric value if the saved result is a scalar
                          that can be interpreted as a number
                r(*name*) = a string containing the first 80 characters (244 for Stata/SE) of the saved
                result otherwise

recode(x,x_1,x_2,...,x_n)
    Domain x: –8e+307 to 8e+307; *missing*
    Domain x_1:   –8e+307 to 8e+307
    Domain x_2: x_1 to 8e+307
    . . .
    Domain x_n: x_{n-1} to 8e+307
    Range: x_1, x_2, ..., x_n; *missing*
    Description: returns *missing* if $x_1,\ldots,x_n$ is not weakly increasing; returns x if x is *missing*;
                x_1 if $x \le x_1$; otherwise, x_2 if $x \le x_2$, ...; otherwise,
                x_n if x is greater than x_1, x_2, ..., x_{n-1}.
                $x_i \ge .$ is interpreted as $x_i = +\infty$.
                Also see [R] **recode** for another style of recode function.

replay()
    Range: integers 0 and 1 meaning *false* and *true*
    Description: returns 1 if the first nonblank character of local macro '0' is a comma
                or if '0' is empty.

This is a function for use by programmers writing estimation commands.

return(*name*)
    Domain: names
    Range: strings, scalars, matrices, and missing
    Description: returns the value of the to-be-saved result return(*name*);
                see [U] **21.8 Accessing results calculated by other programs** and
                [U] **21.10 Saving results**
                return(*name*) = scalar missing if the result does not exist
                return(*name*) = specified matrix if the result is a matrix
                return(*name*) = scalar numeric value if the result is a scalar
                return(*name*) = a string containing the first 80 characters (244 for Stata/SE) of
                the result otherwise

s(*name*)
    Domain: names
    Range: strings, and *missing*
    Description: returns the value of saved result s(*name*);
                see [U] **21.8 Accessing results calculated by other programs**
                s(*name*) = . if the saved result does not exist
                s(*name*) = a string containing the first 80 characters (244 for Stata/SE) of the
                saved result otherwise

scalar(*exp*)
> Domain: any valid expression
> Range: evaluation of *exp*
> Description: restricts name interpretation to scalars and matrices

Names in expressions can refer to names of variables in the dataset, names of matrices, or names of scalars. Matrices and scalars can have the same names as variables in the dataset. In the case of conflict, the default is to assume that you are referring to the name of the variable in the dataset.

matrix() and scalar() explicitly state that you are referring to matrices and scalars. matrix() and scalar() are the same function; scalars and matrices may not have the same names, and so cannot be confused. Typing scalar(x) makes it clear that you are referring to the scalar or matrix named x and not the variable named x, should there happen to be a variable of that name.

Date functions

Stata includes the following *date functions*. These functions are described, with examples, in [U] **27 Commands for dealing with dates**. What follows is a technical description. *s* is used to indicate a string subexpression—a string literal, a string variable, or another string expression—and *e*, *m*, *d*, and *y* are used to indicate numeric subexpressions—numbers, numeric variables, or other numeric expressions. The date functions interpret *e*, *m*, *d*, and *y* as int(*e*), int(*m*), int(*d*), and int(*y*), respectively.

An elapsed date is the number of days from 1jan1960; negative numbers indicate dates prior to 1jan1960. Allowable dates are between 1jan100 and 31dec9999, inclusive, but all functions are based on the Gregorian calendar, and values do not correspond to historical dates prior to Friday, 15oct1582.

d(*l*)
> Domain *l*:   date literals 01jan0100 to 31dec9999
> Range: dates 01jan0100 to 31dec9999 (integers $-679{,}350$ to $2{,}936{,}549$)
> Description: convenience function to make typing dates in expressions easier;
>   e.g., typing d(2jan1960) is equivalent to typing 1

(Continued on next page)

$\text{date}(s_1, s_2 [, y])$

Domain s_1:   strings
Domain s_2:   strings
Domain y: integers 1000 to 9998 (but probably 2001 to 2099)
Range: dates 01jan0100 to 31dec9999 (integers $-679{,}350$ to 2,936,549); *missing*
Description: returns the elapsed date corresponding to s_1 based on s_2 and y

s_1 contains the date, recorded as a string, in virtually any format. Months can be spelled out, abbreviated (to three characters), or indicated as numbers; years can include or exclude the century; blanks and punctuation are allowed.

s_2 is any permutation of m, d, and [##]y, with their order defining the order that month, day, and year occur in s_1. ##, if specified, indicates the default century for 2-digit years in s_1. For instance, $s_2 =$ "md19y" would translate $s_1 =$ "11/15/91" as 15nov1991.

y provides an alternate way of handling two-digit years. y specifies the largest year that is to be returned when a two-digit year is encountered. For instance,

$$\text{date}("1/15/99", "mdy", 2050) = 15\text{jan}1999$$
$$\text{date}("1/15/98", "mdy", 2050) = 15\text{jan}1998$$
$$\vdots$$
$$\text{date}("1/15/51", "mdy", 2050) = 15\text{jan}1951$$
$$\text{date}("1/15/50", "mdy", 2050) = 15\text{jan}2050$$
$$\text{date}("1/15/49", "mdy", 2050) = 15\text{jan}2049$$
$$\vdots$$
$$\text{date}("1/15/01", "mdy", 2050) = 15\text{jan}2001$$
$$\text{date}("1/15/00", "mdy", 2050) = 15\text{jan}2000$$

If neither ## nor y is specified, then date() returns *missing* when it encounters a two-digit year.

$\text{day}(e)$

Domain e: dates 01jan0100 to 31dec9999 (integers $-679{,}350$ to 2,936,549)
Range: integers 1 to 31; *missing*
Description: returns the numeric day of the month corresponding to e

$\text{dow}(e)$

Domain e: dates 01jan0100 to 31dec9999 (integers $-679{,}350$ to 2,936,549)
Range: integers 0 to 6; *missing*
Description: returns the numeric day of the week corresponding to e;
          $0 =$ Sunday, $1 =$ Monday, $\dots$, $6 =$ Saturday

$\text{doy}(e)$

Domain e: dates 01jan0100 to 31dec9999 (integers $-679{,}350$ to 2,936,549)
Range: integers 1 to 366; *missing*
Description: returns the numeric day of the year corresponding to e

$\text{halfyear}(e)$

Domain e: dates 01jan0100 to 31dec9999 (integers $-679{,}350$ to 2,936,549)
Range: integers 1, 2; *missing*
Description: returns the numeric half of the year corresponding to e

$\text{month}(e)$

Domain e: dates 01jan0100 to 31dec9999 (integers $-679{,}350$ to 2,936,549)
Range: integers 1 to 12; *missing*
Description: returns the numeric month corresponding to e

mdy(*m*,*d*,*y*)
    Domain *m*:   integers 1 to 12
    Domain *d*:   integers 1 to 31
    Domain *y*:   integers 100 to 9999 (but probably 1800 to 2100)
    Range: dates 01jan0100 to 31dec9999 (integers $-679{,}350$ to $2{,}936{,}549$); *missing*
    Description: returns the elapsed date corresponding to *m*, *d*, *y*

quarter(*e*)
    Domain *e*:   dates 01jan0100 to 31dec9999 (integers $-679{,}350$ to $2{,}936{,}549$)
    Range: integers 1 to 4; *missing*
    Description: returns the numeric quarter of the year corresponding to *e*

week(*e*)
    Domain *e*:   dates 01jan0100 to 31dec9999 (integers $-679{,}350$ to $2{,}936{,}549$)
    Range: integers 1 to 52; *missing*
    Description: returns the numeric week of the year corresponding to *e*
              (the first week of a year is the first seven days of the year)

year(*e*)
    Domain *e*:   dates 01jan0100 to 31dec9999 (integers $-679{,}350$ to $2{,}936{,}549$)
    Range: integers 100 to 9999 (but probably 1800 to 2100)
    Description: returns the numeric year corresponding to *e*

Time-series functions

In addition to elapsed dates for which $0 = 01jan1960$, Stata provides five other encodings for dates:

Description	Format	Coding
daily	%td	0 = 01jan1960 (same as elapsed date)
weekly	%tw	0 = 1960w1
monthly	%tm	0 = 1960m1
quarterly	%tq	0 = 1960q1
half-yearly	%th	0 = 1960h1
yearly	%ty	1960 = 1960 (records the year itself)

The following functions are for use with %t dates:

d(*l*)
    Domain *l*:   date literals 01jan0100 to 31dec9999
    Range: %td dates 01jan0100 to 31dec9999 (integers $-679{,}350$ to $2{,}936{,}549$)
    Description: convenience function to make typing dates in expressions easier;
              e.g., typing d(2jan1960) is equivalent to typing 1

(Continued on next page)

daily($s_1,s_2\left[,y\right]$)

   Domain s_1:   strings
   Domain s_2:   strings
   Domain y: integers 1000 to 9998 (but probably 2001 to 2099)
   Range: %td dates 01jan0100 to 31dec9999 (integers −679,350 to 2,936,549); *missing*
   Description: returns the elapsed date corresponding to s_1;

   s_1 contains the date stored as a string, and may have a variety of formats.
   s_2 contains a translation string for the date, which is some permutation of "m", "d", and "y" indicating the order of the month, day and year, respectively, in the date string.

   This function is the same as the date() function. For a full explanation of it, please see the entry for date() in [U] **27.2.2.2 The date() function** above.

dofd(e)

   Domain e: %td dates 01jan0100 to 31dec9999 (integers −679,350 to 2,936,549)
   Range: %td dates 01jan0100 to 31dec9999 (integers −679,350 to 2,936,549)
   Description: returns the %td date of e
                   (yes, this is the identity function)

dofh(e_h)

   Domain e_h: %th dates 0100h1 to 9999h2 (integers −3,720 to 16,079)
   Range: %td dates 01jan0100 to 01jul9999 (integers −679,350 to 2,936,366)
   Description: returns the %td date of the start of e_h

dofm(e_m)

   Domain e_m: %tm dates 0100m1 to 9999m12 (integers −22,320 to 96,479)
   Range: %td dates 01jan0100 to 01dec9999 (integers −679,350 to 2,936,519)
   Description: returns the %td date of the start of e_m

dofq(e_q)

   Domain e_q: %tq dates 0100q1 to 9999q4 (integers −7,440 to 32,156)
   Range: %td dates 01jan0100 to 01oct9999 (integers −679,350 to 2,936,458)
   Description: returns the %td date of the start of e_q

dofw(e_w)

   Domain e_w: %tw dates 0100w1 to 9999w52 (integers −96,720 to 418,079)
   Range: %td dates 01jan0100 to 24dec9999 (integers −679,350 to 2,936,542)
   Description: returns the %td date of the start of e_w

dofy(e_y)

   Domain e_y: %ty dates 0100 to 9999 (integers 100 to 9999)
   Range: %td dates 01jan0100 to 01jan9999 (integers −679,350 to 2,936,185)
   Description: returns the %td date of the start of e_y

h(l)

   Domain l: date literals 0100h1 to 9999h2
   Range: %th dates 0100h1 to 9999h2 (integers −3,720 to 16,079)
   Description: convenience function to make typing dates in expressions easier;
                   e.g., typing h(1960h2) is equivalent to typing 1

halfyearly$(s_1, s_2[,y])$

Domain s_1:	strings
Domain s_2:	strings "hy" and "yh"; y may be prefixed with ##
Domain y:	integers 1000 to 9998 (but probably 2001 to 2099)
Range:	%th dates 0100h1 to 9999h2 (integers $-3{,}720$ to 16,079); *missing*
Description:	returns the %th date corresponding to s_1;
	y specifies top year; see date() in [U] **27.2.2.2 The date() function**.

hofd(e_d)

Domain e_d:	%td dates 01jan0100 to 31dec9999 (integers $-679{,}350$ to 2,936,549)
Range:	%th dates 0100h1 to 9999h2 (integers $-3{,}720$ to 16,079)
Description:	returns the %th date containing e_d

m(l)

Domain l:	date literals 0100m1 to 9999m12
Range:	%tm dates 0100m1 to 9999m12 (integers $-22{,}320$ to 96,479)
Description:	convenience function to make typing dates in expressions easier;
	e.g., typing m(1960m2) is equivalent to typing 1

mdy(m, d, y)

Domain m:	integers 1 to 12
Domain d:	integers 1 to 31
Domain y:	integers 100 to 9999 (but probably 1800 to 2100)
Range:	%td dates 01jan0100 to 31dec9999 (integers $-679{,}350$ to 2,936,549); *missing*
Description:	returns the elapsed date corresponding to m, d, y

mofd(e_d)

Domain e_d:	%td dates 01jan0100 to 31dec9999 (integers $-679{,}350$ to 2,936,549)
Range:	%tm dates 0100m1 to 9999m12 (integers $-22{,}320$ to 96,479)
Description:	returns the %tm date containing e_d

monthly$(s_1, s_2[,y])$

Domain s_1:	strings
Domain s_2:	strings "my" and "ym"; y may be prefixed with ##
Domain y:	integers 1000 to 9998 (but probably 2001 to 2099)
Range:	%tm dates 0100m1 to 9999m12 (integers $-22{,}320$ to 96,479); *missing*
Description:	returns the %tm date corresponding to s_1;
	y specifies top year; see date() in [U] **27.2.2.2 The date() function**.

q(l)

Domain l:	date literals 0100q1 to 9999q4
Range:	%tq dates 0100q1 to 9999q4 (integers $-7{,}440$ to 32,156)
Description:	convenience function to make typing dates in expressions easier;
	e.g., typing q(1960q2) is equivalent to typing 1

qofd(e_d)

Domain e_d:	%td dates 01jan0100 to 31dec9999 (integers $-679{,}350$ to 2,936,549)
Range:	%tq dates 0100q1 to 9999q4 (integers $-7{,}440$ to 32,156)
Description:	returns the %tq date containing e_d

quarterly(s_1,s_2[,y])

    Domain s_1:   strings
    Domain s_2:   strings "qy" and "yq"; y may be prefixed with ##
    Domain y: integers 1000 to 9998 (but probably 2001 to 2099)
    Range: %tq dates 0100q1 to 9999q4 (integers −7,440 to 32,156); *missing*
    Description: returns the %tq date corresponding to s_1;
                y specifies top year; see date() in [U] **27.2.2.2 The date() function**.

tin(d_1,d_2)

    Domain d_1: date literals recorded in units of t previously tsset;
    Domain d_2: date literals recorded in units of t previously tsset
    Range: 0 and 1, 1 ⇒ *true*
    Description: *true* if $d_1 \leq t \leq d_2$, where t is the time variable previously tsset

You must have previously tsset the data to use tin(); see [TS] **tsset**. When you tsset the data, you specified a time variable t and the format on t states how it is recorded. You type d_1 and d_2 according to that format.

If t has a %td or %d format, you could type tin(5jan1992, 14apr2002).

If t has a %tw format, you could type tin(1985w1, 2002w15).

If t has a %tm format, you could type tin(1985m1, 2002m4).

If t has a %tq format, you could type tin(1985q1, 2002q2).

If t has a %th format, you could type tin(1985h1, 2002h1).

If t has a %ty format, you could type tin(1985, 2002).

Otherwise, t is just a set of integers and you could type tin(12, 38).

Note that the details of the %t format do not matter. If your t is formatted %tdn/d/y so that 5jan1992 displays as 1/5/92, you would still type the date in day–month–year order: tin(5jan1992, 14apr2002).

twithin(d_1,d_2)

    Domain d_1: date literals recorded in units of t previously tsset
    Domain d_2: date literals recorded in units of t previously tsset
    Range: 0 and 1, 1 ⇒ *true*
    Description: *true* if $d_1 < t < d_2$, where t is the time variable previously tsset;
                see tin() function above; twithin() is similar except the range is exclusive

w(l)

    Domain l: date literals 0100w1 to 9999w52
    Range: %tw dates 0100w1 to 9999w52 (integers −96,720 to 418,079)
    Description: convenience function to make typing dates in expressions easier;
                e.g., typing w(1960w2) is equivalent to typing 1

weekly(s_1,s_2[,y])

    Domain s_1:   strings
    Domain s_2:   strings "wy" and "yw"; y may be prefixed with ##
    Domain y: integers 1000 to 9998 (but probably 2001 to 2099)
    Range: %tw dates 0100w1 to 9999w52 (integers −96,720 to 418,079); *missing*
    Description: returns the %tw date corresponding to s_1;
                y specifies top year; see date() in [U] **27.2.2.2 The date() function**.

wofd(e_d)
  Domain e_d: %td dates 01jan0100 to 31dec9999 (integers −679,350 to 2,936,549)
  Range: %tw dates 0100w1 to 9999w52 (integers −96,720 to 418,079)
  Description: returns the %tw date containing e_d

y(l)
  Domain l: date literals 0100 to 9999
  Range: %ty dates 0100 to 9999 (integers 100 to 9999)
  Description: convenience function to make typing dates in expressions easier;
          e.g., typing y(1961) is equivalent to typing 1961
          Note that y(61) would produce an error message; programmers find this useful.

yearly(s_1,s_2[,y])
  Domain s_1: strings
  Domain s_2: string "y"; y may be prefixed with ##
  Domain y: integers 1000 to 9998 (but probably 2001 to 2099)
  Range: %ty dates 0100 to 9999 (integers 100 to 9999); *missing*
  Description: returns the %ty date corresponding to s_1;
          y specifies top year; see date() in [U] **27.2.2.2 The date() function**.

yh(y,h)
  Domain y: integers 100 to 9999 (but probably 1800 to 2100)
  Domain h: integers 1, 2
  Range: %th dates 0100h1 to 9999h2 (integers −3,720 to 16,079)
  Description: returns the %th date corresponding to year y, half h

ym(y,m)
  Domain y: integers 100 to 9999 (but probably 1800 to 2100)
  Domain m: integers 1 to 12
  Range: %tm dates 0100m1 to 9999m12 (integers −22,320 to 96,479)
  Description: returns the %tm date corresponding to year y, month m

yofd(e_d)
  Domain e_d: %td dates 01jan0100 to 31dec9999 (integers −679,350 to 2,936,549)
  Range: %ty dates 0100 to 9999 (integers 100 to 9999)
  Description: returns the %ty date (year) containing e_d

yq(y,q)
  Domain y: integers 100 to 9999 (but probably 1800 to 2100)
  Domain q: integers 1 to 4
  Range: %tq dates 0100q1 to 9999q4 (integers −7,440 to 32,156)
  Description: returns the %tq date corresponding to year y, quarter q

yw(y,w)
  Domain y: integers 100 to 9999 (but probably 1800 to 2100)
  Domain w: integers 1 to 52
  Range: %tw dates 0100w1 to 9999w52 (integers −96,720 to 418,079)
  Description: returns the %tw date corresponding to year y, week w

Acknowledgments

We thank George Marsaglia of the Florida State University for providing his KISS (Keep It Simple Stupid) random number generator.

We thank John R. Gleason of Syracuse University for directing our attention to Wichura (1988) for calculating the cumulative normal density accurately, for sharing his experiences about techniques with us, and for providing C code to make the calculations.

References

Abramowitz, M. and I. A. Stegun, eds. 1968. *Handbook of Mathematical Functions*, 7th printing. Washington, D.C.: National Bureau of Standards.

Haynam, G. E., Z. Govindarajulu, and F. C. Leone. 1970. Tables of the cumulative noncentral chi-square distribution. In *Selected Tables in Mathematical Statistics*, vol. 1, ed. H. L. Harter and D. B. Owen, 1–78. Providence, RI: American Mathematical Society.

Johnson, N. L., S. Kotz, and N. Balakrishnan. 1995. *Continuous univariate distributions, vol. 2*. 2d ed. New York: Wiley.

Marsaglia, G. 1994. Personal communication.

Moore, R. J. 1982. Derivatives of the gamma integral, algorithm AS 187. *Applied Statistician* 31(3).

Posten, H. O. 1993. An Effective Algorithm for the Noncentral Beta Distribution Function. *The American Statistician* 47: 129-131.

Press, W. H., S. A. Teukolsky, W. T. Vetterling, and B. P. Flannery. 1992. *Numerical Recipes in C: The Art of Scientific Computing*. 2d ed. Cambridge: Cambridge University Press.

Wichura, M. J. 1988. The percentage points of the normal distribution. *Applied Statistics* 37: 454–477.

Also See

Related:	[R] **egen**
Background:	[U] **16.3 Functions**,
	[U] **17.8 Matrix functions**